D1483008

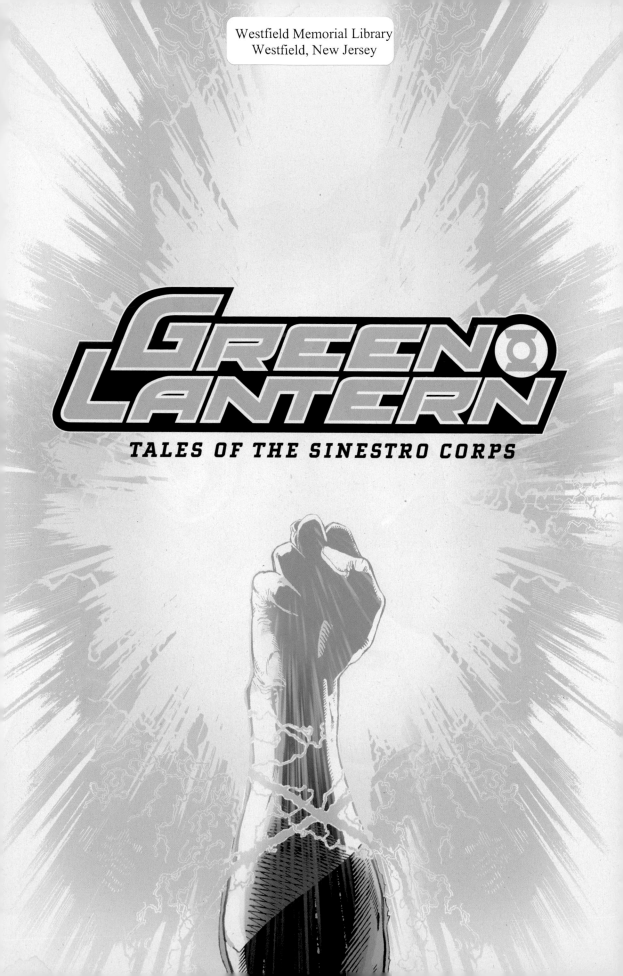

Green Lantern

TALES OF THE SINESTRO CORPS

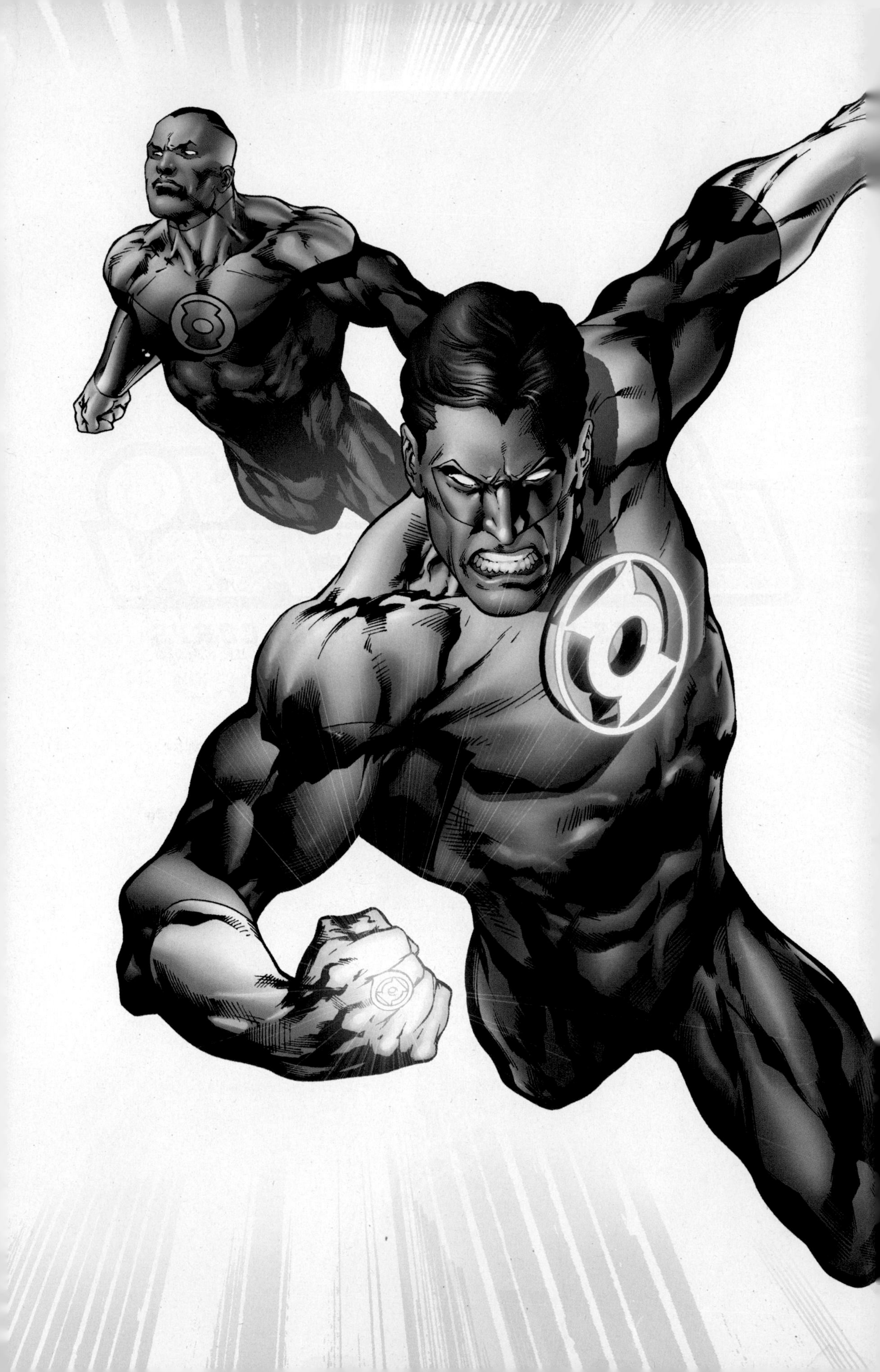

TALES OF THE SINESTRO CORPS

Geoff Johns   Ron Marz   Alan Burnett   Sterling Gates
Writers

**Dave Gibbons   Adriana Melo   Patrick Blaine   Pete Woods
Jerry Ordway   Michel Lacombe   Joe Prado**
Pencillers

**Dave Gibbons   Rodney Ramos   Marlo Alquiza   Jay Leisten
Pete Woods   Jerry Ordway   Michel Lacombe**
Inkers

**Moose Baumann   Jason Wright   David Curiel
Brad Anderson   Jeromy Cox**
Colorists

**Pat Brosseau   Rob Leigh   Jared K. Fletcher
Steve Wands   John J. Hill**
Letterers

DC COMICS

Dan DiDio Senior VP-Executive Editor
Eddie Berganza Peter J. Tomasi Editors-original series
Adam Schlagman Elisabeth V. Gehrlein
Assistant Editors-original series
Bob Joy Editor-collected edition
Robbin Brosterman Senior Art Director
Paul Levitz President & Publisher
Georg Brewer VP-Design & DC Direct Creative
Richard Bruning Senior VP-Creative Director
Patrick Caldon Executive VP-Finance & Operations
Chris Caramalis VP-Finance
John Cunningham VP-Marketing
Terri Cunningham VP-Managing Editor
Alison Gill VP-Manufacturing
David Hyde VP-Publicity
Hank Kanalz VP-General Manager, WildStorm
Jim Lee Editorial Director-WildStorm
Paula Lowitt Senior VP-Business & Legal Affairs
MaryEllen McLaughlin VP-Advertising & Custom Publishing
John Nee Senior VP-Business Development
Gregory Noveck Senior VP-Creative Affairs
Sue Pohja VP-Book Trade Sales
Steve Rotterdam Senior VP-Sales & Marketing
Cheryl Rubin Senior VP-Brand Management
Jeff Trojan VP-Business Development, DC Direct
Bob Wayne VP-Sales

Cover art by Ivan Reis & Oclair Albert with Moose Baumann

**GREEN LANTERN:
TALES OF THE SINESTRO CORPS**

Originally published in single magazine form in GREEN LANTERN 18-20,
GREEN LANTERN: SINESTRO CORPS SPECIAL 1, TALES OF THE
SINESTRO CORPS: PARALLAX 1, TALES OF THE SINESTRO CORPS:
CYBORG SUPERMAN 1, TALES OF THE SINESTRO CORPS:
SUPERMAN-PRIME 1, TALES OF THE SINESTRO CORPS: ION 1,
GREEN LANTERN / SINESTRO CORPS: SECRET FILES 1

DC Comics, 1700 Broadway, New York, NY 10019
A Warner Bros. Entertainment Company
Printed in Canada. First Printing.

Hardcover ISBN: 978-1-4012-1801-0
Softcover ISBN: 978-1-4012-2036-5

Billions of years ago, the Guardians of the Universe created a police force to serve and protect every sector of the galaxy. Recruited for their fearlessness and integrity, these intergalactic peacekeepers serve honorably as the Green Lantern Corps.

Once hailed as the greatest of the Green Lanterns, Sinestro was expelled from the Corps when his pupil Hal Jordan discovered how he kept his space sector in line: with fear. Over the years, he has waged a one-man war against the Corps and its founders, the Guardians of the Universe — and each time he has been defeated.

On the antimatter-universe planet of Qward, Sinestro created thousands of yellow power rings like his own, powered by fear just as the Green Lanterns' rings are fueled by willpower. They were wielded by the universe's most frightening beings, and together this Sinestro Corps attempted to create a new universal order of absolute obedience and abject terror.

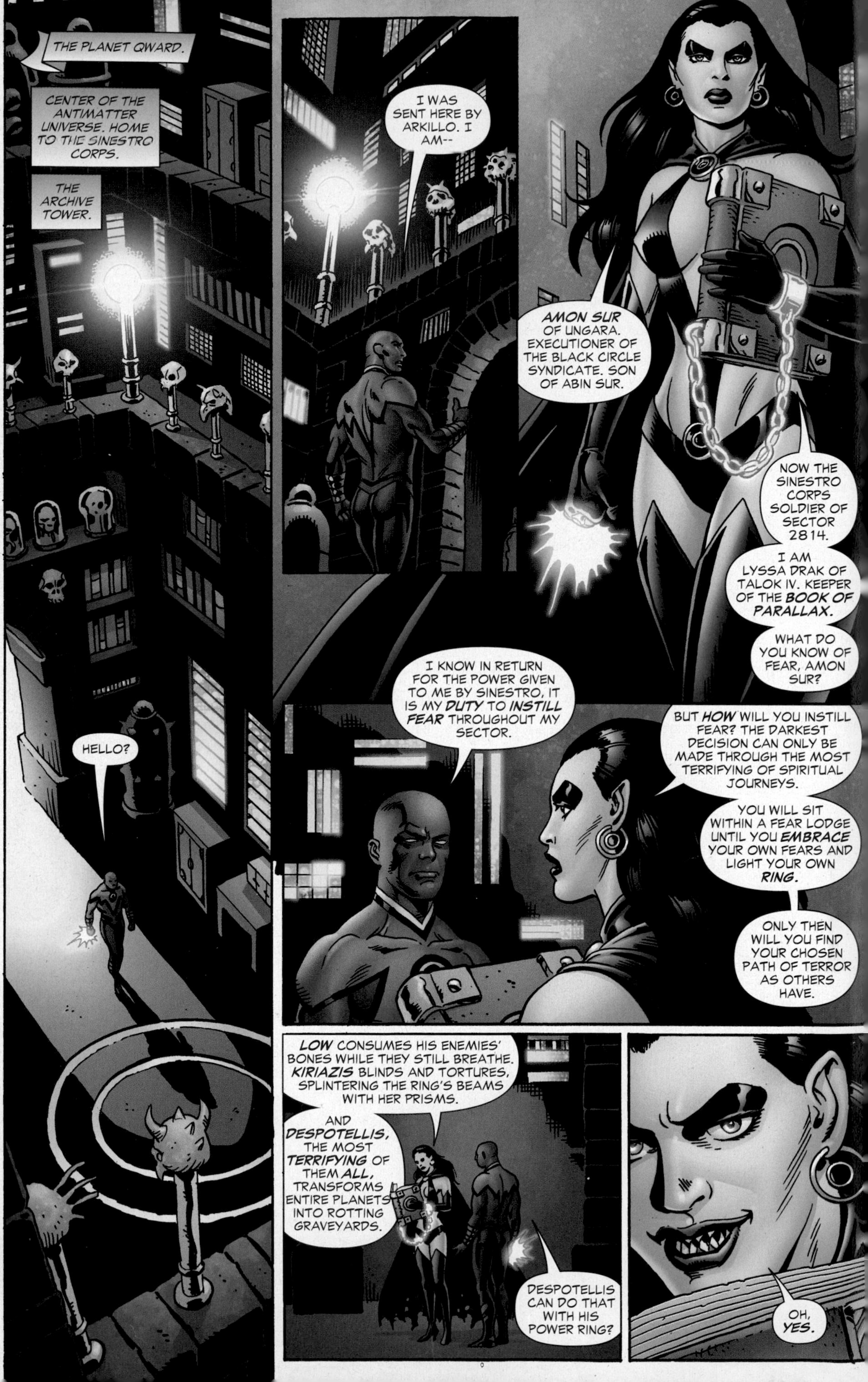
THE PLANET QWARD.
CENTER OF THE ANTIMATTER UNIVERSE. HOME TO THE SINESTRO CORPS.
THE ARCHIVE TOWER.
HELLO?
I WAS SENT HERE BY ARKILLO. I AM--
AMON SUR OF UNGARA. EXECUTIONER OF THE BLACK CIRCLE SYNDICATE. SON OF ABIN SUR.
NOW THE SINESTRO CORPS SOLDIER OF SECTOR 2814.
I AM LYSSA DRAK OF TALOK IV. KEEPER OF THE BOOK OF PARALLAX.
WHAT DO YOU KNOW OF FEAR, AMON SUR?
I KNOW IN RETURN FOR THE POWER GIVEN TO ME BY SINESTRO, IT IS MY DUTY TO INSTILL FEAR THROUGHOUT MY SECTOR.
BUT HOW WILL YOU INSTILL FEAR? THE DARKEST DECISION CAN ONLY BE MADE THROUGH THE MOST TERRIFYING OF SPIRITUAL JOURNEYS.
YOU WILL SIT WITHIN A FEAR LODGE UNTIL YOU EMBRACE YOUR OWN FEARS AND LIGHT YOUR OWN RING.
ONLY THEN WILL YOU FIND YOUR CHOSEN PATH OF TERROR AS OTHERS HAVE.
LOW CONSUMES HIS ENEMIES' BONES WHILE THEY STILL BREATHE. KIRIAZIS BLINDS AND TORTURES, SPLINTERING THE RING'S BEAMS WITH HER PRISMS.
AND DESPOTELLIS, THE MOST TERRIFYING OF THEM ALL, TRANSFORMS ENTIRE PLANETS INTO ROTTING GRAVEYARDS.
DESPOTELLIS CAN DO THAT WITH HIS POWER RING?
OH, YES.

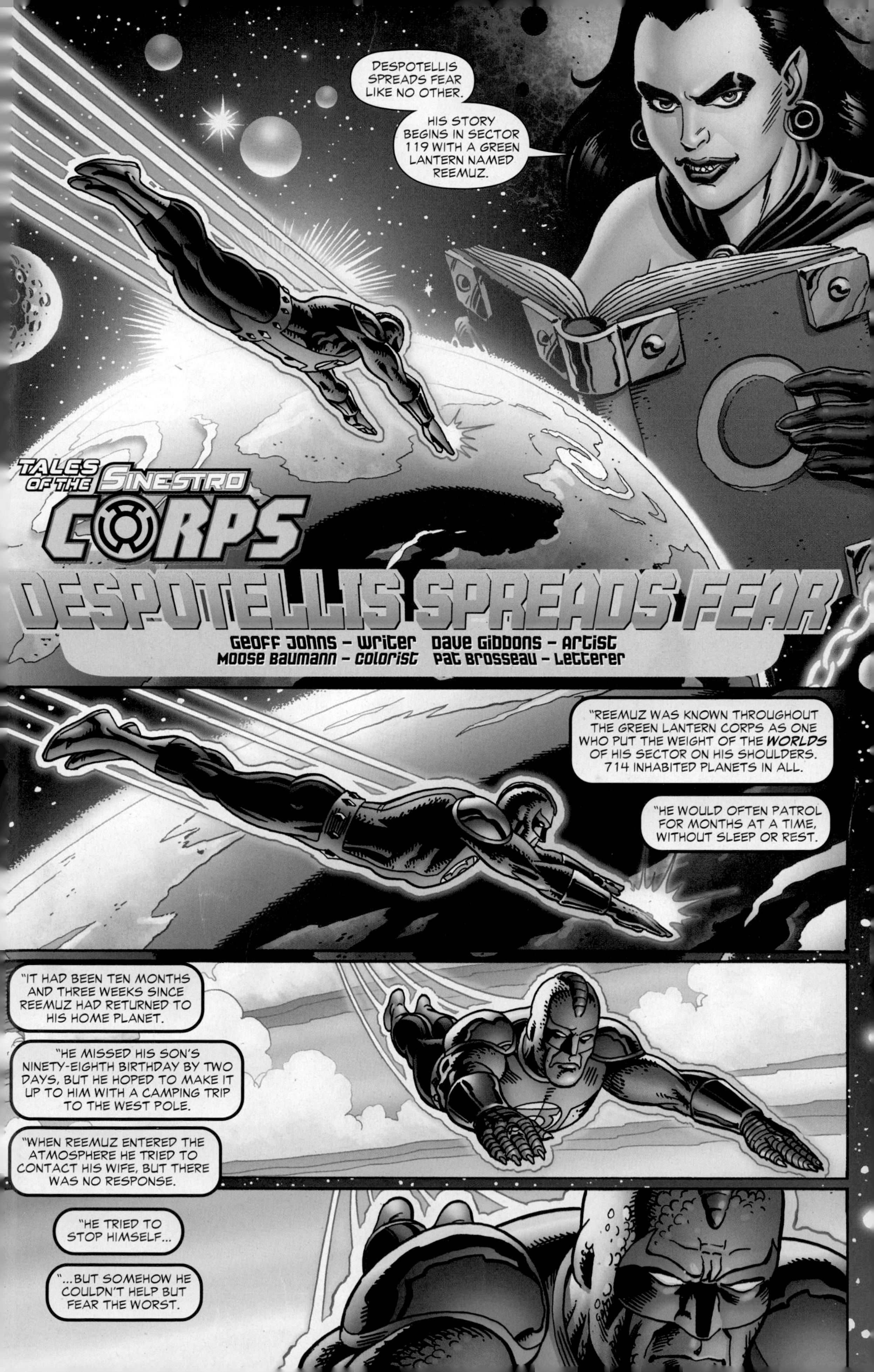
DESPOTELLIS SPREADS FEAR LIKE NO OTHER.
HIS STORY BEGINS IN SECTOR 119 WITH A GREEN LANTERN NAMED REEMUZ.
TALES OF THE SINESTRO CORPS
DESPOTELLIS SPREADS FEAR
GEOFF JOHNS – WRITER DAVE GIBBONS – ARTIST
MOOSE BAUMANN – COLORIST PAT BROSSEAU – LETTERER
"REEMUZ WAS KNOWN THROUGHOUT THE GREEN LANTERN CORPS AS ONE WHO PUT THE WEIGHT OF THE WORLDS OF HIS SECTOR ON HIS SHOULDERS. 714 INHABITED PLANETS IN ALL.
"HE WOULD OFTEN PATROL FOR MONTHS AT A TIME, WITHOUT SLEEP OR REST.
"IT HAD BEEN TEN MONTHS AND THREE WEEKS SINCE REEMUZ HAD RETURNED TO HIS HOME PLANET.
"HE MISSED HIS SON'S NINETY-EIGHTH BIRTHDAY BY TWO DAYS, BUT HE HOPED TO MAKE IT UP TO HIM WITH A CAMPING TRIP TO THE WEST POLE.
"WHEN REEMUZ ENTERED THE ATMOSPHERE HE TRIED TO CONTACT HIS WIFE, BUT THERE WAS NO RESPONSE.
"HE TRIED TO STOP HIMSELF...
"...BUT SOMEHOW HE COULDN'T HELP BUT FEAR THE WORST.

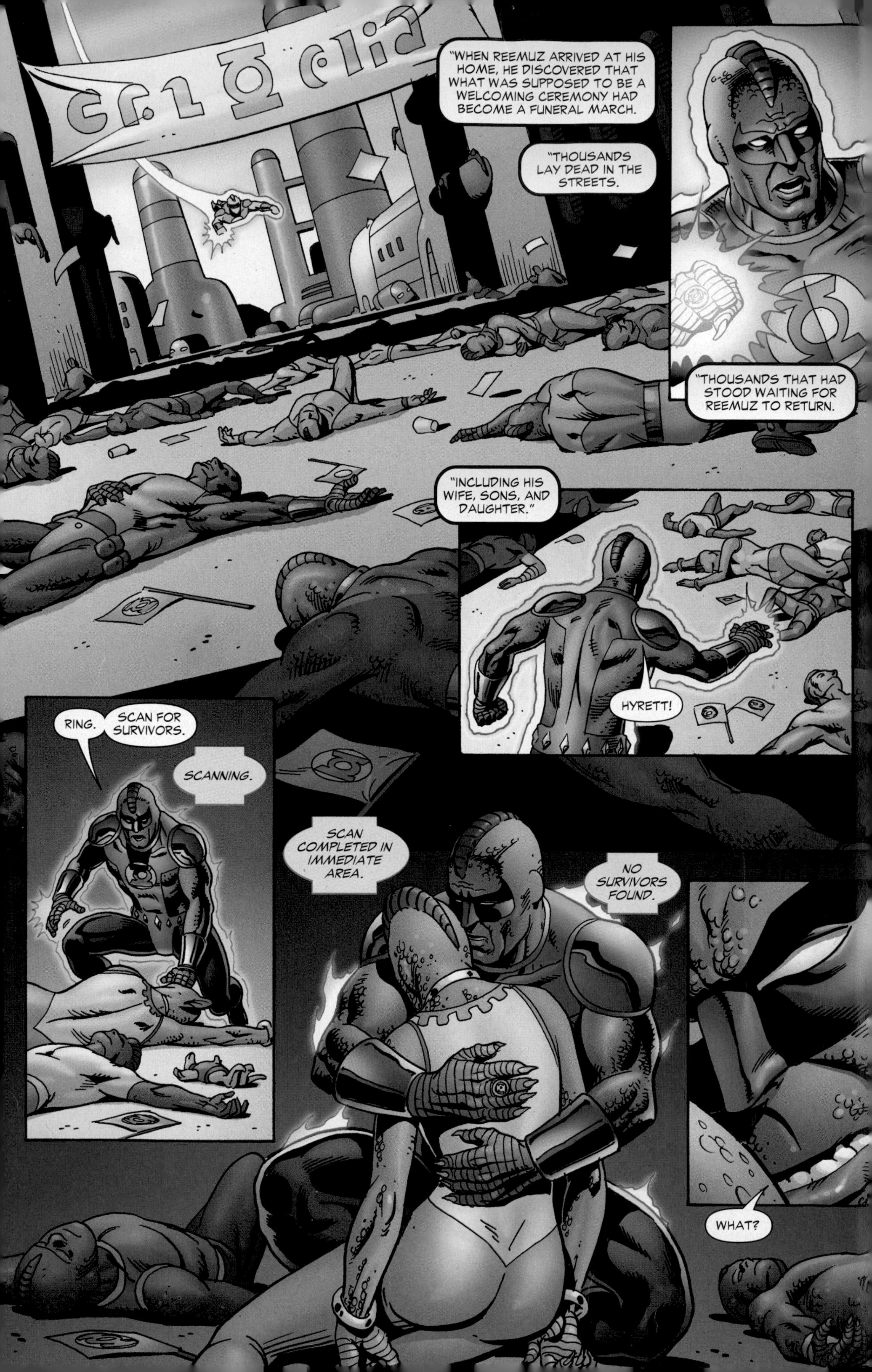
"WHEN REEMUZ ARRIVED AT HIS HOME, HE DISCOVERED THAT WHAT WAS SUPPOSED TO BE A WELCOMING CEREMONY HAD BECOME A FUNERAL MARCH.
"THOUSANDS LAY DEAD IN THE STREETS.
"THOUSANDS THAT HAD STOOD WAITING FOR REEMUZ TO RETURN.
"INCLUDING HIS WIFE, SONS, AND DAUGHTER."
HYRETT!
RING.
SCAN FOR SURVIVORS.
SCANNING.
SCAN COMPLETED IN IMMEDIATE AREA.
NO SURVIVORS FOUND.
WHAT?

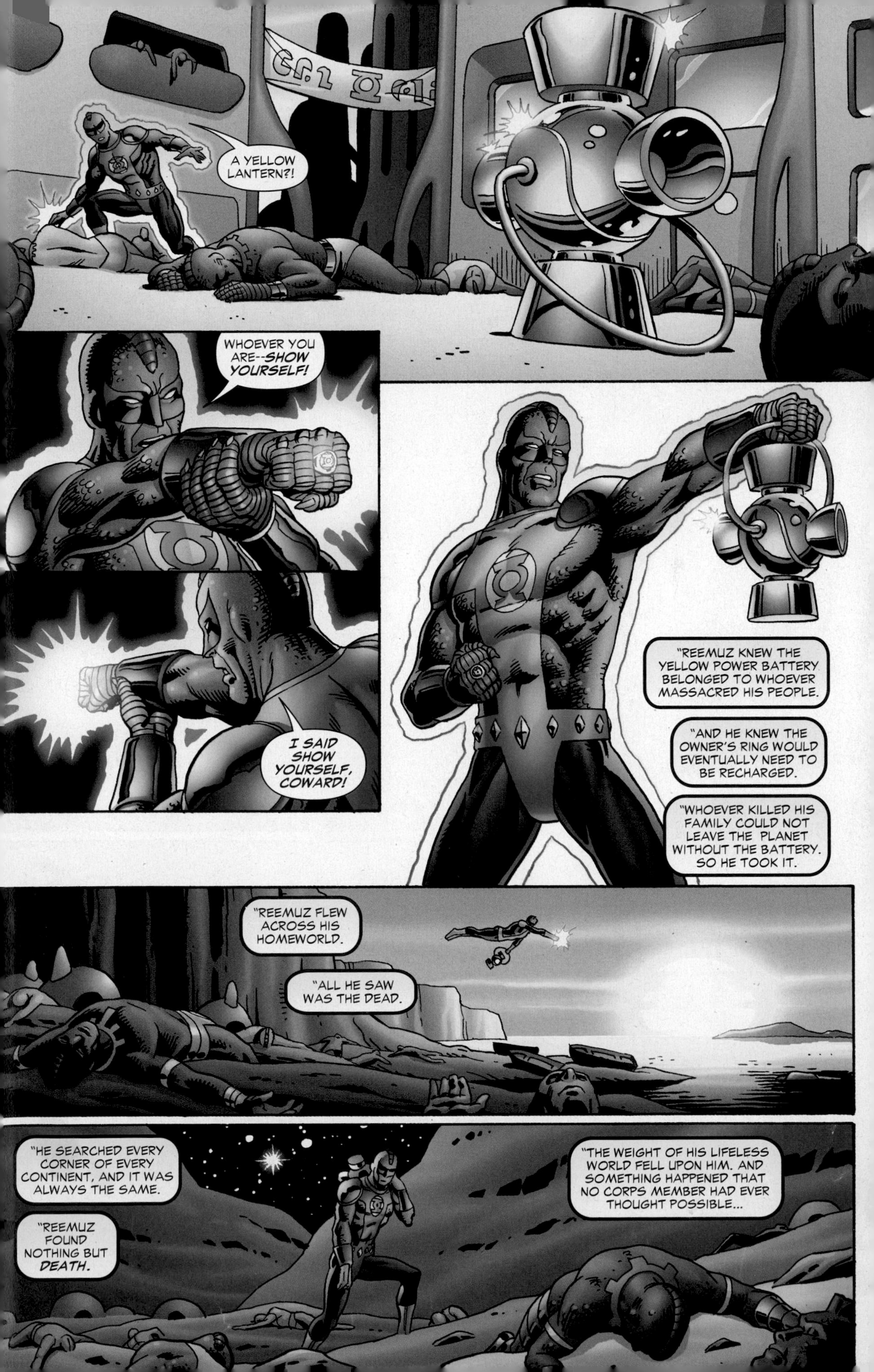
A YELLOW LANTERN?!
WHOEVER YOU ARE--SHOW YOURSELF!
I SAID SHOW YOURSELF, COWARD!
"REEMUZ KNEW THE YELLOW POWER BATTERY BELONGED TO WHOEVER MASSACRED HIS PEOPLE.
"AND HE KNEW THE OWNER'S RING WOULD EVENTUALLY NEED TO BE RECHARGED.
"WHOEVER KILLED HIS FAMILY COULD NOT LEAVE THE PLANET WITHOUT THE BATTERY. SO HE TOOK IT.
"REEMUZ FLEW ACROSS HIS HOMEWORLD.
"ALL HE SAW WAS THE DEAD.
"HE SEARCHED EVERY CORNER OF EVERY CONTINENT, AND IT WAS ALWAYS THE SAME.
"REEMUZ FOUND NOTHING BUT DEATH.
"THE WEIGHT OF HIS LIFELESS WORLD FELL UPON HIM. AND SOMETHING HAPPENED THAT NO CORPS MEMBER HAD EVER THOUGHT POSSIBLE...

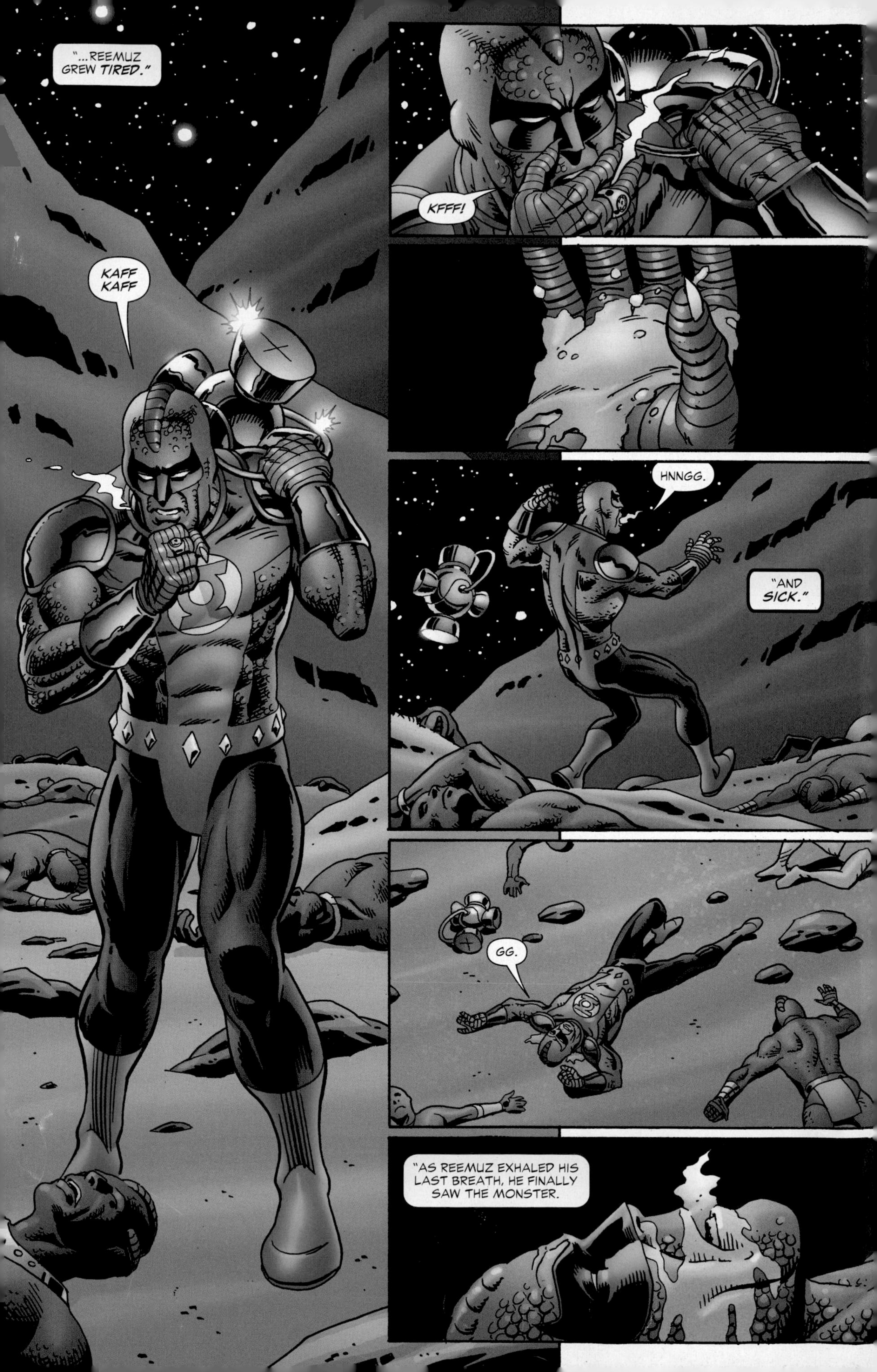
"...REEMUZ GREW TIRED."
KAFF KAFF
KFFF!
HNNGG.
"AND SICK."
GG.
"AS REEMUZ EXHALED HIS LAST BREATH, HE FINALLY SAW THE MONSTER.

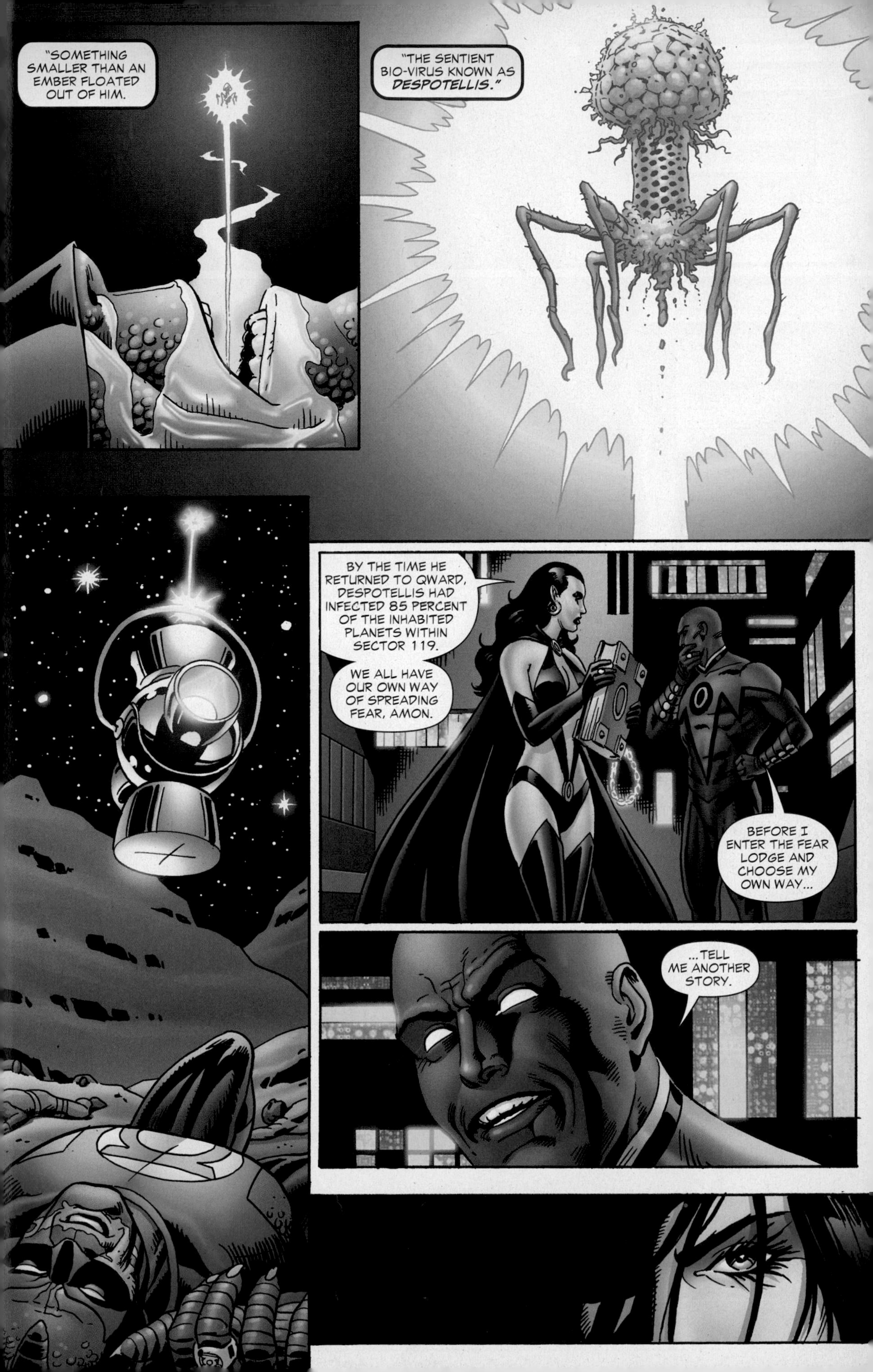
"SOMETHING SMALLER THAN AN EMBER FLOATED OUT OF HIM.
"THE SENTIENT BIO-VIRUS KNOWN AS *DESPOTELLIS*."
BY THE TIME HE RETURNED TO QWARD, DESPOTELLIS HAD INFECTED 85 PERCENT OF THE INHABITED PLANETS WITHIN SECTOR 119.
WE ALL HAVE OUR OWN WAY OF SPREADING FEAR, AMON.
BEFORE I ENTER THE FEAR LODGE AND CHOOSE MY OWN WAY...
...TELL ME ANOTHER STORY.

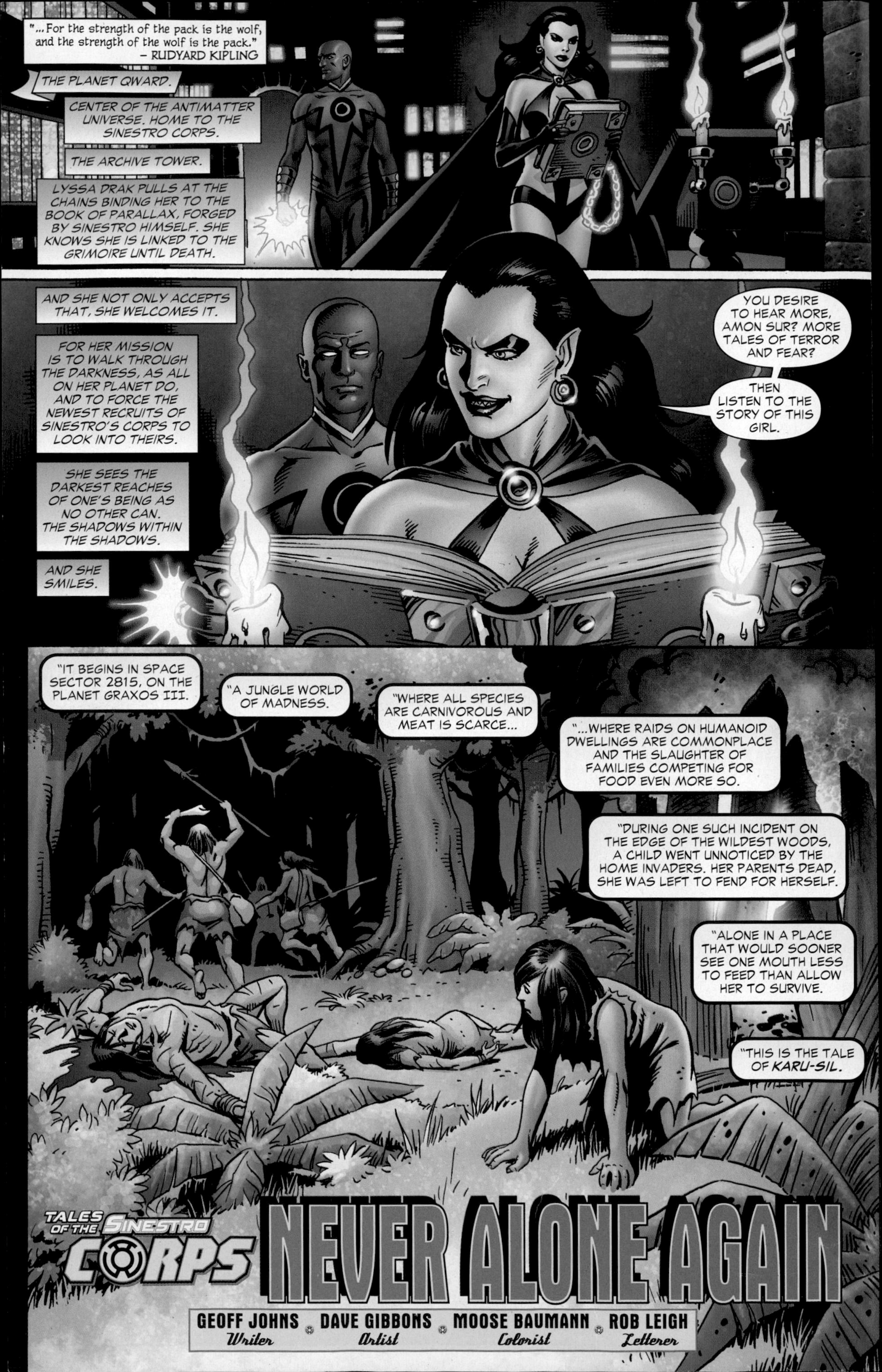
"...For the strength of the pack is the wolf, and the strength of the wolf is the pack."
– RUDYARD KIPLING
THE PLANET QWARD.
CENTER OF THE ANTIMATTER UNIVERSE. HOME TO THE SINESTRO CORPS.
THE ARCHIVE TOWER.
LYSSA DRAK PULLS AT THE CHAINS BINDING HER TO THE BOOK OF PARALLAX, FORGED BY SINESTRO HIMSELF. SHE KNOWS SHE IS LINKED TO THE GRIMOIRE UNTIL DEATH.
AND SHE NOT ONLY ACCEPTS THAT, SHE WELCOMES IT.
FOR HER MISSION IS TO WALK THROUGH THE DARKNESS, AS ALL ON HER PLANET DO, AND TO FORCE THE NEWEST RECRUITS OF SINESTRO'S CORPS TO LOOK INTO THEIRS.
SHE SEES THE DARKEST REACHES OF ONE'S BEING AS NO OTHER CAN. THE SHADOWS WITHIN THE SHADOWS.
AND SHE SMILES.
YOU DESIRE TO HEAR MORE, AMON SUR? MORE TALES OF TERROR AND FEAR?
THEN LISTEN TO THE STORY OF THIS GIRL.
"IT BEGINS IN SPACE SECTOR 2815, ON THE PLANET GRAXOS III.
"A JUNGLE WORLD OF MADNESS.
"WHERE ALL SPECIES ARE CARNIVOROUS AND MEAT IS SCARCE...
"...WHERE RAIDS ON HUMANOID DWELLINGS ARE COMMONPLACE AND THE SLAUGHTER OF FAMILIES COMPETING FOR FOOD EVEN MORE SO.
"DURING ONE SUCH INCIDENT ON THE EDGE OF THE WILDEST WOODS, A CHILD WENT UNNOTICED BY THE HOME INVADERS. HER PARENTS DEAD, SHE WAS LEFT TO FEND FOR HERSELF.
"ALONE IN A PLACE THAT WOULD SOONER SEE ONE MOUTH LESS TO FEED THAN ALLOW HER TO SURVIVE.
"THIS IS THE TALE OF KARU-SIL.
TALES OF THE SINESTRO CORPS
NEVER ALONE AGAIN
GEOFF JOHNS Writer
DAVE GIBBONS Artist
MOOSE BAUMANN Colorist
ROB LEIGH Letterer

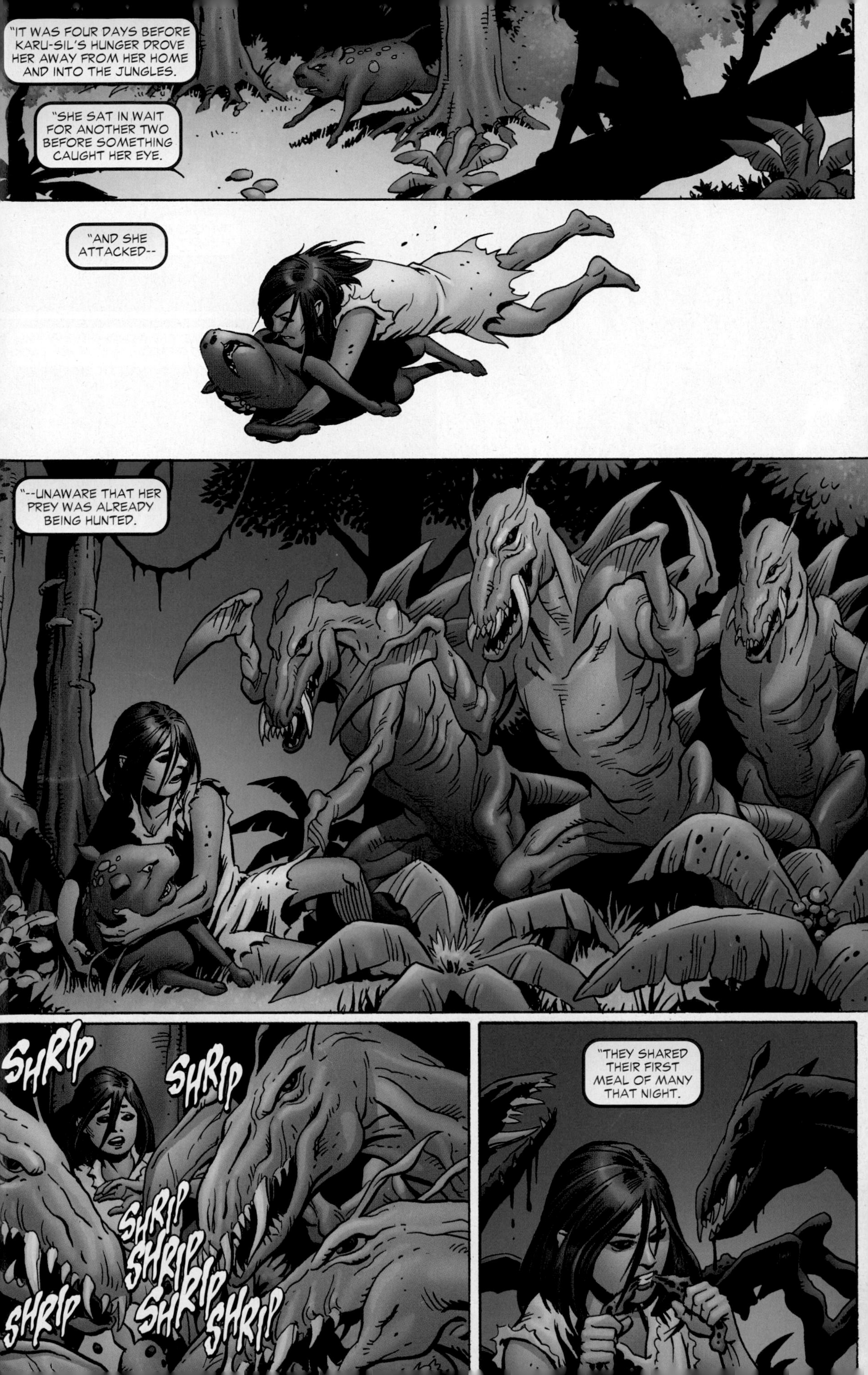
"IT WAS FOUR DAYS BEFORE KARU-SIL'S HUNGER DROVE HER AWAY FROM HER HOME AND INTO THE JUNGLES.
"SHE SAT IN WAIT FOR ANOTHER TWO BEFORE SOMETHING CAUGHT HER EYE.
"AND SHE ATTACKED--
"--UNAWARE THAT HER PREY WAS ALREADY BEING HUNTED.
SHRIP
SHRIP
SHRIP
SHRIP
SHRIP
SHRIP
SHRIP
SHRIP
"THEY SHARED THEIR FIRST MEAL OF MANY THAT NIGHT.

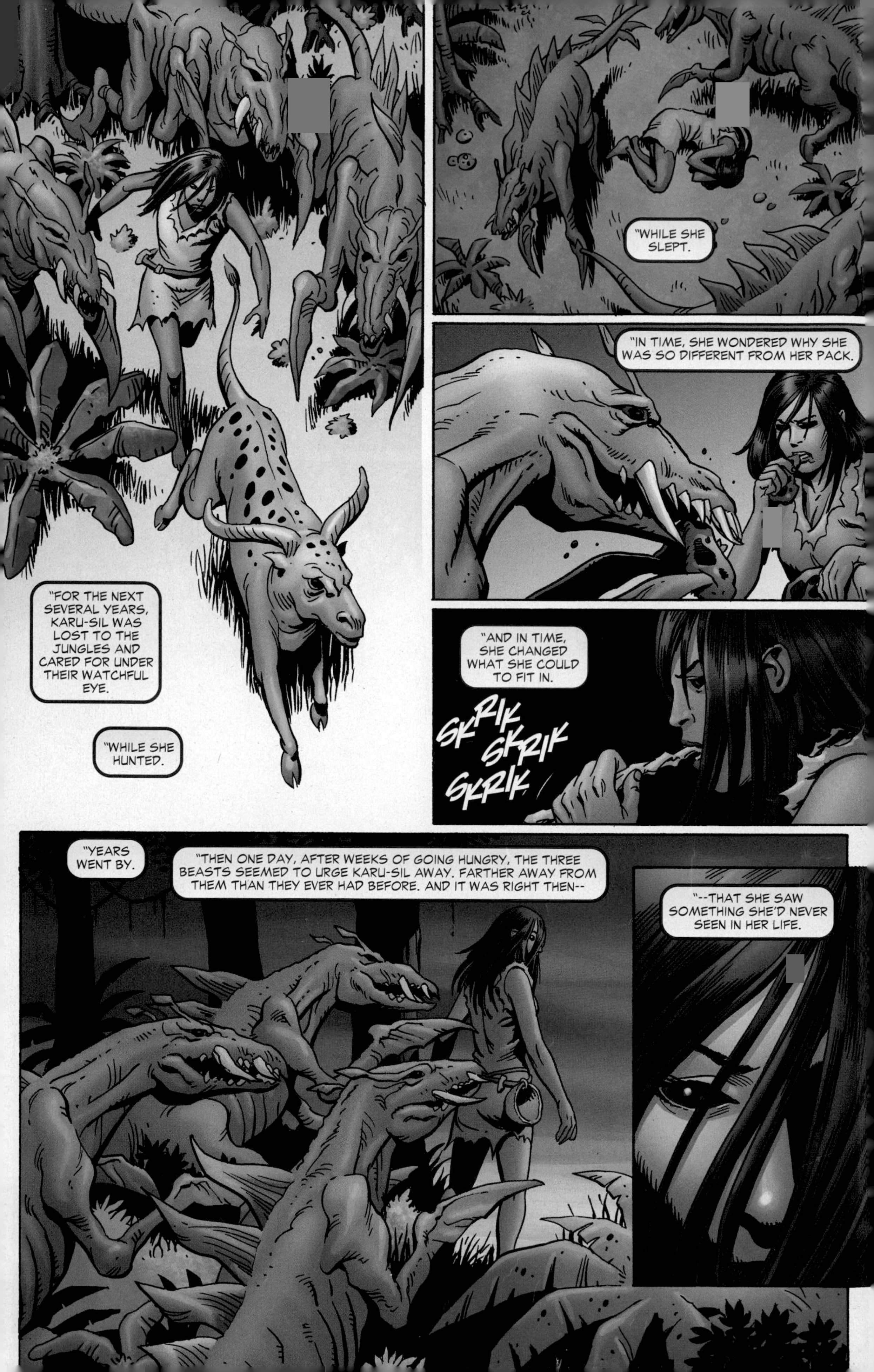
"FOR THE NEXT SEVERAL YEARS, KARU-SIL WAS LOST TO THE JUNGLES AND CARED FOR UNDER THEIR WATCHFUL EYE.
"WHILE SHE HUNTED.
"WHILE SHE SLEPT.
"IN TIME, SHE WONDERED WHY SHE WAS SO DIFFERENT FROM HER PACK.
"AND IN TIME, SHE CHANGED WHAT SHE COULD TO FIT IN.
SKRIK SKRIK SKRIK
"YEARS WENT BY.
"THEN ONE DAY, AFTER WEEKS OF GOING HUNGRY, THE THREE BEASTS SEEMED TO URGE KARU-SIL AWAY. FARTHER AWAY FROM THEM THAN THEY EVER HAD BEFORE. AND IT WAS RIGHT THEN--
"--THAT SHE SAW SOMETHING SHE'D NEVER SEEN IN HER LIFE.

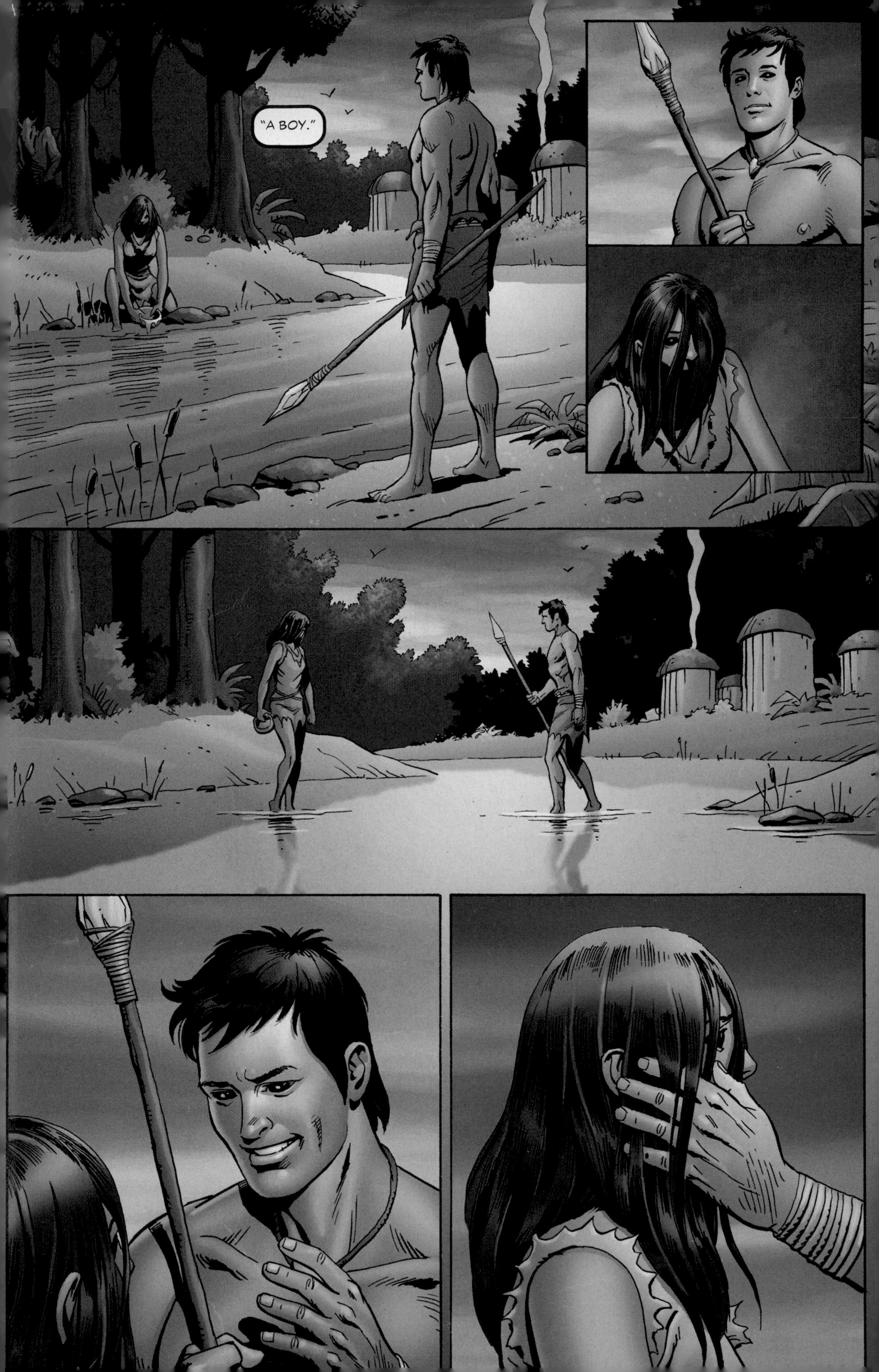
"A BOY."

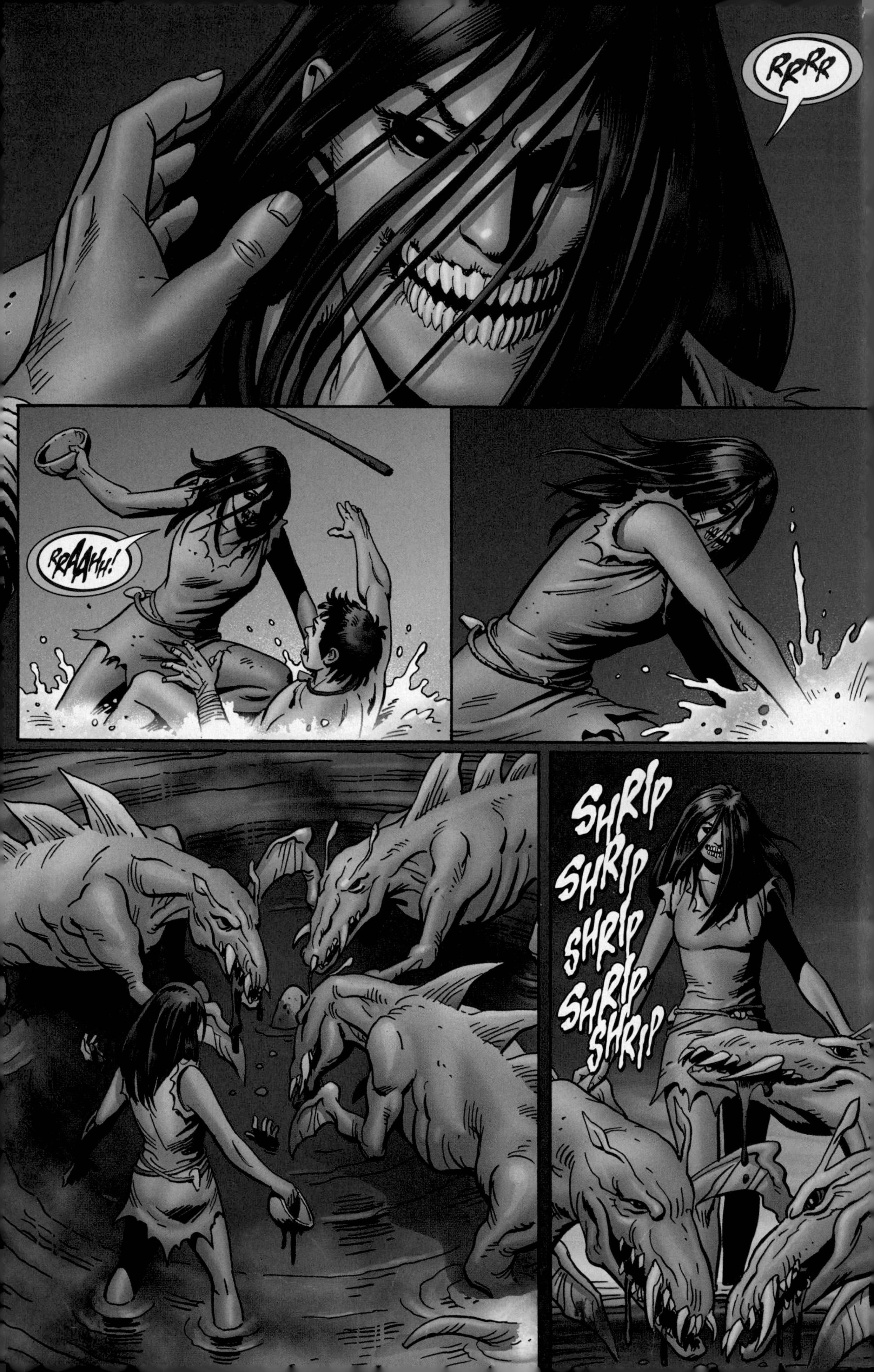
RRRR
RRAAHH!
SHRIP
SHRIP
SHRIP
SHRIP
SHRIP

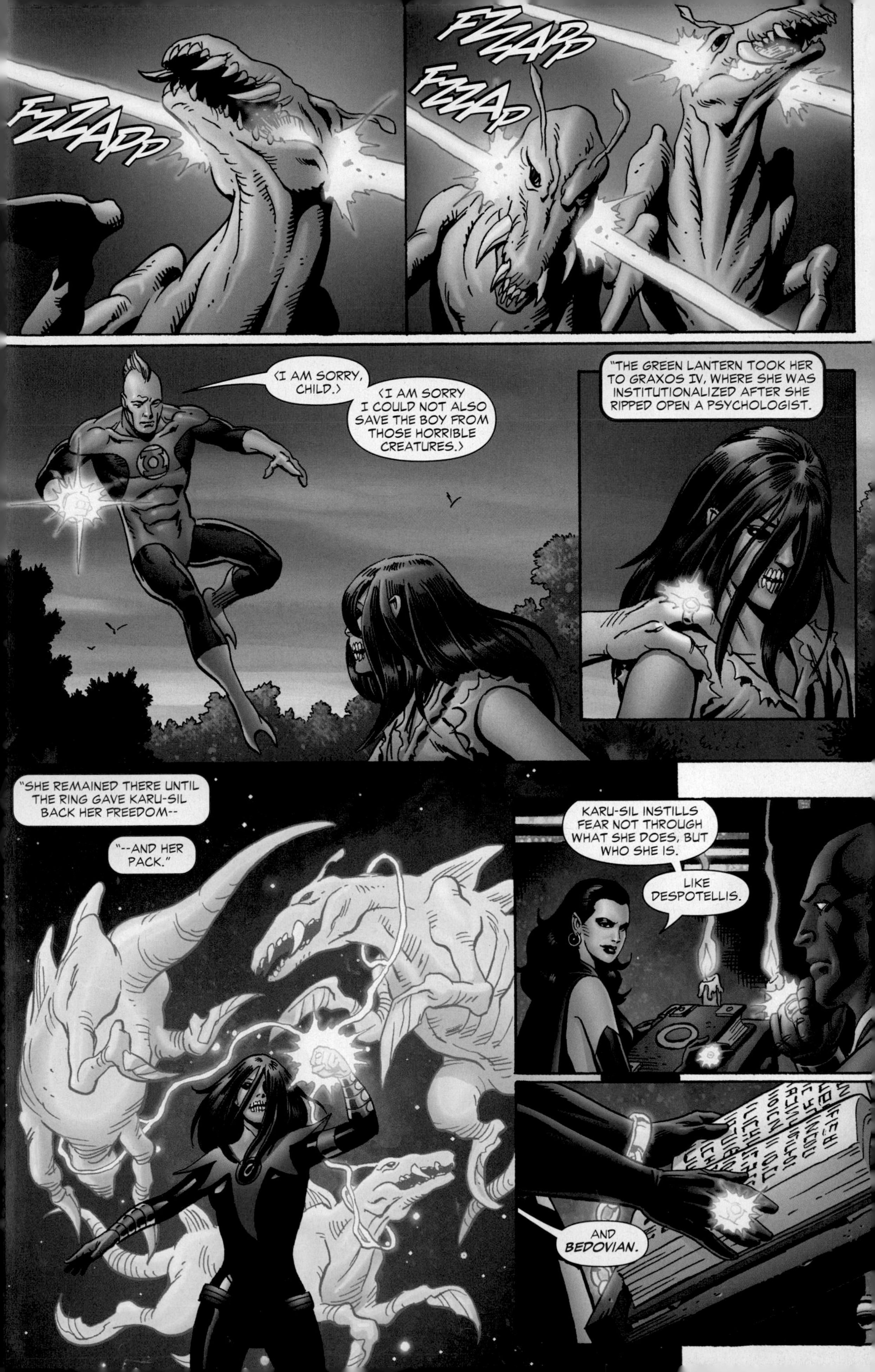
FZZAPP
FZZAPP
FZZAP
⟨I AM SORRY, CHILD.⟩
⟨I AM SORRY I COULD NOT ALSO SAVE THE BOY FROM THOSE HORRIBLE CREATURES.⟩
"THE GREEN LANTERN TOOK HER TO GRAXOS IV, WHERE SHE WAS INSTITUTIONALIZED AFTER SHE RIPPED OPEN A PSYCHOLOGIST.
"SHE REMAINED THERE UNTIL THE RING GAVE KARU-SIL BACK HER FREEDOM--
"--AND HER PACK."
KARU-SIL INSTILLS FEAR NOT THROUGH WHAT SHE DOES, BUT WHO SHE IS.
LIKE DESPOTELLIS.
AND *BEDOVIAN.*

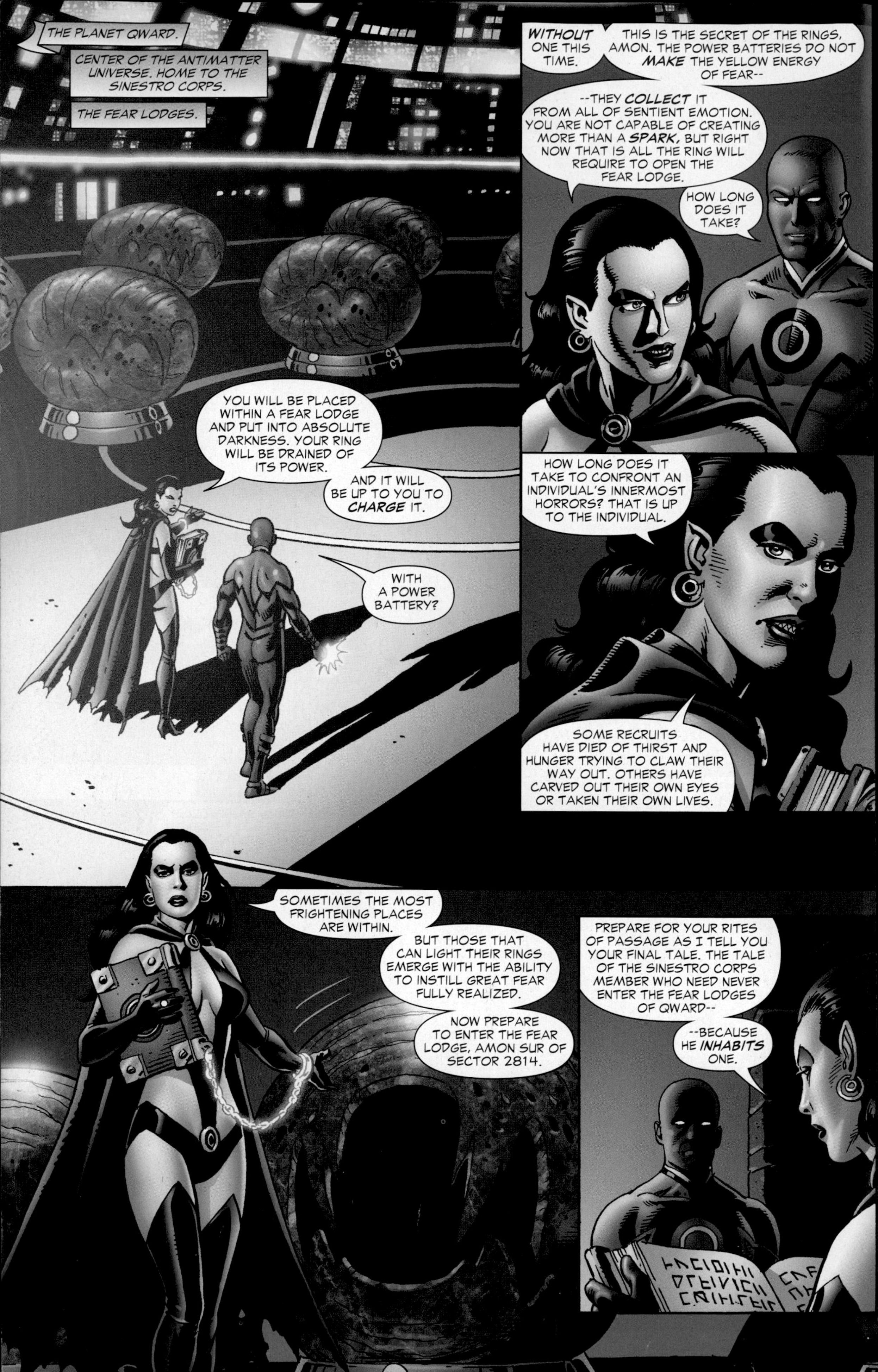
THE PLANET QWARD.
CENTER OF THE ANTIMATTER UNIVERSE. HOME TO THE SINESTRO CORPS.
THE FEAR LODGES.
YOU WILL BE PLACED WITHIN A FEAR LODGE AND PUT INTO ABSOLUTE DARKNESS. YOUR RING WILL BE DRAINED OF ITS POWER.
AND IT WILL BE UP TO YOU TO CHARGE IT.
WITH A POWER BATTERY?
WITHOUT ONE THIS TIME.
THIS IS THE SECRET OF THE RINGS, AMON. THE POWER BATTERIES DO NOT MAKE THE YELLOW ENERGY OF FEAR--
--THEY COLLECT IT FROM ALL OF SENTIENT EMOTION. YOU ARE NOT CAPABLE OF CREATING MORE THAN A SPARK, BUT RIGHT NOW THAT IS ALL THE RING WILL REQUIRE TO OPEN THE FEAR LODGE.
HOW LONG DOES IT TAKE?
HOW LONG DOES IT TAKE TO CONFRONT AN INDIVIDUAL'S INNERMOST HORRORS? THAT IS UP TO THE INDIVIDUAL.
SOME RECRUITS HAVE DIED OF THIRST AND HUNGER TRYING TO CLAW THEIR WAY OUT. OTHERS HAVE CARVED OUT THEIR OWN EYES OR TAKEN THEIR OWN LIVES.
SOMETIMES THE MOST FRIGHTENING PLACES ARE WITHIN.
BUT THOSE THAT CAN LIGHT THEIR RINGS EMERGE WITH THE ABILITY TO INSTILL GREAT FEAR FULLY REALIZED.
NOW PREPARE TO ENTER THE FEAR LODGE, AMON SUR OF SECTOR 2814.
PREPARE FOR YOUR RITES OF PASSAGE AS I TELL YOU YOUR FINAL TALE. THE TALE OF THE SINESTRO CORPS MEMBER WHO NEED NEVER ENTER THE FEAR LODGES OF QWARD--
--BECAUSE HE INHABITS ONE.

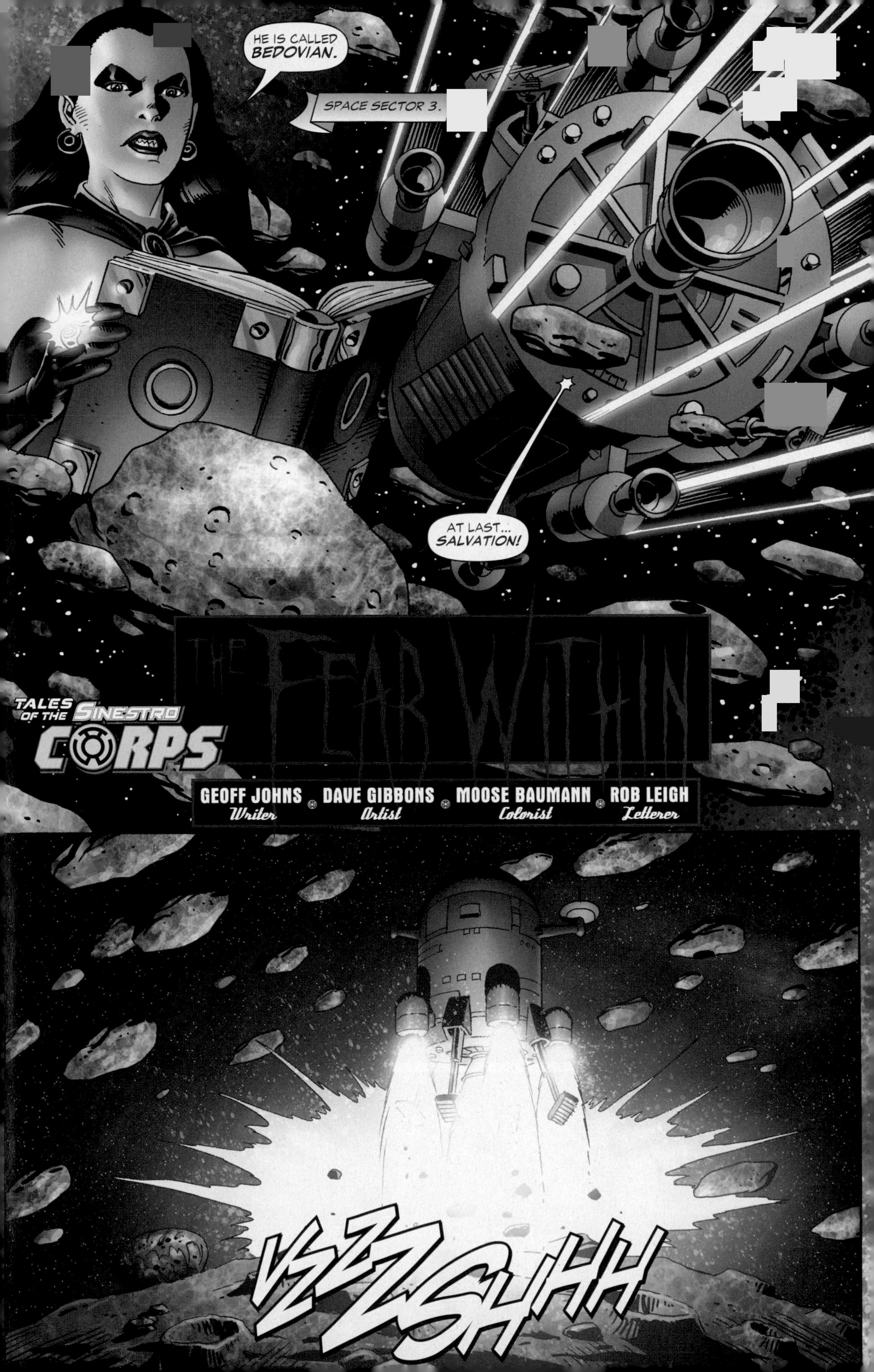
HE IS CALLED BEDOVIAN.
SPACE SECTOR 3.
AT LAST... SALVATION!
TALES OF THE SINESTRO CORPS
THE FEAR WITHIN
GEOFF JOHNS Writer
DAVE GIBBONS Artist
MOOSE BAUMANN Colorist
ROB LEIGH Letterer
VZZSHHH

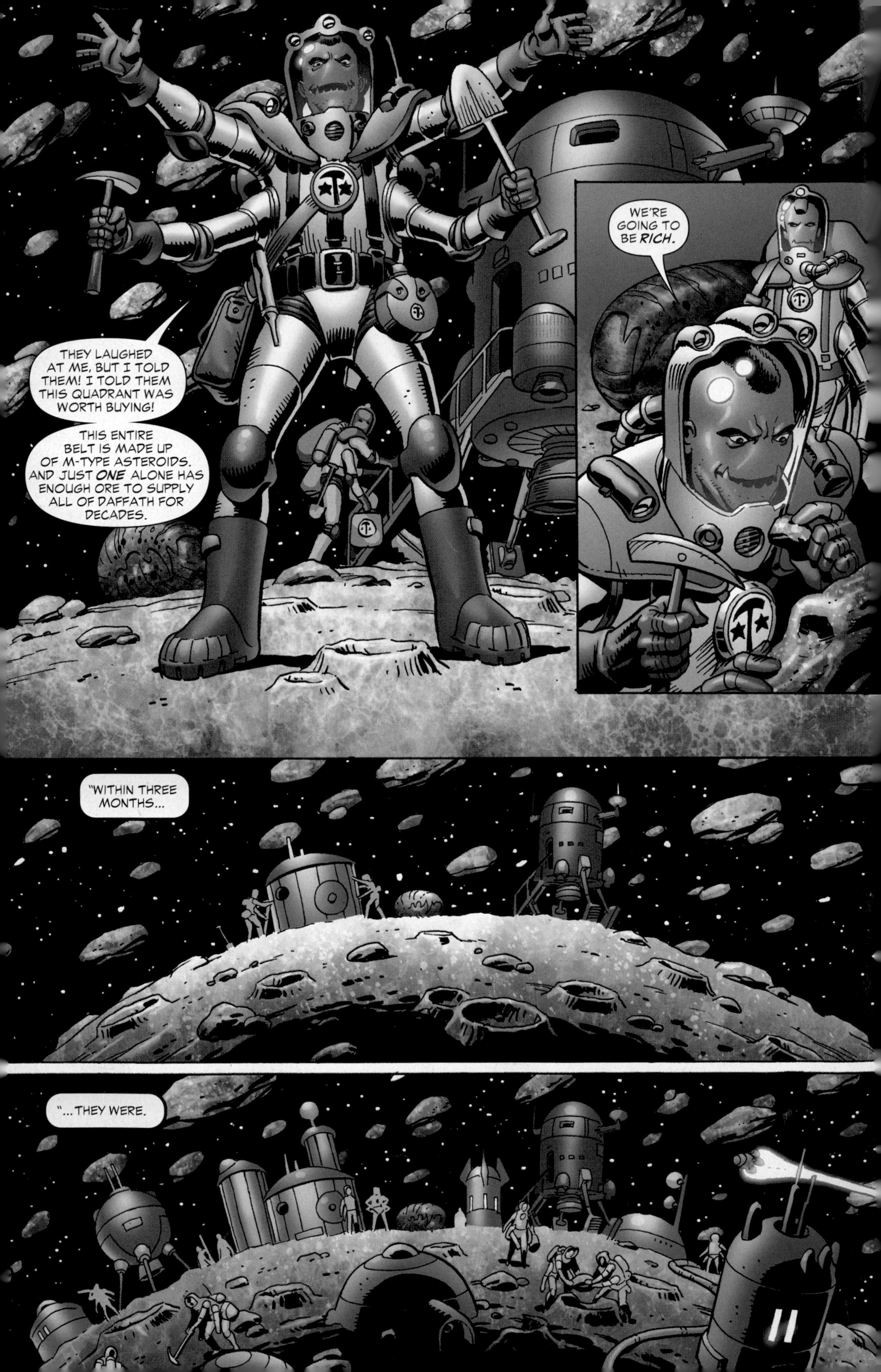
THEY LAUGHED AT ME, BUT I TOLD THEM! I TOLD THEM THIS QUADRANT WAS WORTH BUYING!
THIS ENTIRE BELT IS MADE UP OF M-TYPE ASTEROIDS. AND JUST ONE ALONE HAS ENOUGH ORE TO SUPPLY ALL OF DAFFATH FOR DECADES.
WE'RE GOING TO BE RICH.
"WITHIN THREE MONTHS...
"...THEY WERE.

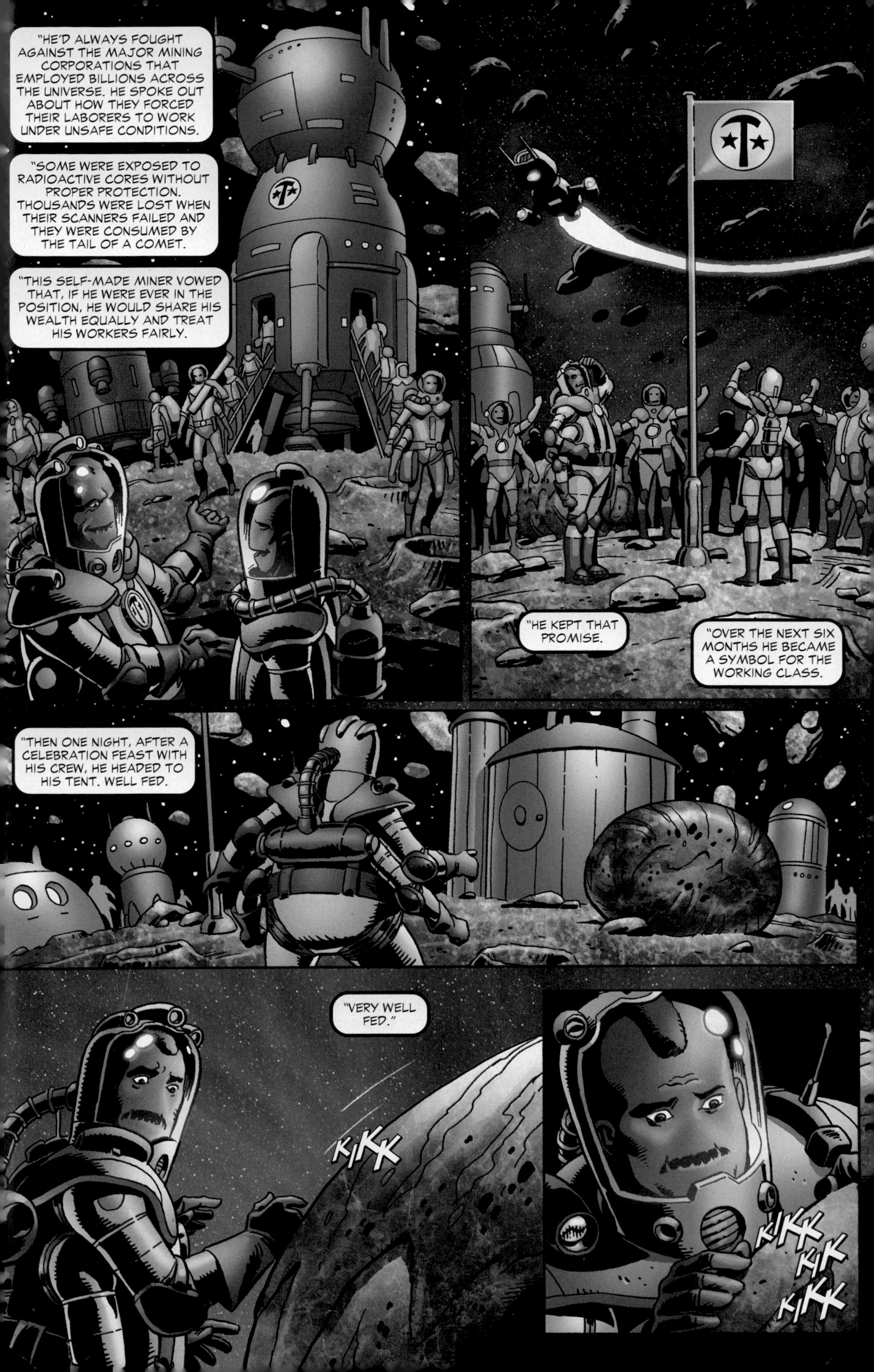
"HE'D ALWAYS FOUGHT AGAINST THE MAJOR MINING CORPORATIONS THAT EMPLOYED BILLIONS ACROSS THE UNIVERSE. HE SPOKE OUT ABOUT HOW THEY FORCED THEIR LABORERS TO WORK UNDER UNSAFE CONDITIONS.
"SOME WERE EXPOSED TO RADIOACTIVE CORES WITHOUT PROPER PROTECTION. THOUSANDS WERE LOST WHEN THEIR SCANNERS FAILED AND THEY WERE CONSUMED BY THE TAIL OF A COMET.
"THIS SELF-MADE MINER VOWED THAT, IF HE WERE EVER IN THE POSITION, HE WOULD SHARE HIS WEALTH EQUALLY AND TREAT HIS WORKERS FAIRLY.
"HE KEPT THAT PROMISE.
"OVER THE NEXT SIX MONTHS HE BECAME A SYMBOL FOR THE WORKING CLASS.
"THEN ONE NIGHT, AFTER A CELEBRATION FEAST WITH HIS CREW, HE HEADED TO HIS TENT. WELL FED.
"VERY WELL FED."
KIKK
KIKK
KIK
KIKK

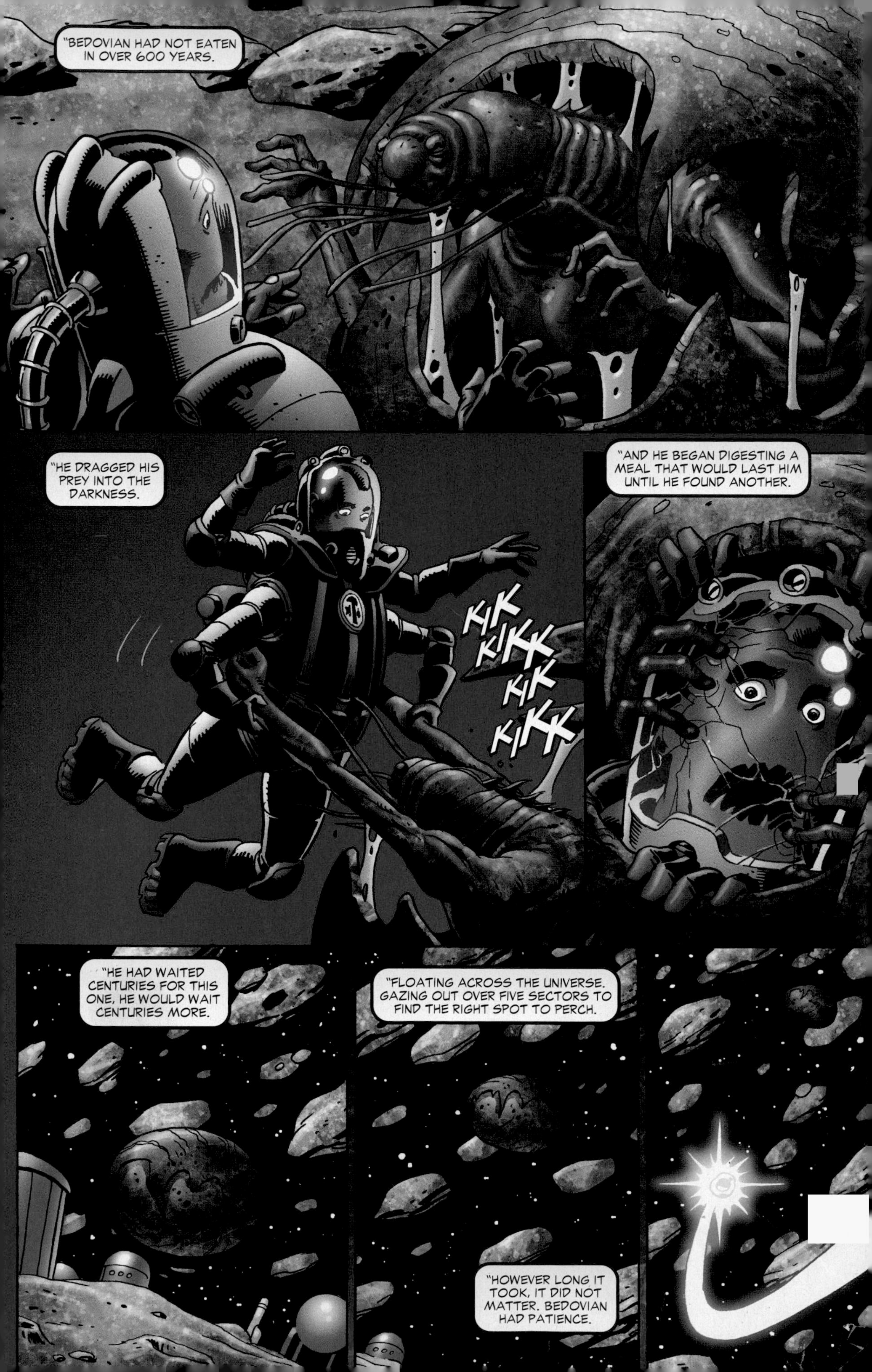
"BEDOVIAN HAD NOT EATEN IN OVER 600 YEARS.
"HE DRAGGED HIS PREY INTO THE DARKNESS.
KIK KIKK KIK KIKK
"AND HE BEGAN DIGESTING A MEAL THAT WOULD LAST HIM UNTIL HE FOUND ANOTHER.
"HE HAD WAITED CENTURIES FOR THIS ONE, HE WOULD WAIT CENTURIES MORE.
"FLOATING ACROSS THE UNIVERSE. GAZING OUT OVER FIVE SECTORS TO FIND THE RIGHT SPOT TO PERCH.
"HOWEVER LONG IT TOOK, IT DID NOT MATTER. BEDOVIAN HAD PATIENCE.

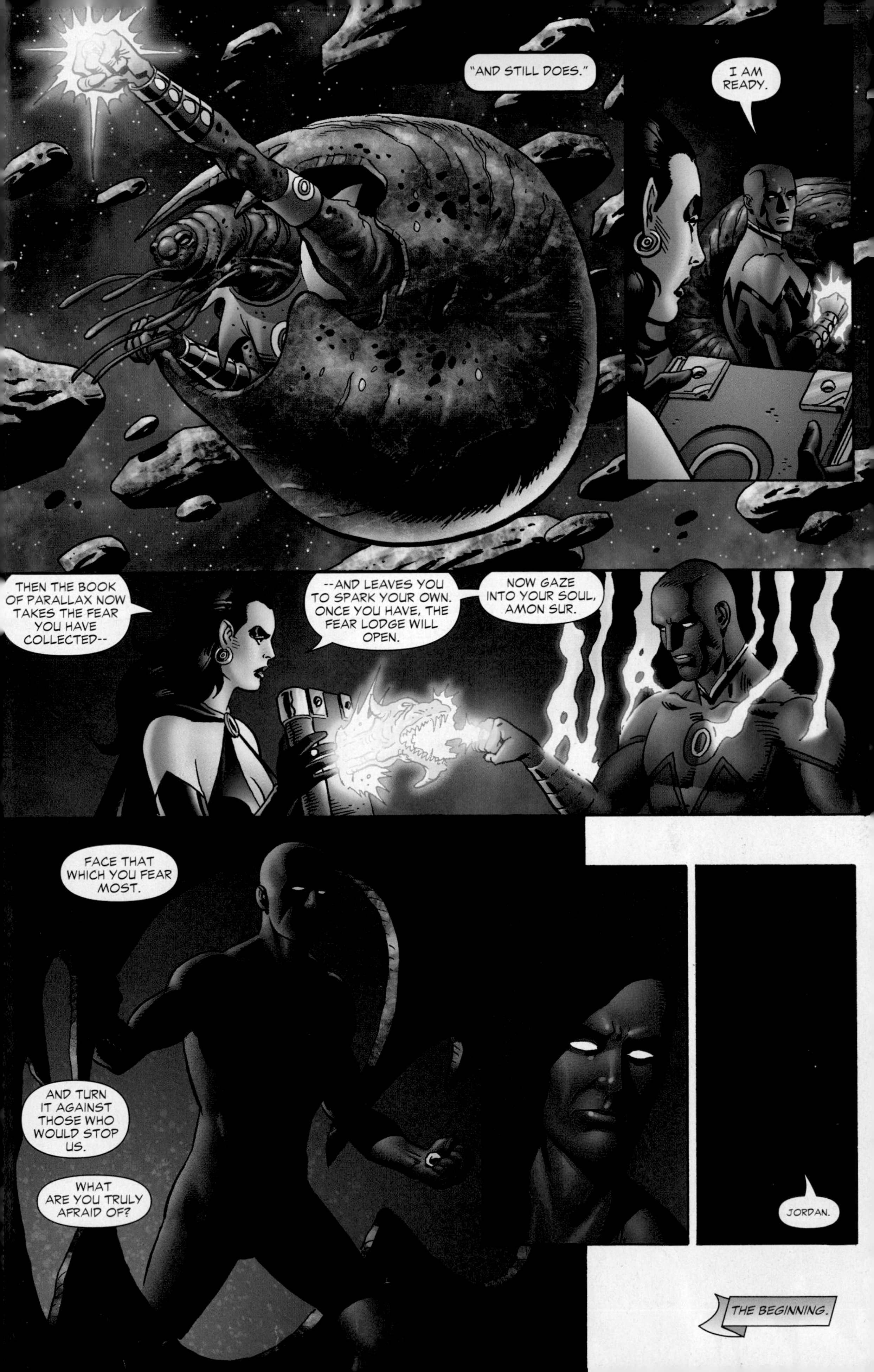
"AND STILL DOES."
I AM READY.
THEN THE BOOK OF PARALLAX NOW TAKES THE FEAR YOU HAVE COLLECTED--
--AND LEAVES YOU TO SPARK YOUR OWN. ONCE YOU HAVE, THE FEAR LODGE WILL OPEN.
NOW GAZE INTO YOUR SOUL, AMON SUR.
FACE THAT WHICH YOU FEAR MOST.
AND TURN IT AGAINST THOSE WHO WOULD STOP US.
WHAT ARE YOU TRULY AFRAID OF?
JORDAN.
THE BEGINNING.

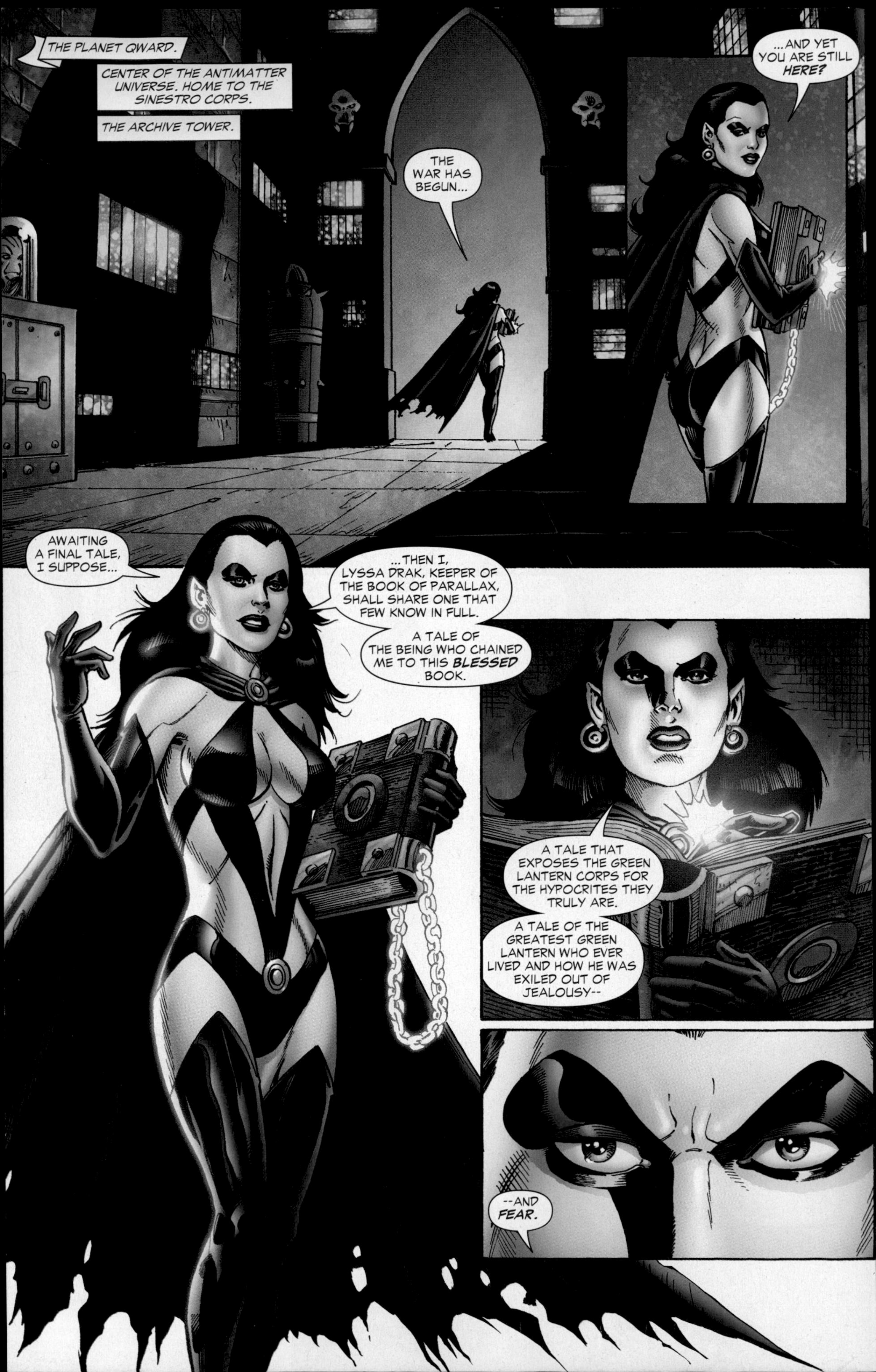
THE PLANET QWARD.
CENTER OF THE ANTIMATTER UNIVERSE. HOME TO THE SINESTRO CORPS.
THE ARCHIVE TOWER.
THE WAR HAS BEGUN...
...AND YET YOU ARE STILL HERE?
AWAITING A FINAL TALE, I SUPPOSE...
...THEN I, LYSSA DRAK, KEEPER OF THE BOOK OF PARALLAX, SHALL SHARE ONE THAT FEW KNOW IN FULL.
A TALE OF THE BEING WHO CHAINED ME TO THIS BLESSED BOOK.
A TALE THAT EXPOSES THE GREEN LANTERN CORPS FOR THE HYPOCRITES THEY TRULY ARE.
A TALE OF THE GREATEST GREEN LANTERN WHO EVER LIVED AND HOW HE WAS EXILED OUT OF JEALOUSY--
--AND FEAR.

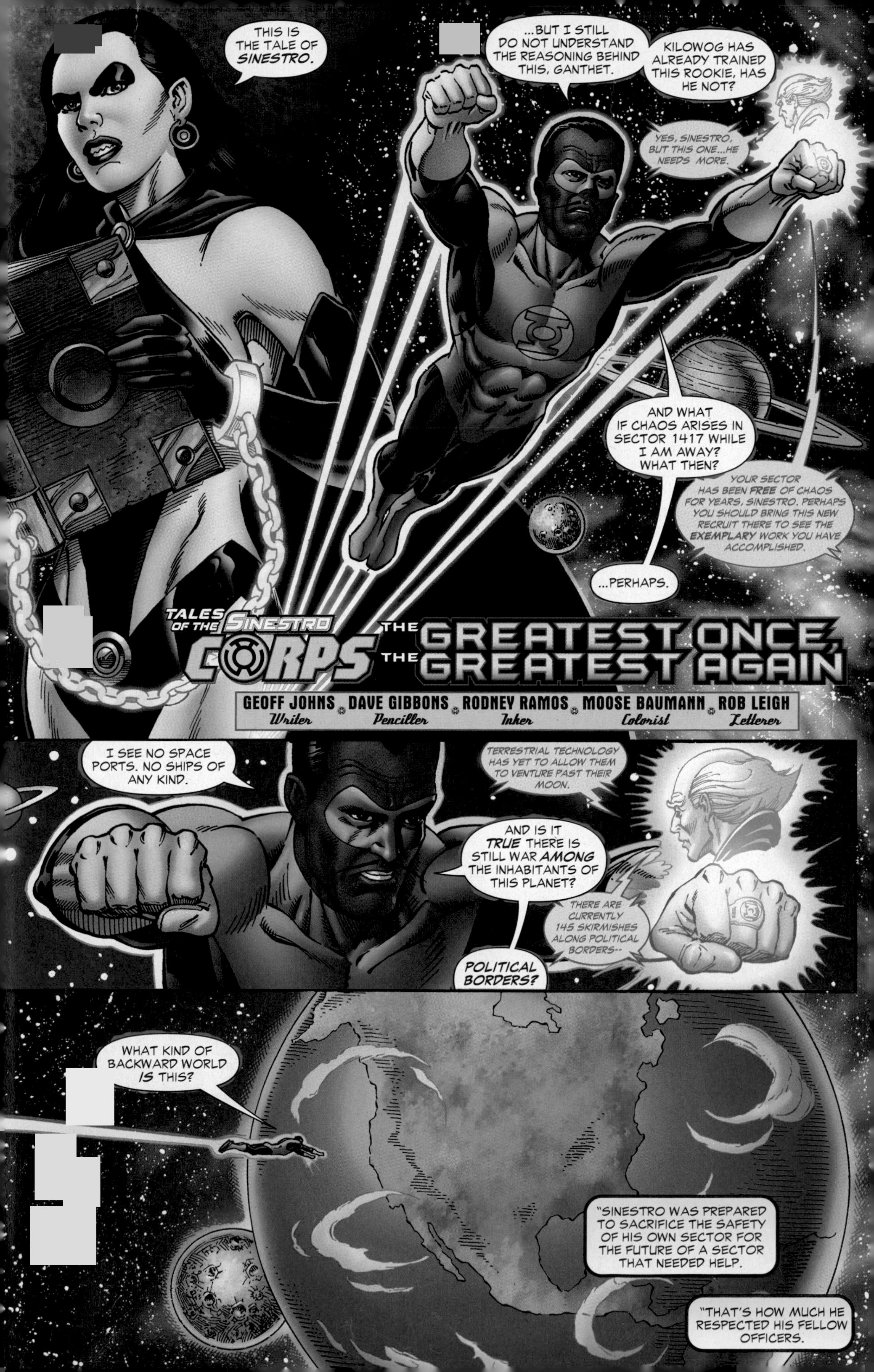
THIS IS THE TALE OF SINESTRO.
...BUT I STILL DO NOT UNDERSTAND THE REASONING BEHIND THIS, GANTHET.
KILOWOG HAS ALREADY TRAINED THIS ROOKIE, HAS HE NOT?
YES, SINESTRO, BUT THIS ONE...HE NEEDS MORE.
AND WHAT IF CHAOS ARISES IN SECTOR 1417 WHILE I AM AWAY? WHAT THEN?
YOUR SECTOR HAS BEEN FREE OF CHAOS FOR YEARS, SINESTRO. PERHAPS YOU SHOULD BRING THIS NEW RECRUIT THERE TO SEE THE EXEMPLARY WORK YOU HAVE ACCOMPLISHED.
...PERHAPS.
TALES OF THE SINESTRO CORPS
THE GREATEST ONCE, THE GREATEST AGAIN
GEOFF JOHNS Writer
DAVE GIBBONS Penciller
RODNEY RAMOS Inker
MOOSE BAUMANN Colorist
ROB LEIGH Letterer
I SEE NO SPACE PORTS. NO SHIPS OF ANY KIND.
TERRESTRIAL TECHNOLOGY HAS YET TO ALLOW THEM TO VENTURE PAST THEIR MOON.
AND IS IT TRUE THERE IS STILL WAR AMONG THE INHABITANTS OF THIS PLANET?
THERE ARE CURRENTLY 145 SKIRMISHES ALONG POLITICAL BORDERS--
POLITICAL BORDERS?
WHAT KIND OF BACKWARD WORLD IS THIS?
"SINESTRO WAS PREPARED TO SACRIFICE THE SAFETY OF HIS OWN SECTOR FOR THE FUTURE OF A SECTOR THAT NEEDED HELP.
"THAT'S HOW MUCH HE RESPECTED HIS FELLOW OFFICERS.

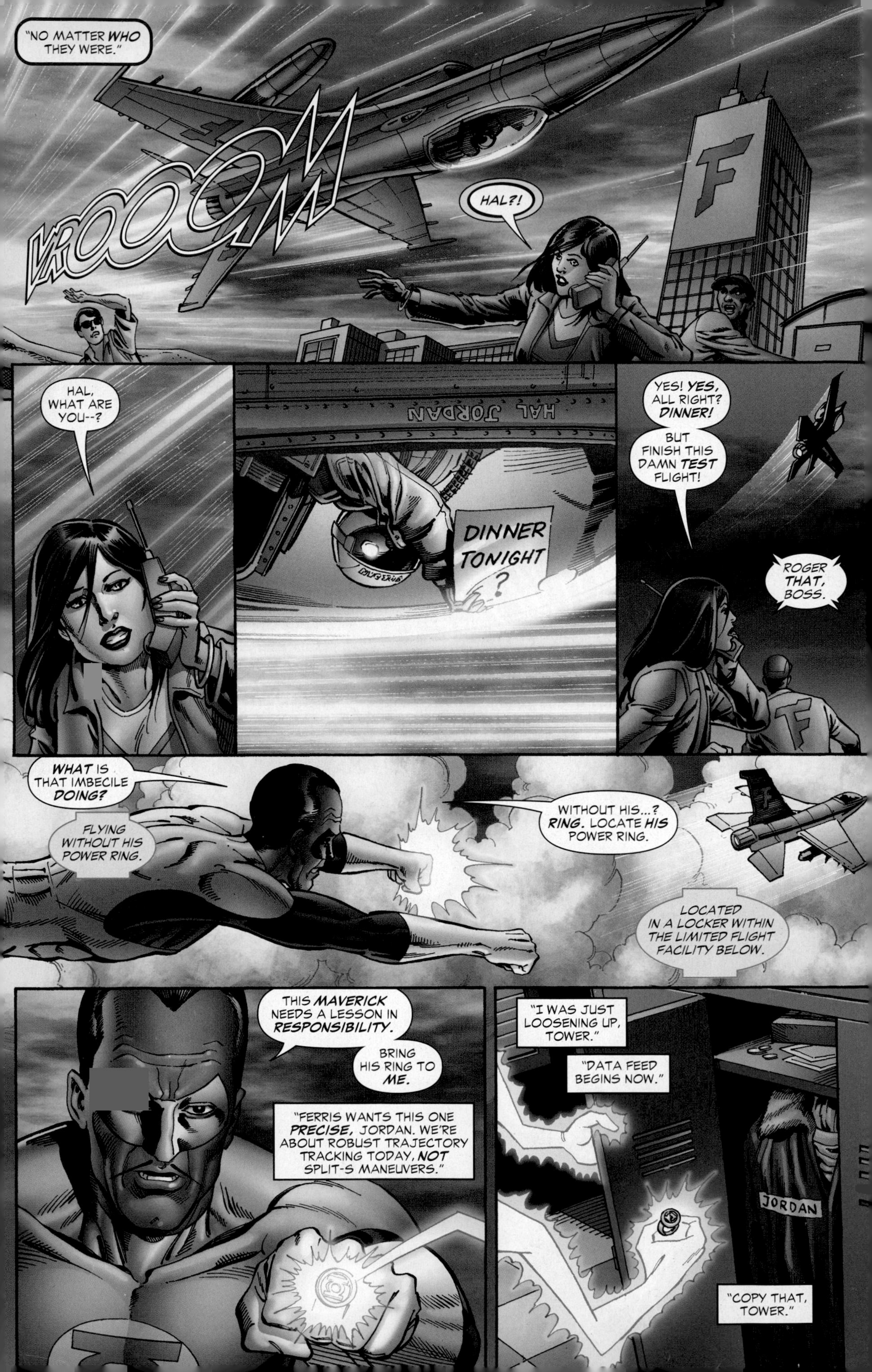
"NO MATTER WHO THEY WERE."
VROOOOM
HAL?!
HAL, WHAT ARE YOU--?
HAL JORDAN
DINNER TONIGHT ?
YES! YES, ALL RIGHT? DINNER!
BUT FINISH THIS DAMN TEST FLIGHT!
ROGER THAT, BOSS.
WHAT IS THAT IMBECILE DOING?
FLYING WITHOUT HIS POWER RING.
WITHOUT HIS...? RING. LOCATE HIS POWER RING.
LOCATED IN A LOCKER WITHIN THE LIMITED FLIGHT FACILITY BELOW.
THIS MAVERICK NEEDS A LESSON IN RESPONSIBILITY.
BRING HIS RING TO ME.
"FERRIS WANTS THIS ONE PRECISE, JORDAN. WE'RE ABOUT ROBUST TRAJECTORY TRACKING TODAY, NOT SPLIT-S MANEUVERS."
"I WAS JUST LOOSENING UP, TOWER."
"DATA FEED BEGINS NOW."
JORDAN
"COPY THAT, TOWER."

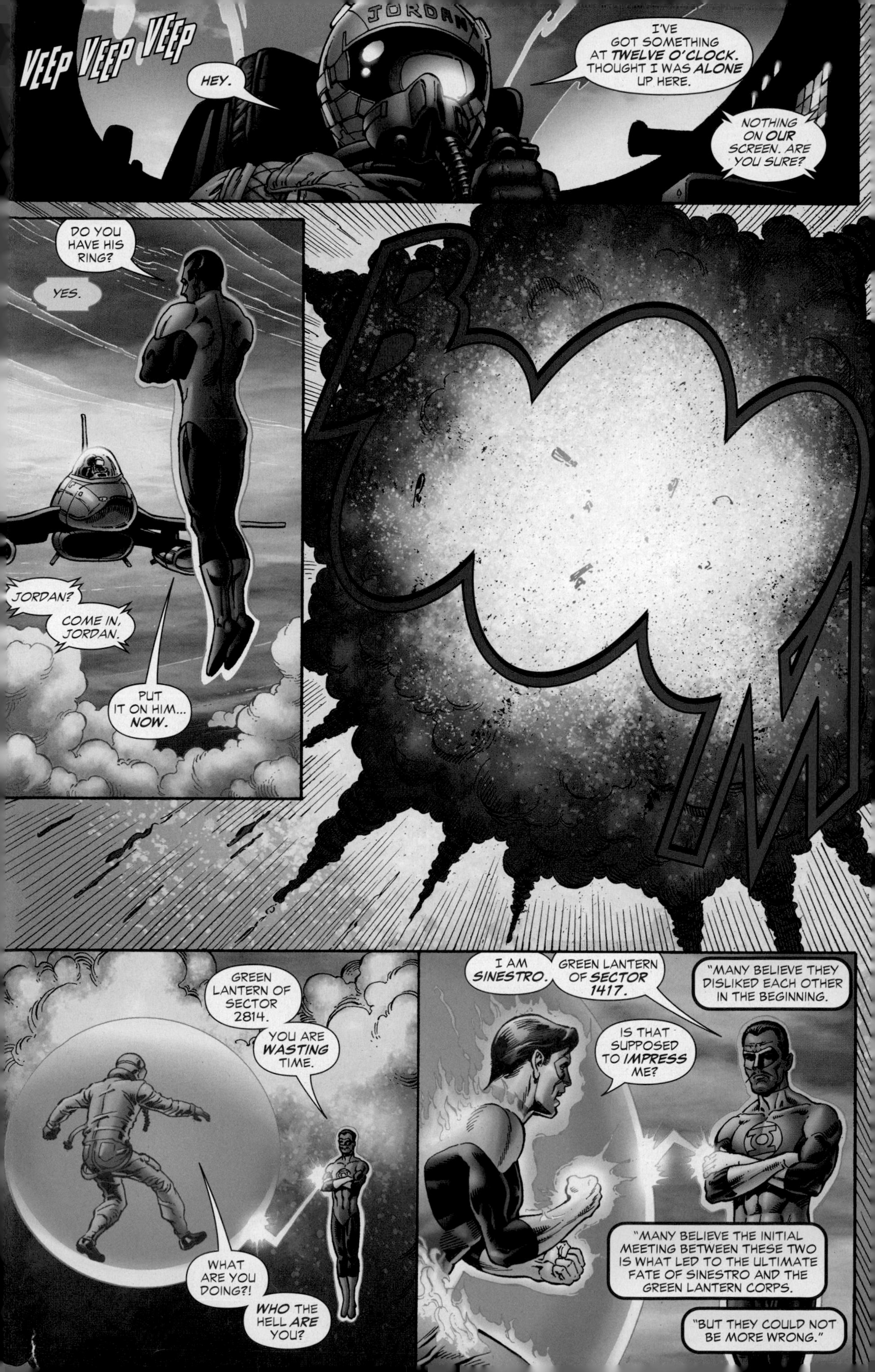

VEEP VEEP VEEP
HEY.
I'VE GOT SOMETHING AT TWELVE O'CLOCK. THOUGHT I WAS ALONE UP HERE.
NOTHING ON OUR SCREEN. ARE YOU SURE?
DO YOU HAVE HIS RING?
YES.
JORDAN?
COME IN, JORDAN.
PUT IT ON HIM... NOW.
BOOM
GREEN LANTERN OF SECTOR 2814.
YOU ARE WASTING TIME.
WHAT ARE YOU DOING?!
WHO THE HELL ARE YOU?
I AM SINESTRO.
GREEN LANTERN OF SECTOR 1417.
IS THAT SUPPOSED TO IMPRESS ME?
"MANY BELIEVE THEY DISLIKED EACH OTHER IN THE BEGINNING.
"MANY BELIEVE THE INITIAL MEETING BETWEEN THESE TWO IS WHAT LED TO THE ULTIMATE FATE OF SINESTRO AND THE GREEN LANTERN CORPS.
"BUT THEY COULD NOT BE MORE WRONG."

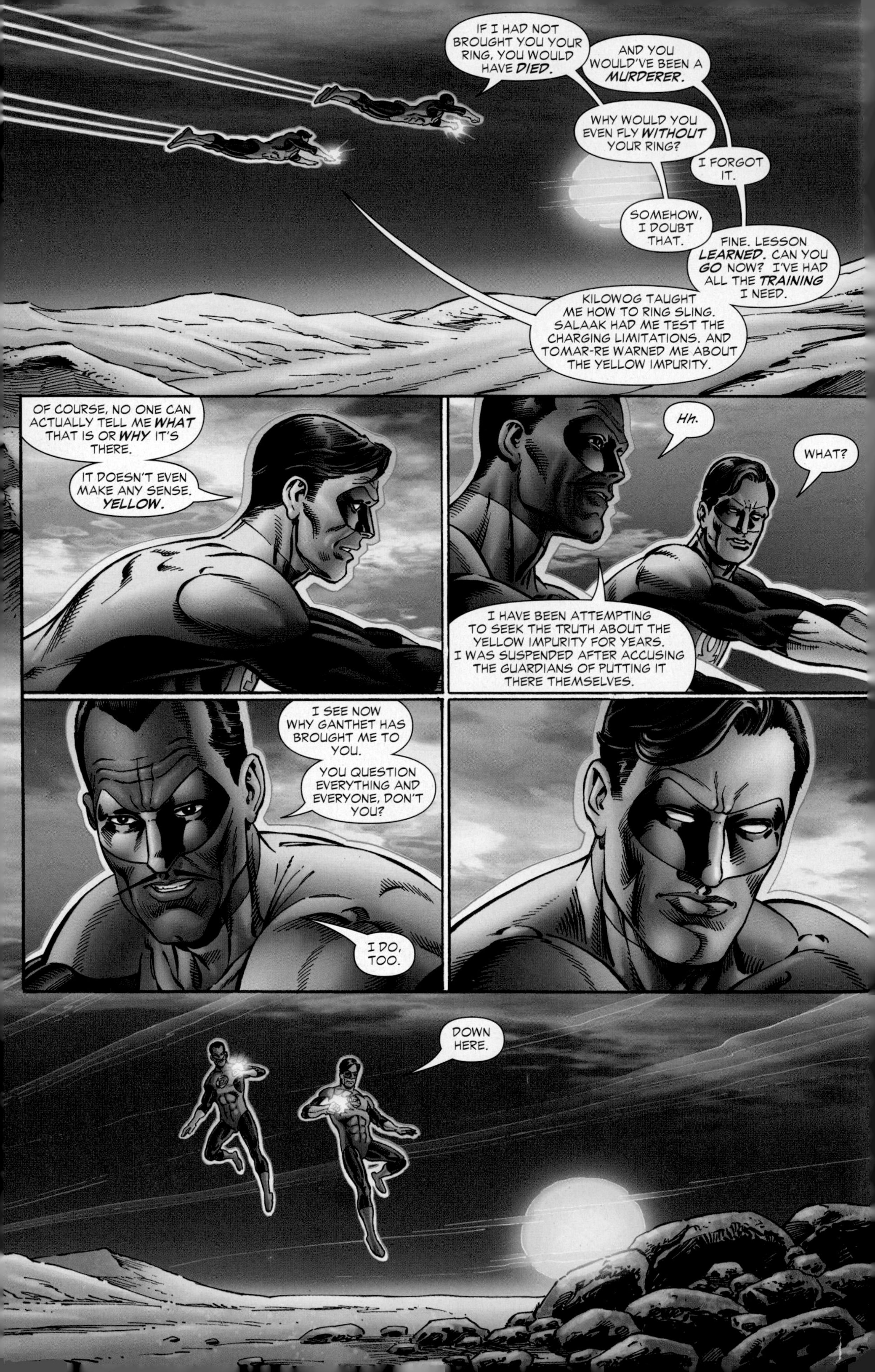
IF I HAD NOT BROUGHT YOU YOUR RING, YOU WOULD HAVE DIED.
AND YOU WOULD'VE BEEN A MURDERER.
WHY WOULD YOU EVEN FLY WITHOUT YOUR RING?
I FORGOT IT.
SOMEHOW, I DOUBT THAT.
FINE. LESSON LEARNED. CAN YOU GO NOW? I'VE HAD ALL THE TRAINING I NEED.
KILOWOG TAUGHT ME HOW TO RING SLING. SALAAK HAD ME TEST THE CHARGING LIMITATIONS. AND TOMAR-RE WARNED ME ABOUT THE YELLOW IMPURITY.
OF COURSE, NO ONE CAN ACTUALLY TELL ME WHAT THAT IS OR WHY IT'S THERE.
IT DOESN'T EVEN MAKE ANY SENSE. YELLOW.
Hh.
WHAT?
I HAVE BEEN ATTEMPTING TO SEEK THE TRUTH ABOUT THE YELLOW IMPURITY FOR YEARS. I WAS SUSPENDED AFTER ACCUSING THE GUARDIANS OF PUTTING IT THERE THEMSELVES.
I SEE NOW WHY GANTHET HAS BROUGHT ME TO YOU.
YOU QUESTION EVERYTHING AND EVERYONE, DON'T YOU?
I DO, TOO.
DOWN HERE.

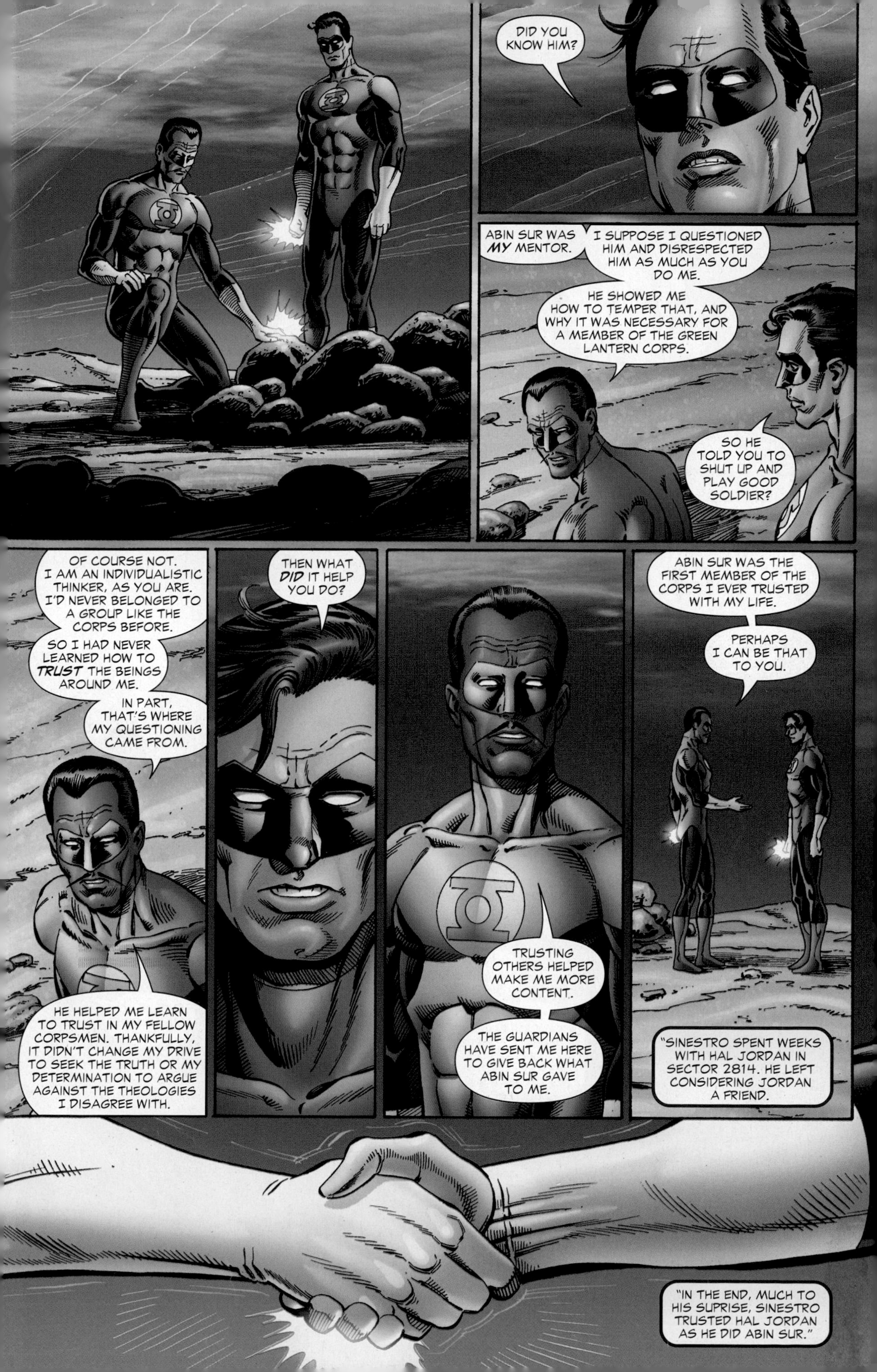
DID YOU KNOW HIM?
ABIN SUR WAS *MY* MENTOR.
I SUPPOSE I QUESTIONED HIM AND DISRESPECTED HIM AS MUCH AS YOU DO ME.
HE SHOWED ME HOW TO TEMPER THAT, AND WHY IT WAS NECESSARY FOR A MEMBER OF THE GREEN LANTERN CORPS.
SO HE TOLD YOU TO SHUT UP AND PLAY GOOD SOLDIER?
OF COURSE NOT. I AM AN INDIVIDUALISTIC THINKER, AS YOU ARE. I'D NEVER BELONGED TO A GROUP LIKE THE CORPS BEFORE.
SO I HAD NEVER LEARNED HOW TO *TRUST* THE BEINGS AROUND ME.
IN PART, THAT'S WHERE MY QUESTIONING CAME FROM.
HE HELPED ME LEARN TO TRUST IN MY FELLOW CORPSMEN. THANKFULLY, IT DIDN'T CHANGE MY DRIVE TO SEEK THE TRUTH OR MY DETERMINATION TO ARGUE AGAINST THE THEOLOGIES I DISAGREE WITH.
THEN WHAT *DID* IT HELP YOU DO?
TRUSTING OTHERS HELPED MAKE ME MORE CONTENT.
THE GUARDIANS HAVE SENT ME HERE TO GIVE BACK WHAT ABIN SUR GAVE TO ME.
ABIN SUR WAS THE FIRST MEMBER OF THE CORPS I EVER TRUSTED WITH MY LIFE.
PERHAPS I CAN BE THAT TO YOU.
"SINESTRO SPENT WEEKS WITH HAL JORDAN IN SECTOR 2814. HE LEFT CONSIDERING JORDAN A FRIEND.
"IN THE END, MUCH TO HIS SUPRISE, SINESTRO TRUSTED HAL JORDAN AS HE DID ABIN SUR."

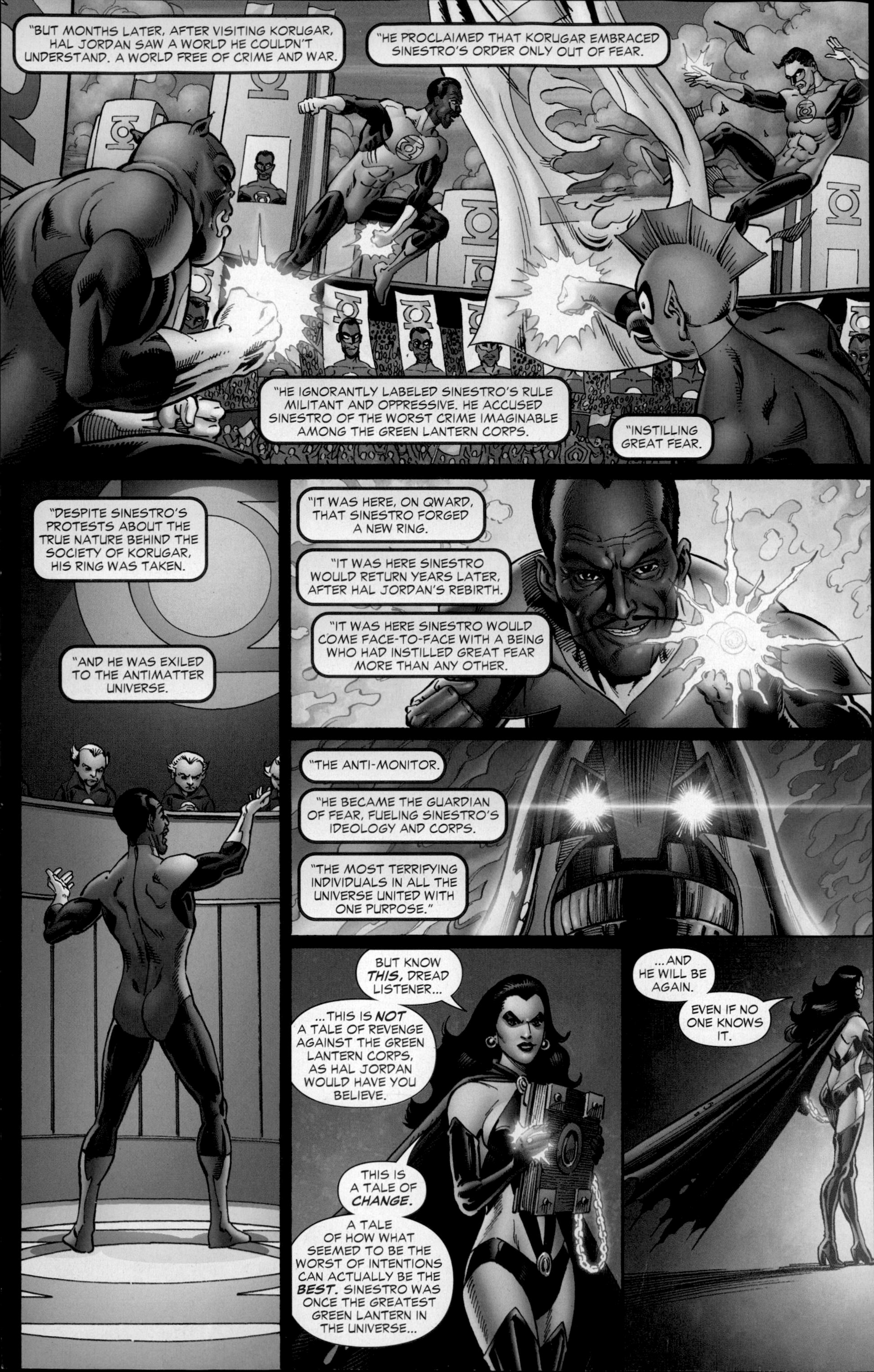

"BUT MONTHS LATER, AFTER VISITING KORUGAR, HAL JORDAN SAW A WORLD HE COULDN'T UNDERSTAND. A WORLD FREE OF CRIME AND WAR.
"HE PROCLAIMED THAT KORUGAR EMBRACED SINESTRO'S ORDER ONLY OUT OF FEAR.
"HE IGNORANTLY LABELED SINESTRO'S RULE MILITANT AND OPPRESSIVE. HE ACCUSED SINESTRO OF THE WORST CRIME IMAGINABLE AMONG THE GREEN LANTERN CORPS.
"INSTILLING GREAT FEAR.
"DESPITE SINESTRO'S PROTESTS ABOUT THE TRUE NATURE BEHIND THE SOCIETY OF KORUGAR, HIS RING WAS TAKEN.
"AND HE WAS EXILED TO THE ANTIMATTER UNIVERSE.
"IT WAS HERE, ON QWARD, THAT SINESTRO FORGED A NEW RING.
"IT WAS HERE SINESTRO WOULD RETURN YEARS LATER, AFTER HAL JORDAN'S REBIRTH.
"IT WAS HERE SINESTRO WOULD COME FACE-TO-FACE WITH A BEING WHO HAD INSTILLED GREAT FEAR MORE THAN ANY OTHER.
"THE ANTI-MONITOR.
"HE BECAME THE GUARDIAN OF FEAR, FUELING SINESTRO'S IDEOLOGY AND CORPS.
"THE MOST TERRIFYING INDIVIDUALS IN ALL THE UNIVERSE UNITED WITH ONE PURPOSE."
BUT KNOW *THIS,* DREAD LISTENER...
...THIS IS *NOT* A TALE OF REVENGE AGAINST THE GREEN LANTERN CORPS, AS HAL JORDAN WOULD HAVE YOU BELIEVE.
THIS IS A TALE OF *CHANGE.*
A TALE OF HOW WHAT SEEMED TO BE THE WORST OF INTENTIONS CAN ACTUALLY BE THE *BEST.* SINESTRO WAS ONCE THE GREATEST GREEN LANTERN IN THE UNIVERSE...
...AND HE WILL BE AGAIN.
EVEN IF NO ONE KNOWS IT.

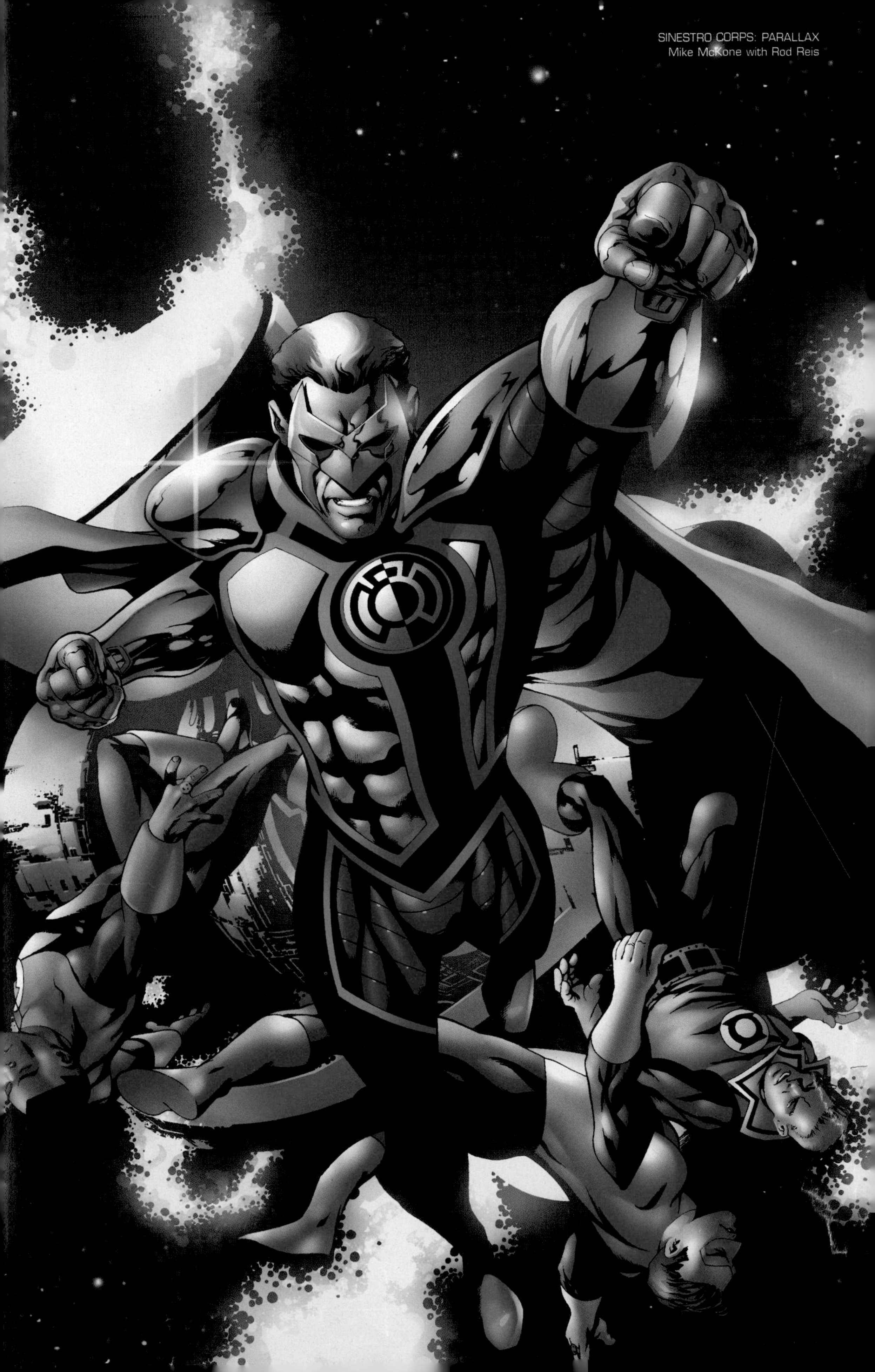

SINESTRO CORPS: PARALLAX
Mike McKone with Rod Reis

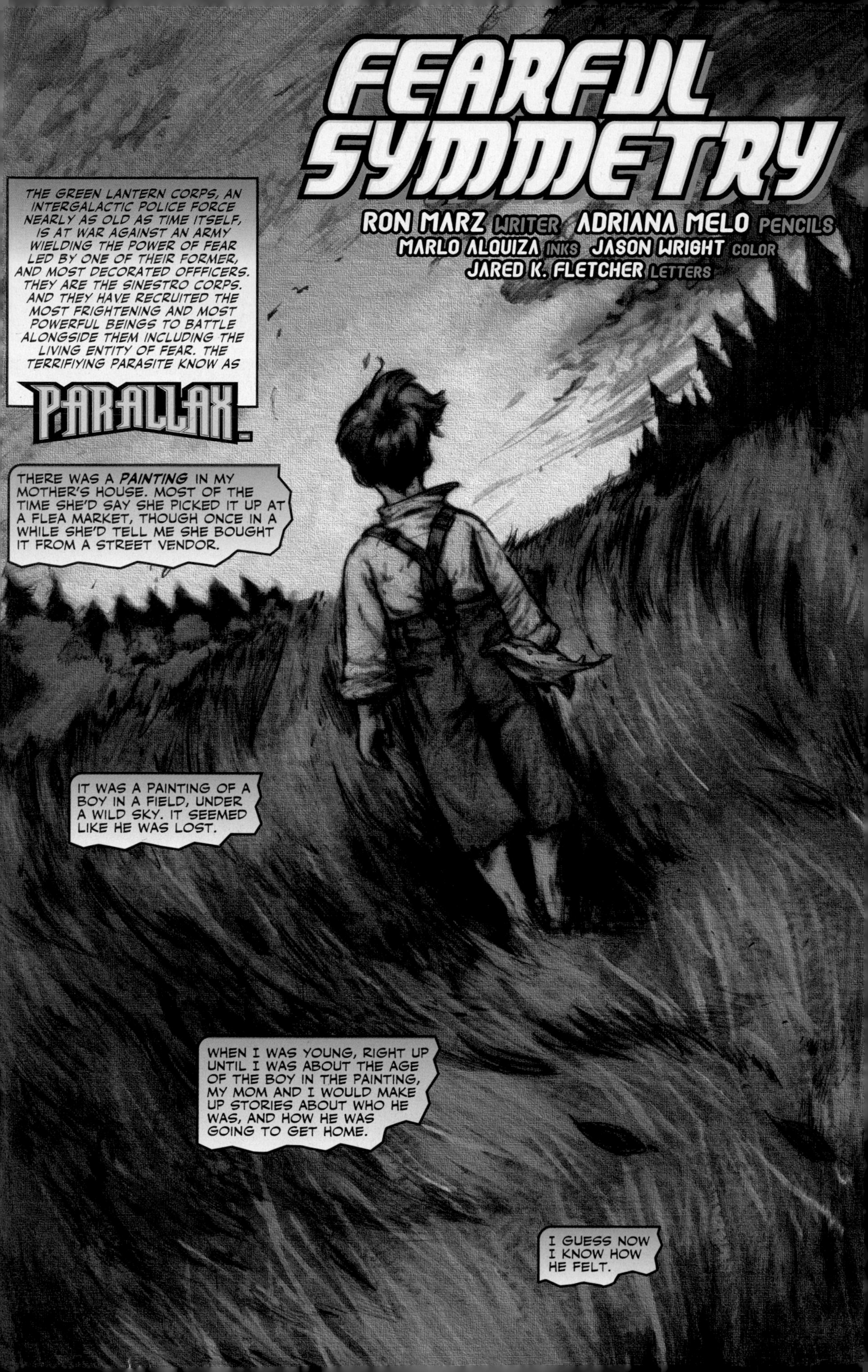
FEARFUL SYMMETRY
RON MARZ WRITER ADRIANA MELO PENCILS
MARLO ALQUIZA INKS JASON WRIGHT COLOR
JARED K. FLETCHER LETTERS
THE GREEN LANTERN CORPS, AN INTERGALACTIC POLICE FORCE NEARLY AS OLD AS TIME ITSELF, IS AT WAR AGAINST AN ARMY WIELDING THE POWER OF FEAR LED BY ONE OF THEIR FORMER, AND MOST DECORATED OFFFICERS. THEY ARE THE SINESTRO CORPS. AND THEY HAVE RECRUITED THE MOST FRIGHTENING AND MOST POWERFUL BEINGS TO BATTLE ALONGSIDE THEM INCLUDING THE LIVING ENTITY OF FEAR. THE TERRIFIYING PARASITE KNOW AS
PARALLAX.
THERE WAS A PAINTING IN MY MOTHER'S HOUSE. MOST OF THE TIME SHE'D SAY SHE PICKED IT UP AT A FLEA MARKET, THOUGH ONCE IN A WHILE SHE'D TELL ME SHE BOUGHT IT FROM A STREET VENDOR.
IT WAS A PAINTING OF A BOY IN A FIELD, UNDER A WILD SKY. IT SEEMED LIKE HE WAS LOST.
WHEN I WAS YOUNG, RIGHT UP UNTIL I WAS ABOUT THE AGE OF THE BOY IN THE PAINTING, MY MOM AND I WOULD MAKE UP STORIES ABOUT WHO HE WAS, AND HOW HE WAS GOING TO GET HOME.
I GUESS NOW I KNOW HOW HE FELT.

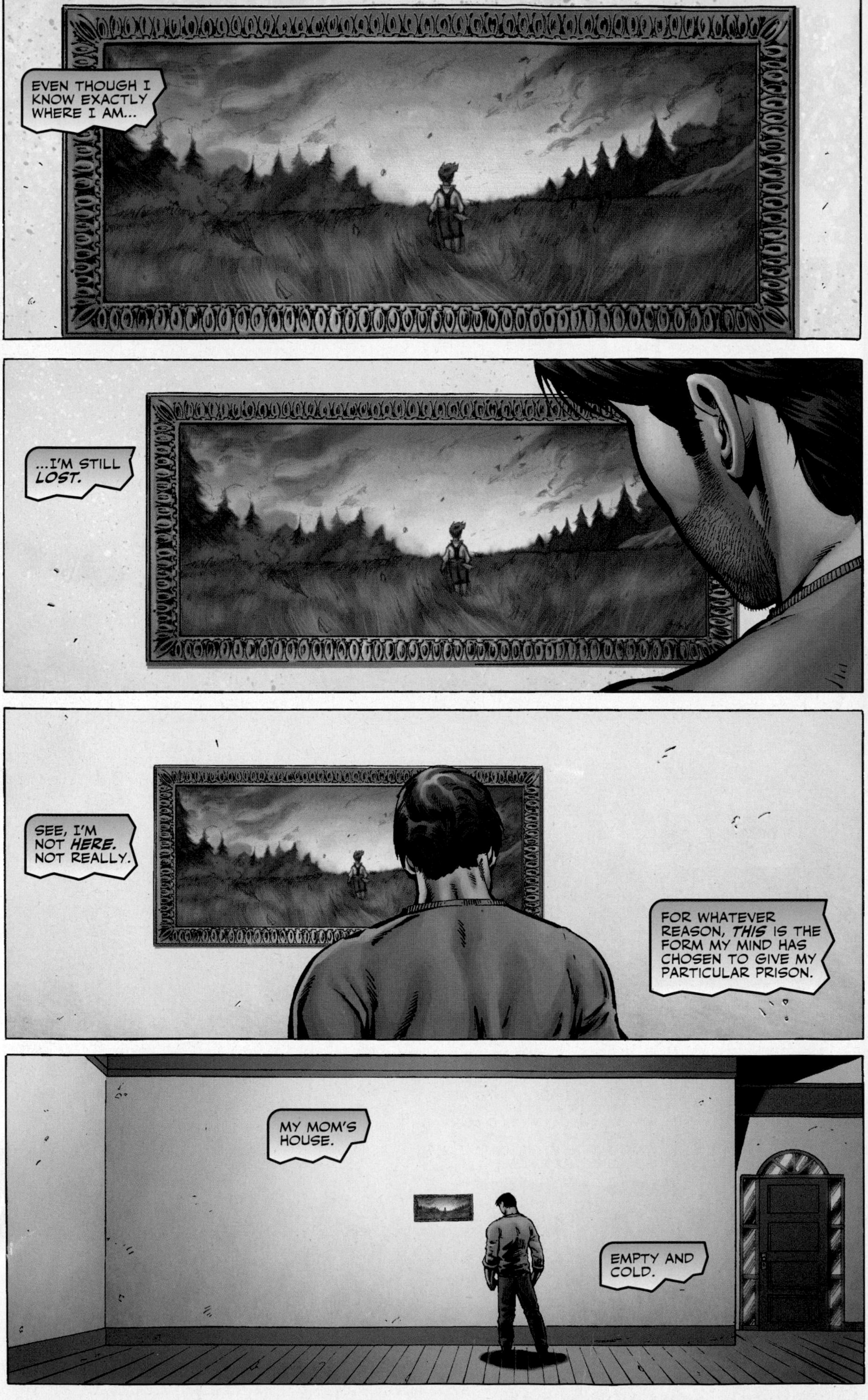
EVEN THOUGH I KNOW EXACTLY WHERE I AM...
...I'M STILL LOST.
SEE, I'M NOT HERE. NOT REALLY.
FOR WHATEVER REASON, THIS IS THE FORM MY MIND HAS CHOSEN TO GIVE MY PARTICULAR PRISON.
MY MOM'S HOUSE.
EMPTY AND COLD.

PARALLAX WAS...

...IS...

...A *FEAR ENTITY.* FIRST IMPRISONED ON OA BY THE GUARDIANS *BILLIONS* OF YEARS AGO.

IT REACHED OUT AND *INFECTED* HAL JORDAN WHEN COAST CITY WAS DESTROYED. CORRUPTED HIM AND LED HIM TO DO... *TERRIBLE THINGS.*

AND NOW PARALLAX IS INSIDE OF *ME*, LIKE SOME PARASITE.

BUT IT FEELS MORE LIKE *I'M* THE ONE TRAPPED INSIDE...

...WITH NO WAY OUT.

I WASN'T STRONG ENOUGH TO KEEP PARALLAX OUT. MY HEART WAS TOO HEAVY FROM MY MOTHER'S DEATH.

AT THE TIME, I HAD NO IDEA THAT *SINESTRO* HAD ORCHESTRATED THE WHOLE THING.

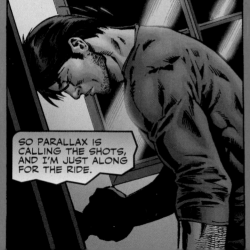

SO PARALLAX IS CALLING THE SHOTS, AND I'M JUST ALONG FOR THE RIDE.

IT'S LIKE BEING A PASSENGER IN AN AIRPLANE. I HAVE NO CONTROL OVER WHAT THE PILOT IS DOING.

ALL I CAN DO IS LOOK OUT THE WINDOW...

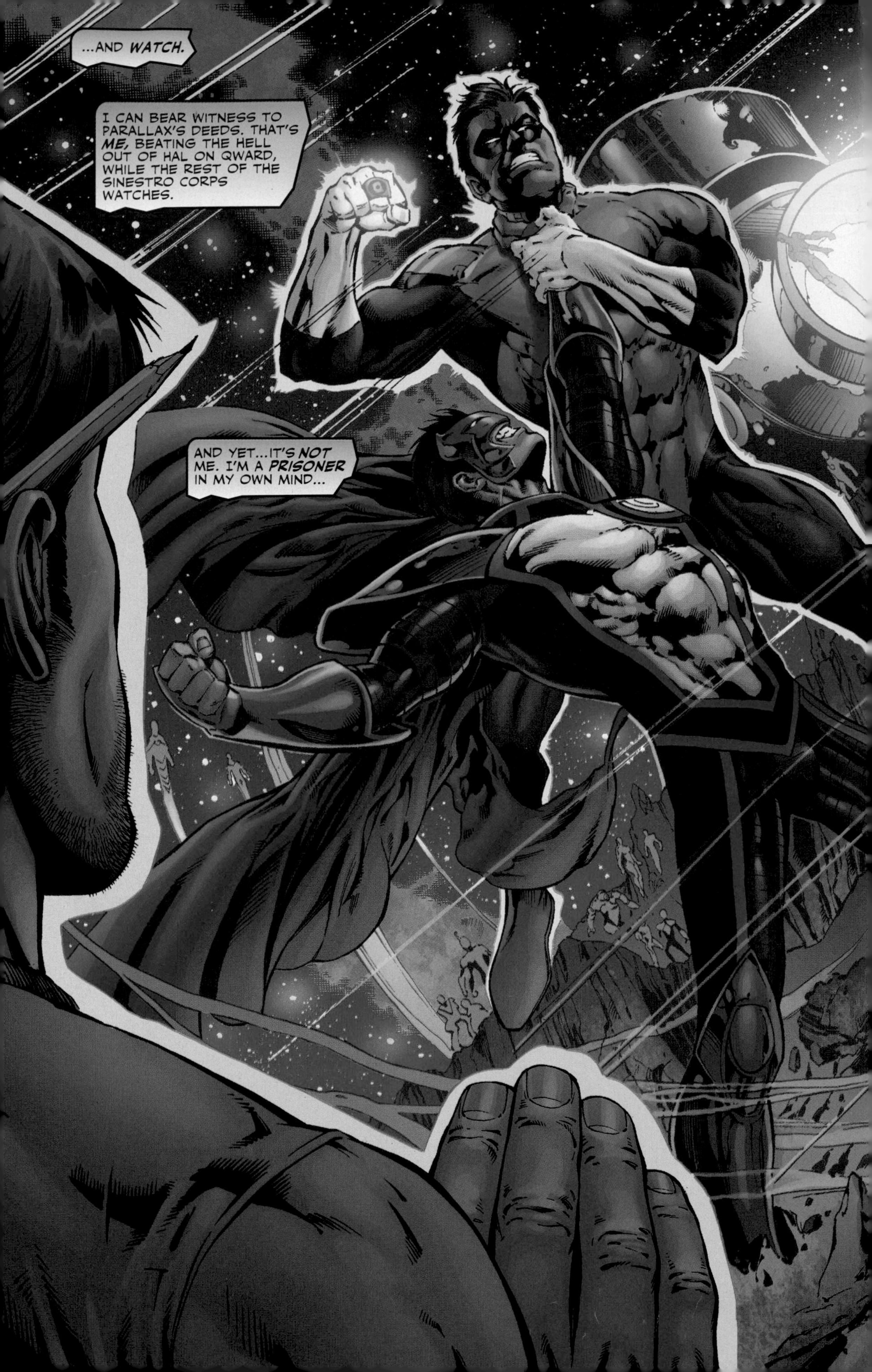
...AND WATCH.
I CAN BEAR WITNESS TO PARALLAX'S DEEDS. THAT'S ME, BEATING THE HELL OUT OF HAL ON QWARD, WHILE THE REST OF THE SINESTRO CORPS WATCHES.
AND YET...IT'S NOT ME. I'M A PRISONER IN MY OWN MIND...

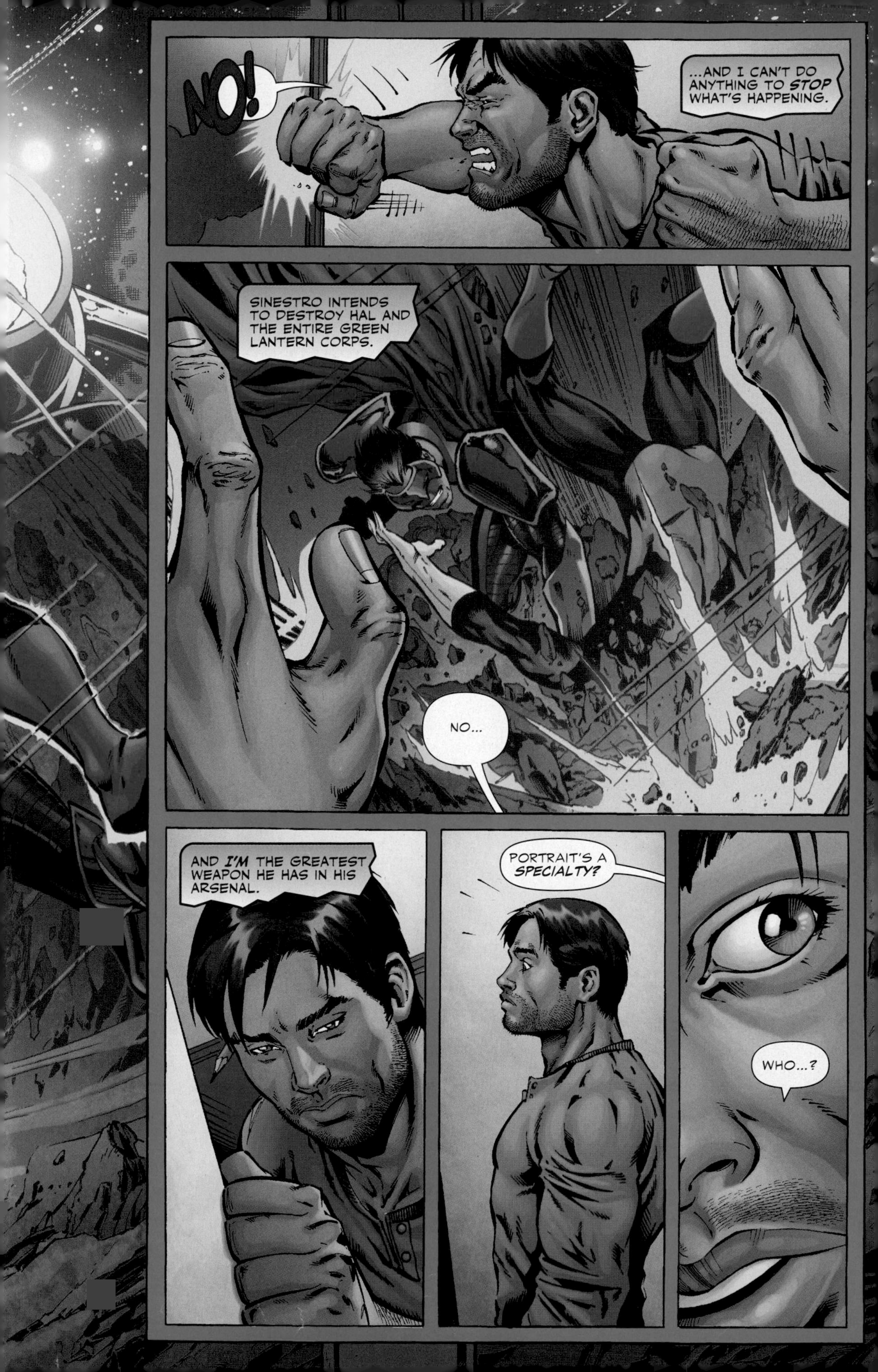
NO!
...AND I CAN'T DO ANYTHING TO STOP WHAT'S HAPPENING.
SINESTRO INTENDS TO DESTROY HAL AND THE ENTIRE GREEN LANTERN CORPS.
NO...
AND I'M THE GREATEST WEAPON HE HAS IN HIS ARSENAL.
PORTRAIT'S A SPECIALTY?
WHO...?

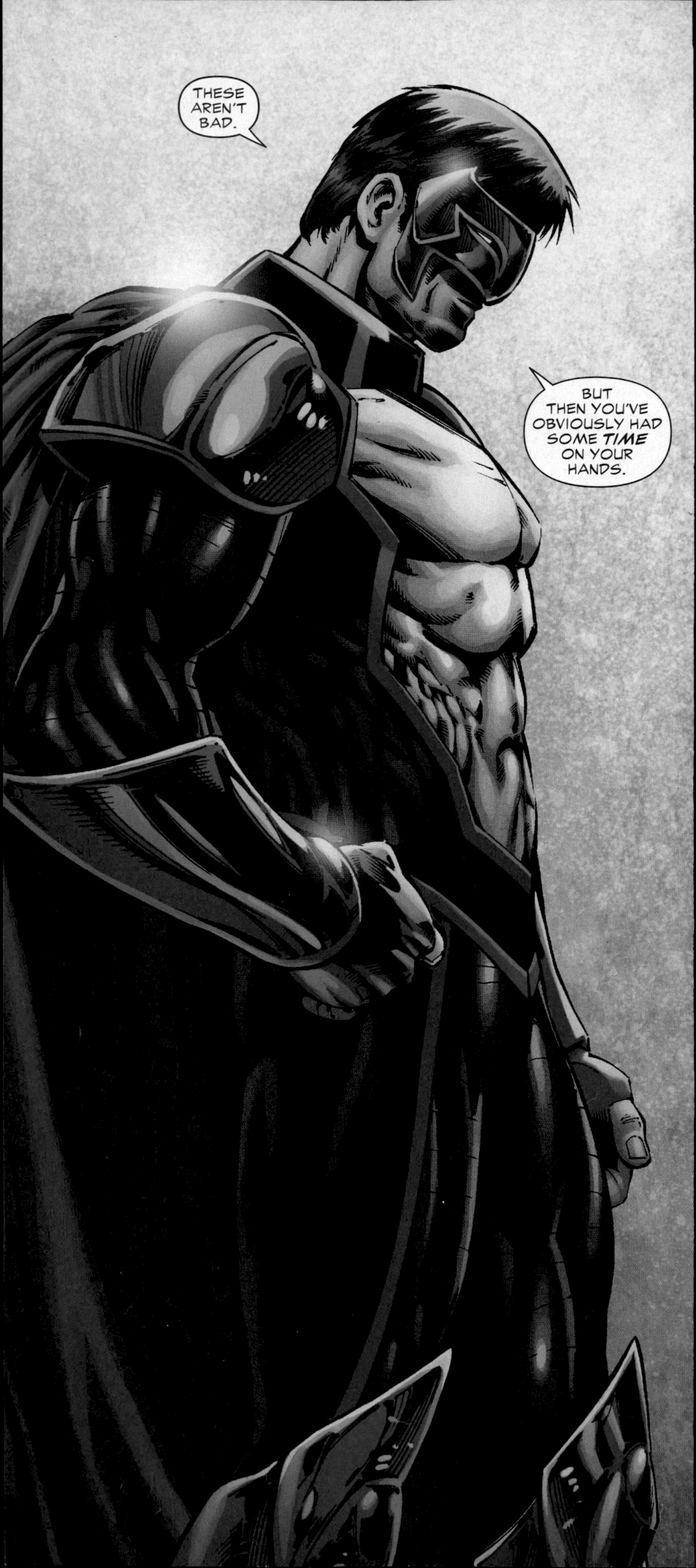
THESE AREN'T BAD.
BUT THEN YOU'VE OBVIOUSLY HAD SOME *TIME* ON YOUR HANDS.
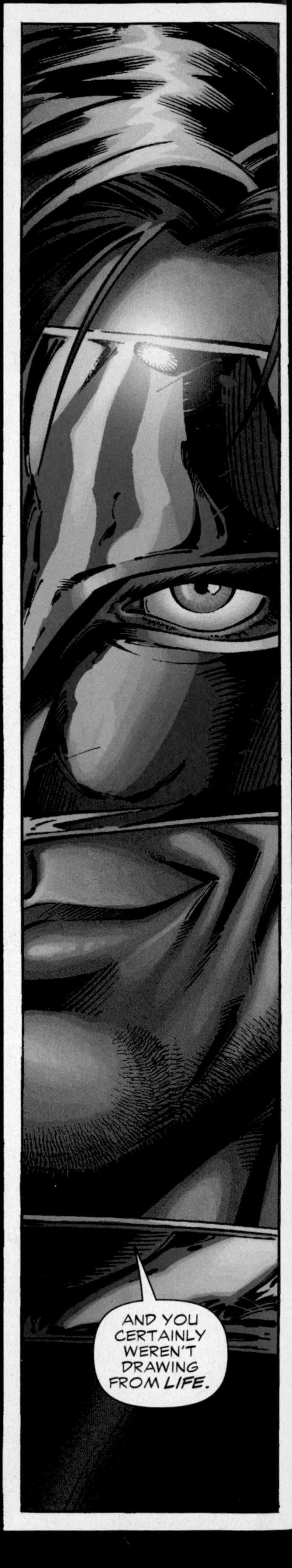
AND YOU CERTAINLY WEREN'T DRAWING FROM *LIFE*.

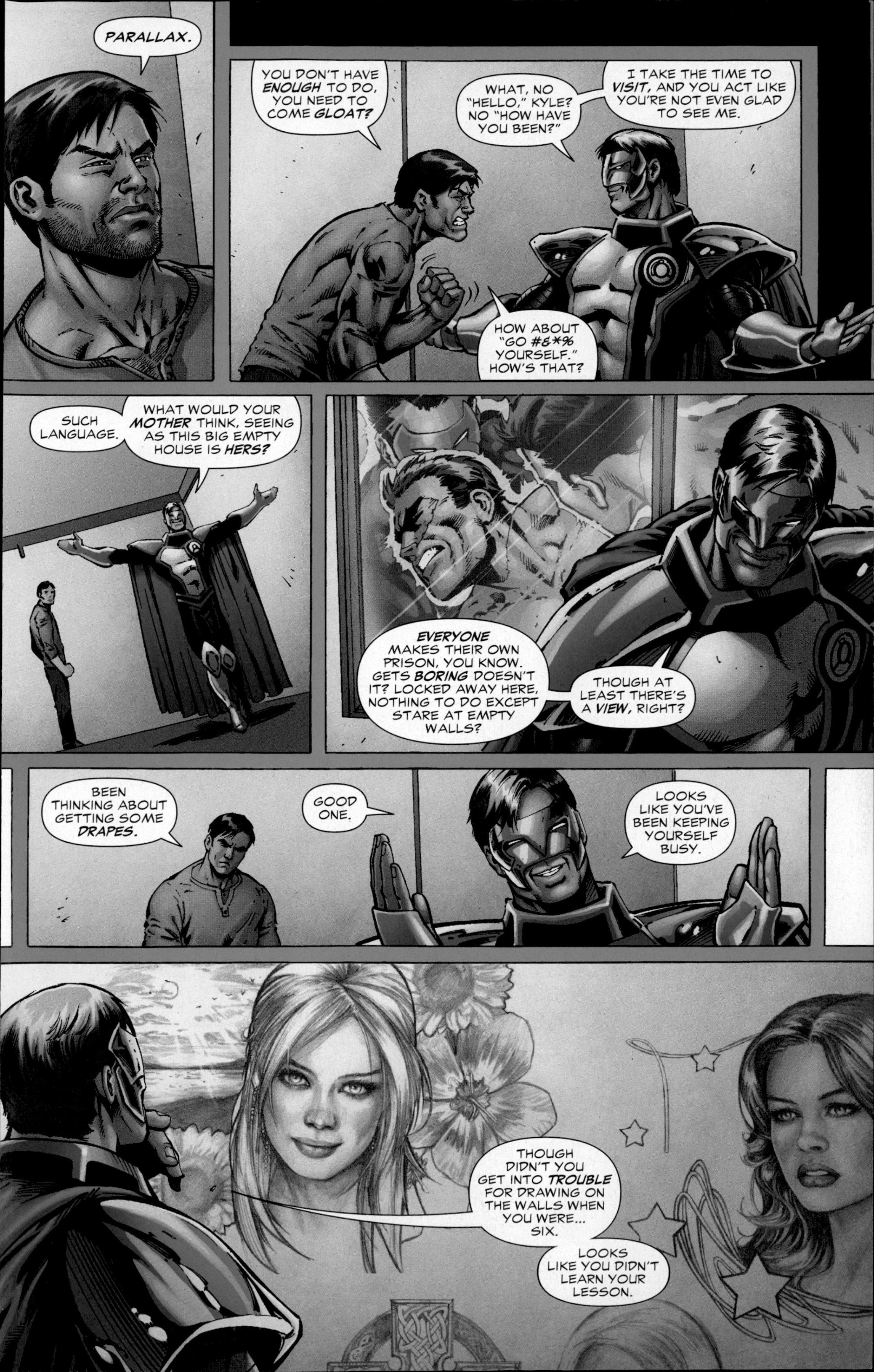
PARALLAX.
YOU DON'T HAVE ENOUGH TO DO, YOU NEED TO COME GLOAT?
WHAT, NO "HELLO," KYLE? NO "HOW HAVE YOU BEEN?"
I TAKE THE TIME TO VISIT, AND YOU ACT LIKE YOU'RE NOT EVEN GLAD TO SEE ME.
HOW ABOUT "GO #&*% YOURSELF." HOW'S THAT?
SUCH LANGUAGE.
WHAT WOULD YOUR MOTHER THINK, SEEING AS THIS BIG EMPTY HOUSE IS HERS?
EVERYONE MAKES THEIR OWN PRISON, YOU KNOW. GETS BORING DOESN'T IT? LOCKED AWAY HERE, NOTHING TO DO EXCEPT STARE AT EMPTY WALLS?
THOUGH AT LEAST THERE'S A VIEW, RIGHT?
BEEN THINKING ABOUT GETTING SOME DRAPES.
GOOD ONE.
LOOKS LIKE YOU'VE BEEN KEEPING YOURSELF BUSY.
THOUGH DIDN'T YOU GET INTO TROUBLE FOR DRAWING ON THE WALLS WHEN YOU WERE... SIX.
LOOKS LIKE YOU DIDN'T LEARN YOUR LESSON.

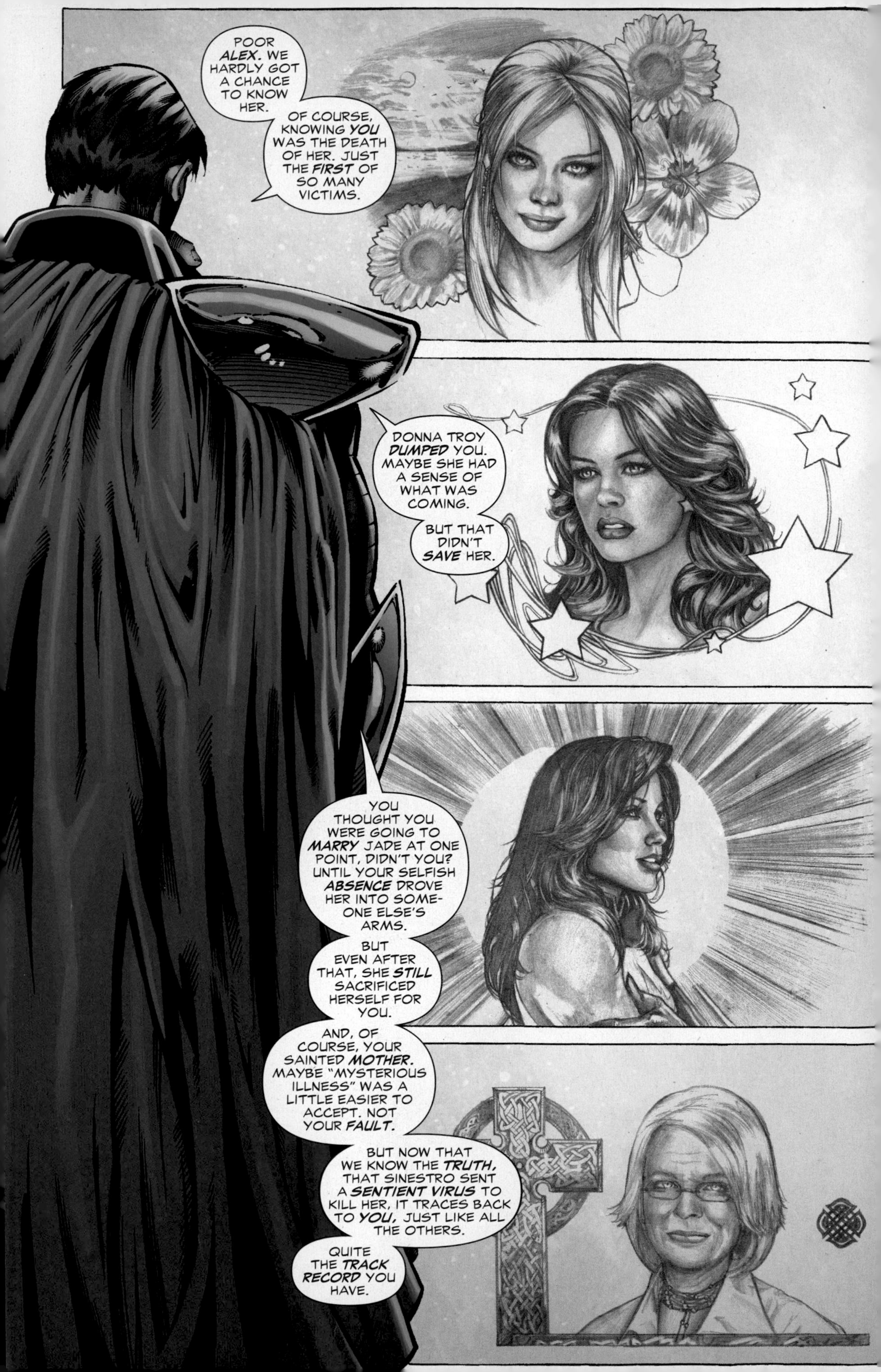
POOR ALEX. WE HARDLY GOT A CHANCE TO KNOW HER.
OF COURSE, KNOWING YOU WAS THE DEATH OF HER. JUST THE FIRST OF SO MANY VICTIMS.
DONNA TROY DUMPED YOU. MAYBE SHE HAD A SENSE OF WHAT WAS COMING.
BUT THAT DIDN'T SAVE HER.
YOU THOUGHT YOU WERE GOING TO MARRY JADE AT ONE POINT, DIDN'T YOU? UNTIL YOUR SELFISH ABSENCE DROVE HER INTO SOME-ONE ELSE'S ARMS.
BUT EVEN AFTER THAT, SHE STILL SACRIFICED HERSELF FOR YOU.
AND, OF COURSE, YOUR SAINTED MOTHER. MAYBE "MYSTERIOUS ILLNESS" WAS A LITTLE EASIER TO ACCEPT. NOT YOUR FAULT.
BUT NOW THAT WE KNOW THE TRUTH, THAT SINESTRO SENT A SENTIENT VIRUS TO KILL HER, IT TRACES BACK TO YOU, JUST LIKE ALL THE OTHERS.
QUITE THE TRACK RECORD YOU HAVE.

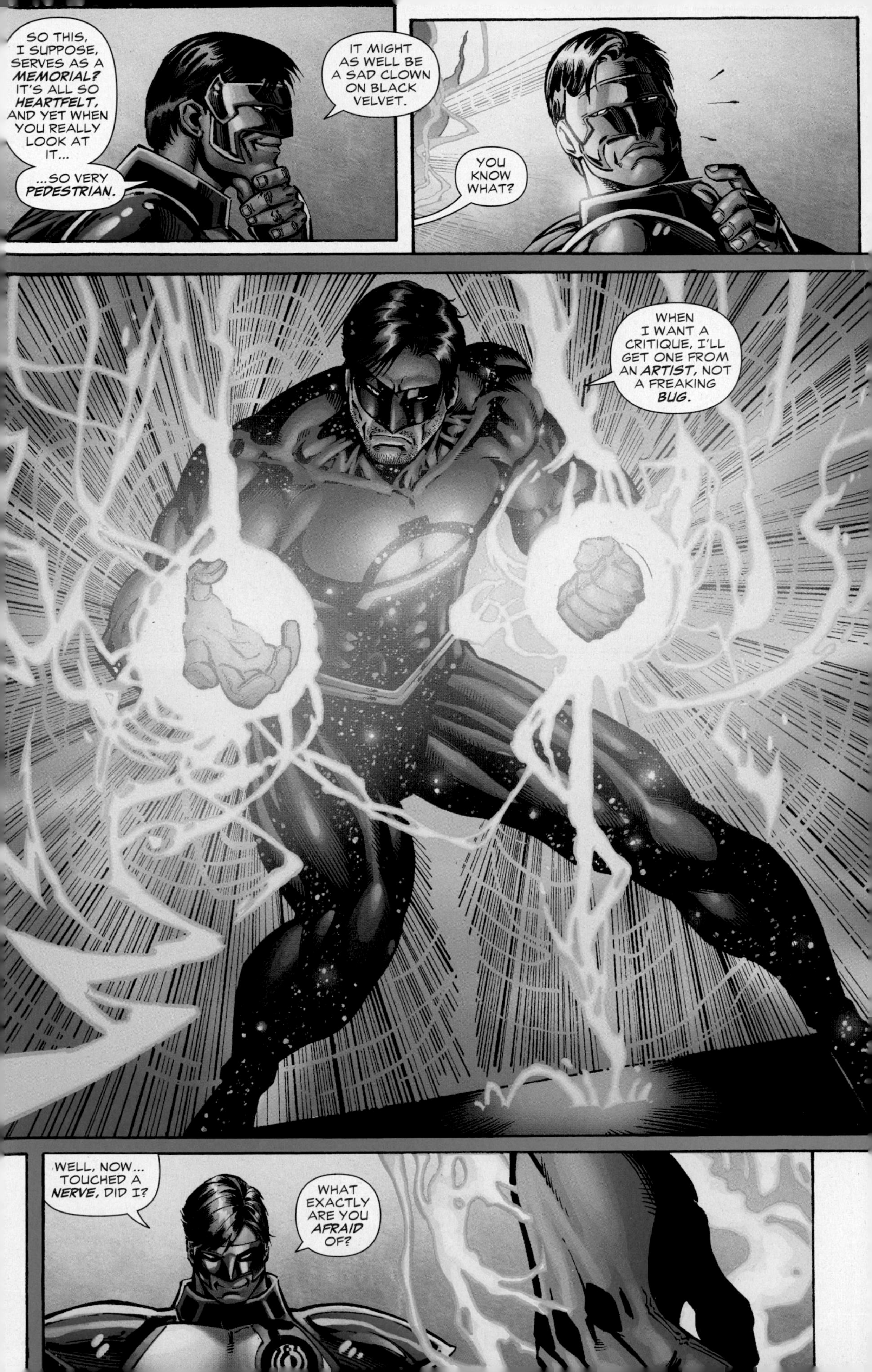
SO THIS, I SUPPOSE, SERVES AS A MEMORIAL? IT'S ALL SO HEARTFELT, AND YET WHEN YOU REALLY LOOK AT IT...
...SO VERY PEDESTRIAN.
IT MIGHT AS WELL BE A SAD CLOWN ON BLACK VELVET.
YOU KNOW WHAT?
WHEN I WANT A CRITIQUE, I'LL GET ONE FROM AN ARTIST, NOT A FREAKING BUG.
WELL, NOW... TOUCHED A NERVE, DID I?
WHAT EXACTLY ARE YOU AFRAID OF?

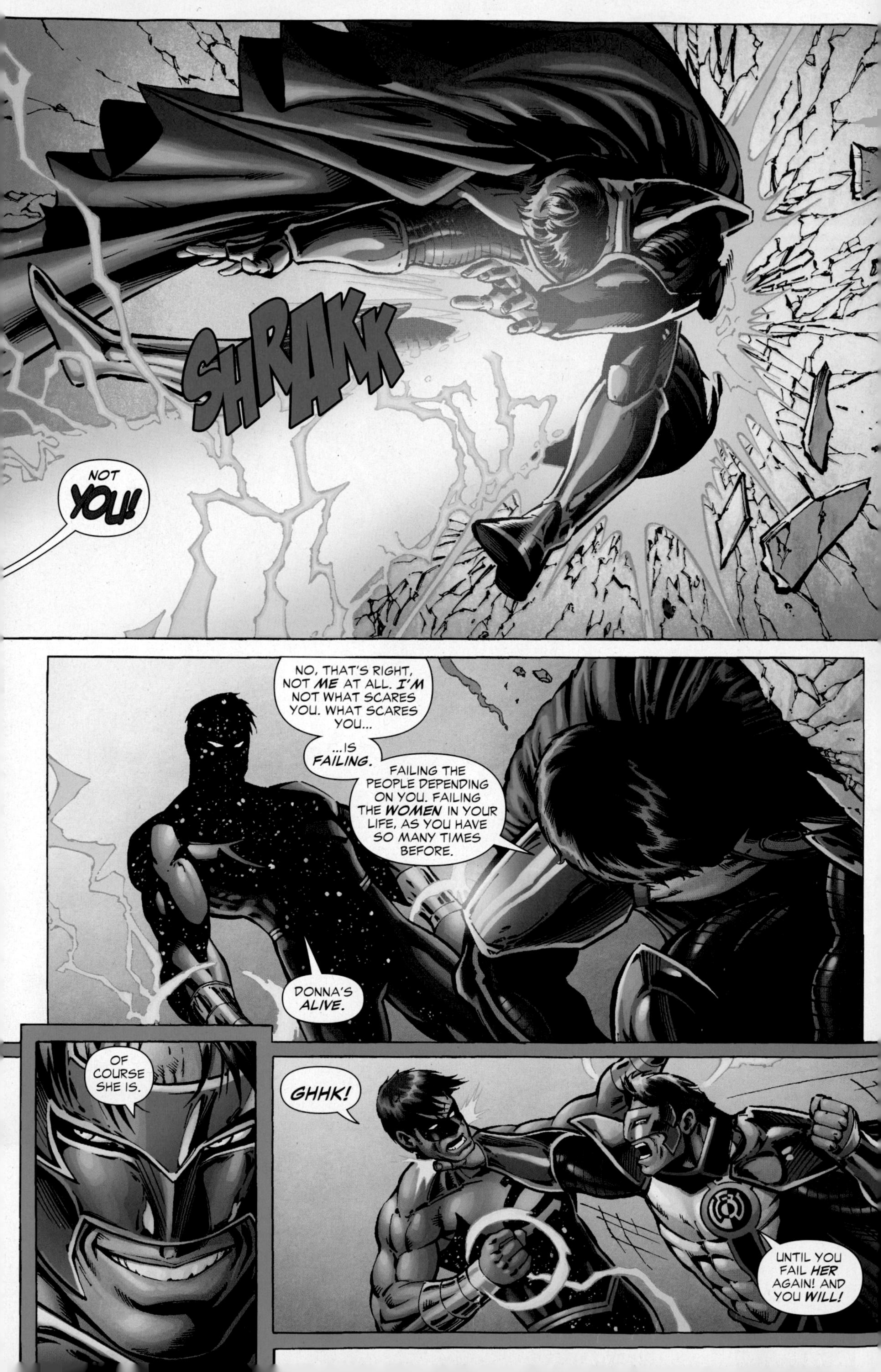
SHRAKK
NOT YOU!
NO, THAT'S RIGHT, NOT ME AT ALL. I'M NOT WHAT SCARES YOU. WHAT SCARES YOU...
...IS FAILING.
FAILING THE PEOPLE DEPENDING ON YOU. FAILING THE WOMEN IN YOUR LIFE, AS YOU HAVE SO MANY TIMES BEFORE.
DONNA'S ALIVE.
OF COURSE SHE IS.
GHHK!
UNTIL YOU FAIL HER AGAIN! AND YOU WILL!

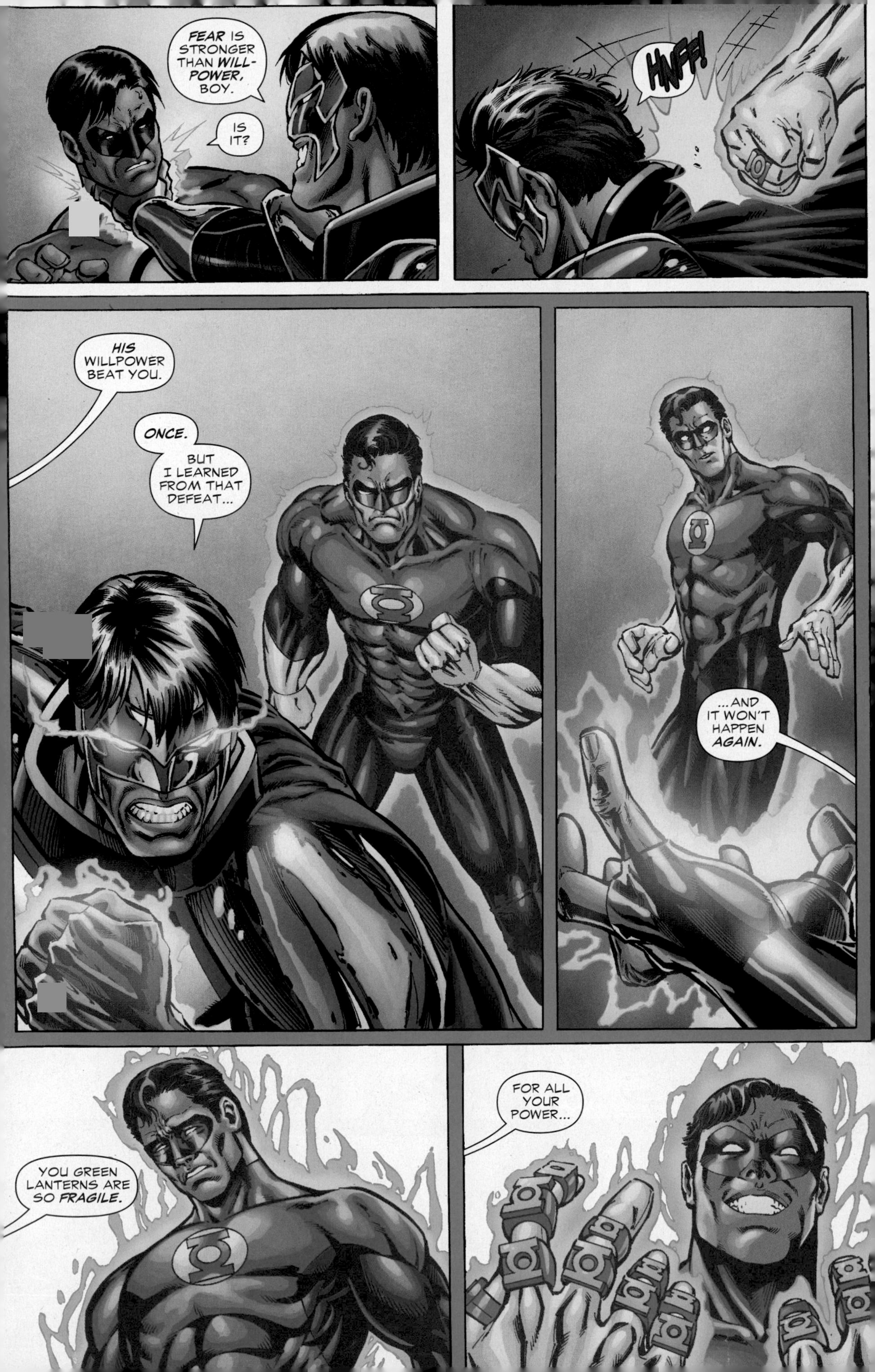
FEAR IS STRONGER THAN WILL-POWER, BOY.
IS IT?
HNFF!
HIS WILLPOWER BEAT YOU.
ONCE.
BUT I LEARNED FROM THAT DEFEAT...
...AND IT WON'T HAPPEN AGAIN.
YOU GREEN LANTERNS ARE SO FRAGILE.
FOR ALL YOUR POWER...

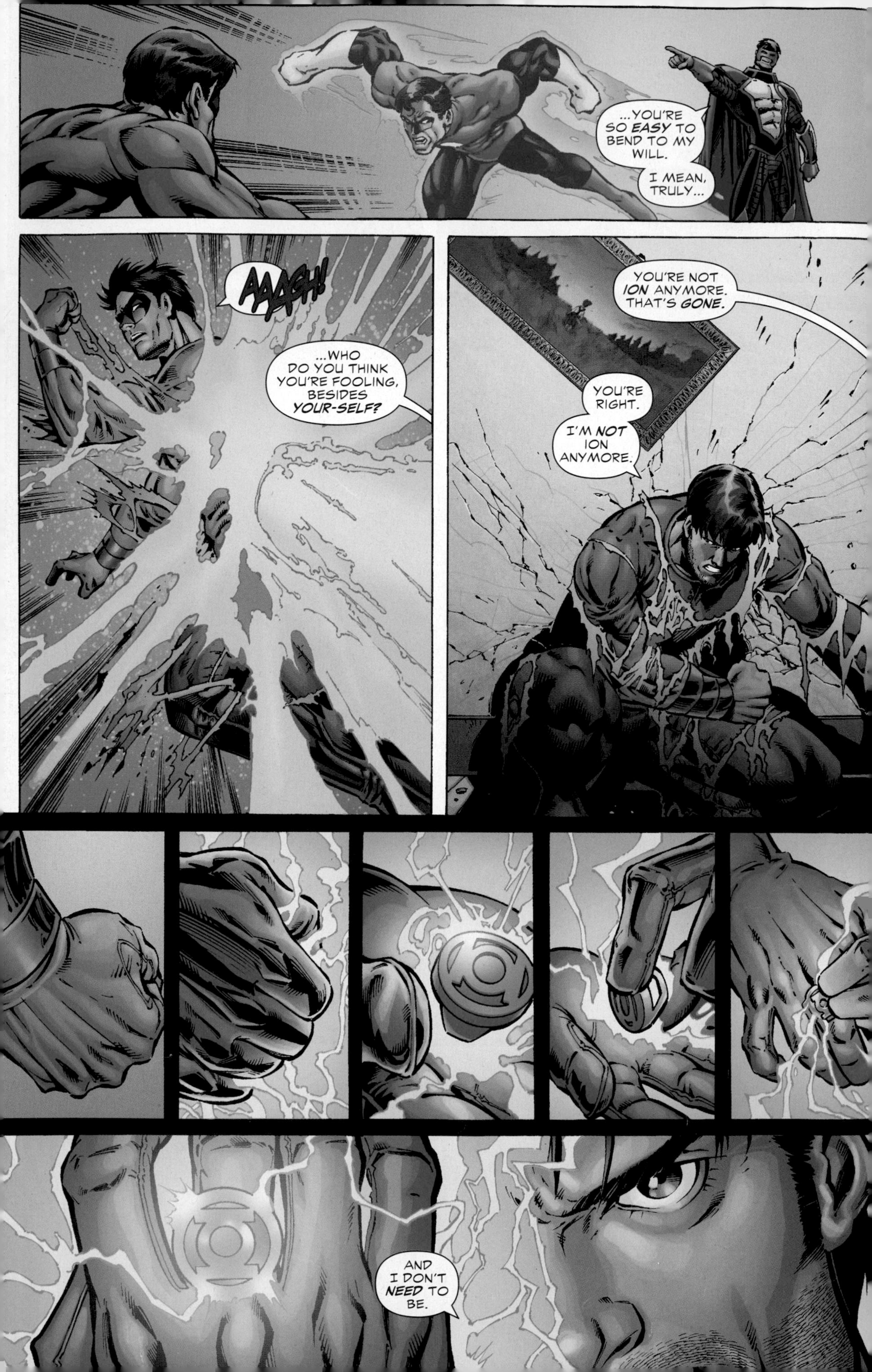
...YOU'RE SO EASY TO BEND TO MY WILL.
I MEAN, TRULY...
AAAGH!
...WHO DO YOU THINK YOU'RE FOOLING, BESIDES YOUR-SELF?
YOU'RE NOT ION ANYMORE. THAT'S GONE.
YOU'RE RIGHT.
I'M NOT ION ANYMORE.
AND I DON'T NEED TO BE.

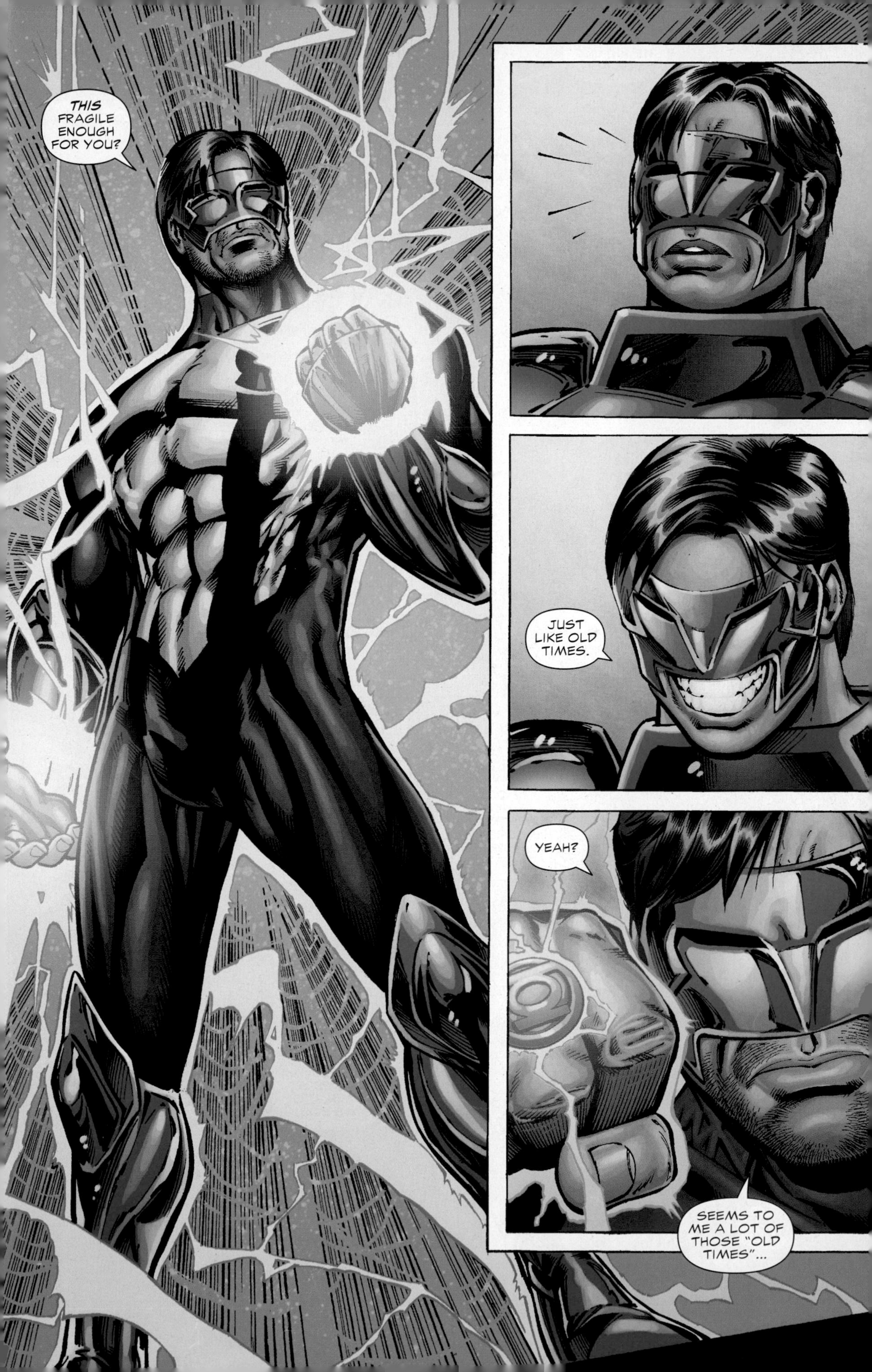
THIS FRAGILE ENOUGH FOR YOU?
JUST LIKE OLD TIMES.
YEAH?
SEEMS TO ME A LOT OF THOSE "OLD TIMES"...

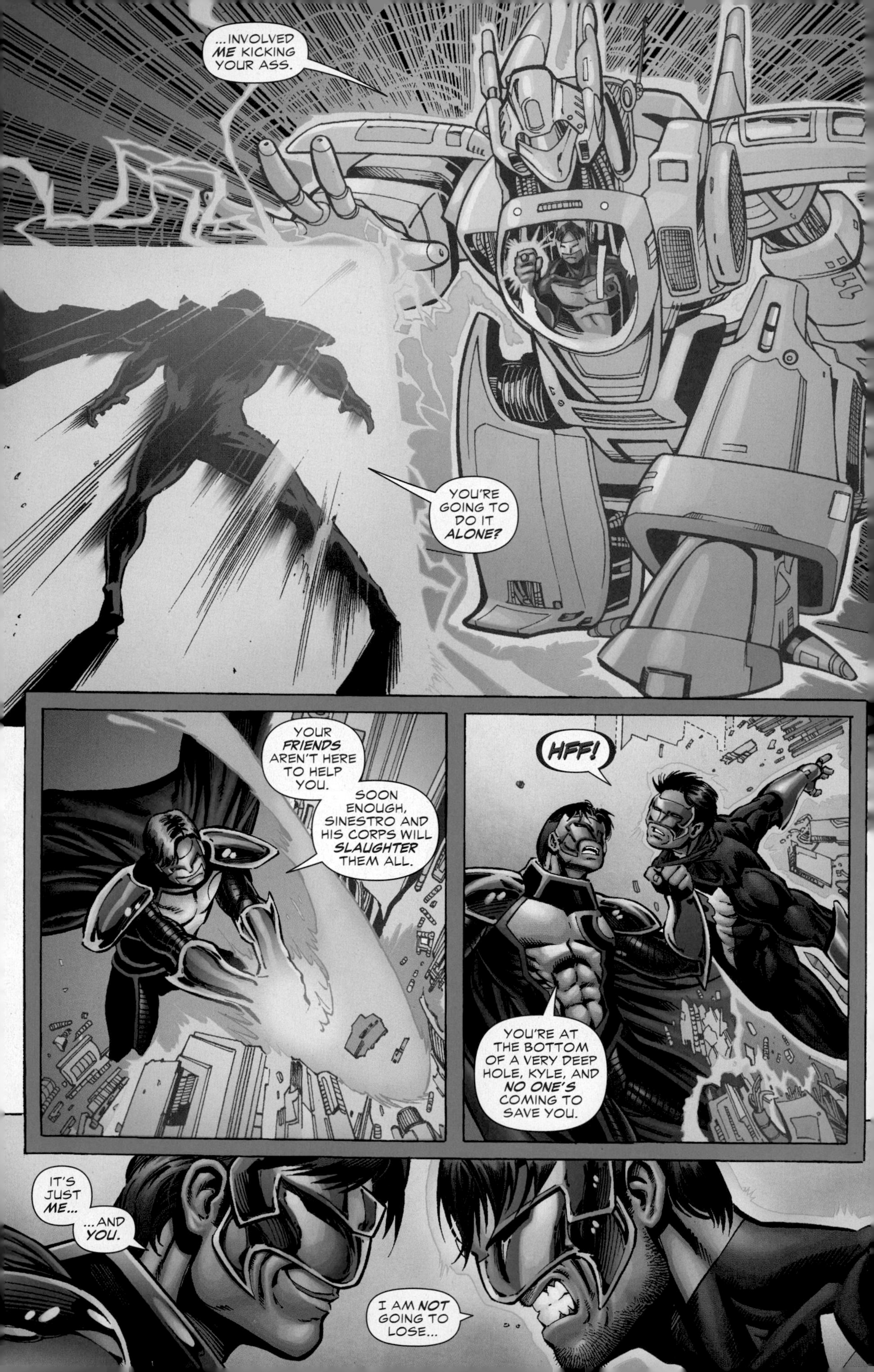
...INVOLVED ME KICKING YOUR ASS.
YOU'RE GOING TO DO IT ALONE?
YOUR FRIENDS AREN'T HERE TO HELP YOU.
SOON ENOUGH, SINESTRO AND HIS CORPS WILL SLAUGHTER THEM ALL.
HFF!
YOU'RE AT THE BOTTOM OF A VERY DEEP HOLE, KYLE, AND NO ONE'S COMING TO SAVE YOU.
IT'S JUST ME...
...AND YOU.
I AM NOT GOING TO LOSE...

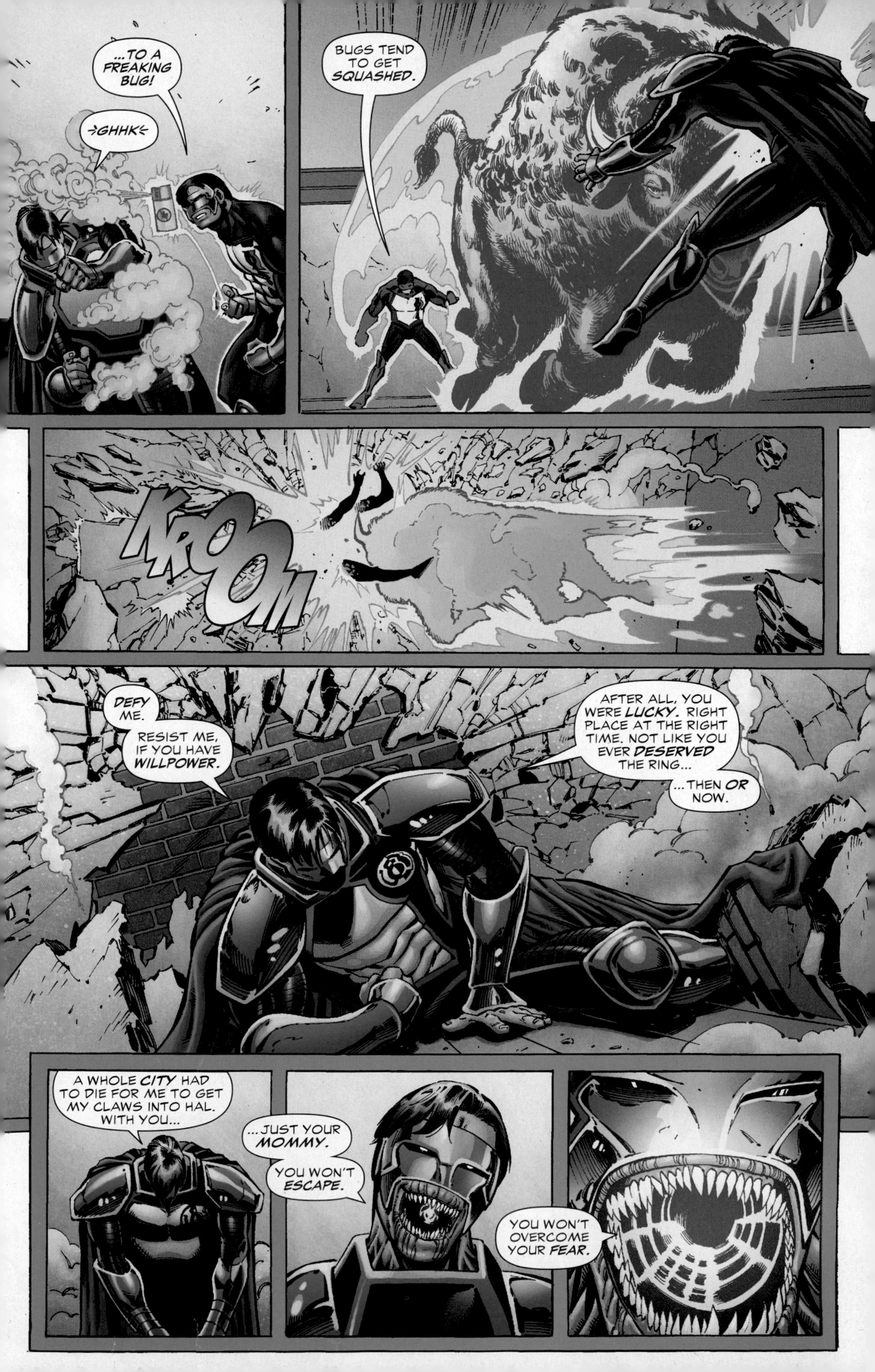
...TO A FREAKING BUG!
→GHHK←
BUGS TEND TO GET SQUASHED.
KROOOM
DEFY ME.
RESIST ME, IF YOU HAVE WILLPOWER.
AFTER ALL, YOU WERE LUCKY. RIGHT PLACE AT THE RIGHT TIME. NOT LIKE YOU EVER DESERVED THE RING...
...THEN OR NOW.
A WHOLE CITY HAD TO DIE FOR ME TO GET MY CLAWS INTO HAL. WITH YOU...
...JUST YOUR MOMMY.
YOU WON'T ESCAPE.
YOU WON'T OVERCOME YOUR FEAR.

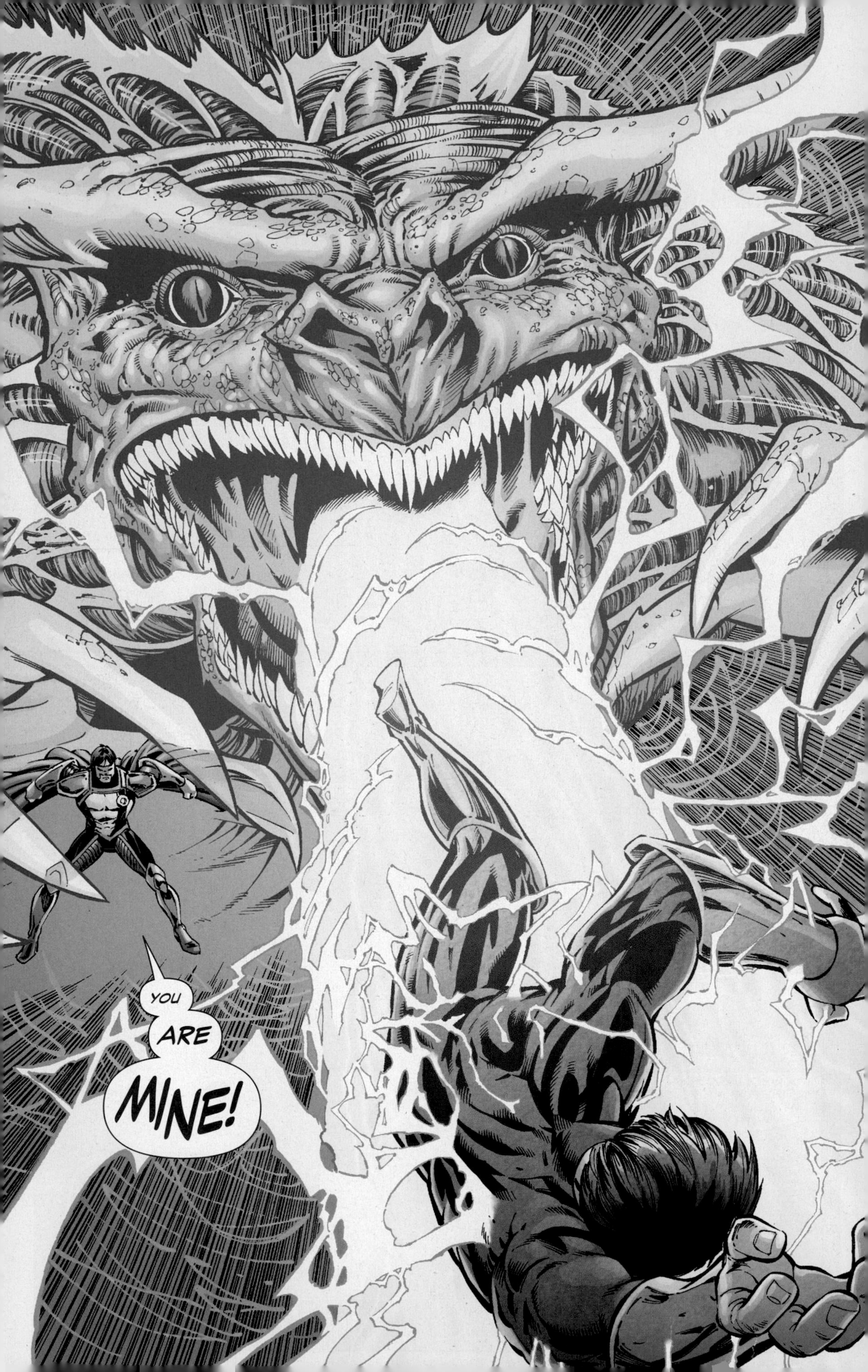
YOU ARE MINE!

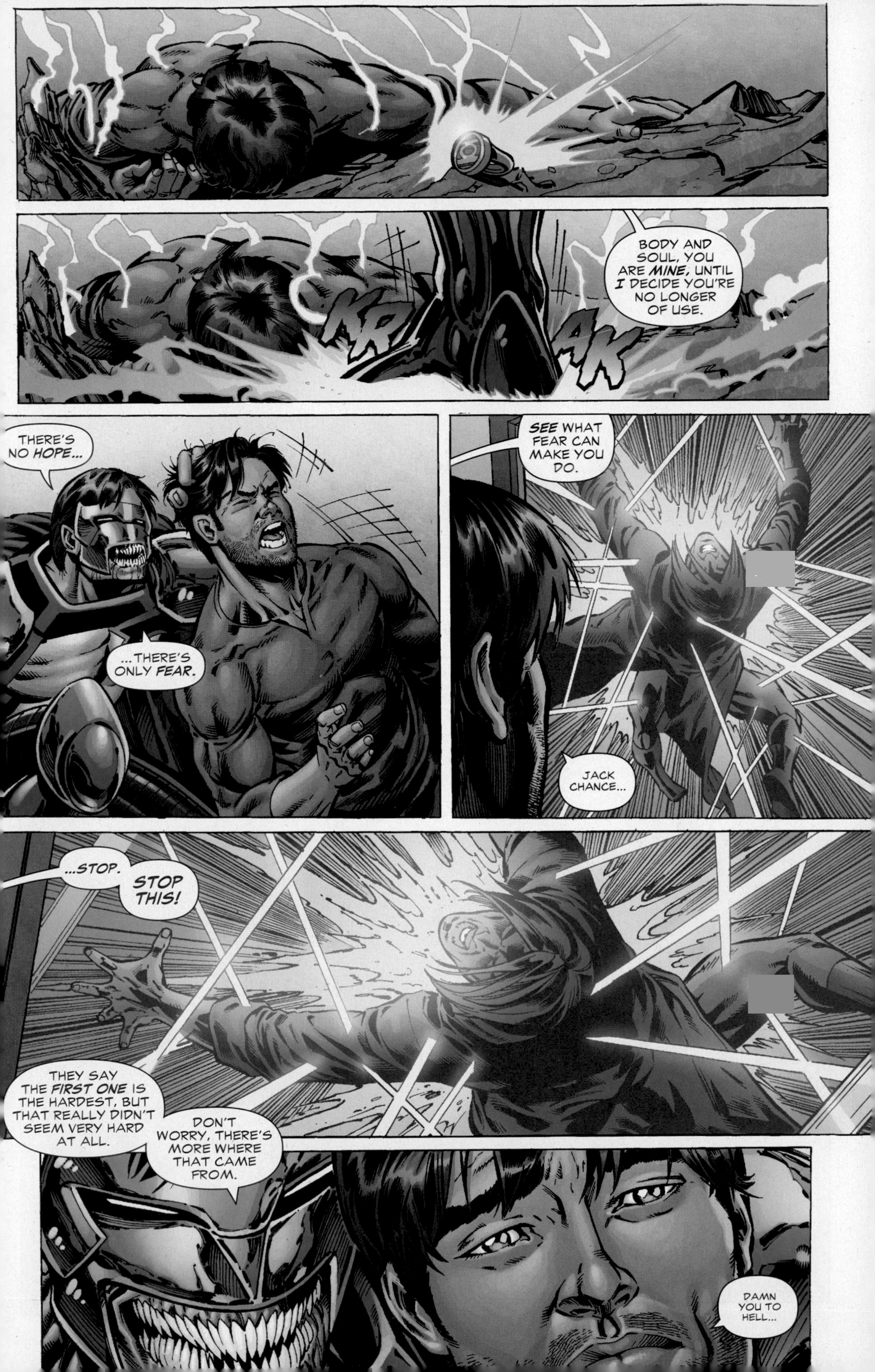
BODY AND SOUL, YOU ARE MINE, UNTIL I DECIDE YOU'RE NO LONGER OF USE.
KRAAK
THERE'S NO HOPE...
...THERE'S ONLY FEAR.
SEE WHAT FEAR CAN MAKE YOU DO.
JACK CHANCE...
...STOP.
STOP THIS!
THEY SAY THE FIRST ONE IS THE HARDEST, BUT THAT REALLY DIDN'T SEEM VERY HARD AT ALL.
DON'T WORRY, THERE'S MORE WHERE THAT CAME FROM.
DAMN YOU TO HELL...

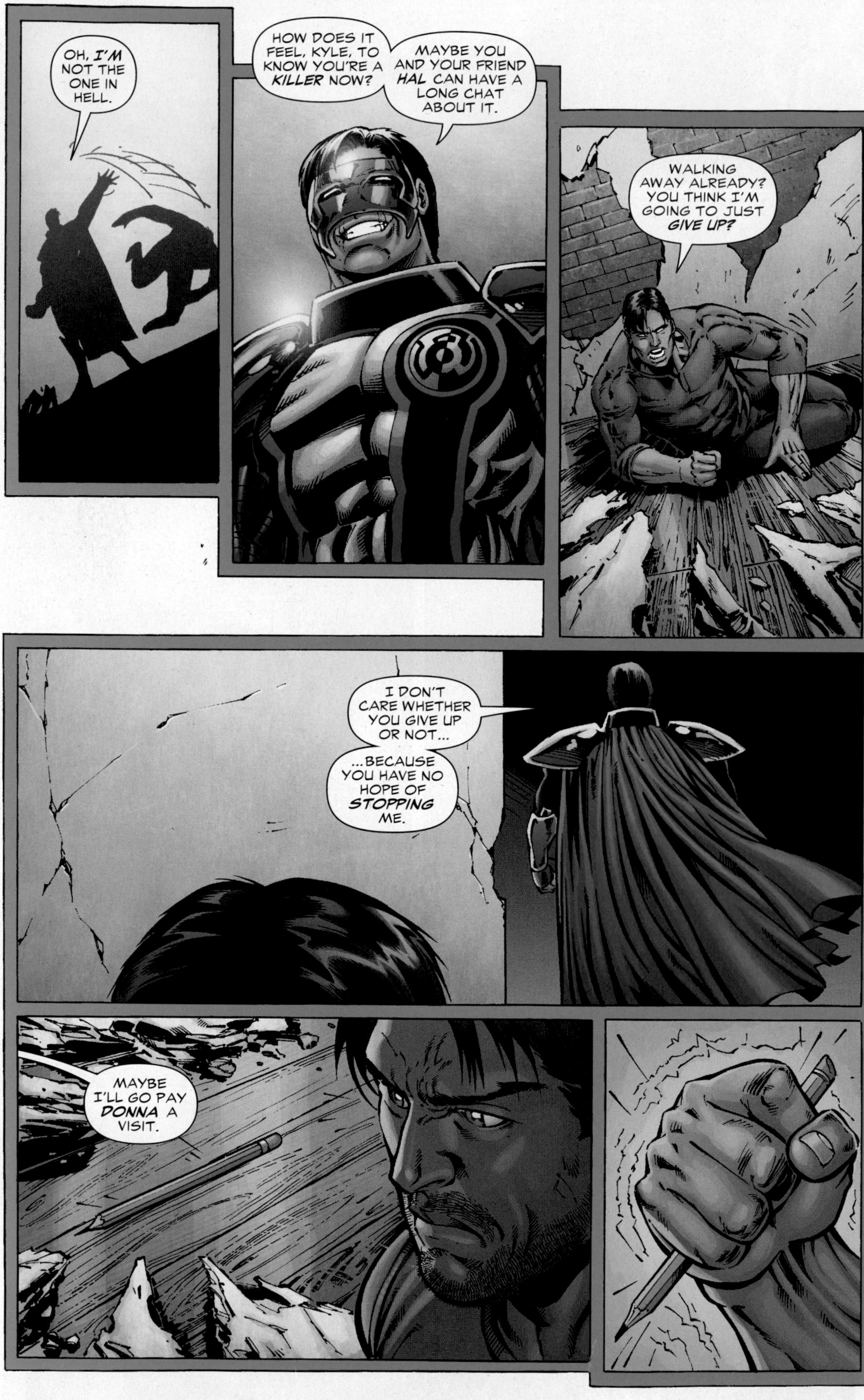
OH, *I'M* NOT THE ONE IN HELL.
HOW DOES IT FEEL, KYLE, TO KNOW YOU'RE A *KILLER* NOW?
MAYBE YOU AND YOUR FRIEND *HAL* CAN HAVE A LONG CHAT ABOUT IT.
WALKING AWAY ALREADY? YOU THINK I'M GOING TO JUST *GIVE UP?*
I DON'T CARE WHETHER YOU GIVE UP OR NOT...
...BECAUSE YOU HAVE NO HOPE OF *STOPPING* ME.
MAYBE I'LL GO PAY *DONNA* A VISIT.

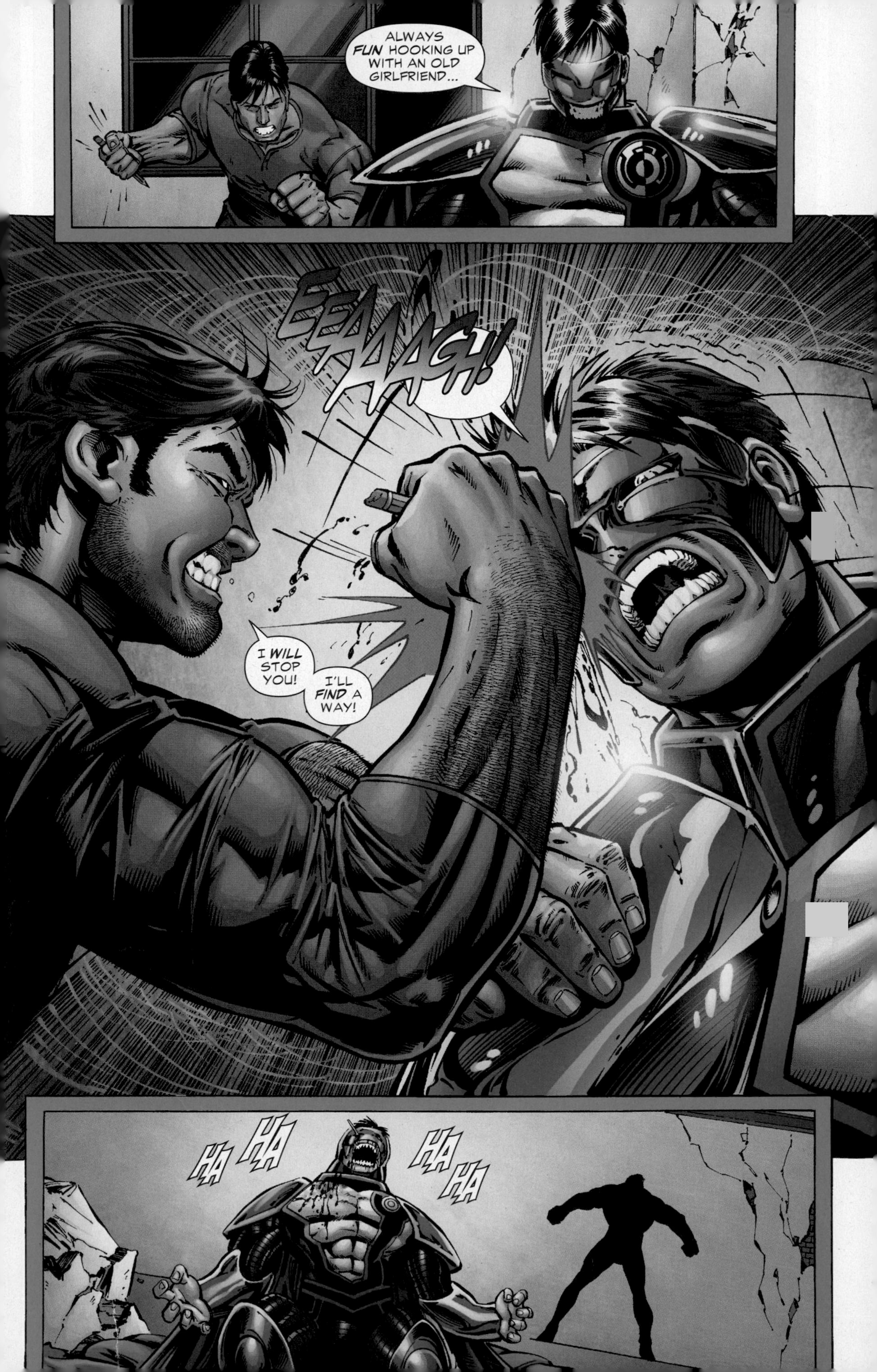
ALWAYS FUN HOOKING UP WITH AN OLD GIRLFRIEND...
EEEAAAGH!
I WILL STOP YOU!
I'LL FIND A WAY!
HA HA
HA HA

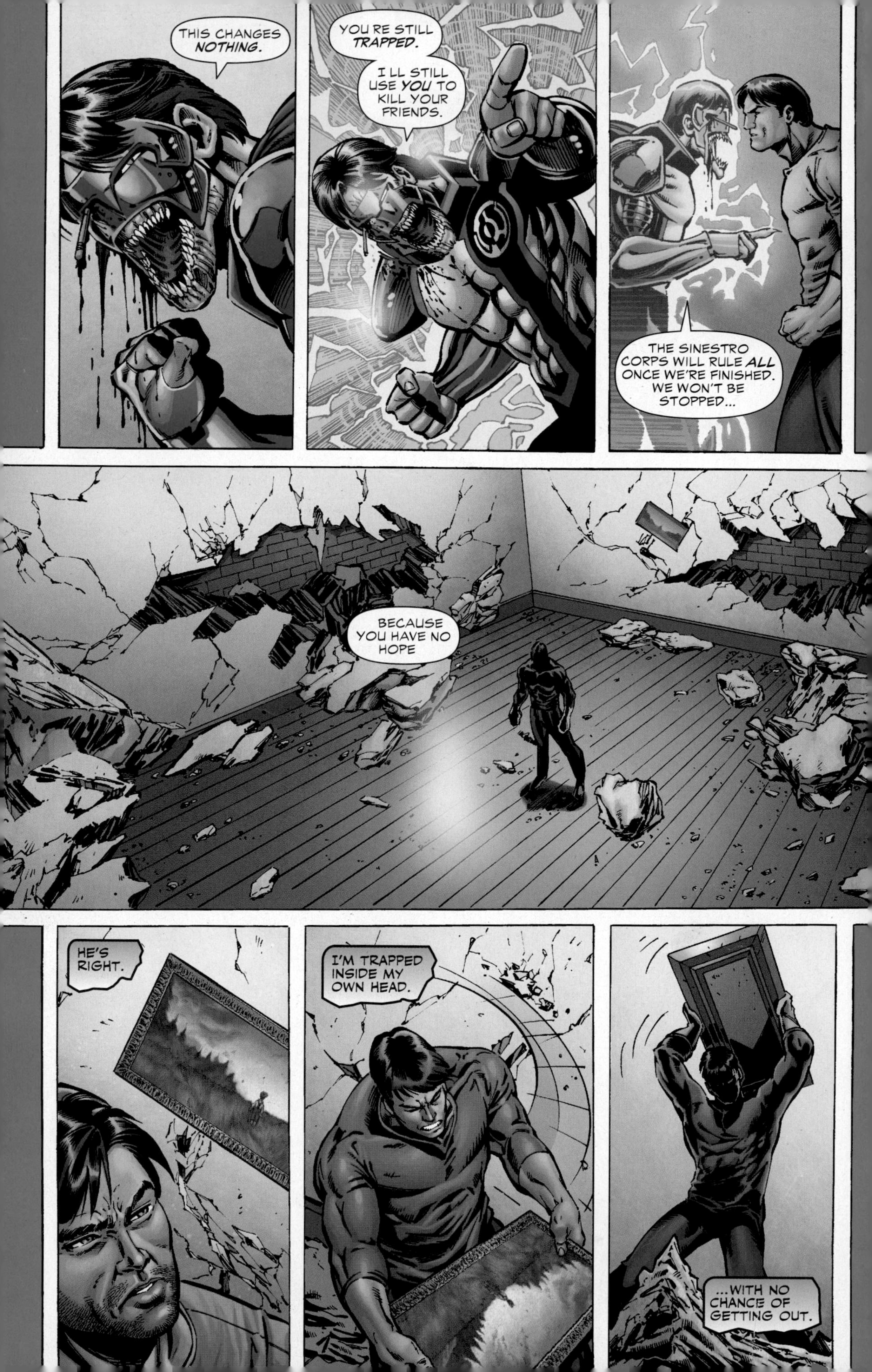
THIS CHANGES NOTHING.
YOU'RE STILL TRAPPED.
I'LL STILL USE YOU TO KILL YOUR FRIENDS.
THE SINESTRO CORPS WILL RULE ALL ONCE WE'RE FINISHED. WE WON'T BE STOPPED...
BECAUSE YOU HAVE NO HOPE
HE'S RIGHT.
I'M TRAPPED INSIDE MY OWN HEAD.
...WITH NO CHANCE OF GETTING OUT.

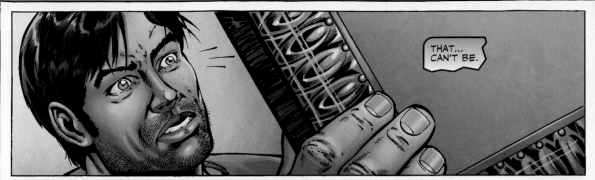

THAT... CAN'T BE.

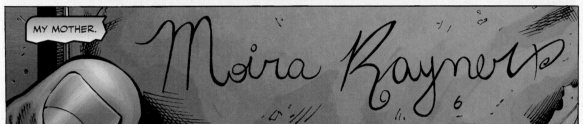

MY MOTHER.

Moira Rayners

MY *MOTHER* PAINTED THIS.

ALL THOSE YEARS, AND SHE DIDN'T TELL ME.

SHE'S GONE, BUT THIS IS HER GIFT TO ME. IT ALWAYS WAS, I JUST NEVER KNEW IT.

I AM WHO I AM...

...I'M ABLE TO DO WHAT I DO...

...BECAUSE OF *HER*.

SHE'S STILL *WITH* ME.

I'M NOT *LOST* ANYMORE...

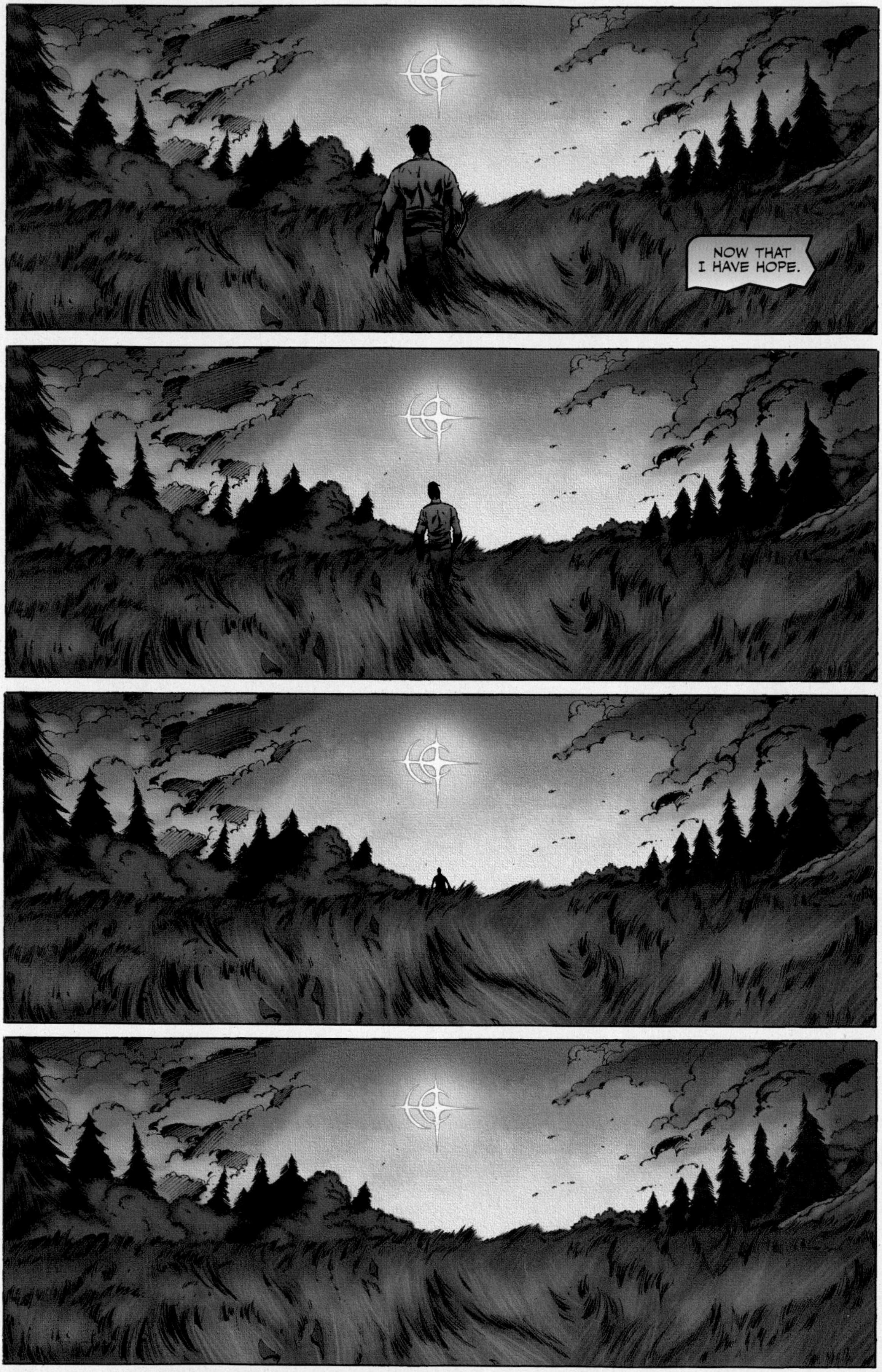
NOW THAT I HAVE HOPE.

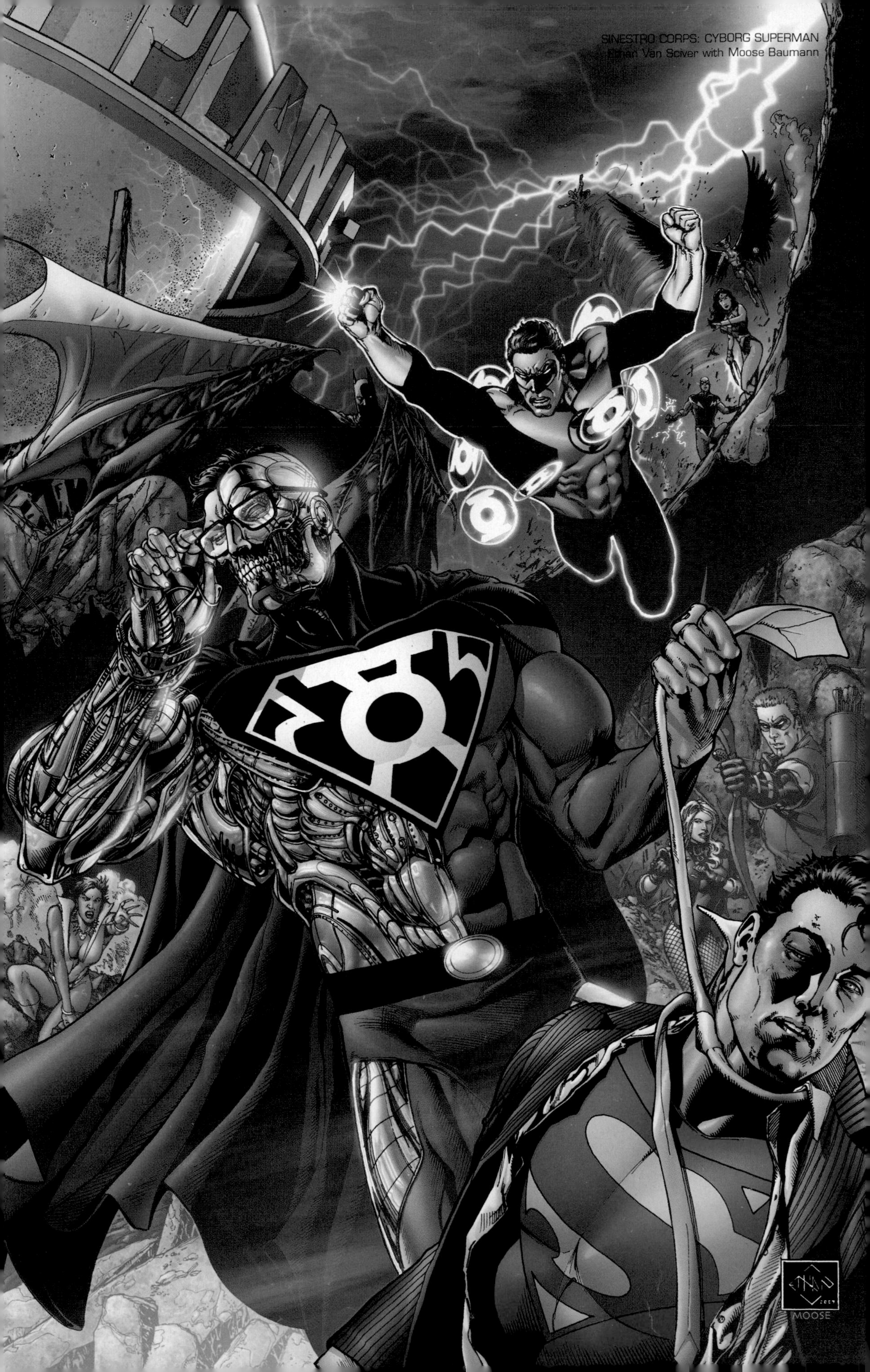
MOOSE

SINESTRO CORPS: CYBORG SUPERMAN
Ethan Van Sciver with Moose Baumann

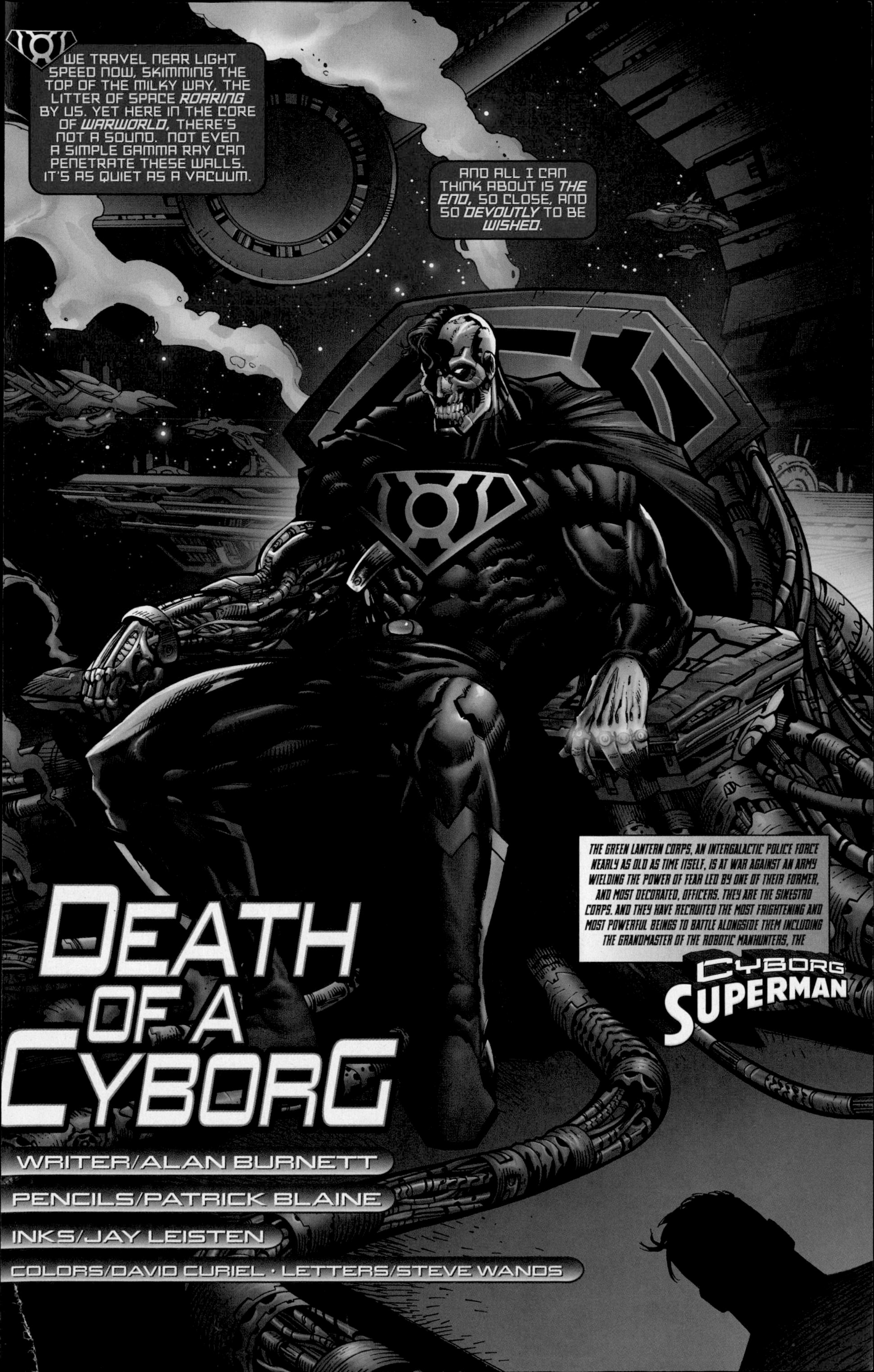
WE TRAVEL NEAR LIGHT SPEED NOW, SKIMMING THE TOP OF THE MILKY WAY, THE LITTER OF SPACE ROARING BY US. YET HERE IN THE CORE OF WARWORLD, THERE'S NOT A SOUND. NOT EVEN A SIMPLE GAMMA RAY CAN PENETRATE THESE WALLS. IT'S AS QUIET AS A VACUUM.
AND ALL I CAN THINK ABOUT IS THE END, SO CLOSE, AND SO DEVOUTLY TO BE WISHED.
THE GREEN LANTERN CORPS, AN INTERGALACTIC POLICE FORCE NEARLY AS OLD AS TIME ITSELF, IS AT WAR AGAINST AN ARMY WIELDING THE POWER OF FEAR LED BY ONE OF THEIR FORMER, AND MOST DECORATED, OFFICERS. THEY ARE THE SINESTRO CORPS. AND THEY HAVE RECRUITED THE MOST FRIGHTENING AND MOST POWERFUL BEINGS TO BATTLE ALONGSIDE THEM INCLUDING THE GRANDMASTER OF THE ROBOTIC MANHUNTERS, THE
CYBORG SUPERMAN
DEATH OF A CYBORG
WRITER/ALAN BURNETT
PENCILS/PATRICK BLAINE
INKS/JAY LEISTEN
COLORS/DAVID CURIEL · LETTERS/STEVE WANDS

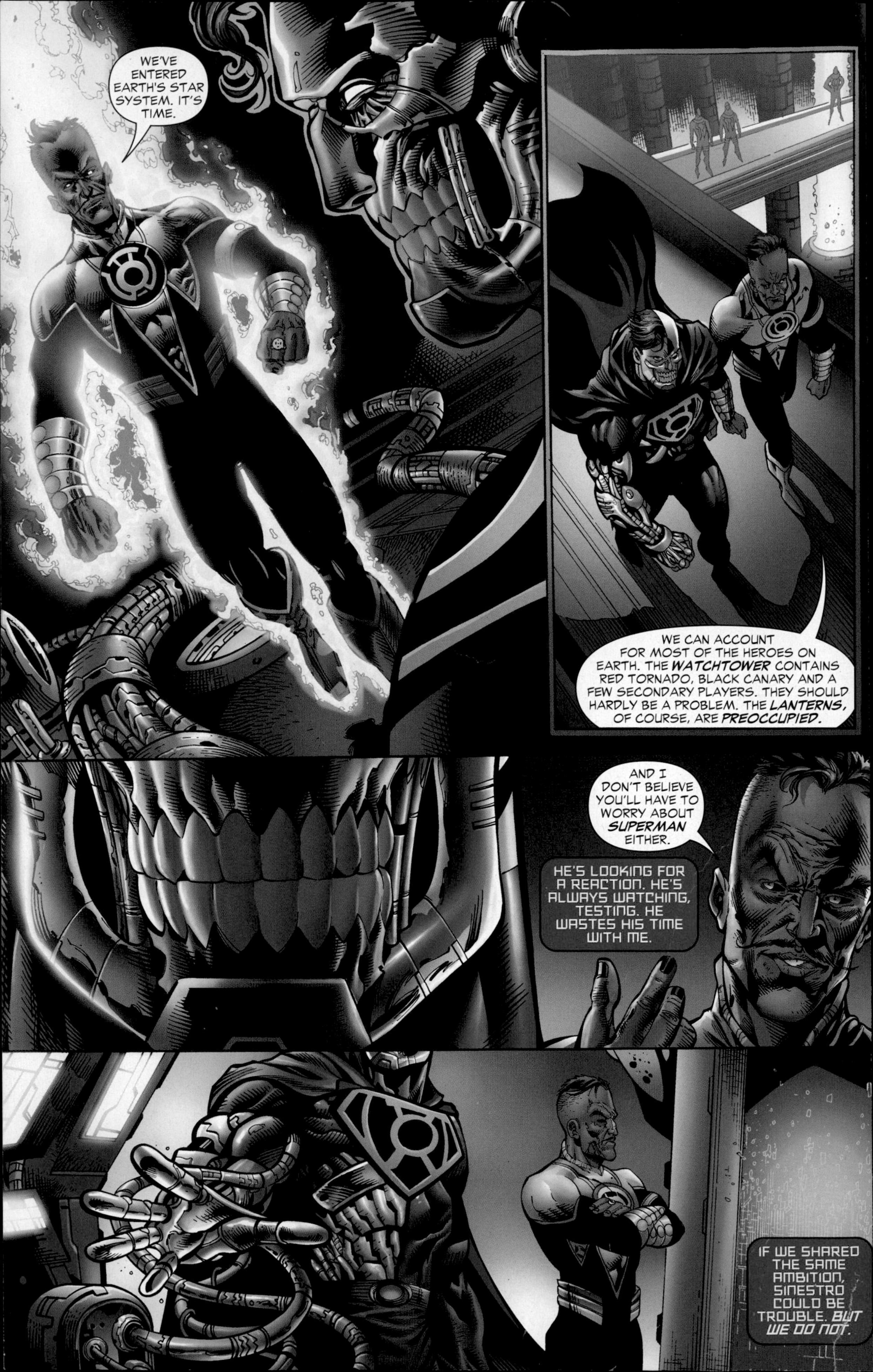
WE'VE ENTERED EARTH'S STAR SYSTEM. IT'S TIME.
WE CAN ACCOUNT FOR MOST OF THE HEROES ON EARTH. THE WATCHTOWER CONTAINS RED TORNADO, BLACK CANARY AND A FEW SECONDARY PLAYERS. THEY SHOULD HARDLY BE A PROBLEM. THE LANTERNS, OF COURSE, ARE PREOCCUPIED.
AND I DON'T BELIEVE YOU'LL HAVE TO WORRY ABOUT SUPERMAN EITHER.
HE'S LOOKING FOR A REACTION. HE'S ALWAYS WATCHING, TESTING. HE WASTES HIS TIME WITH ME.
IF WE SHARED THE SAME AMBITION, SINESTRO COULD BE TROUBLE. BUT WE DO NOT.

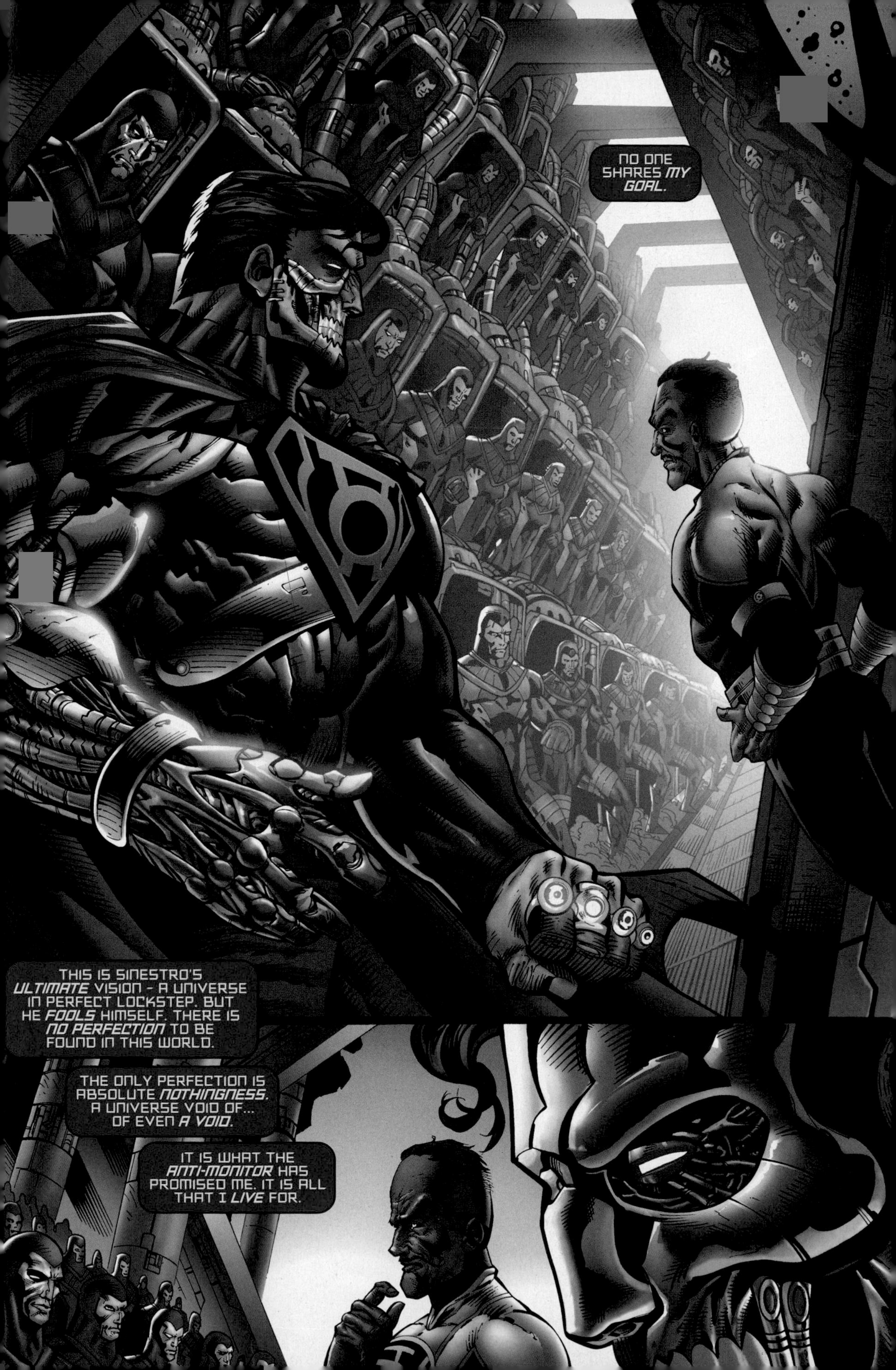
NO ONE SHARES *MY* *GOAL.*
THIS IS SINESTRO'S *ULTIMATE* VISION - A UNIVERSE IN PERFECT LOCKSTEP. BUT HE *FOOLS* HIMSELF. THERE IS *NO PERFECTION* TO BE FOUND IN THIS WORLD.
THE ONLY PERFECTION IS ABSOLUTE *NOTHINGNESS.* A UNIVERSE VOID OF... OF EVEN *A VOID*.
IT IS WHAT THE *ANTI-MONITOR* HAS PROMISED ME. IT IS ALL THAT I *LIVE* FOR.

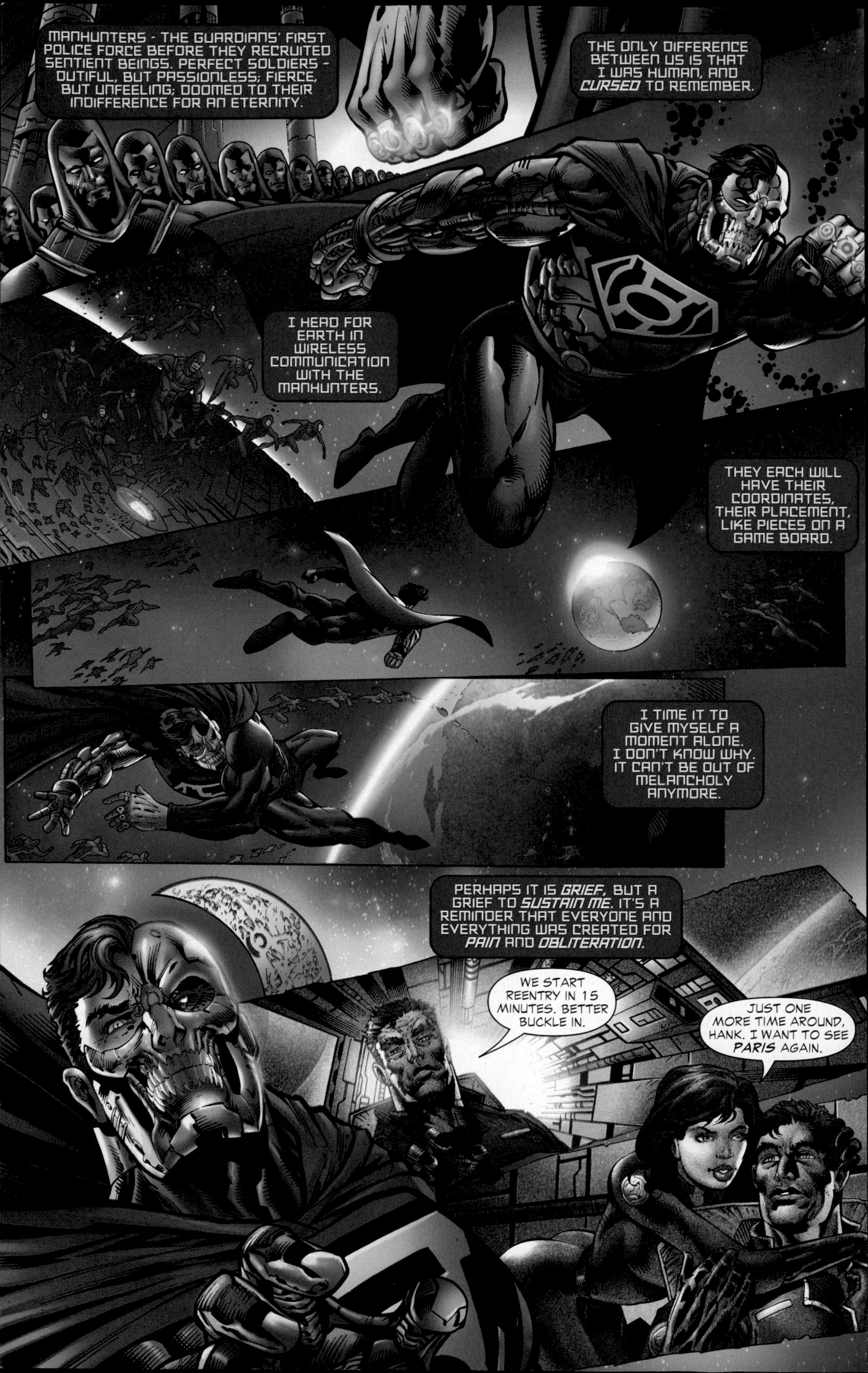
MANHUNTERS - THE GUARDIANS' FIRST POLICE FORCE BEFORE THEY RECRUITED SENTIENT BEINGS. PERFECT SOLDIERS - DUTIFUL, BUT PASSIONLESS; FIERCE, BUT UNFEELING; DOOMED TO THEIR INDIFFERENCE FOR AN ETERNITY.
THE ONLY DIFFERENCE BETWEEN US IS THAT I WAS HUMAN, AND CURSED TO REMEMBER.
I HEAD FOR EARTH IN WIRELESS COMMUNICATION WITH THE MANHUNTERS.
THEY EACH WILL HAVE THEIR COORDINATES, THEIR PLACEMENT, LIKE PIECES ON A GAME BOARD.
I TIME IT TO GIVE MYSELF A MOMENT ALONE. I DON'T KNOW WHY. IT CAN'T BE OUT OF MELANCHOLY ANYMORE.
PERHAPS IT IS GRIEF, BUT A GRIEF TO SUSTAIN ME. IT'S A REMINDER THAT EVERYONE AND EVERYTHING WAS CREATED FOR PAIN AND OBLITERATION.
WE START REENTRY IN 15 MINUTES. BETTER BUCKLE IN.
JUST ONE MORE TIME AROUND, HANK. I WANT TO SEE PARIS AGAIN.

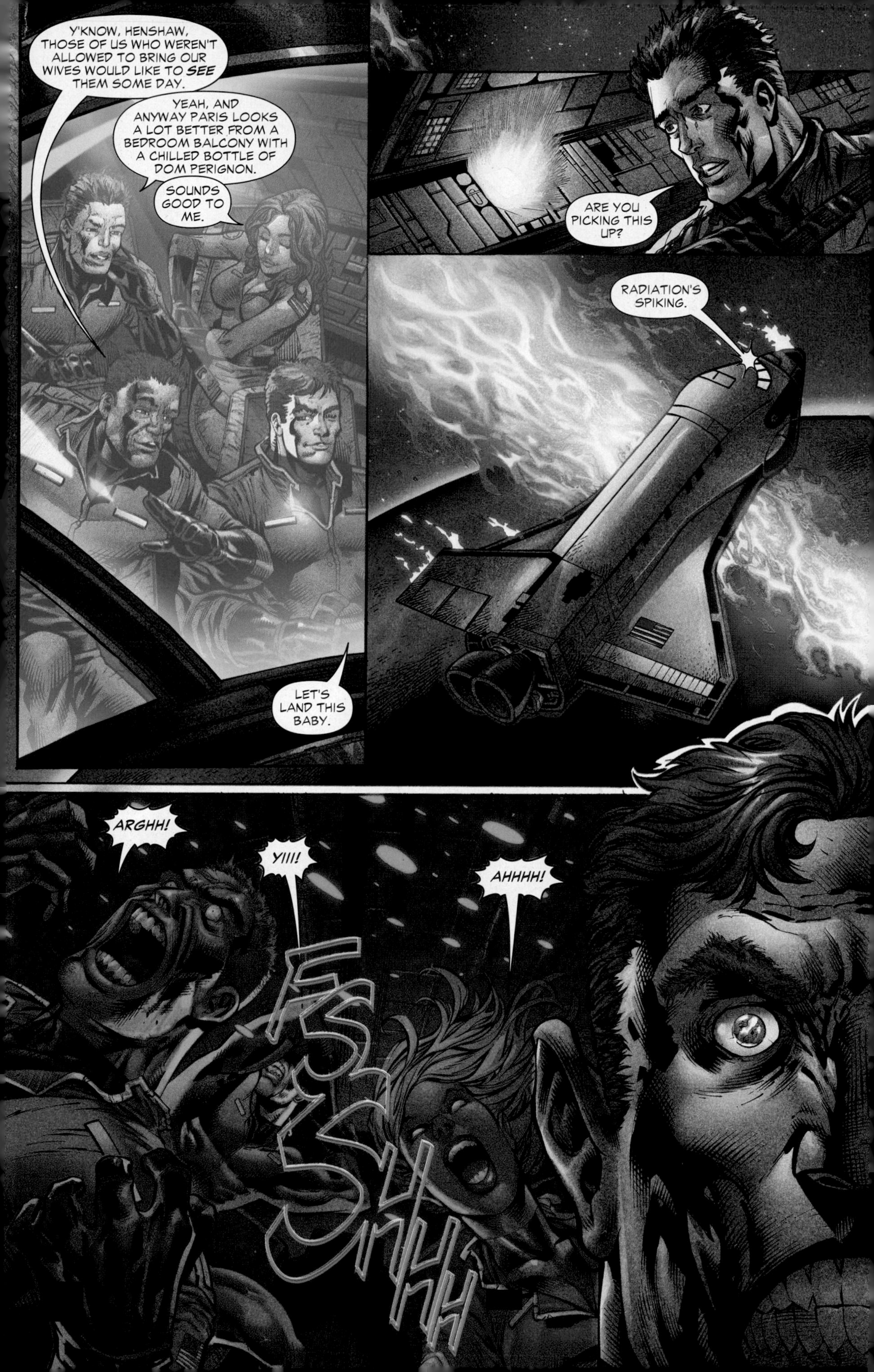
Y'KNOW, HENSHAW, THOSE OF US WHO WEREN'T ALLOWED TO BRING OUR WIVES WOULD LIKE TO SEE THEM SOME DAY.
YEAH, AND ANYWAY PARIS LOOKS A LOT BETTER FROM A BEDROOM BALCONY WITH A CHILLED BOTTLE OF DOM PERIGNON.
SOUNDS GOOD TO ME.
LET'S LAND THIS BABY.
ARE YOU PICKING THIS UP?
RADIATION'S SPIKING.
ARGHH!
YIII!
AHHHH!
FSSSHHH

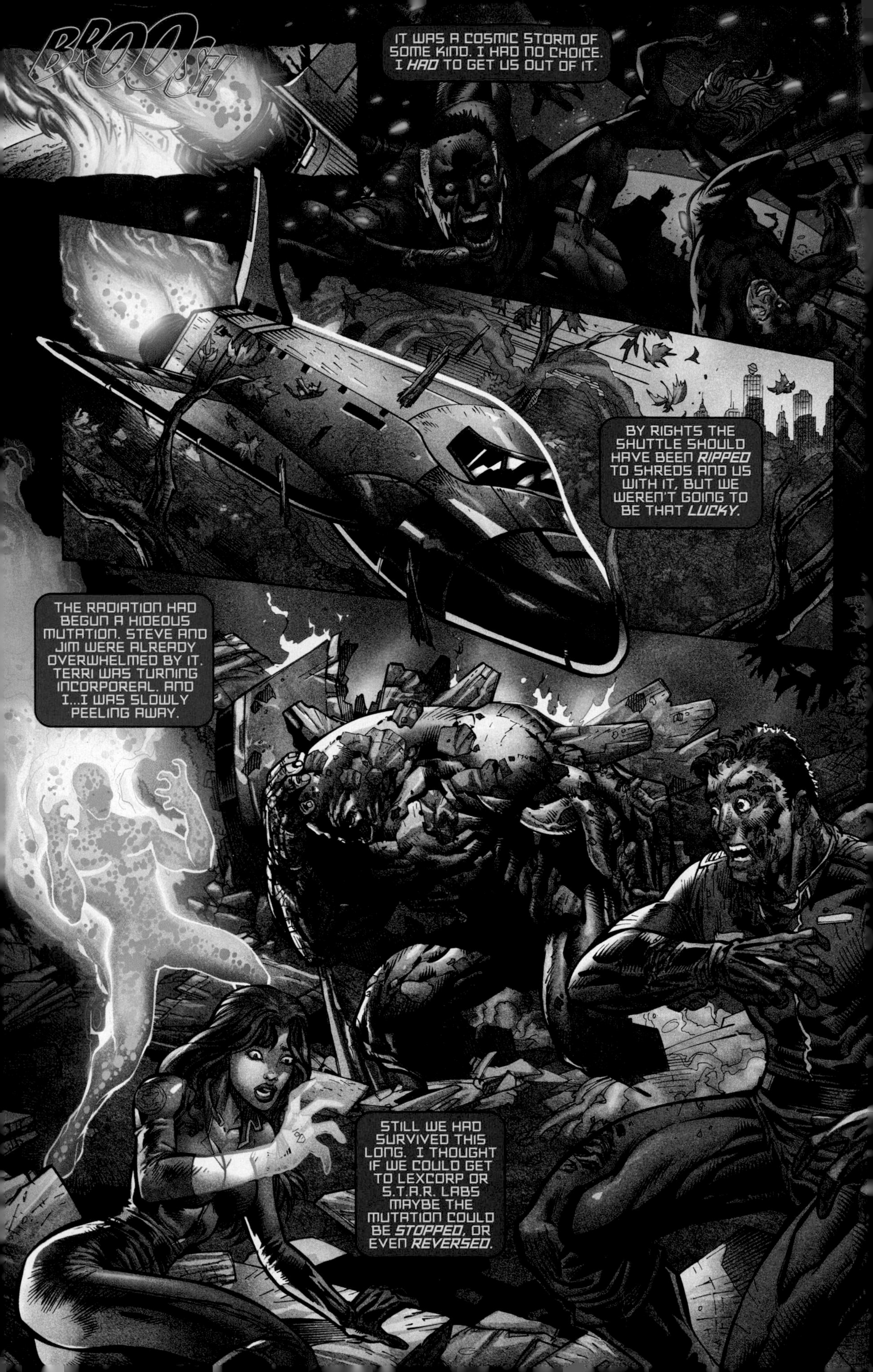
BROOOSH
IT WAS A COSMIC STORM OF SOME KIND. I HAD NO CHOICE. I *HAD* TO GET US OUT OF IT.
BY RIGHTS THE SHUTTLE SHOULD HAVE BEEN *RIPPED* TO SHREDS AND US WITH IT, BUT WE WEREN'T GOING TO BE THAT *LUCKY*.
THE RADIATION HAD BEGUN A HIDEOUS MUTATION. STEVE AND JIM WERE ALREADY OVERWHELMED BY IT. TERRI WAS TURNING INCORPOREAL. AND I...I WAS SLOWLY PEELING AWAY.
STILL WE HAD SURVIVED THIS LONG. I THOUGHT IF WE COULD GET TO LEXCORP OR S.T.A.R. LABS MAYBE THE MUTATION COULD BE *STOPPED*, OR EVEN *REVERSED*.

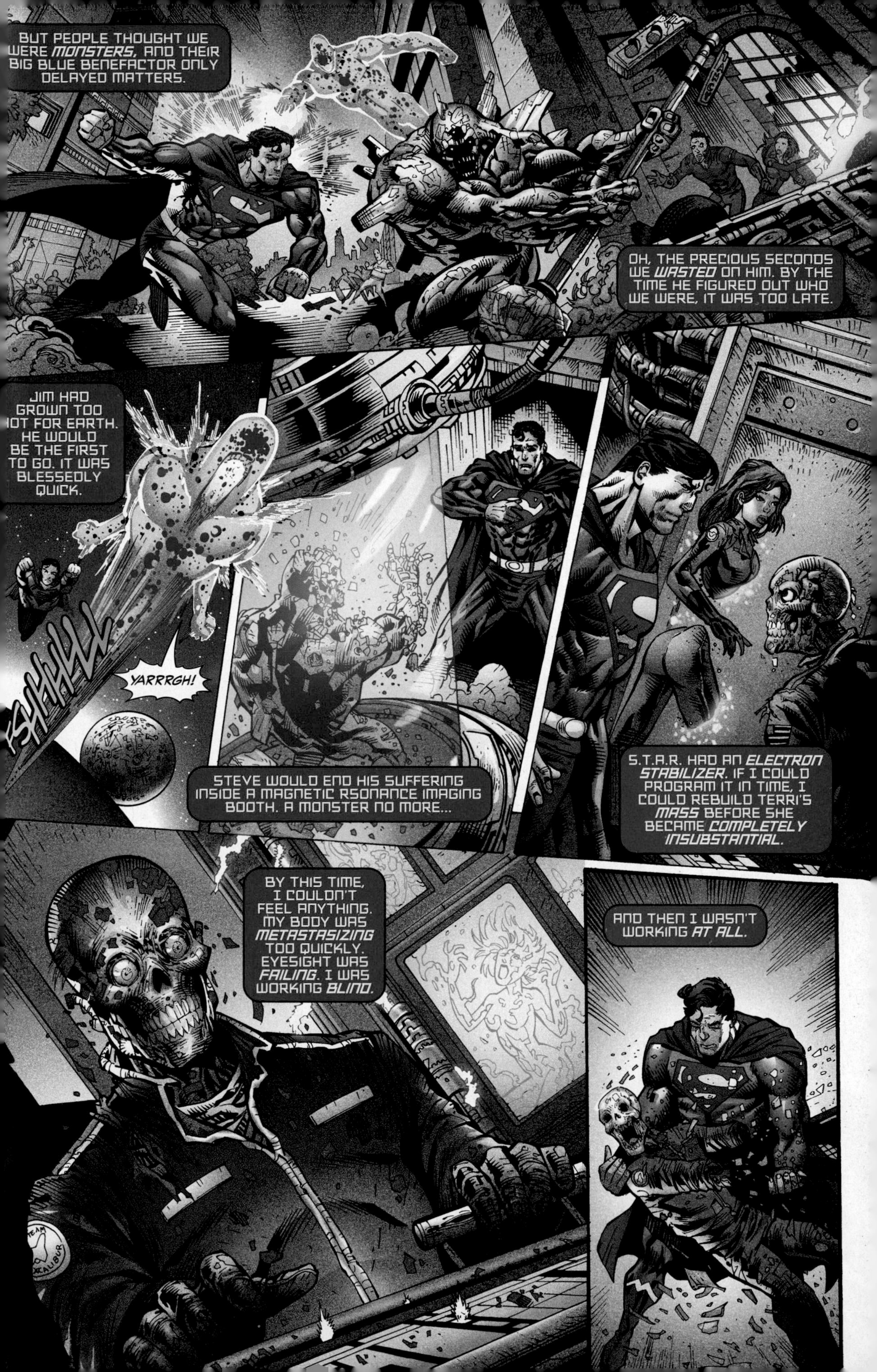
BUT PEOPLE THOUGHT WE WERE MONSTERS, AND THEIR BIG BLUE BENEFACTOR ONLY DELAYED MATTERS.
OH, THE PRECIOUS SECONDS WE WASTED ON HIM. BY THE TIME HE FIGURED OUT WHO WE WERE, IT WAS TOO LATE.
JIM HAD GROWN TOO HOT FOR EARTH. HE WOULD BE THE FIRST TO GO. IT WAS BLESSEDLY QUICK.
SHHHWW
YARRRGH!
STEVE WOULD END HIS SUFFERING INSIDE A MAGNETIC RSONANCE IMAGING BOOTH. A MONSTER NO MORE...
S.T.A.R. HAD AN ELECTRON STABILIZER. IF I COULD PROGRAM IT IN TIME, I COULD REBUILD TERRI'S MASS BEFORE SHE BECAME COMPLETELY INSUBSTANTIAL.
BY THIS TIME, I COULDN'T FEEL ANYTHING. MY BODY WAS METASTASIZING TOO QUICKLY. EYESIGHT WAS FAILING. I WAS WORKING BLIND.
AND THEN I WASN'T WORKING AT ALL.

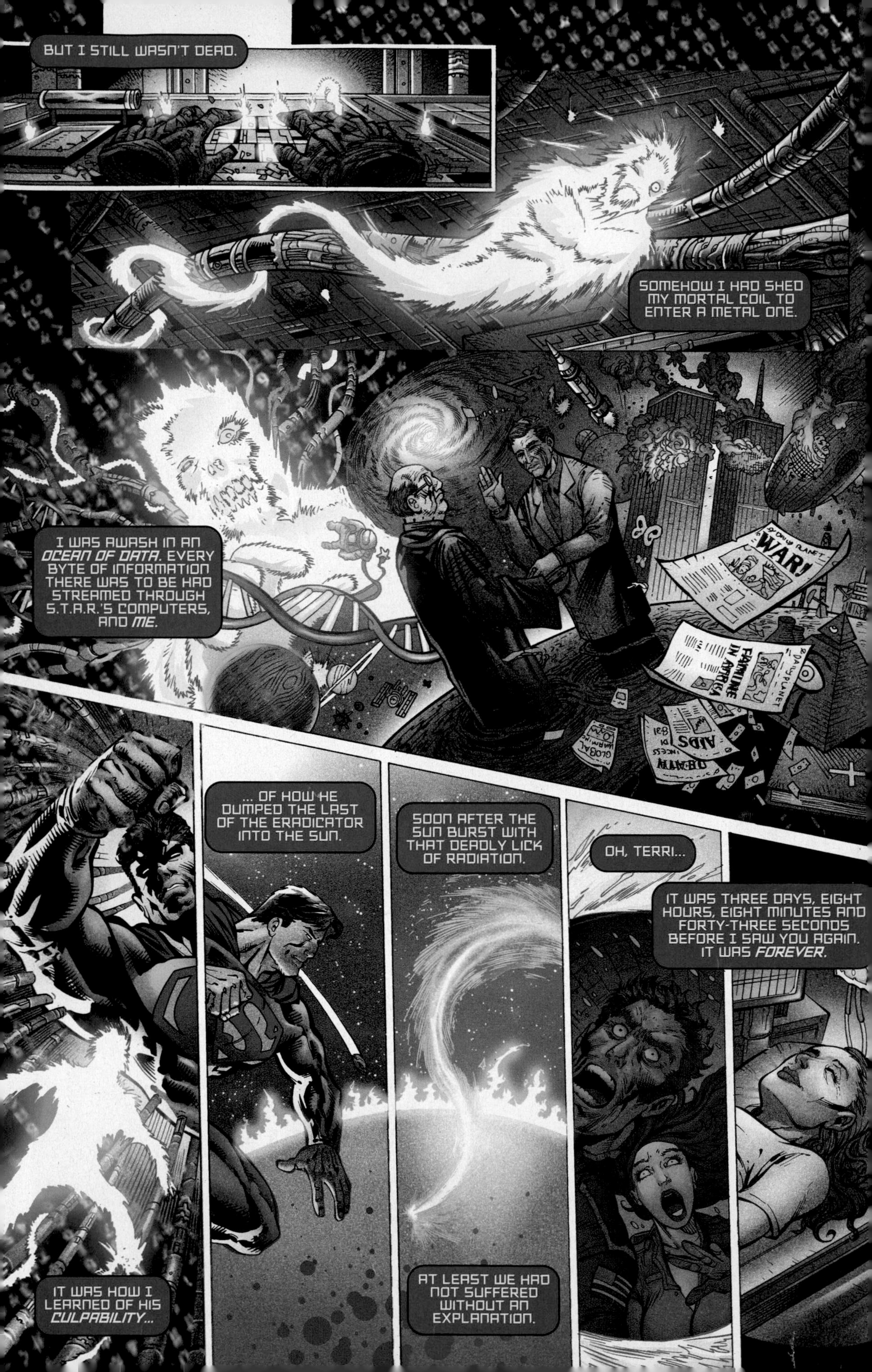
BUT I STILL WASN'T DEAD.
SOMEHOW I HAD SHED MY MORTAL COIL TO ENTER A METAL ONE.
I WAS AWASH IN AN *OCEAN OF DATA.* EVERY BYTE OF INFORMATION THERE WAS TO BE HAD STREAMED THROUGH S.T.A.R.'S COMPUTERS, AND *ME.*
WAR!
FAMINE IN AFRICA
AIDS
GLOBAL WARMING
IT WAS HOW I LEARNED OF HIS *CULPABILITY...*
... OF HOW HE DUMPED THE LAST OF THE ERADICATOR INTO THE SUN.
SOON AFTER THE SUN BURST WITH THAT DEADLY LICK OF RADIATION.
AT LEAST WE HAD NOT SUFFERED WITHOUT AN EXPLANATION.
OH, TERRI...
IT WAS THREE DAYS, EIGHT HOURS, EIGHT MINUTES AND FORTY-THREE SECONDS BEFORE I SAW YOU AGAIN. IT WAS *FOREVER.*

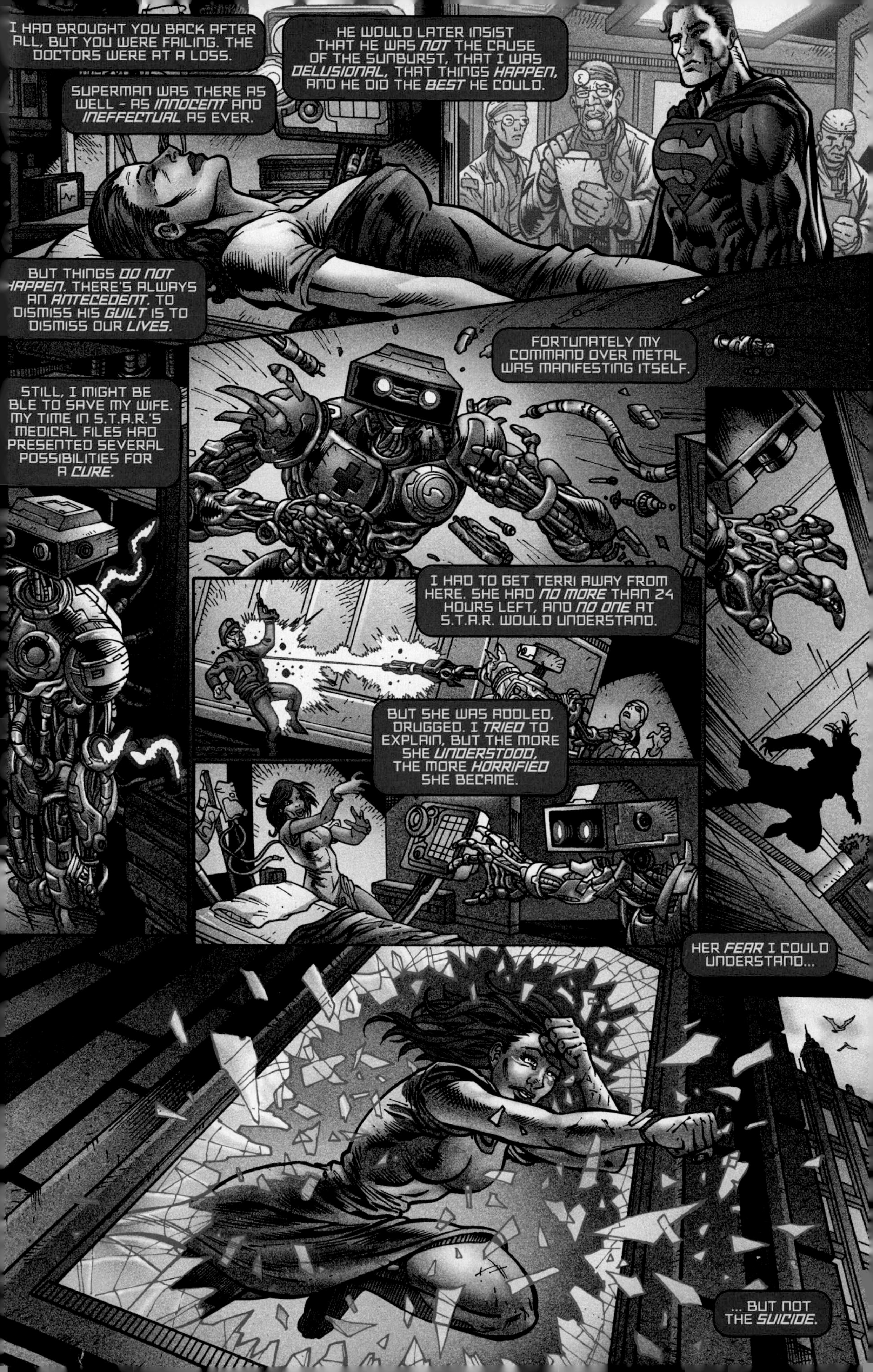

I HAD BROUGHT YOU BACK AFTER ALL, BUT YOU WERE FAILING. THE DOCTORS WERE AT A LOSS.
SUPERMAN WAS THERE AS WELL - AS INNOCENT AND INEFFECTUAL AS EVER.
HE WOULD LATER INSIST THAT HE WAS NOT THE CAUSE OF THE SUNBURST, THAT I WAS DELUSIONAL, THAT THINGS HAPPEN, AND HE DID THE BEST HE COULD.
BUT THINGS DO NOT HAPPEN. THERE'S ALWAYS AN ANTECEDENT. TO DISMISS HIS GUILT IS TO DISMISS OUR LIVES.
STILL, I MIGHT BE BLE TO SAVE MY WIFE. MY TIME IN S.T.A.R.'S MEDICAL FILES HAD PRESENTED SEVERAL POSSIBILITIES FOR A CURE.
FORTUNATELY MY COMMAND OVER METAL WAS MANIFESTING ITSELF.
I HAD TO GET TERRI AWAY FROM HERE. SHE HAD NO MORE THAN 24 HOURS LEFT, AND NO ONE AT S.T.A.R. WOULD UNDERSTAND.
BUT SHE WAS ADDLED, DRUGGED. I TRIED TO EXPLAIN, BUT THE MORE SHE UNDERSTOOD, THE MORE HORRIFIED SHE BECAME.
HER FEAR I COULD UNDERSTAND...
...BUT NOT THE SUICIDE.

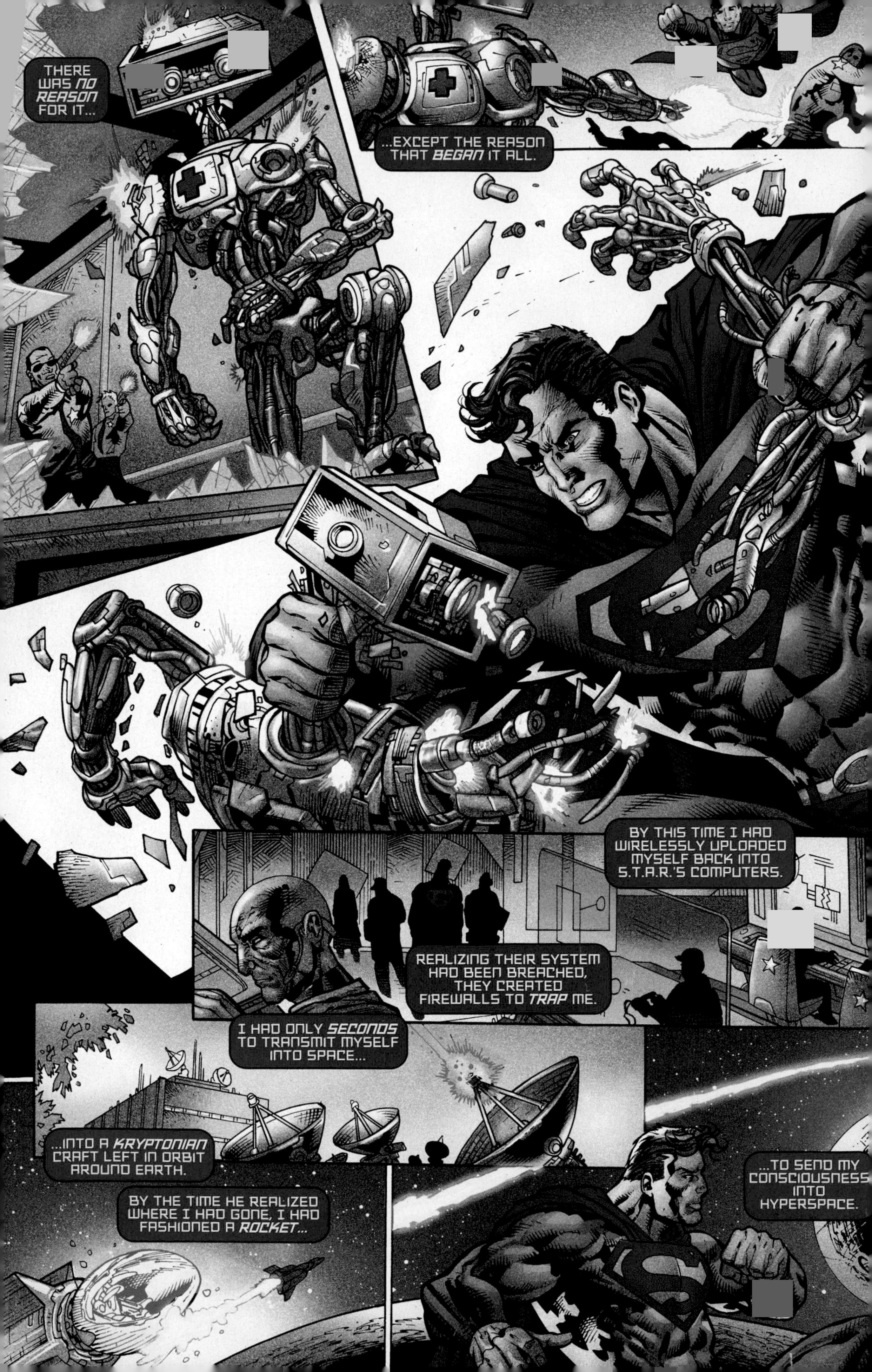
THERE WAS NO REASON FOR IT...
...EXCEPT THE REASON THAT BEGAN IT ALL.
BY THIS TIME I HAD WIRELESSLY UPLOADED MYSELF BACK INTO S.T.A.R.'S COMPUTERS.
REALIZING THEIR SYSTEM HAD BEEN BREACHED, THEY CREATED FIREWALLS TO TRAP ME.
I HAD ONLY SECONDS TO TRANSMIT MYSELF INTO SPACE...
...INTO A KRYPTONIAN CRAFT LEFT IN ORBIT AROUND EARTH.
BY THE TIME HE REALIZED WHERE I HAD GONE, I HAD FASHIONED A ROCKET...
...TO SEND MY CONSCIOUSNESS INTO HYPERSPACE.

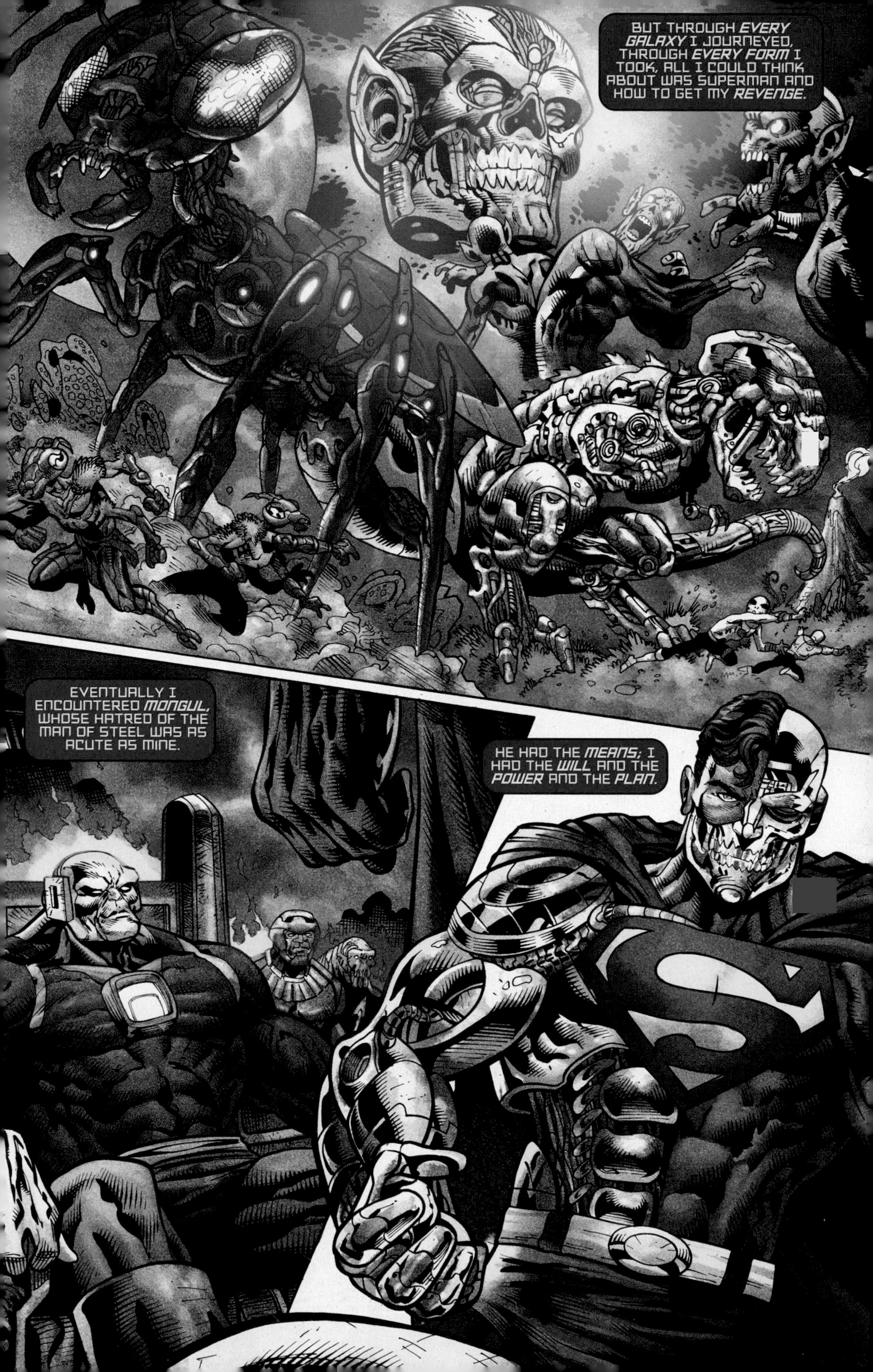
BUT THROUGH EVERY GALAXY I JOURNEYED, THROUGH EVERY FORM I TOOK, ALL I COULD THINK ABOUT WAS SUPERMAN AND HOW TO GET MY REVENGE.
EVENTUALLY I ENCOUNTERED MONGUL, WHOSE HATRED OF THE MAN OF STEEL WAS AS ACUTE AS MINE.
HE HAD THE MEANS; I HAD THE WILL AND THE POWER AND THE PLAN.

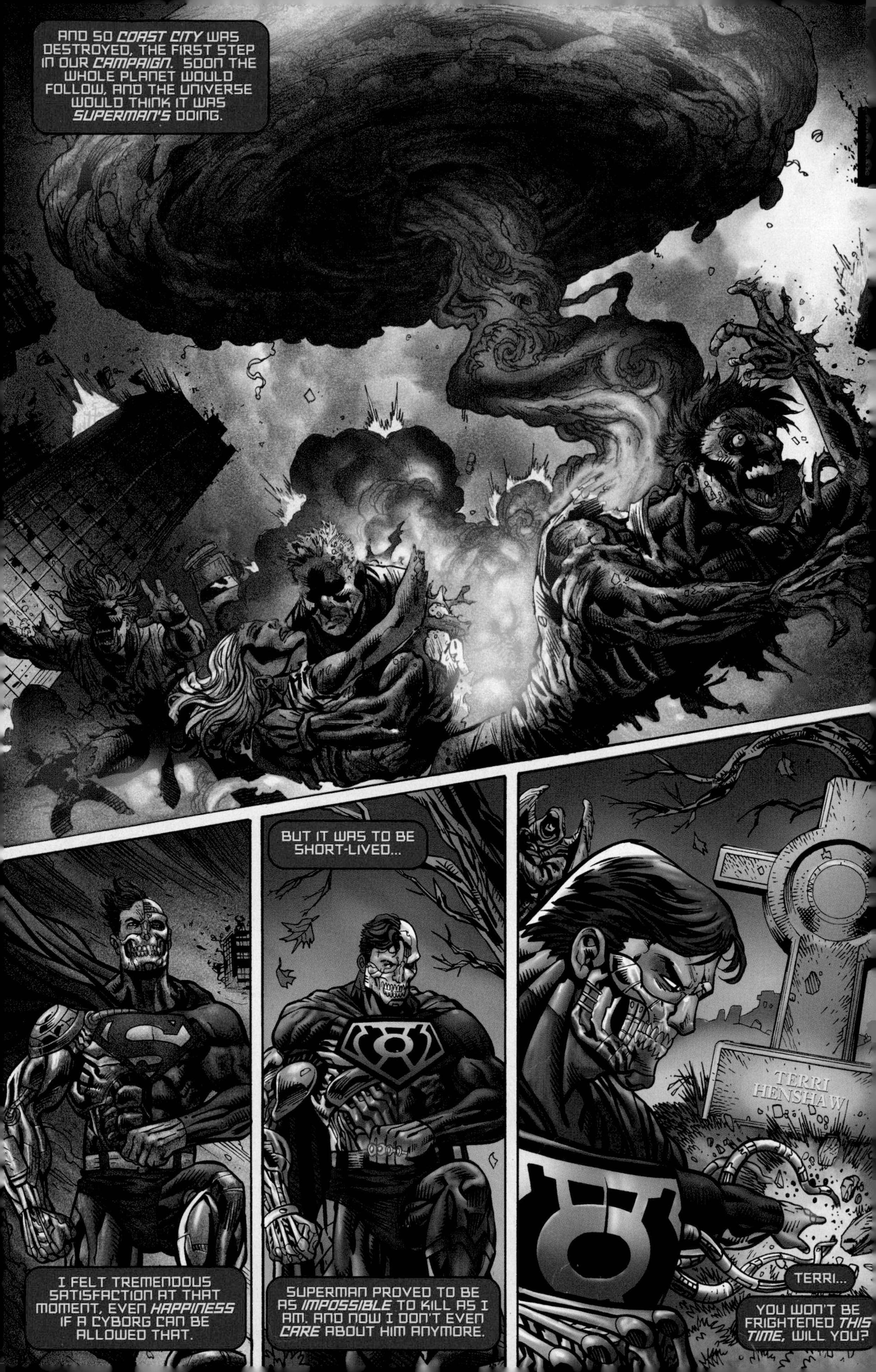
AND SO COAST CITY WAS DESTROYED, THE FIRST STEP IN OUR CAMPAIGN. SOON THE WHOLE PLANET WOULD FOLLOW, AND THE UNIVERSE WOULD THINK IT WAS SUPERMAN'S DOING.
I FELT TREMENDOUS SATISFACTION AT THAT MOMENT, EVEN HAPPINESS IF A CYBORG CAN BE ALLOWED THAT.
BUT IT WAS TO BE SHORT-LIVED...
SUPERMAN PROVED TO BE AS IMPOSSIBLE TO KILL AS I AM. AND NOW I DON'T EVEN CARE ABOUT HIM ANYMORE.
TERRI HENSHAW
TERRI...
YOU WON'T BE FRIGHTENED THIS TIME, WILL YOU?

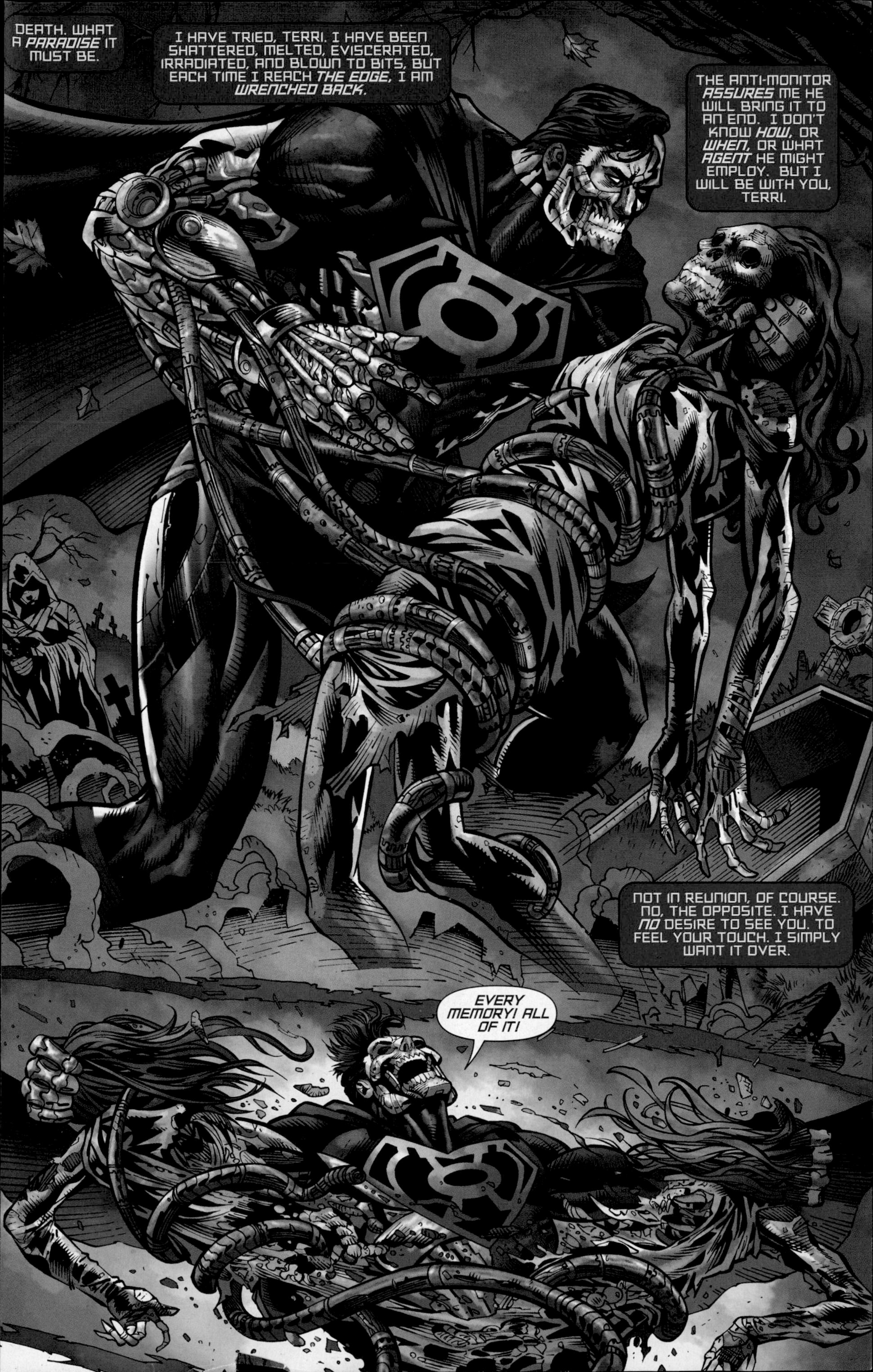
DEATH. WHAT A *PARADISE* IT MUST BE.
I HAVE TRIED, TERRI. I HAVE BEEN SHATTERED, MELTED, EVISCERATED, IRRADIATED, AND BLOWN TO BITS, BUT EACH TIME I REACH *THE EDGE*, I AM *WRENCHED BACK*.
THE ANTI-MONITOR *ASSURES* ME HE WILL BRING IT TO AN END. I DON'T KNOW *HOW*, OR *WHEN*, OR WHAT *AGENT* HE MIGHT EMPLOY. BUT I WILL BE WITH YOU, TERRI.
NOT IN REUNION, OF COURSE. NO, THE OPPOSITE. I HAVE *NO* DESIRE TO SEE YOU. TO FEEL YOUR TOUCH. I SIMPLY WANT IT OVER.
EVERY MEMORY! ALL OF IT!

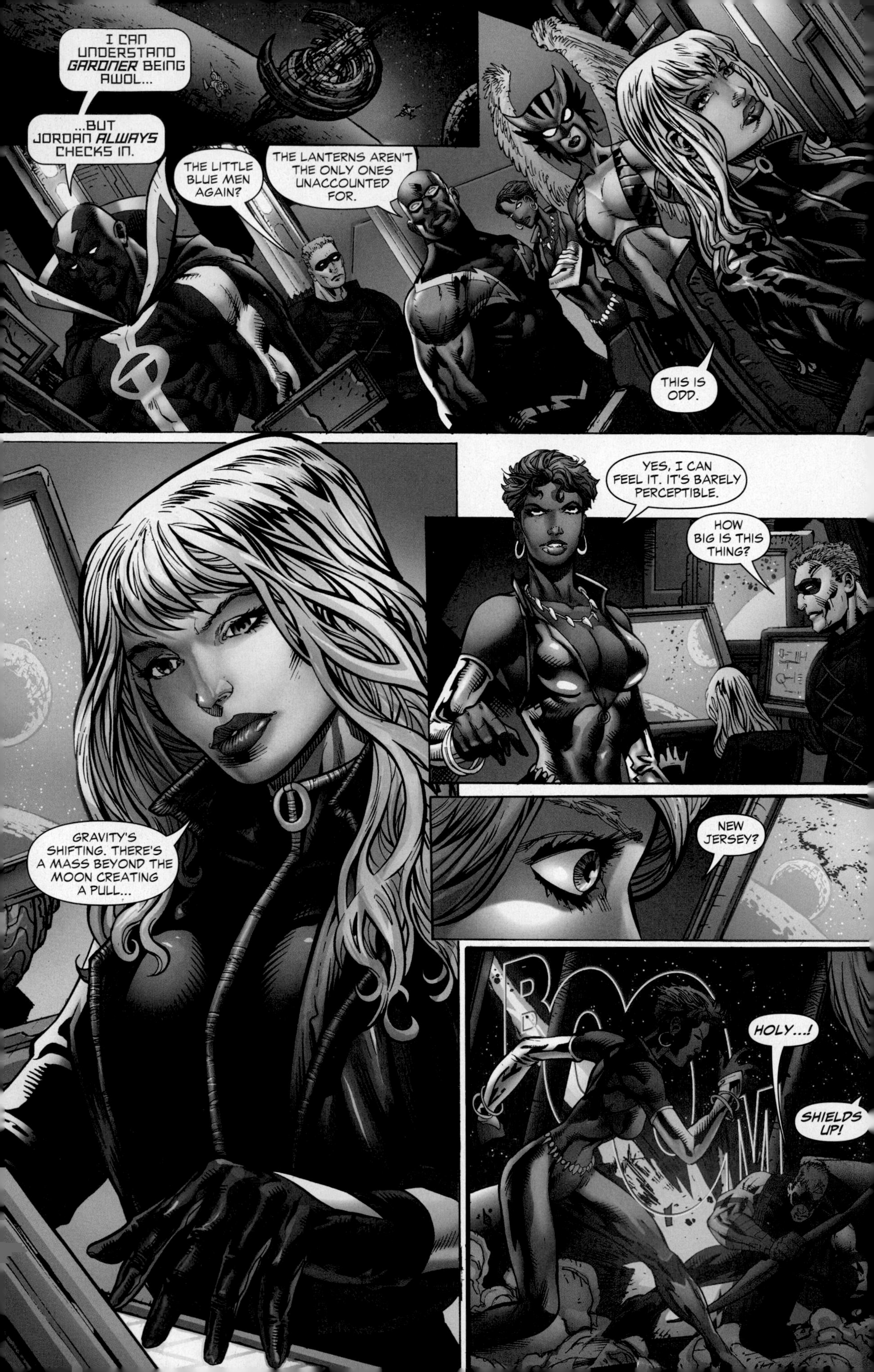
I CAN UNDERSTAND GARDNER BEING AWOL...
...BUT JORDAN ALWAYS CHECKS IN.
THE LITTLE BLUE MEN AGAIN?
THE LANTERNS AREN'T THE ONLY ONES UNACCOUNTED FOR.
THIS IS ODD.
GRAVITY'S SHIFTING. THERE'S A MASS BEYOND THE MOON CREATING A PULL...
YES, I CAN FEEL IT. IT'S BARELY PERCEPTIBLE.
HOW BIG IS THIS THING?
NEW JERSEY?
BOOM
HOLY...!
SHIELDS UP!

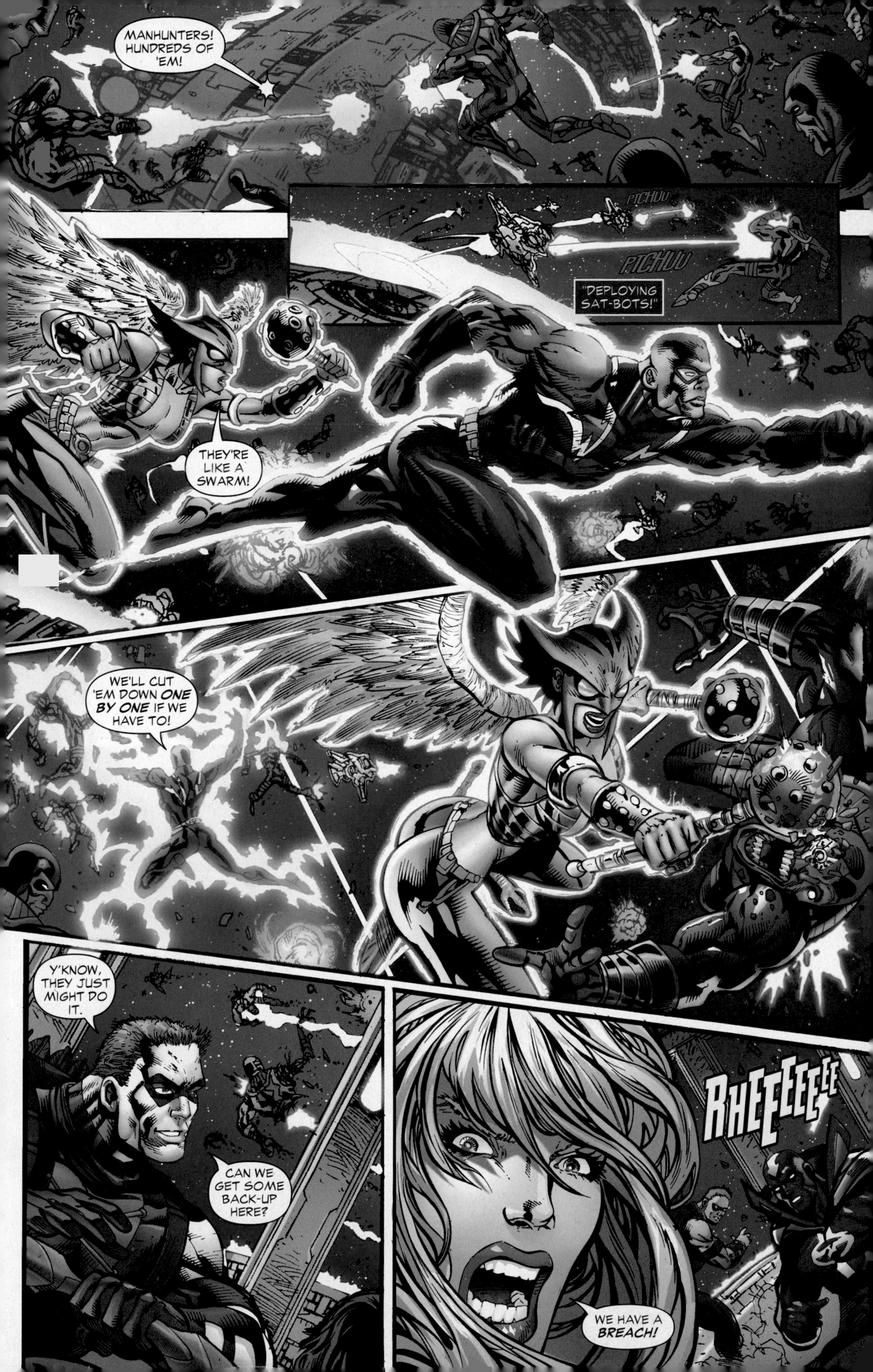

MANHUNTERS! HUNDREDS OF 'EM!
PICHUU
PICHUU
"DEPLOYING SAT-BOTS!"
THEY'RE LIKE A SWARM!
WE'LL CUT 'EM DOWN ONE BY ONE IF WE HAVE TO!
Y'KNOW, THEY JUST MIGHT DO IT.
CAN WE GET SOME BACK-UP HERE?
RHEEEEEEE
WE HAVE A BREACH!

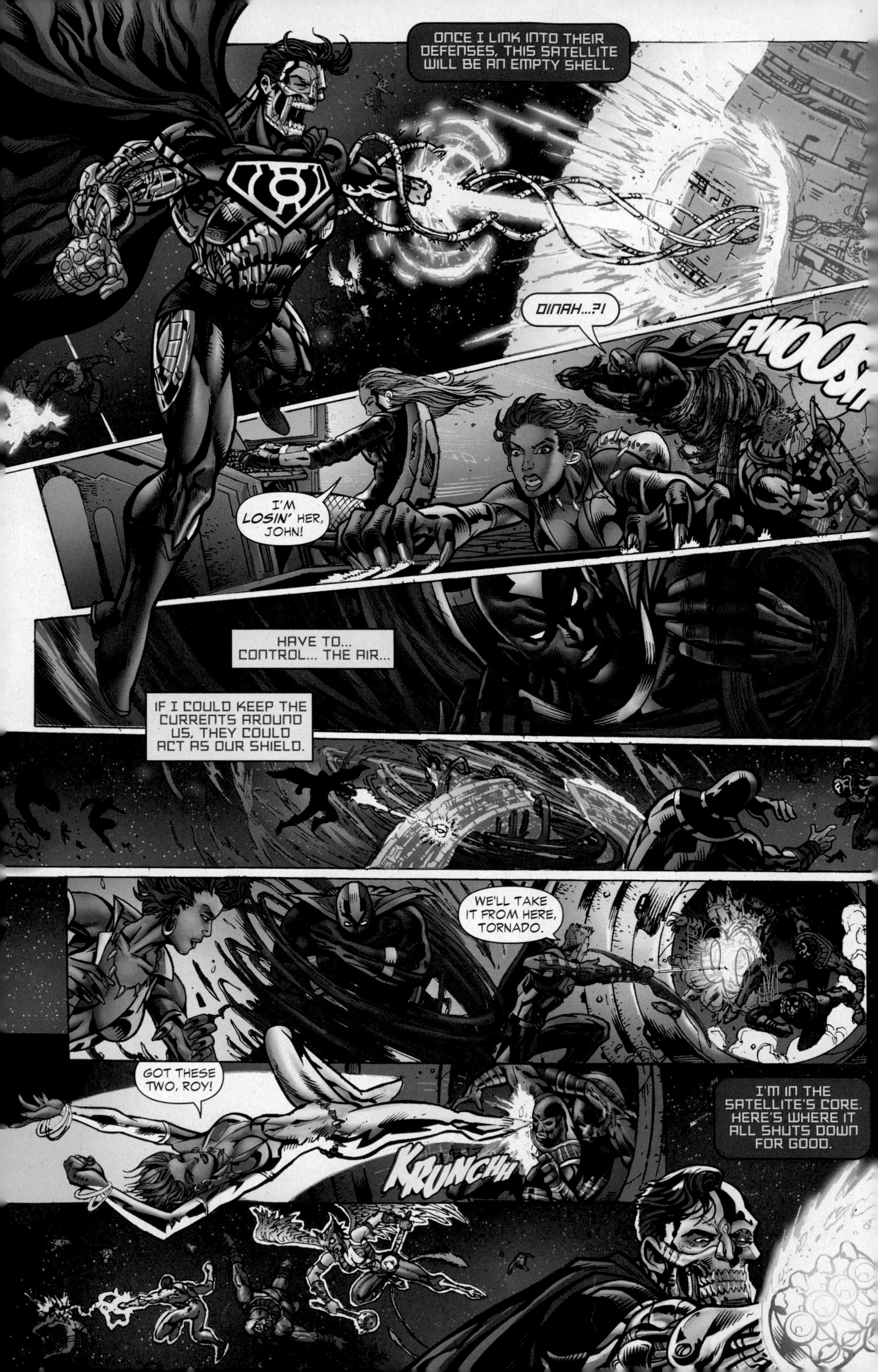
ONCE I LINK INTO THEIR DEFENSES, THIS SATELLITE WILL BE AN EMPTY SHELL.
DINAH...?!
FWOOSH
I'M LOSIN' HER, JOHN!
HAVE TO... CONTROL... THE AIR...
IF I COULD KEEP THE CURRENTS AROUND US, THEY COULD ACT AS OUR SHIELD.
WE'LL TAKE IT FROM HERE, TORNADO.
GOT THESE TWO, ROY!
KRUNCHH
I'M IN THE SATELLITE'S CORE. HERE'S WHERE IT ALL SHUTS DOWN FOR GOOD.

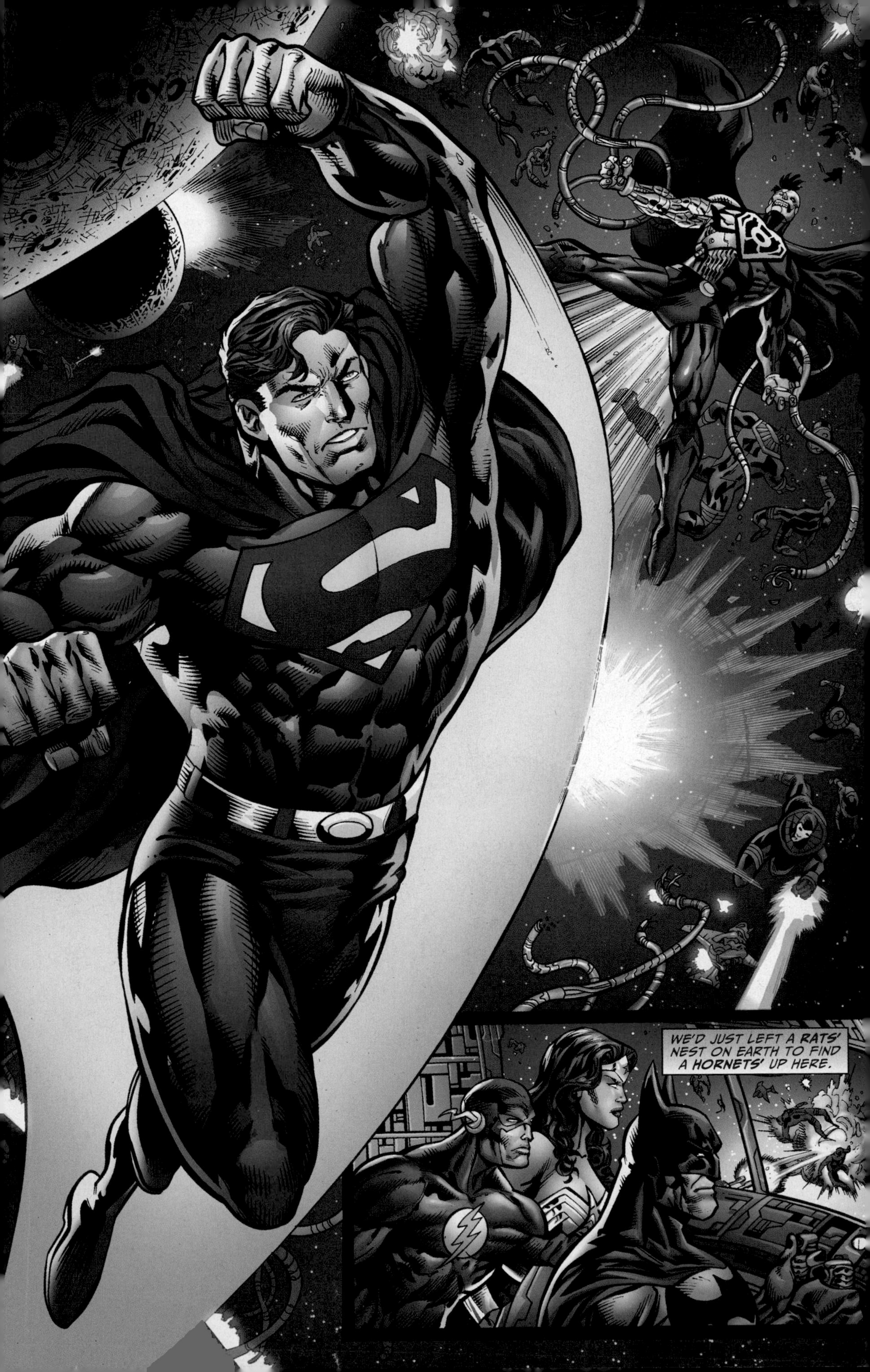
WE'D JUST LEFT A RATS' NEST ON EARTH TO FIND A HORNETS' UP HERE.

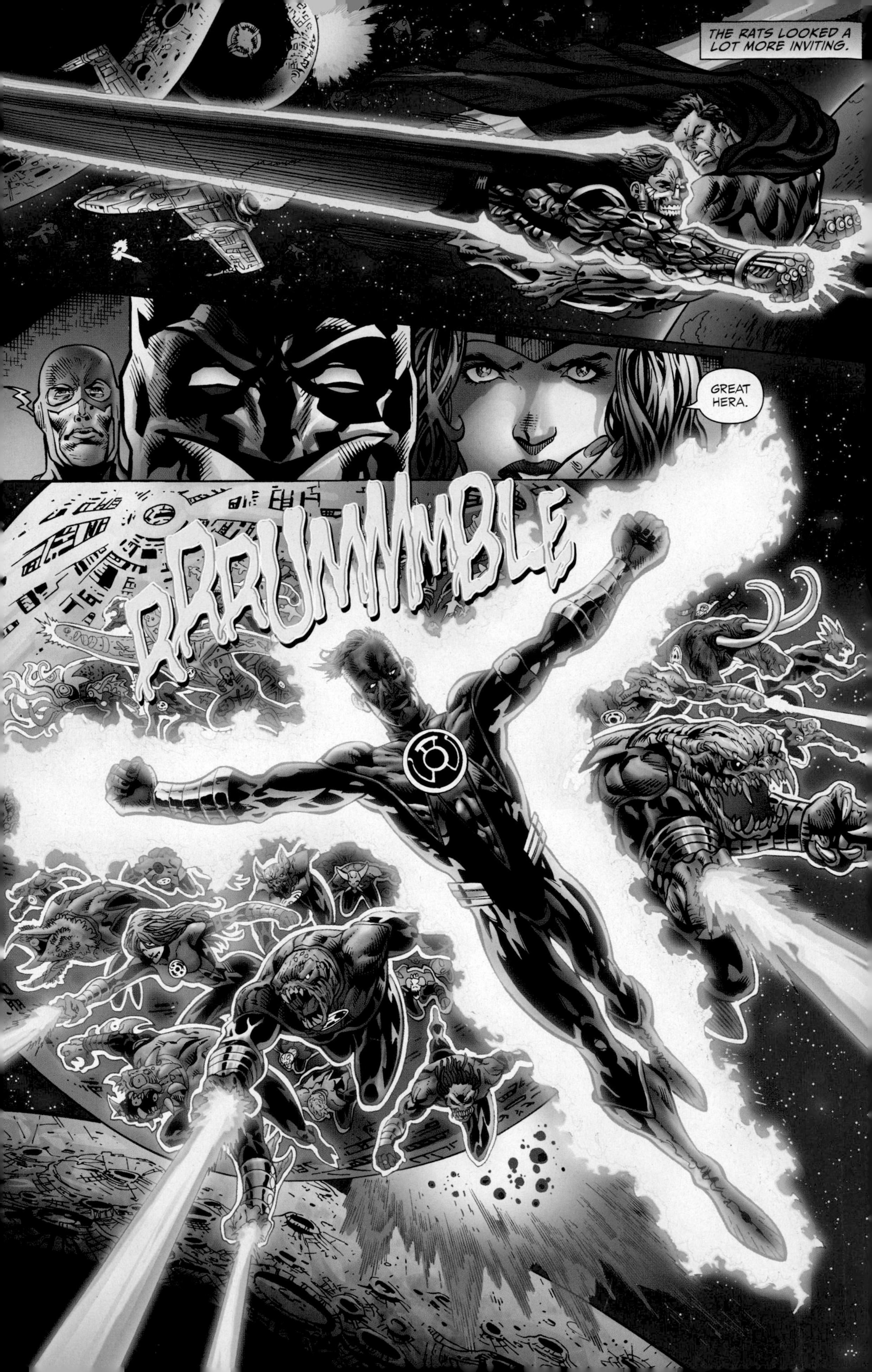
THE RATS LOOKED A LOT MORE INVITING.
GREAT HERA.
RRRUMMMBLE

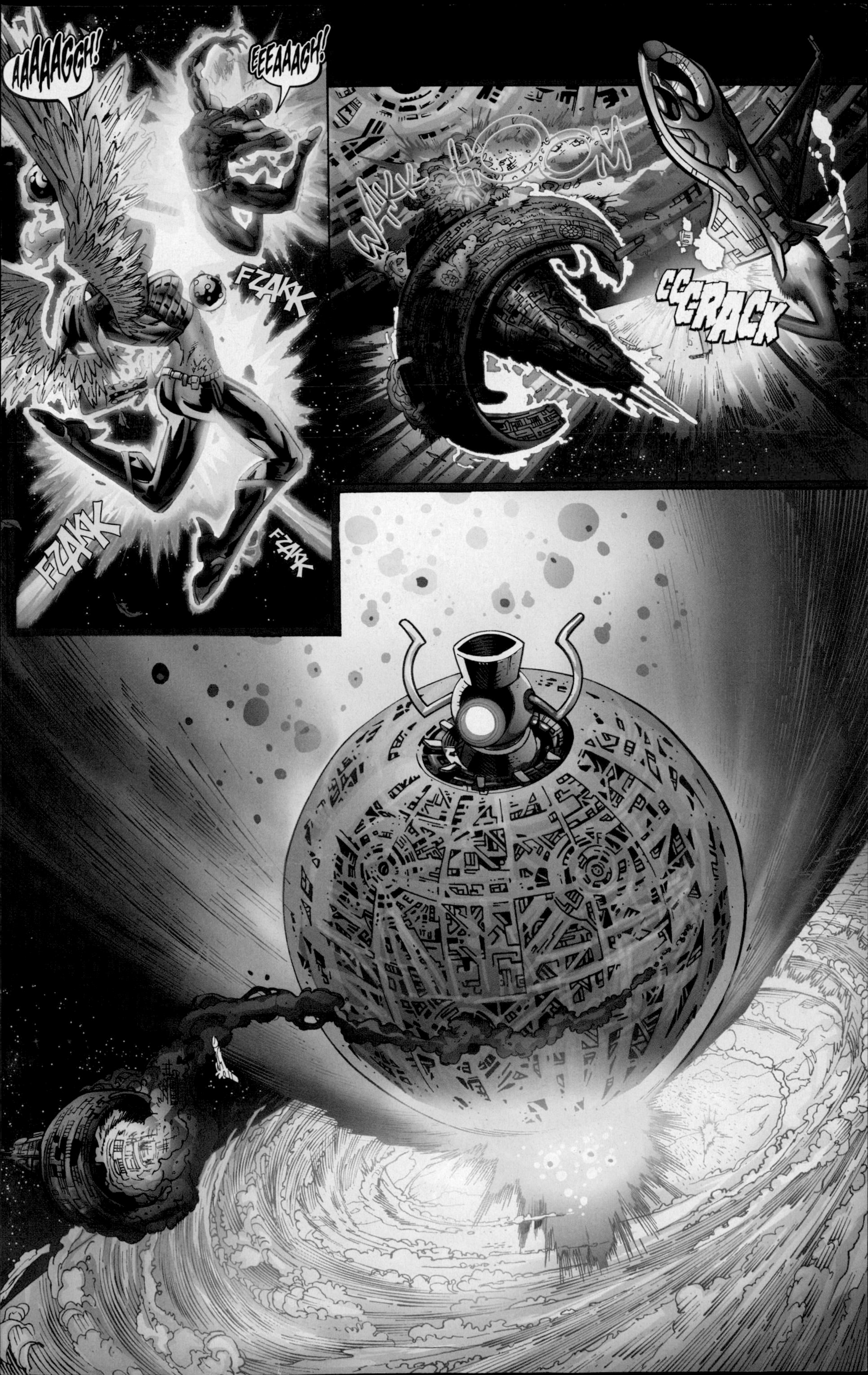
AAAAAGGH!
EEEAAAAGH!
FZAKK
WHAKK
KROOM
CCCRACK
FZAKK
FZAKK

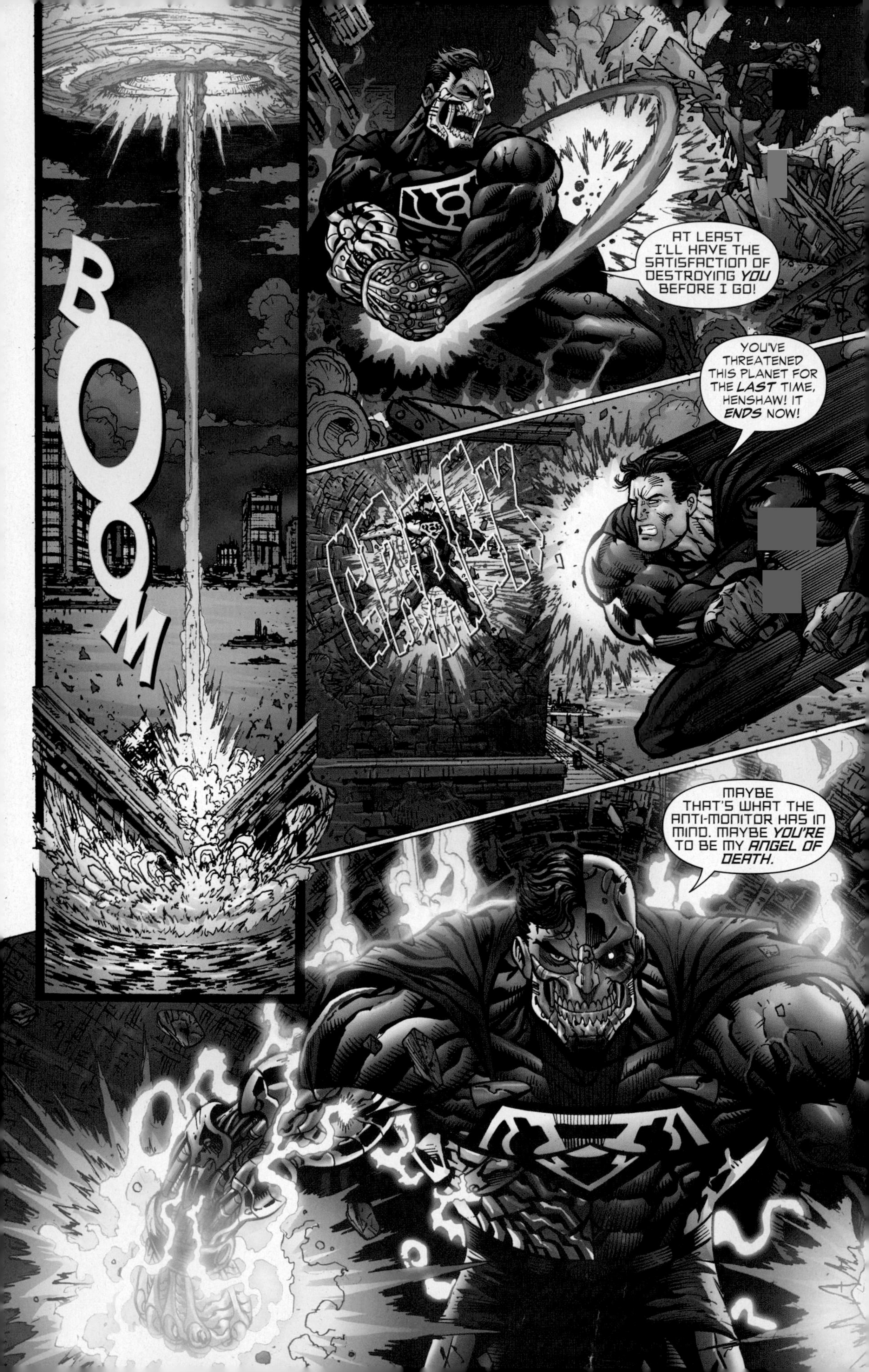
BOOM
AT LEAST I'LL HAVE THE SATISFACTION OF DESTROYING *YOU* BEFORE I GO!
YOU'VE THREATENED THIS PLANET FOR THE *LAST* TIME, HENSHAW! IT ***ENDS*** NOW!
MAYBE THAT'S WHAT THE ANTI-MONITOR HAS IN MIND. MAYBE *YOU'RE* TO BE MY *ANGEL OF DEATH*.

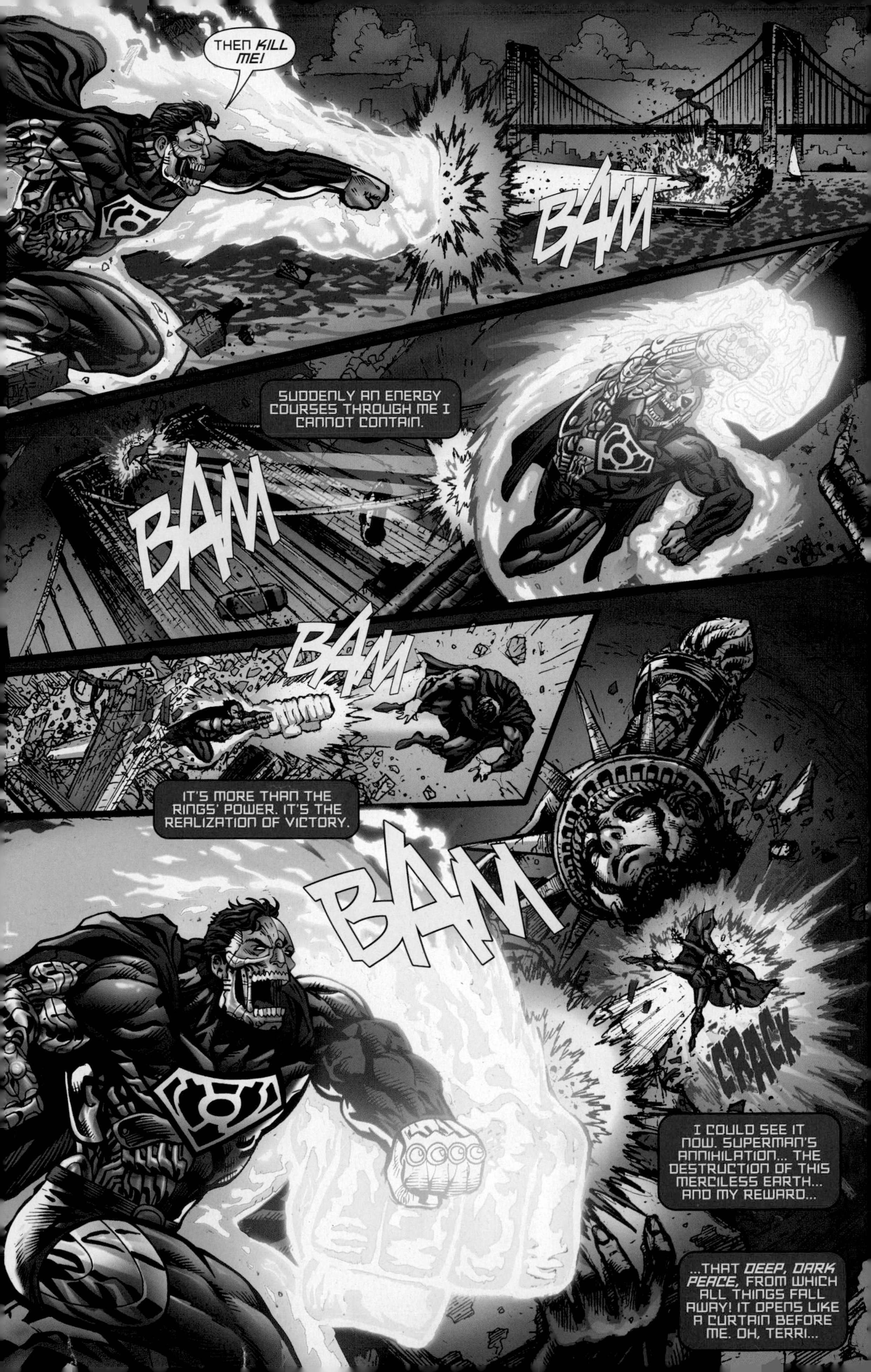
THEN KILL ME!
BAM
SUDDENLY AN ENERGY COURSES THROUGH ME I CANNOT CONTAIN.
BAM
BAM
IT'S MORE THAN THE RINGS' POWER. IT'S THE REALIZATION OF VICTORY.
BAM
CRACK
I COULD SEE IT NOW. SUPERMAN'S ANNIHILATION... THE DESTRUCTION OF THIS MERCILESS EARTH... AND MY REWARD...
...THAT DEEP, DARK PEACE, FROM WHICH ALL THINGS FALL AWAY! IT OPENS LIKE A CURTAIN BEFORE ME. OH, TERRI...

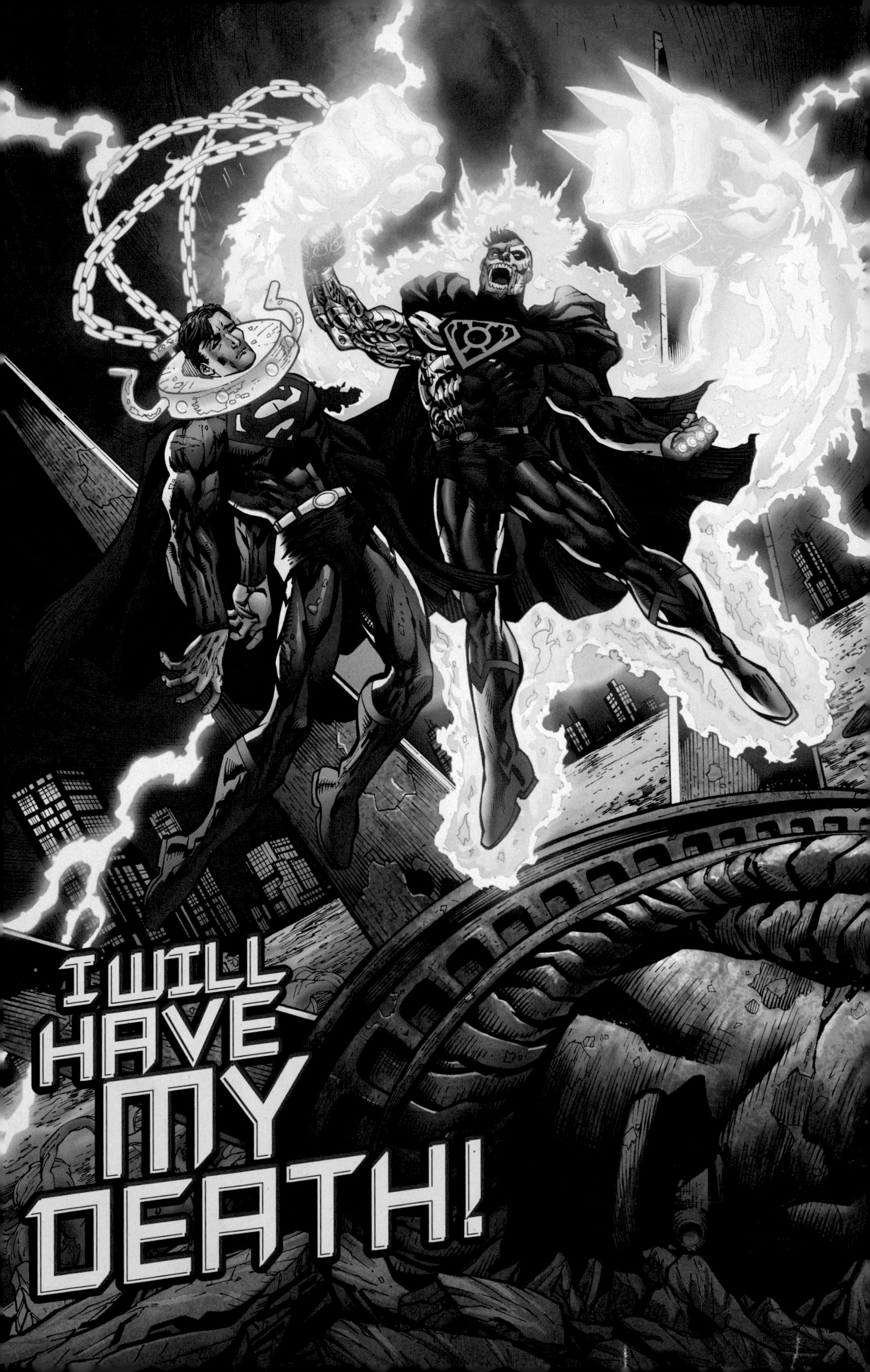
I WILL HAVE MY DEATH!

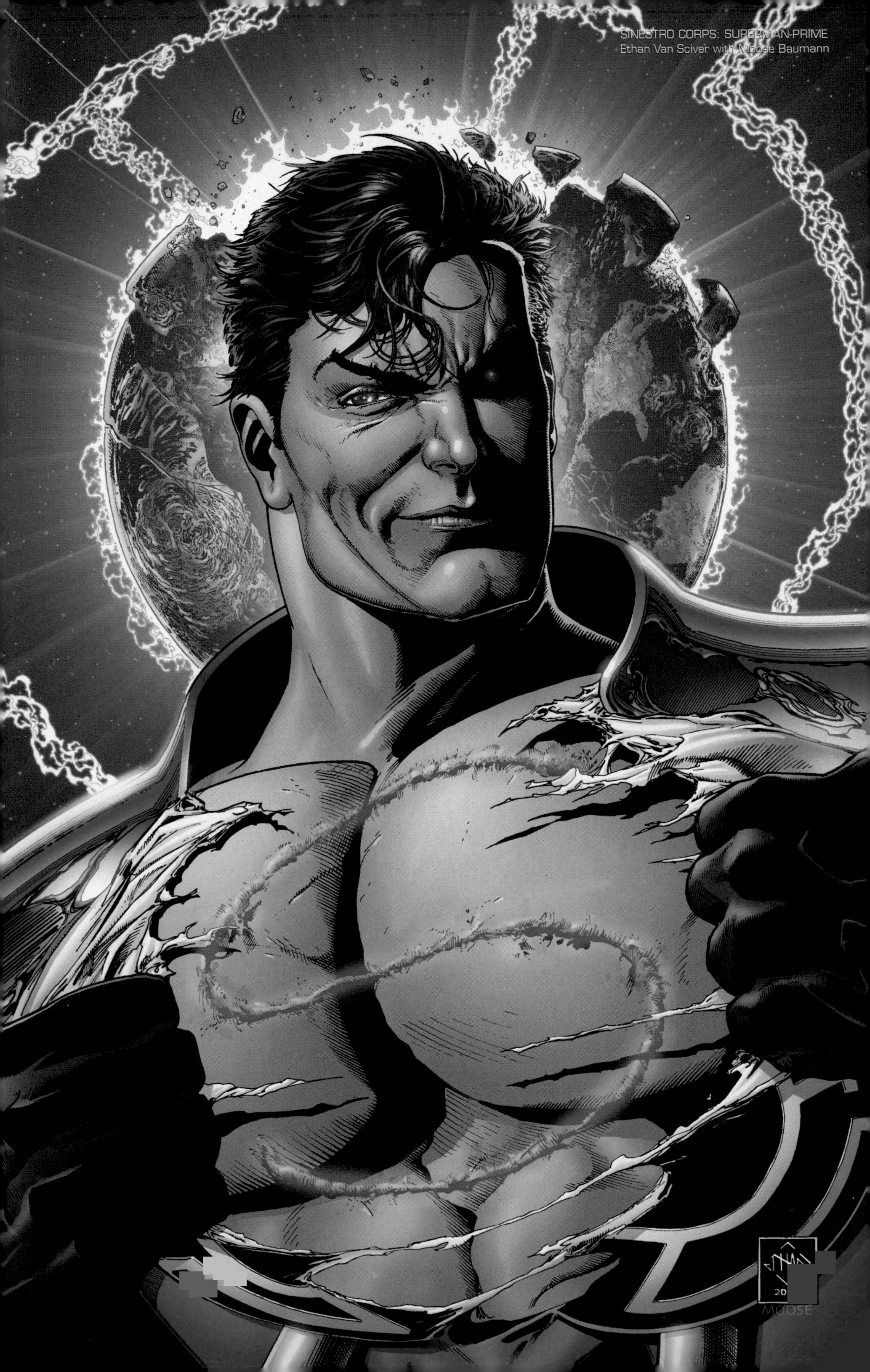

SINESTRO CORPS: SUPERMAN-PRIME
Ethan Van Sciver with Moose Baumann

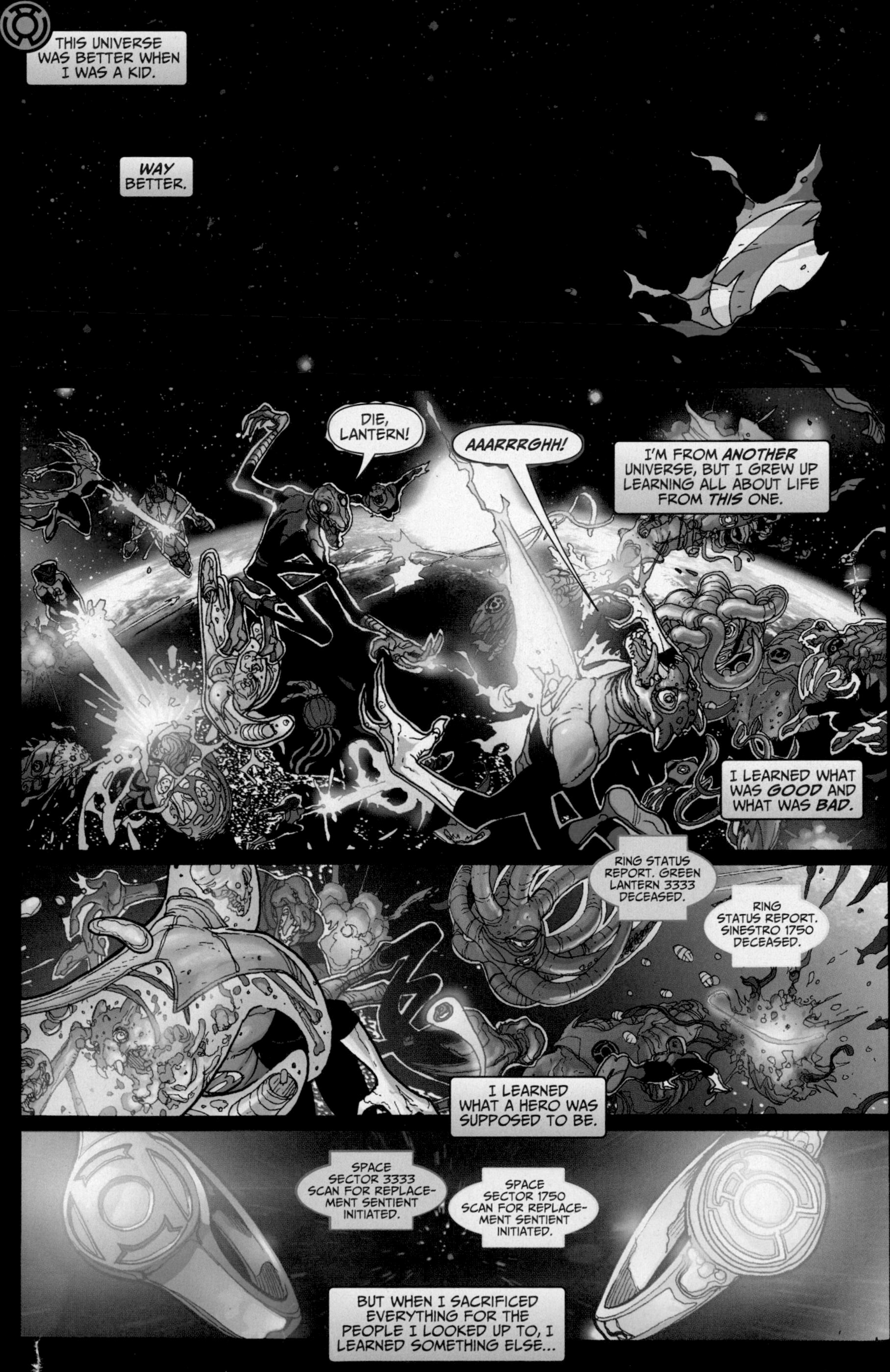
THIS UNIVERSE WAS BETTER WHEN I WAS A KID.
WAY BETTER.
DIE, LANTERN!
AAARRRGHH!
I'M FROM ANOTHER UNIVERSE, BUT I GREW UP LEARNING ALL ABOUT LIFE FROM THIS ONE.
I LEARNED WHAT WAS GOOD AND WHAT WAS BAD.
RING STATUS REPORT. GREEN LANTERN 3333 DECEASED.
RING STATUS REPORT. SINESTRO 1750 DECEASED.
I LEARNED WHAT A HERO WAS SUPPOSED TO BE.
SPACE SECTOR 3333 SCAN FOR REPLACEMENT SENTIENT INITIATED.
SPACE SECTOR 1750 SCAN FOR REPLACEMENT SENTIENT INITIATED.
BUT WHEN I SACRIFICED EVERYTHING FOR THE PEOPLE I LOOKED UP TO, I LEARNED SOMETHING ELSE...

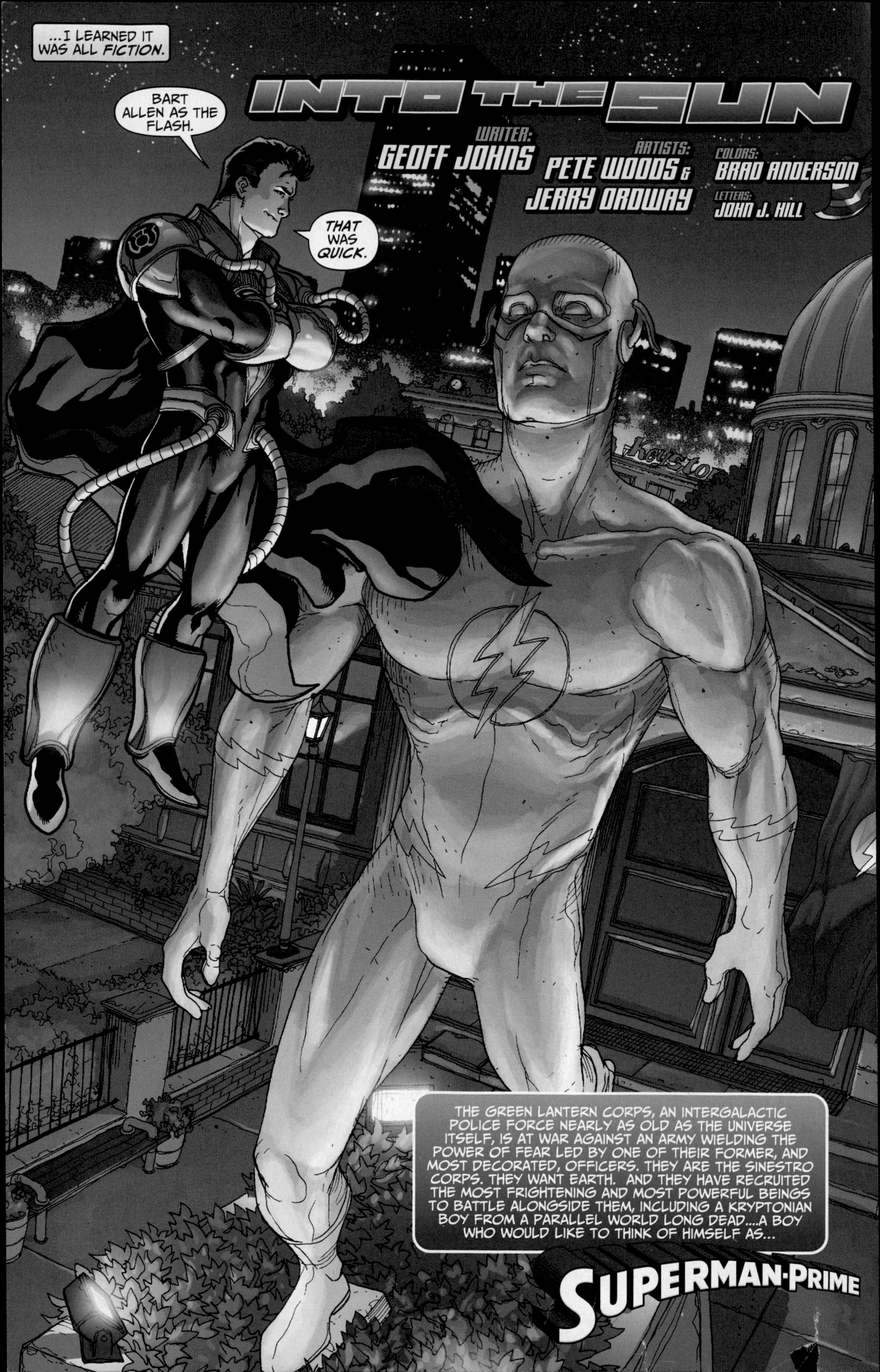

...I LEARNED IT WAS ALL FICTION.
BART ALLEN AS THE FLASH.
INTO THE SUN
WRITER: GEOFF JOHNS
ARTISTS: PETE WOODS & JERRY ORDWAY
COLORS: BRAD ANDERSON
LETTERS: JOHN J. HILL
THAT WAS QUICK.
THE GREEN LANTERN CORPS, AN INTERGALACTIC POLICE FORCE NEARLY AS OLD AS THE UNIVERSE ITSELF, IS AT WAR AGAINST AN ARMY WIELDING THE POWER OF FEAR LED BY ONE OF THEIR FORMER, AND MOST DECORATED, OFFICERS. THEY ARE THE SINESTRO CORPS. THEY WANT EARTH. AND THEY HAVE RECRUITED THE MOST FRIGHTENING AND MOST POWERFUL BEINGS TO BATTLE ALONGSIDE THEM, INCLUDING A KRYPTONIAN BOY FROM A PARALLEL WORLD LONG DEAD....A BOY WHO WOULD LIKE TO THINK OF HIMSELF AS...
SUPERMAN-PRIME

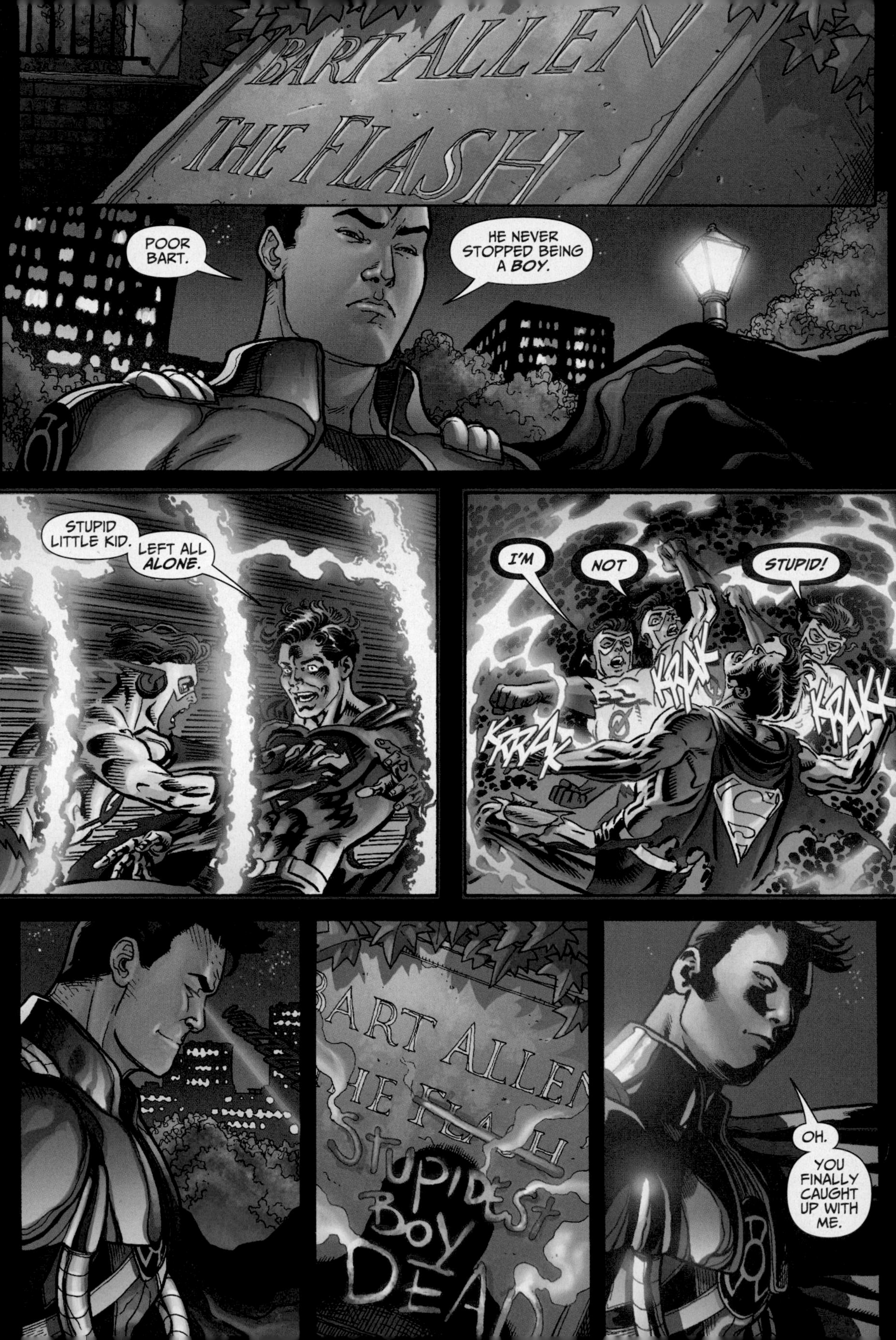
BART ALLEN
THE FLASH
POOR BART.
HE NEVER STOPPED BEING A *BOY*.
STUPID LITTLE KID.
LEFT ALL *ALONE*.
I'M
NOT
STUPID!
KRAK
KRAKK
KRRAK
BART ALLEN
THE FLASH
STUPIDEST BOY DEAD
OH.
YOU FINALLY CAUGHT UP WITH ME.

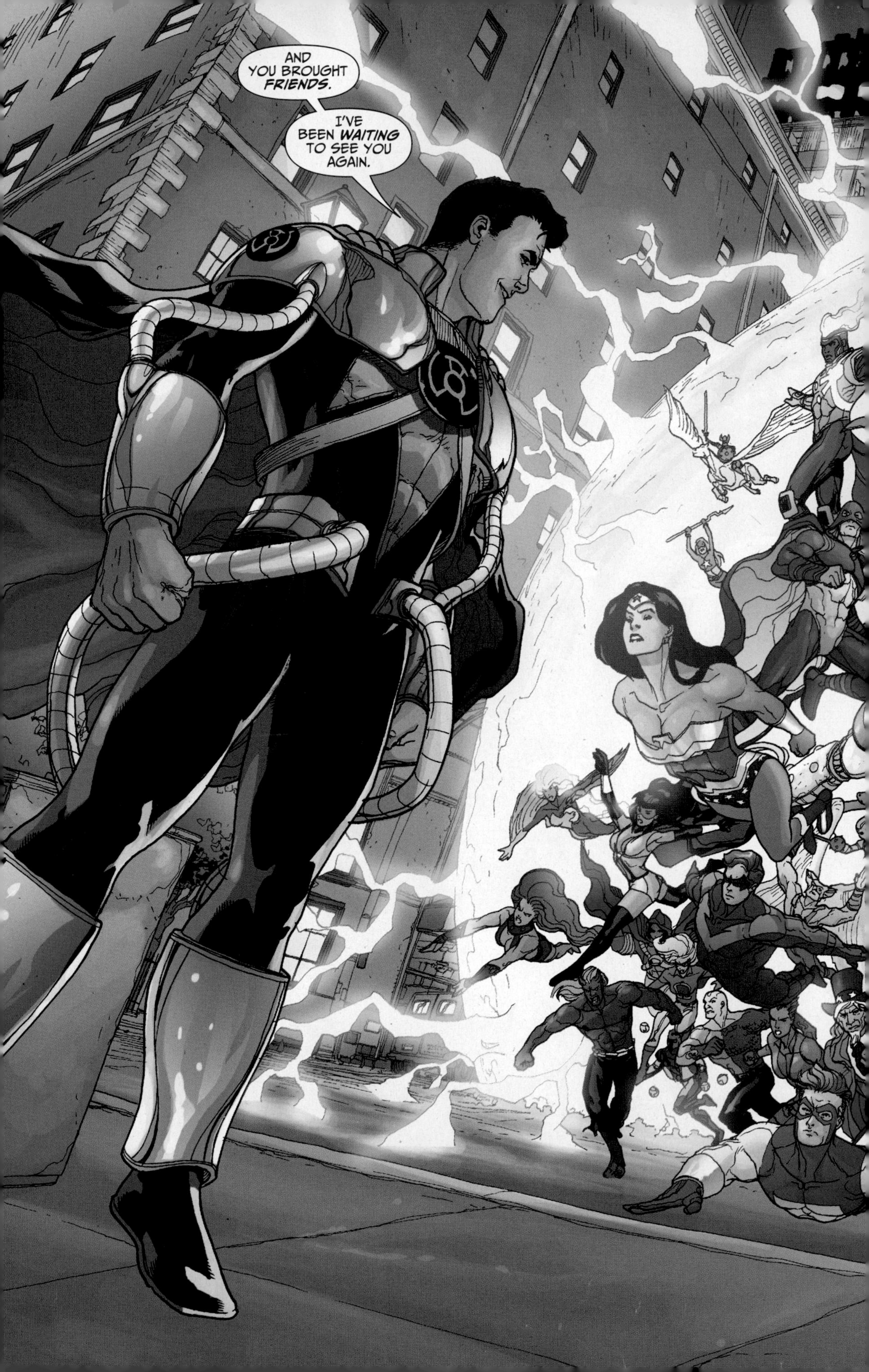
AND YOU BROUGHT *FRIENDS.*
I'VE BEEN *WAITING* TO SEE YOU AGAIN.

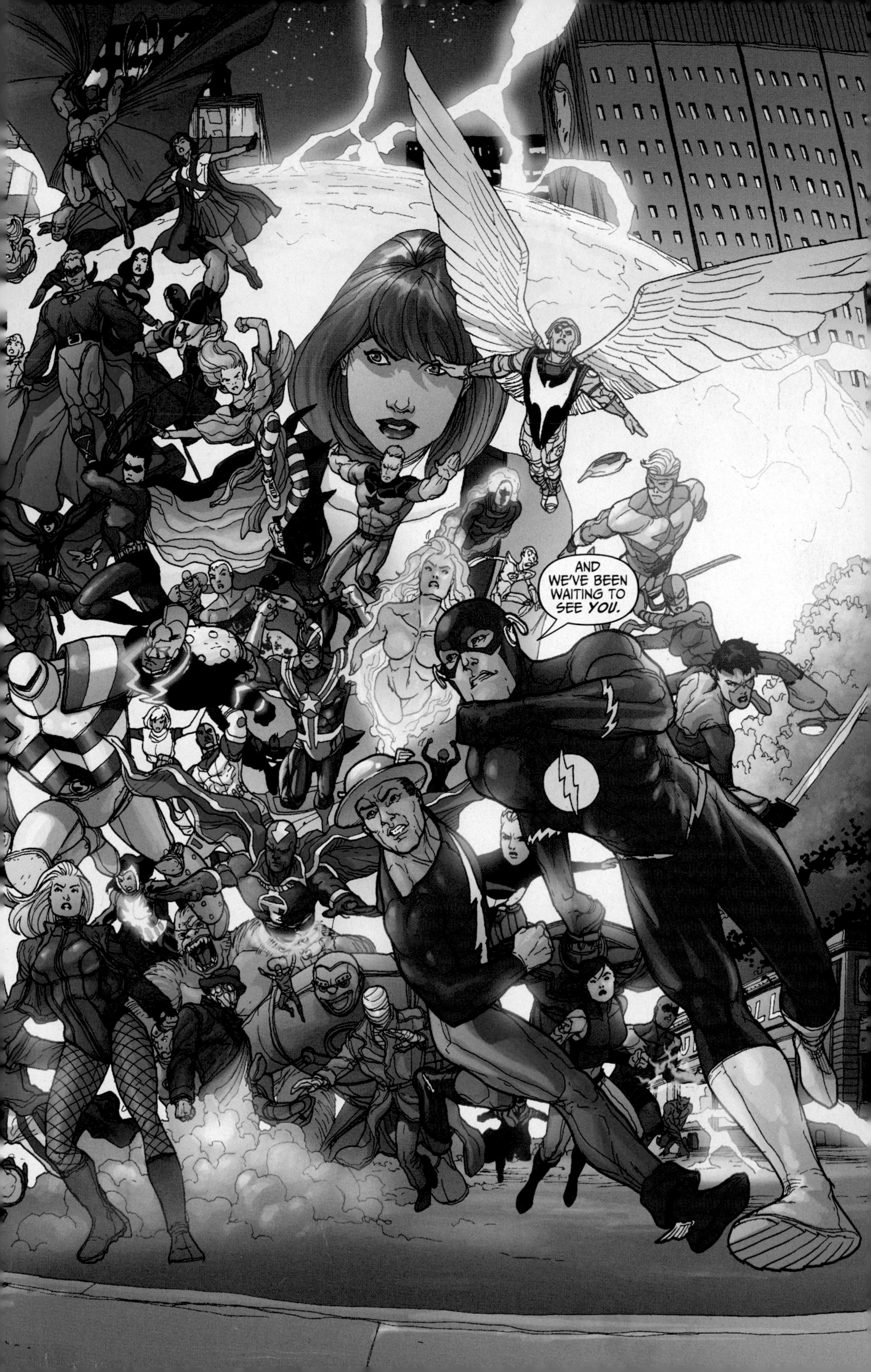
AND WE'VE BEEN WAITING TO SEE YOU.

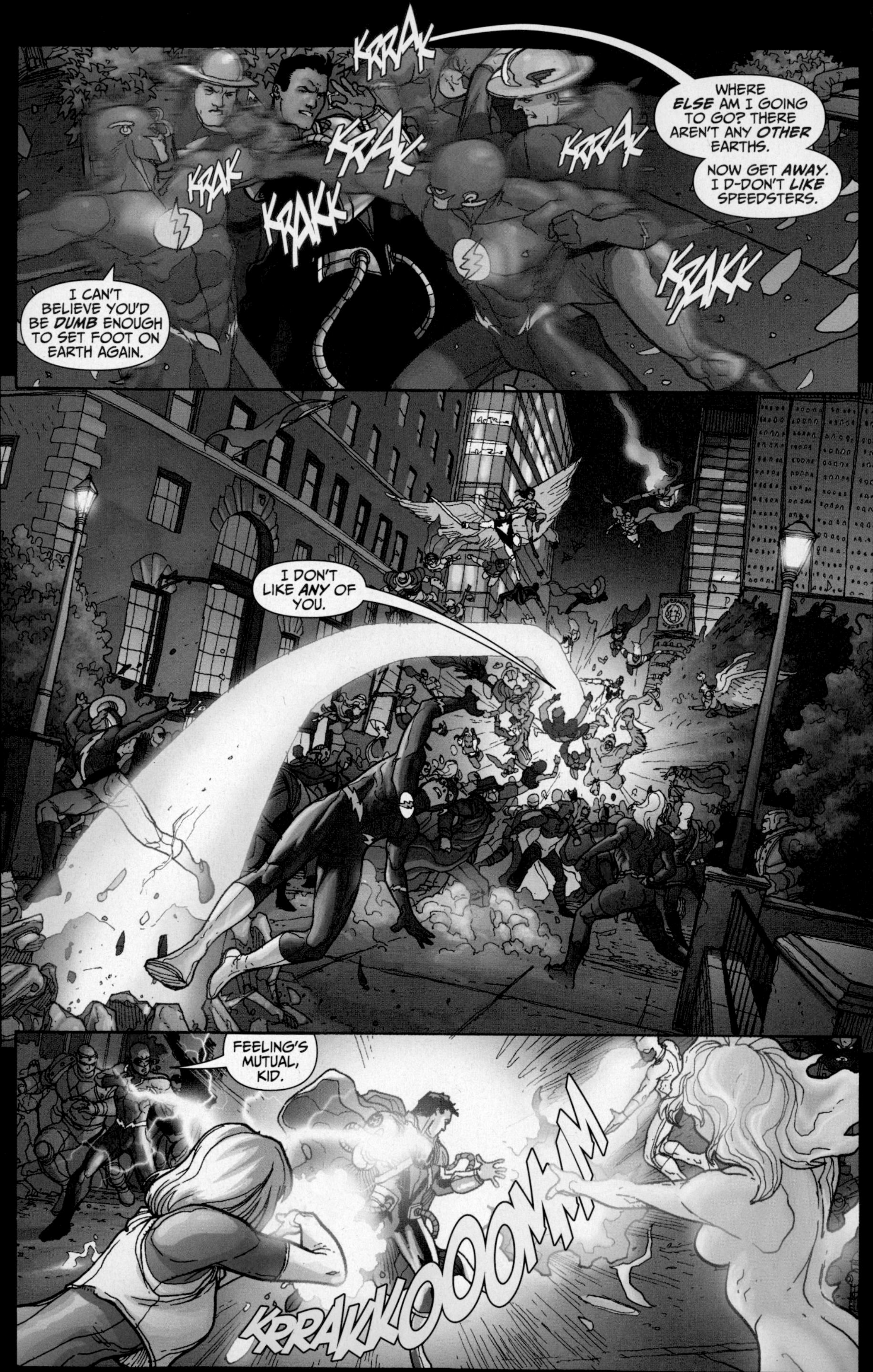

I CAN'T BELIEVE YOU'D BE DUMB ENOUGH TO SET FOOT ON EARTH AGAIN.
KRAK
KRRAK
KRAKK
KRAKK
KRRAK
KRRAK
WHERE ELSE AM I GOING TO GO? THERE AREN'T ANY OTHER EARTHS.
NOW GET AWAY. I D-DON'T LIKE SPEEDSTERS.
I DON'T LIKE ANY OF YOU.
FEELING'S MUTUAL, KID.
KRRAKKOOOMM

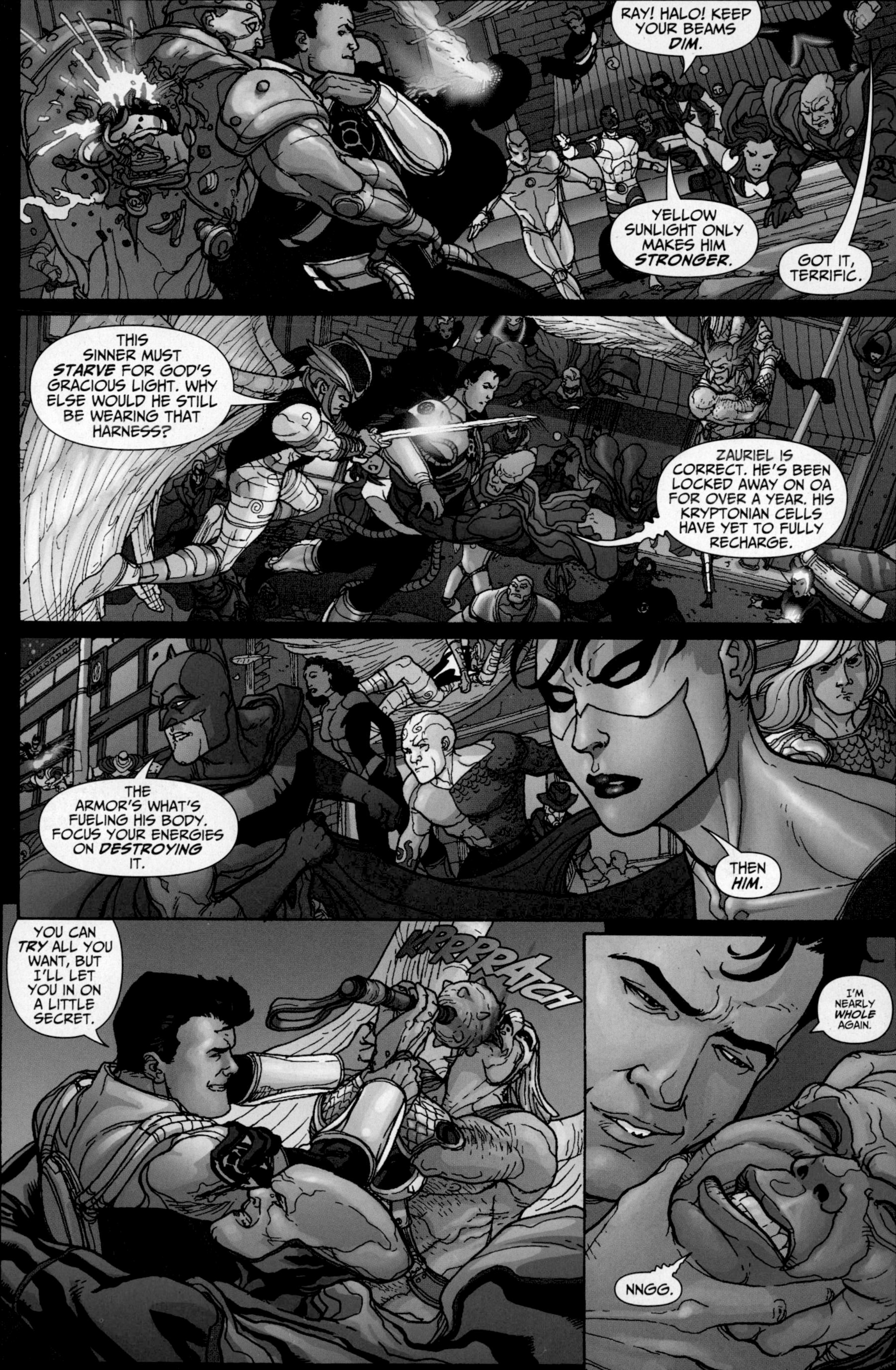
RAY! HALO! KEEP YOUR BEAMS DIM.
YELLOW SUNLIGHT ONLY MAKES HIM STRONGER.
GOT IT, TERRIFIC.
THIS SINNER MUST STARVE FOR GOD'S GRACIOUS LIGHT. WHY ELSE WOULD HE STILL BE WEARING THAT HARNESS?
ZAURIEL IS CORRECT. HE'S BEEN LOCKED AWAY ON OA FOR OVER A YEAR. HIS KRYPTONIAN CELLS HAVE YET TO FULLY RECHARGE.
THE ARMOR'S WHAT'S FUELING HIS BODY. FOCUS YOUR ENERGIES ON DESTROYING IT.
THEN HIM.
YOU CAN TRY ALL YOU WANT, BUT I'LL LET YOU IN ON A LITTLE SECRET.
KRRRRATCH
I'M NEARLY WHOLE AGAIN.
NNGG.

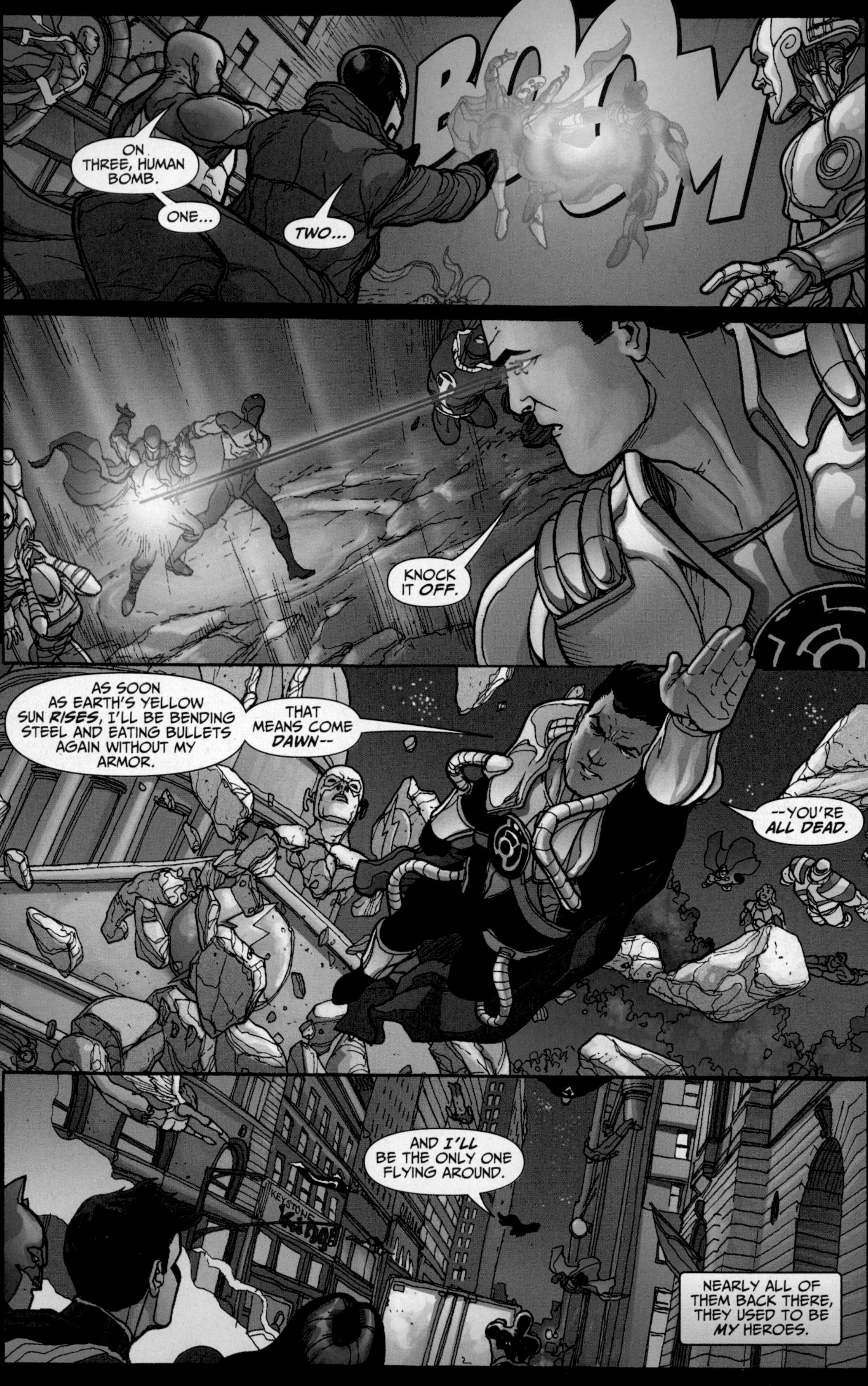
ON THREE, HUMAN BOMB.
ONE...
TWO...
BOOM
KNOCK IT OFF.
AS SOON AS EARTH'S YELLOW SUN RISES, I'LL BE BENDING STEEL AND EATING BULLETS AGAIN WITHOUT MY ARMOR.
THAT MEANS COME DAWN--
--YOU'RE ALL DEAD.
AND I'LL BE THE ONLY ONE FLYING AROUND.
KEYSTONE
NEARLY ALL OF THEM BACK THERE, THEY USED TO BE MY HEROES.

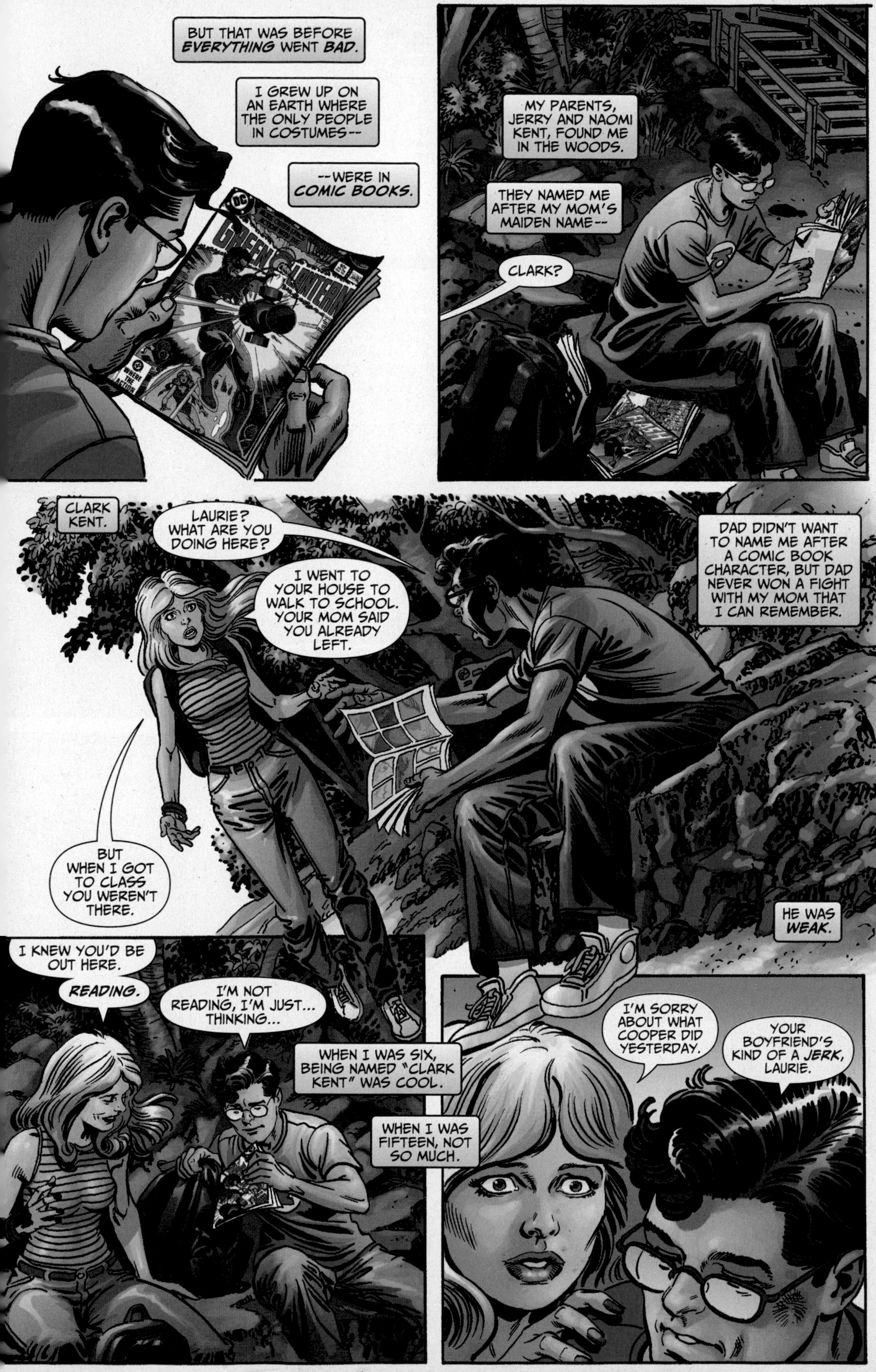
BUT THAT WAS BEFORE EVERYTHING WENT BAD.
I GREW UP ON AN EARTH WHERE THE ONLY PEOPLE IN COSTUMES--
--WERE IN COMIC BOOKS.
MY PARENTS, JERRY AND NAOMI KENT, FOUND ME IN THE WOODS.
THEY NAMED ME AFTER MY MOM'S MAIDEN NAME--
CLARK?
CLARK KENT.
LAURIE? WHAT ARE YOU DOING HERE?
I WENT TO YOUR HOUSE TO WALK TO SCHOOL. YOUR MOM SAID YOU ALREADY LEFT.
DAD DIDN'T WANT TO NAME ME AFTER A COMIC BOOK CHARACTER, BUT DAD NEVER WON A FIGHT WITH MY MOM THAT I CAN REMEMBER.
BUT WHEN I GOT TO CLASS YOU WEREN'T THERE.
HE WAS WEAK.
I KNEW YOU'D BE OUT HERE.
READING.
I'M NOT READING, I'M JUST... THINKING...
WHEN I WAS SIX, BEING NAMED "CLARK KENT" WAS COOL.
WHEN I WAS FIFTEEN, NOT SO MUCH.
I'M SORRY ABOUT WHAT COOPER DID YESTERDAY.
YOUR BOYFRIEND'S KIND OF A JERK, LAURIE.

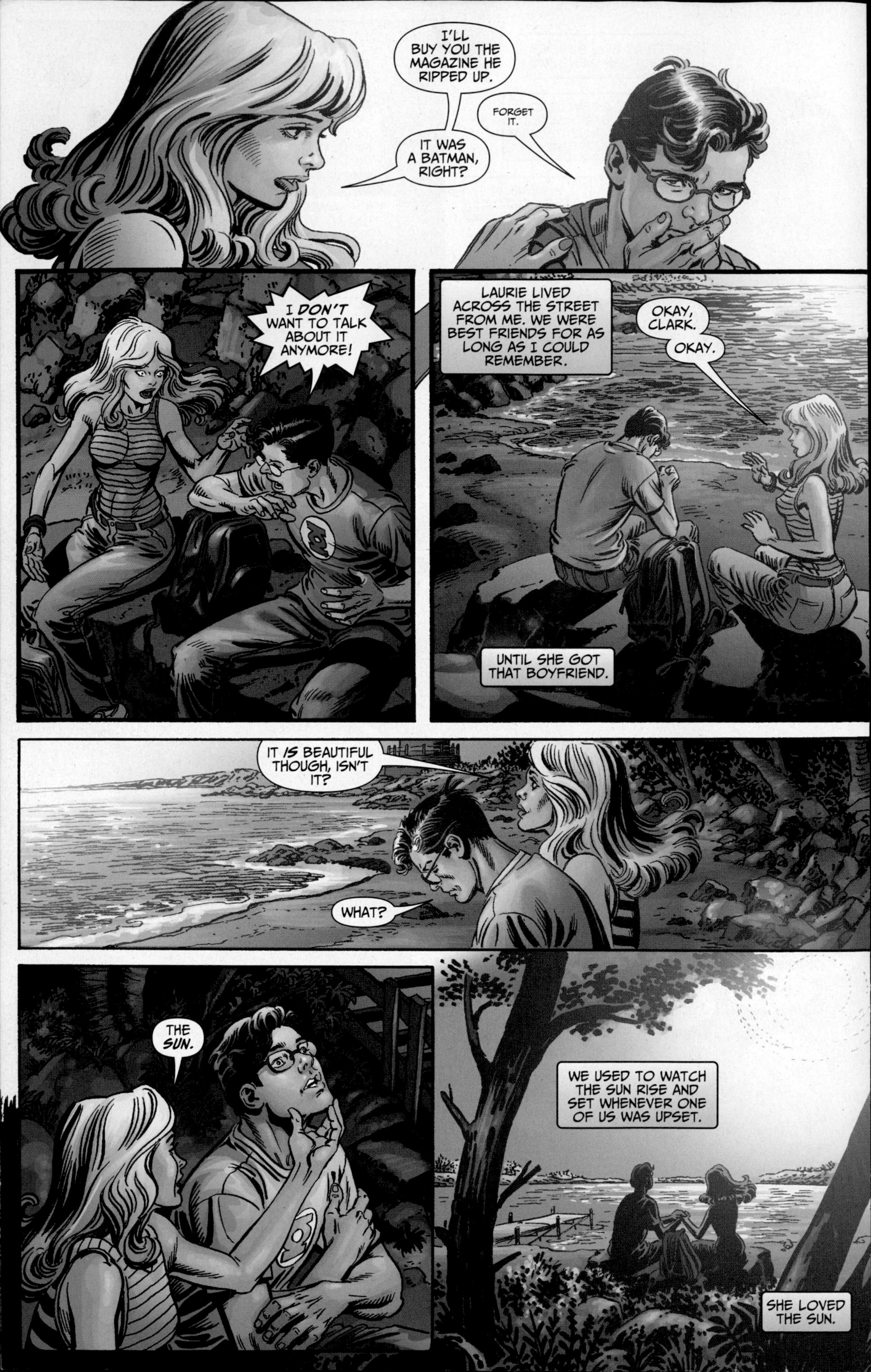
I'LL BUY YOU THE MAGAZINE HE RIPPED UP.
IT WAS A BATMAN, RIGHT?
FORGET IT.
I DON'T WANT TO TALK ABOUT IT ANYMORE!
LAURIE LIVED ACROSS THE STREET FROM ME. WE WERE BEST FRIENDS FOR AS LONG AS I COULD REMEMBER.
OKAY, CLARK.
OKAY.
UNTIL SHE GOT THAT BOYFRIEND.
IT IS BEAUTIFUL THOUGH, ISN'T IT?
WHAT?
THE SUN.
WE USED TO WATCH THE SUN RISE AND SET WHENEVER ONE OF US WAS UPSET.
SHE LOVED THE SUN.

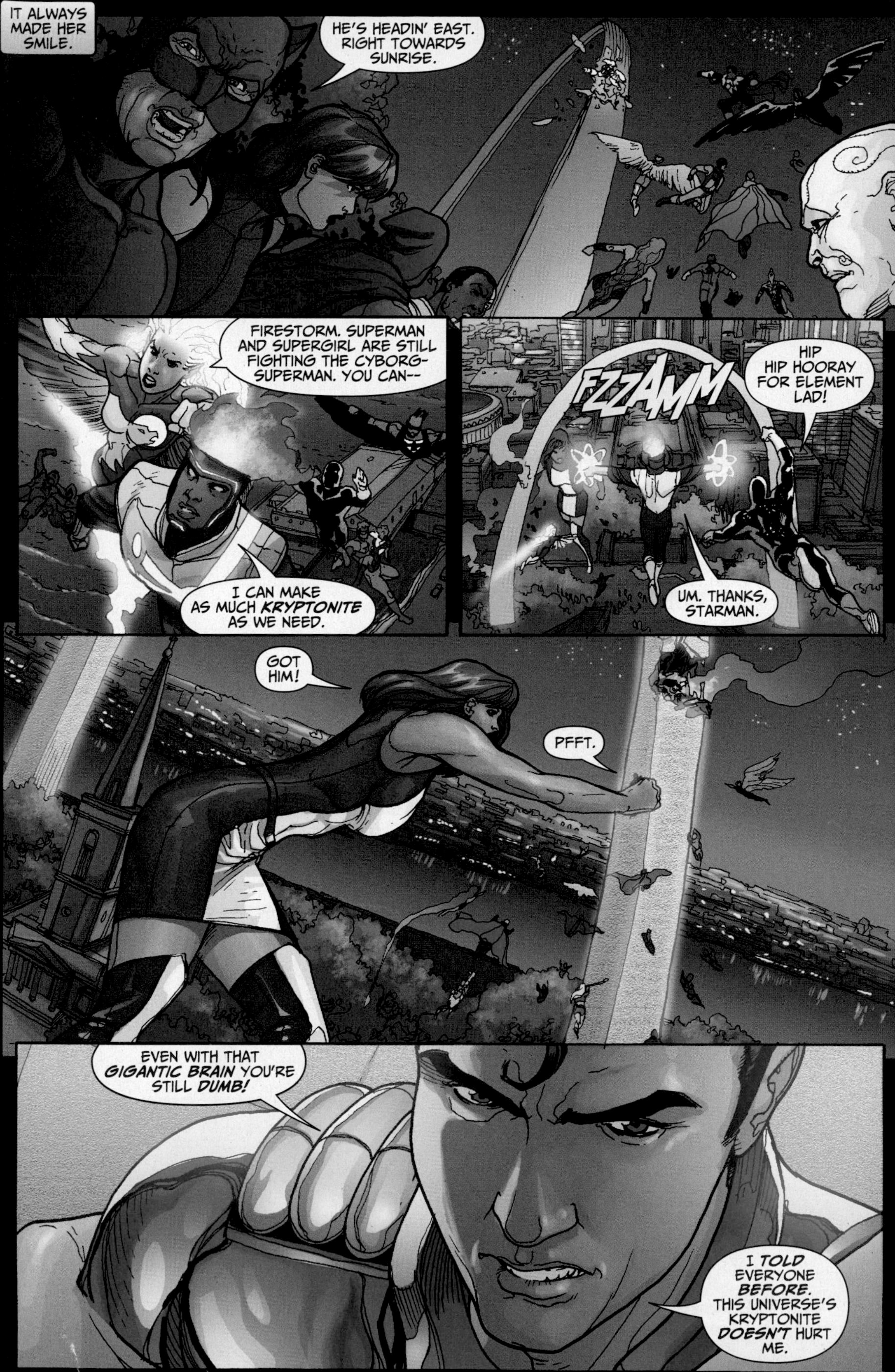
IT ALWAYS MADE HER SMILE.
HE'S HEADIN' EAST. RIGHT TOWARDS SUNRISE.
FIRESTORM. SUPERMAN AND SUPERGIRL ARE STILL FIGHTING THE CYBORG-SUPERMAN. YOU CAN--
I CAN MAKE AS MUCH *KRYPTONITE* AS WE NEED.
FZZAMM
HIP HIP HOORAY FOR ELEMENT LAD!
UM. THANKS, STARMAN.
GOT HIM!
PFFT.
EVEN WITH THAT *GIGANTIC BRAIN* YOU'RE STILL *DUMB!*
I *TOLD* EVERYONE *BEFORE*. THIS UNIVERSE'S KRYPTONITE *DOESN'T* HURT ME.

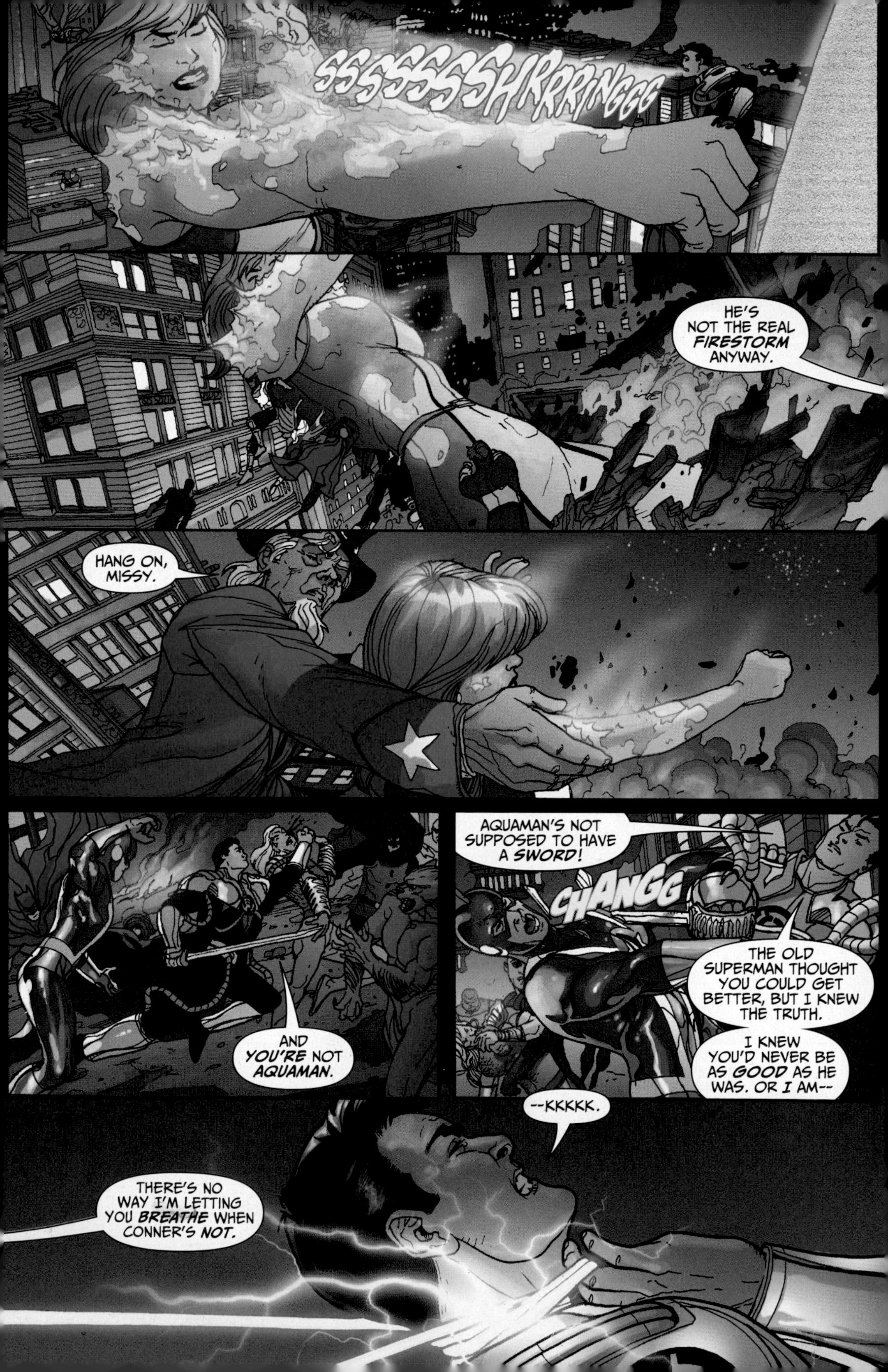
SSSSSSSSHRRRINGGG
HE'S NOT THE REAL FIRESTORM ANYWAY.
HANG ON, MISSY.
AND YOU'RE NOT AQUAMAN.
AQUAMAN'S NOT SUPPOSED TO HAVE A SWORD!
CHANGG
THE OLD SUPERMAN THOUGHT YOU COULD GET BETTER, BUT I KNEW THE TRUTH.
I KNEW YOU'D NEVER BE AS GOOD AS HE WAS. OR I AM--
--KKKKK.
THERE'S NO WAY I'M LETTING YOU BREATHE WHEN CONNER'S NOT.

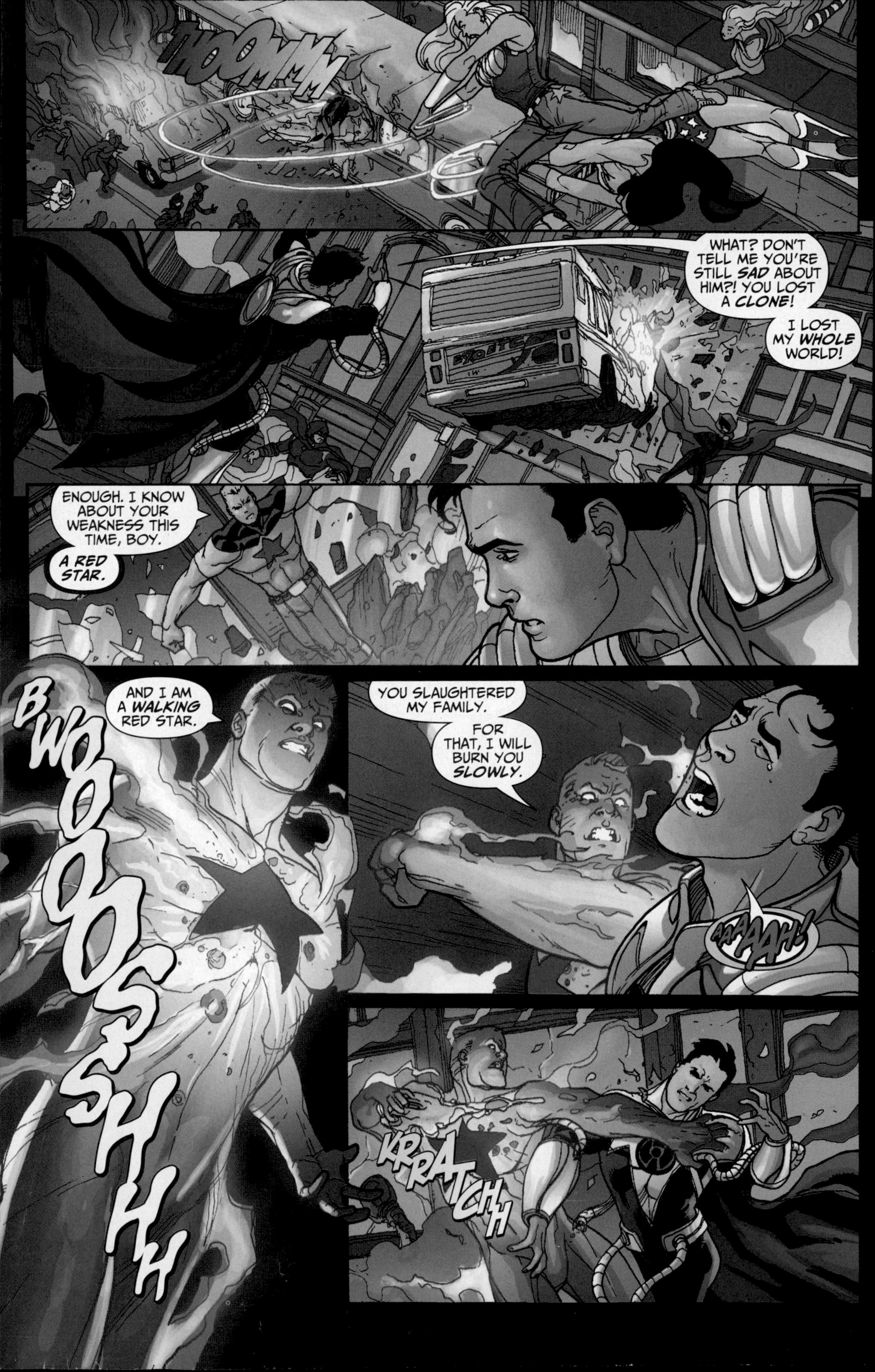
THOOMMM
WHAT? DON'T TELL ME YOU'RE STILL SAD ABOUT HIM?! YOU LOST A CLONE!
I LOST MY WHOLE WORLD!
ENOUGH. I KNOW ABOUT YOUR WEAKNESS THIS TIME, BOY.
A RED STAR.
AND I AM A WALKING RED STAR.
BWOOOOSHHH
YOU SLAUGHTERED MY FAMILY.
FOR THAT, I WILL BURN YOU SLOWLY.
AAAAAH!
KRRATCHH

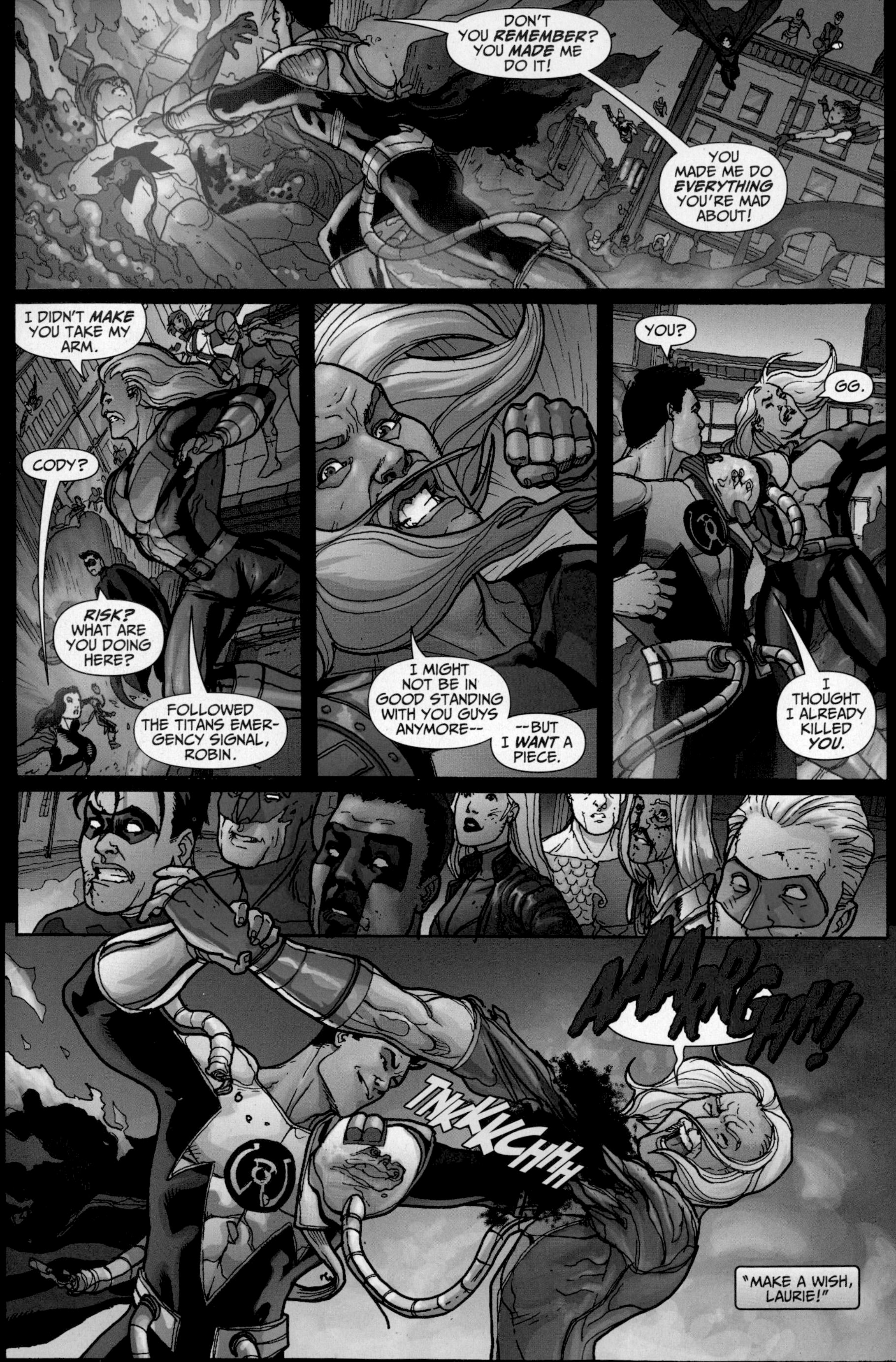
DON'T YOU REMEMBER? YOU MADE ME DO IT!
YOU MADE ME DO EVERYTHING YOU'RE MAD ABOUT!
I DIDN'T MAKE YOU TAKE MY ARM.
CODY?
RISK? WHAT ARE YOU DOING HERE?
FOLLOWED THE TITANS EMERGENCY SIGNAL, ROBIN.
I MIGHT NOT BE IN GOOD STANDING WITH YOU GUYS ANYMORE--
--BUT I WANT A PIECE.
YOU?
GG.
I THOUGHT I ALREADY KILLED YOU.
AAAARGHH!
TNKKKCHHH
"MAKE A WISH, LAURIE!"

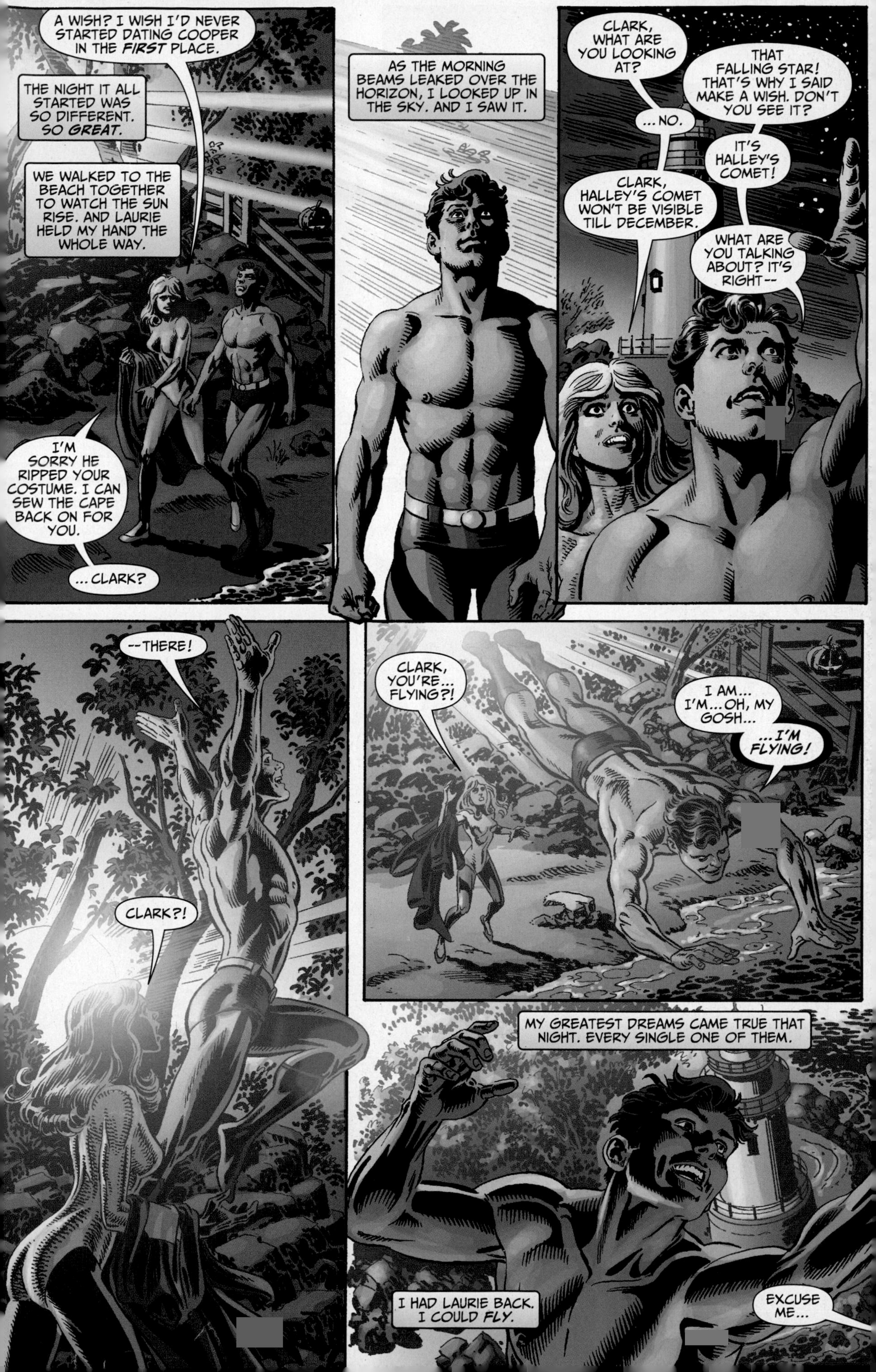
A WISH? I WISH I'D NEVER STARTED DATING COOPER IN THE *FIRST* PLACE.
THE NIGHT IT ALL STARTED WAS SO DIFFERENT. SO *GREAT*.
WE WALKED TO THE BEACH TOGETHER TO WATCH THE SUN RISE. AND LAURIE HELD MY HAND THE WHOLE WAY.
I'M SORRY HE RIPPED YOUR COSTUME. I CAN SEW THE CAPE BACK ON FOR YOU.
...CLARK?
AS THE MORNING BEAMS LEAKED OVER THE HORIZON, I LOOKED UP IN THE SKY. AND I SAW IT.
CLARK, WHAT ARE YOU LOOKING AT?
THAT FALLING STAR! THAT'S WHY I SAID MAKE A WISH. DON'T YOU SEE IT?
...NO.
IT'S HALLEY'S COMET!
CLARK, HALLEY'S COMET WON'T BE VISIBLE TILL DECEMBER.
WHAT ARE YOU TALKING ABOUT? IT'S RIGHT--
--THERE!
CLARK?!
CLARK, YOU'RE... FLYING?!
I AM... I'M...OH, MY GOSH...
...*I'M FLYING!*
MY GREATEST DREAMS CAME TRUE THAT NIGHT. EVERY SINGLE ONE OF THEM.
I HAD LAURIE BACK. I COULD *FLY*.
EXCUSE ME...

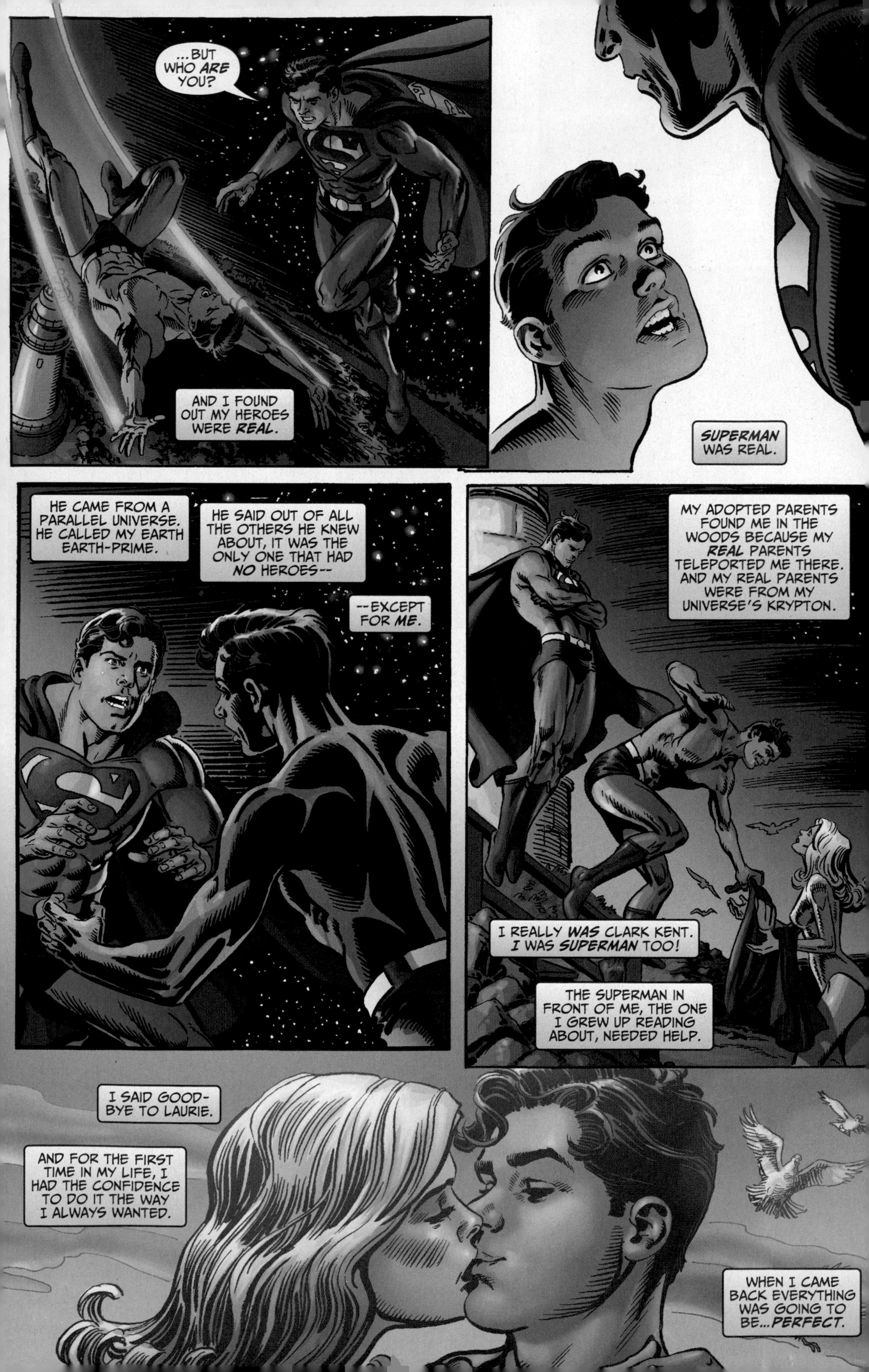
...BUT WHO ARE YOU?
AND I FOUND OUT MY HEROES WERE REAL.
SUPERMAN WAS REAL.
HE CAME FROM A PARALLEL UNIVERSE. HE CALLED MY EARTH EARTH-PRIME.
HE SAID OUT OF ALL THE OTHERS HE KNEW ABOUT, IT WAS THE ONLY ONE THAT HAD NO HEROES--
--EXCEPT FOR ME.
MY ADOPTED PARENTS FOUND ME IN THE WOODS BECAUSE MY REAL PARENTS TELEPORTED ME THERE. AND MY REAL PARENTS WERE FROM MY UNIVERSE'S KRYPTON.
I REALLY WAS CLARK KENT. I WAS SUPERMAN TOO!
THE SUPERMAN IN FRONT OF ME, THE ONE I GREW UP READING ABOUT, NEEDED HELP.
I SAID GOOD-BYE TO LAURIE.
AND FOR THE FIRST TIME IN MY LIFE, I HAD THE CONFIDENCE TO DO IT THE WAY I ALWAYS WANTED.
WHEN I CAME BACK EVERYTHING WAS GOING TO BE...PERFECT.

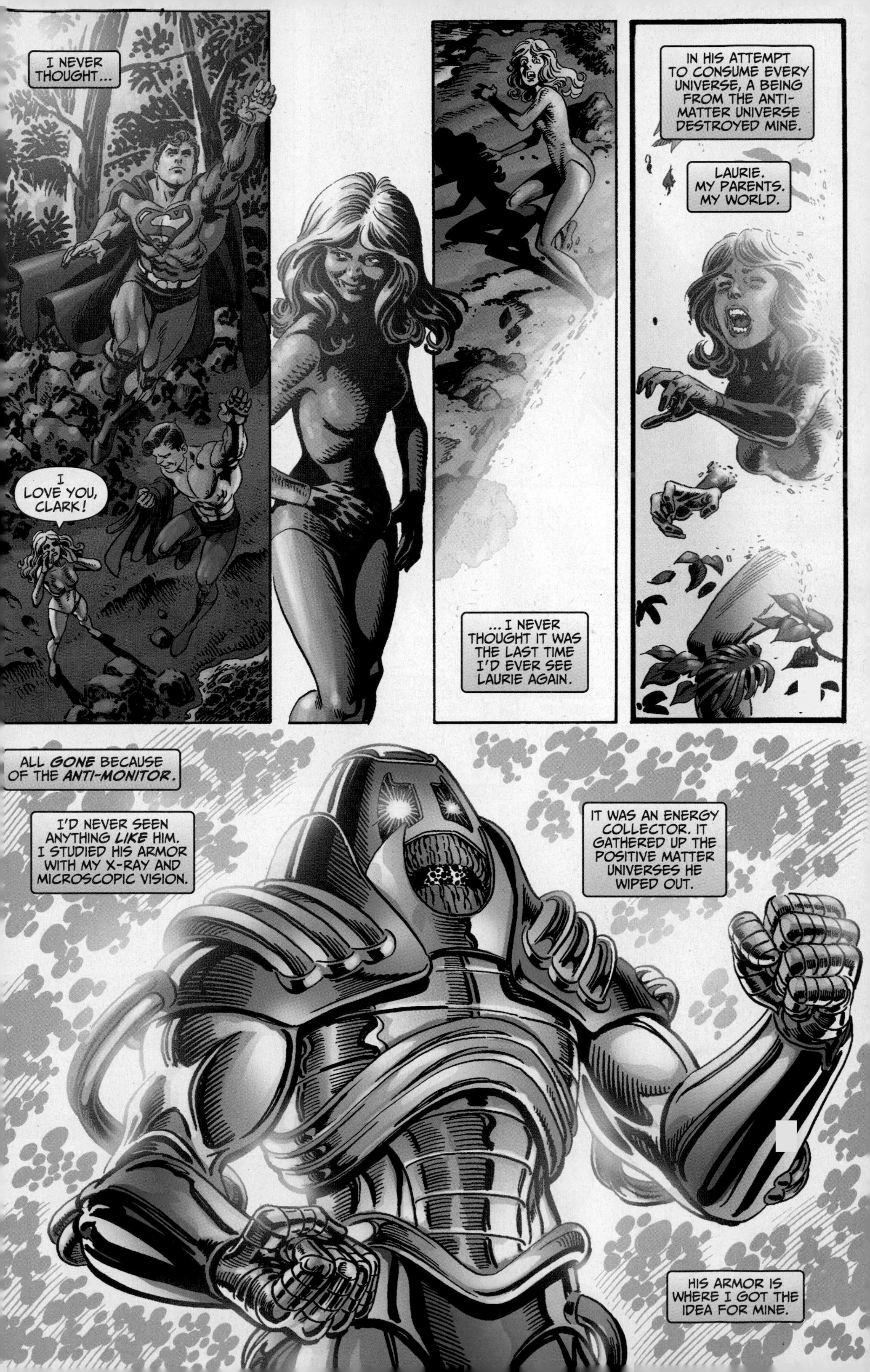

I NEVER THOUGHT...
I LOVE YOU, CLARK!
...I NEVER THOUGHT IT WAS THE LAST TIME I'D EVER SEE LAURIE AGAIN.
IN HIS ATTEMPT TO CONSUME EVERY UNIVERSE, A BEING FROM THE ANTI-MATTER UNIVERSE DESTROYED MINE.
LAURIE. MY PARENTS. MY WORLD.
ALL GONE BECAUSE OF THE ANTI-MONITOR.
I'D NEVER SEEN ANYTHING LIKE HIM. I STUDIED HIS ARMOR WITH MY X-RAY AND MICROSCOPIC VISION.
IT WAS AN ENERGY COLLECTOR. IT GATHERED UP THE POSITIVE MATTER UNIVERSES HE WIPED OUT.
HIS ARMOR IS WHERE I GOT THE IDEA FOR MINE.

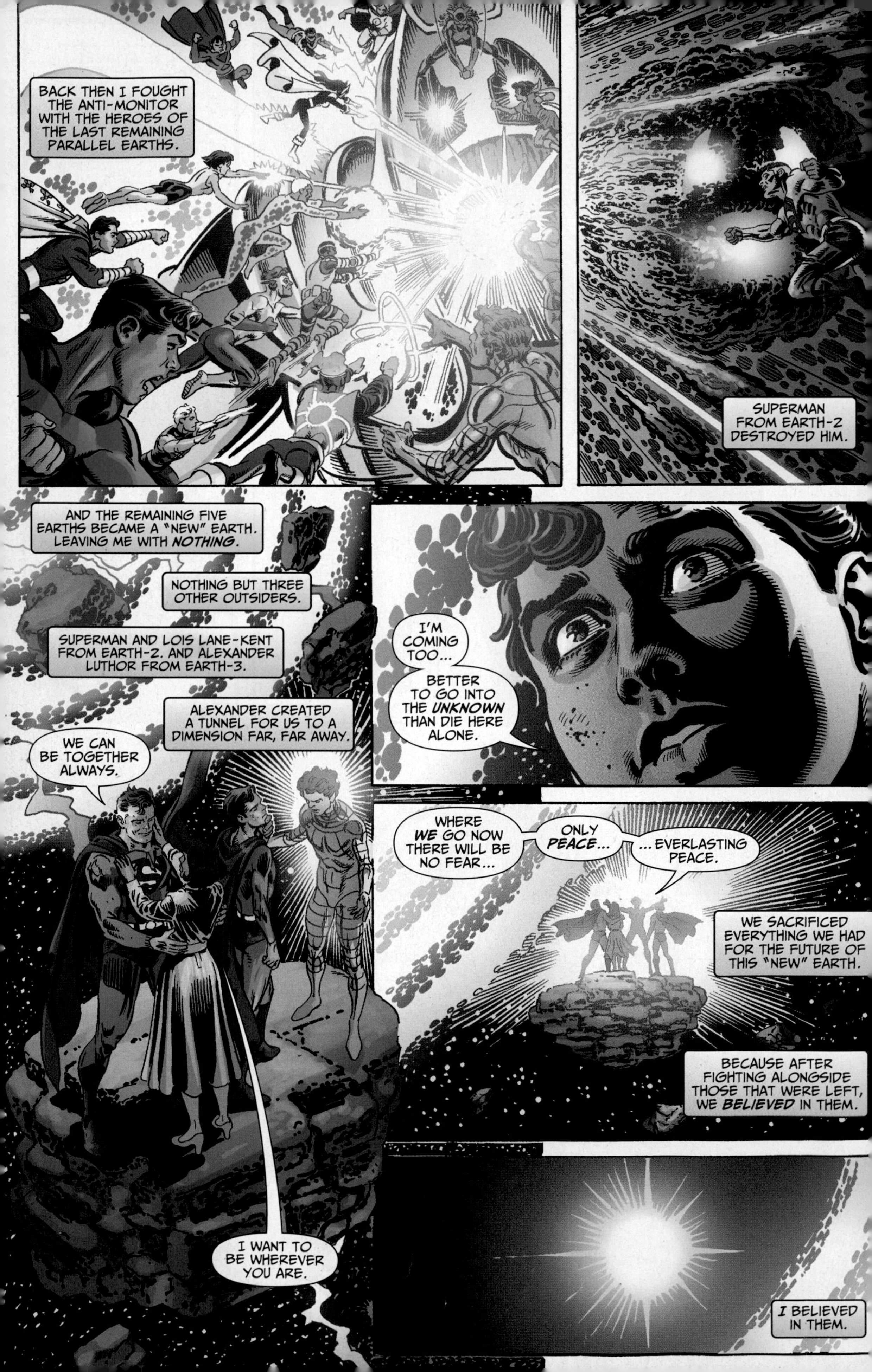
BACK THEN I FOUGHT THE ANTI-MONITOR WITH THE HEROES OF THE LAST REMAINING PARALLEL EARTHS.
SUPERMAN FROM EARTH-2 DESTROYED HIM.
AND THE REMAINING FIVE EARTHS BECAME A "NEW" EARTH. LEAVING ME WITH NOTHING.
NOTHING BUT THREE OTHER OUTSIDERS.
SUPERMAN AND LOIS LANE-KENT FROM EARTH-2. AND ALEXANDER LUTHOR FROM EARTH-3.
ALEXANDER CREATED A TUNNEL FOR US TO A DIMENSION FAR, FAR AWAY.
WE CAN BE TOGETHER ALWAYS.
I WANT TO BE WHEREVER YOU ARE.
I'M COMING TOO...
BETTER TO GO INTO THE UNKNOWN THAN DIE HERE ALONE.
WHERE WE GO NOW THERE WILL BE NO FEAR...
ONLY PEACE...
...EVERLASTING PEACE.
WE SACRIFICED EVERYTHING WE HAD FOR THE FUTURE OF THIS "NEW" EARTH.
BECAUSE AFTER FIGHTING ALONGSIDE THOSE THAT WERE LEFT, WE BELIEVED IN THEM.
I BELIEVED IN THEM.

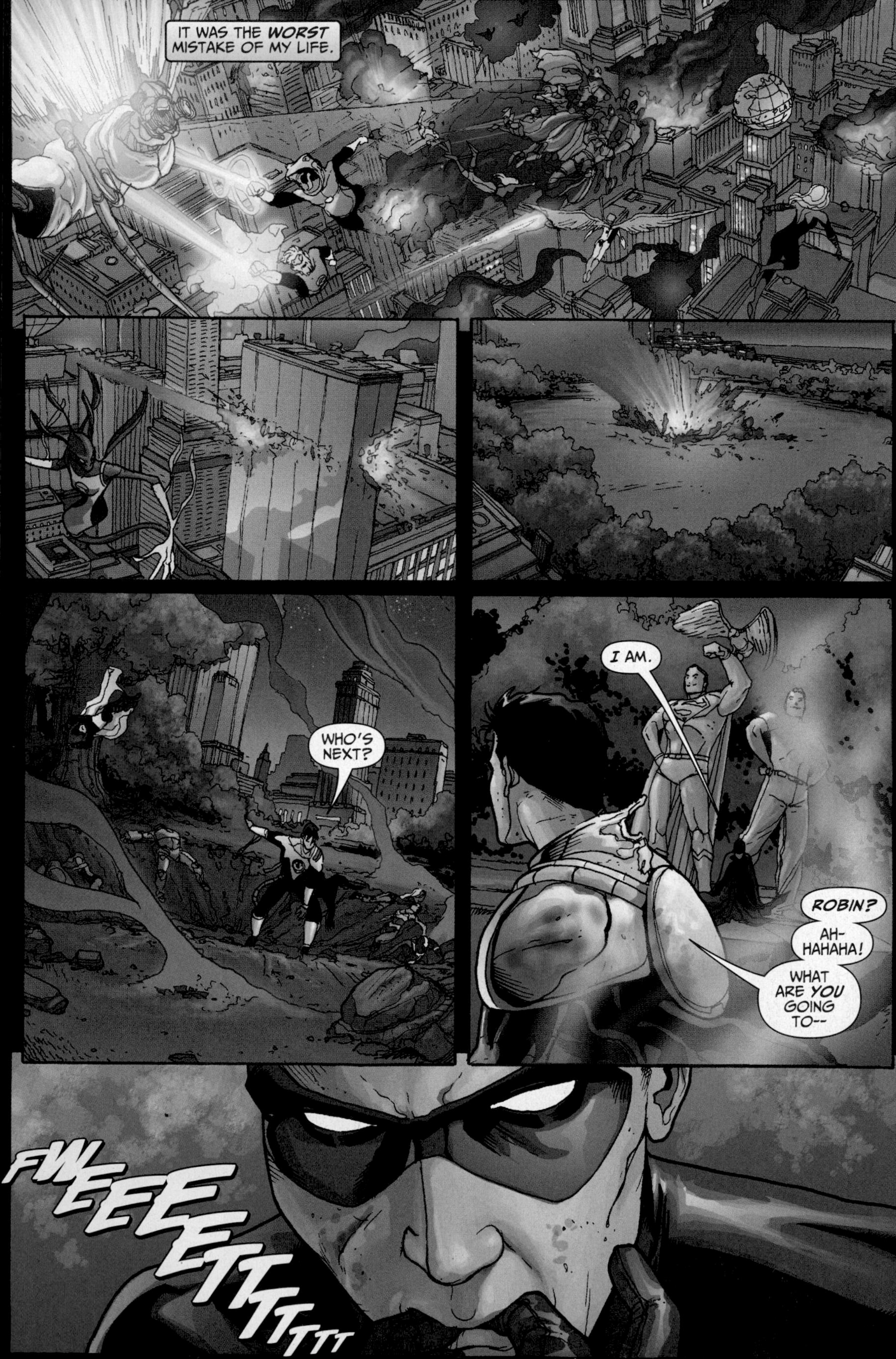
IT WAS THE WORST MISTAKE OF MY LIFE.
WHO'S NEXT?
I AM.
ROBIN? AH-HAHAHA! WHAT ARE YOU GOING TO--
FWEEEETTTTTTT

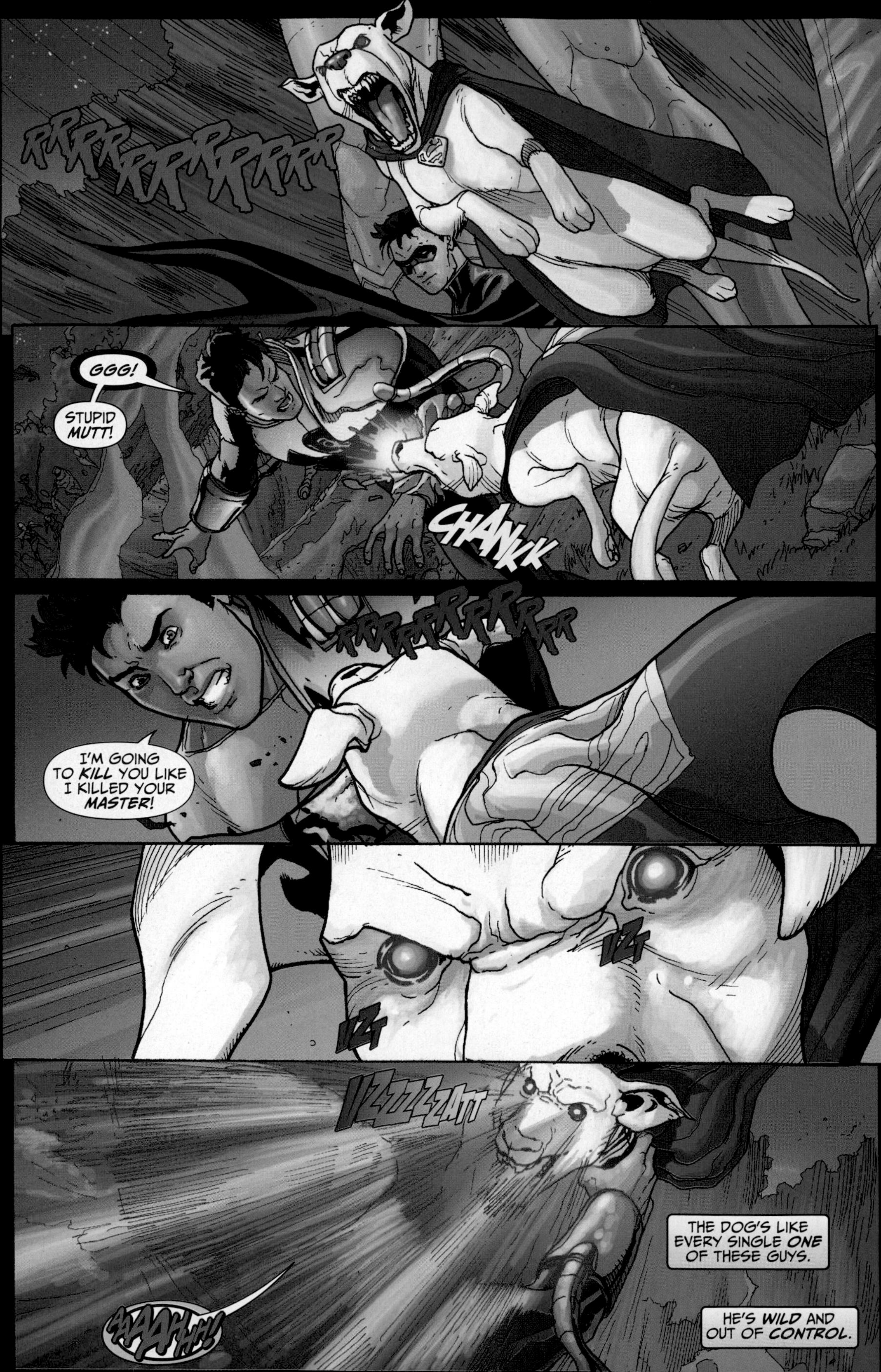
RRRRRRRRRRRRRRRR
GGG!
STUPID MUTT!
CHANKK
RRRRRRRRRRRR
I'M GOING TO KILL YOU LIKE I KILLED YOUR MASTER!
VZT
VZT
VZZZZZATT
THE DOG'S LIKE EVERY SINGLE ONE OF THESE GUYS.
AAAAHHH!
HE'S WILD AND OUT OF CONTROL.

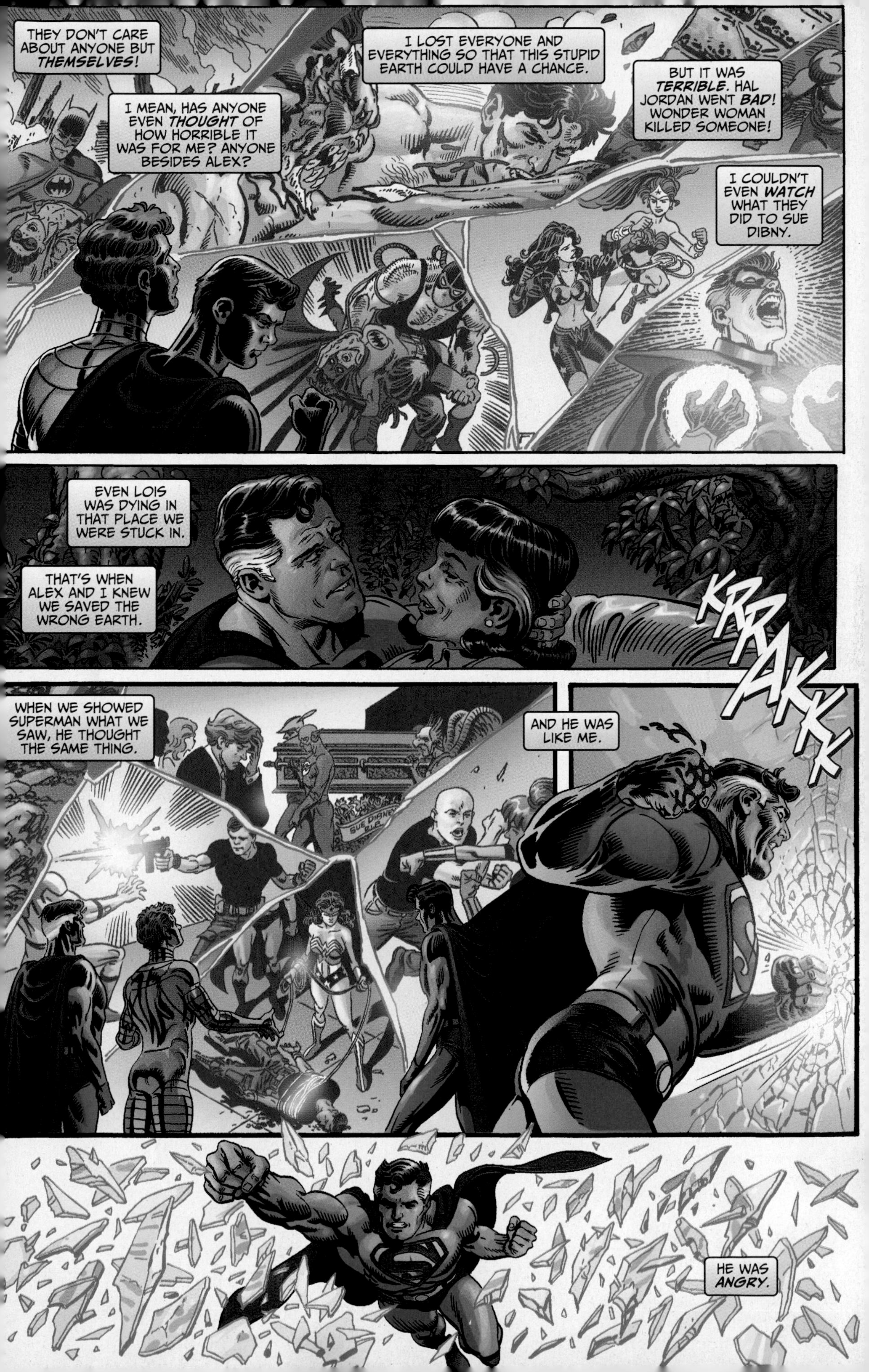
THEY DON'T CARE ABOUT ANYONE BUT *THEMSELVES*!
I LOST EVERYONE AND EVERYTHING SO THAT THIS STUPID EARTH COULD HAVE A CHANCE.
I MEAN, HAS ANYONE EVEN *THOUGHT* OF HOW HORRIBLE IT WAS FOR ME? ANYONE BESIDES ALEX?
BUT IT WAS *TERRIBLE*. HAL JORDAN WENT *BAD*! WONDER WOMAN KILLED SOMEONE!
I COULDN'T EVEN *WATCH* WHAT THEY DID TO SUE DIBNY.
EVEN LOIS WAS DYING IN THAT PLACE WE WERE STUCK IN.
THAT'S WHEN ALEX AND I KNEW WE SAVED THE WRONG EARTH.
KRRAKKK
WHEN WE SHOWED SUPERMAN WHAT WE SAW, HE THOUGHT THE SAME THING.
SUE DIBNY R.I.P.
AND HE WAS LIKE ME.
HE WAS *ANGRY*.

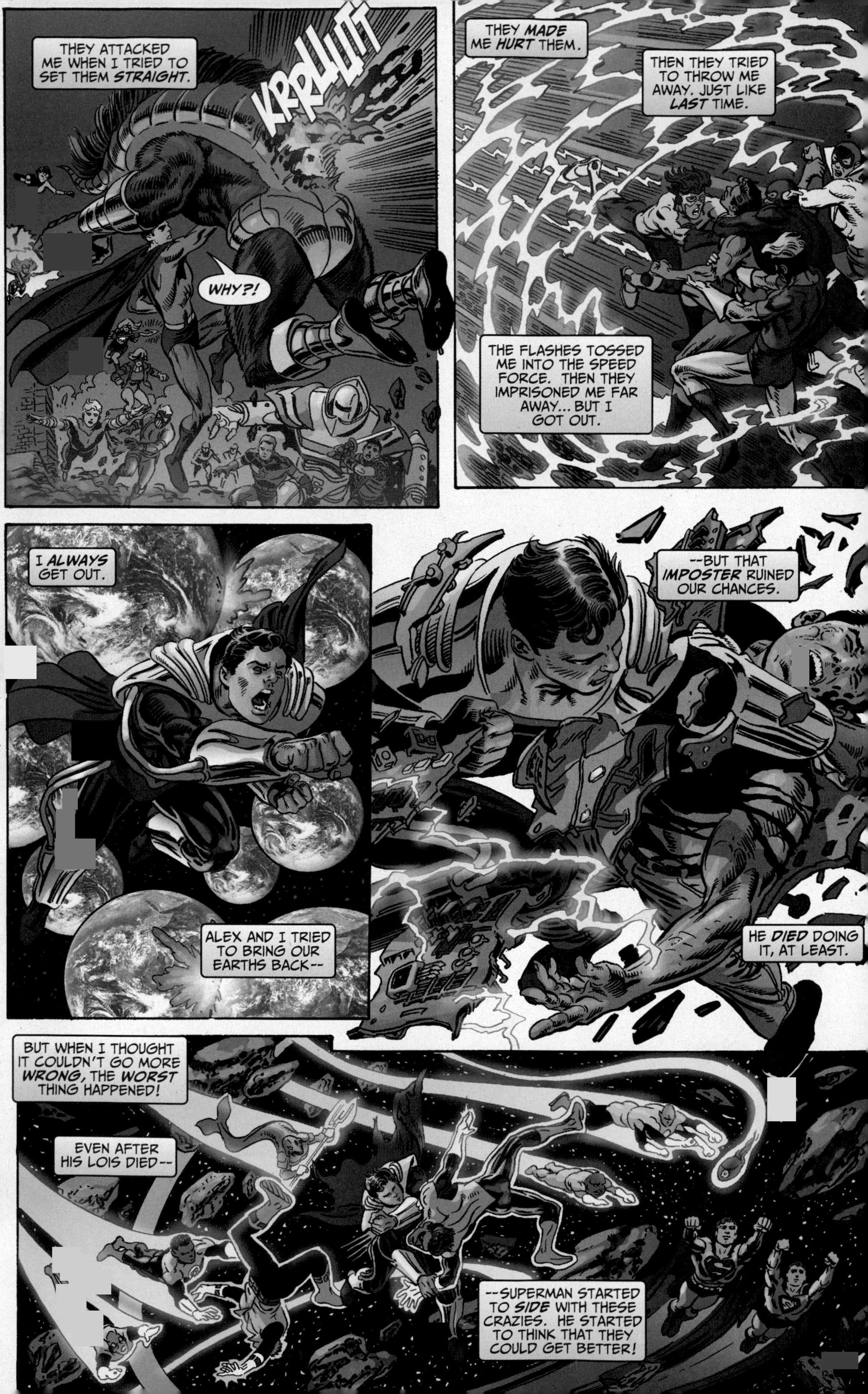
THEY ATTACKED ME WHEN I TRIED TO SET THEM STRAIGHT.
KRRUUT
WHY?!
THEY MADE ME HURT THEM.
THEN THEY TRIED TO THROW ME AWAY. JUST LIKE LAST TIME.
THE FLASHES TOSSED ME INTO THE SPEED FORCE. THEN THEY IMPRISONED ME FAR AWAY... BUT I GOT OUT.
I ALWAYS GET OUT.
ALEX AND I TRIED TO BRING OUR EARTHS BACK--
--BUT THAT IMPOSTER RUINED OUR CHANCES.
HE DIED DOING IT, AT LEAST.
BUT WHEN I THOUGHT IT COULDN'T GO MORE WRONG, THE WORST THING HAPPENED!
EVEN AFTER HIS LOIS DIED--
--SUPERMAN STARTED TO SIDE WITH THESE CRAZIES. HE STARTED TO THINK THAT THEY COULD GET BETTER!

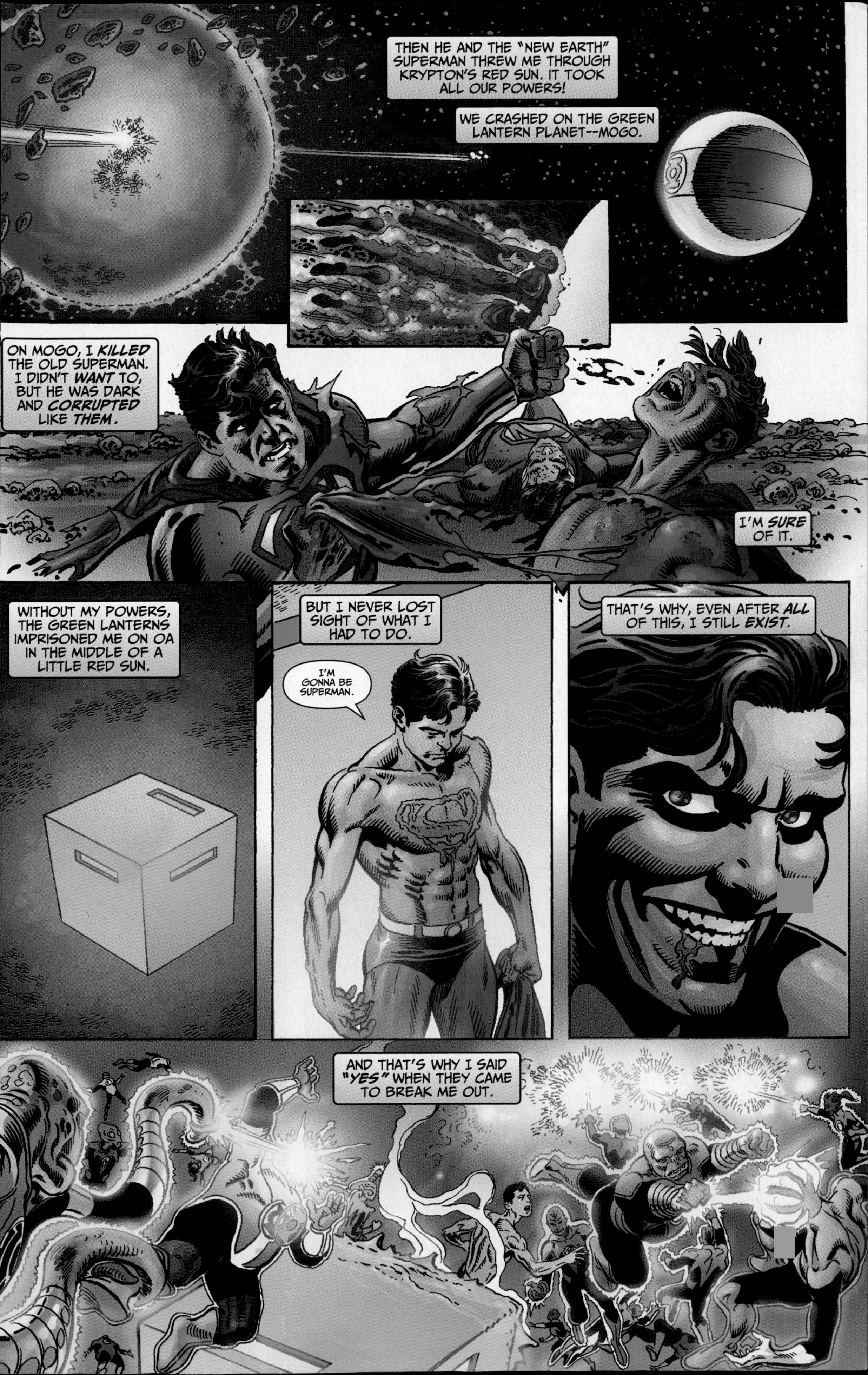

THEN HE AND THE "NEW EARTH" SUPERMAN THREW ME THROUGH KRYPTON'S RED SUN. IT TOOK ALL OUR POWERS!
WE CRASHED ON THE GREEN LANTERN PLANET--MOGO.
ON MOGO, I KILLED THE OLD SUPERMAN. I DIDN'T WANT TO, BUT HE WAS DARK AND CORRUPTED LIKE THEM.
I'M SURE OF IT.
WITHOUT MY POWERS, THE GREEN LANTERNS IMPRISONED ME ON OA IN THE MIDDLE OF A LITTLE RED SUN.
BUT I NEVER LOST SIGHT OF WHAT I HAD TO DO.
I'M GONNA BE SUPERMAN.
THAT'S WHY, EVEN AFTER ALL OF THIS, I STILL EXIST.
AND THAT'S WHY I SAID "YES" WHEN THEY CAME TO BREAK ME OUT.

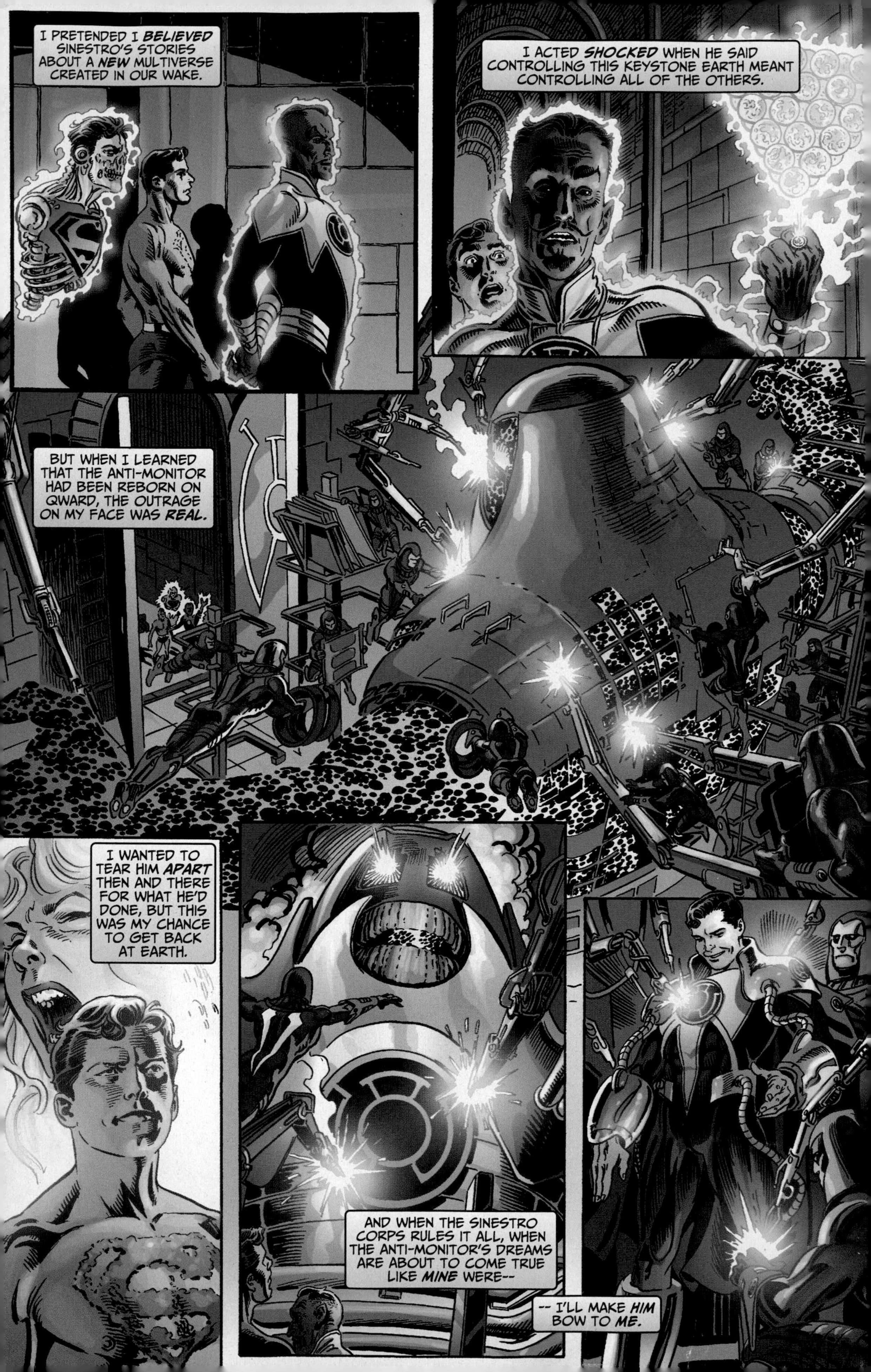
I PRETENDED I *BELIEVED* SINESTRO'S STORIES ABOUT A *NEW* MULTIVERSE CREATED IN OUR WAKE.
I ACTED *SHOCKED* WHEN HE SAID CONTROLLING THIS KEYSTONE EARTH MEANT CONTROLLING ALL OF THE OTHERS.
BUT WHEN I LEARNED THAT THE ANTI-MONITOR HAD BEEN REBORN ON QWARD, THE OUTRAGE ON MY FACE WAS *REAL*.
I WANTED TO TEAR HIM *APART* THEN AND THERE FOR WHAT HE'D DONE, BUT THIS WAS MY CHANCE TO GET BACK AT EARTH.
AND WHEN THE SINESTRO CORPS RULES IT ALL, WHEN THE ANTI-MONITOR'S DREAMS ARE ABOUT TO COME TRUE LIKE *MINE* WERE--
-- I'LL MAKE *HIM* BOW TO *ME*.

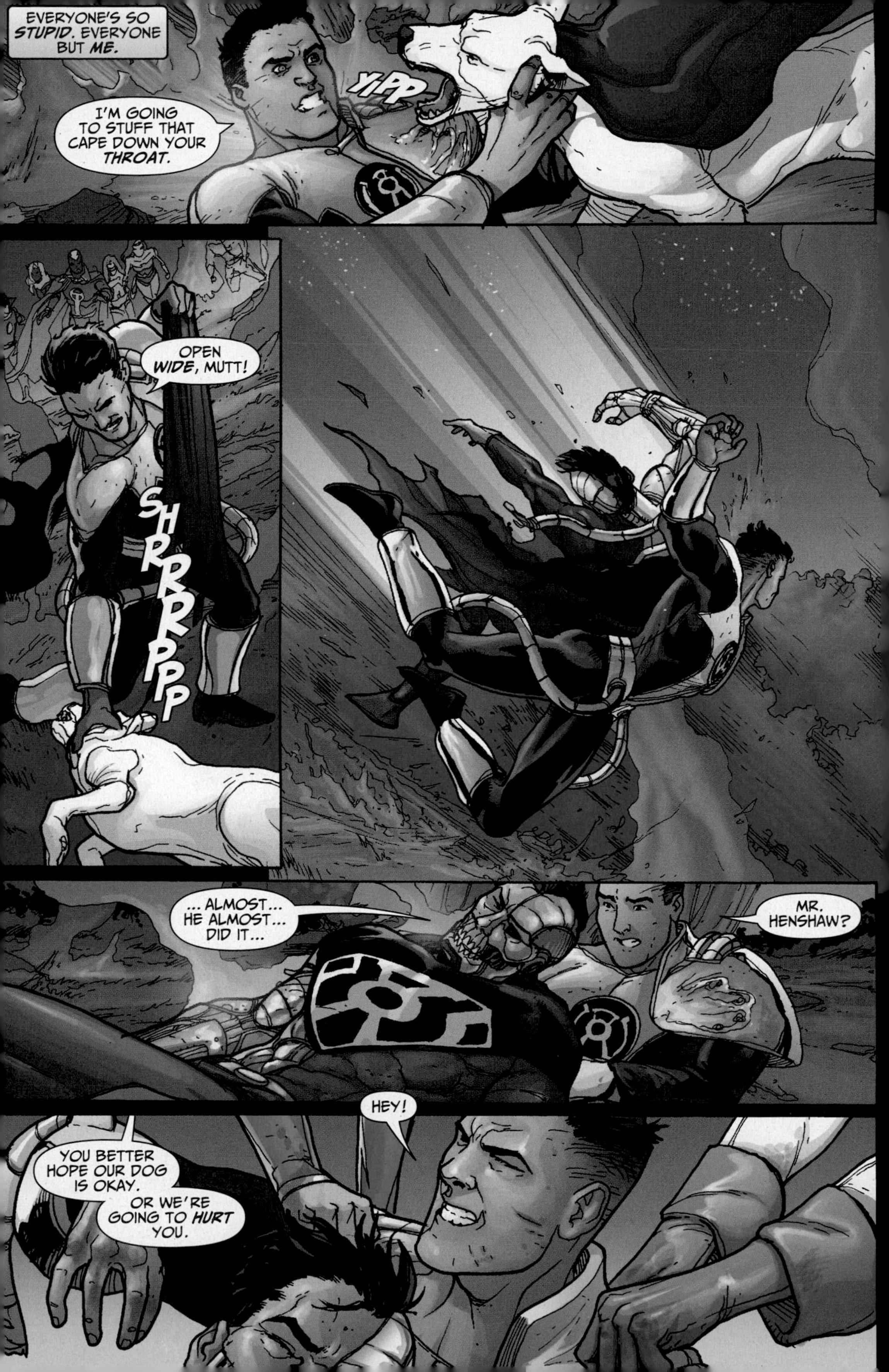
EVERYONE'S SO STUPID. EVERYONE BUT ME.
YIPP
I'M GOING TO STUFF THAT CAPE DOWN YOUR THROAT.
OPEN WIDE, MUTT!
SHRRRPPP
... ALMOST... HE ALMOST... DID IT...
MR. HENSHAW?
HEY!
YOU BETTER HOPE OUR DOG IS OKAY.
OR WE'RE GOING TO HURT YOU.

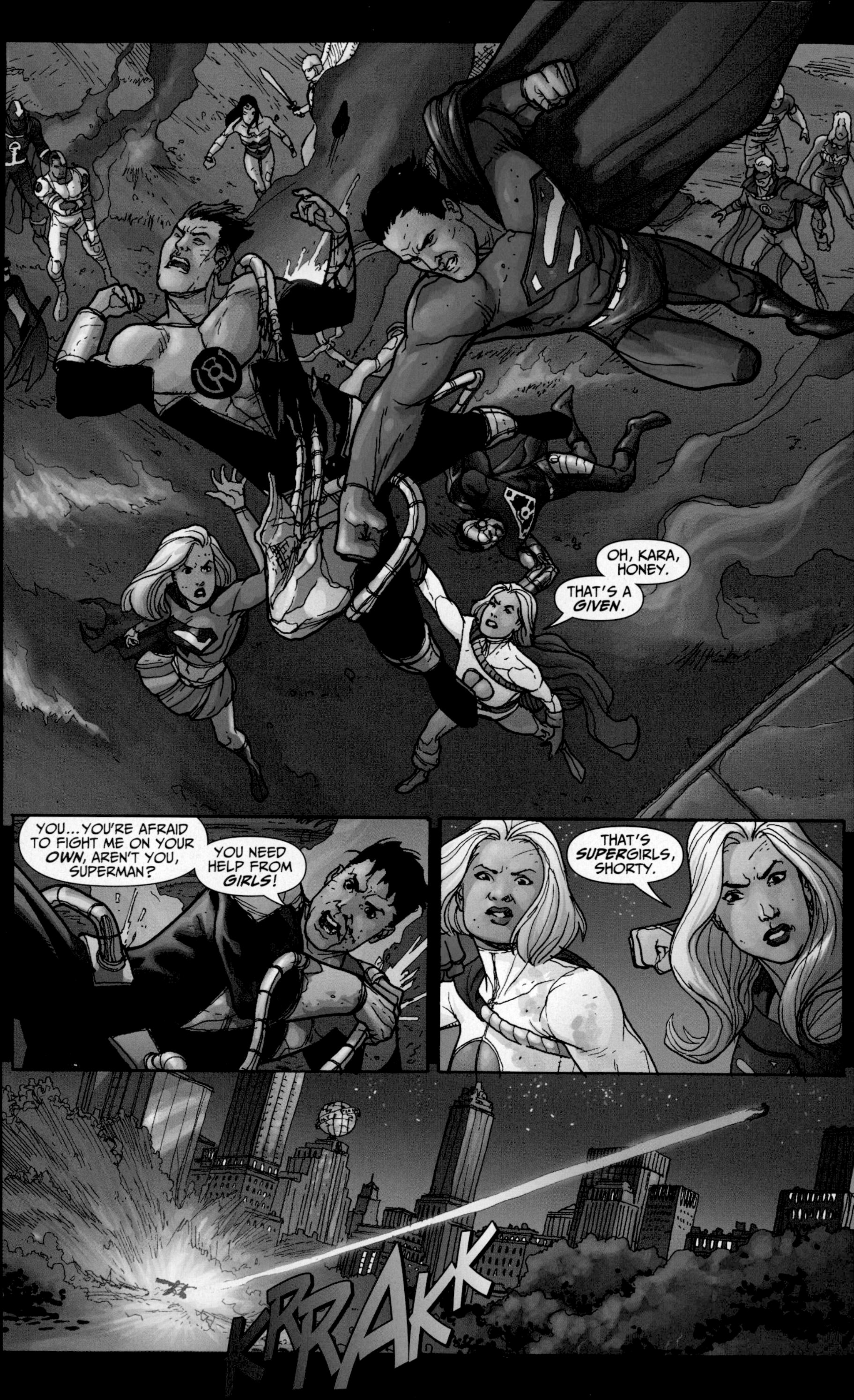
OH, KARA, HONEY.
THAT'S A *GIVEN*.
YOU... YOU'RE AFRAID TO FIGHT ME ON YOUR *OWN*, AREN'T YOU, SUPERMAN?
YOU NEED HELP FROM *GIRLS*!
THAT'S *SUPER*GIRLS, SHORTY.
KRRAKK

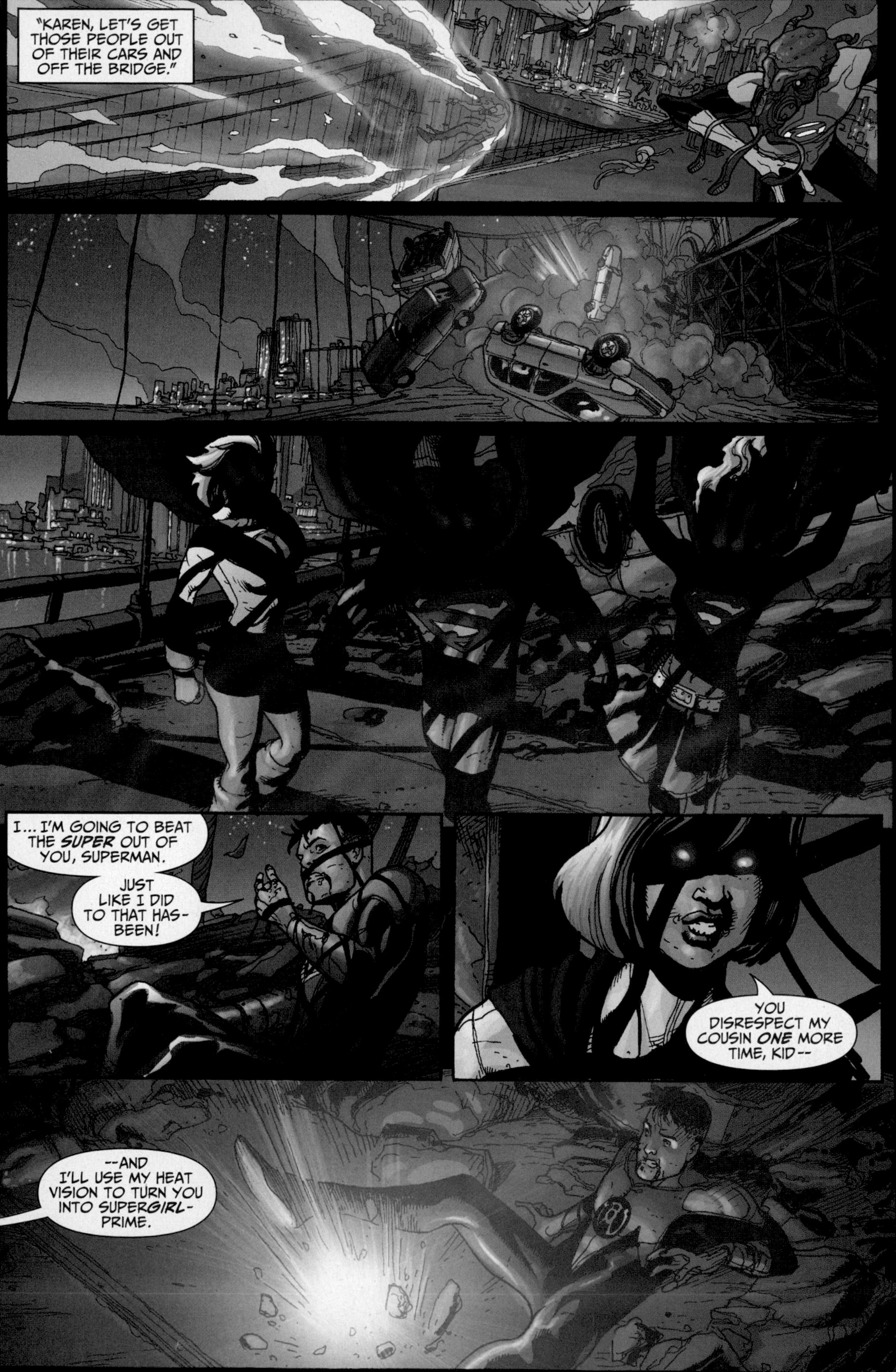
"KAREN, LET'S GET THOSE PEOPLE OUT OF THEIR CARS AND OFF THE BRIDGE."
I... I'M GOING TO BEAT THE SUPER OUT OF YOU, SUPERMAN.
JUST LIKE I DID TO THAT HAS-BEEN!
YOU DISRESPECT MY COUSIN ONE MORE TIME, KID--
--AND I'LL USE MY HEAT VISION TO TURN YOU INTO SUPERGIRL-PRIME.

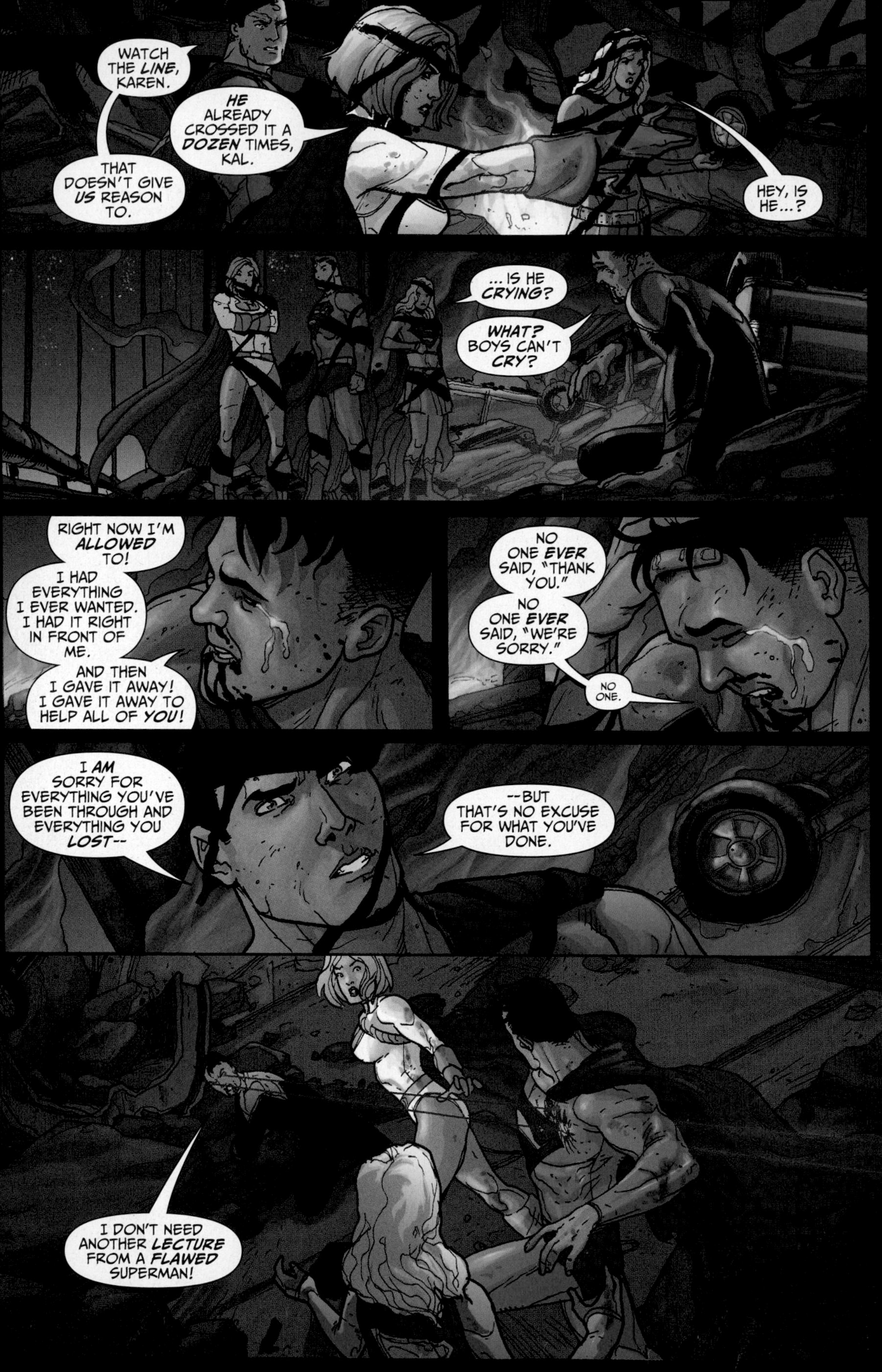
WATCH THE LINE, KAREN.
HE ALREADY CROSSED IT A DOZEN TIMES, KAL.
THAT DOESN'T GIVE US REASON TO.
HEY, IS HE...?
... IS HE CRYING?
WHAT? BOYS CAN'T CRY?
RIGHT NOW I'M ALLOWED TO!
I HAD EVERYTHING I EVER WANTED. I HAD IT RIGHT IN FRONT OF ME.
AND THEN I GAVE IT AWAY! I GAVE IT AWAY TO HELP ALL OF YOU!
NO ONE EVER SAID, "THANK YOU."
NO ONE EVER SAID, "WE'RE SORRY."
NO ONE.
I AM SORRY FOR EVERYTHING YOU'VE BEEN THROUGH AND EVERYTHING YOU LOST--
--BUT THAT'S NO EXCUSE FOR WHAT YOU'VE DONE.
I DON'T NEED ANOTHER LECTURE FROM A FLAWED SUPERMAN!

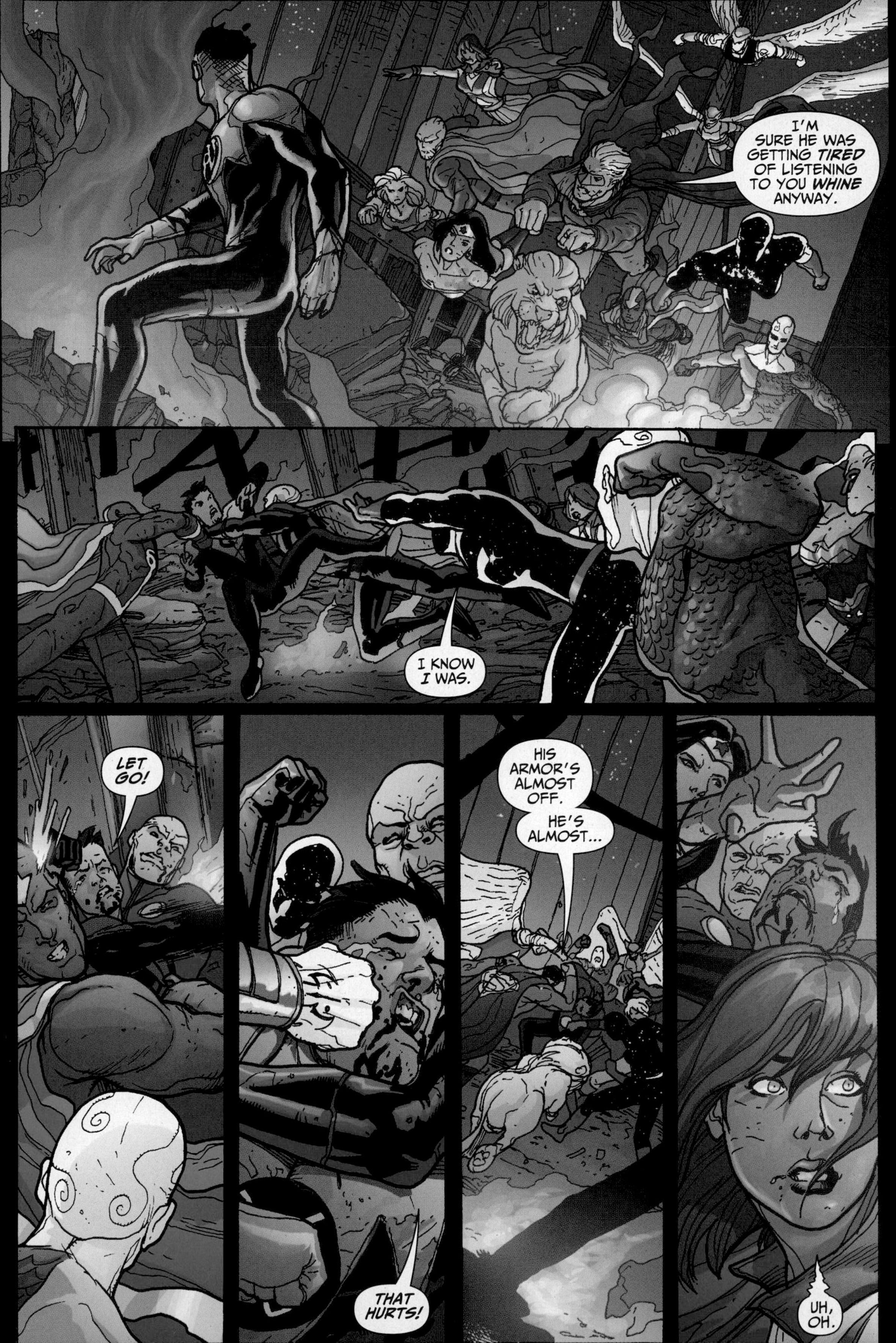
I'M SURE HE WAS GETTING *TIRED* OF LISTENING TO YOU *WHINE* ANYWAY.
I KNOW *I* WAS.
LET GO!
THAT HURTS!
HIS ARMOR'S ALMOST OFF.
HE'S ALMOST...
UH, OH.

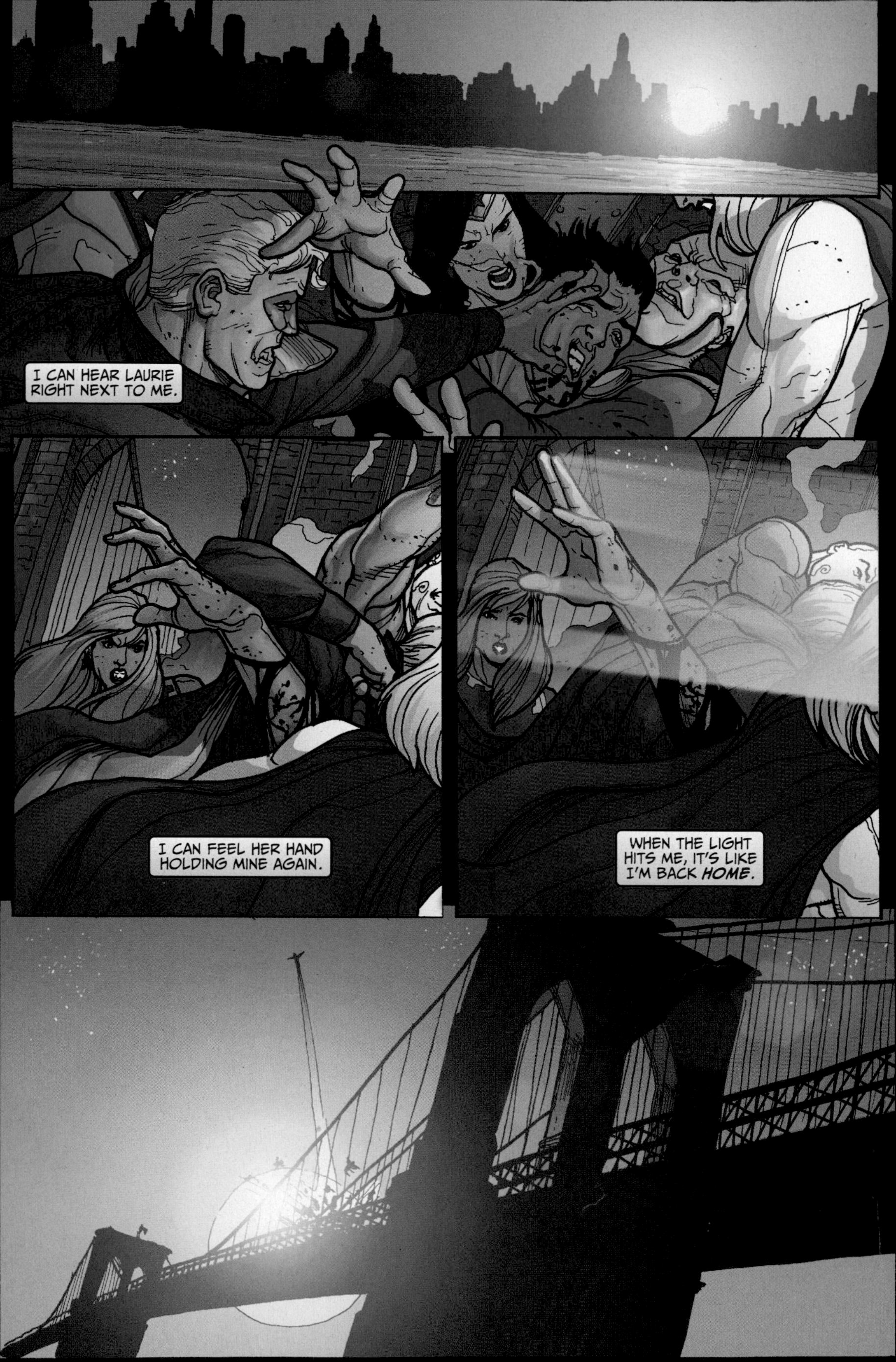
I CAN HEAR LAURIE RIGHT NEXT TO ME.
I CAN FEEL HER HAND HOLDING MINE AGAIN.
WHEN THE LIGHT HITS ME, IT'S LIKE I'M BACK *HOME*.

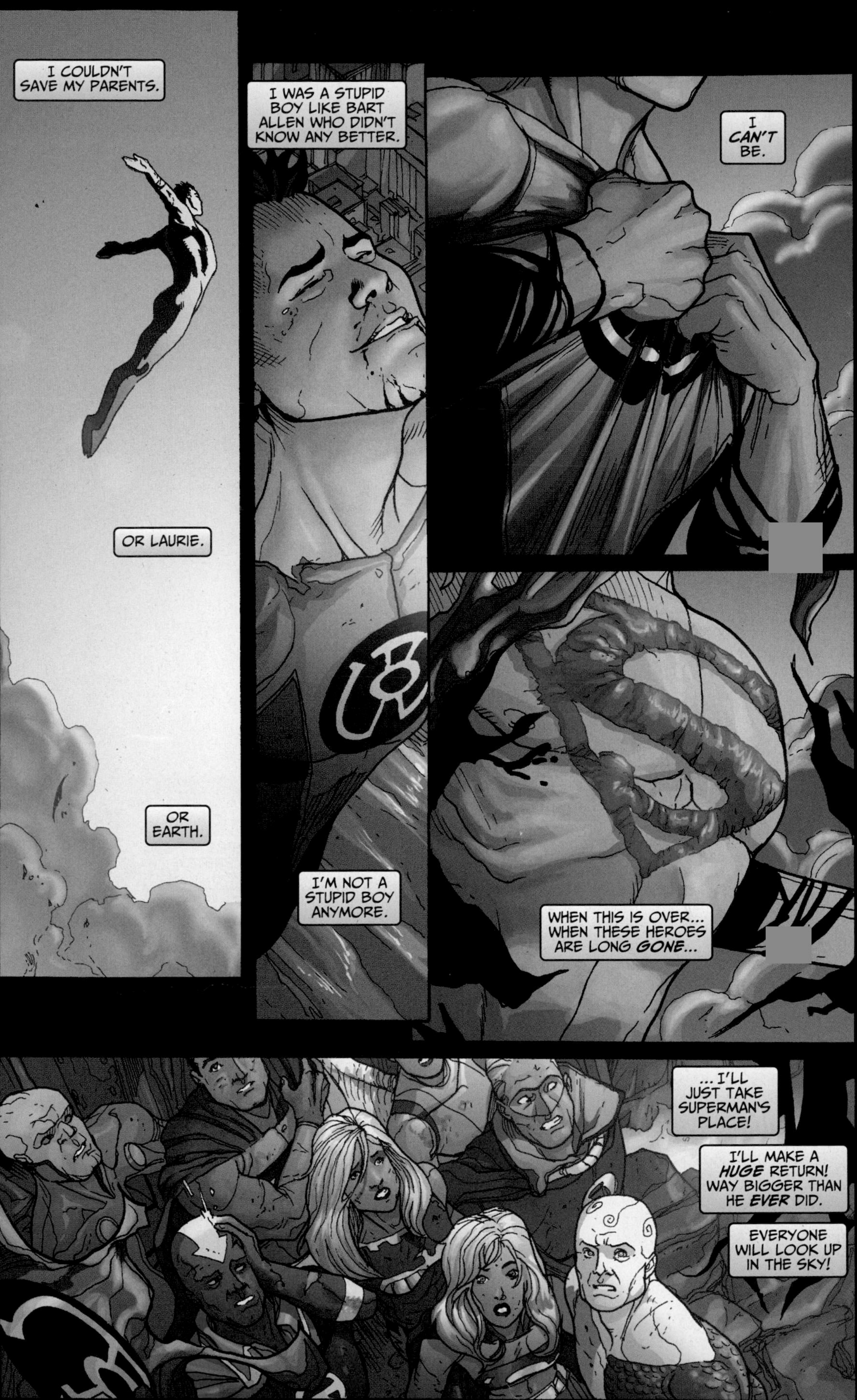
I COULDN'T SAVE MY PARENTS.
I WAS A STUPID BOY LIKE BART ALLEN WHO DIDN'T KNOW ANY BETTER.
I CAN'T BE.
OR LAURIE.
OR EARTH.
I'M NOT A STUPID BOY ANYMORE.
WHEN THIS IS OVER... WHEN THESE HEROES ARE LONG GONE...
... I'LL JUST TAKE SUPERMAN'S PLACE!
I'LL MAKE A HUGE RETURN! WAY BIGGER THAN HE EVER DID.
EVERYONE WILL LOOK UP IN THE SKY!

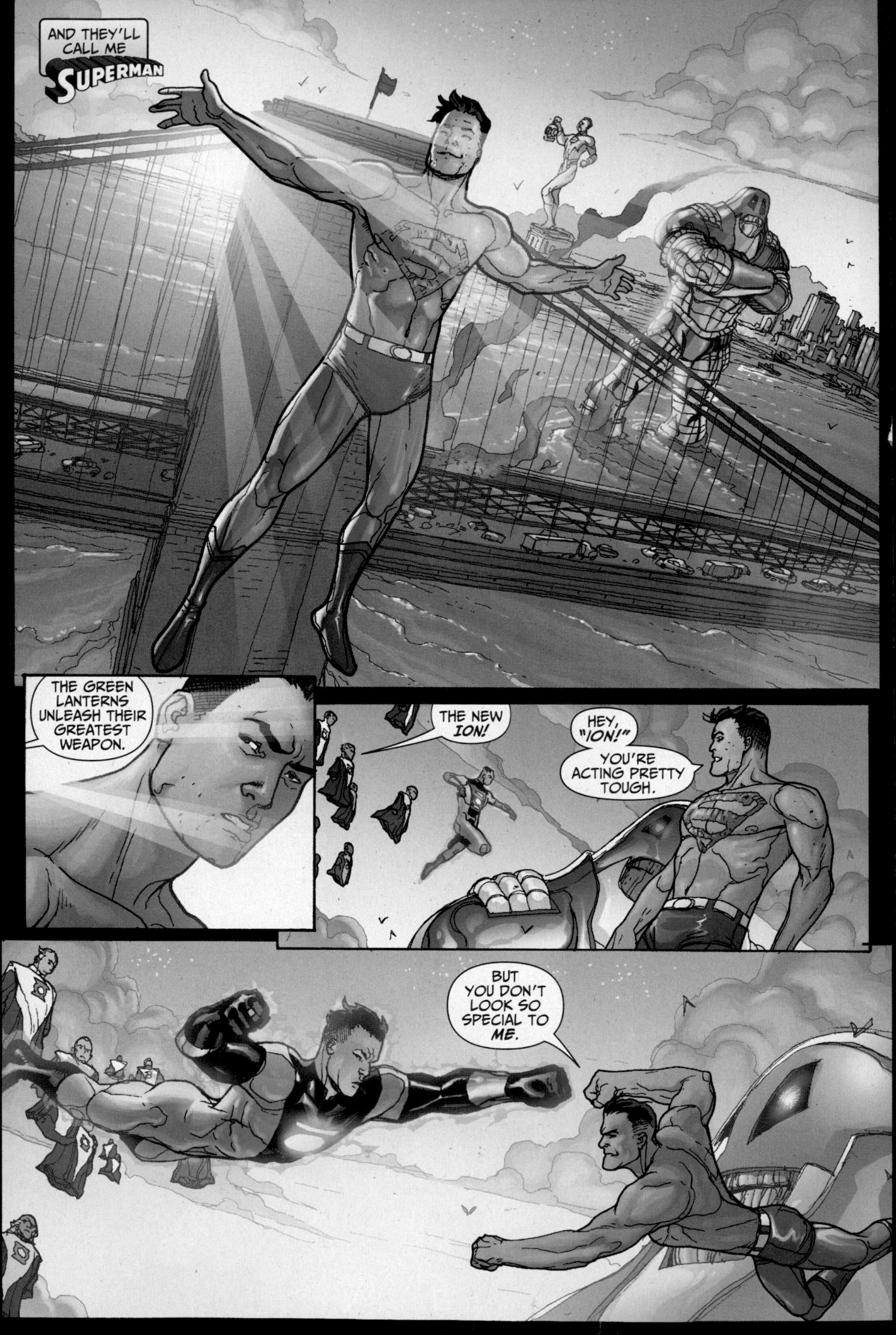
AND THEY'LL CALL ME SUPERMAN
THE GREEN LANTERNS UNLEASH THEIR GREATEST WEAPON.
THE NEW ION!
HEY, "ION!"
YOU'RE ACTING PRETTY TOUGH.
BUT YOU DON'T LOOK SO SPECIAL TO ME.

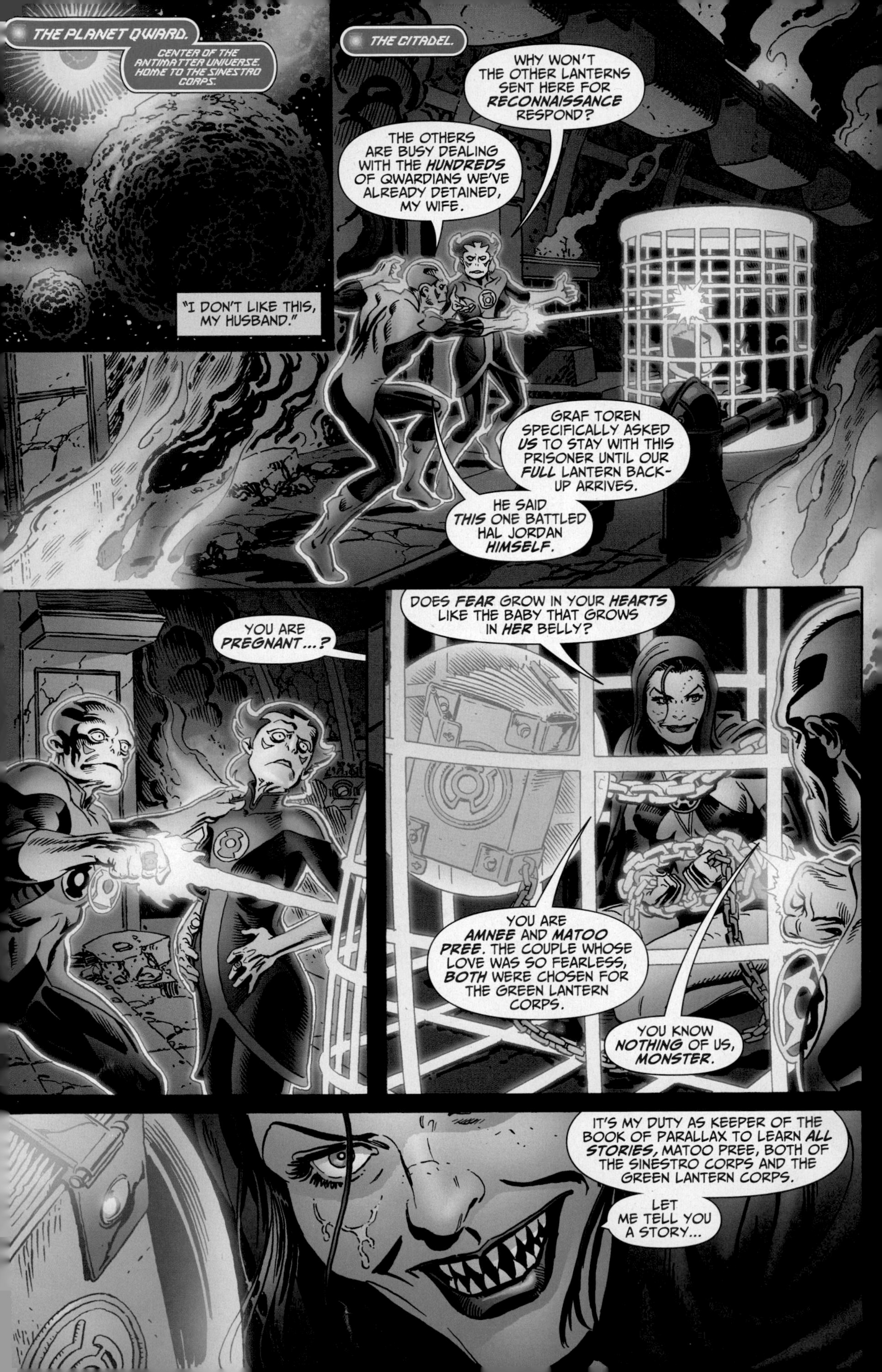
THE PLANET QWARD.
CENTER OF THE ANTIMATTER UNIVERSE. HOME TO THE SINESTRO CORPS.
"I DON'T LIKE THIS, MY HUSBAND."
THE CITADEL.
WHY WON'T THE OTHER LANTERNS SENT HERE FOR RECONNAISSANCE RESPOND?
THE OTHERS ARE BUSY DEALING WITH THE HUNDREDS OF QWARDIANS WE'VE ALREADY DETAINED, MY WIFE.
GRAF TOREN SPECIFICALLY ASKED US TO STAY WITH THIS PRISONER UNTIL OUR FULL LANTERN BACK-UP ARRIVES.
HE SAID THIS ONE BATTLED HAL JORDAN HIMSELF.
YOU ARE PREGNANT...?
DOES FEAR GROW IN YOUR HEARTS LIKE THE BABY THAT GROWS IN HER BELLY?
YOU ARE AMNEE AND MATOO PREE. THE COUPLE WHOSE LOVE WAS SO FEARLESS, BOTH WERE CHOSEN FOR THE GREEN LANTERN CORPS.
YOU KNOW NOTHING OF US, MONSTER.
IT'S MY DUTY AS KEEPER OF THE BOOK OF PARALLAX TO LEARN ALL STORIES, MATOO PREE, BOTH OF THE SINESTRO CORPS AND THE GREEN LANTERN CORPS.
LET ME TELL YOU A STORY...

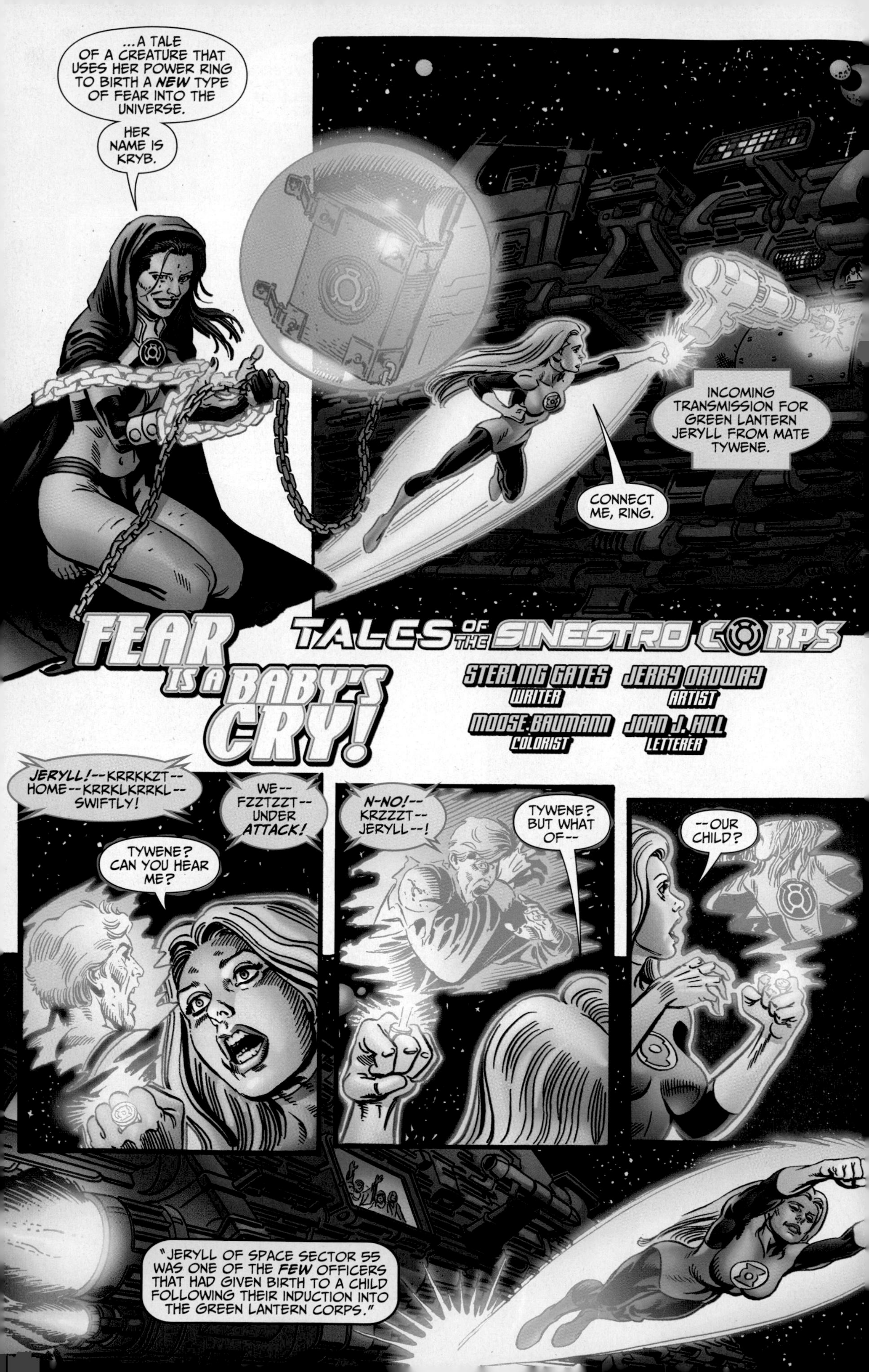

...A TALE OF A CREATURE THAT USES HER POWER RING TO BIRTH A NEW TYPE OF FEAR INTO THE UNIVERSE.
HER NAME IS KRYB.
INCOMING TRANSMISSION FOR GREEN LANTERN JERYLL FROM MATE TYWENE.
CONNECT ME, RING.
FEAR IS A BABY'S CRY!
TALES OF THE SINESTRO CORPS
STERLING GATES WRITER
JERRY ORDWAY ARTIST
MOOSE BAUMANN COLORIST
JOHN J. HILL LETTERER
JERYLL!--KRRKKZT--HOME--KRRRKLKRRKL--SWIFTLY!
WE--FZZTZZT--UNDER ATTACK!
TYWENE? CAN YOU HEAR ME?
N-NO!--KRZZZT--JERYLL--!
TYWENE? BUT WHAT OF--
--OUR CHILD?
"JERYLL OF SPACE SECTOR 55 WAS ONE OF THE FEW OFFICERS THAT HAD GIVEN BIRTH TO A CHILD FOLLOWING THEIR INDUCTION INTO THE GREEN LANTERN CORPS."

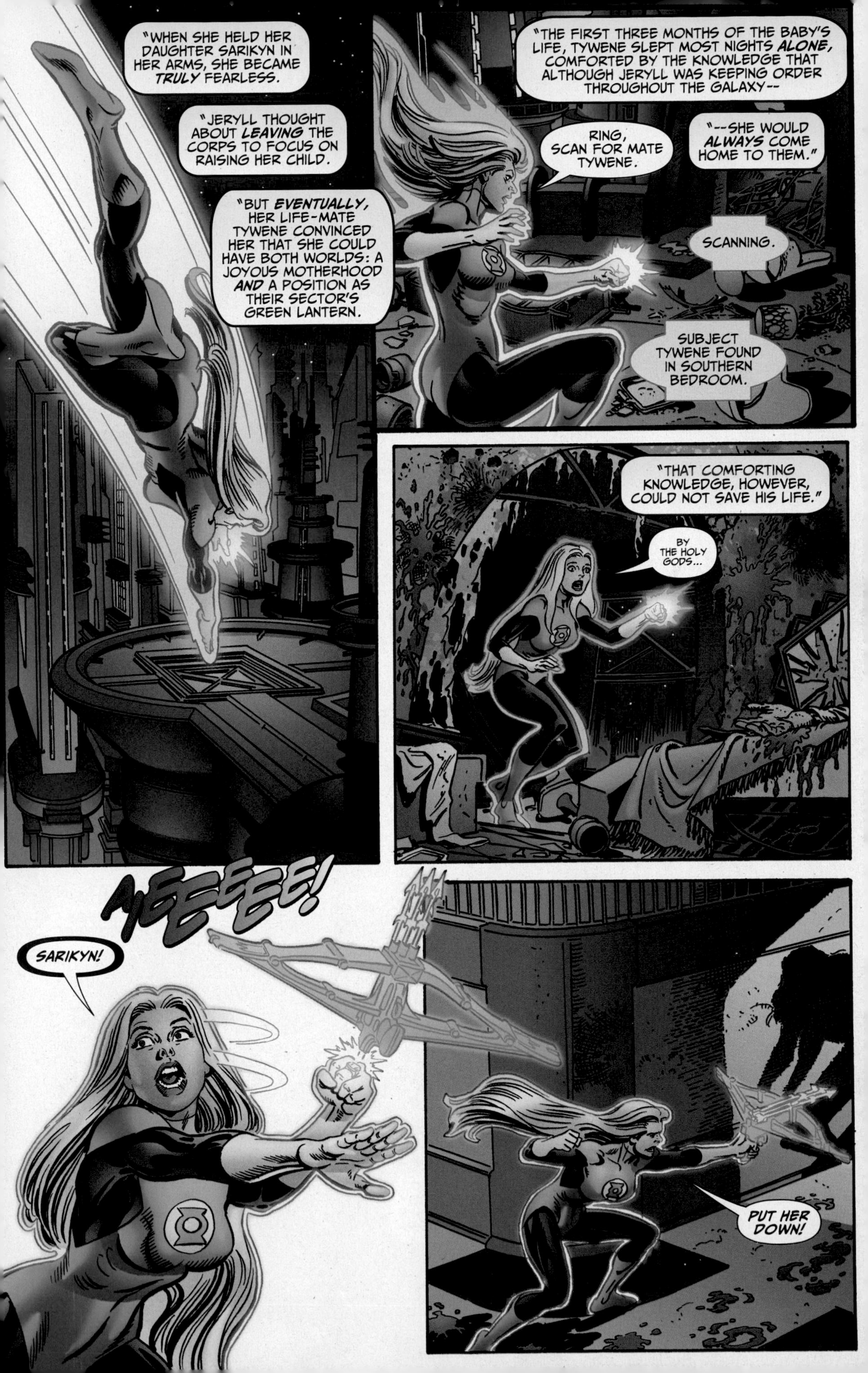
"WHEN SHE HELD HER DAUGHTER SARIKYN IN HER ARMS, SHE BECAME TRULY FEARLESS.
"JERYLL THOUGHT ABOUT LEAVING THE CORPS TO FOCUS ON RAISING HER CHILD.
"BUT EVENTUALLY, HER LIFE-MATE TYWENE CONVINCED HER THAT SHE COULD HAVE BOTH WORLDS: A JOYOUS MOTHERHOOD AND A POSITION AS THEIR SECTOR'S GREEN LANTERN.
"THE FIRST THREE MONTHS OF THE BABY'S LIFE, TYWENE SLEPT MOST NIGHTS ALONE, COMFORTED BY THE KNOWLEDGE THAT ALTHOUGH JERYLL WAS KEEPING ORDER THROUGHOUT THE GALAXY--
RING, SCAN FOR MATE TYWENE.
"--SHE WOULD ALWAYS COME HOME TO THEM."
SCANNING.
SUBJECT TYWENE FOUND IN SOUTHERN BEDROOM.
"THAT COMFORTING KNOWLEDGE, HOWEVER, COULD NOT SAVE HIS LIFE."
BY THE HOLY GODS...
AEEEEEE!
SARIKYN!
PUT HER DOWN!

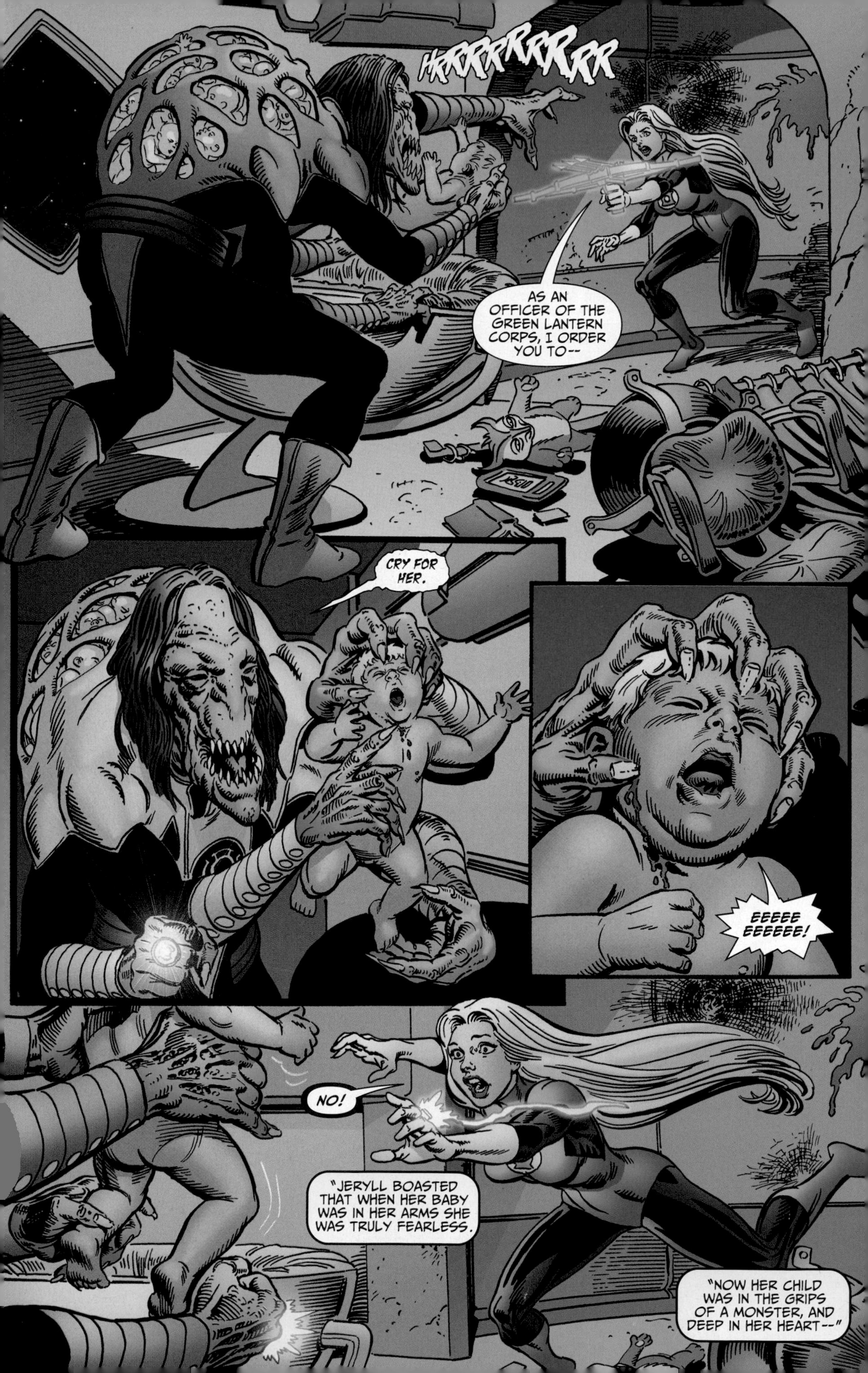
HRRRRRRRRRRR
AS AN OFFICER OF THE GREEN LANTERN CORPS, I ORDER YOU TO--
CRY FOR HER.
EEEEE EEEEEE!
NO!
"JERYLL BOASTED THAT WHEN HER BABY WAS IN HER ARMS SHE WAS TRULY FEARLESS.
"NOW HER CHILD WAS IN THE GRIPS OF A MONSTER, AND DEEP IN HER HEART--"

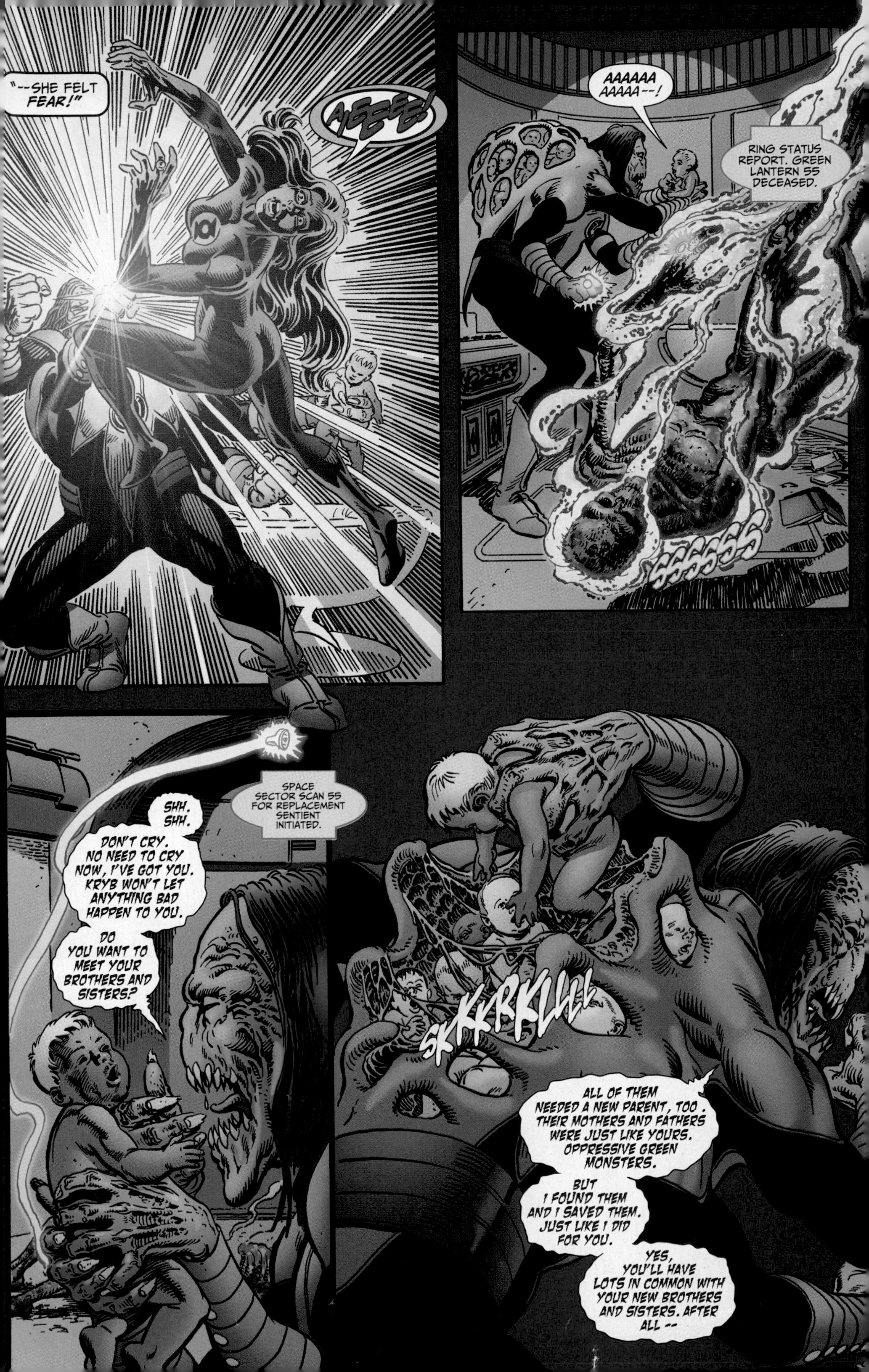
"--SHE FELT FEAR!"
AIEEEE!
AAAAAA AAAAA--!
RING STATUS REPORT. GREEN LANTERN 55 DECEASED.
SSSSSS
SPACE SECTOR SCAN 55 FOR REPLACEMENT SENTIENT INITIATED.
SHH. SHH.
DON'T CRY. NO NEED TO CRY NOW, I'VE GOT YOU. KRYB WON'T LET ANYTHING BAD HAPPEN TO YOU.
DO YOU WANT TO MEET YOUR BROTHERS AND SISTERS?
SKKKRKLLL
ALL OF THEM NEEDED A NEW PARENT, TOO. THEIR MOTHERS AND FATHERS WERE JUST LIKE YOURS. OPPRESSIVE GREEN MONSTERS.
BUT I FOUND THEM AND I SAVED THEM. JUST LIKE I DID FOR YOU.
YES, YOU'LL HAVE LOTS IN COMMON WITH YOUR NEW BROTHERS AND SISTERS. AFTER ALL --

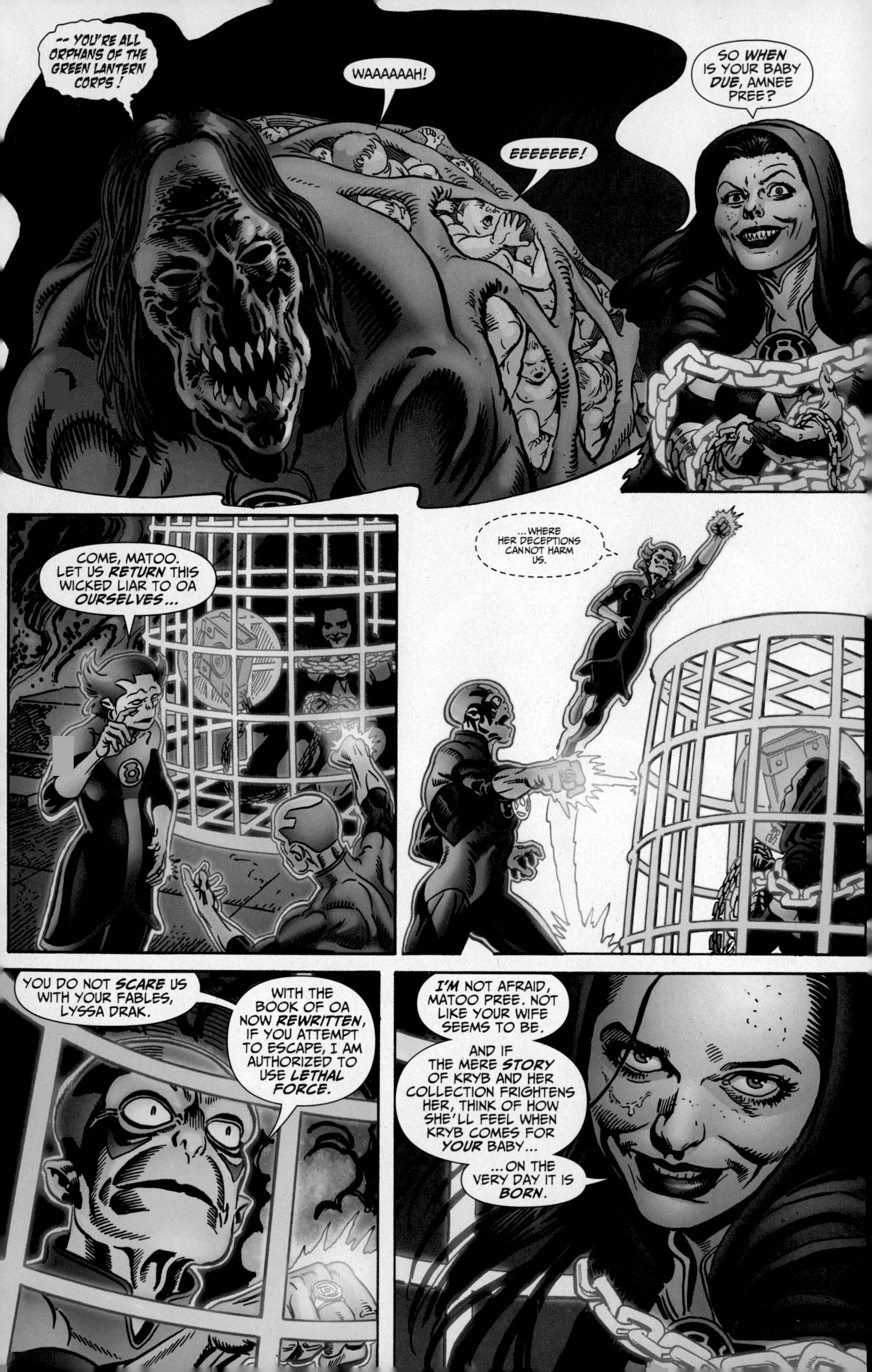
-- YOU'RE ALL ORPHANS OF THE GREEN LANTERN CORPS!
WAAAAAAH!
EEEEEEE!
SO WHEN IS YOUR BABY DUE, AMNEE PREE?
COME, MATOO. LET US RETURN THIS WICKED LIAR TO OA OURSELVES...
...WHERE HER DECEPTIONS CANNOT HARM US.
YOU DO NOT SCARE US WITH YOUR FABLES, LYSSA DRAK.
WITH THE BOOK OF OA NOW REWRITTEN, IF YOU ATTEMPT TO ESCAPE, I AM AUTHORIZED TO USE LETHAL FORCE.
I'M NOT AFRAID, MATOO PREE. NOT LIKE YOUR WIFE SEEMS TO BE.
AND IF THE MERE STORY OF KRYB AND HER COLLECTION FRIGHTENS HER, THINK OF HOW SHE'LL FEEL WHEN KRYB COMES FOR YOUR BABY...
...ON THE VERY DAY IT IS BORN.

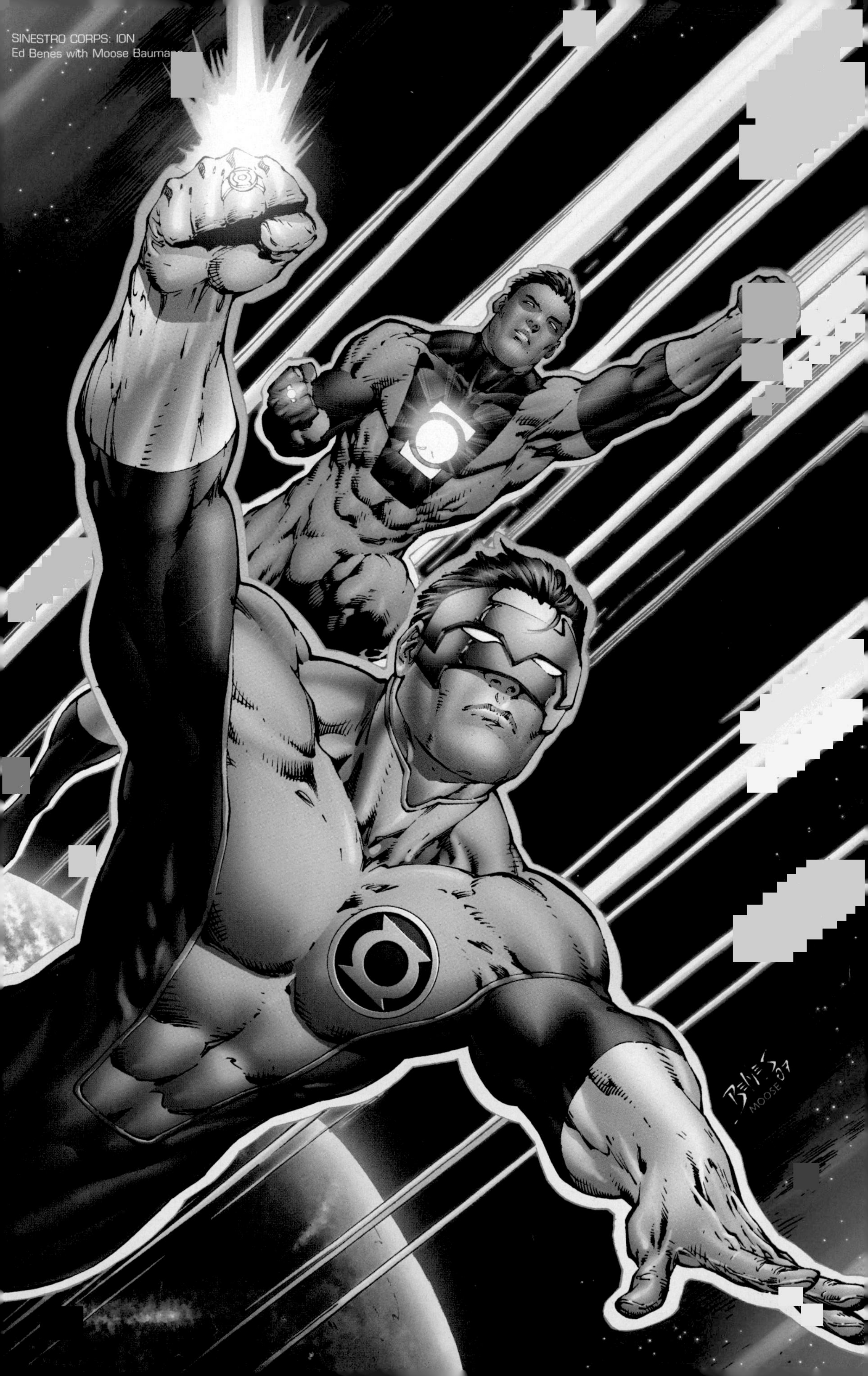

SINESTRO CORPS: ION
Ed Benes with Moose Baumann

Once so powerful that he single handedly re-created the Green Lantern Corps, Kyle Rayner was possessed by the evil Parallax and forced to fight against his allies. Now Kyle must come to terms with what has happened and find a new place within the Corps…

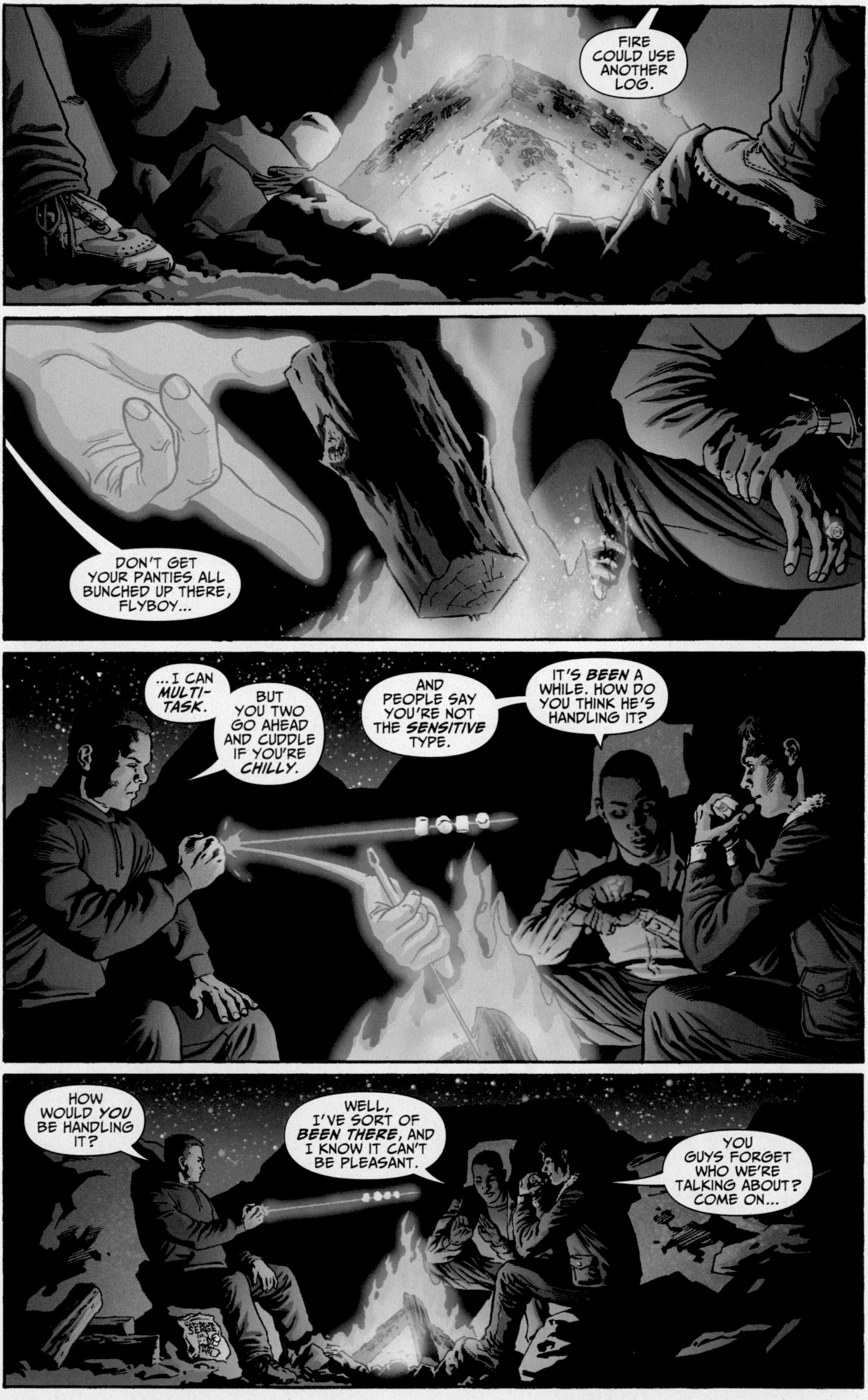
FIRE COULD USE ANOTHER LOG.
DON'T GET YOUR PANTIES ALL BUNCHED UP THERE, FLYBOY...
...I CAN MULTI-TASK.
BUT YOU TWO GO AHEAD AND CUDDLE IF YOU'RE CHILLY.
AND PEOPLE SAY YOU'RE NOT THE SENSITIVE TYPE.
IT'S BEEN A WHILE. HOW DO YOU THINK HE'S HANDLING IT?
HOW WOULD YOU BE HANDLING IT?
WELL, I'VE SORT OF BEEN THERE, AND I KNOW IT CAN'T BE PLEASANT.
YOU GUYS FORGET WHO WE'RE TALKING ABOUT? COME ON...

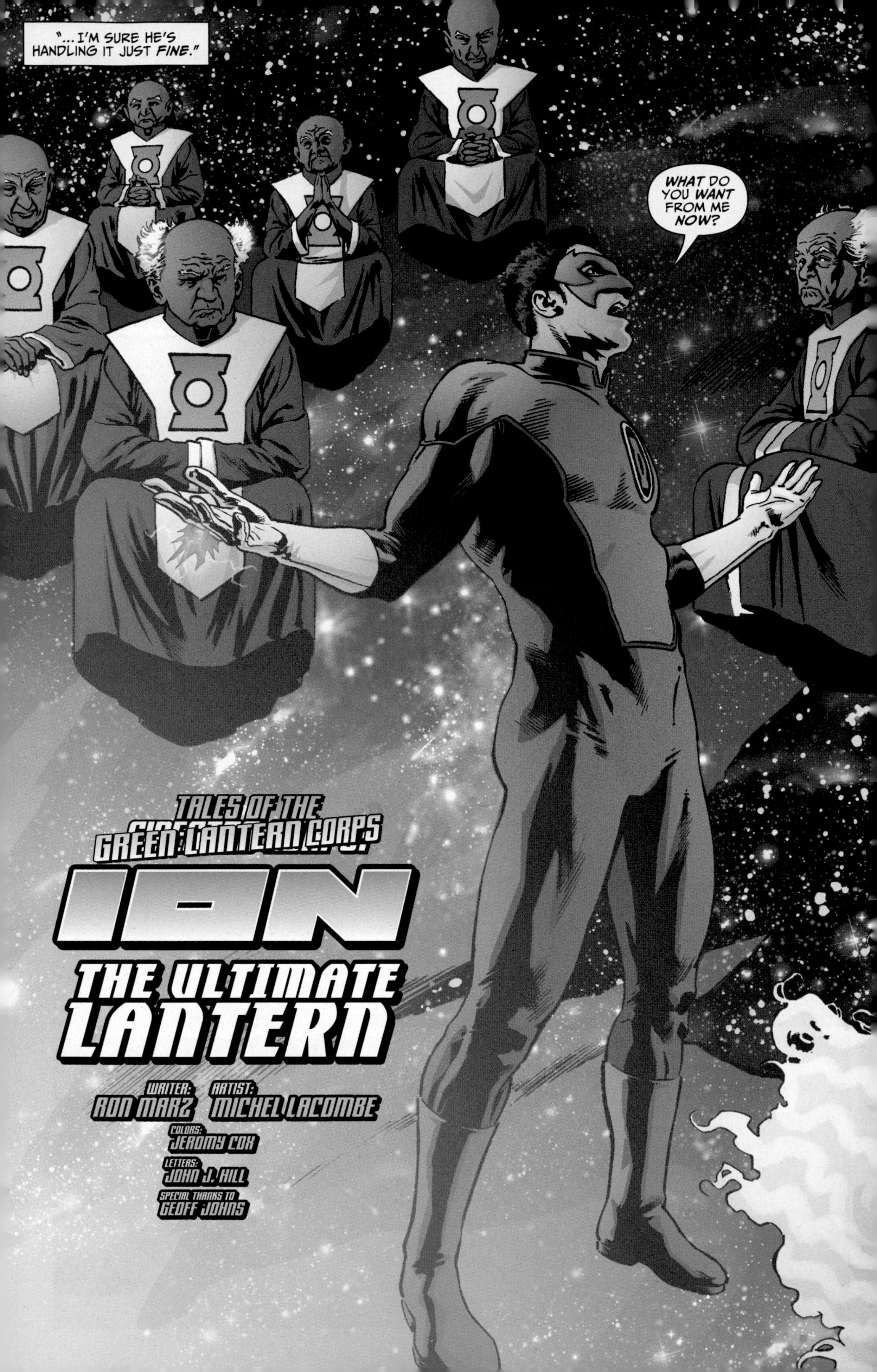
"... I'M SURE HE'S HANDLING IT JUST FINE."
WHAT DO YOU WANT FROM ME NOW?
TALES OF THE GREEN LANTERN CORPS
ION
THE ULTIMATE LANTERN
WRITER: RON MARZ
ARTIST: MICHEL LACOMBE
COLORS: JEROMY COX
LETTERS: JOHN J. HILL
SPECIAL THANKS TO GEOFF JOHNS

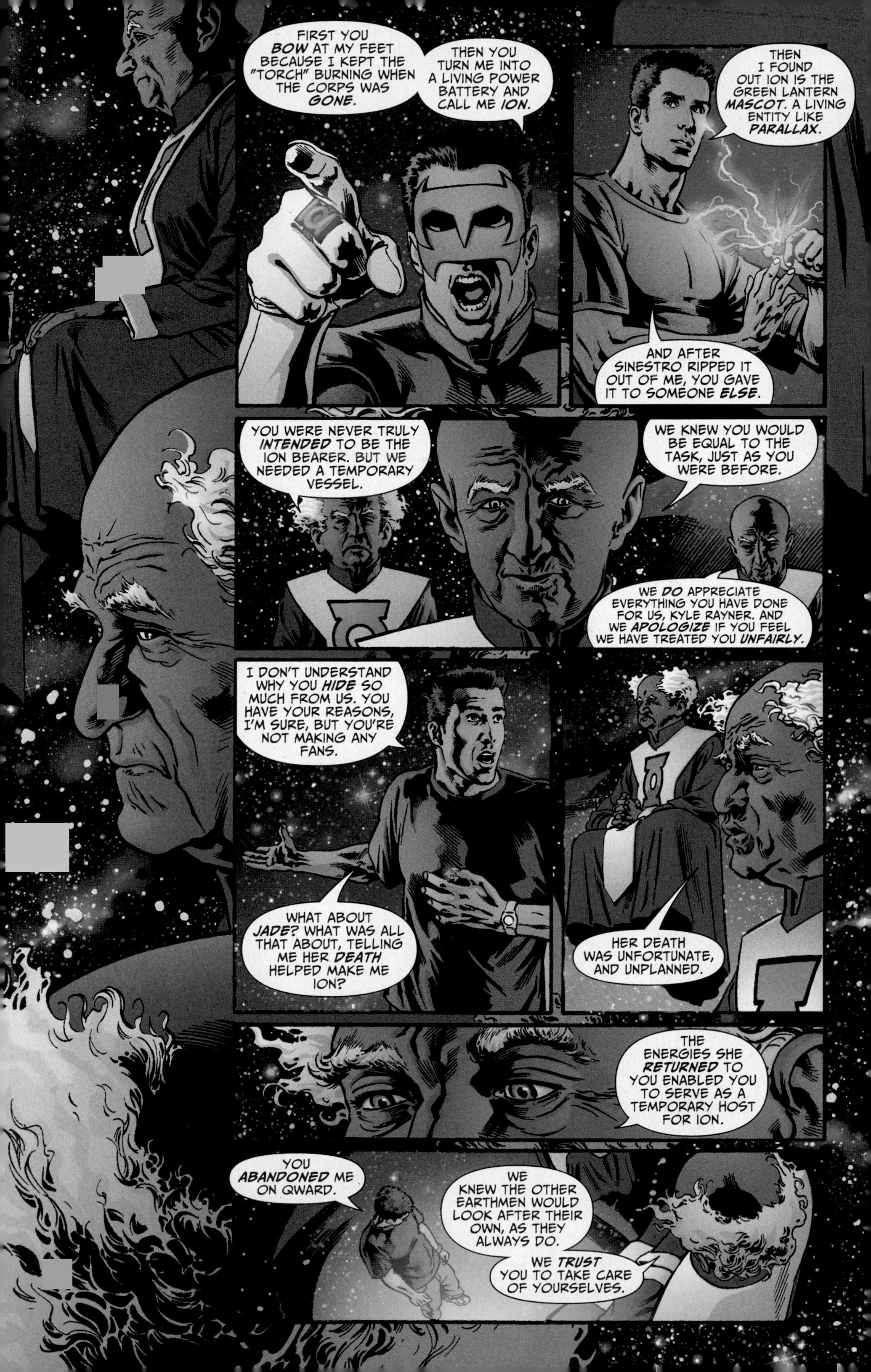
FIRST YOU BOW AT MY FEET BECAUSE I KEPT THE "TORCH" BURNING WHEN THE CORPS WAS GONE.
THEN YOU TURN ME INTO A LIVING POWER BATTERY AND CALL ME ION.
THEN I FOUND OUT ION IS THE GREEN LANTERN MASCOT. A LIVING ENTITY LIKE PARALLAX.
AND AFTER SINESTRO RIPPED IT OUT OF ME, YOU GAVE IT TO SOMEONE ELSE.
YOU WERE NEVER TRULY INTENDED TO BE THE ION BEARER. BUT WE NEEDED A TEMPORARY VESSEL.
WE KNEW YOU WOULD BE EQUAL TO THE TASK, JUST AS YOU WERE BEFORE.
WE DO APPRECIATE EVERYTHING YOU HAVE DONE FOR US, KYLE RAYNER. AND WE APOLOGIZE IF YOU FEEL WE HAVE TREATED YOU UNFAIRLY.
I DON'T UNDERSTAND WHY YOU HIDE SO MUCH FROM US. YOU HAVE YOUR REASONS, I'M SURE, BUT YOU'RE NOT MAKING ANY FANS.
WHAT ABOUT JADE? WHAT WAS ALL THAT ABOUT, TELLING ME HER DEATH HELPED MAKE ME ION?
HER DEATH WAS UNFORTUNATE, AND UNPLANNED.
THE ENERGIES SHE RETURNED TO YOU ENABLED YOU TO SERVE AS A TEMPORARY HOST FOR ION.
YOU ABANDONED ME ON QWARD.
WE KNEW THE OTHER EARTHMEN WOULD LOOK AFTER THEIR OWN, AS THEY ALWAYS DO.
WE TRUST YOU TO TAKE CARE OF YOURSELVES.

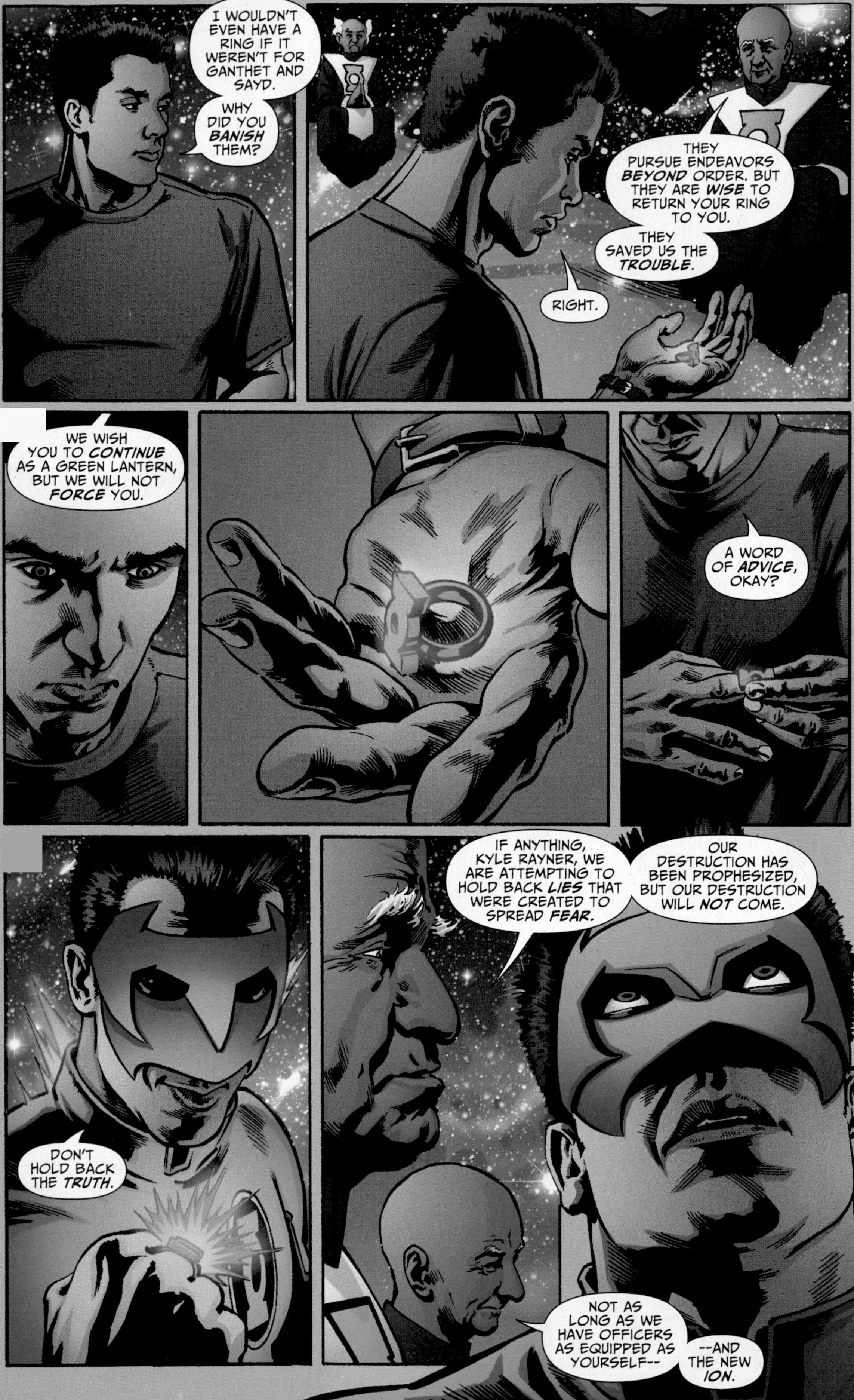

I WOULDN'T EVEN HAVE A RING IF IT WEREN'T FOR GANTHET AND SAYD.
WHY DID YOU *BANISH* THEM?
THEY PURSUE ENDEAVORS *BEYOND* ORDER. BUT THEY ARE *WISE* TO RETURN YOUR RING TO YOU.
THEY SAVED US THE *TROUBLE*.
RIGHT.
WE WISH YOU TO *CONTINUE* AS A GREEN LANTERN, BUT WE WILL NOT *FORCE* YOU.
A WORD OF *ADVICE*, OKAY?
DON'T HOLD BACK THE *TRUTH*.
IF ANYTHING, KYLE RAYNER, WE ARE ATTEMPTING TO HOLD BACK *LIES* THAT WERE CREATED TO SPREAD *FEAR*.
OUR DESTRUCTION HAS BEEN PROPHESIZED, BUT OUR DESTRUCTION WILL *NOT* COME.
NOT AS LONG AS WE HAVE OFFICERS AS EQUIPPED AS YOURSELF--
--AND THE NEW *ION*.

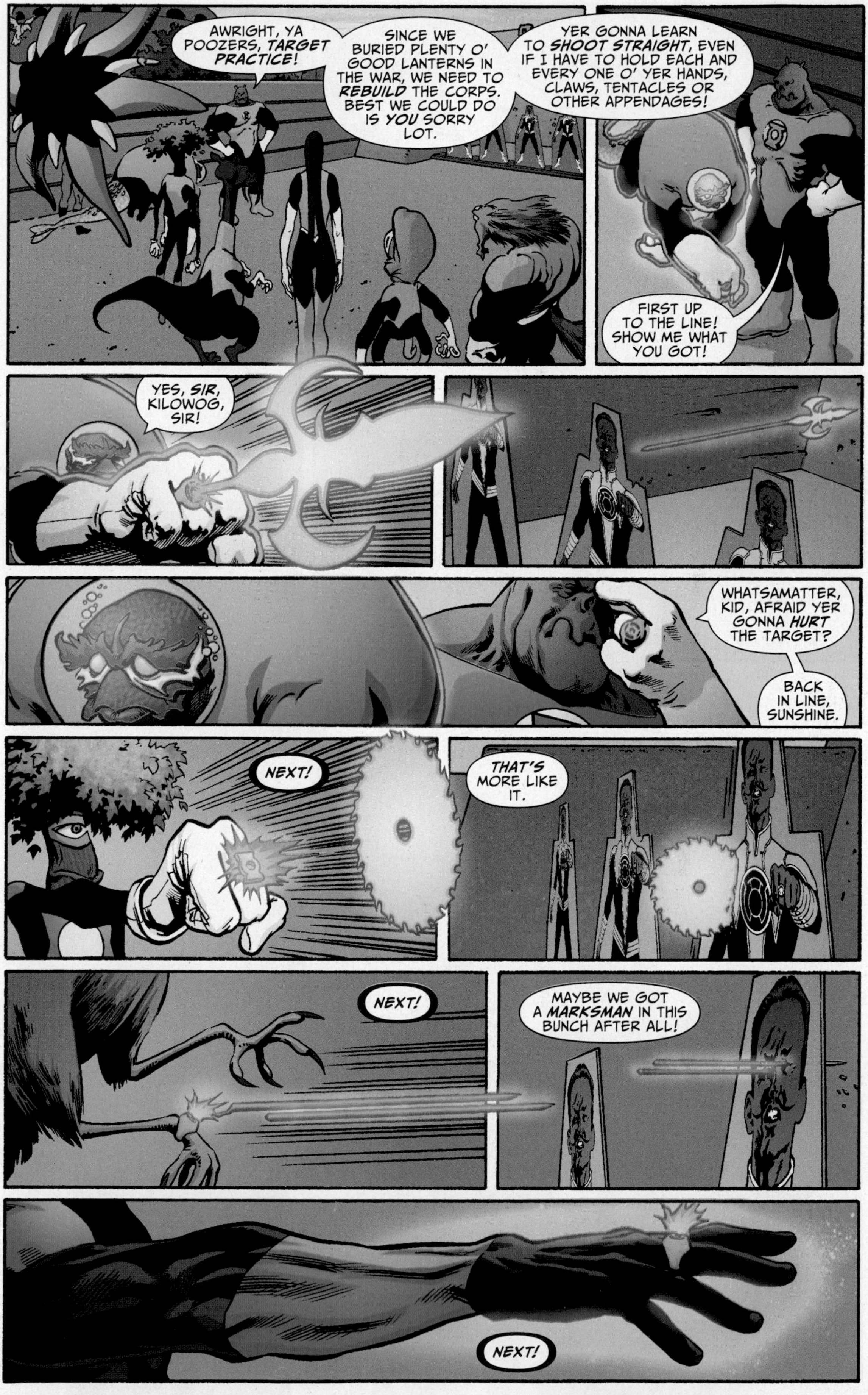
AWRIGHT, YA POOZERS, TARGET PRACTICE!
SINCE WE BURIED PLENTY O' GOOD LANTERNS IN THE WAR, WE NEED TO REBUILD THE CORPS. BEST WE COULD DO IS YOU SORRY LOT.
YER GONNA LEARN TO SHOOT STRAIGHT, EVEN IF I HAVE TO HOLD EACH AND EVERY ONE O' YER HANDS, CLAWS, TENTACLES OR OTHER APPENDAGES!
FIRST UP TO THE LINE! SHOW ME WHAT YOU GOT!
YES, SIR, KILOWOG, SIR!
WHATSAMATTER, KID, AFRAID YER GONNA HURT THE TARGET?
BACK IN LINE, SUNSHINE.
NEXT!
THAT'S MORE LIKE IT.
NEXT!
MAYBE WE GOT A MARKSMAN IN THIS BUNCH AFTER ALL!
NEXT!

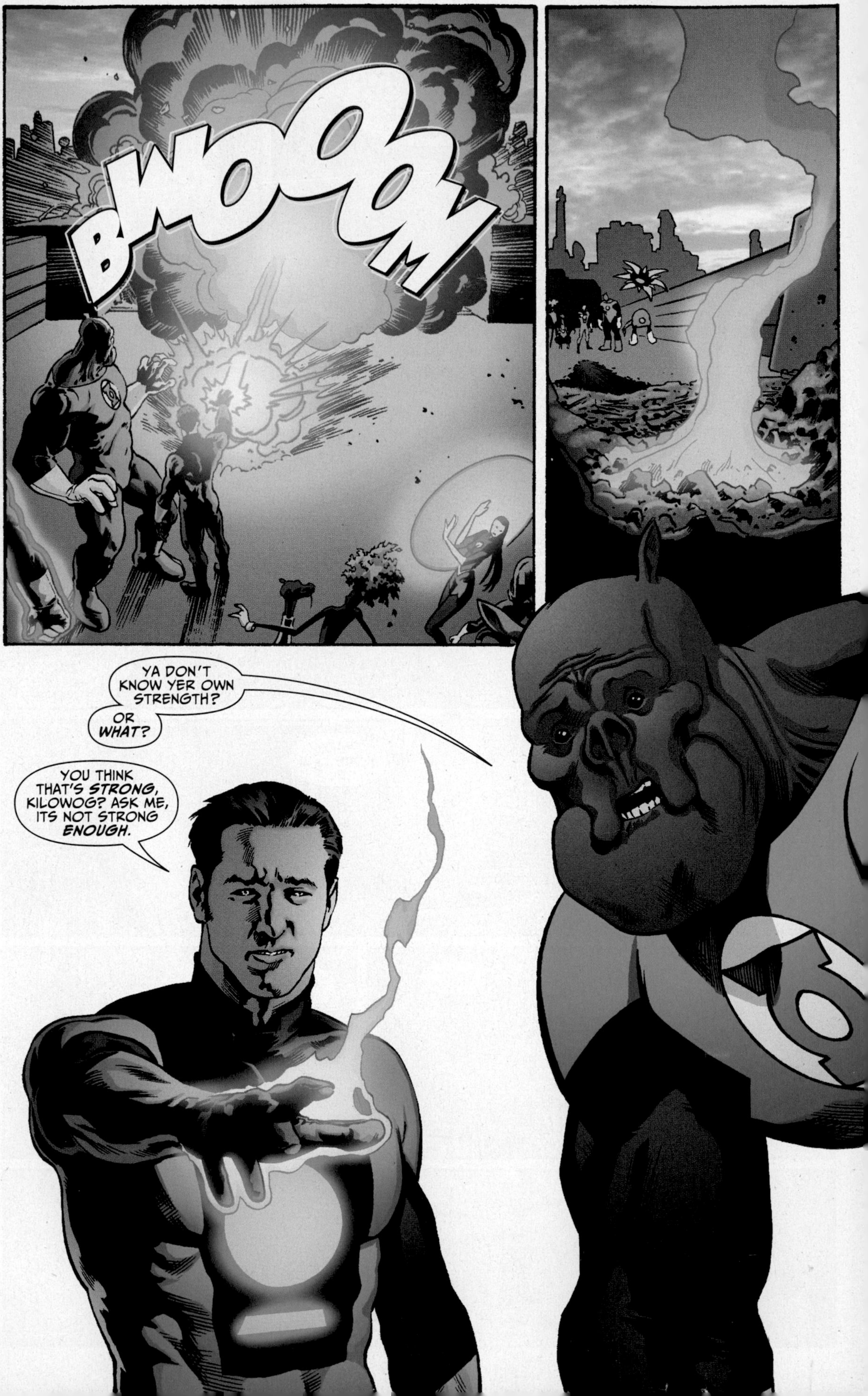
BWOOOM
YA DON'T KNOW YER OWN STRENGTH?
OR WHAT?
YOU THINK THAT'S STRONG, KILOWOG? ASK ME, ITS NOT STRONG ENOUGH.

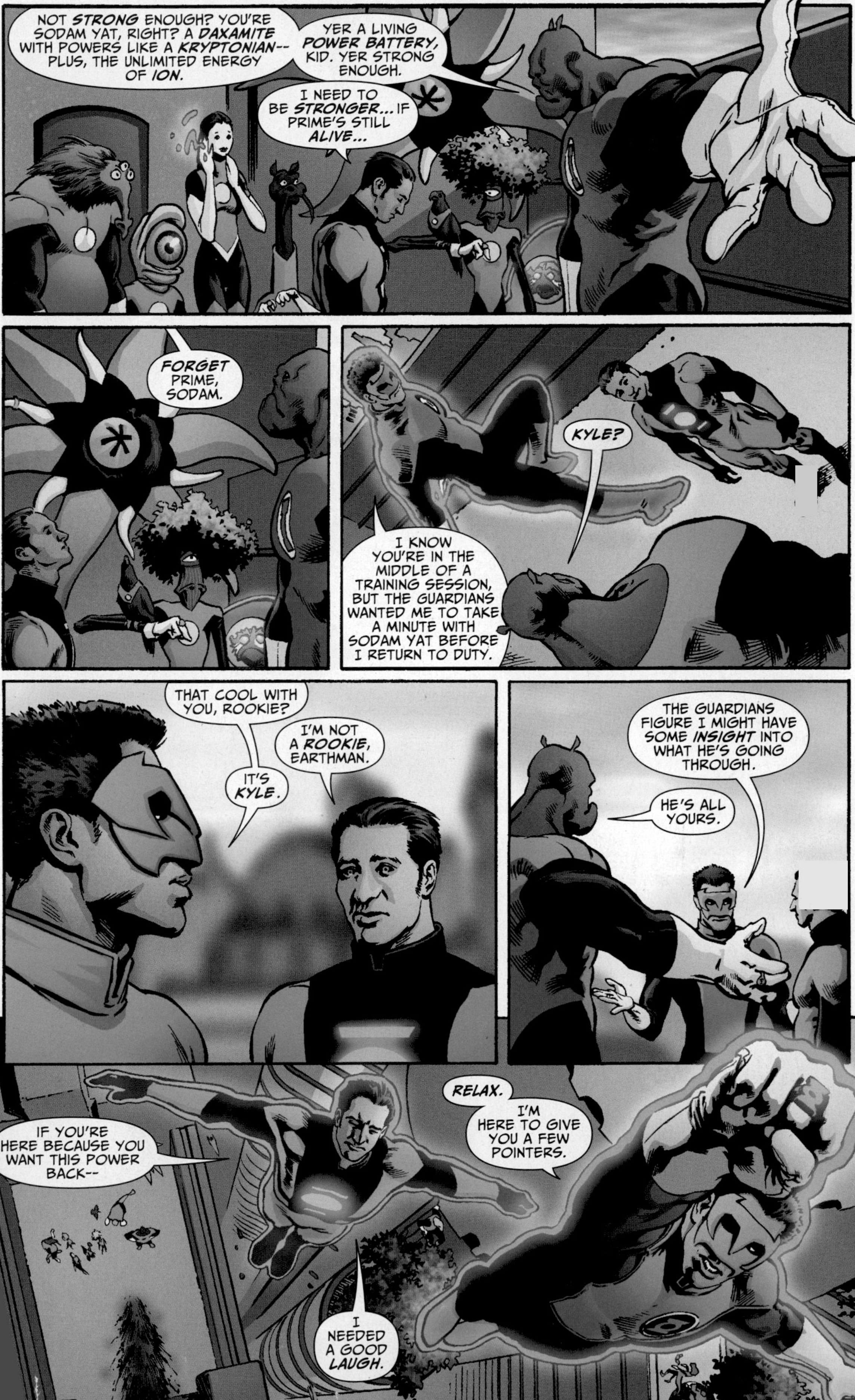
NOT STRONG ENOUGH? YOU'RE SODAM YAT, RIGHT? A DAXAMITE WITH POWERS LIKE A KRYPTONIAN-- PLUS, THE UNLIMITED ENERGY OF ION.
YER A LIVING POWER BATTERY, KID. YER STRONG ENOUGH.
I NEED TO BE STRONGER... IF PRIME'S STILL ALIVE...
FORGET PRIME, SODAM.
KYLE?
I KNOW YOU'RE IN THE MIDDLE OF A TRAINING SESSION, BUT THE GUARDIANS WANTED ME TO TAKE A MINUTE WITH SODAM YAT BEFORE I RETURN TO DUTY.
THAT COOL WITH YOU, ROOKIE?
I'M NOT A ROOKIE, EARTHMAN.
IT'S KYLE.
THE GUARDIANS FIGURE I MIGHT HAVE SOME INSIGHT INTO WHAT HE'S GOING THROUGH.
HE'S ALL YOURS.
IF YOU'RE HERE BECAUSE YOU WANT THIS POWER BACK--
RELAX.
I'M HERE TO GIVE YOU A FEW POINTERS.
I NEEDED A GOOD LAUGH.

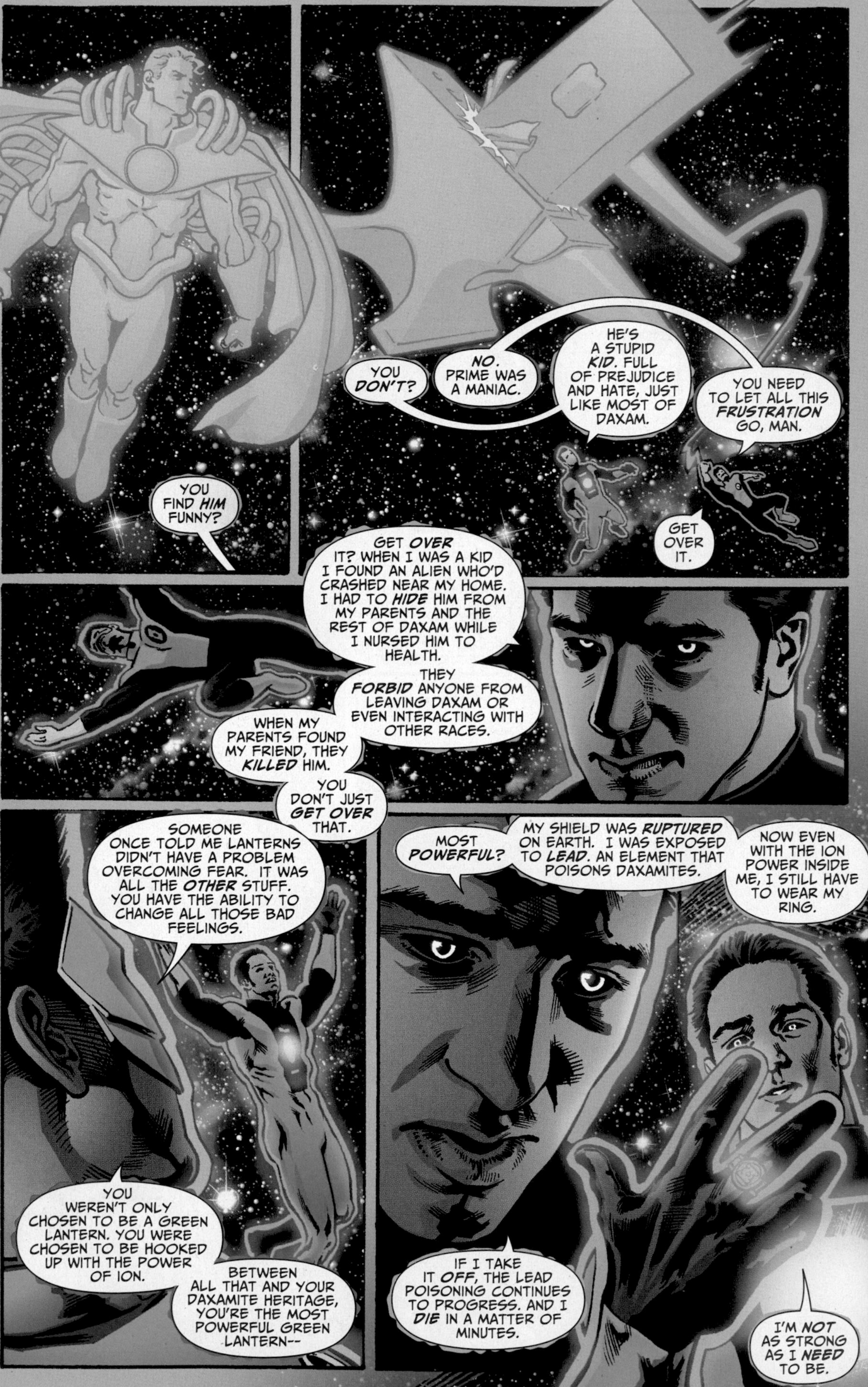
YOU FIND HIM FUNNY?
YOU DON'T?
NO. PRIME WAS A MANIAC.
HE'S A STUPID KID. FULL OF PREJUDICE AND HATE, JUST LIKE MOST OF DAXAM.
YOU NEED TO LET ALL THIS FRUSTRATION GO, MAN.
GET OVER IT.
GET OVER IT? WHEN I WAS A KID I FOUND AN ALIEN WHO'D CRASHED NEAR MY HOME. I HAD TO HIDE HIM FROM MY PARENTS AND THE REST OF DAXAM WHILE I NURSED HIM TO HEALTH.
THEY FORBID ANYONE FROM LEAVING DAXAM OR EVEN INTERACTING WITH OTHER RACES.
WHEN MY PARENTS FOUND MY FRIEND, THEY KILLED HIM.
YOU DON'T JUST GET OVER THAT.
SOMEONE ONCE TOLD ME LANTERNS DIDN'T HAVE A PROBLEM OVERCOMING FEAR. IT WAS ALL THE OTHER STUFF. YOU HAVE THE ABILITY TO CHANGE ALL THOSE BAD FEELINGS.
YOU WEREN'T ONLY CHOSEN TO BE A GREEN LANTERN. YOU WERE CHOSEN TO BE HOOKED UP WITH THE POWER OF ION.
BETWEEN ALL THAT AND YOUR DAXAMITE HERITAGE, YOU'RE THE MOST POWERFUL GREEN LANTERN--
MOST POWERFUL?
MY SHIELD WAS RUPTURED ON EARTH. I WAS EXPOSED TO LEAD. AN ELEMENT THAT POISONS DAXAMITES.
NOW EVEN WITH THE ION POWER INSIDE ME, I STILL HAVE TO WEAR MY RING.
IF I TAKE IT OFF, THE LEAD POISONING CONTINUES TO PROGRESS. AND I DIE IN A MATTER OF MINUTES.
I'M NOT AS STRONG AS I NEED TO BE.

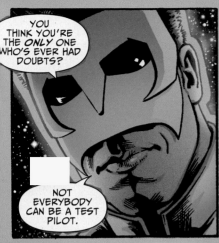

YOU THINK YOU'RE THE *ONLY* ONE WHO'S EVER HAD DOUBTS?

NOT EVERYBODY CAN BE A TEST PILOT.

TEST... PILOT? I DON'T UNDERSTAND.

NEVER MIND.

POINT IS, YOU CAN HAVE DOUBTS, BUT YOU CAN'T LET THEM *OVERWHELM* YOU. BECAUSE ONCE *THAT* HAPPENS...

...WHAT GOOD IS YOUR *WILLPOWER*?

WILLPOWER ISN'T A PROBLEM FOR SOMETHING LIKE *THIS*.

VERY COOL.

THANK YOU.

BUT *THIS* ISN'T LIFE OR DEATH. IT'S ANOTHER THING *ENTIRELY* WHEN SOMEONE'S *LIFE* IS IN YOUR HANDS.

WELL...

...CRAP.

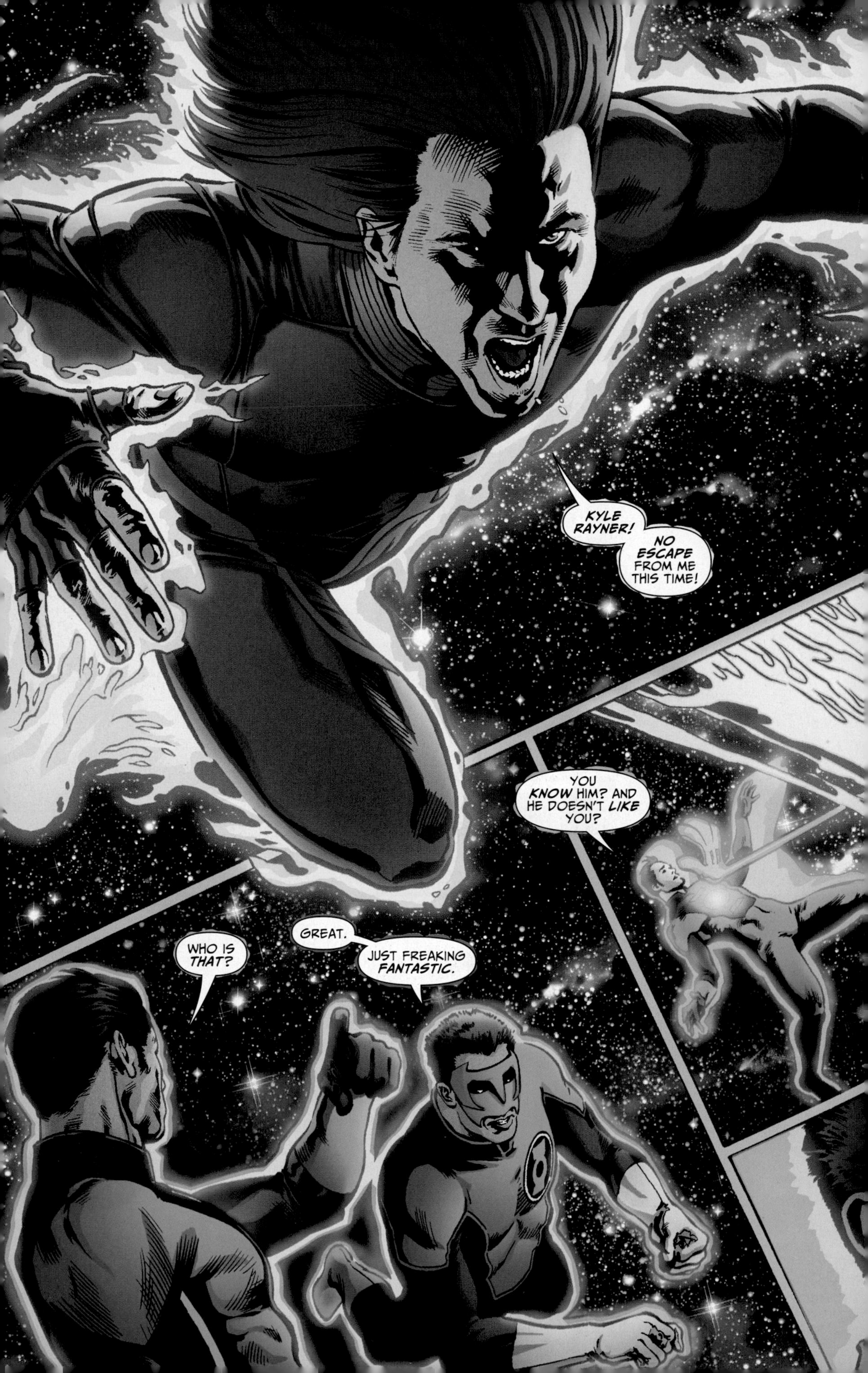
KYLE RAYNER!
NO ESCAPE FROM ME THIS TIME!
YOU KNOW HIM? AND HE DOESN'T LIKE YOU?
WHO IS THAT?
GREAT.
JUST FREAKING FANTASTIC.

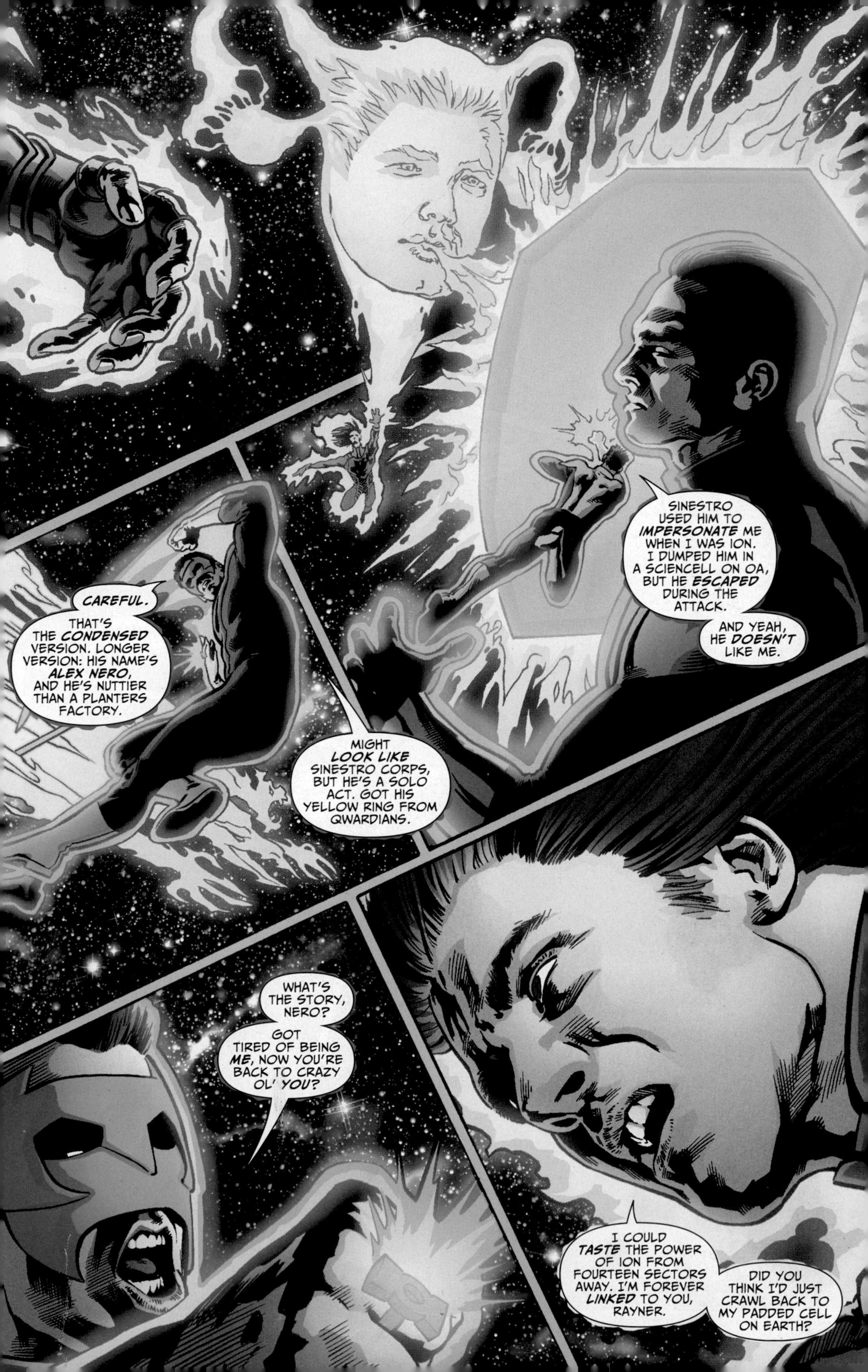
SINESTRO USED HIM TO *IMPERSONATE* ME WHEN I WAS ION. I DUMPED HIM IN A SCIENCELL ON OA, BUT HE *ESCAPED* DURING THE ATTACK.
AND YEAH, HE *DOESN'T* LIKE ME.
CAREFUL.
THAT'S THE *CONDENSED* VERSION. LONGER VERSION: HIS NAME'S *ALEX NERO*, AND HE'S NUTTIER THAN A PLANTERS FACTORY.
MIGHT *LOOK LIKE* SINESTRO CORPS, BUT HE'S A SOLO ACT. GOT HIS YELLOW RING FROM QWARDIANS.
WHAT'S THE STORY, NERO?
GOT TIRED OF BEING *ME*, NOW YOU'RE BACK TO CRAZY OL' *YOU*?
I COULD *TASTE* THE POWER OF ION FROM FOURTEEN SECTORS AWAY. I'M FOREVER *LINKED* TO YOU, RAYNER.
DID YOU THINK I'D JUST CRAWL BACK TO MY PADDED CELL ON EARTH?

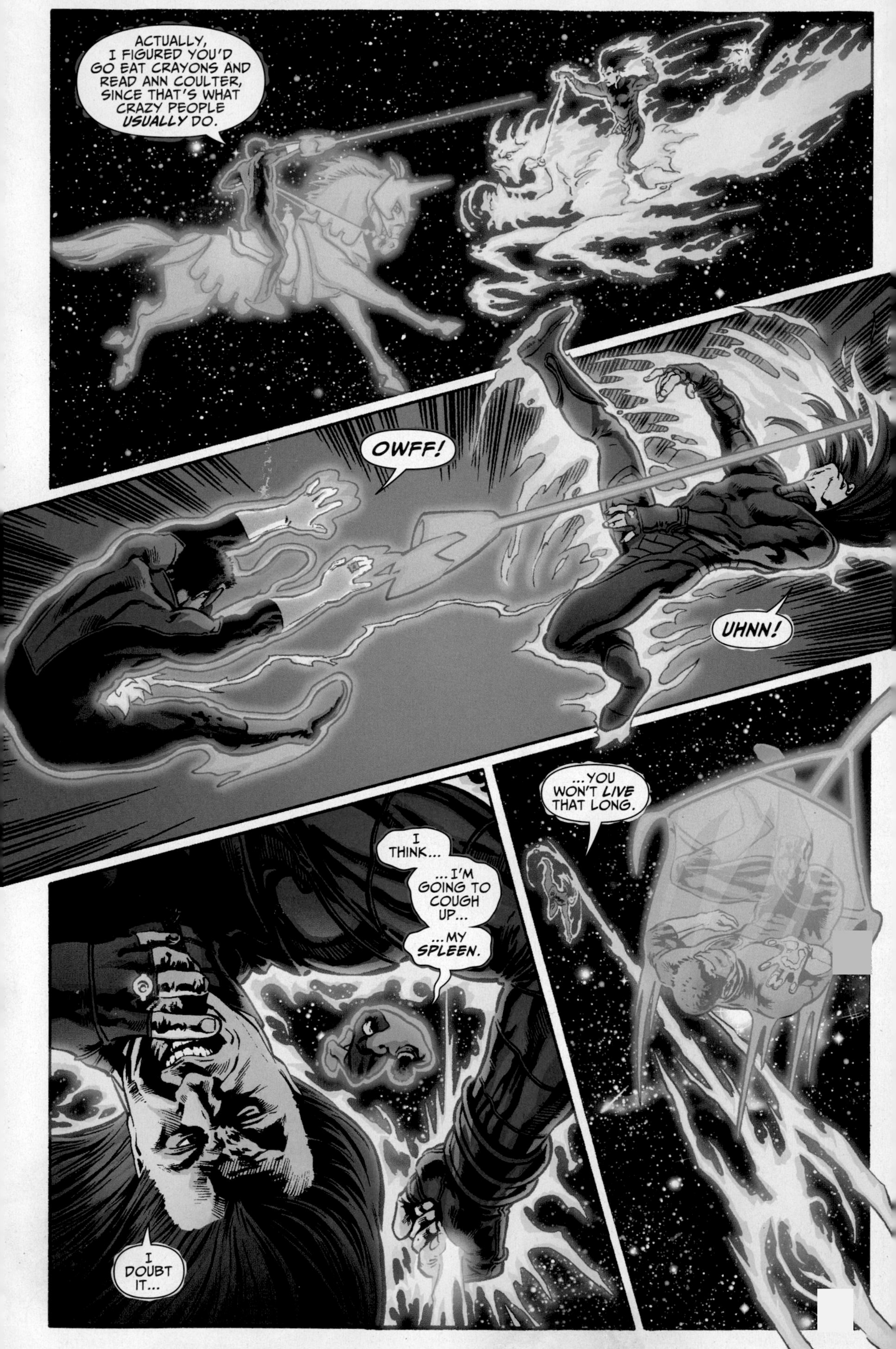
ACTUALLY, I FIGURED YOU'D GO EAT CRAYONS AND READ ANN COULTER, SINCE THAT'S WHAT CRAZY PEOPLE USUALLY DO.
OWFF!
UHNN!
I THINK...
...I'M GOING TO COUGH UP...
...MY SPLEEN.
I DOUBT IT...
...YOU WON'T LIVE THAT LONG.

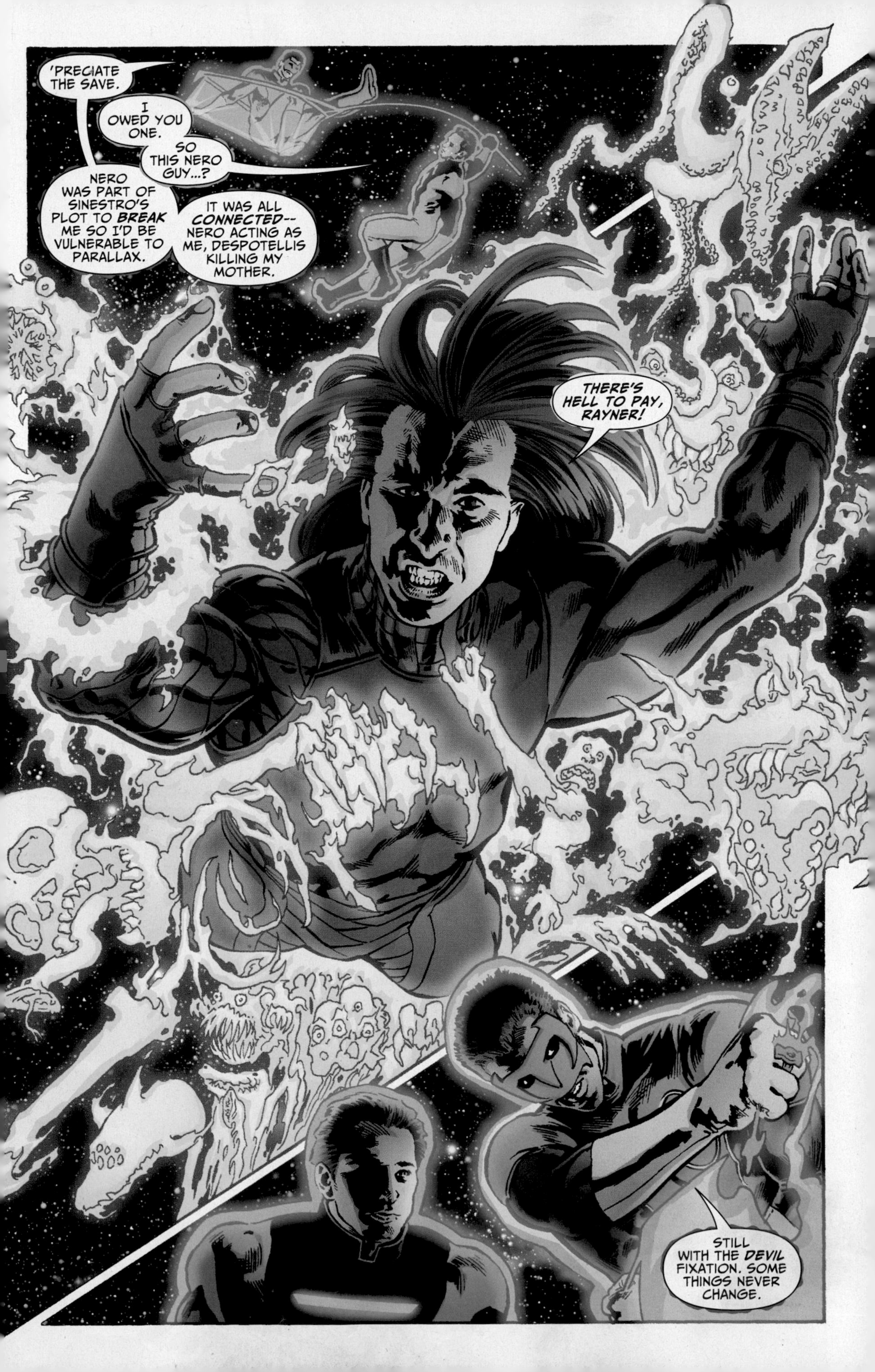
'PRECIATE THE SAVE.
I OWED YOU ONE.
SO THIS NERO GUY...?
NERO WAS PART OF SINESTRO'S PLOT TO BREAK ME SO I'D BE VULNERABLE TO PARALLAX.
IT WAS ALL CONNECTED-- NERO ACTING AS ME, DESPOTELLIS KILLING MY MOTHER.
THERE'S HELL TO PAY, RAYNER!
STILL WITH THE DEVIL FIXATION. SOME THINGS NEVER CHANGE.

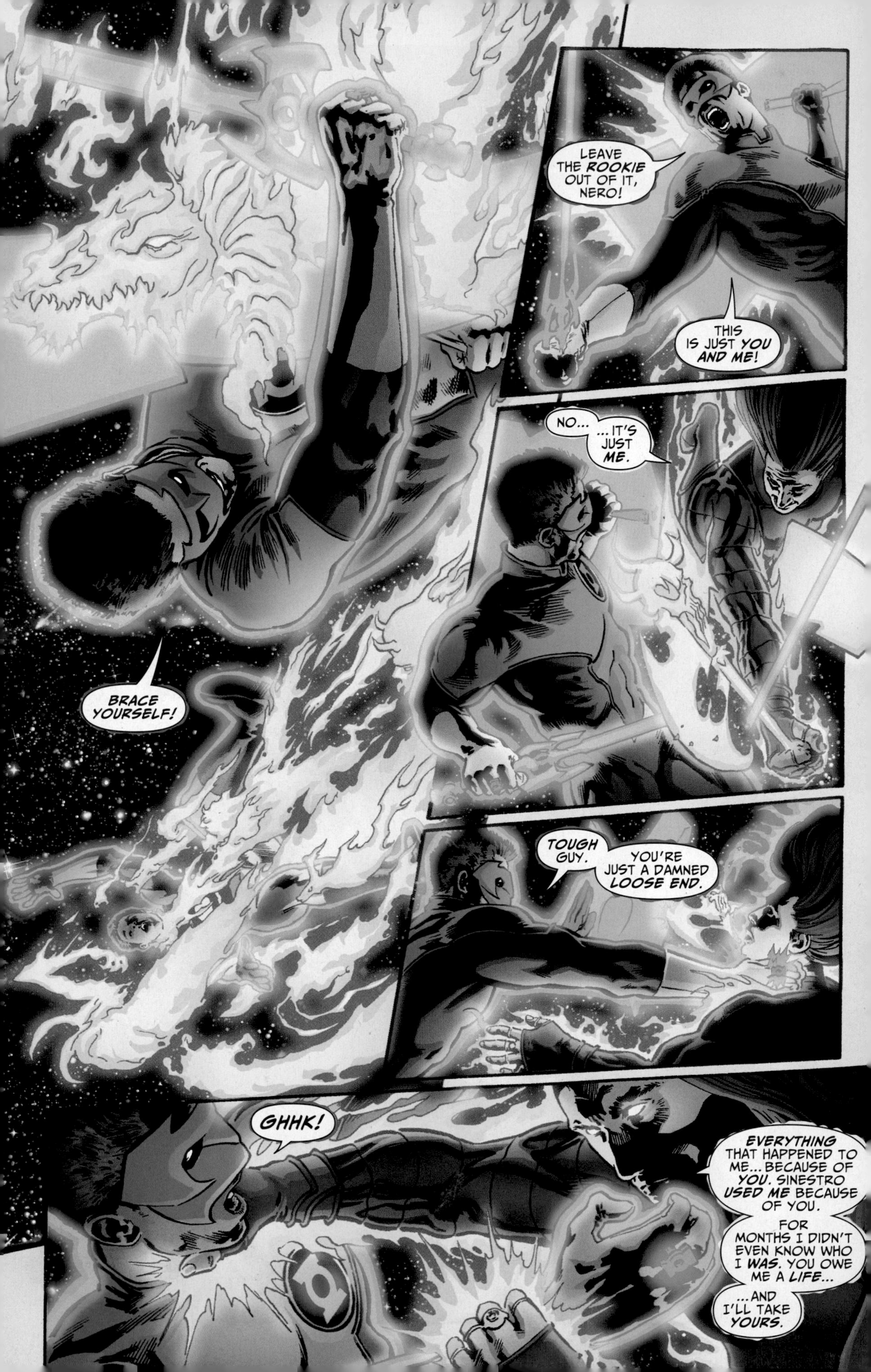
LEAVE THE ROOKIE OUT OF IT, NERO!
THIS IS JUST YOU AND ME!
NO...
...IT'S JUST ME.
BRACE YOURSELF!
TOUGH GUY.
YOU'RE JUST A DAMNED LOOSE END.
GHHK!
EVERYTHING THAT HAPPENED TO ME... BECAUSE OF YOU. SINESTRO USED ME BECAUSE OF YOU.
FOR MONTHS I DIDN'T EVEN KNOW WHO I WAS. YOU OWE ME A LIFE...
...AND I'LL TAKE YOURS.

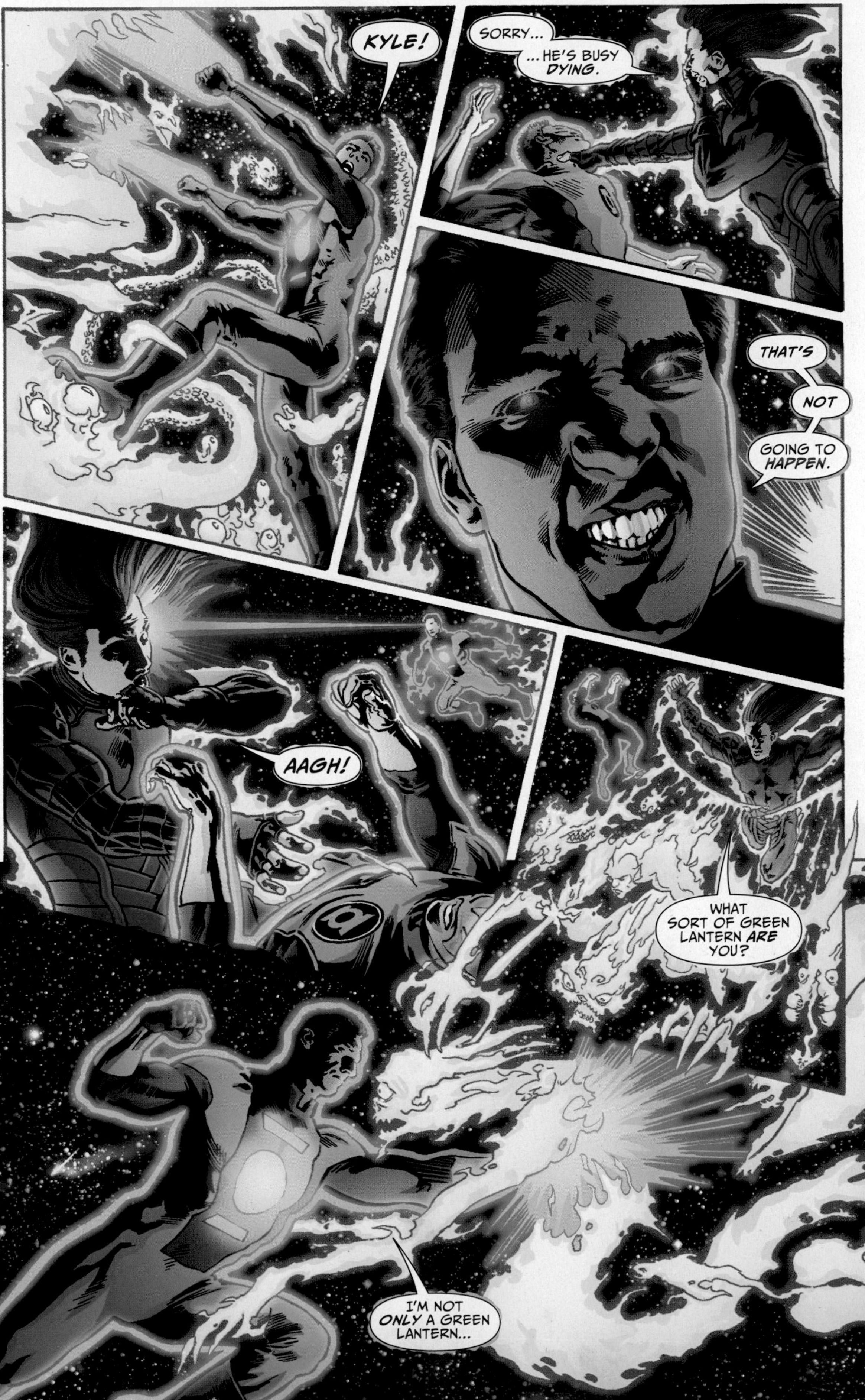
KYLE!
SORRY...
...HE'S BUSY DYING.
THAT'S
NOT
GOING TO HAPPEN.
AAGH!
WHAT SORT OF GREEN LANTERN ARE YOU?
I'M NOT ONLY A GREEN LANTERN...

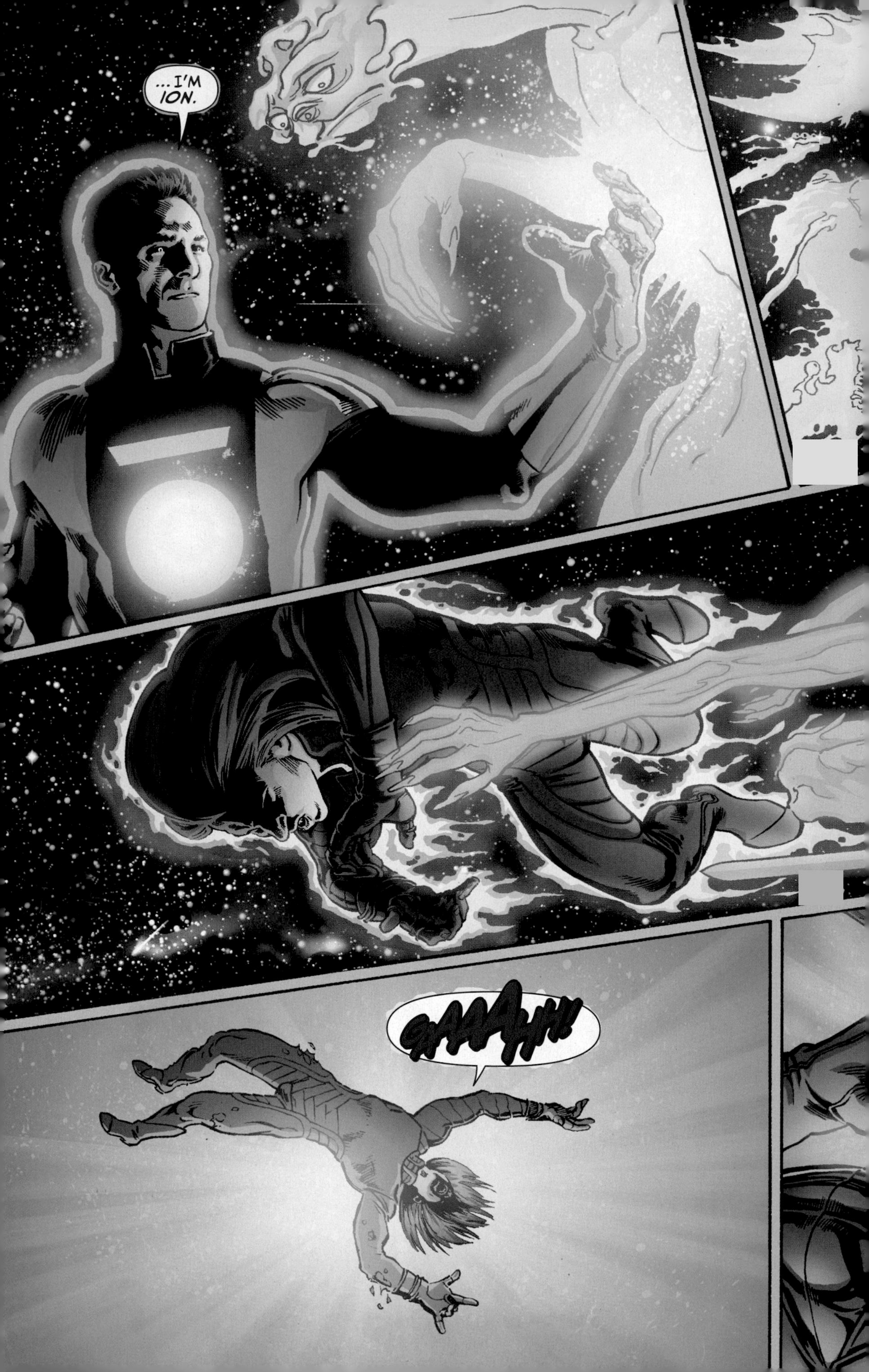
...I'M ION.
GAAAAHH!

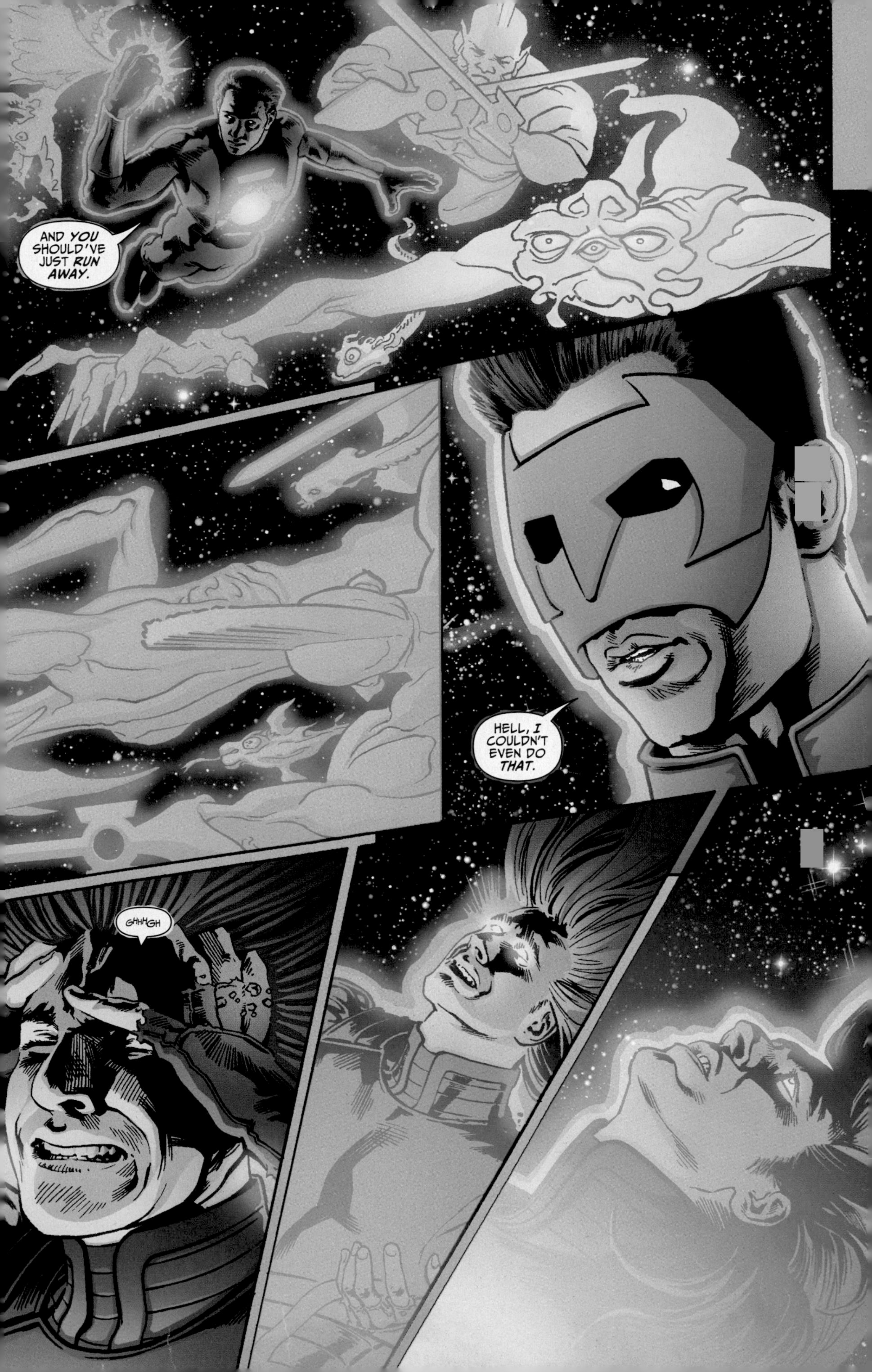
AND YOU SHOULD'VE JUST RUN AWAY.
HELL, I COULDN'T EVEN DO THAT.
GHHHGH

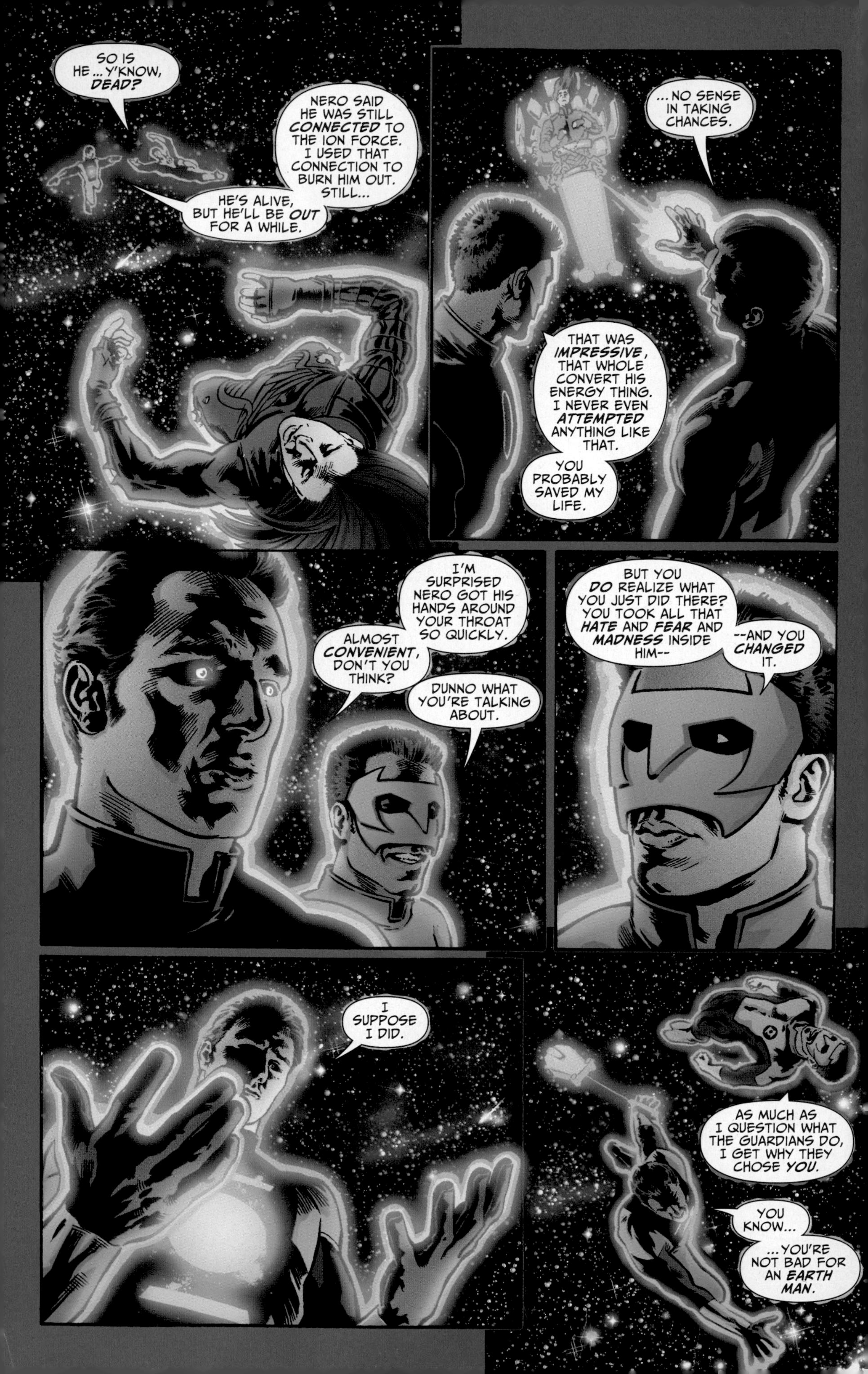
SO IS HE ... Y'KNOW, DEAD?
NERO SAID HE WAS STILL CONNECTED TO THE ION FORCE. I USED THAT CONNECTION TO BURN HIM OUT. STILL...
HE'S ALIVE, BUT HE'LL BE OUT FOR A WHILE.
... NO SENSE IN TAKING CHANCES.
THAT WAS IMPRESSIVE, THAT WHOLE CONVERT HIS ENERGY THING. I NEVER EVEN ATTEMPTED ANYTHING LIKE THAT.
YOU PROBABLY SAVED MY LIFE.
I'M SURPRISED NERO GOT HIS HANDS AROUND YOUR THROAT SO QUICKLY.
ALMOST CONVENIENT, DON'T YOU THINK?
DUNNO WHAT YOU'RE TALKING ABOUT.
BUT YOU DO REALIZE WHAT YOU JUST DID THERE? YOU TOOK ALL THAT HATE AND FEAR AND MADNESS INSIDE HIM--
--AND YOU CHANGED IT.
I SUPPOSE I DID.
AS MUCH AS I QUESTION WHAT THE GUARDIANS DO, I GET WHY THEY CHOSE YOU.
YOU KNOW...
... YOU'RE NOT BAD FOR AN EARTH MAN.

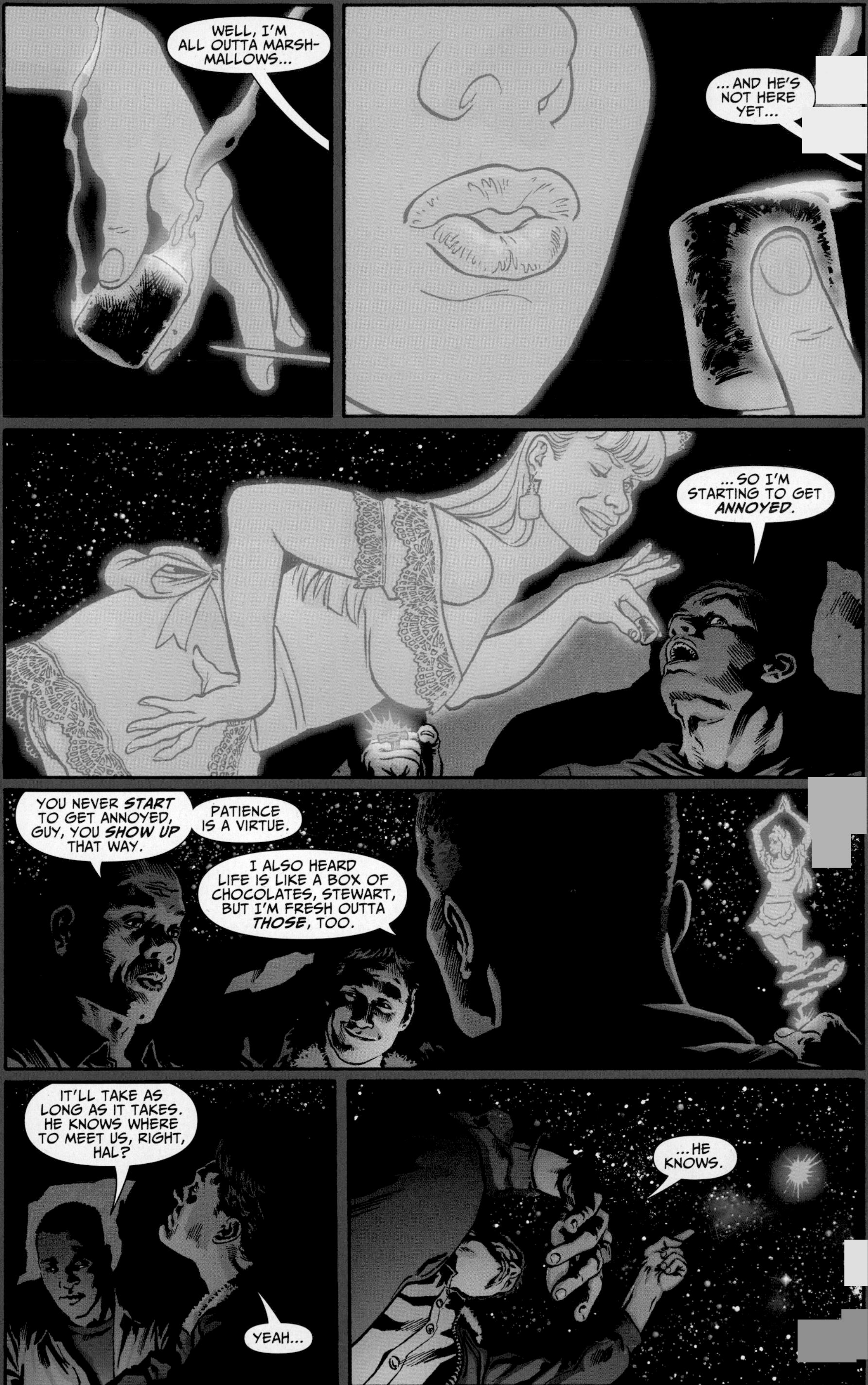
WELL, I'M ALL OUTTA MARSH-MALLOWS...
...AND HE'S NOT HERE YET...
...SO I'M STARTING TO GET ANNOYED.
YOU NEVER START TO GET ANNOYED, GUY, YOU SHOW UP THAT WAY.
PATIENCE IS A VIRTUE.
I ALSO HEARD LIFE IS LIKE A BOX OF CHOCOLATES, STEWART, BUT I'M FRESH OUTTA THOSE, TOO.
IT'LL TAKE AS LONG AS IT TAKES. HE KNOWS WHERE TO MEET US, RIGHT, HAL?
YEAH...
...HE KNOWS.

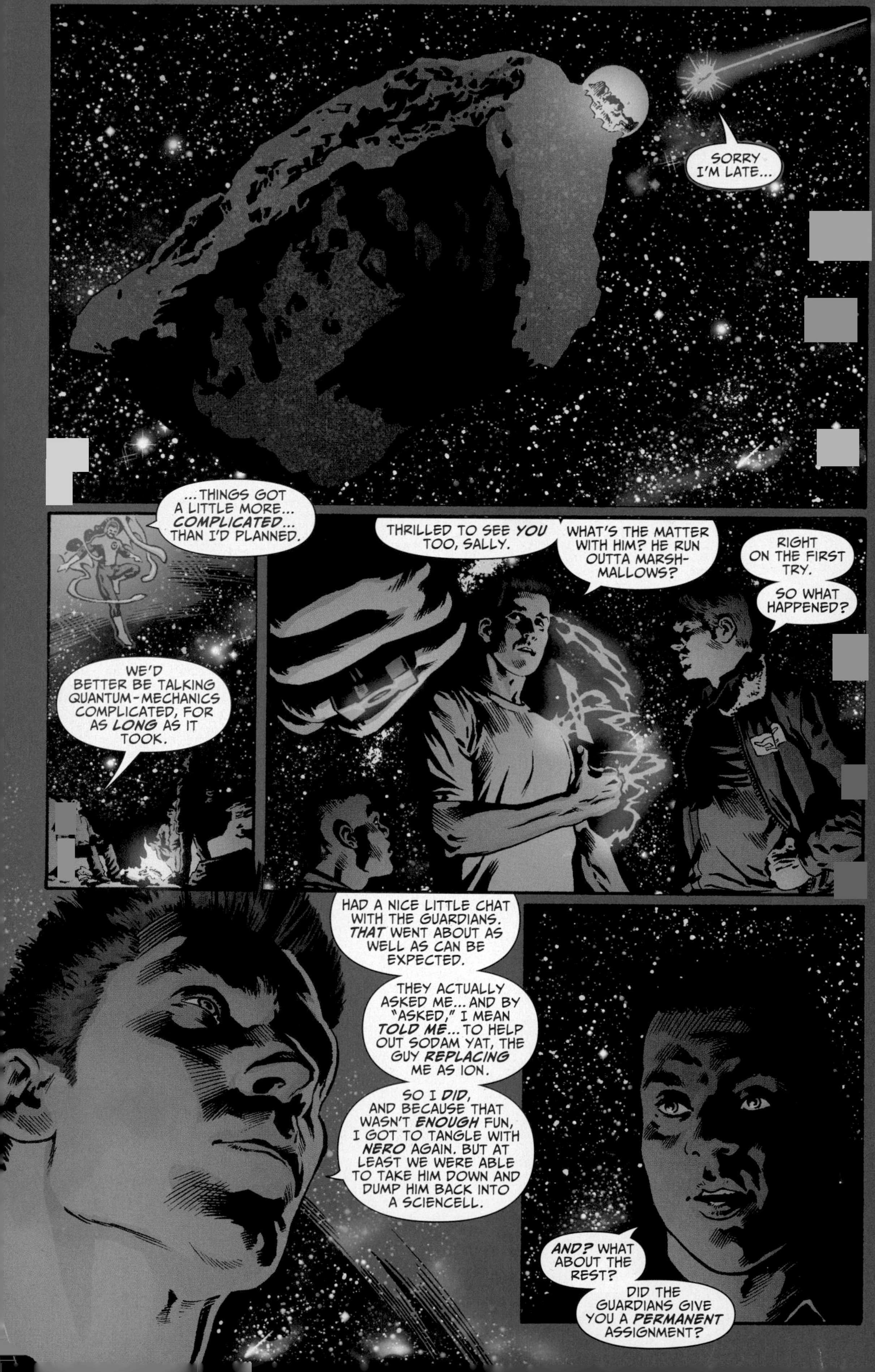
SORRY I'M LATE...
...THINGS GOT A LITTLE MORE... COMPLICATED... THAN I'D PLANNED.
WE'D BETTER BE TALKING QUANTUM-MECHANICS COMPLICATED, FOR AS LONG AS IT TOOK.
THRILLED TO SEE YOU TOO, SALLY.
WHAT'S THE MATTER WITH HIM? HE RUN OUTTA MARSH-MALLOWS?
RIGHT ON THE FIRST TRY.
SO WHAT HAPPENED?
HAD A NICE LITTLE CHAT WITH THE GUARDIANS. THAT WENT ABOUT AS WELL AS CAN BE EXPECTED.
THEY ACTUALLY ASKED ME... AND BY "ASKED," I MEAN TOLD ME... TO HELP OUT SODAM YAT, THE GUY REPLACING ME AS ION.
SO I DID, AND BECAUSE THAT WASN'T ENOUGH FUN, I GOT TO TANGLE WITH NERO AGAIN. BUT AT LEAST WE WERE ABLE TO TAKE HIM DOWN AND DUMP HIM BACK INTO A SCIENCELL.
AND? WHAT ABOUT THE REST?
DID THE GUARDIANS GIVE YOU A PERMANENT ASSIGNMENT?

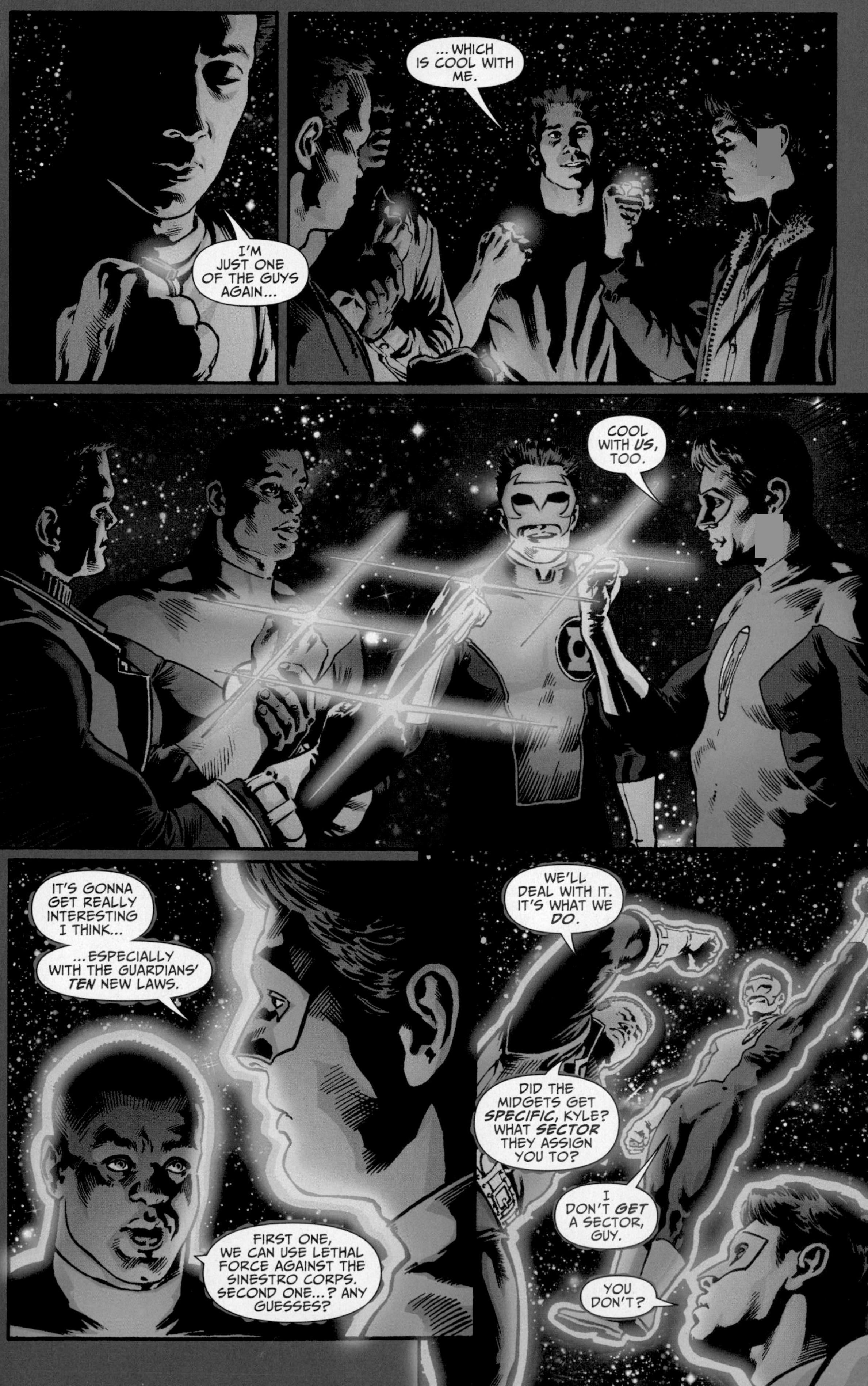
I'M JUST ONE OF THE GUYS AGAIN...
...WHICH IS COOL WITH ME.
COOL WITH US, TOO.
IT'S GONNA GET REALLY INTERESTING I THINK...
...ESPECIALLY WITH THE GUARDIANS' TEN NEW LAWS.
FIRST ONE, WE CAN USE LETHAL FORCE AGAINST THE SINESTRO CORPS. SECOND ONE...? ANY GUESSES?
WE'LL DEAL WITH IT. IT'S WHAT WE DO.
DID THE MIDGETS GET SPECIFIC, KYLE? WHAT SECTOR THEY ASSIGN YOU TO?
I DON'T GET A SECTOR, GUY.
YOU DON'T?

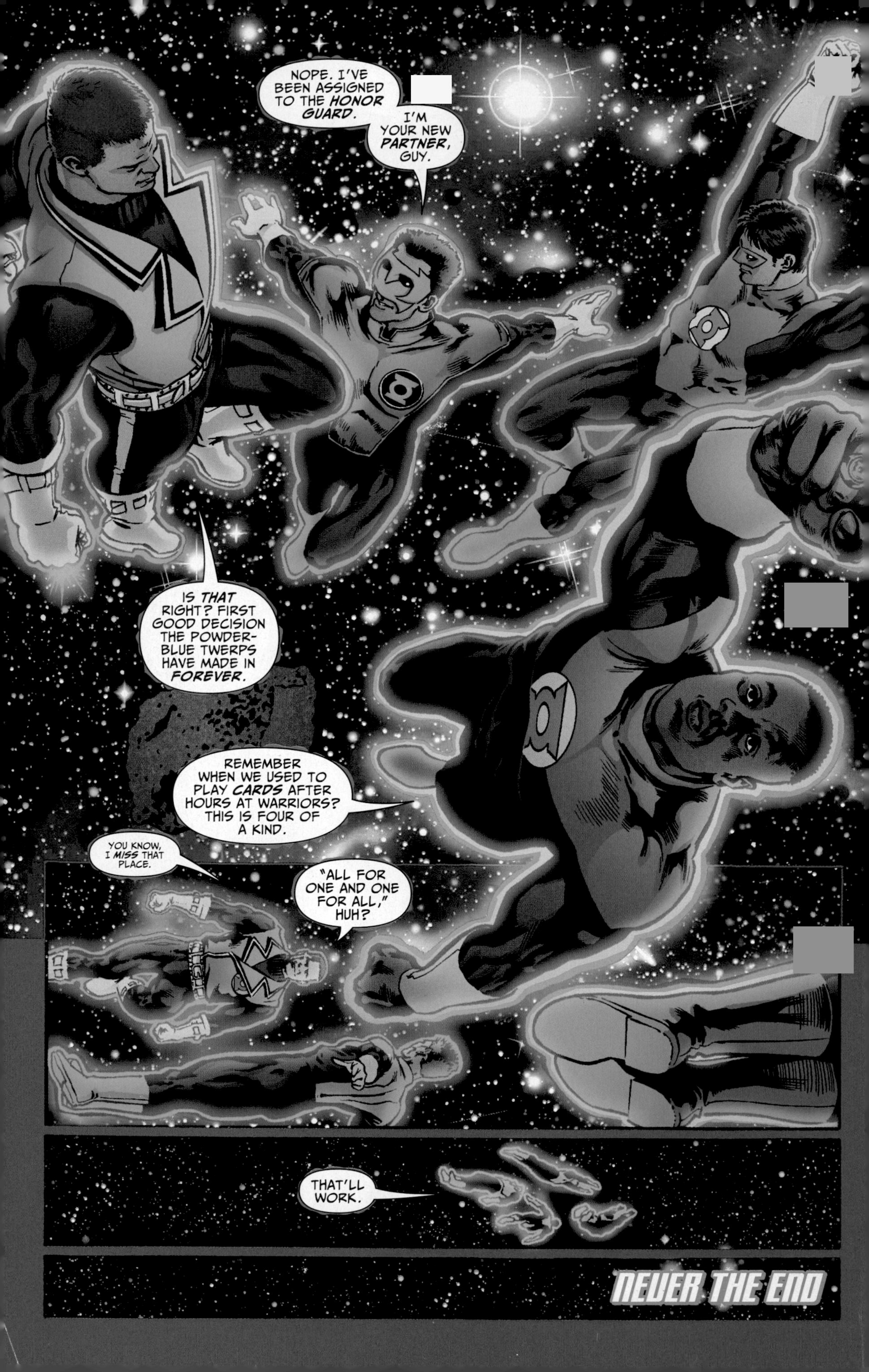

NOPE. I'VE BEEN ASSIGNED TO THE HONOR GUARD.
I'M YOUR NEW PARTNER, GUY.
IS THAT RIGHT? FIRST GOOD DECISION THE POWDER-BLUE TWERPS HAVE MADE IN FOREVER.
REMEMBER WHEN WE USED TO PLAY CARDS AFTER HOURS AT WARRIORS? THIS IS FOUR OF A KIND.
YOU KNOW, I MISS THAT PLACE.
"ALL FOR ONE AND ONE FOR ALL," HUH?
THAT'LL WORK.
NEVER THE END

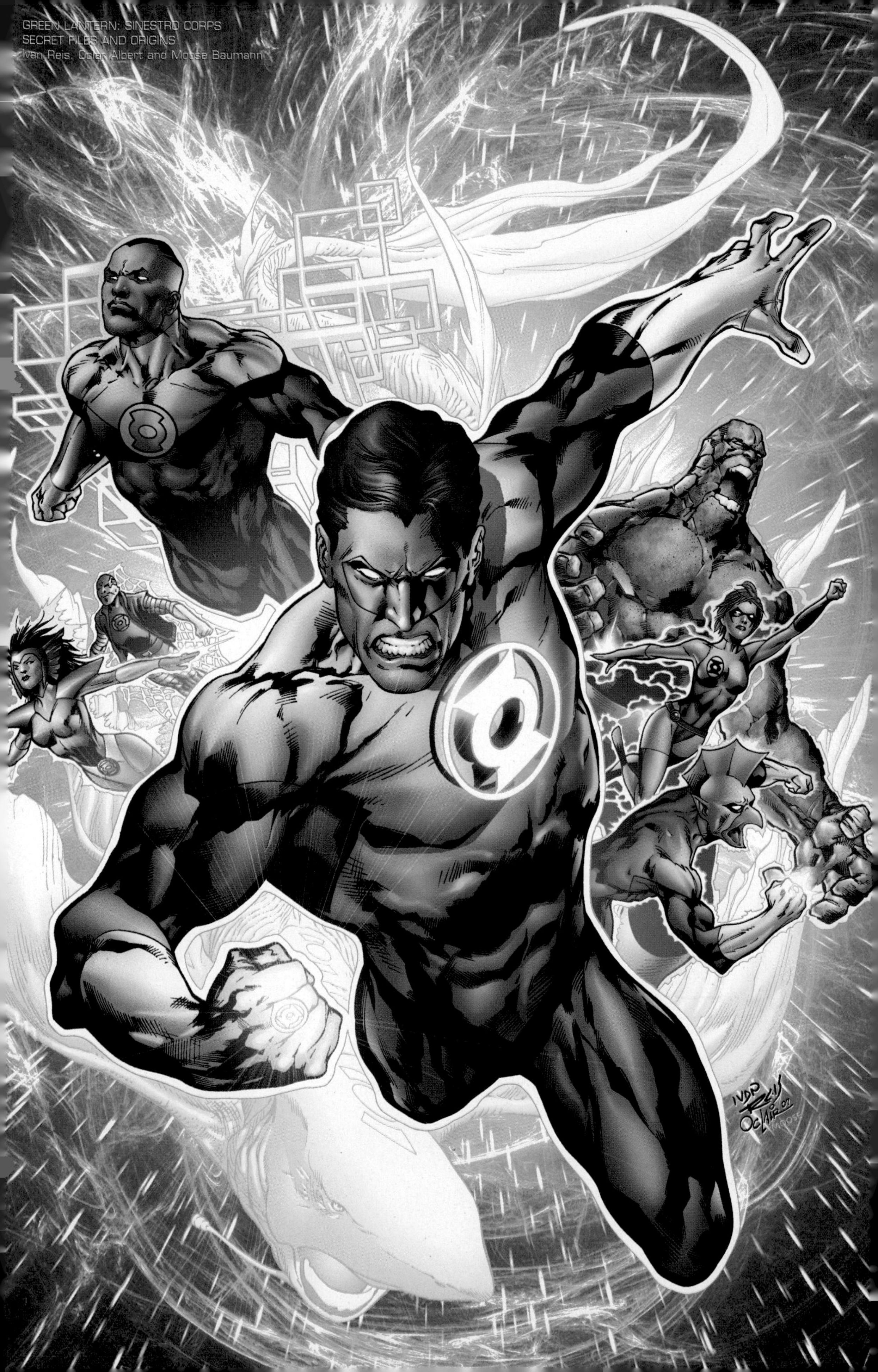

GREEN LANTERN: SINESTRO CORPS
SECRET FILES AND ORIGINS
Ivan Reis, Oclair Albert and Moose Baumann

Billions of years ago, the oldest and most powerful beings in existence, the Guardians of the Universe, created a police force to serve and protect every sector of space. Recruited for their bravery and courage, from planets across the universe, the best and brightest serve proudly as members of the intergalactic peacekeepers known as the

GREEN LANTERN CORPS

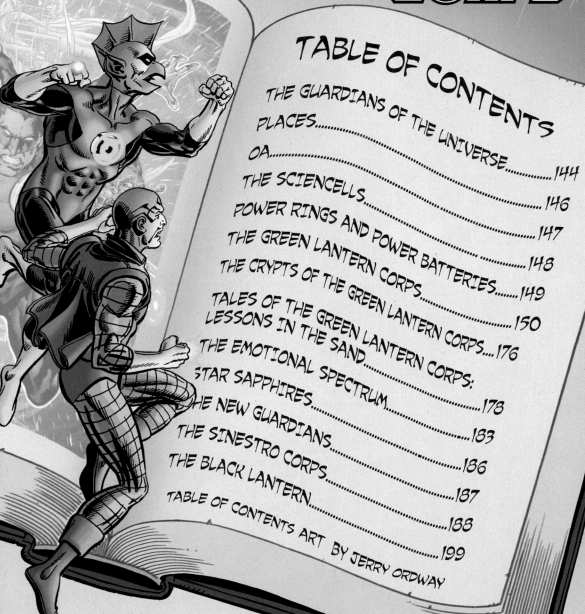

TABLE OF CONTENTS

THE GUARDIANS OF THE UNIVERSE

PLACES...144

OA...146

THE SCIENCELLS..147

POWER RINGS AND POWER BATTERIES.......148

THE GREEN LANTERN CORPS.........................149

THE CRYPTS OF THE GREEN LANTERN CORPS....150

TALES OF THE GREEN LANTERN CORPS:
LESSONS IN THE SAND....................................176

THE EMOTIONAL SPECTRUM

STAR SAPPHIRES...178

THE NEW GUARDIANS......................................183

THE SINESTRO CORPS......................................186

THE BLACK LANTERN.......................................187

TABLE OF CONTENTS.......................................188

TABLE OF CONTENTS ART BY JERRY ORDWAY....199

Written by Geoff Johns & Sterling Gates
Cover: Oclair Albert & Ivan Reis w/Moose Baumann
Color: JD Smith, Art Lyon, Moose Baumann, Digikore, & Guru EFX
Designed by: Hank Manfra

The Guardians of the Universe

FIRST APPEARANCE: GREEN LANTERN V. 2 #1

BIO: AN IMMORTAL RACE AS ANCIENT AS LIFE ITSELF, THE BENEVOLENT GUARDIANS OF THE UNIVERSE DESIRE A PEACEFUL, ORDERLY EXISTENCE FOR ALL LIVING BEINGS, AS WELL THE PURSUIT OF THEIR OWN ENIGMATIC AGENDAS. THEY NEVER ALLOW EMOTIONS TO INFECT THEIR THOUGHTS AND ACTIONS.

THE GUARDIANS CREATED THE GREEN LANTERN CORPS, AN INTERSTELLAR POLICE FORCE THAT NOW PATROLS THE UNIVERSE'S 3600 SPACE SECTORS. EACH SECTOR IS DESIGNATED TWO GREEN LANTERNS, TOTALING 7200 OFFICERS.

THERE ARE CURRENTLY NINE GUARDIANS ON THE COUNCIL, FOUR MALE AND FIVE FEMALES. ONE FEMALE HAS BEEN LEFT SCARRED BY HER RECENT ENCOUNTER WITH THE ANTI-MONITOR.

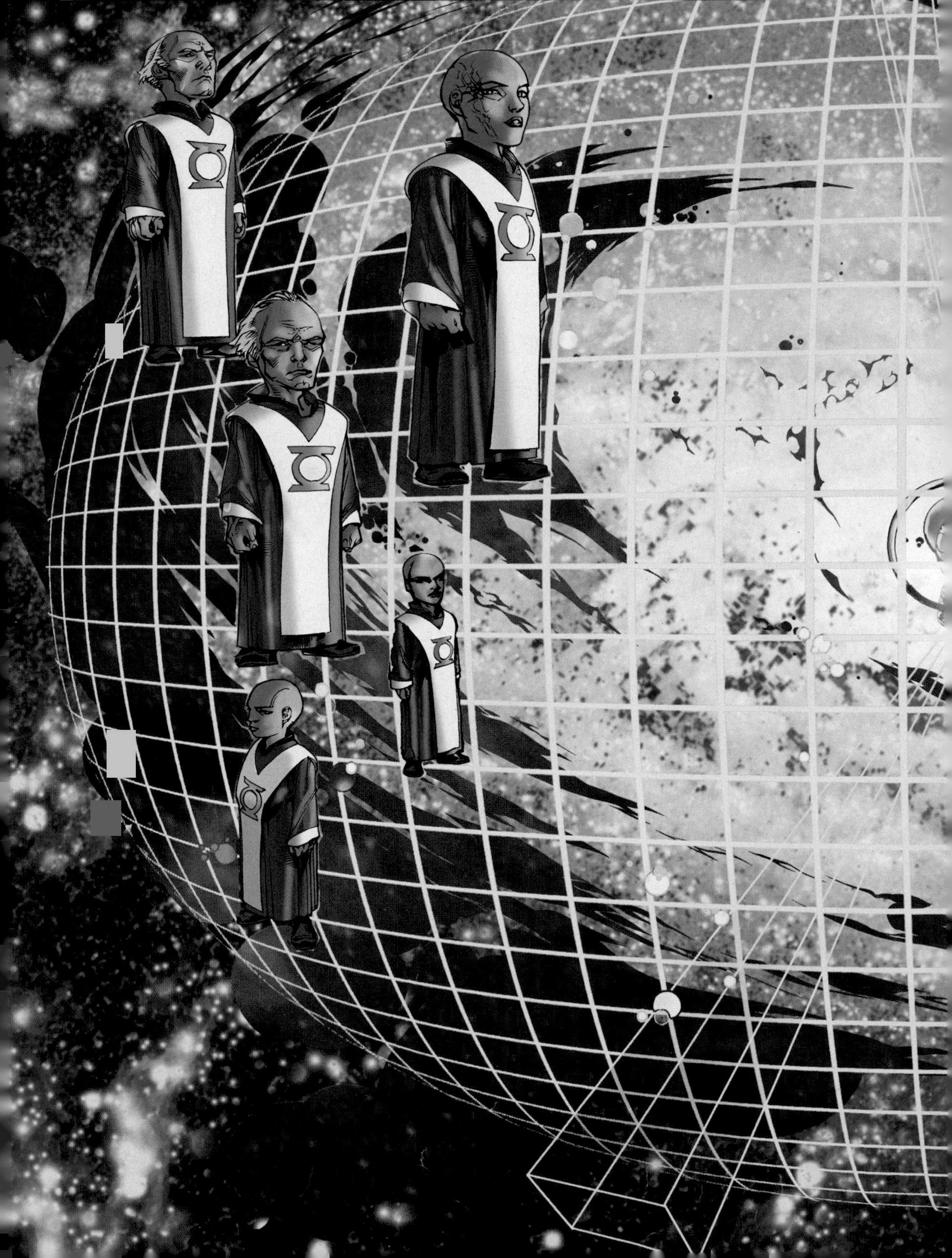

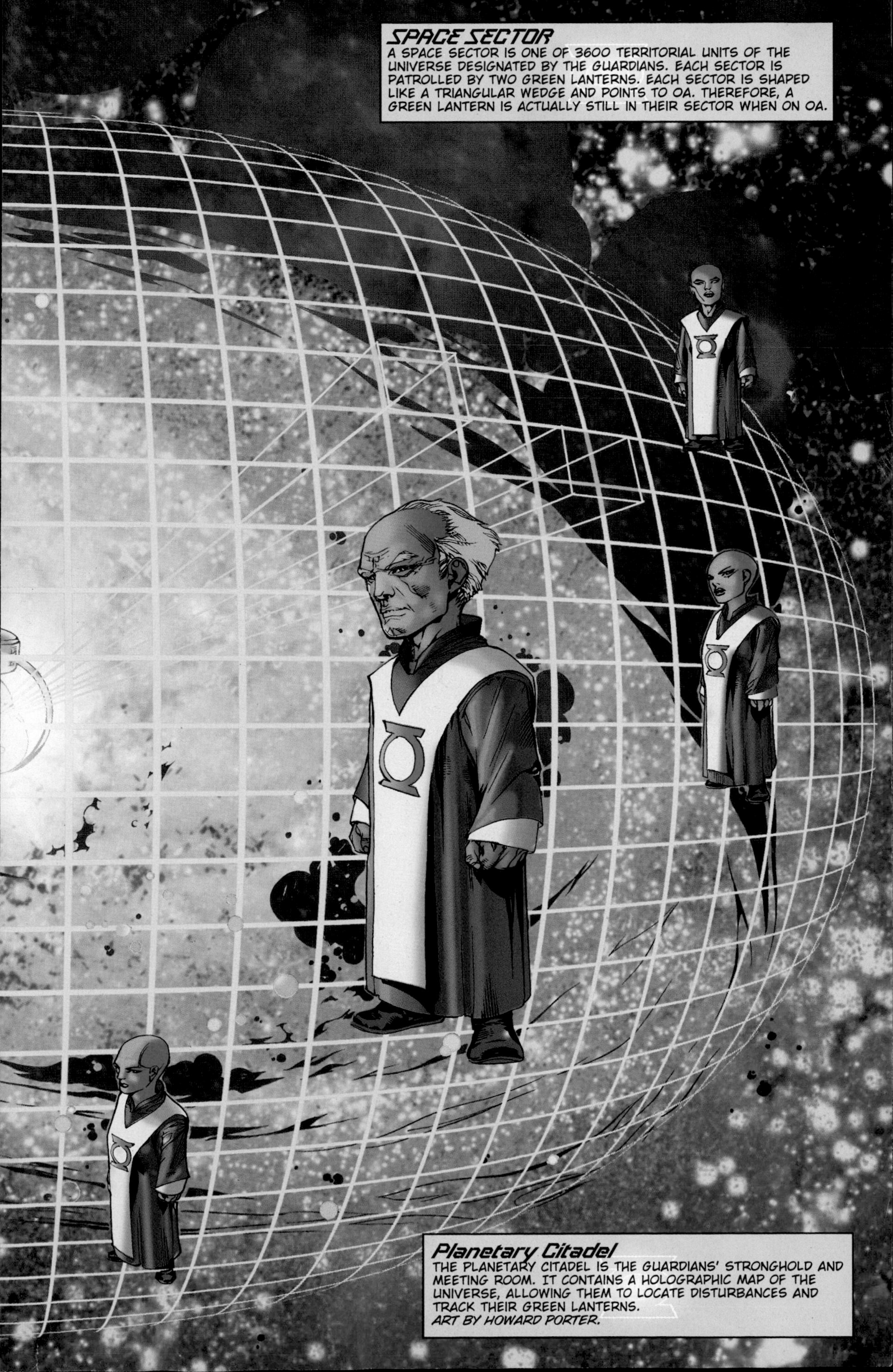
SPACE SECTOR
A SPACE SECTOR IS ONE OF 3600 TERRITORIAL UNITS OF THE UNIVERSE DESIGNATED BY THE GUARDIANS. EACH SECTOR IS PATROLLED BY TWO GREEN LANTERNS. EACH SECTOR IS SHAPED LIKE A TRIANGULAR WEDGE AND POINTS TO OA. THEREFORE, A GREEN LANTERN IS ACTUALLY STILL IN THEIR SECTOR WHEN ON OA.
Planetary Citadel
THE PLANETARY CITADEL IS THE GUARDIANS' STRONGHOLD AND MEETING ROOM. IT CONTAINS A HOLOGRAPHIC MAP OF THE UNIVERSE, ALLOWING THEM TO LOCATE DISTURBANCES AND TRACK THEIR GREEN LANTERNS.
ART BY HOWARD PORTER.

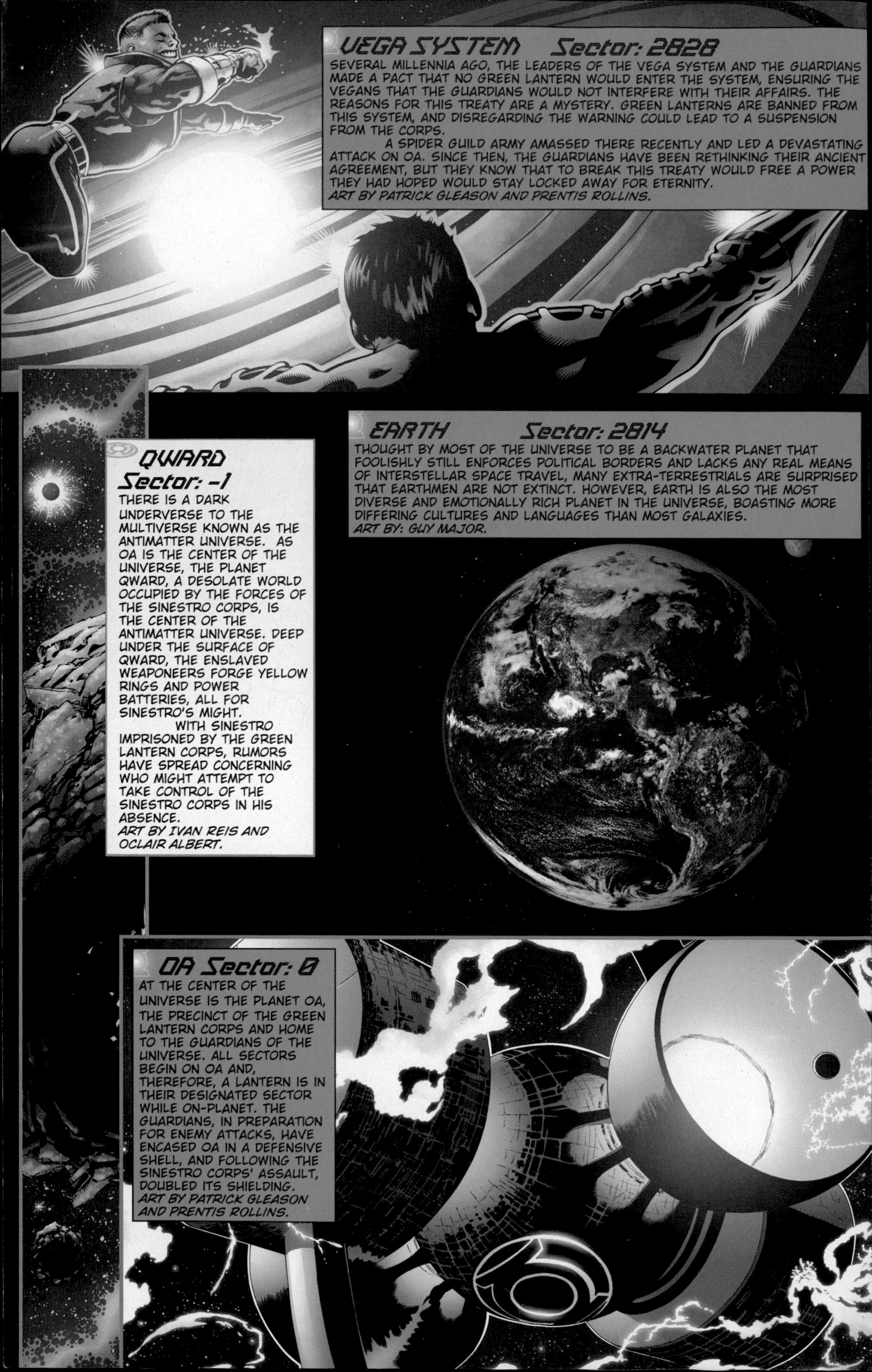
VEGA SYSTEM Sector: 2828
SEVERAL MILLENNIA AGO, THE LEADERS OF THE VEGA SYSTEM AND THE GUARDIANS MADE A PACT THAT NO GREEN LANTERN WOULD ENTER THE SYSTEM, ENSURING THE VEGANS THAT THE GUARDIANS WOULD NOT INTERFERE WITH THEIR AFFAIRS. THE REASONS FOR THIS TREATY ARE A MYSTERY. GREEN LANTERNS ARE BANNED FROM THIS SYSTEM, AND DISREGARDING THE WARNING COULD LEAD TO A SUSPENSION FROM THE CORPS.
A SPIDER GUILD ARMY AMASSED THERE RECENTLY AND LED A DEVASTATING ATTACK ON OA. SINCE THEN, THE GUARDIANS HAVE BEEN RETHINKING THEIR ANCIENT AGREEMENT, BUT THEY KNOW THAT TO BREAK THIS TREATY WOULD FREE A POWER THEY HAD HOPED WOULD STAY LOCKED AWAY FOR ETERNITY.
ART BY PATRICK GLEASON AND PRENTIS ROLLINS.
QWARD Sector: -1
THERE IS A DARK UNDERVERSE TO THE MULTIVERSE KNOWN AS THE ANTIMATTER UNIVERSE. AS OA IS THE CENTER OF THE UNIVERSE, THE PLANET QWARD, A DESOLATE WORLD OCCUPIED BY THE FORCES OF THE SINESTRO CORPS, IS THE CENTER OF THE ANTIMATTER UNIVERSE. DEEP UNDER THE SURFACE OF QWARD, THE ENSLAVED WEAPONEERS FORGE YELLOW RINGS AND POWER BATTERIES, ALL FOR SINESTRO'S MIGHT.
WITH SINESTRO IMPRISONED BY THE GREEN LANTERN CORPS, RUMORS HAVE SPREAD CONCERNING WHO MIGHT ATTEMPT TO TAKE CONTROL OF THE SINESTRO CORPS IN HIS ABSENCE.
ART BY IVAN REIS AND OCLAIR ALBERT.
EARTH Sector: 2814
THOUGHT BY MOST OF THE UNIVERSE TO BE A BACKWATER PLANET THAT FOOLISHLY STILL ENFORCES POLITICAL BORDERS AND LACKS ANY REAL MEANS OF INTERSTELLAR SPACE TRAVEL, MANY EXTRA-TERRESTRIALS ARE SURPRISED THAT EARTHMEN ARE NOT EXTINCT. HOWEVER, EARTH IS ALSO THE MOST DIVERSE AND EMOTIONALLY RICH PLANET IN THE UNIVERSE, BOASTING MORE DIFFERING CULTURES AND LANGUAGES THAN MOST GALAXIES.
ART BY: GUY MAJOR.
OA Sector: 0
AT THE CENTER OF THE UNIVERSE IS THE PLANET OA, THE PRECINCT OF THE GREEN LANTERN CORPS AND HOME TO THE GUARDIANS OF THE UNIVERSE. ALL SECTORS BEGIN ON OA AND, THEREFORE, A LANTERN IS IN THEIR DESIGNATED SECTOR WHILE ON-PLANET. THE GUARDIANS, IN PREPARATION FOR ENEMY ATTACKS, HAVE ENCASED OA IN A DEFENSIVE SHELL, AND FOLLOWING THE SINESTRO CORPS' ASSAULT, DOUBLED ITS SHIELDING.
ART BY PATRICK GLEASON AND PRENTIS ROLLINS.

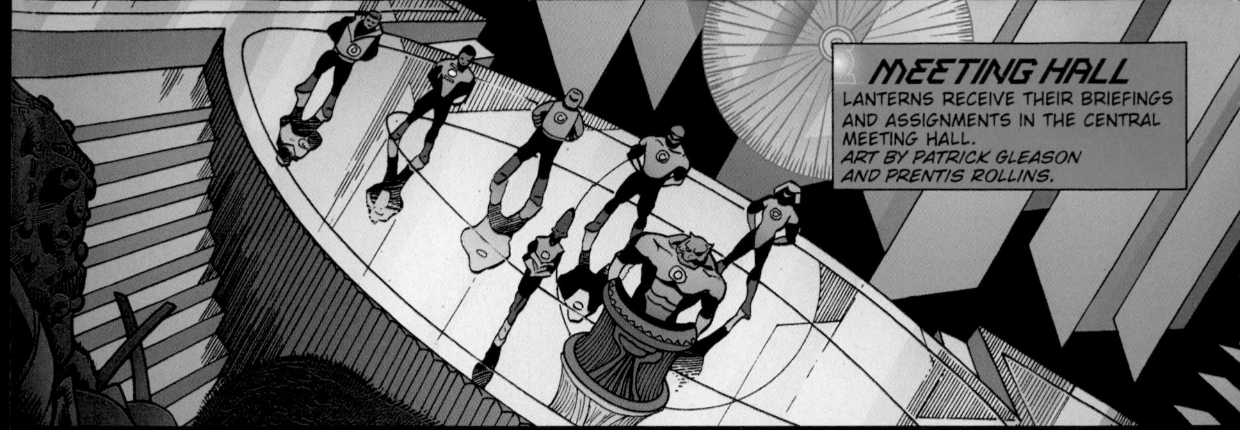

MEETING HALL

LANTERNS RECEIVE THEIR BRIEFINGS AND ASSIGNMENTS IN THE CENTRAL MEETING HALL.
ART BY PATRICK GLEASON AND PRENTIS ROLLINS.

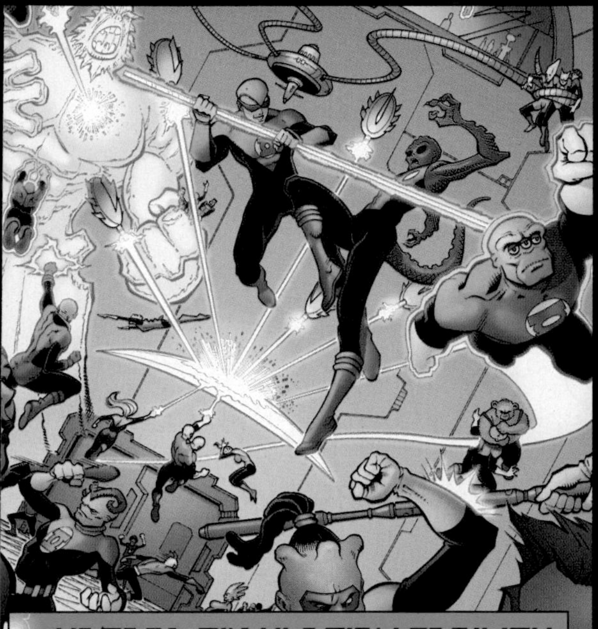

HAZARD SIMULATION FACILITY

ALL ROOKIE GREEN LANTERNS ENDURE A SERIES OF TESTS TO DETERMINE THEIR VIABILITY IN THE FIELD. THE HAZARD SIMULATION FACILITY ALLOWS FOR SAFE, NON-LETHAL TRAINING SCENARIOS TO BE ENACTED.
ART BY TOM NGUYEN.

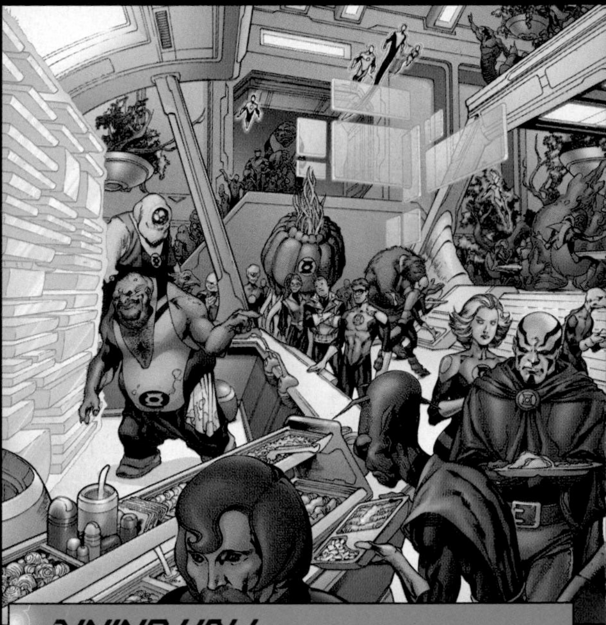

DINING HALL

THE DINING HALL CAN ACCOMMODATE ANY GREEN LANTERN'S NUTRITIONAL NEEDS. THE EXECUTIVE CHEF, GREET, SPECIALIZES IN REPLICATING DISHES FROM ACROSS THE UNIVERSE. HE, UNFORTUNATELY, HAS TROUBLE REPLICATING THE VAST NUMBER OF FOODS FROM EARTH.
ART BY IVAN REIS AND OCLAIR ALBERT.

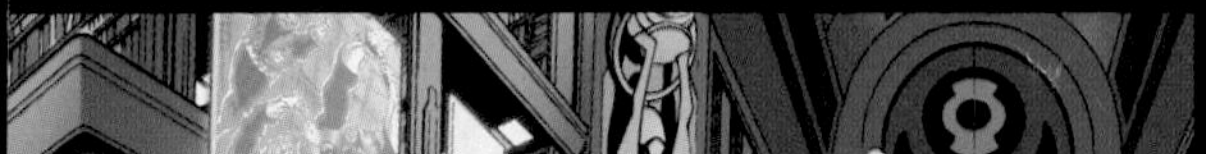

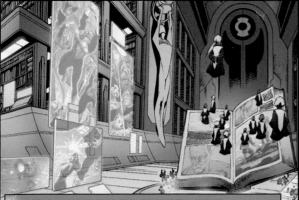

HALL OF GREAT SERVICE

HOUSING THE MASSIVE BOOK OF OA - THE CORPS LAWBOOK AND BIBLE - THE HALL OF GREAT SERVICE IS A LIBRARY OF THE STORIES AND DEEDS OF THE FINEST GREEN LANTERNS OF ALL TIME. LIKE HIS FATHER BEFORE HIM, TOMAR-TU RECENTLY TOOK THE POSITION OF ARCHIVIST SUPERIOR, FILING EVERY TALE AS IT COMES IN. THE BOOK OF OA HAS BEEN DESIGNATED OFF-LIMITS AFTER BEING REWRITTEN BY THE GUARDIANS OF THE UNIVERSE TO INCLUDE TEN NEW LAWS.

THE FIRST NEW LAW: LETHAL FORCE IS APPROVED AGAINST ANY MEMBER OF THE SINESTRO CORPS.
ART BY IVAN REIS AND OCLAIR ALBERT.

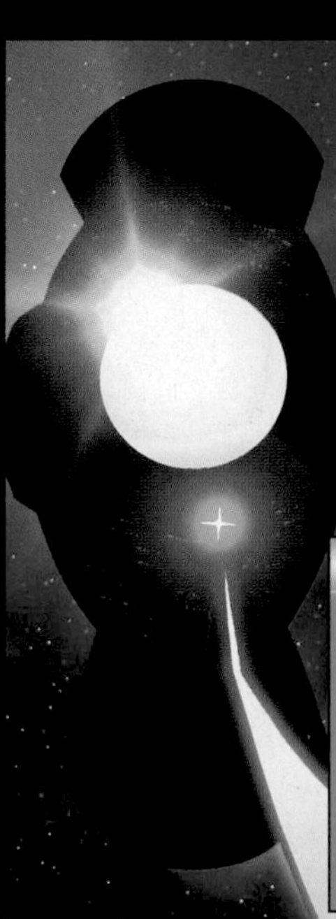

SECTOR HOUSES

THESE SAFE HOUSES ALLOW LANTERNS TO HOLD CRIMINALS AS THEY AWAIT ESCORT BACK TO THE OAN SCIENCELLS. LIMITED RECREATIONAL FACILITIES ARE AVAILABLE TO ACCOMMODATE GREEN LANTERNS IN THEIR TRAVELS.
ART BY PATRICK GLEASON AND PRENTIS ROLLINS.

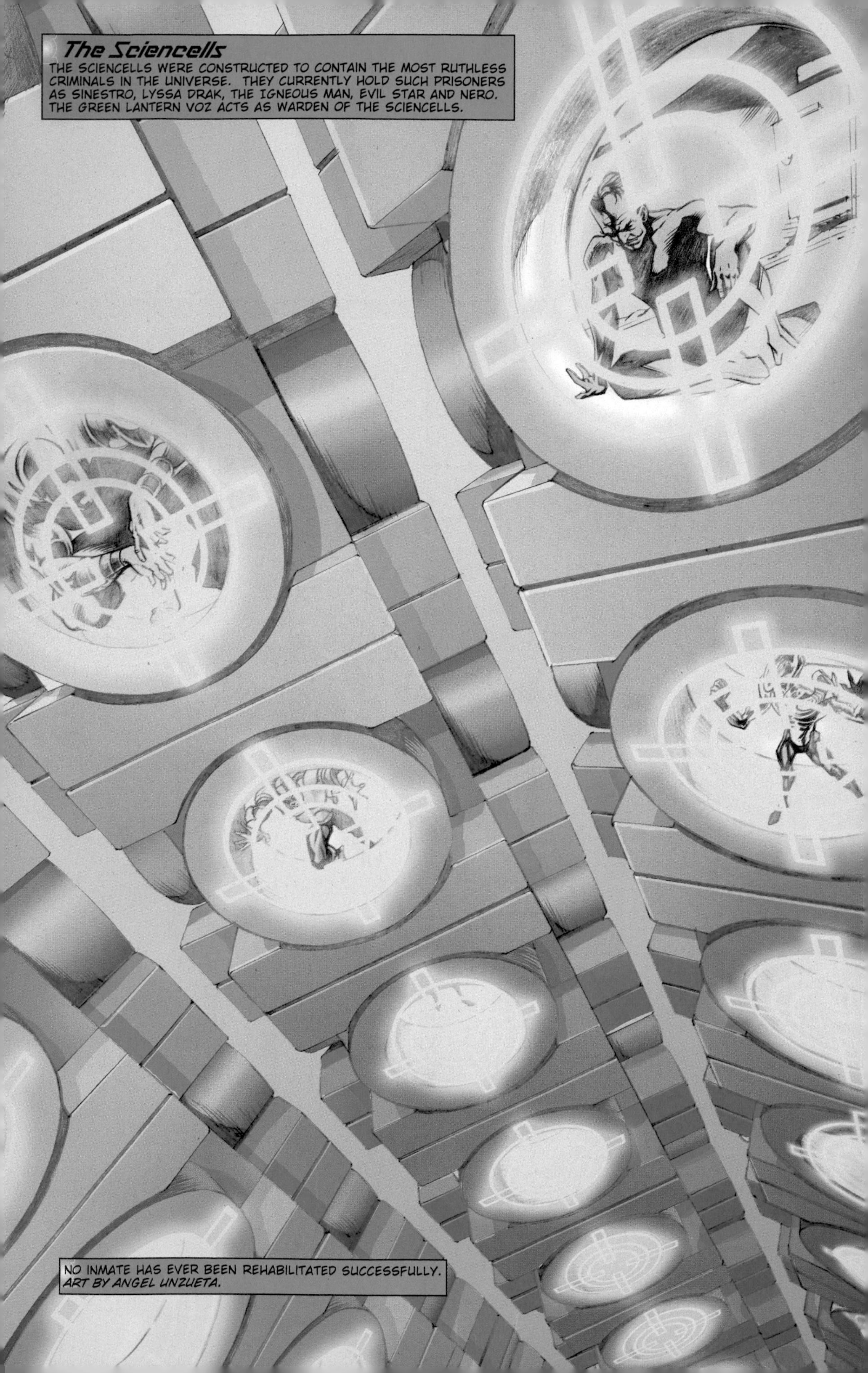
The Sciencells
THE SCIENCELLS WERE CONSTRUCTED TO CONTAIN THE MOST RUTHLESS CRIMINALS IN THE UNIVERSE. THEY CURRENTLY HOLD SUCH PRISONERS AS SINESTRO, LYSSA DRAK, THE IGNEOUS MAN, EVIL STAR AND NERO. THE GREEN LANTERN VOZ ACTS AS WARDEN OF THE SCIENCELLS.
NO INMATE HAS EVER BEEN REHABILITATED SUCCESSFULLY.
ART BY ANGEL UNZUETA.

Power Rings

A GREEN LANTERN'S STANDARD WEAPON, THE POWER RING IS CONTROLLED BY THE USER'S WILLPOWER. IT TAPS INTO WILLPOWER CREATED BY SENTIENT BEINGS THROUGHOUT THE UNIVERSE AND COLLECTED ON OA IN THE GUARDIANS' CENTRAL POWER BATTERY.

THE RING GENERATES A STANDARD-ISSUE POLICE UNIFORM, WHICH IS OFTEN ALTERED BY THE BEARER'S INDIVIDUAL THOUGHTS, A FORCE FIELD, AND GIVES ITS USER FLIGHT CAPABILITIES. THE RINGS PROVIDE COMMUNICATION WITH A LANTERN'S FELLOW OFFICERS AS WELL AS ANY LOCALIZED COMMUNICATION SYSTEMS (CELL PHONES, FOR EXAMPLE). THEY ALSO TRANSFORM THE LANTERN BADGE INTO A FLASHING "SIREN" WHILE IN HOT PURSUIT. THE RING'S ULTIMATE POWER COMES IN GRANTING THE USER THE ABILITY TO CREATE CONSTRUCTS OF GREEN ENERGY IN ANY GIVEN SHAPE BY THE USER'S MIND.

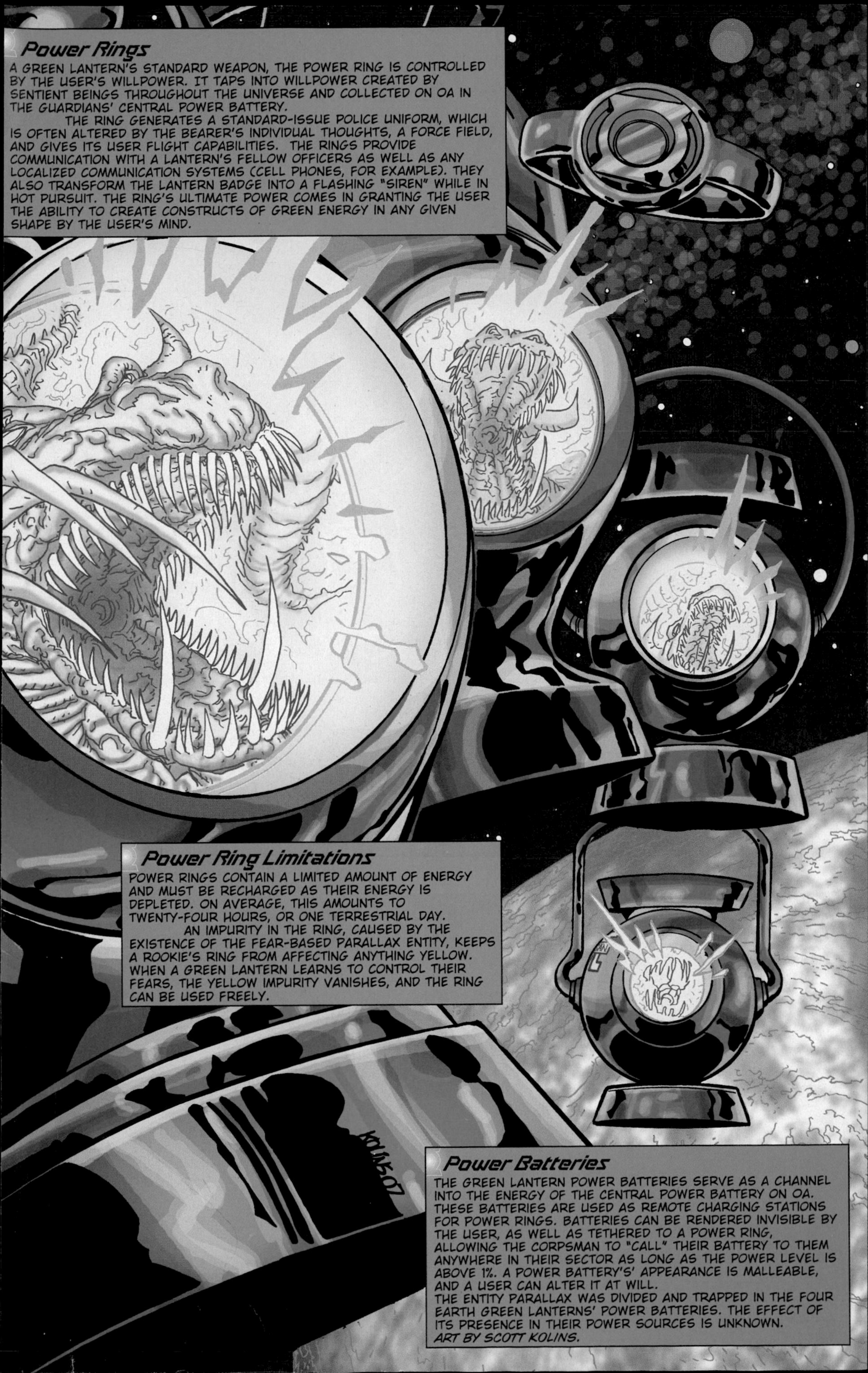

Power Ring Limitations

POWER RINGS CONTAIN A LIMITED AMOUNT OF ENERGY AND MUST BE RECHARGED AS THEIR ENERGY IS DEPLETED. ON AVERAGE, THIS AMOUNTS TO TWENTY-FOUR HOURS, OR ONE TERRESTRIAL DAY.

AN IMPURITY IN THE RING, CAUSED BY THE EXISTENCE OF THE FEAR-BASED PARALLAX ENTITY, KEEPS A ROOKIE'S RING FROM AFFECTING ANYTHING YELLOW. WHEN A GREEN LANTERN LEARNS TO CONTROL THEIR FEARS, THE YELLOW IMPURITY VANISHES, AND THE RING CAN BE USED FREELY.

Power Batteries

THE GREEN LANTERN POWER BATTERIES SERVE AS A CHANNEL INTO THE ENERGY OF THE CENTRAL POWER BATTERY ON OA. THESE BATTERIES ARE USED AS REMOTE CHARGING STATIONS FOR POWER RINGS. BATTERIES CAN BE RENDERED INVISIBLE BY THE USER, AS WELL AS TETHERED TO A POWER RING, ALLOWING THE CORPSMAN TO "CALL" THEIR BATTERY TO THEM ANYWHERE IN THEIR SECTOR AS LONG AS THE POWER LEVEL IS ABOVE 1%. A POWER BATTERY'S' APPEARANCE IS MALLEABLE, AND A USER CAN ALTER IT AT WILL.

THE ENTITY PARALLAX WAS DIVIDED AND TRAPPED IN THE FOUR EARTH GREEN LANTERNS' POWER BATTERIES. THE EFFECT OF ITS PRESENCE IN THEIR POWER SOURCES IS UNKNOWN.

ART BY SCOTT KOLINS.

THE GREEN LANTERN CORPS

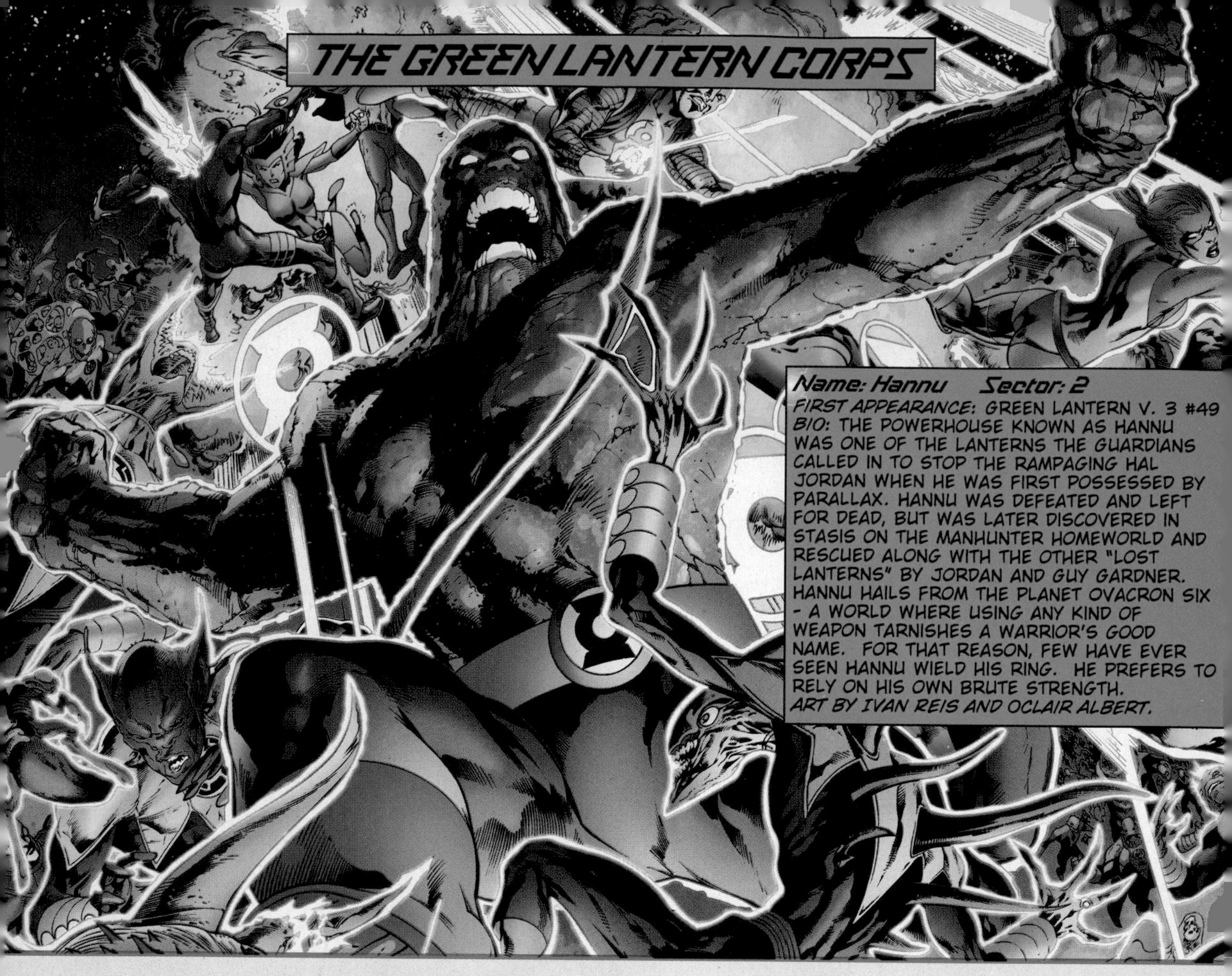

Name: Hannu Sector: 2

FIRST APPEARANCE: GREEN LANTERN V. 3 #49

BIO: THE POWERHOUSE KNOWN AS HANNU WAS ONE OF THE LANTERNS THE GUARDIANS CALLED IN TO STOP THE RAMPAGING HAL JORDAN WHEN HE WAS FIRST POSSESSED BY PARALLAX. HANNU WAS DEFEATED AND LEFT FOR DEAD, BUT WAS LATER DISCOVERED IN STASIS ON THE MANHUNTER HOMEWORLD AND RESCUED ALONG WITH THE OTHER "LOST LANTERNS" BY JORDAN AND GUY GARDNER. HANNU HAILS FROM THE PLANET OVACRON SIX - A WORLD WHERE USING ANY KIND OF WEAPON TARNISHES A WARRIOR'S GOOD NAME. FOR THAT REASON, FEW HAVE EVER SEEN HANNU WIELD HIS RING. HE PREFERS TO RELY ON HIS OWN BRUTE STRENGTH.

ART BY IVAN REIS AND OCLAIR ALBERT.

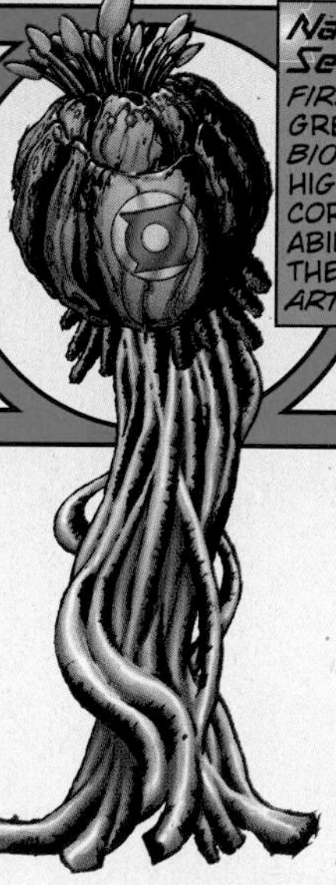

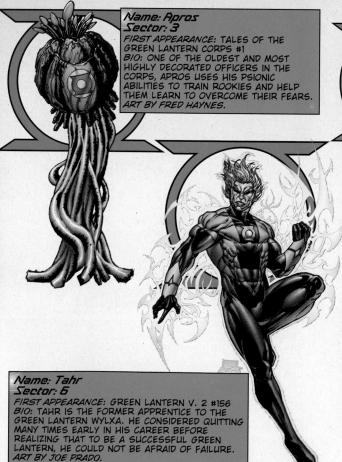

Name: Apros
Sector: 3

FIRST APPEARANCE: TALES OF THE GREEN LANTERN CORPS #1

BIO: ONE OF THE OLDEST AND MOST HIGHLY DECORATED OFFICERS IN THE CORPS, APROS USES HIS PSIONIC ABILITIES TO TRAIN ROOKIES AND HELP THEM LEARN TO OVERCOME THEIR FEARS.

ART BY FRED HAYNES.

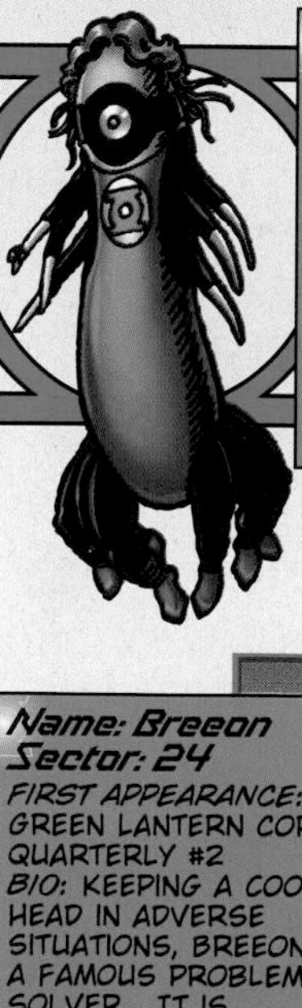

Name: Larvox
Sector: 17

FIRST APPEARANCE: GREEN LANTERN V. 2 #9

BIO: THE ASEXUAL BEING KNOWN AS LARVOX SERVED AS A FIERCE GUARDIAN OF HIS SECTOR FOR YEARS, AND WHEN THE GREEN LANTERN CORPS RE-FORMED, LARVOX RETURNED TO DUTY. LARVOX IS UNABLE TO SPEAK AND COMMUNICATES USING HIS POWER RING.

ART BY PAT BRODERICK.

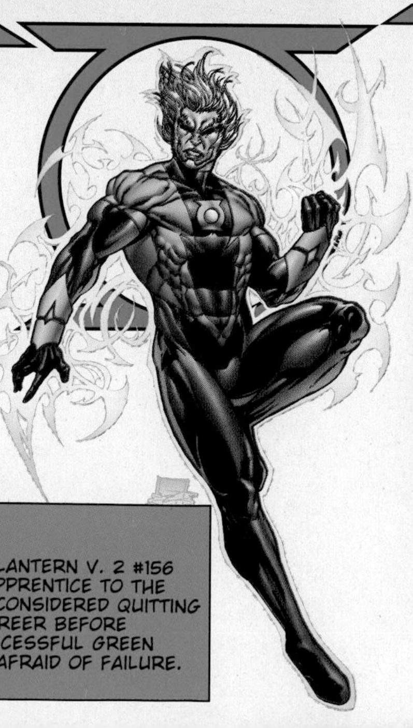

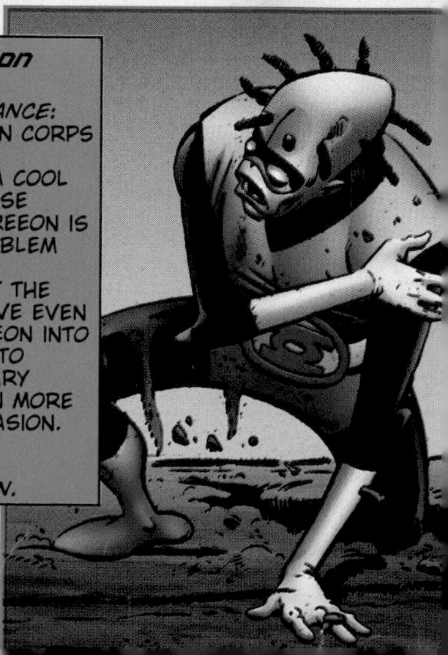

Name: Breeon
Sector: 24

FIRST APPEARANCE: GREEN LANTERN CORPS QUARTERLY #2

BIO: KEEPING A COOL HEAD IN ADVERSE SITUATIONS, BREEON IS A FAMOUS PROBLEM SOLVER. IT IS RUMORED THAT THE GUARDIANS HAVE EVEN BROUGHT BREEON INTO THEIR CITADEL TO DISCUSS MILITARY STRATEGIES ON MORE THAN ONE OCCASION.

ART BY TY TEMPLETON AND AL GORDON.

Name: Tahr
Sector: 6

FIRST APPEARANCE: GREEN LANTERN V. 2 #156

BIO: TAHR IS THE FORMER APPRENTICE TO THE GREEN LANTERN WYLXA. HE CONSIDERED QUITTING MANY TIMES EARLY IN HIS CAREER BEFORE REALIZING THAT TO BE A SUCCESSFUL GREEN LANTERN, HE COULD NOT BE AFRAID OF FAILURE.

ART BY JOE PRADO.

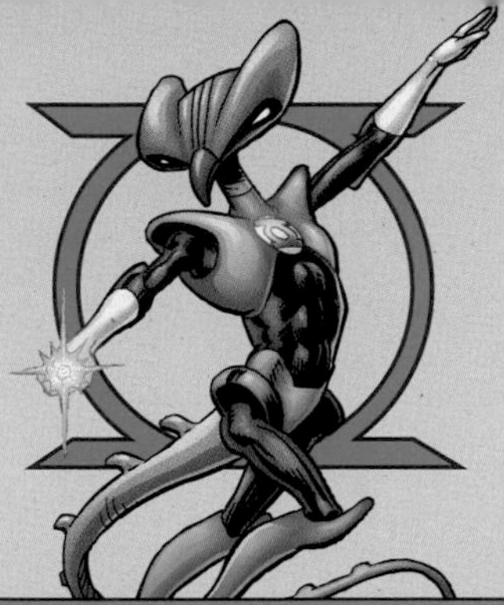

Name: Norchavius Sector: 26

FIRST APPEARANCE: GREEN LANTERN/SINESTRO CORPS SECRET FILES #1

BIO: NORCHAVIUS IS A RENOWNED SCULPTOR THROUGHOUT HIS SECTOR. HE WAS A GOOD FRIEND OF THE LANTERN ARCHON Z'GMORA, WHOSE DEATH HE COMMEMORATED WITH THE CREATION OF A STUNNING TRIBUTE. MUCH OF THE STATUARY THROUGHOUT OA'S GREAT GARDENS IS THE WORK OF NORCHAVIUS.

ART BY DAVE GIBBONS.

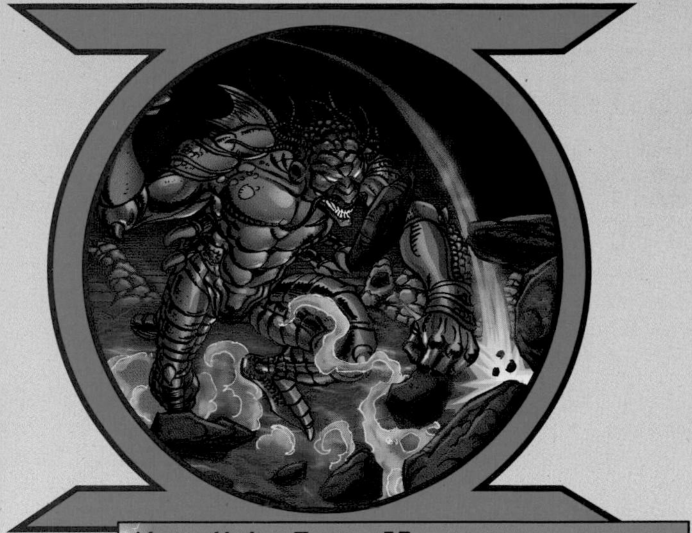

Name: Umitu Sector: 28

FIRST APPEARANCE: GREEN LANTERN CORPS QUARTERLY #4

BIO: UMITU HAS EARNED MORE DEMERITS AND SUSPENSIONS FOR EMPLOYING EXCESSIVE FORCE THAN ANY OTHER GREEN LANTERN. HE HAS BEEN INFORMED THAT ONE MORE SUSPENSION WILL RESULT IN HIS EXPULSION FROM THE CORPS. UMITU IS SAVING HIS FINAL OUTBURST FOR WHEN IT IS NEEDED MOST.

ART BY ROMEO TANGHAL.

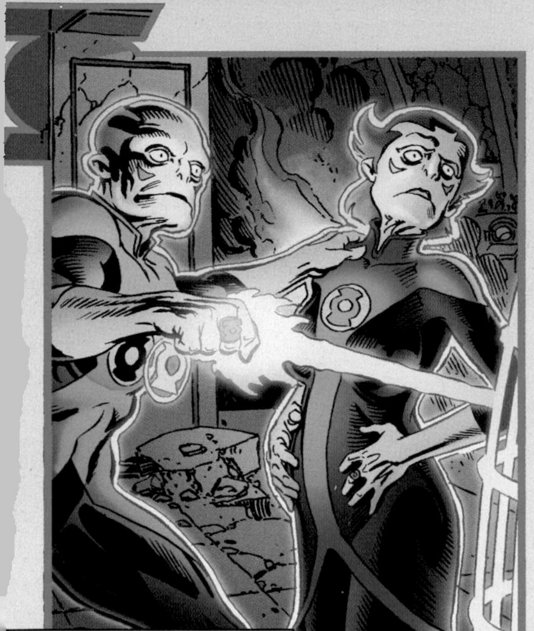

Name: Matoo and Amnee Pree Sector: 35

FIRST APPEARANCE: SUPERMAN-PRIME SPECIAL #1

BIO: AMNEE AND HER HUSBAND, MATOO PREE, WERE CHOSEN TOGETHER TO BE GREEN LANTERNS ON THEIR WEDDING DAY. THEY ARE EXPECTING THEIR FIRST CHILD SOON AND, FOR THAT REASON, ARE LEADING THE HUNT FOR THE SINESTRO CORPS MEMBER KRYB.

ART BY JERRY ORDWAY.

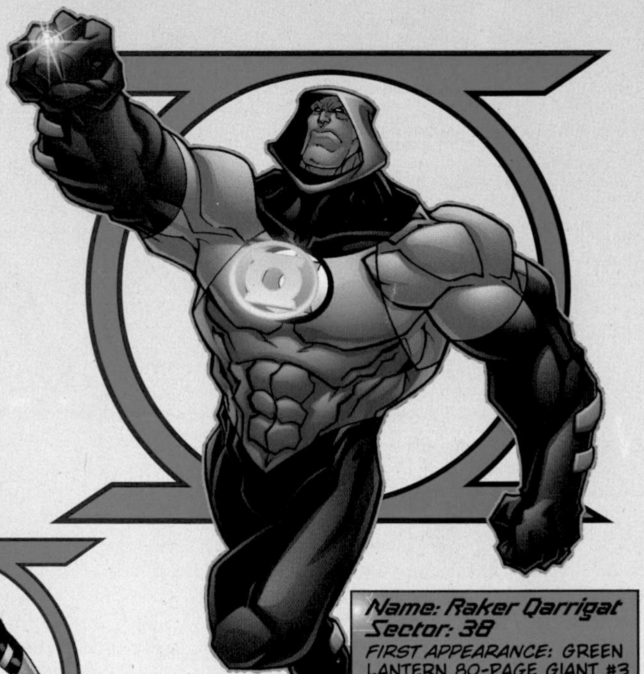

Name: Raker Qarrigat Sector: 38

FIRST APPEARANCE: GREEN LANTERN 80-PAGE GIANT #3

BIO: OPERATING IN AND AROUND APOKOLIPS FOR CENTURIES, RAKER QARRIGAT WAS CAPTURED BY DARKSEID AND PUBLICLY TORTURED FOR YEARS TO CRUSH ANY SENSE OF HOPE. RECENTLY, HIS NEW SECTOR PARTNER, KRAKEN, FREED RAKER FROM DESAAD'S DUNGEONS. HE STRUGGLES TO RECUPERATE FROM HIS YEARS OF PHYSICAL AND PSYCHOLOGICAL TORTURE. HE HAS YET TO SLEEP THROUGH THE NIGHT.

ART BY JONBOY MEYERS.

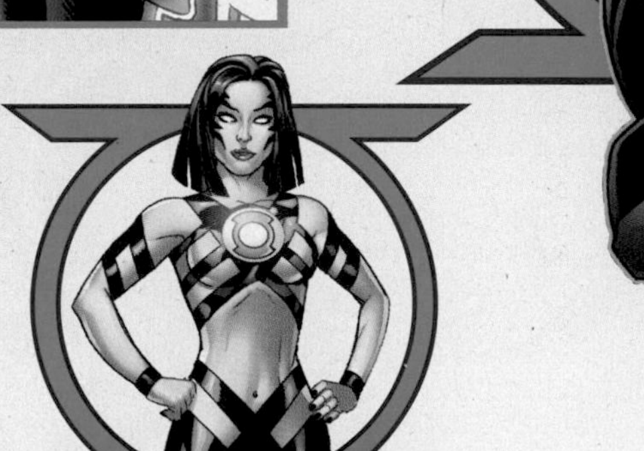

Name: Kraken Sector: 38

FIRST APPEARANCE: GREEN LANTERN V. 4 #25

BIO: LITTLE IS KNOWN ABOUT THE ENIGMATIC GREEN LANTERN CALLED KRAKEN, SAVE FOR HER DARING RESCUE OF RAKER QARRIGAT FROM DARKSEID'S CLUTCHES AND HER DESIRE TO SEE JUSTICE SERVED. IT IS RUMORED THAT KRAKEN HAS BEEN TARGETED BY THE FEMALE FURIES OF APOKOLIPS.

ART BY MIKE MCKONE.

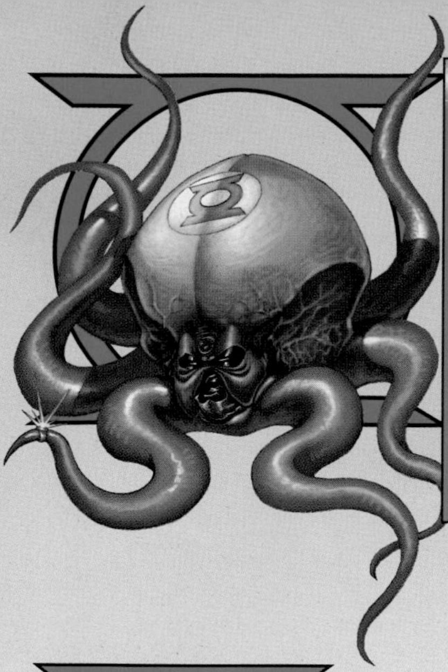

Name: Shorm
Sector: 40
FIRST APPEARANCE: GREEN LANTERN CORPS: RECHARGE #1
BIO: SHORM IS THE ACTING DESK SERGEANT FOR THE GREEN LANTERN CORPS, WHOSE DUTIES INCLUDE MANAGING THE DISTRIBUTION OF GREEN LANTERN STANDARD GEAR TO ALL ROOKIES. SHORM AND SALAAK OFTEN SPEND HOURS COMPLAINING ABOUT THE LACK OF PROFESSIONALISM AMONG THE EARTH GREEN LANTERNS. SHORM IS STRONGLY OPPOSED TO THE GUARDIANS' ALPHA LANTERN PROJECT, BUT HAS THUS FAR KEPT HIS OPINIONS TO HIMSELF.
ART BY ANGEL UNZUETA.

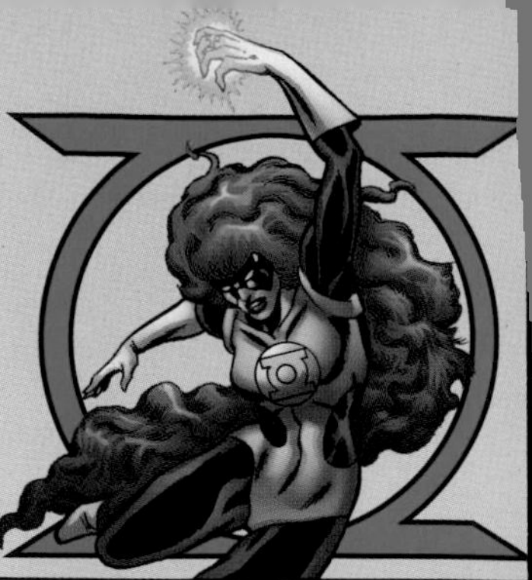

Name: Lysandra Sector: 47
FIRST APPEARANCE: GREEN LANTERN V. 2 #168
BIO: A SPIRITUAL GUIDE ON HER HOME PLANET, LYSANDRA MADE THE SACRED VOW NEVER TO LEAVE HER WORLD. SHE WAS EXCOMMUNICATED AFTER SHE WAS FORCED TO GO OFF-PLANET BECAUSE OF HER DUTIES AS A GREEN LANTERN. SHE RETURNED TO HER PLANET AND NOW REFUSES TO LEAVE, BUT SHE HAS YET TO BE WELCOMED BACK INTO HER CHURCH.
ART BY JEROME MOORE AND SAL TRAPANI.

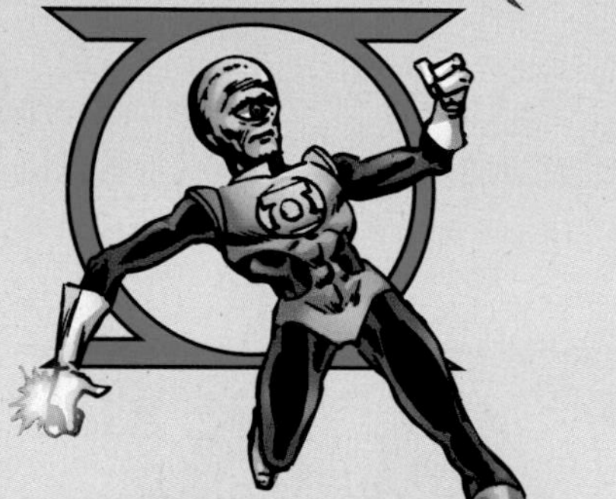

Name: Spol
Sector: 47
FIRST APPEARANCE: GREEN LANTERN V. 2 #168
BIO: SPOL'S PARTNER, LYSANDRA, CANNOT LEAVE HER PLANET BECAUSE OF HER RELIGIOUS BELIEFS. AN ATHEIST, SPOL RESENTS HIS PARTNER'S ABSENCE AND CONTINUALLY REQUESTS A NEW ONE.
ART BY JEROME MOORE AND SAL TRAPANI.

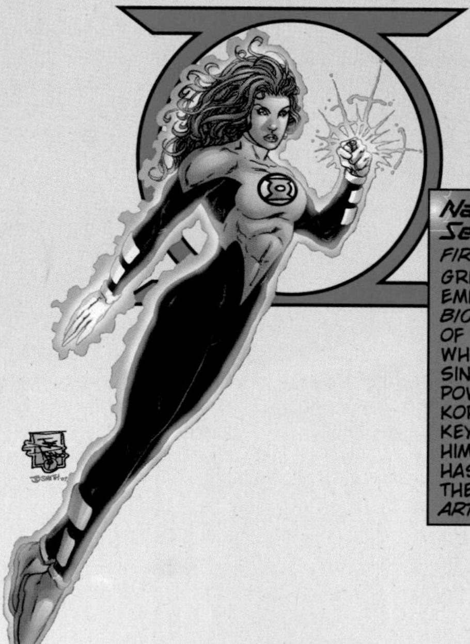

Name: Tomy-Fai
Sector: 56
FIRST APPEARANCE: GREEN LANTERN: EMERALD DAWN #5
BIO: TOMY-FAI WAS ONE OF THE GREEN LANTERNS WHO INVESTIGATED SINESTRO'S MISUSE OF POWER ON THE PLANET KORUGAR, AND WAS A KEY WITNESS AGAINST HIM IN HIS TRIAL. SHE HAS BEEN MISSING FOR THE LAST SIX MONTHS.
ART BY JOE PRADO

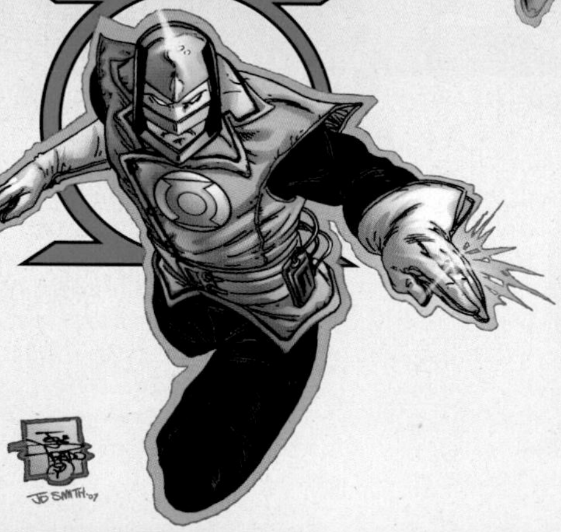

Name: Varix Sector: 69
FIRST APPEARANCE: TALES OF THE GREEN LANTERN CORPS ANNUAL #2
BIO: VARIX IS A VENERABLE LAW ENFORCEMENT OFFICER ON THE PLANET NAKTOS. HE WAS GIVEN HIS RING BY THE AGING GREEN LANTERN GHRELK AFTER GHRELK WAS FORCED TO RETIRE DUE TO A MYSTERIOUS ILLNESS THAT DESTROYED HIS BRAIN. VARIX IS A HYPOCHONDRIAC. IN ADDITION TO HIS PREDECESSOR'S FALL TO DISEASE, HALF OF HIS WORLD WAS DECIMATED BY THE YELLOW PLAGUE OF GHERA.
ART BY JOE PRADO.

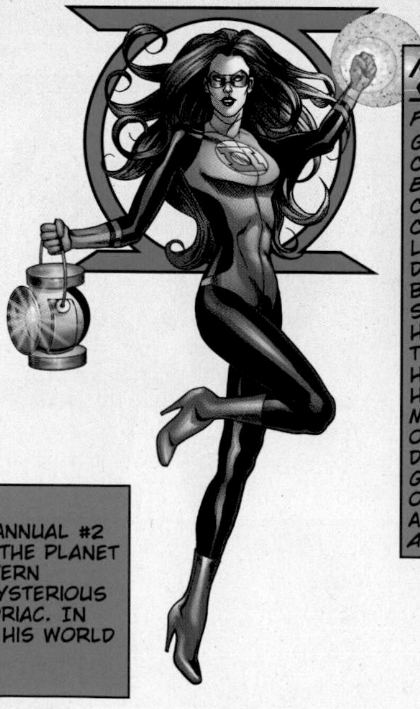

Name: Sendrina
Sector: 73
FIRST APPEARANCE: GREEN LANTERN/SINESTR CORPS SECRET FILES #1
BIO: SENDRINA WAS CHTHOS-CHTHAS CHTHATIS'S PARTNER, A LANTERN WHO FELL DURING THE GREAT WAR BETWEEN MOGO AND RA SENDRINA BLAMES HERSELF FOR NOT BEING THERE AND HAS DEDICAT HER LIFE TO CONTINUIN HER FALLEN PARTNER'S MISSION TO ERADICATE OF THE UNIVERSE'S DEADLIEST TERRORIST GROUPS - THE CHILDRE OF THE WHITE LOBE.
ART BY ALECIA RODRIG AND REBECCA BUCHMA

Name: Bynai Bruun
Sector: 83

FIRST APPEARANCE: TALES OF THE GREEN LANTERN CORPS ANNUAL #3
BIO: FROM THE PLANET ZYMIA, BRUUN BLAMED THE GREEN LANTERN CORPS' INACTION FOR HER HUSBAND'S DEATH DURING A MANHUNTER ATTACK. AFTER BECOMING A GREEN LANTERN HERSELF, BRUUN FORGAVE THE CORPS AND NOW LEADS A STRIKE TEAM THAT SEEKS TO CAPTURE AND DEACTIVATE ALL MANHUNTERS.
ART BY DAVE GIBBONS.

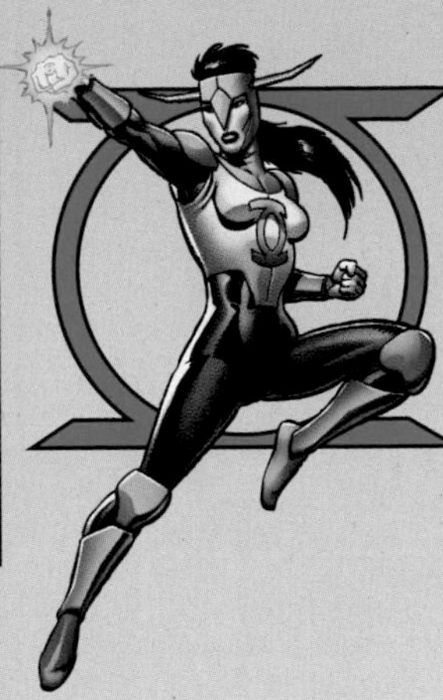

Name: Malet Dasim
Sector: 103

FIRST APPEARANCE: GREEN LANTERN V. 2 #130
BIO: MALET DASIM IS THE MASTER DISTRICT ATTORNEY OF HIS HOME PLANET, DLIST, AS WELL AS THE CHIEF PROSECUTOR FOR THE GREEN LANTERNS. MALET IS COMMITTED TO UTILIZING THE NEW LAWS WRITTEN INTO THE BOOK OF OA IN HIS CASES AGAINST THE CRIMINALS OF THE UNIVERSE.
ART BY MARK ROBINSON.

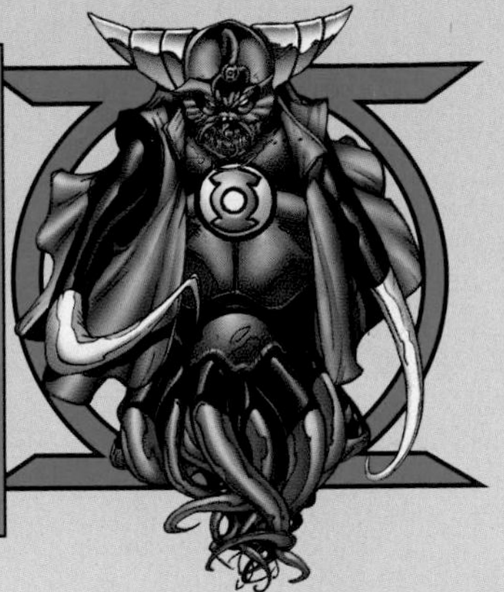

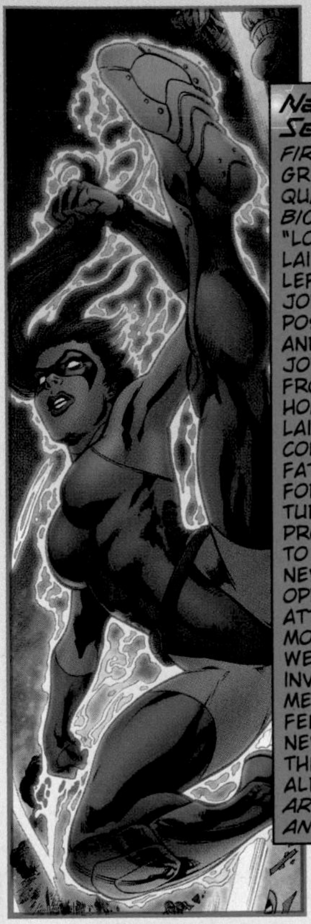

Name: Laira
Sector: 112

FIRST APPEARANCE: GREEN LANTERN CORPS QUARTERLY #6
BIO: LIKE HER FELLOW "LOST LANTERN" HANNU, LAIRA WAS DEFEATED AND LEFT FOR DEAD BY HAL JORDAN WHEN HE WAS POSSESSED BY PARALLAX AND LATER RESCUED BY JORDAN AND GUY GARDNER FROM THE MANHUNTER HOMEWORLD. AS A ROOKIE, LAIRA WAS FORCED TO CONFRONT HER OWN FATHER, KENTOR OMOTO, A FORMER GREEN LANTERN TURNED OVERLORD, TO PROVE HER FEARLESSNESS TO THE GUARDIANS. LAIRA NEVER LOOKS AT AN OPPONENT WHEN SHE ATTACKS, MAKING EVERY MOVE A SURPRISE. THERE WERE RUMORS SHE WAS INVOLVED WITH HER MENTOR, KE'HAAN, BUT HER FEELINGS FOR HIM WERE NEVER ACTED UPON DUE TO THE FACT THAT KE'HAAN ALREADY HAD A FAMILY.
ART BY IVAN REIS AND OCLAIR ALBERT.

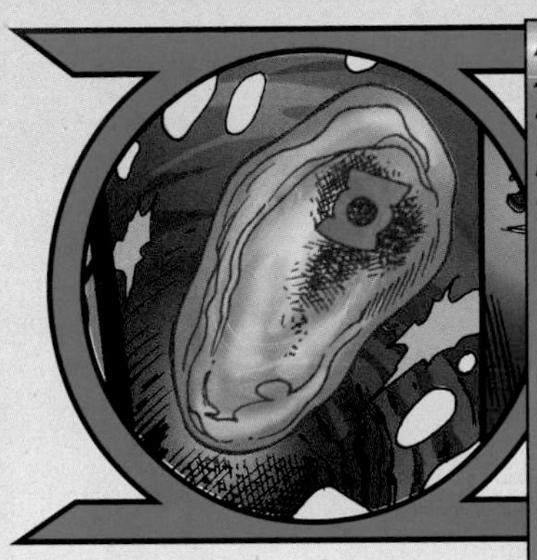

Name: Leezle Pon
Sector: 119

FIRST APPEARANCE: GREEN LANTERN V. 4 #25
BIO: LEEZLE PON IS A MICROSCOPIC SENTIENT SMALLPOX VIRUS SENT ON BIOLOGICAL MISSIONS WHERE OTHER GREEN LANTERNS CAN'T GO. LEEZLE PON WAS DISTRAUGHT OVER THE DEATH OF HIS LONG-TIME SECTOR PARTNER, REEMUZ, AND NOW SEEKS TO ERADICATE ANY REMNANT OF THE DISEASE DESPOTELLIS FROM THE UNIVERSE.
ART BY IVAN REIS AND OCLAIR ALBERT.

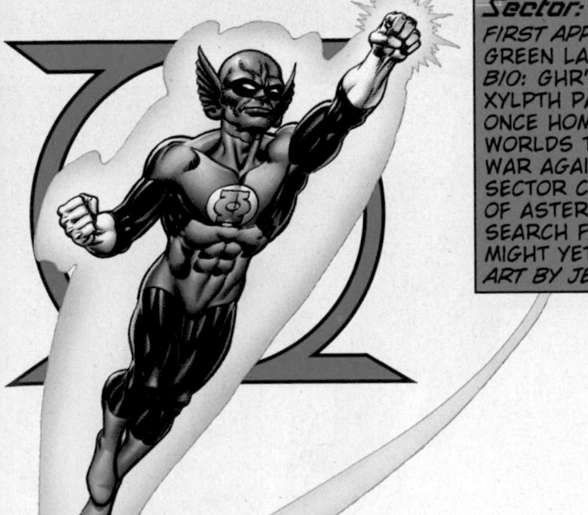

Name: Ghr'll and Xylpth
Sector: 151

FIRST APPEARANCE: GREEN LANTERN V. 2 #151
BIO: GHR'LL AND HIS PARTNER XYLPTH PATROL SECTOR 151, A SECTOR ONCE HOME TO A VAST NETWORK OF WORLDS THAT WERE DESTROYED IN A WAR AGAINST MONGUL. NOW, IN THIS SECTOR COMPOSED ALMOST ENTIRELY OF ASTEROIDS, GHR'LL AND XYLPTH SEARCH FOR ANY SIGNS OF LIFE THEY MIGHT YET PROTECT.
ART BY JERRY ORDWAY.

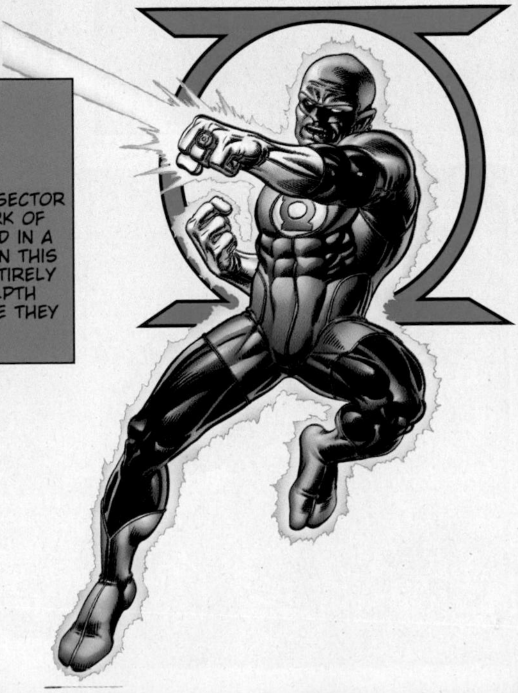

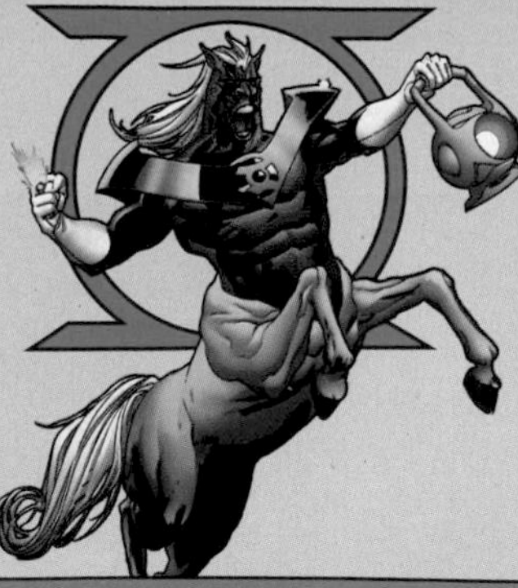

Name: Relok Hag Sector: 173
FIRST APPEARANCE:
GREEN LANTERN/SINESTRO CORPS SECRET FILES #1
BIO: FROM A PRIMITIVE WORLD, RELOK HAG WAS A FIERCE BARBARIAN WHO, UPON RECEIVING HIS GREEN LANTERN RING, WAGED A ONE-MAN WAR AGAINST THE DOMINATORS WHO HAD ENSLAVED AND EXPERIMENTED ON HIS PEOPLE FOR DECADES. BELIEVED TO HAVE BEEN KILLED BATTLING THE DOMINATORS, RELOK HAG WAS LATER FOUND HELD IN STASIS ON THE MANHUNTER WORLD, BIOT, AND SET FREE.
ART BY RYAN SOOK.

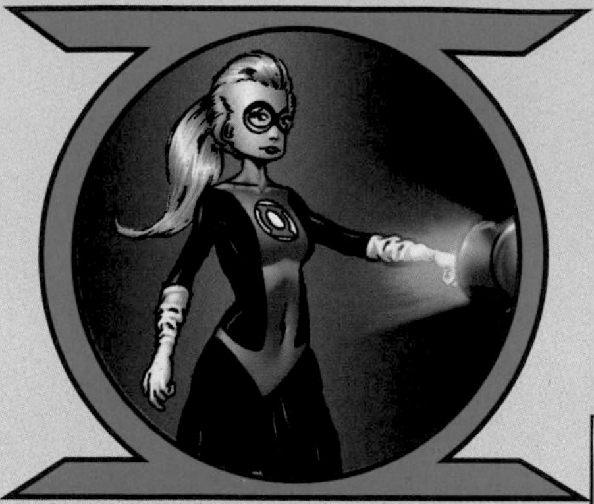

Name: KT21 Sector: 181
FIRST APPEARANCE: GREEN LANTERN V. 2 #187
BIO: KT21 WAS PREGNANT WHEN SHE WAS INDUCTED INTO THE CORPS, AND HAS HAD TO RAISE HER SON WHILE BOTH A GREEN LANTERN AND A SINGLE MOTHER. WHEN NEWS REACHED HER THAT THE SINESTRO CORPS MEMBER KRYB WAS TARGETING THE CHILDREN OF GREEN LANTERNS, SHE JOINED AMNEE AND MATOO PREE IN THEIR HUNT FOR THE MONSTER.
ART BY MARSHALL ROGERS.

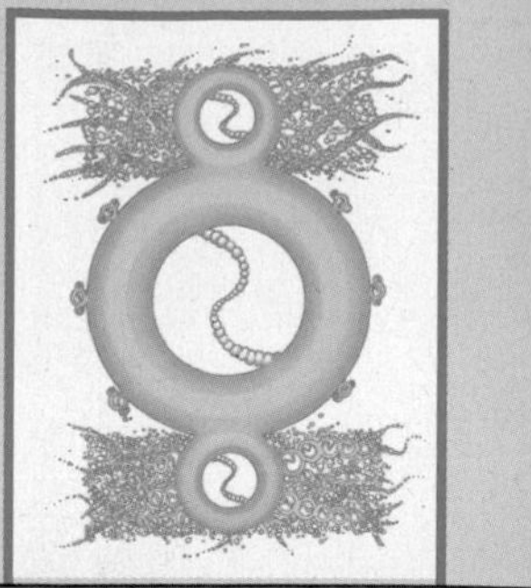

Name: Dkrtzy RRR Sector: 18
FIRST APPEARANCE:
GREEN LANTERN/SINESTRO CORPS SECRET FILES #1
BIO: DKRTZY RRR IS A BIO-SENTIENT MATHEMATICAL EQUATION FIRST DISCOVERED BY THE MAD MATHEMATICIAN TIMPH RYE, WHO SOUGHT TO PROVE THAT WILLPOWER COULD BE DERIVED FORMULAICALLY. DKRTZY HAS BEEN KNOWN TO INVADE THE BRAINS OF HIS ENEMIES AND ERAS THEM, A SUBJECT OF MUCH DEBATE ACROSS OA.
ART BY JOE PRADO.

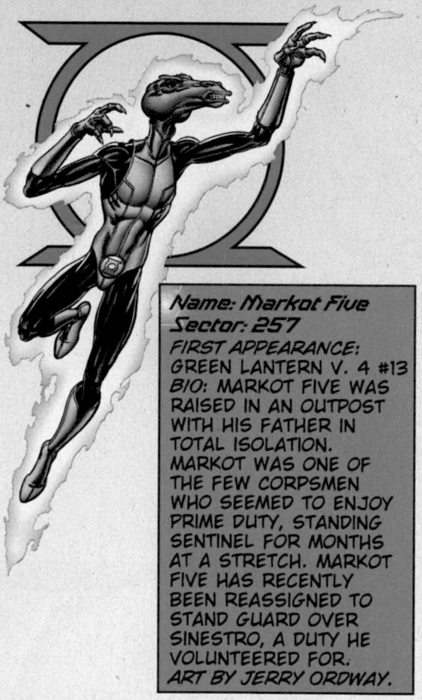

Name: Markot Five Sector: 257
FIRST APPEARANCE:
GREEN LANTERN V. 4 #13
BIO: MARKOT FIVE WAS RAISED IN AN OUTPOST WITH HIS FATHER IN TOTAL ISOLATION. MARKOT WAS ONE OF THE FEW CORPSMEN WHO SEEMED TO ENJOY PRIME DUTY, STANDING SENTINEL FOR MONTHS AT A STRETCH. MARKOT FIVE HAS RECENTLY BEEN REASSIGNED TO STAND GUARD OVER SINESTRO, A DUTY HE VOLUNTEERED FOR.
ART BY JERRY ORDWAY.

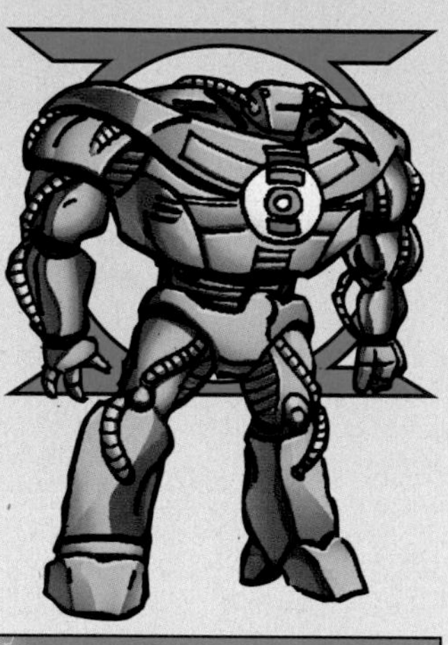

Name: RRU-9-2 Sector: 279
FIRST APPEARANCE:
GUY GARDNER #11
BIO: RRU-9-2 IS A ROBOTIC LAW ENFORCEMENT UNIT. COLD AND STERILE, RRU-9-2 IS RUMORED TO HAVE BEEN A MANHUNTER. THOSE RUMORS ARE WIDELY BELIEVED TO BE TRUE, AND FEW TRUST OR AGREE TO WORK WITH RRU-9-2.
ART BY JOE STATON AND TERRY BEATTY.

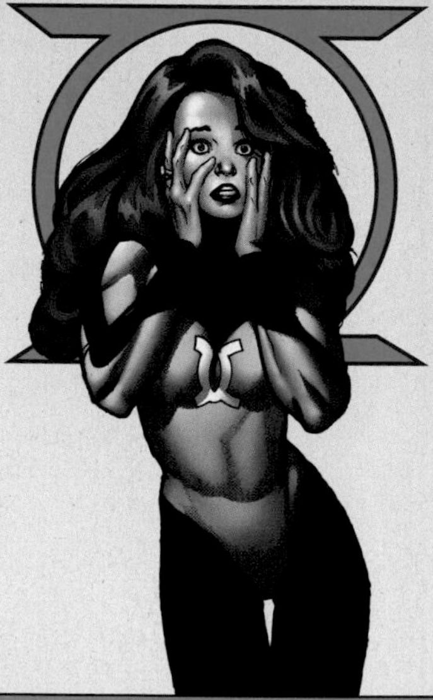

Name: Alia Sector: 281
FIRST APPEARANCE: VALOR #5
BIO: ALIA IS A BEING OF PURE ENERGY. AFTER A HORRIFIC CONFRONTATION WITH A CREATURE KNOWN AS THE UNIMAGINABLE LEFT HER MORTALLY WOUNDED, ALIA RETREATED INTO HER RING. SHE NOW INHABITS HER POWER RING.
ART BY ADAM HUGHES.

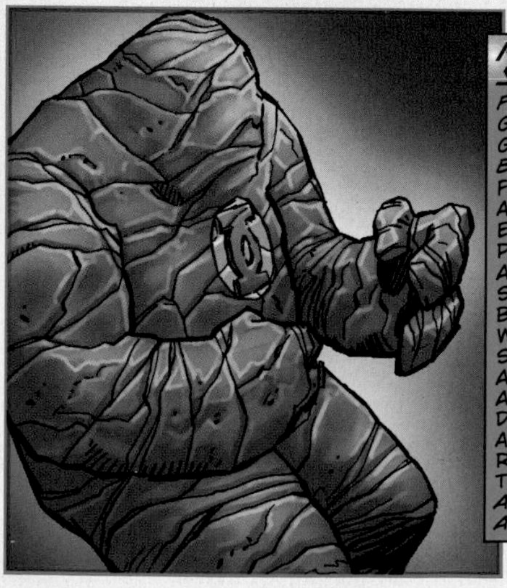

Name: Ash-Pak-Glif Sector: 312
FIRST APPEARANCE:
GREEN LANTERN 80-PAGE GIANT #3
BIO: LIVING ON A FRAGMENTARY WORLD, ASH-PAK-GLIF WAS ENLISTED TO FIGHT AS PART OF A CORPS ARMY ATTACKING APOKOLIPS. HE SURVIVED THE ATTEMPT BUT IS OFTEN FOUND WANDERING OUT OF HIS SECTOR PURSUING AND ATTACKING PARADEMONS AND OTHER SERVANTS TO DARKSEID. FOR THIS, ASH-PAK-GLIF HAS BEEN REPRIMANDED SEVERAL TIMES.
ART BY GRAHAM NOLAN AND KEITH AIKEN.

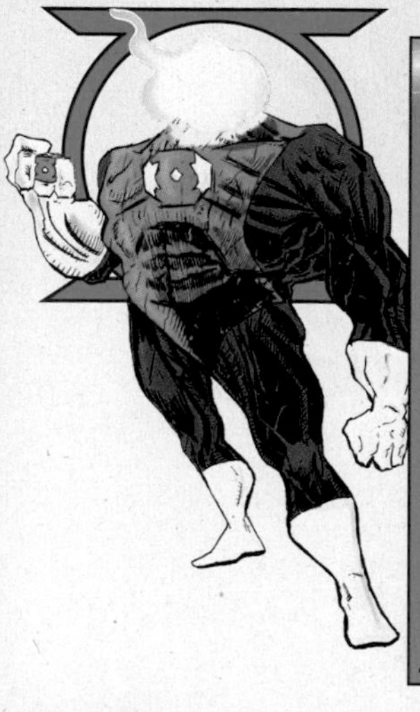

Name: Volk Sector: 315
FIRST APPEARANCE:
GREEN LANTERN V. 2 #190
BIO: SPRINGING FROM THE VOLCANIC FIELDS OF MAAG, VOLK IS LIVING LAVA INSIDE A SHELL OF ORGANIC ROCK. BECAUSE OF THE MASSIVE HEAT HE GENERATES, VOLK MUST PLACE A PROTECTIVE SHIELD AROUND HIMSELF WHILE WORKING WITH OTHER LANTERNS. THE BOUNTY HUNTER KNOWN AS THE IGNEOUS MAN HAILS FROM VOLK'S SECTOR.
ART BY DEZI SIENTY.

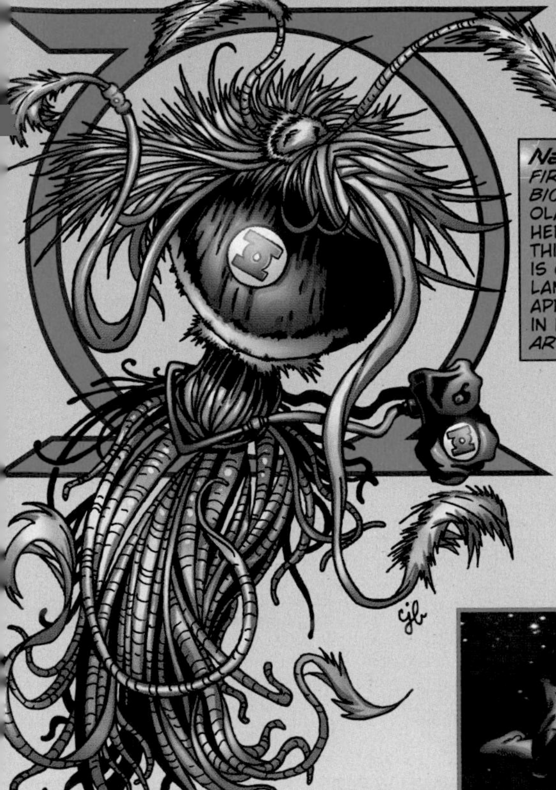

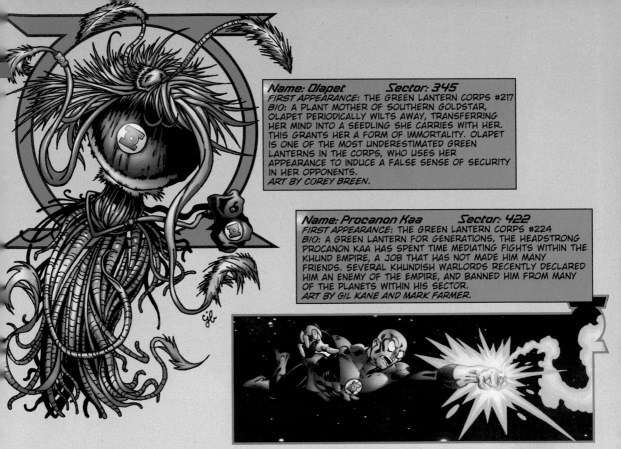

Name: Olapet **Sector: 345**
FIRST APPEARANCE: THE GREEN LANTERN CORPS #217
BIO: A PLANT MOTHER OF SOUTHERN GOLDSTAR, OLAPET PERIODICALLY WILTS AWAY, TRANSFERRING HER MIND INTO A SEEDLING SHE CARRIES WITH HER. THIS GRANTS HER A FORM OF IMMORTALITY. OLAPET IS ONE OF THE MOST UNDERESTIMATED GREEN LANTERNS IN THE CORPS, WHO USES HER APPEARANCE TO INDUCE A FALSE SENSE OF SECURITY IN HER OPPONENTS.
ART BY COREY BREEN.

Name: Procanon Kaa **Sector: 422**
FIRST APPEARANCE: THE GREEN LANTERN CORPS #224
BIO: A GREEN LANTERN FOR GENERATIONS, THE HEADSTRONG PROCANON KAA HAS SPENT TIME MEDIATING FIGHTS WITHIN THE KHUND EMPIRE, A JOB THAT HAS NOT MADE HIM MANY FRIENDS. SEVERAL KHUNDISH WARLORDS RECENTLY DECLARED HIM AN ENEMY OF THE EMPIRE, AND BANNED HIM FROM MANY OF THE PLANETS WITHIN HIS SECTOR.
ART BY GIL KANE AND MARK FARMER.

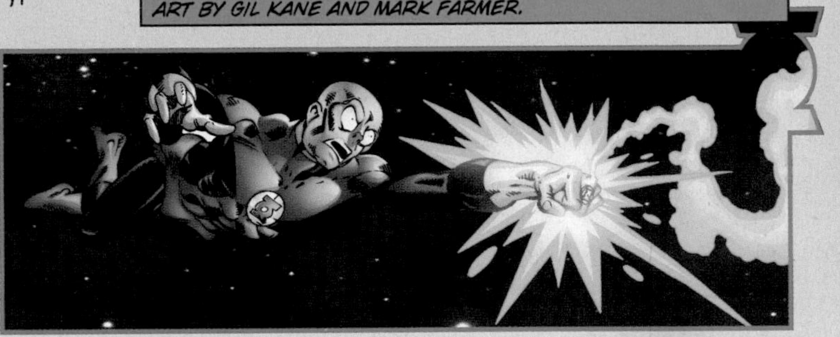

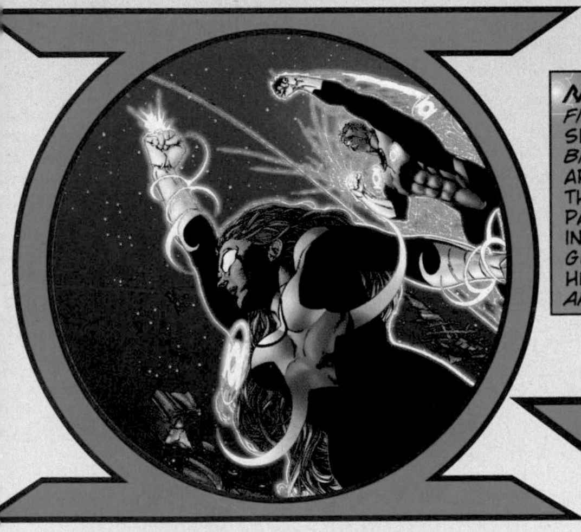

Name: Vode-M **Sector: 424**
FIRST APPEARANCE: GREEN LANTERN: SINESTRO CORPS SPECIAL #1
BIO: VODE-M IS GRAF TOREN'S APPRENTICE AND NEW TO HER STUDIES IN THE LIGHT. WHEN SHE BECAME GRAF'S PARTNER, SHE WAS OVERLY AGGRESSIVE IN THE ONGOING JIHAD WITH THE SPIDER GUILD, AND HAS BEEN FORCED TO PUT HER FRIENDS AND FAMILY INTO HIDING.
ART BY ETHAN VAN SCIVER.

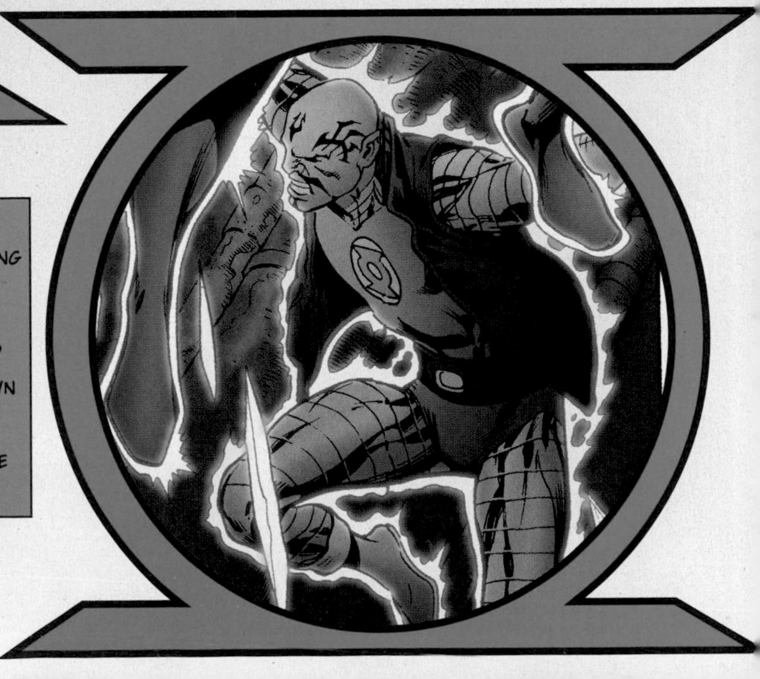

Name: Graf Toren **Sector: 424**
FIRST APPEARANCE: GUY GARDNER #11
BIO: GRAF IS A KARAXIAN LIGHT MONK, DEVOTING AS MUCH OF HIS LIFE STUDYING THE WAYS OF THE LIGHT AS HE SPENDS STRIVING TO DEFEAT THE SPIDER GUILD. HE IS SKILLED IN ANCIENT TEXTS AND UNIVERSAL HISTORY. THOUGHT KILLED BY PARALLAX, GRAF TOREN WAS FOUND BEING HELD IN STASIS ON THE MANHUNTER WORLD, BIOT, AND SET FREE. IT IS WELL KNOWN THAT THE PRICE PUT ON THE HEAD OF GRAF TOREN BY THE SPIDER GUILD EXCEEDS EVERY OTHER KNOWN PRICE ON A GREEN LANTERN. GRAF WEAVES HIS CONSTRUCTS MUCH LIKE THE SPIDER GUILD WEAVES THEIR WEBS.
ART BY IVAN REIS AND OCLAIR ALBERT.

Name: Charqwep **Sector:** 501
FIRST APPEARANCE: GREEN LANTERN V. 2 #150
BIO: CHARQWEP ONCE INVADED QWARD TO STOP A GROUP OF ROGUE WEAPONEERS. DURING THEIR BATTLE, ONE OF HIS MIND-PODS WAS DAMAGED, AND HE HAS HAD TROUBLE CONTROLLING HIS RING CONSTRUCTS EVER SINCE.
ART BY JOE STATON AND MIKE DECARLO.

Name: Arx **Sector:** 488
FIRST APPEARANCE: GREEN LANTERN CORPS #1
BIO: BORN A TWIN ON THE PLANET THORR'G, THE MUSCLE BOUND ARX WAS DELIGHTED WHEN HIS BROTHER WAS NOT CHOSEN TO BE A GREEN LANTERN BECAUSE THAT SELECTION ALLOWED HIM TO SURPASS HIS BROTHER IN YET ANOTHER AREA. HIS COMPETITIVE SPIRIT GAVE ARX A MASSIVE EDGE WHEN TRAINING TO BECOME A GREEN LANTERN, BUT HE HAS YET TO LEARN THE MEANING OF CAMARADERIE.
ART BY ANGEL UNZUETA.

Name: Rees-Van **Sector:** 567
FIRST APPEARANCE: GREEN LANTERN V. 4 #11
BIO: OFTEN MISTAKEN AS UNINTELLIGENT BECAUSE OF HIS APPEARANCE, THE MASSIVE REES-VAN IS A SCHOLAR OF 10TH LEVEL INTELLIGENCE, SPECIALIZING IN THE HISTORY OF THE GREEN LANTERN CORPS. REES-VAN HAS BEEN PETITIONING FOR AN AUDIENCE WITH THE GUARDIANS RECENTLY BECAUSE OF RUMORS REGARDING THEIR REMOVAL OF PAGES FROM THE SACRED BOOK OF OA.
ART BY ANGEL UNZUETA.

Name: Voz **Sector:** 571
FIRST APPEARANCE: GUY GARDNER #11
BIO: AFTER HELPING TO BRING THE MALEVOLENT ALIEN RACE KNOWN AS THE DRAAL TO JUSTICE, VOZ DECIDED HE WOULD TAKE ON MORE OA-CENTRIC RESPONSIBILITY, AND HE NOW OPERATES AS THE WARDEN OF THE NEW SCIENCELLS. THE INMATES WILL GENERALLY SPEAK OUT TO VOX ONCE AND THEN QUICKLY LEARN THEIR LESSON.
ART BY RYAN SOOK.

Name: Medphyll
Sector: 586
FIRST APPEARANCE: GREEN LANTERN V. 2 #11
BIO: A SENTIENT PLANT, MEDPHYLL IS A HIGHLY EXPERIENCED AND LAUDED GREEN LANTERN. MEDPHYLL POSSESSES A NATURAL ABILITY TO TRANSFER HIS THOUGHT-ESSENCE TO ANY NEARBY PLANT LIFE, A USEFUL TALENT WHEN IT COMES TO BATTLING THE INHABITANTS OF HIS SECTOR, THE WARRING APPELLAXIANS.
ART BY PARIS CULLINS AND RODIN RODRIGUEZ.

Name: Ash **Sector:** 650
FIRST APPEARANCE: GREEN LANTERN CORPS QUARTERLY #7
BIO: ASH WAS A FARMER BEFORE HIS WIFE WAS MURDERED BY A VAMPIRE. WHEN HE WAS CHOSEN FOR THE CORPS, ASH BEGAN HIS CRUSADE AGAINST VAMPIRES. ASH EVENTUALLY DISCOVERED THAT HIS WIFE'S KILLER WAS A DISCIPLE OF THE SPACE VAMPIRE STARBREAKER, AND HE HAS SWORN REVENGE ON HIM AND ALL OF HIS FOLLOWERS.
ART BY TONY HARRIS.

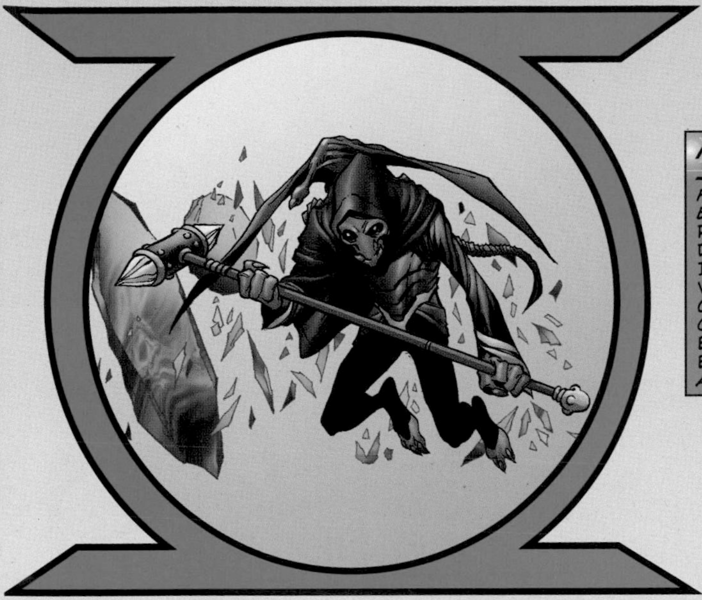

Name: Morro
Sector: 666
FIRST APPEARANCE: GREEN LANTERN V. 4 #12
BIO: MORRO COMES FROM THE DESERT PLANET SARC. HIS FOUR PETS, CALLED DRATURES, ARE ALSO NATIVE TO HIS PLANET. IT IS WHISPERED IN THE HALLWAYS THAT HE VOLUNTEERED FOR HIS DUTY AS CRYPT-KEEPER OF THE GREEN LANTERN CORPS, BUT SO FAR NO SUPPORTING EVIDENCE HAS BEEN DISCOVERED. MORRO EATS LUNCH ALONE.
ART BY IVAN REIS AND OCLAIR ALBERT.

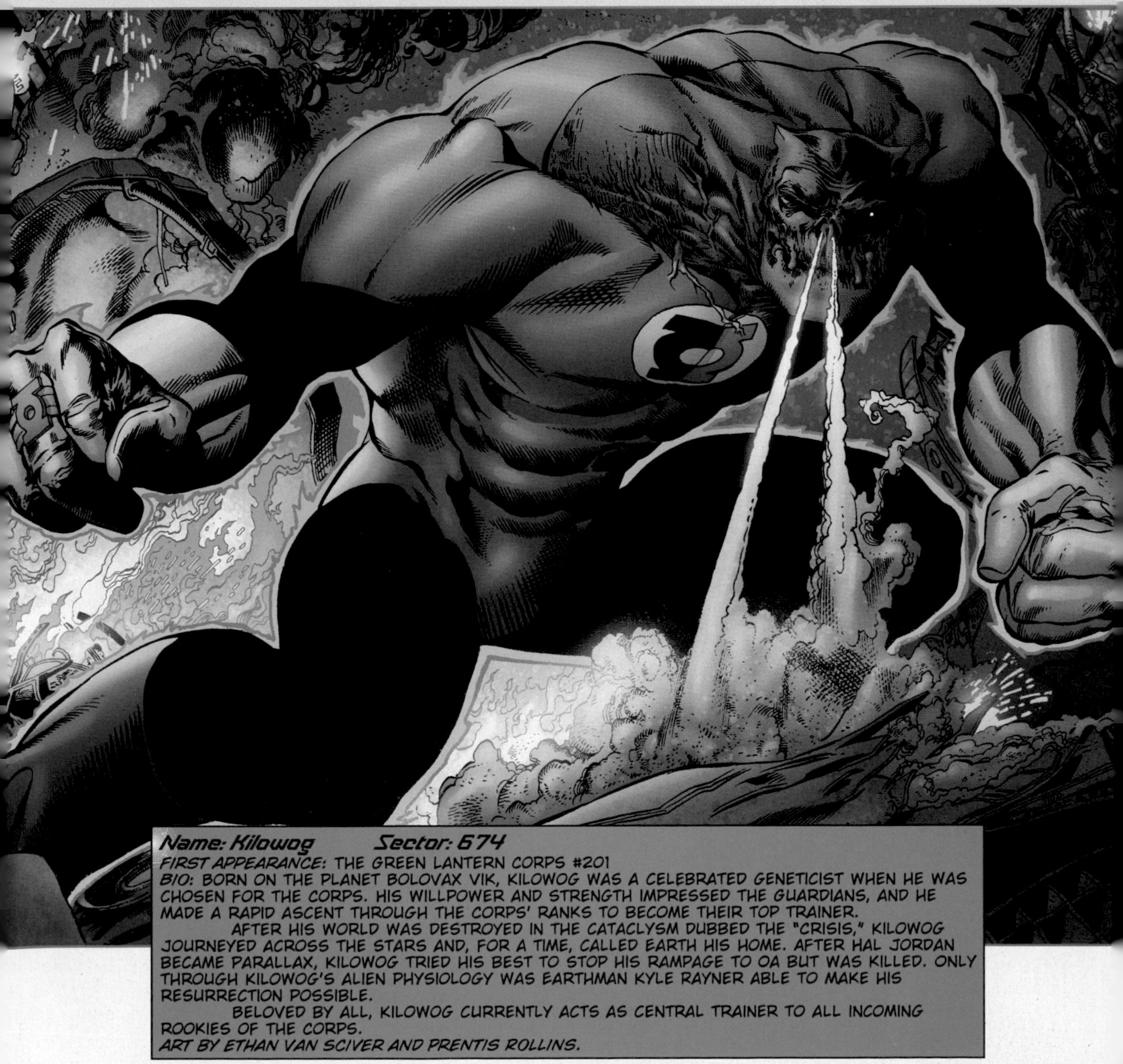

Name: Kilowog ***Sector: 674***
FIRST APPEARANCE: THE GREEN LANTERN CORPS #201
BIO: BORN ON THE PLANET BOLOVAX VIK, KILOWOG WAS A CELEBRATED GENETICIST WHEN HE WAS CHOSEN FOR THE CORPS. HIS WILLPOWER AND STRENGTH IMPRESSED THE GUARDIANS, AND HE MADE A RAPID ASCENT THROUGH THE CORPS' RANKS TO BECOME THEIR TOP TRAINER.

AFTER HIS WORLD WAS DESTROYED IN THE CATACLYSM DUBBED THE "CRISIS," KILOWOG JOURNEYED ACROSS THE STARS AND, FOR A TIME, CALLED EARTH HIS HOME. AFTER HAL JORDAN BECAME PARALLAX, KILOWOG TRIED HIS BEST TO STOP HIS RAMPAGE TO OA BUT WAS KILLED. ONLY THROUGH KILOWOG'S ALIEN PHYSIOLOGY WAS EARTHMAN KYLE RAYNER ABLE TO MAKE HIS RESURRECTION POSSIBLE.

BELOVED BY ALL, KILOWOG CURRENTLY ACTS AS CENTRAL TRAINER TO ALL INCOMING ROOKIES OF THE CORPS.
ART BY ETHAN VAN SCIVER AND PRENTIS ROLLINS.

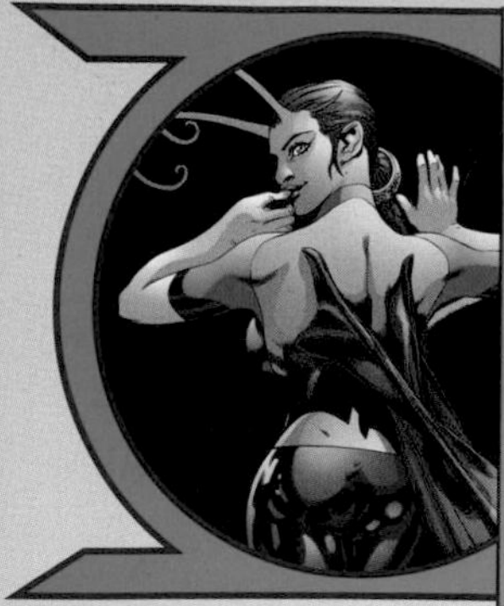

Name: R'amey Holl
Sector: 700

FIRST APPEARANCE: GREEN LANTERN CORPS #7
BIO: R'AMEY HOLL SERVED AS A LAW OFFICER ON THE PLANET PAPILLIOX BEFORE BECOMING A MEMBER OF THE COVERT GREEN LANTERN GROUP NAMED "THE CORPSE." LAST SEEN BY GUY GARDNER, SHE HASN'T BEEN HEARD FROM IN ALMOST A YEAR, BUT GIVEN THE DEEP UNDERCOVER WORK THE CORPSE DOES, NO ONE HAS YET BEGUN SEARCHING FOR HER.
ART BY PATRICK GLEASON AND WAYNE FAUCHER.

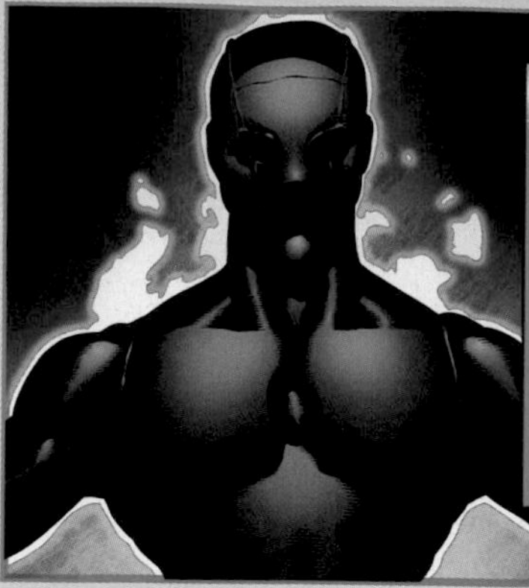

Name: Von Daggle
Sector: 700

FIRST APPEARANCE: GREEN LANTERN CORPS #7
BIO: A FOUNDING MEMBER OF THE COVERT GREEN LANTERN GROUP CALLED "THE CORPSE," VON DAGGLE ACTS IN DEEP COVER, USING HIS NATURAL DURLAN SHAPE-SHIFTING ABILITIES TO DISGUISE HIMSELF.
ART BY PATRICK GLEASON AND PRENTIS ROLLINS.

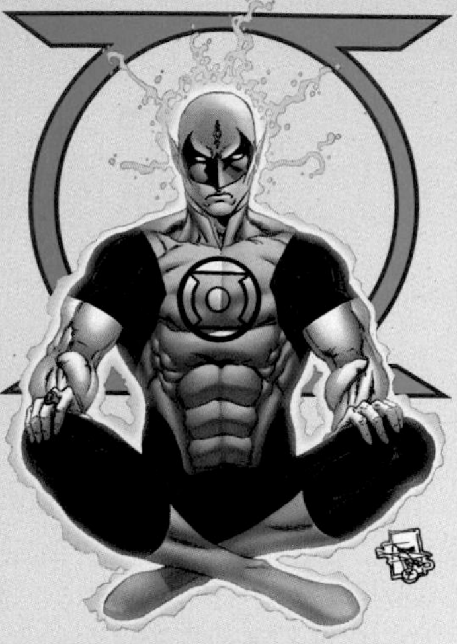

Name: Saarek
Sector: 773

FIRST APPEARANCE: GREEN LANTERN V. 2 #90
BIO: SAAREK RELENTLESSLY HUNTS FOR SECRETS OF DEATH IN THE UNIVERSE AND HAS BEEN AWAY FROM OA FOR YEARS, KEEPING IN CONTACT WITH ONLY THE GUARDIANS VIA HIS NATURAL TELEPATHY. HE CLAIMS TO HAVE USED HIS TELEPATHY TO MAKE CONTACT WITH THE DEAD. MOST DISMISS HIS CLAIMS AS THOSE OF A MADMAN.
ART BY JOE PRADO.

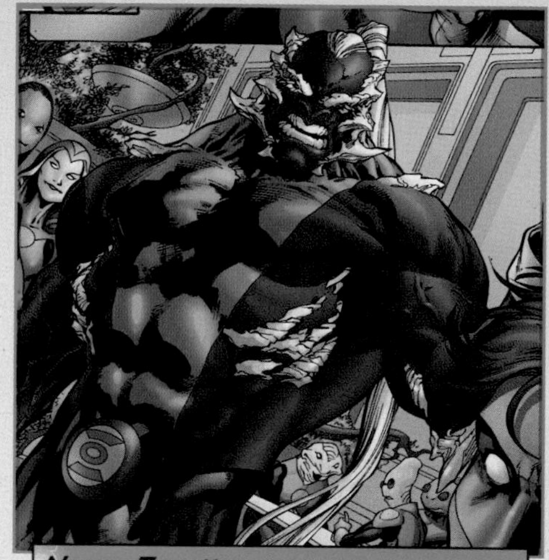

Name: Turytt
Sector: 786

FIRST APPEARANCE: GREEN LANTERN V. 4 #11
BIO: THE MASSIVE TURYTT IS KE'HAAN'S SUCCESSOR AND STILL HARBORS A DEEP RESENTMENT AGAINST HAL JORDAN FOR KE'HAAN'S LONG-TERM DISAPPEARANCE, A FACT HE REMINDS JORDAN OF EVERY TIME HE SEES HIM. ALTHOUGH KE'HAAN DIED AT THE HANDS OF THE ANTI-MONITOR, TURYTT STILL BLAMES JORDAN FOR HIS DEATH. TURYTT LED A VIGIL FOR ALL OF THE FALLEN CORPSMEN THE NIGHT AFTER SINESTRO WAS DEFEATED.
ART BY IVAN REIS AND OCLAIR ALBERT.

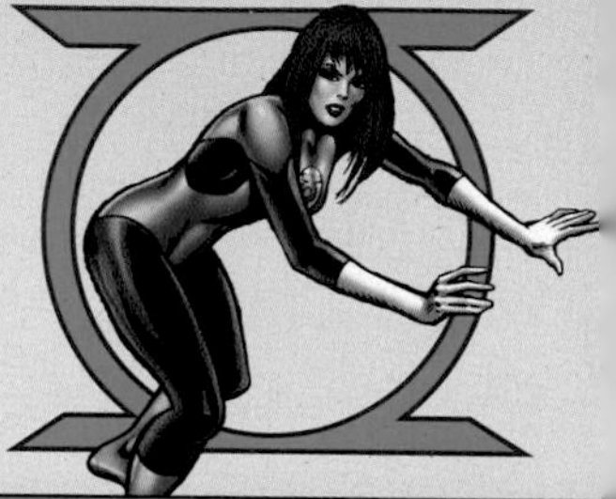

Name: Krista X Sector: 863

FIRST APPEARANCE: GREEN LANTERN V. 2 #166
BIO: KRISTA X WAS ONCE PART OF A SECRET PSYCHOLOGICAL TESTING DIVISION OF THE GREEN LANTERN CORPS, BUT AFTER SEEING SEVERAL OF THE GUARDIANS' "PSYCHODRAMAS" FAIL AND BACKFIRE, SHE QUIT IN DISGUST. THE GUARDIANS HAVE REPEATEDLY ORDERED KRISTA TO RETURN TO HER POSITION, BUT SHE REFUSES, AND SHE NOW AVOIDS OA ALTOGETHER, RETURNING ONLY AT THE CALLING OF A CODE ZERO, A DIRECT ATTACK ON THE PLANET ITSELF.
ART BY GEORGE TUSKA AND FRANK MCLAUGHLIN.

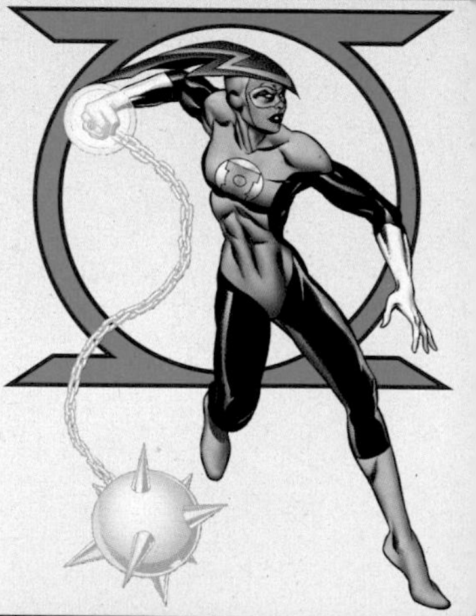

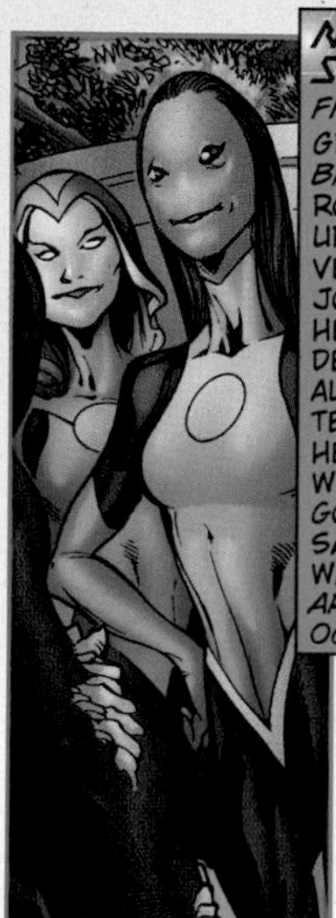

Name: Horoq Nnot
Sector: 885

FIRST APPEARANCE: GREEN LANTERN V. 4 #11
BIO: HOROQ NNOT WAS A ROOKIE LANTERN SWEPT UP IN TURYTT'S PERSONAL VENDETTA AGAINST HAL JORDAN. SHE EARNED HERSELF SEVENTY DEMERITS IN THE PROCESS. ALTHOUGH SHE HAS SINCE TEMPERED HER BEHAVIOR, HER TENDENCY TO RUN WITH THE PACK HAS NOT GONE UNNOTICED BY SALAAK, WHO KEEPS A WATCHFUL EYE ON HER.
ART BY IVAN REIS AND OCLAIR ALBERT.

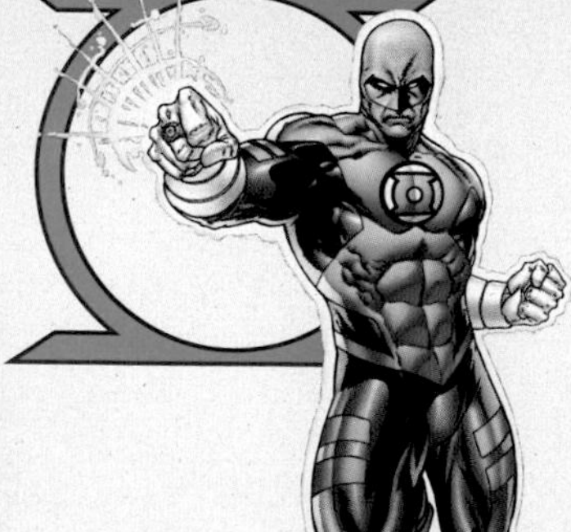

Name: Aa Sector: 904

FIRST APPEARANCE: GREEN LANTERN V. 3 #21
BIO: AA OF STONEWORLD ONCE LEFT THE CORPS BECAUSE OF IDEOLOGICAL DIFFERENCES, BUT RETURNED AS A GREEN LANTERN IN ORDER TO SHARE DIFFERING VIEWPOINTS AND IDEAS WITH FELLOW CORPSMEN. AA'S BODY IS COMPLETELY SOLID, WITH NO INTERNAL ORGANS TO SPEAK OF. THIS IS NOT AS UNCOMMON AS ONE MIGHT IMAGINE.
ART BY JOE PRADO.

Name: Brik Sector: 904

FIRST APPEARANCE: GREEN LANTERN V. 3 #12
BIO: BRIK COMES FROM THE PLANET DRYAD AND, LIKE HER SECTOR PARTNER, IS COMPOSED ENTIRELY OF ORGANIC ROCK. ORIGINALLY RECRUITED BY HAL JORDAN, BRIK WAS ONE OF HUNDREDS OF VETERAN GREEN LANTERNS TO RETURN TO ACTIVE SERVICE UPON THE RECENT RESTORATION OF THE GREEN LANTERN CORPS. BRIK ONCE HAD FEELINGS FOR JORDAN, AND HER PARTNER, AA, SUSPECTS THAT SHE STILL MIGHT. IN TRUTH, HER FEELINGS ARE FOR ANOTHER EARTHMAN.
ART BY ALECIA RODRIGUEZ AND PRENTIS ROLLINS.

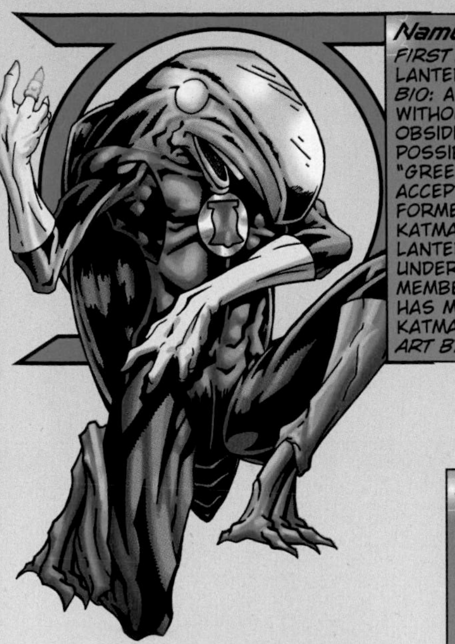

Name: Rot Lop Fan Sector: 911

FIRST APPEARANCE: TALES OF THE GREEN LANTERN CORPS ANNUAL #3

BIO: A BLIND INHABITANT OF A PLACE WITHOUT COLOR OR LIGHT CALLED THE OBSIDIAN DEEPS, ROT LOP FAN COULDN'T POSSIBLY UNDERSTAND THE CONCEPT OF A "GREEN LANTERN" AND WAS UNABLE TO ACCEPT RECRUITMENT INTO THE CORPS. THE FORMER GREEN LANTERN OF KORUGAR, KATMA TUI, INGENIOUSLY ALTERED THE LANTERN TO BE A CONCEPT FAN COULD UNDERSTAND, AND NOW HE'S THE ONLY MEMBER OF THE F-SHARP BELL CORPS. FAN HAS MADE PILGRIMAGE TO KORUGAR IN KATMA TUI'S NAME SEVERAL TIMES.

ART BY COREY BREEN.

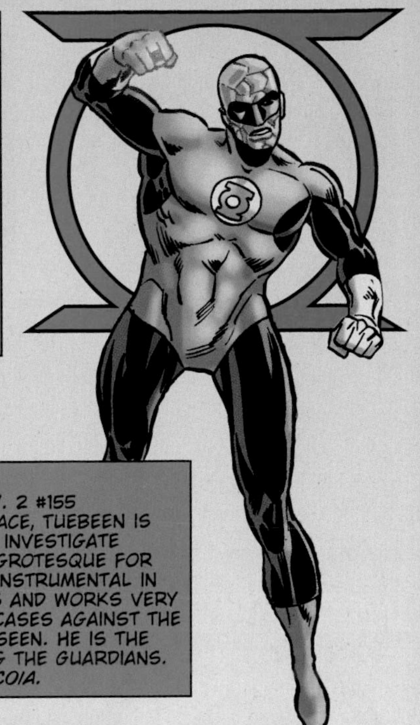

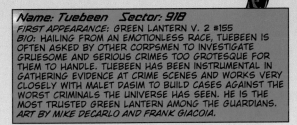

Name: Tuebeen Sector: 918

FIRST APPEARANCE: GREEN LANTERN V. 2 #155

BIO: HAILING FROM AN EMOTIONLESS RACE, TUEBEEN IS OFTEN ASKED BY OTHER CORPSMEN TO INVESTIGATE GRUESOME AND SERIOUS CRIMES TOO GROTESQUE FOR THEM TO HANDLE. TUEBEEN HAS BEEN INSTRUMENTAL IN GATHERING EVIDENCE AT CRIME SCENES AND WORKS VERY CLOSELY WITH MALET DASIM TO BUILD CASES AGAINST THE WORST CRIMINALS THE UNIVERSE HAS SEEN. HE IS THE MOST TRUSTED GREEN LANTERN AMONG THE GUARDIANS.

ART BY MIKE DECARLO AND FRANK GIACOIA.

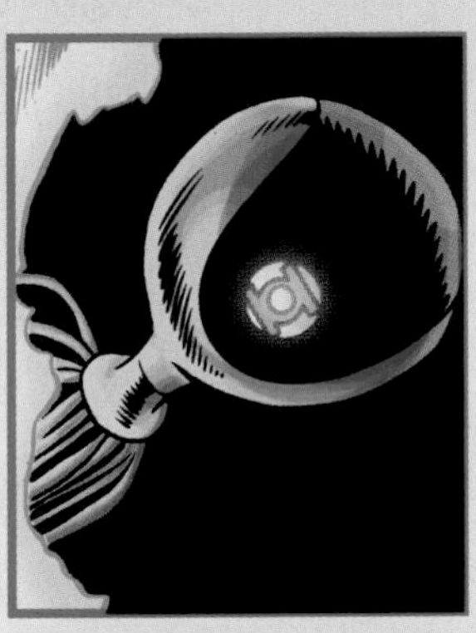

Name: Brokk
Sector: 981

FIRST APPEARANCE: TALES OF THE GREEN LANTERN CORPS #1

BIO: BROKK USES ITS LONG, EMPATHIC TENTACLES TO AID IT IN ITS DUTY AS A "LIVING AMBULANCE," SOOTHING THE INJURED AS IT CARRIES THEM FROM THE BATTLEFIELD TO SAFETY. BROKK WORKED OVERTIME RECENTLY AFTER THE SINESTRO CORPS' OAN INVASION AND WAS RESPONSIBLE FOR SAVING THE LIVES OF HUNDREDS OF CORPSMEN.

ART BY JOE STATON AND FRANK MCLAUGHLIN.

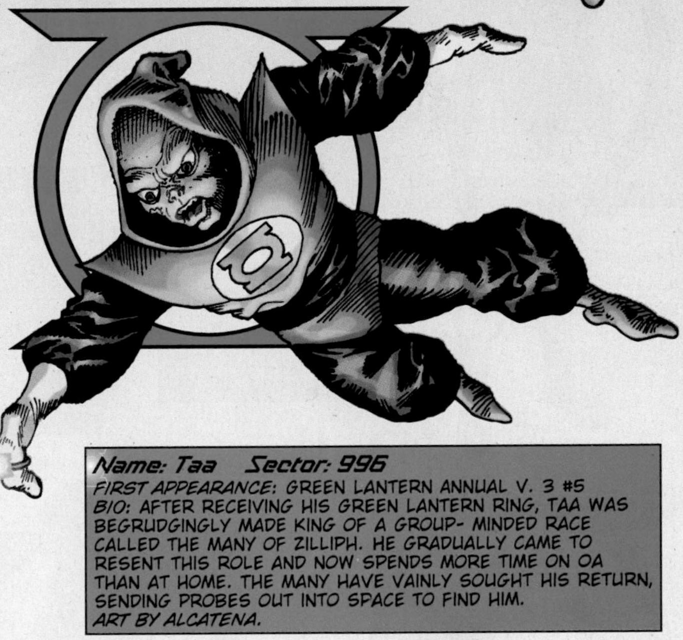

Name: Taa Sector: 996

FIRST APPEARANCE: GREEN LANTERN ANNUAL V. 3 #5

BIO: AFTER RECEIVING HIS GREEN LANTERN RING, TAA WAS BEGRUDGINGLY MADE KING OF A GROUP- MINDED RACE CALLED THE MANY OF ZILLIPH. HE GRADUALLY CAME TO RESENT THIS ROLE AND NOW SPENDS MORE TIME ON OA THAN AT HOME. THE MANY HAVE VAINLY SOUGHT HIS RETURN, SENDING PROBES OUT INTO SPACE TO FIND HIM.

ART BY ALCATENA.

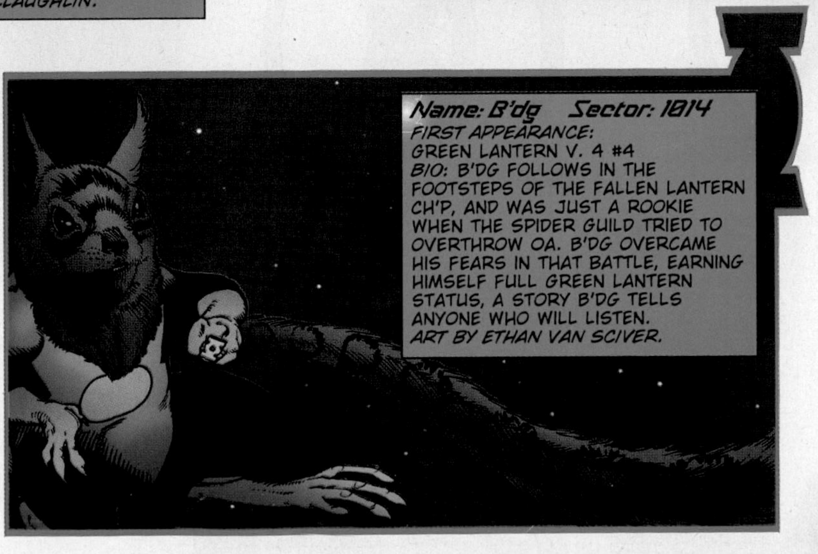

Name: B'dg Sector: 1014

FIRST APPEARANCE: GREEN LANTERN V. 4 #4

BIO: B'DG FOLLOWS IN THE FOOTSTEPS OF THE FALLEN LANTERN CH'P, AND WAS JUST A ROOKIE WHEN THE SPIDER GUILD TRIED TO OVERTHROW OA. B'DG OVERCAME HIS FEARS IN THAT BATTLE, EARNING HIMSELF FULL GREEN LANTERN STATUS, A STORY B'DG TELLS ANYONE WHO WILL LISTEN.

ART BY ETHAN VAN SCIVER.

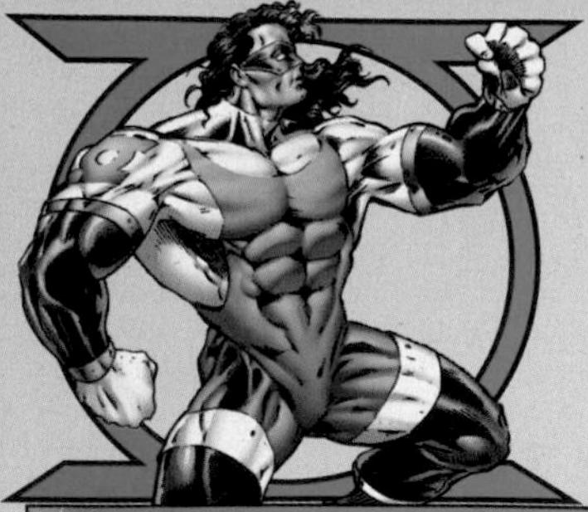

Name: Sir Deeter Sector: 1110
FIRST APPEARANCE: GREEN LANTERN V. 2 #162
BIO: DEETER SPENT THE FORMATIVE YEARS OF HIS LIFE WORKING AS APPRENTICE UNDER HIS MASTER OKONOKO. AFTER EARNING HIS GREEN LANTERN STATUS, DEETER HELPED PRINCESS ORYNA OVERTHROW HER TYRANNICAL FATHER, KING GARZOUM. THE TWO FELL IN LOVE AND MARRIED, AND DEETER WAS KNIGHTED SOON AFTER. OF LATE, SIR DEETER HAS ELECTED TO SPEND MORE TIME AT HOME AFTER HEARING RUMORS OF A RESURGENCE OF GARZOUM'S FORCES.
ART BY TOM FEISTER.

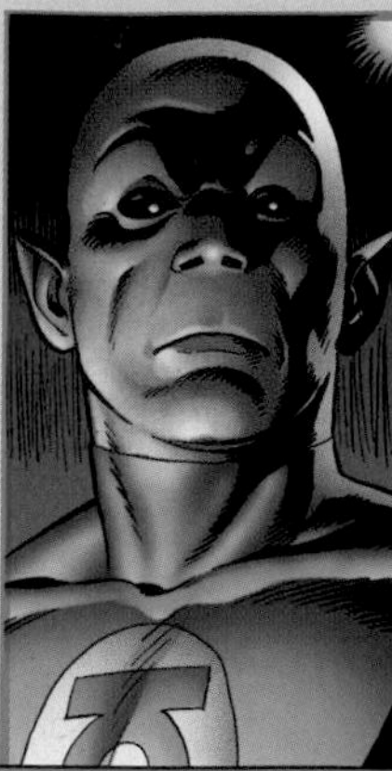

Name: Adam Sector: 1055
FIRST APPEARANCE:
GREEN LANTERN CORPS QUARTERLY #5
BIO: ADAM IS THE ONLY KNOWN MEMBER OF A RACE THAT REINCARNATES OVER AND OVER ENDLESSLY AFTER EACH DEATH. UNFORTUNATELY, MEMORIES DON'T TRANSFER FROM REGENERATION TO REGENERATION, SO ADAM HAS PROGRAMMED HIS POWER RING TO FILL HIM IN EVERY TIME HE'S REBORN. THE NEWEST INCARNATION OF ADAM, HOWEVER, HAS YET TO REPORT BACK TO OA AFTER BEING DESTROYED BY THE ANTI-MONITOR ON EARTH.
ART BY FRANCHESCO.

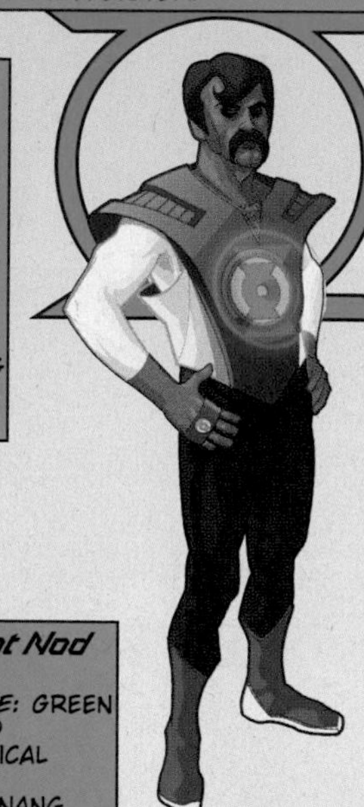

Name: Okonoko Sector: 1110
FIRST APPEARANCE: GREEN LANTERN V. 2 #162
BIO: A HIGHLY DECORATED CORPSMAN, OKONOKO SPENT YEARS TRAINING HIS APPRENTICE, DEETER, TO BE AN EVEN BETTER GREEN LANTERN THAN HE. OKONOKO RETIRED WHEN DEETER EARNED HIS LANTERN STATUS, BUT WAS HAPPILY RECRUITED BACK INTO THE CORPS WHEN THEY RETURNED. IT WAS A LIFE HE HAD MISSED. HE WAS HORRIFIED TO LEARN OF THE SINESTRO CORPS' CREATION, AND HAS VOLUNTEERED TO TRACK THE YELLOW RINGS SEARCHING FOR NEW RECRUITS THROUGHOUT HIS SECTOR.
ART BY DAVE GIBBONS.

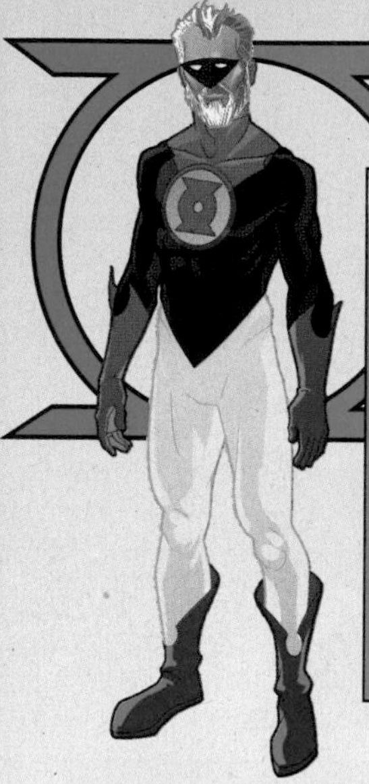

Name: Remnant Nod
Sector: 1132
FIRST APPEARANCE: GREEN LANTERN V. 2 #170
BIO: ONCE A POLITICAL PRISONER ON HIS HOMEWORLD OF Z'NANG, REMNANT STOOD FOR TRUTH, JUSTICE, AND DIGNITY EVEN IN THE FACE OF HIS OPPRESSORS. HE BECAME A GREEN LANTERN FOLLOWING THE DEATH OF MEENO MORAK AND HAS SINCE BEEN USING HIS POWER RING TO LEAD POLITICAL UPRISINGS TO RESTORE THE GOVERNMENT OF Z'NANG.
ART BY TOM FEISTER.

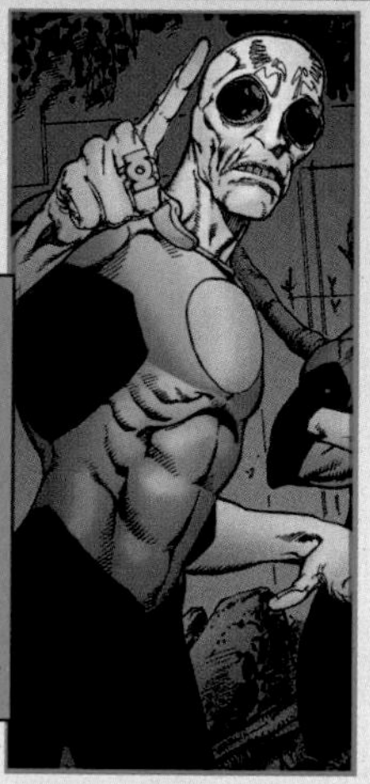

Name: Grumb
Sector: 1198
FIRST APPEARANCE:
GREEN LANTERN V. 4 #4
BIO: GRUMB WAS A SOLDIER IN THE NAMELESS ARMY WHEN HE WAS DRAFTED INTO THE CORPS, AND FOR THE FIRST FEW MONTHS OF HIS LIFE AS A GREEN LANTERN, HE DIDN'T EVEN HAVE A NAME. GRUMB HAS DREAMS OF WORKING ALONGSIDE KILOWOG AS A TRAINER.
ART BY ETHAN VAN SCIVER.

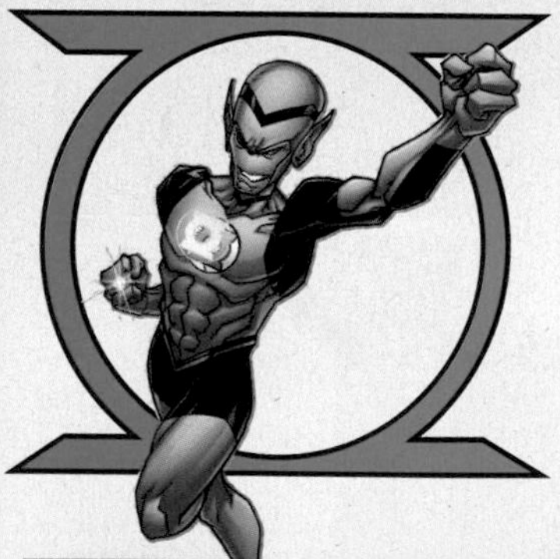

Name: Rori Stroh
Sector: 1234
FIRST APPEARANCE: GREEN LANTERN V. 2 #9
BIO: RORI STROH WAS BORN ON ROJIRA, ONE OF THE MOST ADVANCED SCIENTIFIC CIVILIZATIONS IN THE UNIVERSE. RORI'S PARENTS NAMED HIM AFTER RORI DAG, ONE OF THE FOUNDING GREEN LANTERNS, AND RORI STROH DOES HIS BEST TO LIVE UP TO HIS NAMESAKE. HIS ONGOING EXPERIMENTS WITH BLACK HOLES HAVE CAUSED WAVES IN THE SCIENTIFIC COMMUNITY, SOME CLAIMING HE IS PLAYING WITH FORCES BIGGER THAN THE GUARDIANS THEMSELVES. IF THEY LET THEMSELVES FEEL EMOTION, THE GUARDIANS WOULD FIND THIS HUMOROUS.
ART BY JONBOY MEYER.

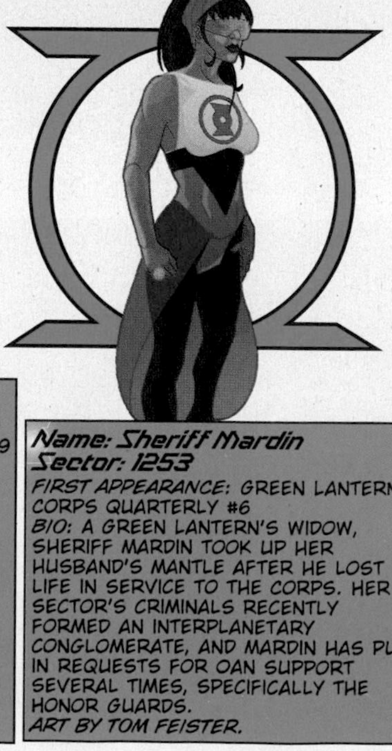

Name: Sheriff Mardin
Sector: 1253
FIRST APPEARANCE: GREEN LANTERN CORPS QUARTERLY #6
BIO: A GREEN LANTERN'S WIDOW, SHERIFF MARDIN TOOK UP HER HUSBAND'S MANTLE AFTER HE LOST HIS LIFE IN SERVICE TO THE CORPS. HER SECTOR'S CRIMINALS RECENTLY FORMED AN INTERPLANETARY CONGLOMERATE, AND MARDIN HAS PUT IN REQUESTS FOR OAN SUPPORT SEVERAL TIMES, SPECIFICALLY THE HONOR GUARDS.
ART BY TOM FEISTER.

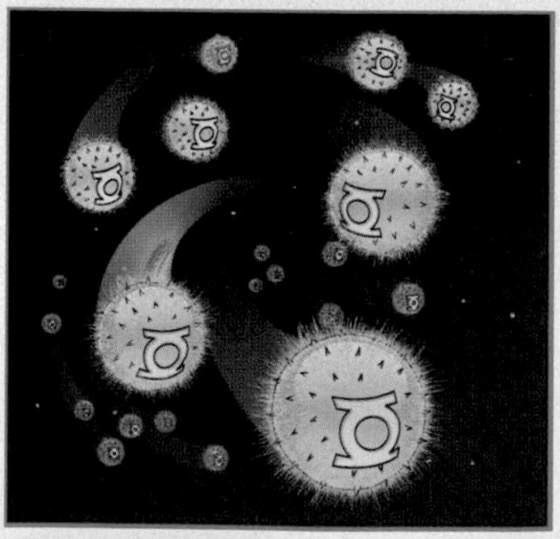

Name: The Collective
Sector: 1287
FIRST APPEARANCE: TALES OF THE GREEN LANTERN CORPS ANNUAL #3
BIO: THE COLLECTIVE IS A MASSIVE GROUP OF FLOATING ORBS THAT WERE GIVEN SENTIENT THOUGHT AND A POWER BATTERY BY THE DYING GREEN LANTERN TO-T-UK. THE COLLECTIVE EXPANDED ACROSS THEIR SECTOR, AND THEIR WIDESPREAD PRESENCE HAS MADE SECTOR 1287 ONE OF THE SAFEST IN THE UNIVERSE.
ART BY SONIA CHOI.

Name: T-Cher
Sector: 1324

FIRST APPEARANCE:
GREEN LANTERN V. 2 #167
BIO: T-CHER PRIVATELY TUTORED THE CHILDREN OF THE GREEN LANTERN BRIN FOR YEARS BEFORE THE GUARDIANS APPEARED AND CHOSE HIM TO JOIN THE CORPS AND TRAIN NEW RECRUITS. T-CHER NOW TRAINS POWER RING STRATEGIES, WORKING IN UNISON WITH APROS AND KILOWOG. HE WAS QUITE PLEASED TO SEE HOW WELL HIS STUDENTS FARED DURING THE SINESTRO CORPS WAR, BUT HAS SPENT TIME GRIEVING THE HEAVY LOSSES OF HIS FORMER STUDENTS.
ART BY DAVE GIBBONS.

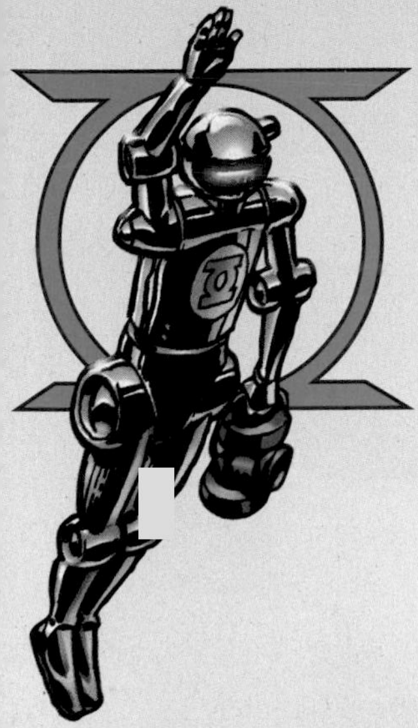

Name: Penelops
Sector: 1355

FIRST APPEARANCE: TALES OF THE GREEN LANTERN CORPS #3
BIO: PENELOPS IS A VETERAN GREEN LANTERN RE-RECRUITED WHEN THE CORPS RETURNED. HE'S A BEING OF EXTREME WILLPOWER, FAMOUS AROUND THE CORPS FOR USING HIS RING TO CHANGE HIS PLANET'S ORBIT WITH ONLY A STRAY THOUGHT. SEVERAL CORPSMEN HAVE ASKED PENELOPS TO TRAIN THEM PRIVATELY IN HOW TO USE THEIR WILLPOWER TO THE FULLEST, BUT PENELOPS HAS POLITELY REFUSED.
ART BY JEROME MOORE AND RODIN RODRIGUEZ.

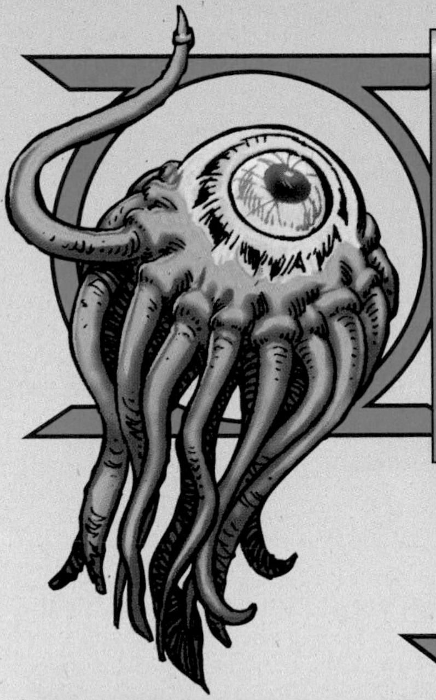

Name: Gk'd
Sector: 1337

FIRST APPEARANCE:
TALES OF THE GREEN LANTERN CORPS #1
BIO: GK'D OF FP'Y IS A FP'YAN EVALUATOR OF THE HIGHEST ORDER, AND IS SENT BY THE GUARDIANS TO ASSESS GREEN LANTERNS WHEN THEIR PERFORMANCE MIGHT NOT BE UP TO PAR. HE HAS GROWN TO DETEST THE EARTH GREEN LANTERNS, AS THEY ALL IMPATIENTLY SEND HIM AWAY EVERY TIME HE TRIES TO RUN AN EVALUATION.
ART BY JOE STATON AND FRANK MCLAUGHLIN.

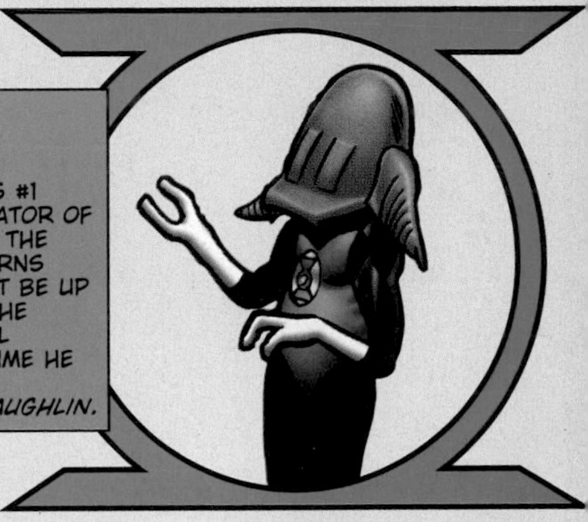

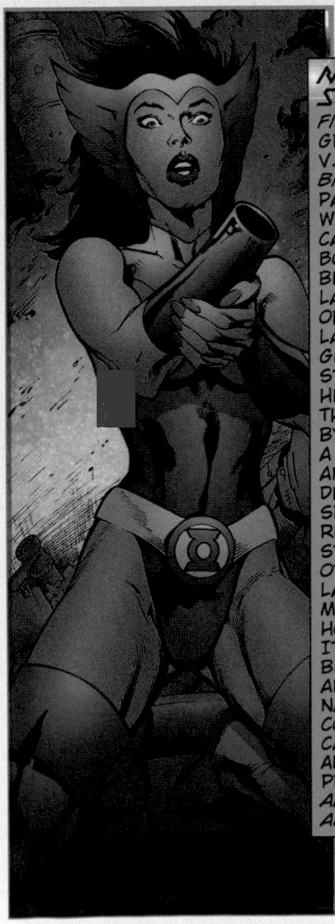

Name: Boodikka
Sector: 1414

FIRST APPEARANCE:
GREEN LANTERN V. 3 #20
BIO: BOODIKKA WAS PART OF A GROUP OF WARRIOR WOMEN CALLED THE BELLATRIX BOMBERS BEFORE BECOMING A GREEN LANTERN. SHE WAS ONE OF THE GREEN LANTERNS THE GUARDIANS CHOSE TO STOP HAL JORDAN AS HE RAMPAGED THROUGH THE GALAXY POSSESSED BY PARALLAX. SHE LOST A HAND IN THAT BATTLE, AND WAS LEFT FOR DEAD FLOATING IN SPACE. SHE WAS RECENTLY FOUND IN STASIS ALONGSIDE THE OTHER "LOST LANTERNS" ON THE MANHUNTER HOMEWORLD OF BIOT. IT'S RUMORED THAT BECAUSE OF HER GRUFF AND INQUISITIVE NATURE, THE GUARDIANS CONSIDER HER A PRIME CANDIDATE FOR THEIR ALPHA LANTERNS PROJECT.
ART BY IVAN REIS AND OCLAIR ALBERT.

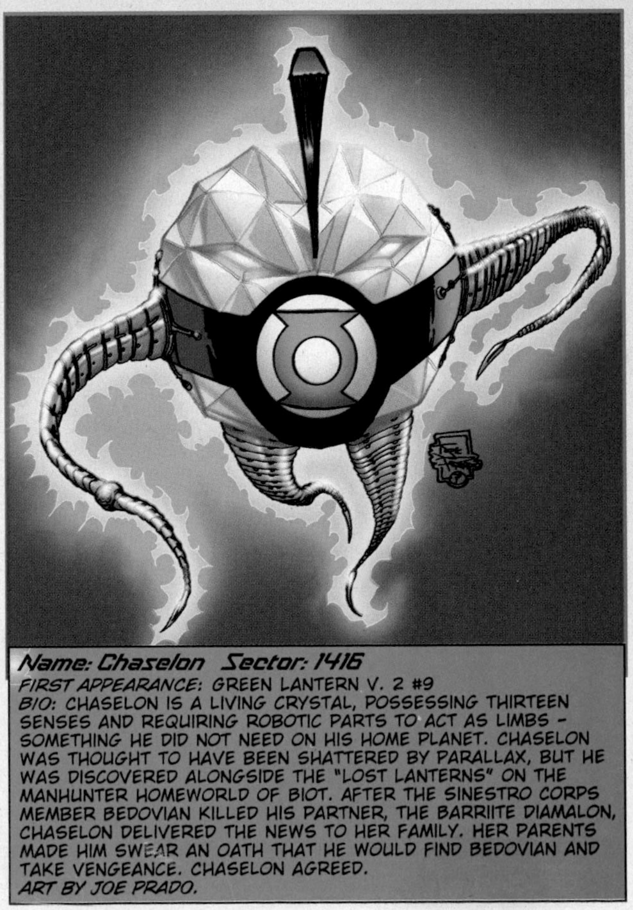

Name: Chaselon Sector: 1416

FIRST APPEARANCE: GREEN LANTERN V. 2 #9
BIO: CHASELON IS A LIVING CRYSTAL, POSSESSING THIRTEEN SENSES AND REQUIRING ROBOTIC PARTS TO ACT AS LIMBS - SOMETHING HE DID NOT NEED ON HIS HOME PLANET. CHASELON WAS THOUGHT TO HAVE BEEN SHATTERED BY PARALLAX, BUT HE WAS DISCOVERED ALONGSIDE THE "LOST LANTERNS" ON THE MANHUNTER HOMEWORLD OF BIOT. AFTER THE SINESTRO CORPS MEMBER BEDOVIAN KILLED HIS PARTNER, THE BARRIITE DIAMALON, CHASELON DELIVERED THE NEWS TO HER FAMILY. HER PARENTS MADE HIM SWEAR AN OATH THAT HE WOULD FIND BEDOVIAN AND TAKE VENGEANCE. CHASELON AGREED.
ART BY JOE PRADO.

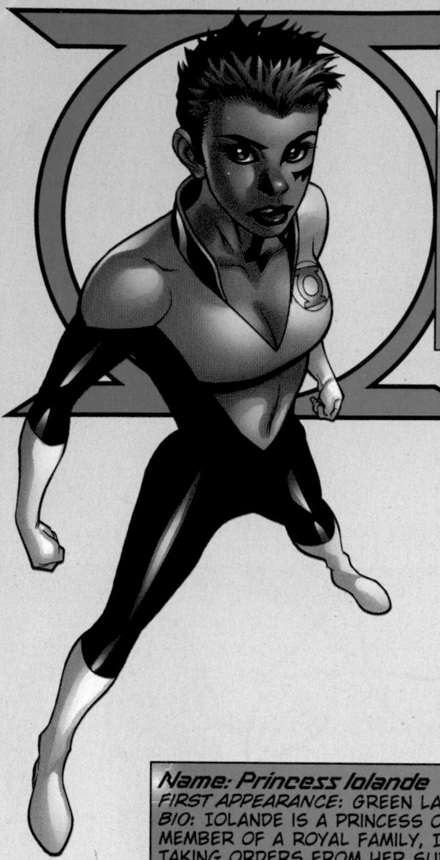

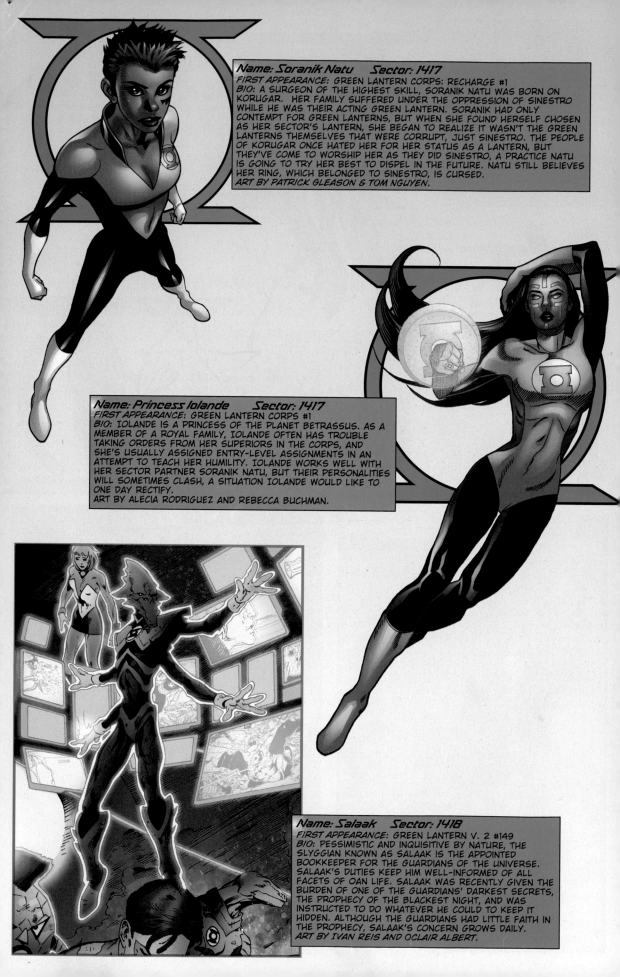

Name: Soranik Natu Sector: 1417

FIRST APPEARANCE: GREEN LANTERN CORPS: RECHARGE #1

BIO: A SURGEON OF THE HIGHEST SKILL, SORANIK NATU WAS BORN ON KORUGAR. HER FAMILY SUFFERED UNDER THE OPPRESSION OF SINESTRO WHILE HE WAS THEIR ACTING GREEN LANTERN. SORANIK HAD ONLY CONTEMPT FOR GREEN LANTERNS, BUT WHEN SHE FOUND HERSELF CHOSEN AS HER SECTOR'S LANTERN, SHE BEGAN TO REALIZE IT WASN'T THE GREEN LANTERNS THEMSELVES THAT WERE CORRUPT, JUST SINESTRO. THE PEOPLE OF KORUGAR ONCE HATED HER FOR HER STATUS AS A LANTERN, BUT THEY'VE COME TO WORSHIP HER AS THEY DID SINESTRO, A PRACTICE NATU IS GOING TO TRY HER BEST TO DISPEL IN THE FUTURE. NATU STILL BELIEVES HER RING, WHICH BELONGED TO SINESTRO, IS CURSED.

ART BY PATRICK GLEASON & TOM NGUYEN.

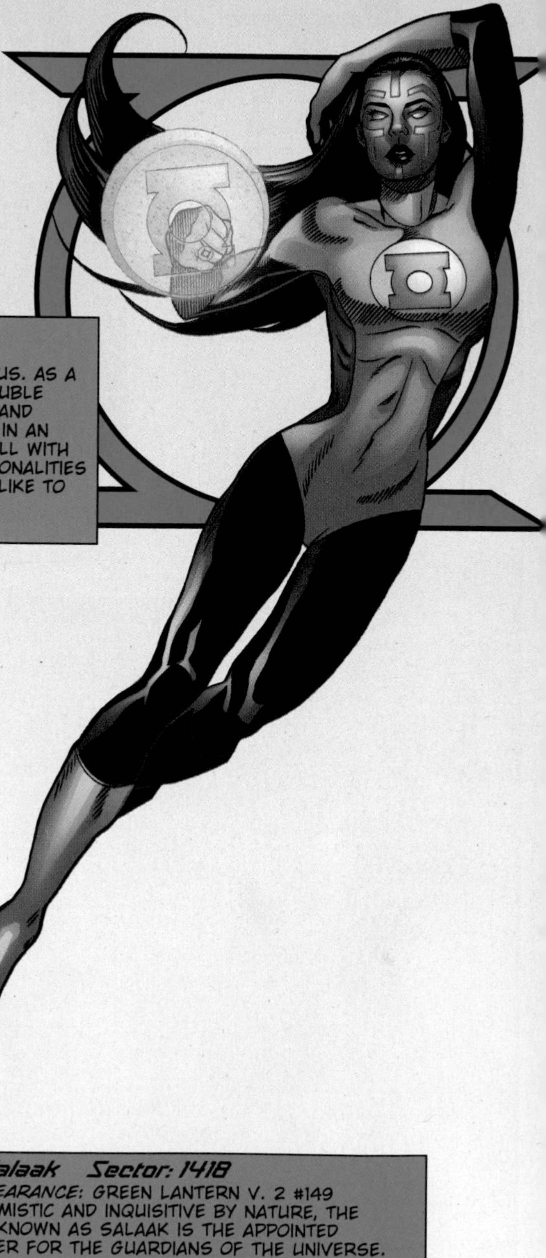

Name: Princess Iolande Sector: 1417

FIRST APPEARANCE: GREEN LANTERN CORPS #1

BIO: IOLANDE IS A PRINCESS OF THE PLANET BETRASSUS. AS A MEMBER OF A ROYAL FAMILY, IOLANDE OFTEN HAS TROUBLE TAKING ORDERS FROM HER SUPERIORS IN THE CORPS, AND SHE'S USUALLY ASSIGNED ENTRY-LEVEL ASSIGNMENTS IN AN ATTEMPT TO TEACH HER HUMILITY. IOLANDE WORKS WELL WITH HER SECTOR PARTNER SORANIK NATU, BUT THEIR PERSONALITIES WILL SOMETIMES CLASH, A SITUATION IOLANDE WOULD LIKE TO ONE DAY RECTIFY.

ART BY ALECIA RODRIGUEZ AND REBECCA BUCHMAN.

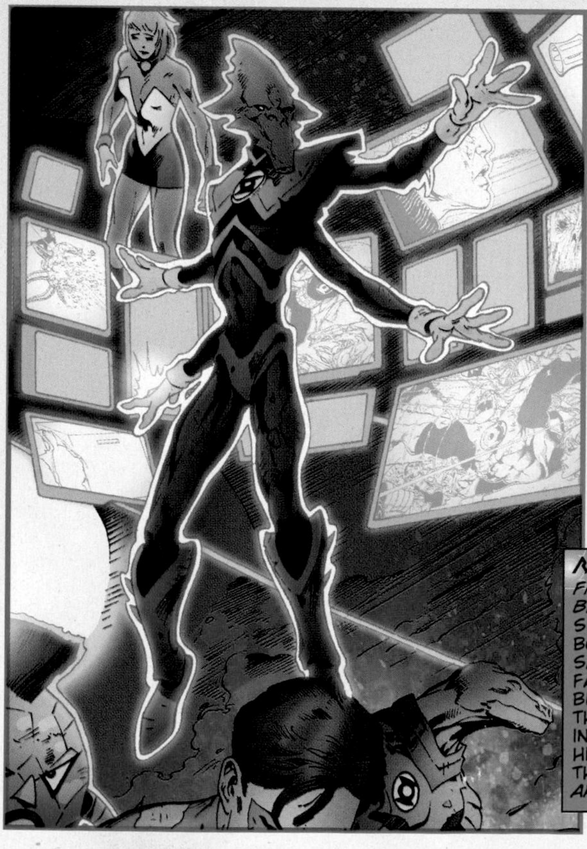

Name: Salaak Sector: 1418

FIRST APPEARANCE: GREEN LANTERN V. 2 #149

BIO: PESSIMISTIC AND INQUISITIVE BY NATURE, THE SLYGGIAN KNOWN AS SALAAK IS THE APPOINTED BOOKKEEPER FOR THE GUARDIANS OF THE UNIVERSE. SALAAK'S DUTIES KEEP HIM WELL-INFORMED OF ALL FACETS OF OAN LIFE. SALAAK WAS RECENTLY GIVEN THE BURDEN OF ONE OF THE GUARDIANS' DARKEST SECRETS, THE PROPHECY OF THE BLACKEST NIGHT, AND WAS INSTRUCTED TO DO WHATEVER HE COULD TO KEEP IT HIDDEN. ALTHOUGH THE GUARDIANS HAD LITTLE FAITH IN THE PROPHECY, SALAAK'S CONCERN GROWS DAILY.

ART BY IVAN REIS AND OCLAIR ALBERT.

Name: *Lin Canar   Sector: 1582*
FIRST APPEARANCE: GREEN LANTERN CORPS QUARTERLY #3
BIO: A GREEN LANTERN HAILING FROM THE OCEAN PLANET FLUVIAN, LIN CANAR IS A FAMED OCEANOGRAPHER, SPECIALIZING IN UNDERWATER ENERGY EXPULSION PHENOMENA. AS A RESULT OF ONE OF LIN'S EXPERIMENTS, AN UNDERWATER DISEASE WAS UNLEASHED, WHICH QUICKLY SPREAD THROUGH THE WATER. LIN CANAR QUARANTINED HIS HOME PLANET WHILE HE ATTEMPTS TO FIND A CURE.
ART BY DAVE COCKRUM AND BRAD VANCATA.

Name: *Kaylark   Sector: 1721*
FIRST APPEARANCE: GREEN LANTERN V. 2 #166
BIO: PARTICIPATING IN A PSYCHIC TEST DONE ON HAL JORDAN, KAYLARK ONCE POSED AS A GREEN LANTERN GONE MAD WITH POWER. JORDAN PASSED HER EVALUATION AND KAYLARK CONTINUED HER STUDIES INTO THE PSYCHE OF THE VARIOUS MEMBERS OF THE GREEN LANTERN CORPS. SHE WAS SHAKEN TO LEARN OF JORDAN'S DESCENT INTO THE SINISTER ENTITY KNOWN AS PARALLAX, AND SINCE REJOINING THE CORPS, SHE'S COME TO REALIZE THAT HE IS HER GREATEST FEAR.
ART BY GEORGE TUSKA AND FRANK MCLAUGHLIN.

Name: *Sodam Yat   Sector: 1760*
FIRST APPEARANCE: TALES OF THE GREEN LANTERN CORPS ANNUAL #2
BIO: A BOY WHO ONCE DREAMED OF WHAT WAS BEYOND THE STARS WAS FORBIDDEN TO LEAVE HIS HOME PLANET. AFTER DISCOVERING AN ALIEN CRASHED NEAR HIS HOME, SODAM HELPED FEED THE ALIEN AND BRING HIM BACK TO HEALTH. HIS PARENTS DISCOVERED THE ALIEN AND KILLED IT. SODAM SPENT THE REST OF HIS CHILDHOOD ATTEMPTING TO REBUILD THE ALIEN'S CRAFT AND LEAVE DAXAM. IRONICALLY, THE MOMENT HE FINISHED THE CRAFT, HE WAS CHOSEN TO BE A GREEN LANTERN. SODAM PROVED HIS MERIT TO THE GUARDIANS AND, NOTING HE WAS PROPHESIED TO BE THE ULTIMATE GREEN LANTERN, THEY EMPOWERED HIM WITH THE ION FORCE – THE LIVING EMBODIMENT OF WILLPOWER. DUE TO HIS EXPOSURE TO LEAD ON EARTH, EVEN WITH THE ION FORCE INSIDE HIM SODAM IS NOW REQUIRED TO WEAR A RING THAT HE CAN NEVER REMOVE. IF HE DOES, HE WILL DIE FROM LEAD POISONING WITHIN MINUTES.
ART BY PATRICK GLEASON.

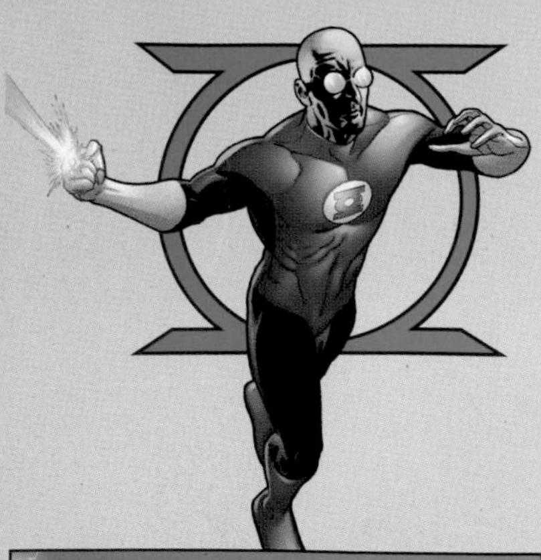

Name: Meadlux
Sector: 1776
FIRST APPEARANCE:
GREEN LANTERN V. 2 #169
BIO: A PSYCHOLOGICAL DOCTOR OF THE SIXTH DEGREE, MEADLUX IS EMPLOYED BY THE GUARDIANS TO HEAL ANY PSYCHIC DAMAGE THAT A GREEN LANTERN MIGHT HAVE SUFFERED IN THEIR TRAVELS. MEADLUX HAS PETITIONED THE GUARDIANS SEVERAL TIMES TO STUDY BOTH KYLE RAYNER AND HAL JORDAN AFTER THEIR EXPOSURE TO THE FEAR-BASED PARALLAX ENTITY, BUT THEY CONTINUALLY DENY HIS REQUEST.
ART BY RYAN SOOK.

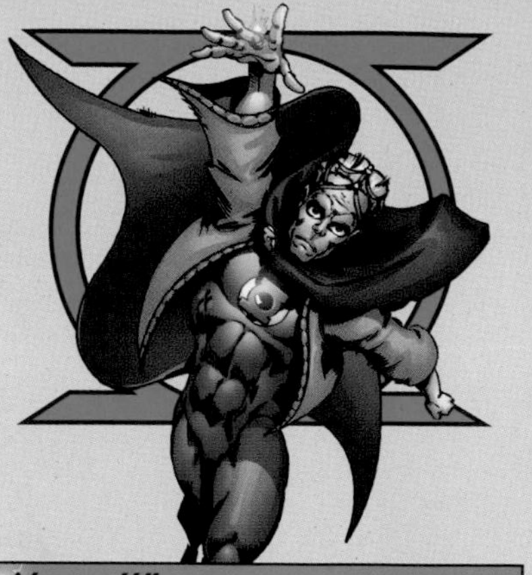

Name: Wissen
Sector: 1915
FIRST APPEARANCE: TALES OF THE GREEN LANTERN CORPS ANNUAL #3
BIO: WISSEN IS THE ELDERLY GREEN LANTERN FROM THE PLANET VELTRE. AFTER STOPPING A PLANETARY CIVIL WAR, HIS PEOPLE CAME TO THINK OF HIM AS A GOD. WISSEN CONVINCED THEM OF HIS HUMANITY AND RETURNED TO PATROLLING HIS SECTOR, UNCOMFORTABLE AT THE THOUGHT OF SOMEONE WORSHIPPING A BEING AS UNWORTHY AS HE.
ART BY NICK NAPOLITANO.

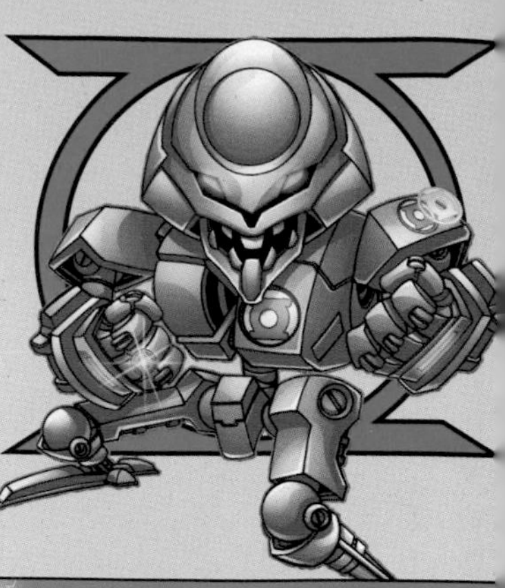

Name: Krydel-4
Sector: 2106
FIRST APPEARANCE:
GREEN LANTERN CORPS #1
BIO: IN THE FAR REACHES OF SECTOR 2106, A FORCE CALLED THE BLIGHT WAS OVERTAKING THE PLANETS, ASSIMILATING EVERY CIVILIZATION INTO THEIR ROBOTIC DRONE ARMY. KRYDEL-4 WAS SUCH A DRONE UNTIL HIS MIND WAS ABLE TO OVERCOME THE BLIGHT'S PROGRAMMING, AND HE LED A GROUP OF FREEDOM FIGHTERS THAT SEEMINGLY ENDED THE SCOURGE OF THE BLIGHT.
ART BY JONBOY MEYERS.

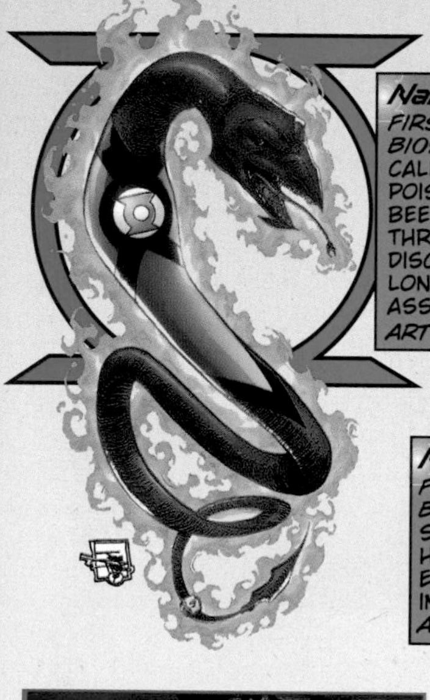

Name: Oliversity Sector: 2111
FIRST APPEARANCE: THE GREEN LANTERN CORPS #222
BIO: A MEMBER OF A RACE LONG THOUGHT EXTINCT CALLED SNARE SNAKES, OLIVERSITY IS ONE OF THE MOST POISONOUS REPTILES IN THE GALAXY. HIS VENOM HAS BEEN USED TO CREATE ANTITOXINS TO COMBAT DISEASE THROUGHOUT HIS SECTOR, BUT SOME SCIENTISTS HAVE DISCOVERED THAT THE ANTITOXINS MIGHT HAVE LONG-TERM HARMFUL EFFECTS ON ITS RECIPIENTS, AN ASSERTION OLIVERSITY IS STILL EXPLORING.
ART BY JOE PRADO.

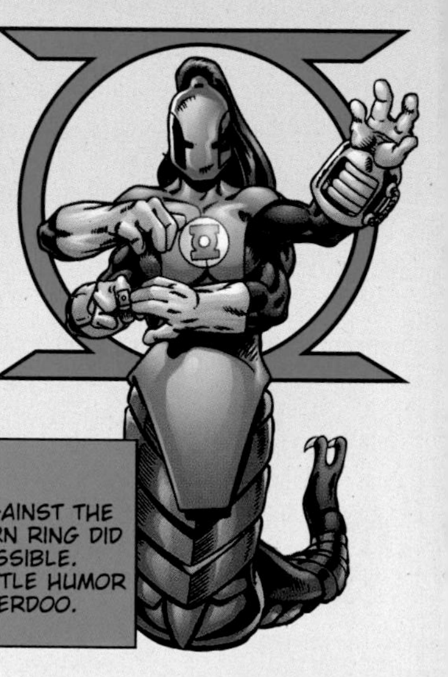

Name: El'qa Squa Zreenah Sector: 2234
FIRST APPEARANCE: GREEN LANTERN ANNUAL V. 3 #5
BIO: EL'QA SQUA ZREENAH SPENT HIS LIFE FIGHTING AGAINST THE STATEJIANS. ONLY WHEN HE RECEIVED A GREEN LANTERN RING DID HE REALIZE THAT THEIR DEFEAT MIGHT ACTUALLY BE POSSIBLE. EL'QA TAKES LIFE EXTREMELY SERIOUSLY AND FINDS LITTLE HUMOR IN IT, AN IDEA THAT BAFFLES HIS UNSTABLE PARTNER, PERDOO.
ART BY BILL WILLINGHAM AND ROBERT CAMPANELLA.

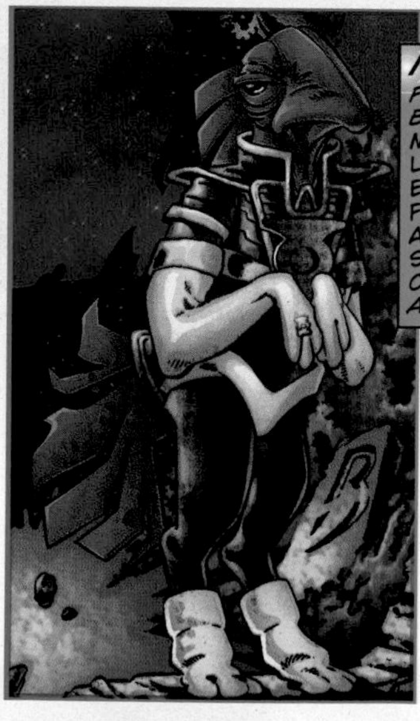

Name: Perdoo Sector: 2234
FIRST APPEARANCE: GREEN LANTERN ANNUAL V. 3 #5
BIO: HAVING SPENT MOST OF HIS LIFE CONFINED TO A MENTAL ASYLUM, THE GREEN LANTERN PERDOO WAS LEFT COMPLETELY WITHOUT FEAR FROM HIS EXPERIENCES THERE. OTHER LANTERNS SHY AWAY FROM HIM IN BATTLE, THOUGH, AS HIS CONSTRUCTS ARE OFTEN WILDLY UNPREDICTABLE AND HAVE BEEN SAID TO TURN AGAINST HIS FELLOW CORPSMEN, A CLAIM THAT IS MOST LIKELY AN EXAGGERATION.
ART BY BILL WILLINGHAM AND ROBERT CAMPANELLA.

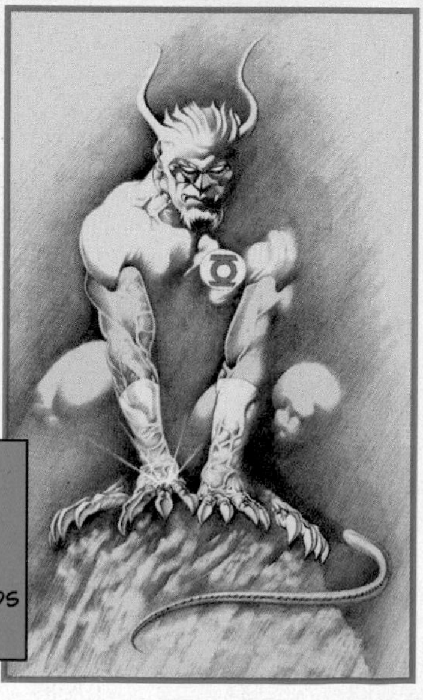

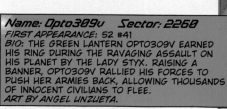

Name: Opto309v Sector: 2260
FIRST APPEARANCE: 52 #41
BIO: THE GREEN LANTERN OPTO309V EARNED HIS RING DURING THE RAVAGING ASSAULT ON HIS PLANET BY THE LADY STYX. RAISING A BANNER, OPTO309V RALLIED HIS FORCES TO PUSH HER ARMIES BACK, ALLOWING THOUSANDS OF INNOCENT CIVILIANS TO FLEE.
ART BY ANGEL UNZUETA.

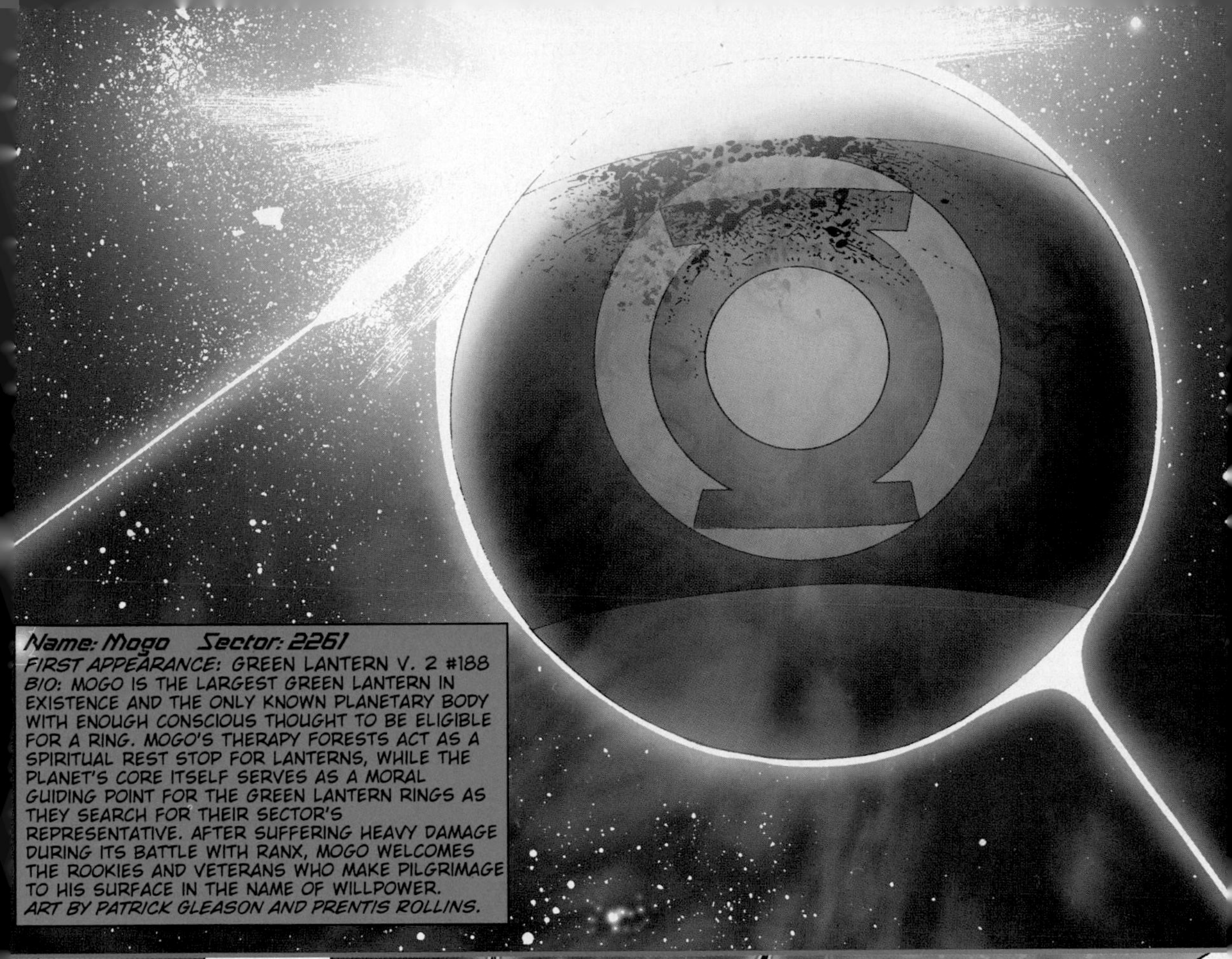
Name: Mogo Sector: 2261
FIRST APPEARANCE: GREEN LANTERN V. 2 #188
BIO: MOGO IS THE LARGEST GREEN LANTERN IN EXISTENCE AND THE ONLY KNOWN PLANETARY BODY WITH ENOUGH CONSCIOUS THOUGHT TO BE ELIGIBLE FOR A RING. MOGO'S THERAPY FORESTS ACT AS A SPIRITUAL REST STOP FOR LANTERNS, WHILE THE PLANET'S CORE ITSELF SERVES AS A MORAL GUIDING POINT FOR THE GREEN LANTERN RINGS AS THEY SEARCH FOR THEIR SECTOR'S REPRESENTATIVE. AFTER SUFFERING HEAVY DAMAGE DURING ITS BATTLE WITH RANX, MOGO WELCOMES THE ROOKIES AND VETERANS WHO MAKE PILGRIMAGE TO HIS SURFACE IN THE NAME OF WILLPOWER.
ART BY PATRICK GLEASON AND PRENTIS ROLLINS.

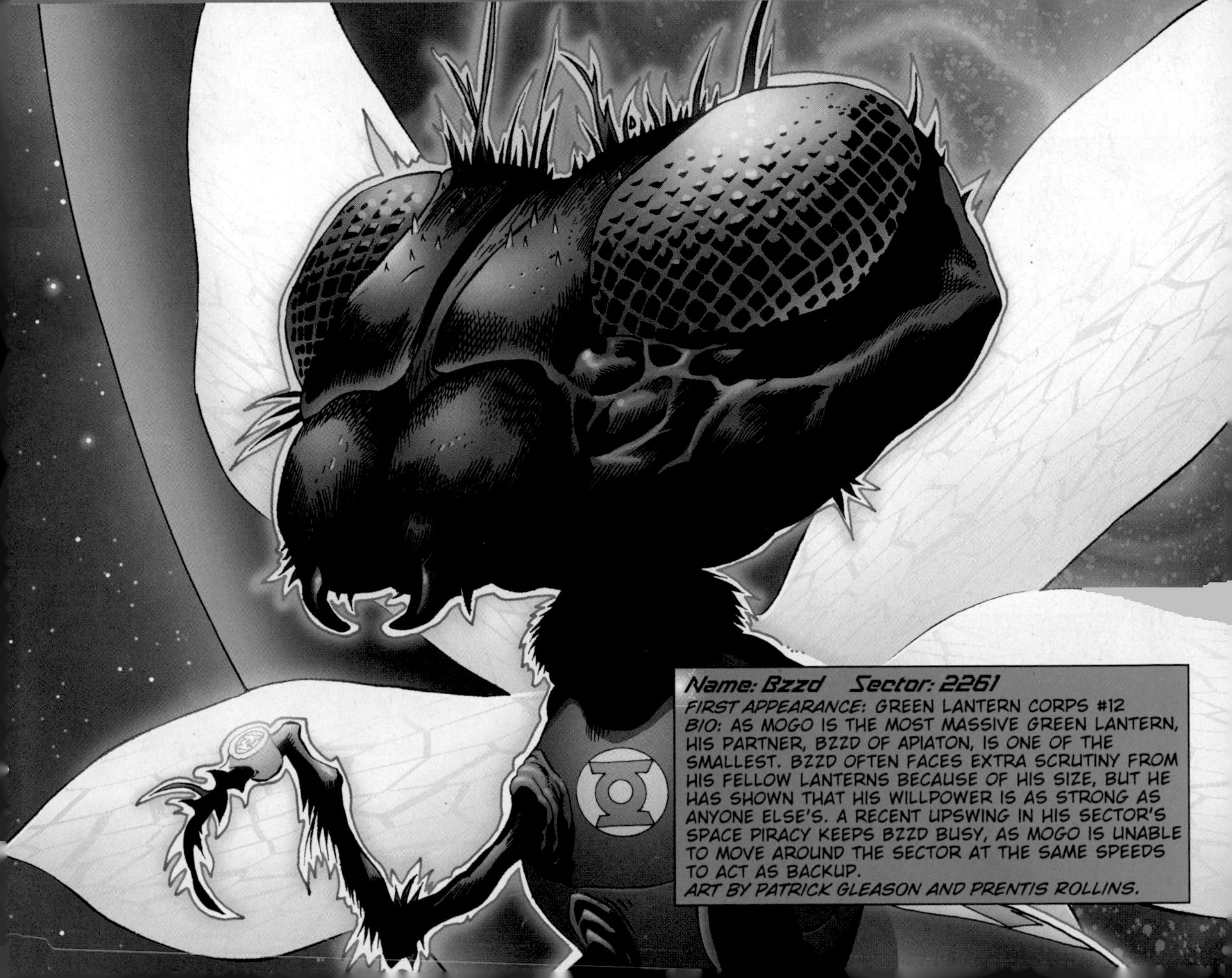
Name: Bzzd Sector: 2261
FIRST APPEARANCE: GREEN LANTERN CORPS #12
BIO: AS MOGO IS THE MOST MASSIVE GREEN LANTERN, HIS PARTNER, BZZD OF APIATON, IS ONE OF THE SMALLEST. BZZD OFTEN FACES EXTRA SCRUTINY FROM HIS FELLOW LANTERNS BECAUSE OF HIS SIZE, BUT HE HAS SHOWN THAT HIS WILLPOWER IS AS STRONG AS ANYONE ELSE'S. A RECENT UPSWING IN HIS SECTOR'S SPACE PIRACY KEEPS BZZD BUSY, AS MOGO IS UNABLE TO MOVE AROUND THE SECTOR AT THE SAME SPEEDS TO ACT AS BACKUP.
ART BY PATRICK GLEASON AND PRENTIS ROLLINS.

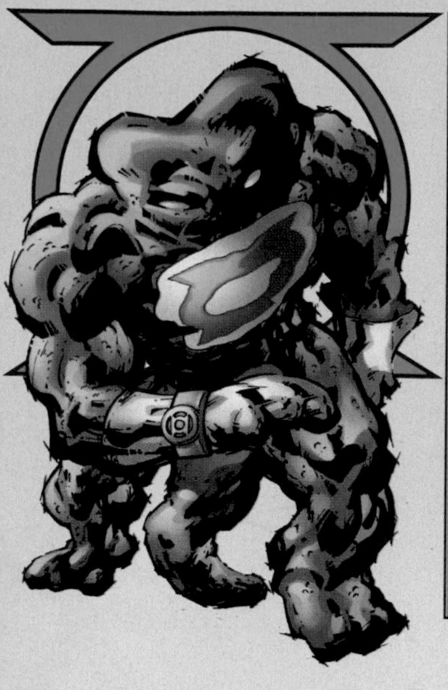

Name: Talmadge
Sector: 2471

FIRST APPEARANCE:
GREEN LANTERN V. 2 #190
BIO: A JANITOR IN AN ENERGY PRODUCTION PLANT ON HIS HOMEWORLD, TALMADGE NEVER THOUGHT HE WOULD AMOUNT TO ANYTHING. WHILE TRYING TO STOP AN EXPLOSION THAT WOULD VAPORIZE HIS CITY, THE WORLD WENT GREEN. TALMADGE THOUGHT HE WAS DEAD...UNTIL HE OPENED HIS EYES TO FIND HIMSELF AND HIS CITY STILL IN ONE PIECE, A GREEN AURA SURROUNDING HIM. HIS NEWLY-SENT POWER RING HAD STOPPED THE EXPLOSION. NOW A VETERAN MEMBER OF THE CORPS, THE MUSCLEBOUND TALMADGE PREFERS TO BE SENT INTO SITUATIONS THAT NEED TO BE "CLEANED UP."
ART BY FRED HAYNES.

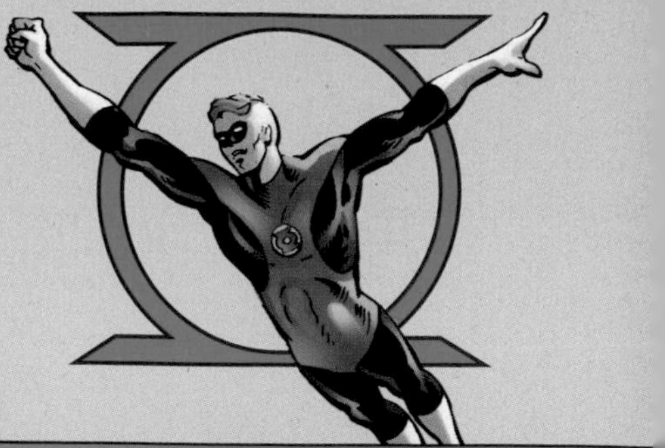

Name: Symon Terrynce **Sector: 2515**

FIRST APPEARANCE: GREEN LANTERN V. 2 #190
BIO: SYMON WAS EXILED FROM HIS HOMEWORLD OF TANJENT BECAUSE HE LACKED PSIONIC ABILITIES LIKE THE REST OF HIS PEOPLE. IN ACTUALITY, THEY WERE SLOW TO MANIFEST, AND NOW SYMON POSSESSES FULL TELEPATHY AND TELEKINESIS, AS WELL AS LIMITED PRECOGNITION. SYMON HAS TRIED TO TEST THE FULL LIMITS OF HIS POWERS, GOING SO FAR AS TRYING TO MIND-READ THE GUARDIANS, BUT HIS ABILITIES ARE NOT YET STRONG ENOUGH TO PENETRATE THEIR FORMIDABLE PSYCHIC DEFENSES. SYMON HOPES THAT SOMEDAY THEY WILL BE. HE WILL REGRET THE DAY THEY ARE.
ART BY HOWARD SIMPSON AND GARY MARTIN.

Name: Isamot Kol **Sector: 2682**

FIRST APPEARANCE: GREEN LANTERN CORPS: RECHARGE #1
BIO: ISAMOT KOL WAS JUST ANOTHER SOLDIER FIGHTING RANNIANS IN THE IMPERIAL THANAGARIAN ARMY WHEN HIS SUPERIOR ORDERED HIS SQUAD TO SURRENDER. RATHER THAN LET HIS SQUADRON BE NEEDLESSLY KILLED, KOL KILLED HIS SUPERIOR AND TOOK CONTROL OF THE SQUAD. AFTER THE BATTLE WAS WON, KOL TOOK RESPONSIBILITY FOR HIS ACTIONS. HE WAS ABOUT TO BE BEHEADED FOR TREASON WHEN THE POWER RING APPEARED AND BROUGHT HIM TO OA. HE HAS AN UNEASY TRUCE WITH VATH SARN, HIS RANNIAN PARTNER, BUT THEIR FRIENDSHIP GROWS WITH EACH MISSION THEY UNDERTAKE.
ART BY PATRICK GLEASON & TOM NGUYEN.

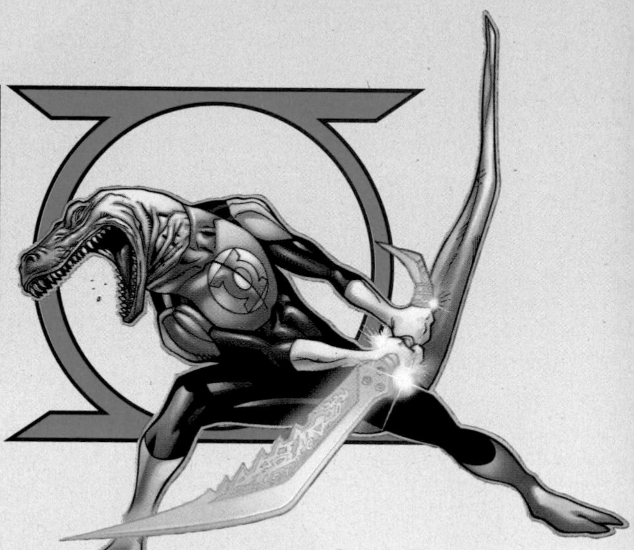

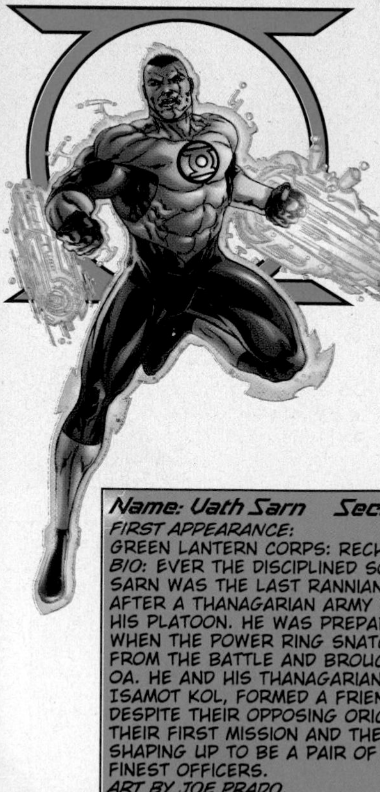

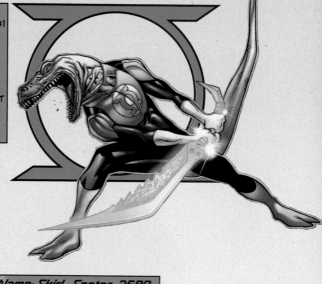

Name: Vath Sarn **Sector: 2682**

FIRST APPEARANCE:
GREEN LANTERN CORPS: RECHARGE #1
BIO: EVER THE DISCIPLINED SOLDIER, VATH SARN WAS THE LAST RANNIAN STANDING AFTER A THANAGARIAN ARMY CORNERED HIS PLATOON. HE WAS PREPARING TO DIE WHEN THE POWER RING SNATCHED HIM FROM THE BATTLE AND BROUGHT HIM TO OA. HE AND HIS THANAGARIAN PARTNER, ISAMOT KOL, FORMED A FRIENDSHIP DESPITE THEIR OPPOSING ORIGINS DURING THEIR FIRST MISSION AND THE TWO ARE SHAPING UP TO BE A PAIR OF THE CORPS' FINEST OFFICERS.
ART BY JOE PRADO.

Name: Skirl **Sector: 2689**

FIRST APPEARANCE:
GREEN LANTERN V. 2 #222
BIO: BORN INTO THE JUNGLE WAR OF NIRDOOR, SKIRL GREW UP SURROUNDED BY DEATH. HE HAS SINCE BECOME AN ACTIVIST FOR PACIFISM AND IS ONE OF NIRDOOR'S MOST VOCAL ANTI-WAR PROPONENTS. HIS INDUCTION INTO THE GREEN LANTERN CORPS LOST HIM SUPPORT, HOWEVER, AS MANY NIRDOOREANS SEE THE GROUP AS A UNIVERSAL TOOL OF OPPRESSION. SKIRL IS TRYING TO DISPEL THIS NEGATIVE IMAGE OF THE CORPS BUT SEEMS TO LOSE GROUND EVERY TIME HE COMES FLYING OUT OF THE SKY, GREEN LANTERN EMBLEM FLASHING ON HIS CHEST.
ART BY JOE PRADO.

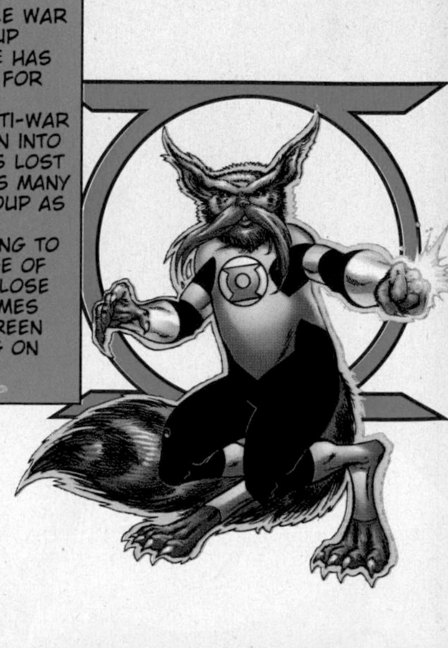

Name: M'Dahna   Sector: 2751
FIRST APPEARANCE: TALES OF THE GREEN LANTERN CORPS #2
BIO: M'DAHNA HAS BEEN A GREEN LANTERN FOR OVER A
MILLENNIUM, AND FOUGHT ALONGSIDE ITS FELLOW CORPSMEN IN
SOME OF THEIR BIGGEST BATTLES. FOLLOWING THE
TRISTRAM-ZANNER IMPERIAL WAR, M'DAHNA'S RACE DISAPPEARED
FROM THE COSMOS, LEAVING M'DAHNA TO PATROL ITS SECTOR
WHILE SEARCHING FOR ANY REMNANT OF ITS PEOPLE.
ART BY ANGEL UNZUETA.

**Name: Tagort
Sector: 2812**
FIRST APPEARANCE:
GREEN LANTERN V. 4 #6
BIO: HIS BODY OVERGROWN DUE
TO REPEATED EVOLUTIONARY
EXPERIMENTATION BY
KROLOTEAN GREMLINS, TAGORT
WAS PART OF A MASSIVE
REFUGEE CAMP THAT WAS
FREED BY THE GREEN LANTERN
VENIZZ. SOON AFTER, TAGORT
RECEIVED HIS POWER RING, AND
THE PAIR HAVE SINCE GONE
HUNTING, FLUSHING OUT AND
ARRESTING KROLOTEAN
GREMLINS BEFORE THEY CAN
EXPERIMENT ON OTHER
LIFEFORMS. THEIR PROGRESS IN
THIS ENDEAVOR HAS BEEN
NEGLIGIBLE.
ART BY SIMONE BIANCHI.

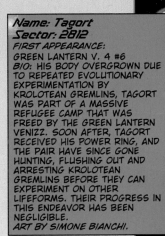

Name: Venizz   Sector: 2812
FIRST APPEARANCE: GREEN LANTERN V. 4 #6
BIO: VENIZZ WAS ONE OF THE MOST CELEBRATED FIGURES ON HER HOME PLANET
EVEN BEFORE SHE WAS CHOSEN TO BE A GREEN LANTERN. A POLITICAL ACTIVIST,
VENIZZ WAS SHOCKED WHEN SHE LEARNED OF THE PLAGUE OF THE KROLOTEAN
GREMLINS, A RACE THAT STEALS AWAY A SPECIES' EVOLUTIONARY RIGHTS. TOGETHER
WITH HER PARTNER TAGORT, VENIZZ SCOURS HER SECTOR FOR ANY TRACE OF THE
GREMLINS. LATELY, THEIR SEARCH HAS BEGUN TO SPILL INTO OTHER SECTORS AS
THE GREMLINS FIND WAYS INTO OTHER PARTS OF THE UNIVERSE, MOST OFTEN
PLANETS RIPE WITH EVOLUTIONARY POSSIBILITIES SUCH AS EARTH.
ART BY SIMONE BIANCHI.

Name: Dalor   Sector: 2813
FIRST APPEARANCE:
GREEN LANTERN V. 2 #154
BIO: ONCE FALSELY ACCUSED OF
ABUSING HIS POWER BY A FELLOW
GREEN LANTERN, DALOR IS NOW A
RECLUSE, AVOIDING CONTACT WITH
OTHER GREEN LANTERNS UNLESS IT IS
ABSOLUTELY NECESSARY. HIS
ABSENCE WAS NOTICED WHEN HIS
PRESUMED DEAD SECTOR PARTNER
TOMAR-TU RETURNED, AND HE DID NOT
VENTURE TO OA FOR THE
CELEBRATIONS. TOMAR-TU HAS
SCANNED THE SECTOR FOR HIM
SEVERAL TIMES, BUT SOMEHOW
DALOR STAYS HIDDEN.
ART BY JOE STATON.

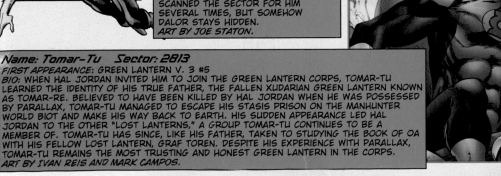

Name: Tomar-Tu   Sector: 2813
FIRST APPEARANCE: GREEN LANTERN V. 3 #5
BIO: WHEN HAL JORDAN INVITED HIM TO JOIN THE GREEN LANTERN CORPS, TOMAR-TU
LEARNED THE IDENTITY OF HIS TRUE FATHER, THE FALLEN XUDARIAN GREEN LANTERN KNOWN
AS TOMAR-RE. BELIEVED TO HAVE BEEN KILLED BY HAL JORDAN WHEN HE WAS POSSESSED
BY PARALLAX, TOMAR-TU MANAGED TO ESCAPE HIS STASIS PRISON ON THE MANHUNTER
WORLD BIOT AND MAKE HIS WAY BACK TO EARTH. HIS SUDDEN APPEARANCE LED HAL
JORDAN TO THE OTHER "LOST LANTERNS," A GROUP TOMAR-TU CONTINUES TO BE A
MEMBER OF. TOMAR-TU HAS SINCE, LIKE HIS FATHER, TAKEN TO STUDYING THE BOOK OF OA
WITH HIS FELLOW LOST LANTERN, GRAF TOREN. DESPITE HIS EXPERIENCE WITH PARALLAX,
TOMAR-TU REMAINS THE MOST TRUSTING AND HONEST GREEN LANTERN IN THE CORPS.
ART BY IVAN REIS AND MARK CAMPOS.

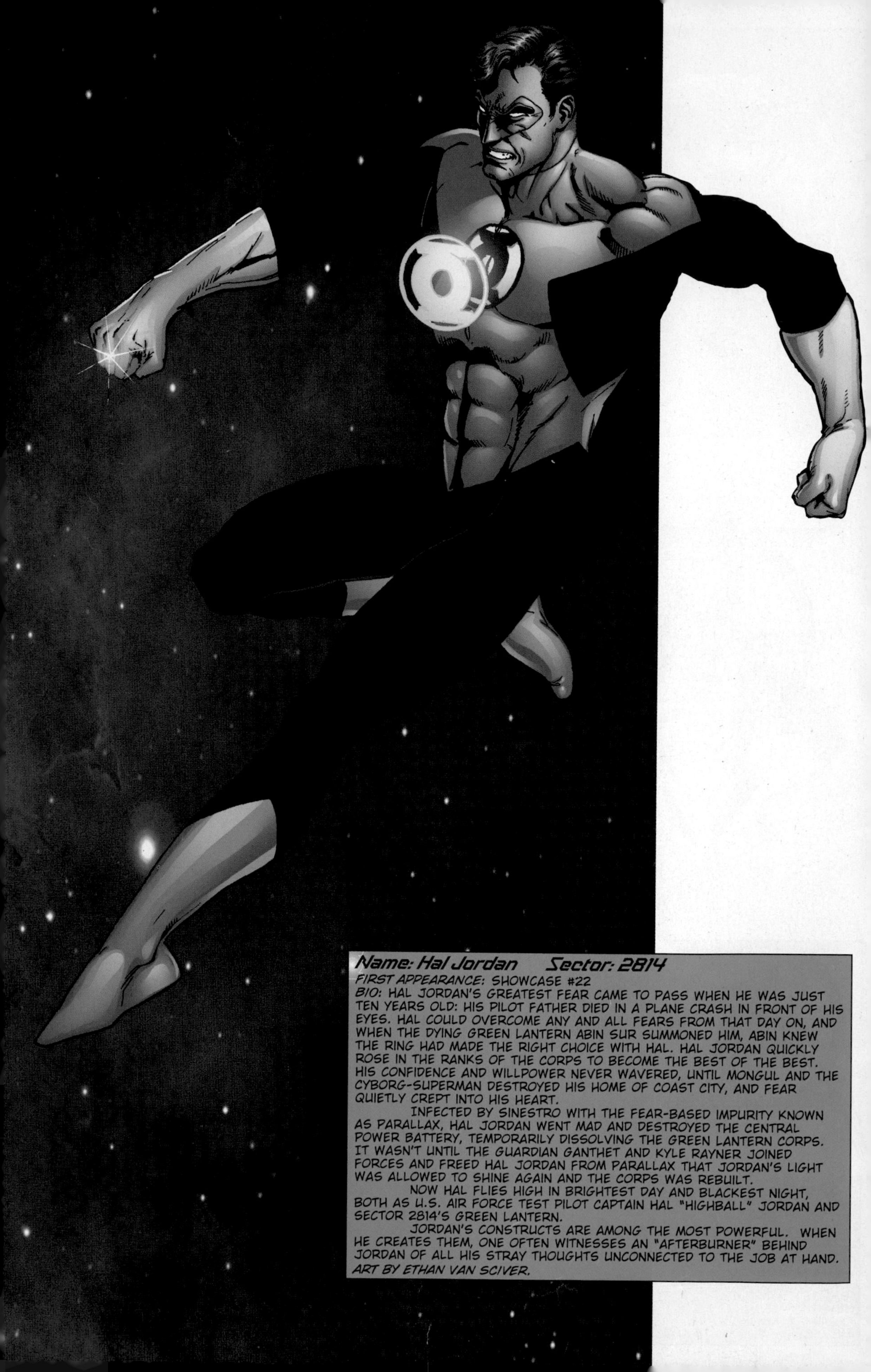

Name: Hal Jordan **Sector: 2814**

FIRST APPEARANCE: SHOWCASE #22

BIO: HAL JORDAN'S GREATEST FEAR CAME TO PASS WHEN HE WAS JUST TEN YEARS OLD: HIS PILOT FATHER DIED IN A PLANE CRASH IN FRONT OF HIS EYES. HAL COULD OVERCOME ANY AND ALL FEARS FROM THAT DAY ON, AND WHEN THE DYING GREEN LANTERN ABIN SUR SUMMONED HIM, ABIN KNEW THE RING HAD MADE THE RIGHT CHOICE WITH HAL. HAL JORDAN QUICKLY ROSE IN THE RANKS OF THE CORPS TO BECOME THE BEST OF THE BEST. HIS CONFIDENCE AND WILLPOWER NEVER WAVERED, UNTIL MONGUL AND THE CYBORG-SUPERMAN DESTROYED HIS HOME OF COAST CITY, AND FEAR QUIETLY CREPT INTO HIS HEART.

INFECTED BY SINESTRO WITH THE FEAR-BASED IMPURITY KNOWN AS PARALLAX, HAL JORDAN WENT MAD AND DESTROYED THE CENTRAL POWER BATTERY, TEMPORARILY DISSOLVING THE GREEN LANTERN CORPS. IT WASN'T UNTIL THE GUARDIAN GANTHET AND KYLE RAYNER JOINED FORCES AND FREED HAL JORDAN FROM PARALLAX THAT JORDAN'S LIGHT WAS ALLOWED TO SHINE AGAIN AND THE CORPS WAS REBUILT.

NOW HAL FLIES HIGH IN BRIGHTEST DAY AND BLACKEST NIGHT, BOTH AS U.S. AIR FORCE TEST PILOT CAPTAIN HAL "HIGHBALL" JORDAN AND SECTOR 2814'S GREEN LANTERN.

JORDAN'S CONSTRUCTS ARE AMONG THE MOST POWERFUL. WHEN HE CREATES THEM, ONE OFTEN WITNESSES AN "AFTERBURNER" BEHIND JORDAN OF ALL HIS STRAY THOUGHTS UNCONNECTED TO THE JOB AT HAND.

ART BY ETHAN VAN SCIVER.

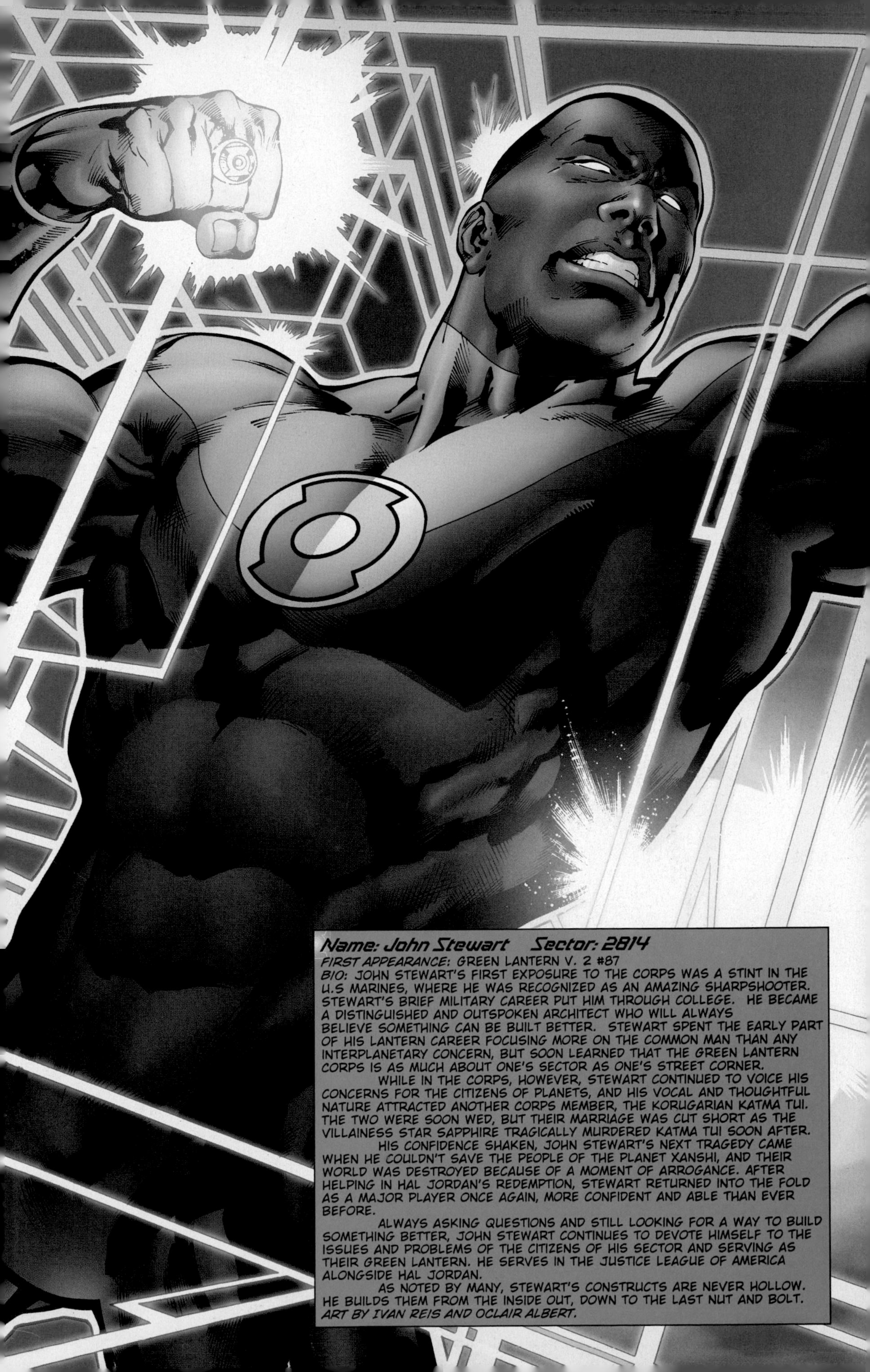

Name: John Stewart   Sector: 2814

FIRST APPEARANCE: GREEN LANTERN V. 2 #87

BIO: JOHN STEWART'S FIRST EXPOSURE TO THE CORPS WAS A STINT IN THE U.S MARINES, WHERE HE WAS RECOGNIZED AS AN AMAZING SHARPSHOOTER. STEWART'S BRIEF MILITARY CAREER PUT HIM THROUGH COLLEGE. HE BECAME A DISTINGUISHED AND OUTSPOKEN ARCHITECT WHO WILL ALWAYS BELIEVE SOMETHING CAN BE BUILT BETTER. STEWART SPENT THE EARLY PART OF HIS LANTERN CAREER FOCUSING MORE ON THE COMMON MAN THAN ANY INTERPLANETARY CONCERN, BUT SOON LEARNED THAT THE GREEN LANTERN CORPS IS AS MUCH ABOUT ONE'S SECTOR AS ONE'S STREET CORNER.

WHILE IN THE CORPS, HOWEVER, STEWART CONTINUED TO VOICE HIS CONCERNS FOR THE CITIZENS OF PLANETS, AND HIS VOCAL AND THOUGHTFUL NATURE ATTRACTED ANOTHER CORPS MEMBER, THE KORUGARIAN KATMA TUI. THE TWO WERE SOON WED, BUT THEIR MARRIAGE WAS CUT SHORT AS THE VILLAINESS STAR SAPPHIRE TRAGICALLY MURDERED KATMA TUI SOON AFTER.

HIS CONFIDENCE SHAKEN, JOHN STEWART'S NEXT TRAGEDY CAME WHEN HE COULDN'T SAVE THE PEOPLE OF THE PLANET XANSHI, AND THEIR WORLD WAS DESTROYED BECAUSE OF A MOMENT OF ARROGANCE. AFTER HELPING IN HAL JORDAN'S REDEMPTION, STEWART RETURNED INTO THE FOLD AS A MAJOR PLAYER ONCE AGAIN, MORE CONFIDENT AND ABLE THAN EVER BEFORE.

ALWAYS ASKING QUESTIONS AND STILL LOOKING FOR A WAY TO BUILD SOMETHING BETTER, JOHN STEWART CONTINUES TO DEVOTE HIMSELF TO THE ISSUES AND PROBLEMS OF THE CITIZENS OF HIS SECTOR AND SERVING AS THEIR GREEN LANTERN. HE SERVES IN THE JUSTICE LEAGUE OF AMERICA ALONGSIDE HAL JORDAN.

AS NOTED BY MANY, STEWART'S CONSTRUCTS ARE NEVER HOLLOW. HE BUILDS THEM FROM THE INSIDE OUT, DOWN TO THE LAST NUT AND BOLT.

ART BY IVAN REIS AND OCLAIR ALBERT.

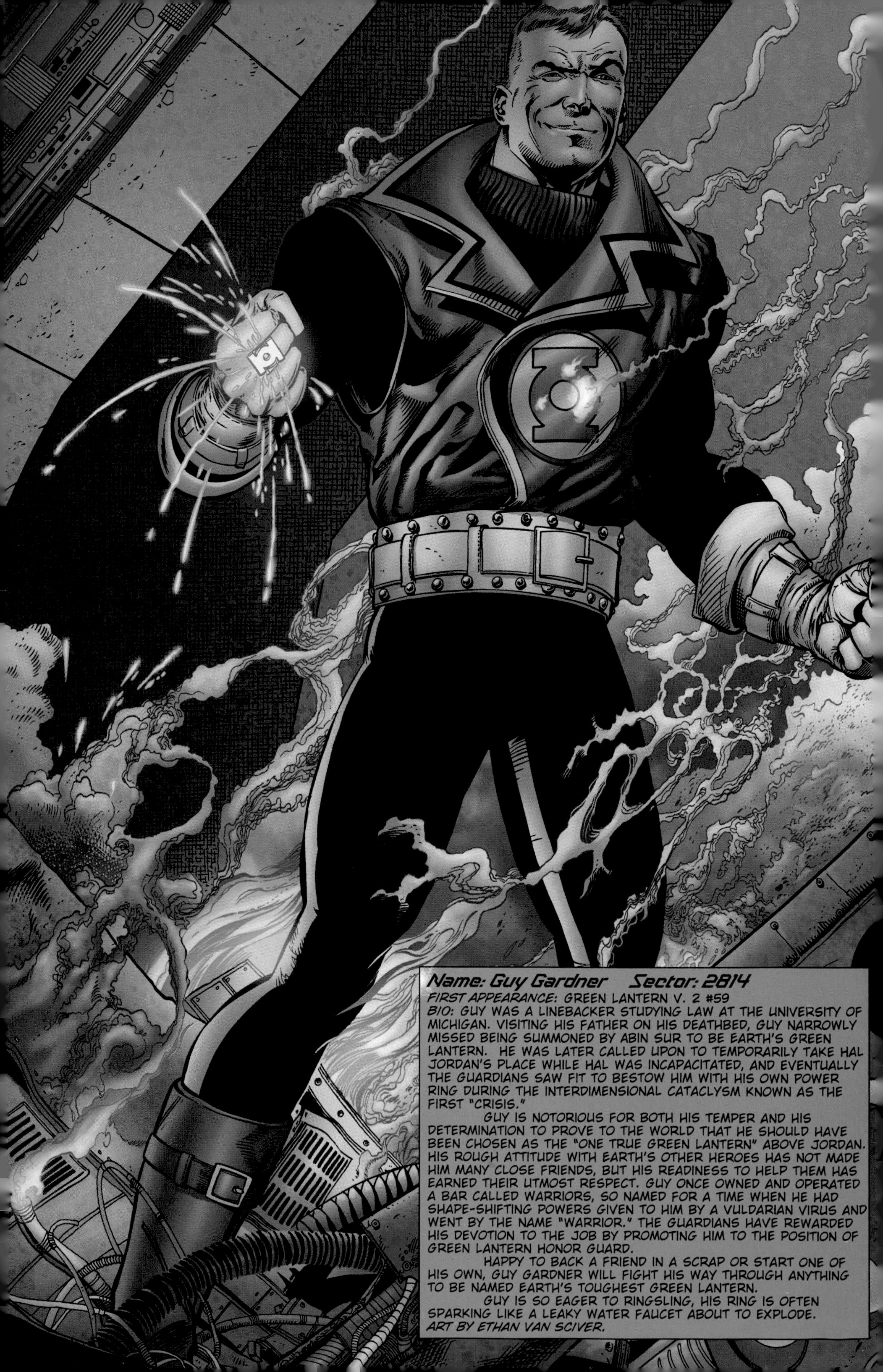
Name: Guy Gardner Sector: 2814
FIRST APPEARANCE: GREEN LANTERN V. 2 #59
BIO: GUY WAS A LINEBACKER STUDYING LAW AT THE UNIVERSITY OF MICHIGAN. VISITING HIS FATHER ON HIS DEATHBED, GUY NARROWLY MISSED BEING SUMMONED BY ABIN SUR TO BE EARTH'S GREEN LANTERN. HE WAS LATER CALLED UPON TO TEMPORARILY TAKE HAL JORDAN'S PLACE WHILE HAL WAS INCAPACITATED, AND EVENTUALLY THE GUARDIANS SAW FIT TO BESTOW HIM WITH HIS OWN POWER RING DURING THE INTERDIMENSIONAL CATACLYSM KNOWN AS THE FIRST "CRISIS."
GUY IS NOTORIOUS FOR BOTH HIS TEMPER AND HIS DETERMINATION TO PROVE TO THE WORLD THAT HE SHOULD HAVE BEEN CHOSEN AS THE "ONE TRUE GREEN LANTERN" ABOVE JORDAN. HIS ROUGH ATTITUDE WITH EARTH'S OTHER HEROES HAS NOT MADE HIM MANY CLOSE FRIENDS, BUT HIS READINESS TO HELP THEM HAS EARNED THEIR UTMOST RESPECT. GUY ONCE OWNED AND OPERATED A BAR CALLED WARRIORS, SO NAMED FOR A TIME WHEN HE HAD SHAPE-SHIFTING POWERS GIVEN TO HIM BY A VULDARIAN VIRUS AND WENT BY THE NAME "WARRIOR." THE GUARDIANS HAVE REWARDED HIS DEVOTION TO THE JOB BY PROMOTING HIM TO THE POSITION OF GREEN LANTERN HONOR GUARD.
HAPPY TO BACK A FRIEND IN A SCRAP OR START ONE OF HIS OWN, GUY GARDNER WILL FIGHT HIS WAY THROUGH ANYTHING TO BE NAMED EARTH'S TOUGHEST GREEN LANTERN.
GUY IS SO EAGER TO RINGSLING, HIS RING IS OFTEN SPARKING LIKE A LEAKY WATER FAUCET ABOUT TO EXPLODE.
ART BY ETHAN VAN SCIVER.

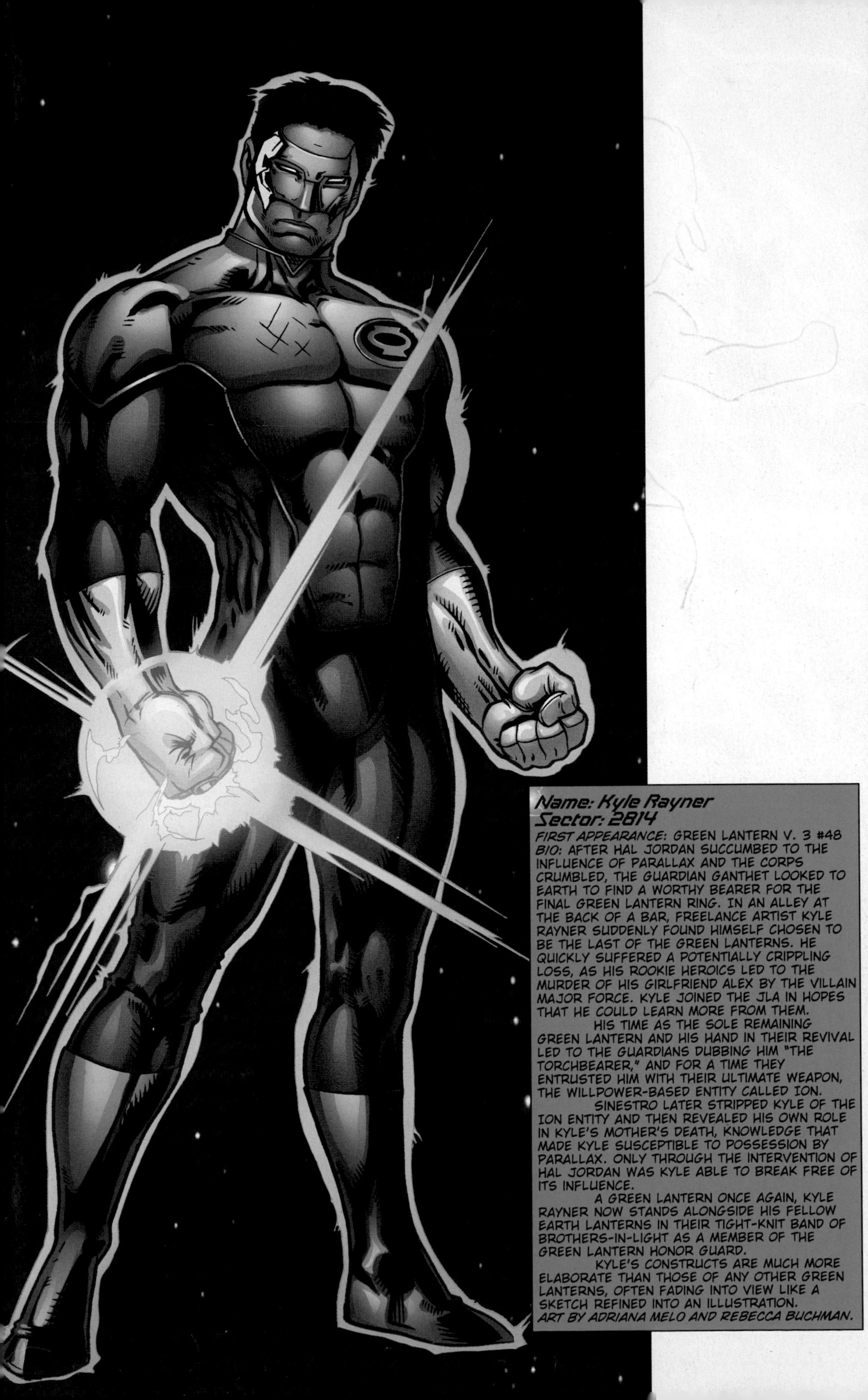

Name: Kyle Rayner
Sector: 2814

FIRST APPEARANCE: GREEN LANTERN V. 3 #48
BIO: AFTER HAL JORDAN SUCCUMBED TO THE INFLUENCE OF PARALLAX AND THE CORPS CRUMBLED, THE GUARDIAN GANTHET LOOKED TO EARTH TO FIND A WORTHY BEARER FOR THE FINAL GREEN LANTERN RING. IN AN ALLEY AT THE BACK OF A BAR, FREELANCE ARTIST KYLE RAYNER SUDDENLY FOUND HIMSELF CHOSEN TO BE THE LAST OF THE GREEN LANTERNS. HE QUICKLY SUFFERED A POTENTIALLY CRIPPLING LOSS, AS HIS ROOKIE HEROICS LED TO THE MURDER OF HIS GIRLFRIEND ALEX BY THE VILLAIN MAJOR FORCE. KYLE JOINED THE JLA IN HOPES THAT HE COULD LEARN MORE FROM THEM.

HIS TIME AS THE SOLE REMAINING GREEN LANTERN AND HIS HAND IN THEIR REVIVAL LED TO THE GUARDIANS DUBBING HIM "THE TORCHBEARER," AND FOR A TIME THEY ENTRUSTED HIM WITH THEIR ULTIMATE WEAPON, THE WILLPOWER-BASED ENTITY CALLED ION.

SINESTRO LATER STRIPPED KYLE OF THE ION ENTITY AND THEN REVEALED HIS OWN ROLE IN KYLE'S MOTHER'S DEATH, KNOWLEDGE THAT MADE KYLE SUSCEPTIBLE TO POSSESSION BY PARALLAX. ONLY THROUGH THE INTERVENTION OF HAL JORDAN WAS KYLE ABLE TO BREAK FREE OF ITS INFLUENCE.

A GREEN LANTERN ONCE AGAIN, KYLE RAYNER NOW STANDS ALONGSIDE HIS FELLOW EARTH LANTERNS IN THEIR TIGHT-KNIT BAND OF BROTHERS-IN-LIGHT AS A MEMBER OF THE GREEN LANTERN HONOR GUARD.

KYLE'S CONSTRUCTS ARE MUCH MORE ELABORATE THAN THOSE OF ANY OTHER GREEN LANTERNS, OFTEN FADING INTO VIEW LIKE A SKETCH REFINED INTO AN ILLUSTRATION.

ART BY ADRIANA MELO AND REBECCA BUCHMAN.

Name: Arisia   Sector: 2815

FIRST APPEARANCE: TALES OF THE GREEN LANTERN CORPS #1

BIO: HAVING TRAINED UNDER HER FATHER, FENTARA, TO BE A GREEN LANTERN, ARISIA WAS DELIGHTED WHEN SHE GOT THE CALL TO JOIN. AFTER A FLIRTATIOUS RELATIONSHIP WITH HAL JORDAN (SHE IS OVER TWO-HUNDRED EARTH YEARS HIS SENIOR), ARISIA WAS SEEMINGLY KILLED BY MAJOR FORCE. HOWEVER, HER GRAXONITE PHYSIOLOGY SAVED HER, PUTTING HER IN AN EXTENDED HIBERNATION. THE MANHUNTERS FOUND HER AND TOOK HER BACK TO BIOT, WHERE HAL JORDAN EVENTUALLY SET HER FREE, AND THE TWO OF THEM DEFEATED THE CYBORG-SUPERMAN AND HIS MANHUNTER ARMY. ARISIA IS ONE OF THE MOST DECORATED OFFICERS OF THE GREEN LANTERN CORPS AND IT IS RUMORED SHE WAS CONSIDERED AS THE VESSEL FOR THE NEXT ION BEFORE SODAM YAT ARRIVED ON THE SCENE. SHE RECENTLY WAS ASKED TO EVALUATE HIS PERFORMANCE, MOST LIKELY TO BE AVAILABLE IN CASE HE FAILED.

ART BY IVAN REIS AND OCLAIR ALBERT.

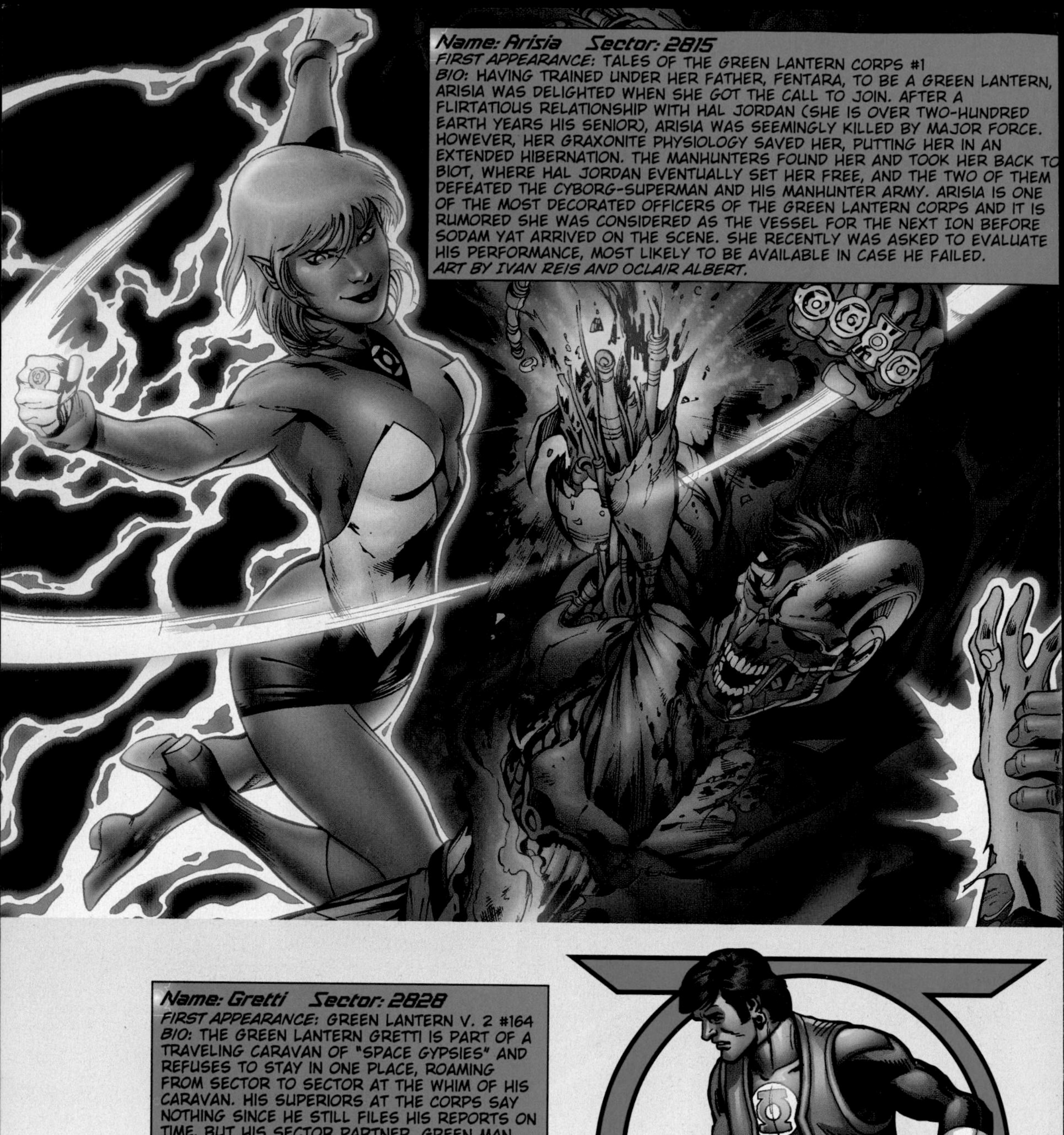

Name: Gretti   Sector: 2828

FIRST APPEARANCE: GREEN LANTERN V. 2 #164

BIO: THE GREEN LANTERN GRETTI IS PART OF A TRAVELING CARAVAN OF "SPACE GYPSIES" AND REFUSES TO STAY IN ONE PLACE, ROAMING FROM SECTOR TO SECTOR AT THE WHIM OF HIS CARAVAN. HIS SUPERIORS AT THE CORPS SAY NOTHING SINCE HE STILL FILES HIS REPORTS ON TIME, BUT HIS SECTOR PARTNER, GREEN MAN, HAS LATELY BEEN LESS AND LESS PLEASED WITH THE SITUATION.

ART BY DAVE GIBBONS.

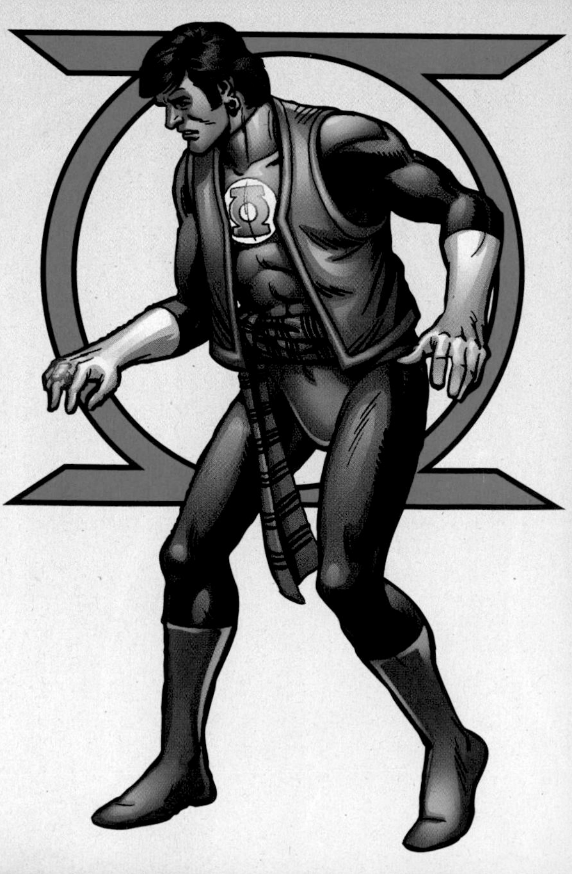

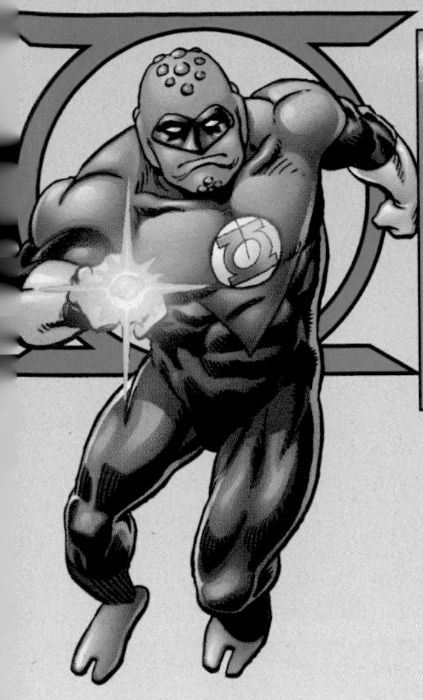

Name: Green Man Sector: 2828

FIRST APPEARANCE: GREEN LANTERN V. 2 #164
BIO: GREEN MAN SPENT HIS LIFE ON THE PLANET UXOR WISHING TO LEARN HOW TO BECOME AN INDIVIDUAL, OF WHICH THERE ARE NONE. GREEN MAN SERVED FAITHFULLY AS A GREEN LANTERN FOR YEARS, THEN SPENT TIME TRAVELING WITH THE GROUP KNOWN AS THE OMEGA MEN BEFORE BEING RECRUITED BACK INTO THE GREEN LANTERN CORPS. IT IS RARE FOR GREEN MAN TO SEE HIS SECTOR PARTNER, THE "SPACE GYPSY" GRETTI, SO GREEN MAN HAS ADOPTED ANOTHER PARTNER BY NECESSITY, THE ROBOTIC LIFE FORM CALLED STEL.
ART BY DAVE GIBBONS.

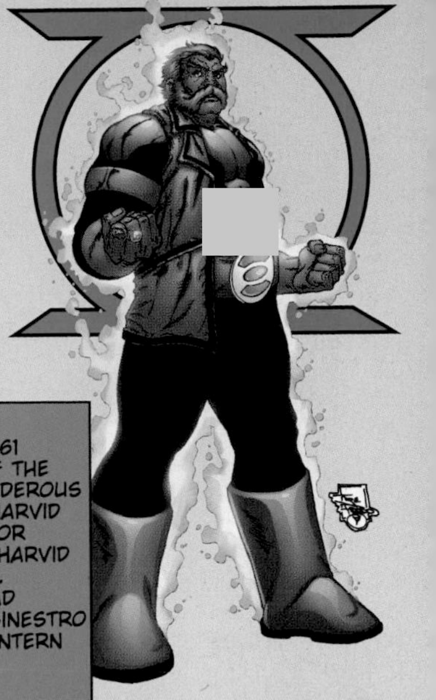

Name: Harvid Sector: 2937

FIRST APPEARANCE: GREEN LANTERN V. 2 #161
BIO: HARVID WAS AN EXEMPLARY OFFICER OF THE GREEN LANTERN CORPS, BUT AFTER HIS MURDEROUS SUPER-POWERED BROTHER WENT MAD AND HARVID COMMITTED HIM TO A SCIENCELL, HE OPTED FOR RETIREMENT. WHEN THE CORPS RESTARTED, HARVID INITIALLY REJECTED THEIR OFFER TO RETURN. HOWEVER, AFTER LEARNING HIS BROTHER HAD ESCAPED THE SCIENCELLS AND JOINED THE SINESTRO CORPS, HARVID RETURNED TO THE GREEN LANTERN CORPS. HE NOW HUNTS FOR HIS BROTHER.
ART BY JOE PRADO.

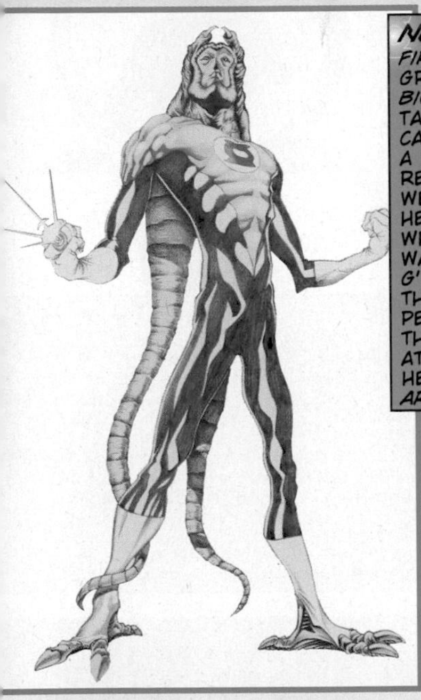

Name: G'Hu Sector: 2937

FIRST APPEARANCE:
GREEN LANTERN CORPS #1
BIO: G'HU WAS A PRISON GUARD ON TAKRON-GALTOS WHEN HE WAS CAPTURED BY THE INMATES AND USED AS A HOSTAGE TO NEGOTIATE THEIR RELEASE. BY THE TIME THE GUARDS WERE ABLE TO FREE HIM, THEY FOUND HE'D ALREADY TAKEN DOWN THE INMATES WHO WERE HOLDING HIM AND WAS JUST WAITING FOR THEM TO OPEN THE DOOR. G'HU IS A CONFIDENT, ABLE OFFICER IN THE CORPS, AND SALAAK HAS TAKEN A PERSONAL INTEREST IN HIS MOVEMENT THROUGH THE RANKS. VOZ IS CURRENTLY ATTEMPTING TO RECRUIT HIM AS THE HEAD GUARD OF THE SCIENCELLS.
ART BY ANGEL UNZUETA.

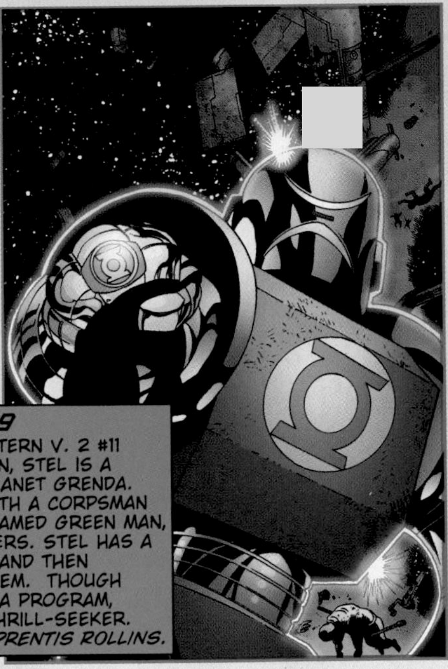

Name: Stel Sector: 3009

FIRST APPEARANCE: GREEN LANTERN V. 2 #11
BIO: A LONGTIME GREEN LANTERN, STEL IS A ROBOTIC LIFEFORM FROM THE PLANET GRENDA. STEL FREQUENTLY PARTNERS WITH A CORPSMAN FROM A NEIGHBORING SECTOR NAMED GREEN MAN, AND THE TWO ARE MODEL OFFICERS. STEL HAS A HABIT OF COMPUTING THE ODDS AND THEN IMMEDIATELY TRYING TO BEAT THEM. THOUGH EVERYONE ELSE WOULD CALL IT A PROGRAM, GREEN MAN CLAIMS STEL IS A THRILL-SEEKER.
ART BY PATRICK GLEASON AND PRENTIS ROLLINS.

Name: Barreer Wot
Sector: 3014

FIRST APPEARANCE:
GREEN LANTERN V. 4 #4
BIO: HIS SPECIES ENDANGERED, BARREER WOT FACES MUCH MORE THAN THE REGULAR CORPSMAN. NOT ONLY MUST HE CONTEND WITH THE USUAL MISCREANTS ATTEMPTING TO DESTROY THE GREEN LANTERN CORPS, HE'S ALSO THE MAIN TARGET FOR A UNIVERSAL POACHING GROUP. HIS TOOMEAN HIDE IS WORTH MORE THAN SOME PLANETS ARE ON THE BLACK MARKET. THIS COULD BE BECAUSE HIS RACE EATS ITS FALLEN COMRADES AS AN HONOR.
ART BY ETHAN VAN SCIVER.

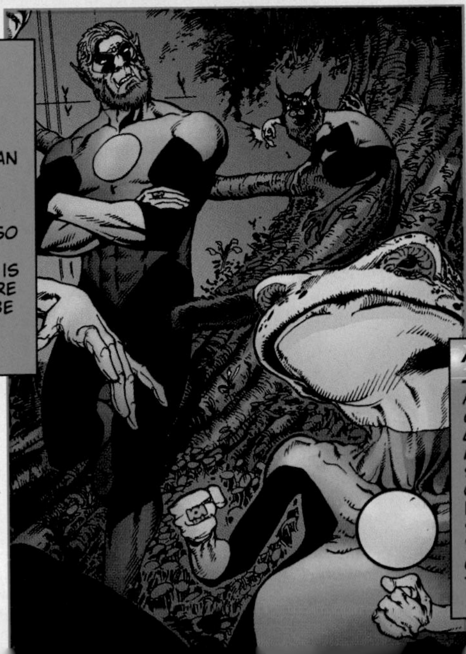

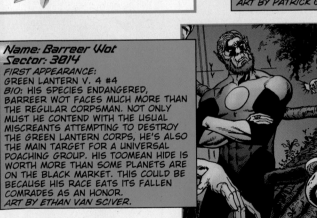

Name: Lok Neboora
Sector: 3014

FIRST APPEARANCE:
GREEN LANTERN V. 4 #4
BIO: LOK NEBOORA IS OF A MULTI-EVOLUTIONARY AMPHIBIOUS SPECIES THAT IS CONSTANTLY CHANGING OVER HIS OR HER OWN LIFETIME. LOK IS IN THE FOURTH STAGE OF HIS FIVE STAGES OF EVOLUTION. IT IS UNKNOWN WHAT HIS NEXT FORM WILL LOOK LIKE, OR IF IT WILL STILL DESIRE TO REMAIN IN THE CORPS AFTERWARDS.
ART BY ETHAN VAN SCIVER.

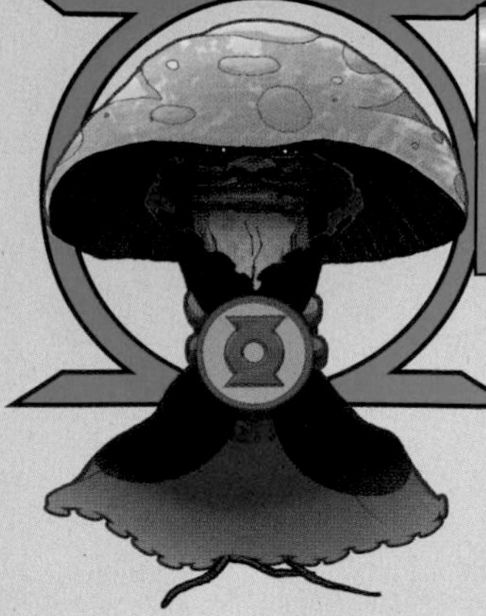

Name: Amanita **Sector: 3100**
FIRST APPEARANCE: GREEN LANTERN V. 3 #20
BIO: AMANITA IS A FUNGUS FROM THE PLANET MUSCARIA. IT IS SAID IN THE HALLWAYS OF OA THAT AMANITA IS OLDER THAN THE GUARDIANS THEMSELVES AND POSSESSES A KIND OF "COSMIC AWARENESS," BUT THOSE CLAIMS SEEM UNFOUNDED.
ART BY TOM FEISTER.

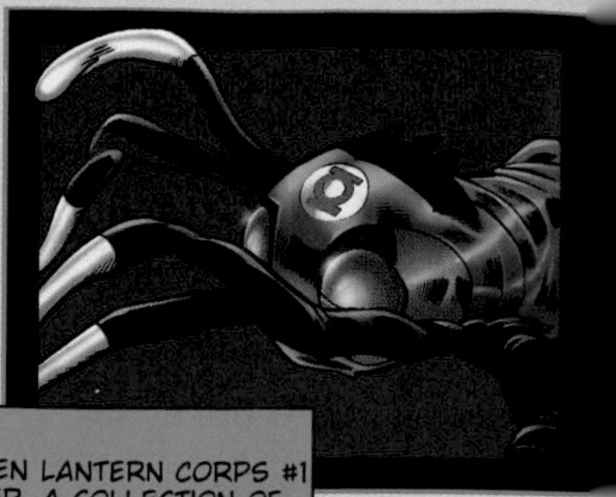

Name: Skyrd **Sector: 3181**
FIRST APPEARANCE: TALES OF THE GREEN LANTERN CORPS #1
BIO: SKYRD IS FROM THE MULTU CLUSTER, A COLLECTION OF PLANETS IN THE BACK OF A BLEAK AND DARK SECTOR. YEARS AGO, SKYRD WAS INJURED WHEN A POWER BATTERY EXPLODED. HE WAS REVIVED BY TOMAR-RE. HE SWORE A LIFE-DEBT TO HIM, BUT AFTER TOMAR-RE'S PASSING, HE TRANSFERRED THAT DEBT TO HIS SON, TOMAR-TU. TOMAR-TU RELEASED SKYRD FROM ANY DEBT.
ART BY JOE STATON AND FRANK MCLAUGHLIN.

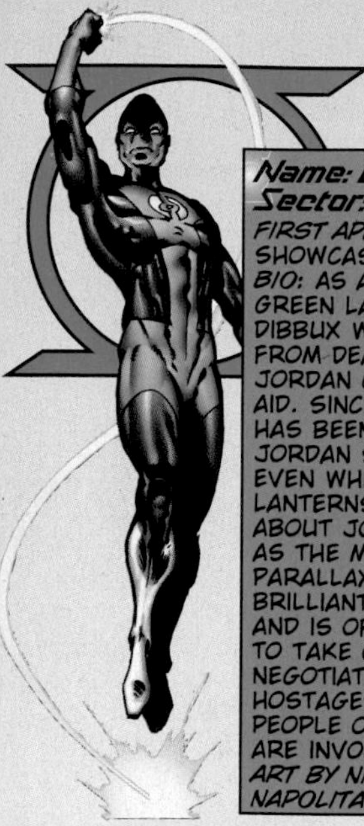

Name: Lan Dibbux
Sector: 3192
FIRST APPEARANCE: SHOWCASE '93 #12
BIO: AS A ROOKIE GREEN LANTERN, LAN DIBBUX WAS SAVED FROM DEATH WHEN HAL JORDAN CAME TO HIS AID. SINCE THEN, HE HAS BEEN A VOCAL HAL JORDAN SUPPORTER, EVEN WHEN THE OTHER LANTERNS WHISPER ABOUT JORDAN'S TIME AS THE MONSTER PARALLAX. LAN IS A BRILLIANT NEGOTIATOR AND IS OFTEN ASKED TO TAKE OVER NEGOTIATIONS WHEN HOSTAGES, BE THEY PEOPLE OR PLANETS, ARE INVOLVED.
ART BY NICK NAPOLITANO.

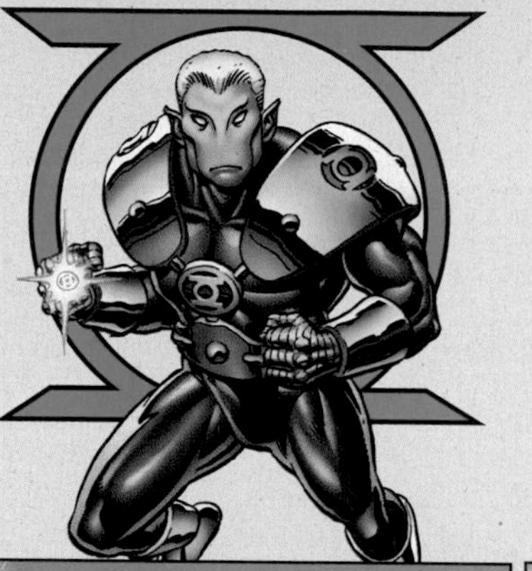

Name: Vandor **Sector: 3212**
FIRST APPEARANCE: GREEN LANTERN CORPS #1
BIO: VANDOR GREW UP FIGHTING FOR HIS LIFE IN THE GLADIATORIAL RINGS OF THE PLANET YDOC. AFTER WINNING HIS HUNDREDTH DEATH MATCH, HE WAS FREED FROM BEING A GLADIATORIAL SLAVE. HIS LATER COURAGEOUS DEPOSING OF THE WORLD'S GLADIATORIAL MASTERS EARNED HIM A RIGHT TO A POWER RING.
ART BY DAVE GIBBONS.

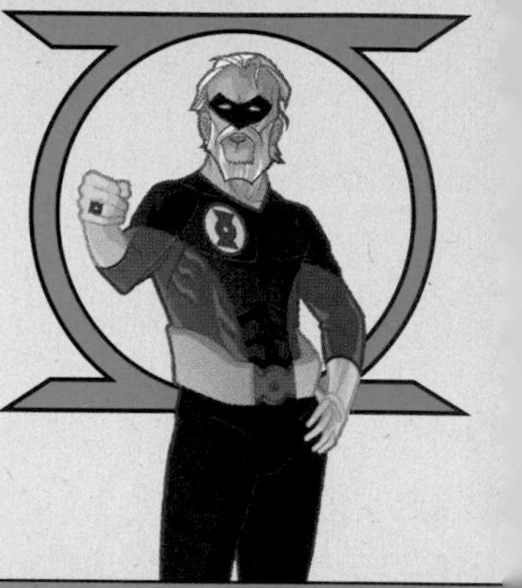

Name: Penn Maricc **Sector: 333**
FIRST APPERANCE: TALES OF THE GREEN LANTERN CORPS ANN. #2
BIO: WITH A TENDENCY TO TELL HYPERBOLIC TALL TALES ABOUT HIS LIFE AS HE SWILLS THE FINEST ALE, THE MERCENARY PENN MARICC IS A GREEN LANTERN WHO PUNCHES FIRST AND SCANS FOR ANSWERS LATER. SOME TIME AGO, PENN MADE A LIFELONG ENEMY OF GUY GARDNER. SEVERAL PEOPLE HAVE ASKED WHAT CAUSED THE RIFT BETWEEN THEM, BUT ONLY THEY KNOW THE TRUTH.
ART BY TOM FEISTER.

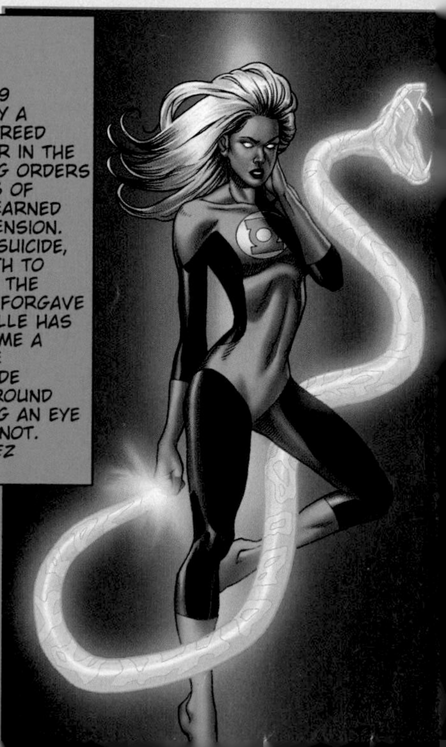

Name: Droxelle
Sector: 3411
FIRST APPEARANCE: GREEN LANTERN V. 2 #169
BIO: DROXELLE WAS ONLY A ROOKIE WHEN SHE DISAGREED WITH A SUPERIOR OFFICER IN THE LINE OF DUTY. DISOBEYING ORDERS RESULTED IN THE DEATHS OF SEVERAL CIVILIANS AND EARNED DROXELLE A LONG SUSPENSION. SHE NEARLY COMMITTED SUICIDE, BUT FOUND THE STRENGTH TO FORGIVE HERSELF AFTER THE FAMILIES OF THE FALLEN FORGAVE HER. SINCE THEN, DROXELLE HAS DONE HER BEST TO BECOME A VOICE OF REASON TO THE LANTERNS WHO HAVE MADE ERRORS IN JUDGMENT AROUND HER. SHE'S BEEN KEEPING AN EYE ON THE ROOKIE HOROQ NNOT.
ART BY ALECIA RODRIGUEZ AND REBECCA BUCHMAN.

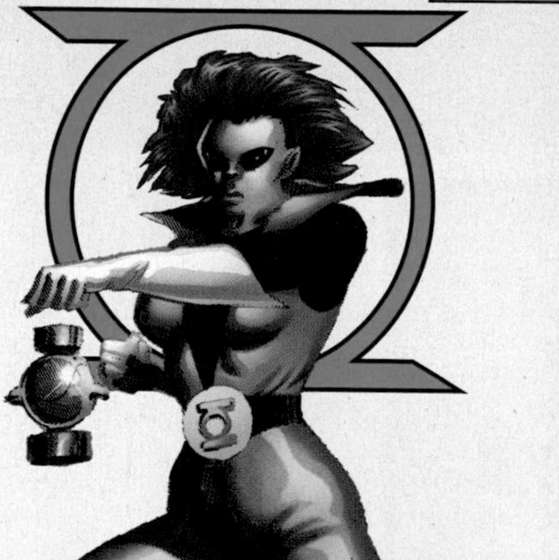

Name: Shilandra Thane **Sector: 3399**
FIRST APPEARANCE: GREEN LANTERN CORPS QUARTERLY #1
BIO: LONE SURVIVOR OF A PLANET RAVAGED BY NUCLEAR WAR, SHILANDRA THANE PATROLS HER SECTOR RELENTLESSLY, MEDIATING ANY DISPUTES THAT MIGHT ARISE AND SPREADING A BENEVOLENT MESSAGE OF PEACE AND UNDERSTANDING. WITH THE NEW LAWS OF OA NOW IMPLEMENTED, SHILANDRA HAS ATTEMPTED TO START A MOVEMENT AGAINST LETHAL FORCE, BUT HAS THUS FAR FAILED.
ART BY PAUL GULACY AND JOHN BEATTY.

Name: Greet
Sector: 3443
FIRST APPEARANCE: GREEN LANTERN V. 4 #11
BIO: MANAGER OF OA'S CAFETERIA, GREET IS ONE OF THE MOST RESPECTED CULINARY MASTERS IN THE UNIVERSE. HIS MANY ATTEMPTS TO RECREATE TERRAN CUISINE HAVE BEEN CONSTANTLY DERIDED BY GUY GARDNER. GREET SPENDS MOST OF HIS TIME ON OA AND HAS FILED SEVERAL TIMES TO MOVE HIS FAMILY THERE SO HE CAN SPEND MORE TIME WITH THEM. ART BY IVAN REIS AND OCLAIR ALBERT.

Name: Lashorr
Sector: 3453
FIRST APPEARANCE: GREEN LANTERN/SINESTRO CORPS SECRET FILES #1
BIO: AFTER HAVING A BRIEF AFFAIR WITH A ROOKIE SALAAK, LASHORR WAS THOUGHT TO HAVE BEEN KILLED FIGHTING THE DOMINATORS IN THE BATTLE OF BREATHWIT-MARNE, AND HER BODY LOST TO SPACE. SHE WAS LATER FOUND HELD IN STASIS ON THE MANHUNTER HOME PLANET BIOT. LASHORR WAS SET FREE AND RETURNED TO HER HOME SECTOR TO REBUILD HER LIFE. SALAAK HAS ATTEMPTED TO REKINDLE THEIR RELATIONSHIP, BUT LASHORR STILL SUFFERS FROM POST-TRAUMATIC STRESS AND HAS REFUSED HIS COMPANY. ART BY RYAN SOOK.

Name: Gpaak
Sector: 3515
FIRST APPEARANCE: GUY GARDNER #11
BIO: HELD CAPTIVE FOR YEARS BY AN ALIEN RACE CALLED THE DRAAL, GPAAK WAS RESCUED BY GUY GARDNER. AFTERWARDS, HE SWORE HE WOULD NEVER BE CAGED AGAIN, SO GPAAK MASTERED CONTROL OF HIS LIQUID BODY. HIS LIQUID BRAIN ALLOWS GPAAK TO THOROUGHLY THINK THROUGH ANY COMPLICATED SITUATION, INCLUDING A RECENT DISPUTE ABOUT PRISONER'S RIGHTS ON OA. GPAAK'S ESCAPE SKILLS ARE CONSIDERED EQUAL TO THOSE OF THE FAMED NEW GOD, MR. MIRACLE. ART BY JOE STATON AND TERRY BEATTY.

Name: Garmin Vid
Sector: 3521
FIRST APPEARANCE: ION #1
BIO: A FORMER MASTER THIEF WHO ORGANIZED THE INFAMOUS TRAGGAL SYSTEM HEIST, GARMIN VID IS OFTEN CALLED UPON TO ANALYZE AND EVEN PREDICT THE CRIMINAL ACTIONS OF OTHERS. VID'S FORMER CRIMINAL ASSOCIATES ACT AS HIS INFORMANTS. VID IS CURRENTLY INVESTIGATING THE HEADMAGE OF THE NECROMANCERS OF THE BLACK CIRCLE. ART BY GREG TOCCHINI AND JAY LEISTEN.

Name: Torquemada
Sector: 3521
FIRST APPEARANCE: GREEN LANTERN CORPS QUARTERLY #4
BIO: A MASTER OF MYSTICAL ARTS, TORQUEMADA BEGAN HIS STUDIES FOLLOWING THE DEATHS OF HIS LIFEMATE AND CHILDREN. STUDYING ALL COLORS OF MAGIC, FROM BLACK TO YELLOW, TORQUEMADA USES HIS KNOWLEDGE TO COMBAT THE NECROMANCERS OF THE BLACK CIRCLE, A GROUP OF MALEVOLENT BEINGS WHO TERRORIZE HIS SECTOR. TORQUEMADA HAS OFFERED TO ADVISE ANY GREEN LANTERN IN NEED OF MAGICAL CONSULTATION, THOUGH TO HIS FRUSTRATION HE HAS YET TO BE CALLED UPON. ART BY MICHEL LACOMBE.

Name: Palaqua
Sector: 3587
FIRST APPEARANCE: TALES OF THE GREEN LANTERN CORPS ANNUAL #2
BIO: PALAQUA WAS PART OF A FORCE SENT TO STOP THE MAD GOD OF SECTOR 3600 AND WAS BELIEVED KILLED IN THE CONFRONTATION. RECENTLY HE RETURNED, ALONG WITH FIVE OTHER LANTERNS THOUGHT KILLED BY THE MAD GOD, AND THE SIX HAVE TOLD ONLY THE GUARDIANS WHAT HAPPENED TO THEM. ART BY NICK NAPOLITANO.

Name: Cimfet Tau
Sector: 3588
FIRST APPEARANCE: TALES OF THE GREEN LANTERN CORPS ANNUAL #2
BIO: CIMFET TAU WAS PART OF A FORCE SENT TO STOP THE MAD GOD OF SECTOR 3600. ALL WERE THOUGHT KILLED IN ACTION, THEIR RINGS LOST FOR GOOD. RECENTLY HE RETURNED ALONG WITH FIVE OTHER LANTERNS THOUGHT KILLED BY THE MAD GOD, AND THE SIX HAVE TOLD ONLY THE GUARDIANS OF THE SECRETS THEY LEARNED. ART BY FRED HAYNES.

Name: Zghithii
Sector: 3599
FIRST APPEARANCE: GREEN LANTERN V. 2 #190
BIO: ZGHITHII IS A HOJIAN SILKWORM WHO SPINS SOME OF THE FINEST STORY-TAPESTRIES IN THE UNIVERSE. A FIERCELY LOYAL FRIEND AND FIGHTER, ZGHITHII ONCE FOUGHT COURAGEOUSLY WITH HIS BEST FRIEND AND FELLOW LANTERN XAX AGAINST THE SPIDER GUILD'S INVASION OF XAOS. HE WAS DISTRAUGHT WHEN HE LEARNED OF XAX'S DEATH AT THE HANDS OF LADY STYX, AND HAS SINCE RETREATED INTO SECLUSION. ART BY COREY BREEN.

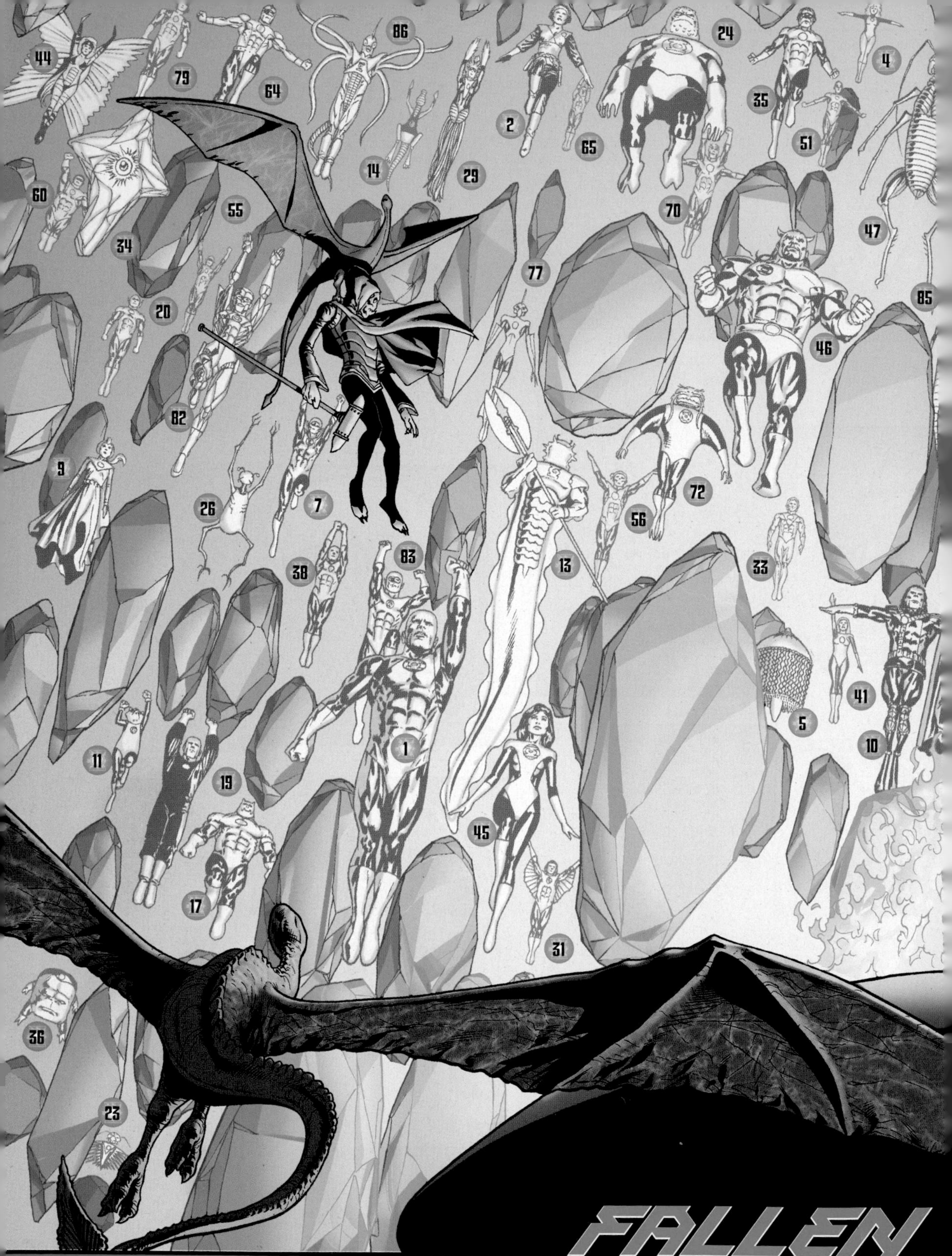
FALLEN

1 Abin Sur - 2814
2 Adara - 62
3 Ahtier - 83
4 Alisand'r - 2828
5 AR-N-D-Q - 1287
6 Archon Z'gmora - 26
7 Ard Rennat
8 Arkkis Chummuck - 1313
9 Avir - 1632
10 Ayria - 3112
11 B'rr - 1014
12 B'shi - 312
13 Barin - 1415
14 Bivvix - 3391
15 Blish - 2815
16 Bogosar - 777
17 Branwilla - 674
18 Brin - 1324
19 Bruks - 1867
20 Burkett - 3143
21 Ch'p - 1014
22 Cherniss - 344
23 Chogar - 2349
24 Chthos-Chthos Chthatis - 73
25 Cundiff Cood
26 D'Aran Tuu - 2284
27 Dava Yull - 2345
28 Diamalon - 1416
29 Dob Zagil - 1582
30 Driq - 3567
31 Ebikar Hrui - 2815
32 Eddore - 1419
33 Fentara - 2815
34 Flodo Span - 875
35 Gala De - 3214
36 Galius Zed - 3335
37 General Kreon - 2002
38 Ghrelk - 69
39 Hollika Rahn - 1632
40 Jack T. Chance - 17
41 Jeryll - 55
42 Jewelius Blak - 1417
43 Joanquin - 53
44 K'ryssma - 1890
45 Katma Tui - 1417
46 Ke'Haan - 786
47 Kendotha Kr'nek
48 Kentor Omoto - 112
49 Khen-To - 2090
50 Ki-Nilg - 1965
51 Kwo Varrikk - 24
52 Kworri - 904
53 Laham - 2814
54 Lodar Monak - 432
55 Meeno Monak - 1132

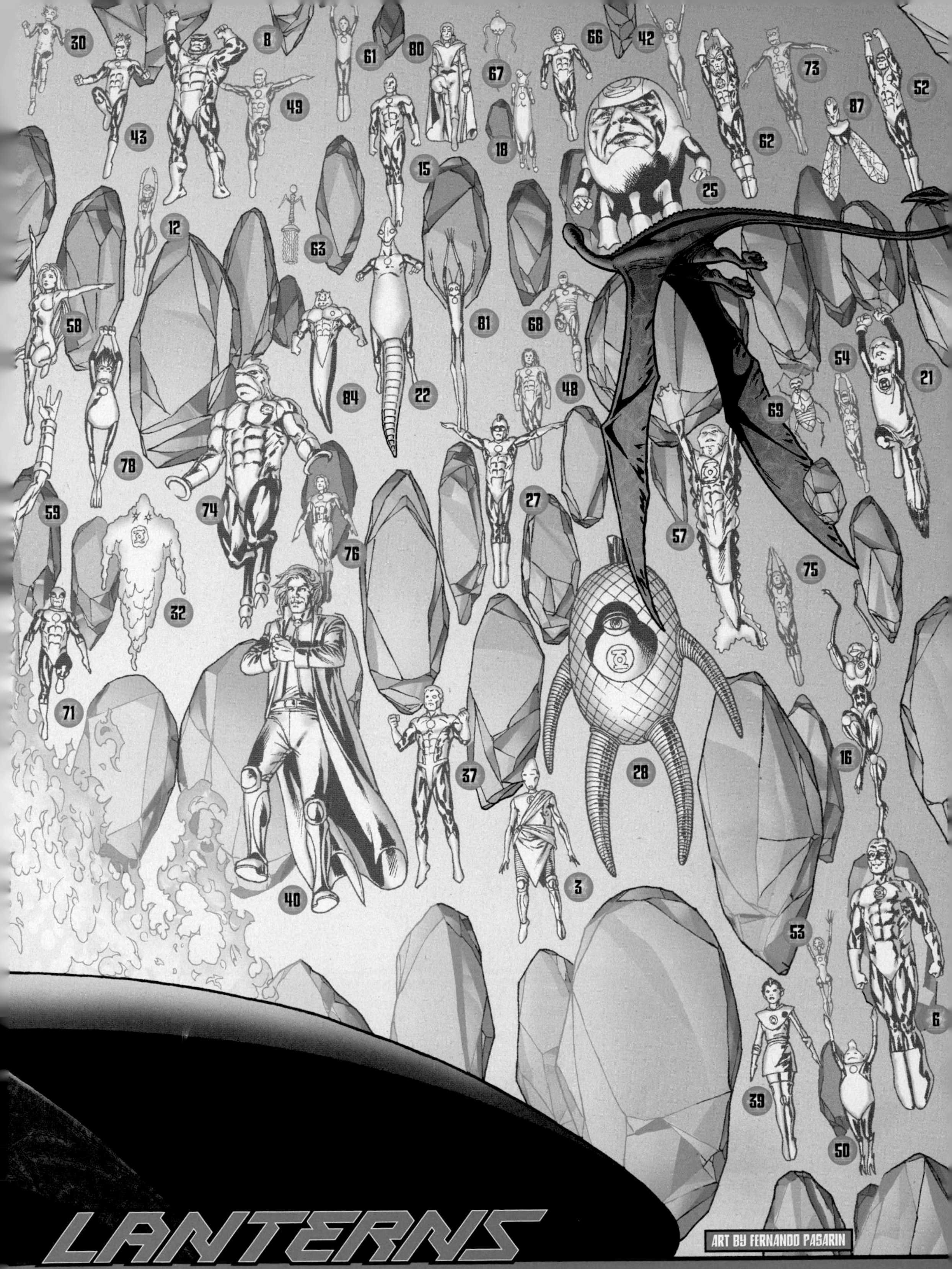
30
8
61
80
67
66
42
73
52
43
49
18
15
87
62
25
12
63
58
81
68
54
21
84
22
48
69
78
74
27
59
57
76
75
32
71
28
37
16
40
3
53
6
39
50
LANTERNS
ART BY FERNANDO PASARIN

56 Myrrt - 1417
57 Pathavim Seth-Ottarak - 17
58 Pelle - 2240
59 Priest - 1634
60 Quarzz Teranh - 3451
61 Quond - 2684
62 Rak Arranya - 996
63 Rosa Nekroy - 3600
64 Reemuz - 119
65 Reever - 1313
66 Rori Dag - 1234

67 Sandra Batorn - 181
68 Shingo Wol - 897
69 Shr'kl - 119
70 Spak Drom - 3145
71 Squagga - 1995
72 Starkadr - 2814
73 Steppe
74 Tanakata Z - 2684
75 Tarkus Whin - 1417
76 Thormon Toxzz - 3500
77 TO-T-U-K - 1287

78 Tylot - 2666
79 Waverly Sayre - 2814
80 Wylxa - 6
81 Xax - 3500
82 Yron - 3009
83 Zac Ares Bandet - 2167
84 Zaneth - 2277
85 Zborra
86 Zharan Pel - 2813
87 The Unknown Lantern

PRESUMED DEAD

- G'Nort
- Gion
- Ekron of Vengar
- Probert
- Charlie Vicker
- Naut Ke Loi

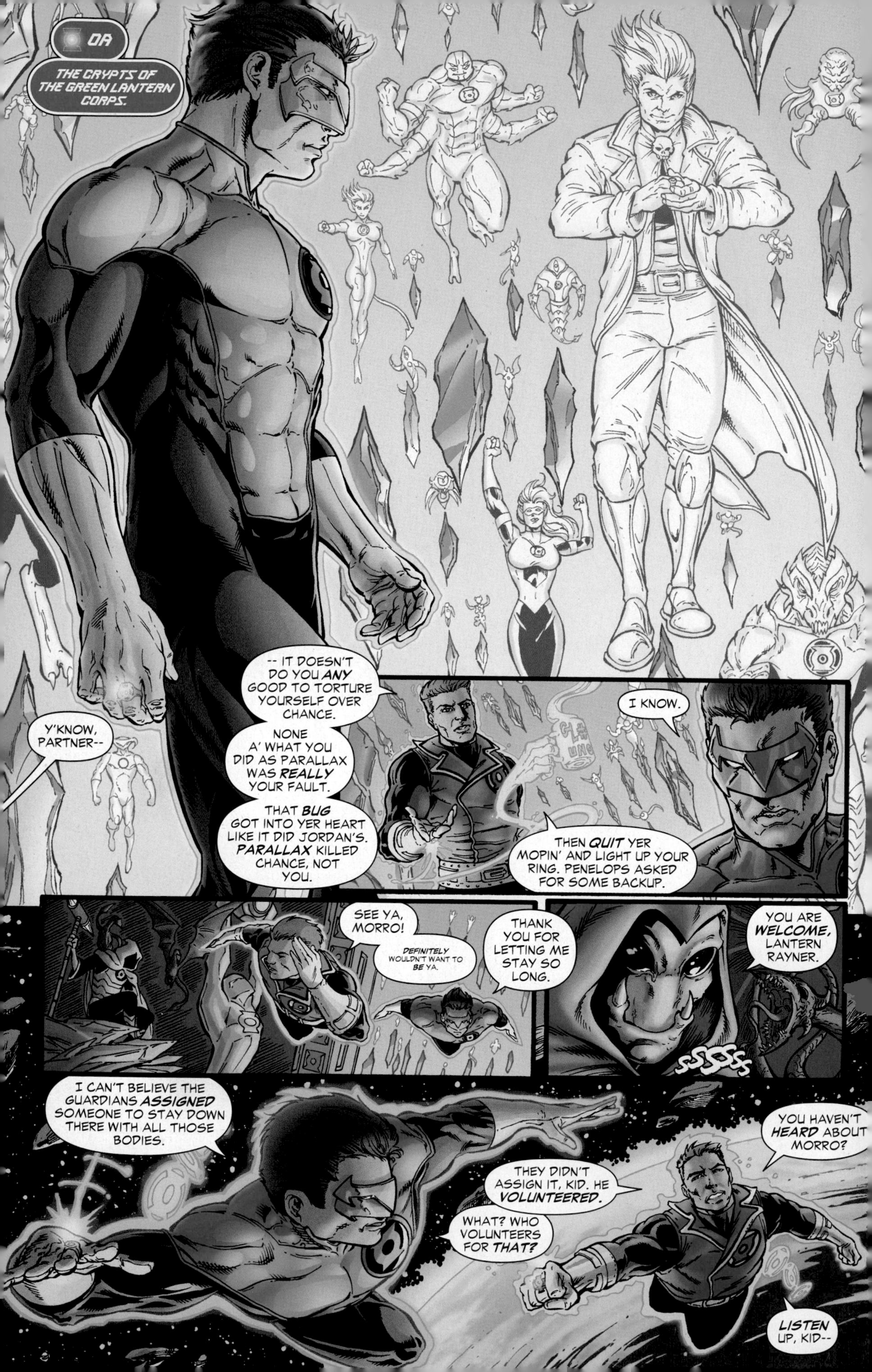
OA
THE CRYPTS OF THE GREEN LANTERN CORPS.
Y'KNOW, PARTNER--
-- IT DOESN'T DO YOU ANY GOOD TO TORTURE YOURSELF OVER CHANCE.
NONE A' WHAT YOU DID AS PARALLAX WAS REALLY YOUR FAULT.
THAT BUG GOT INTO YER HEART LIKE IT DID JORDAN'S. PARALLAX KILLED CHANCE, NOT YOU.
I KNOW.
THEN QUIT YER MOPIN' AND LIGHT UP YOUR RING. PENELOPS ASKED FOR SOME BACKUP.
SEE YA, MORRO!
DEFINITELY WOULDN'T WANT TO BE YA.
THANK YOU FOR LETTING ME STAY SO LONG.
YOU ARE WELCOME, LANTERN RAYNER.
SSSSS
I CAN'T BELIEVE THE GUARDIANS ASSIGNED SOMEONE TO STAY DOWN THERE WITH ALL THOSE BODIES.
YOU HAVEN'T HEARD ABOUT MORRO?
THEY DIDN'T ASSIGN IT, KID. HE VOLUNTEERED.
WHAT? WHO VOLUNTEERS FOR THAT?
LISTEN UP, KID--

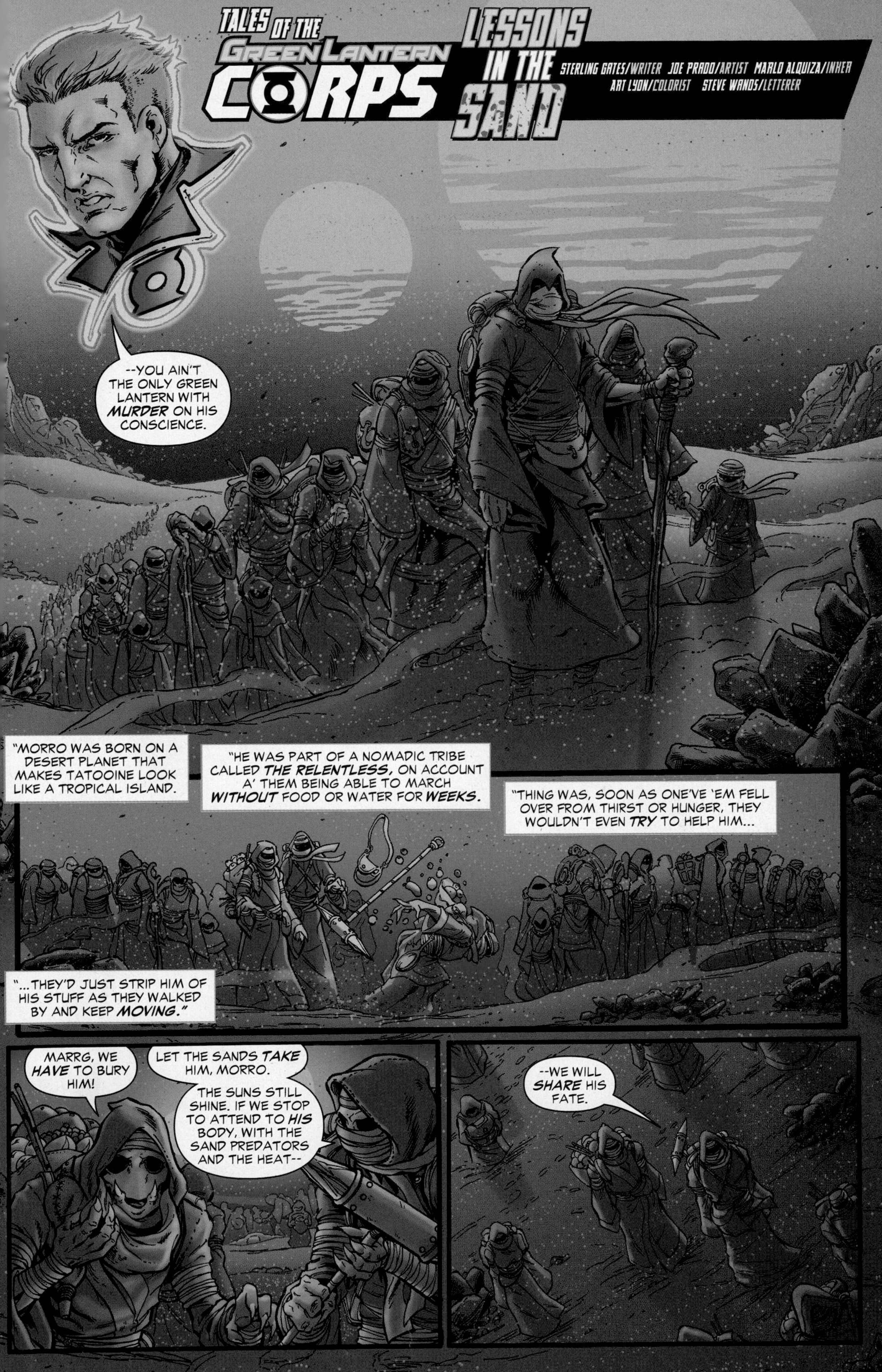
TALES OF THE GREEN LANTERN CORPS
LESSONS IN THE SAND
STERLING GATES/WRITER JOE PRADO/ARTIST MARLO ALQUIZA/INKER
ART LYON/COLORIST STEVE WANDS/LETTERER
--YOU AIN'T THE ONLY GREEN LANTERN WITH MURDER ON HIS CONSCIENCE.
"MORRO WAS BORN ON A DESERT PLANET THAT MAKES TATOOINE LOOK LIKE A TROPICAL ISLAND.
"HE WAS PART OF A NOMADIC TRIBE CALLED THE RELENTLESS, ON ACCOUNT A' THEM BEING ABLE TO MARCH WITHOUT FOOD OR WATER FOR WEEKS.
"THING WAS, SOON AS ONE'VE 'EM FELL OVER FROM THIRST OR HUNGER, THEY WOULDN'T EVEN TRY TO HELP HIM...
"...THEY'D JUST STRIP HIM OF HIS STUFF AS THEY WALKED BY AND KEEP MOVING."
MARRG, WE HAVE TO BURY HIM!
LET THE SANDS TAKE HIM, MORRO.
THE SUNS STILL SHINE. IF WE STOP TO ATTEND TO HIS BODY, WITH THE SAND PREDATORS AND THE HEAT--
--WE WILL SHARE HIS FATE.

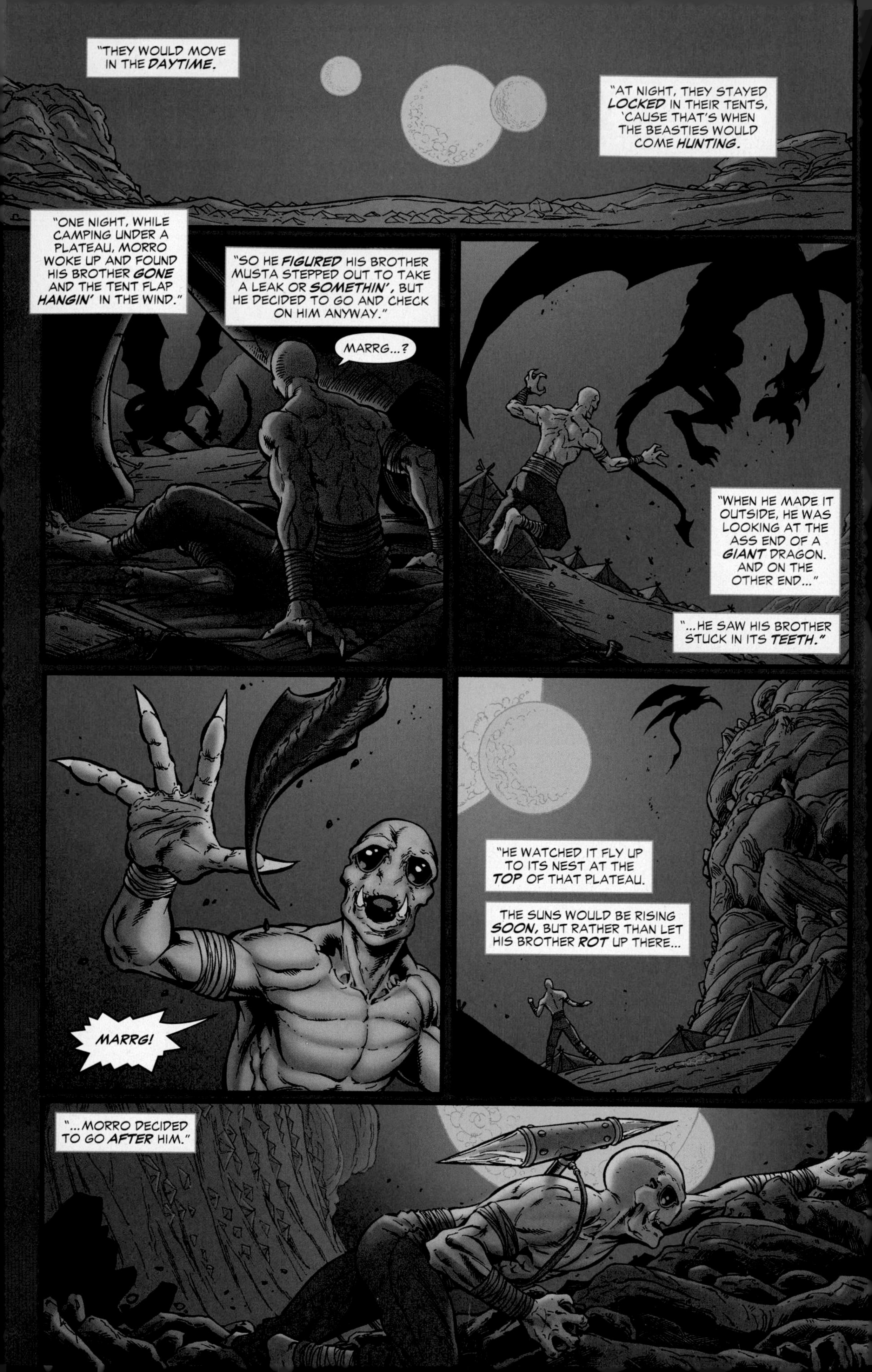
"THEY WOULD MOVE IN THE DAYTIME.
"AT NIGHT, THEY STAYED LOCKED IN THEIR TENTS, 'CAUSE THAT'S WHEN THE BEASTIES WOULD COME HUNTING.
"ONE NIGHT, WHILE CAMPING UNDER A PLATEAU, MORRO WOKE UP AND FOUND HIS BROTHER GONE AND THE TENT FLAP HANGIN' IN THE WIND."
"SO HE FIGURED HIS BROTHER MUSTA STEPPED OUT TO TAKE A LEAK OR SOMETHIN', BUT HE DECIDED TO GO AND CHECK ON HIM ANYWAY."
MARRG...?
"WHEN HE MADE IT OUTSIDE, HE WAS LOOKING AT THE ASS END OF A GIANT DRAGON. AND ON THE OTHER END..."
"...HE SAW HIS BROTHER STUCK IN ITS TEETH."
MARRG!
"HE WATCHED IT FLY UP TO ITS NEST AT THE TOP OF THAT PLATEAU.
THE SUNS WOULD BE RISING SOON, BUT RATHER THAN LET HIS BROTHER ROT UP THERE...
"...MORRO DECIDED TO GO AFTER HIM."

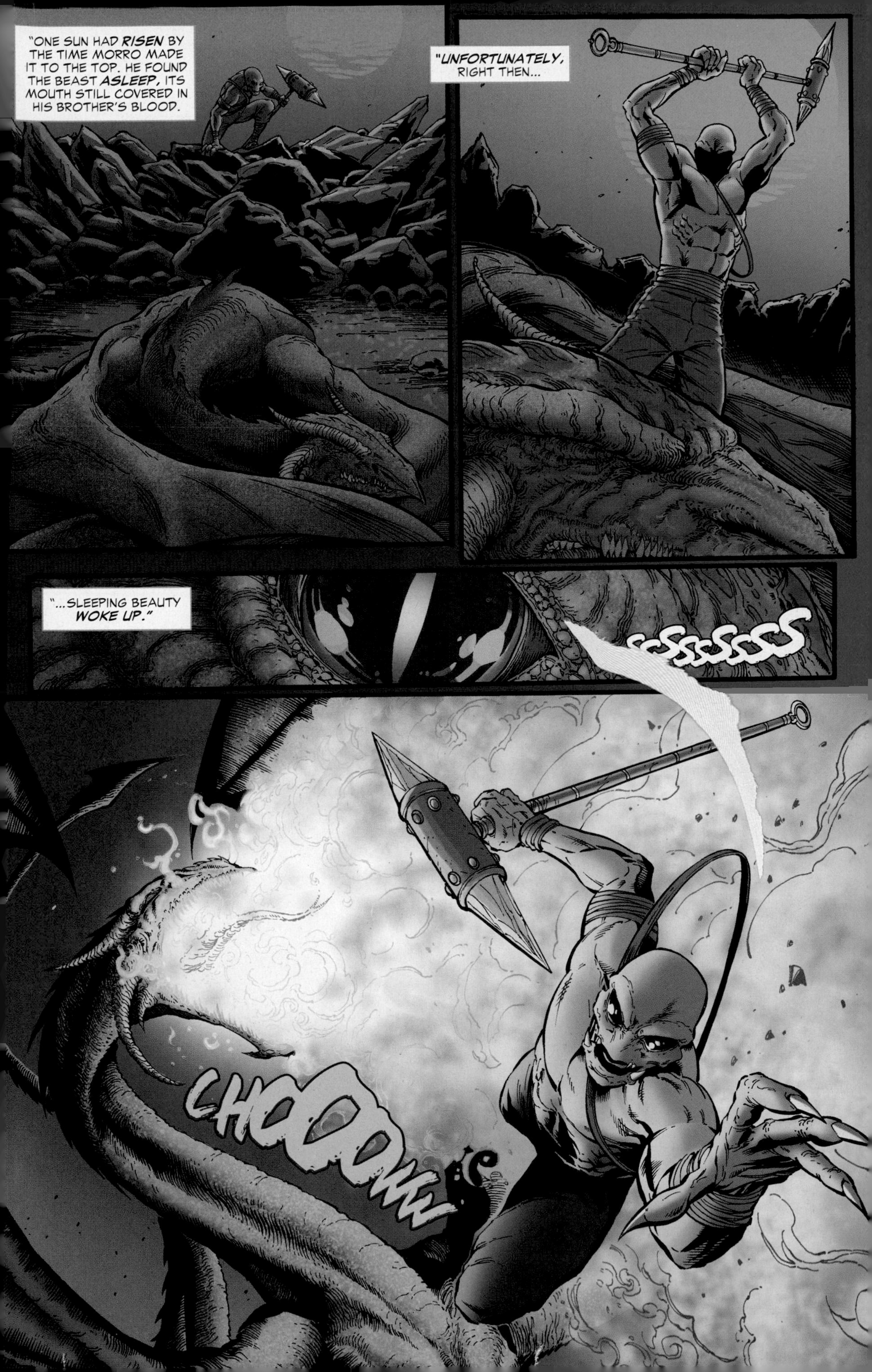
"ONE SUN HAD RISEN BY THE TIME MORRO MADE IT TO THE TOP. HE FOUND THE BEAST ASLEEP, ITS MOUTH STILL COVERED IN HIS BROTHER'S BLOOD.
"UNFORTUNATELY, RIGHT THEN...
"...SLEEPING BEAUTY WOKE UP."
SSSSSSSSS
CHOOOM

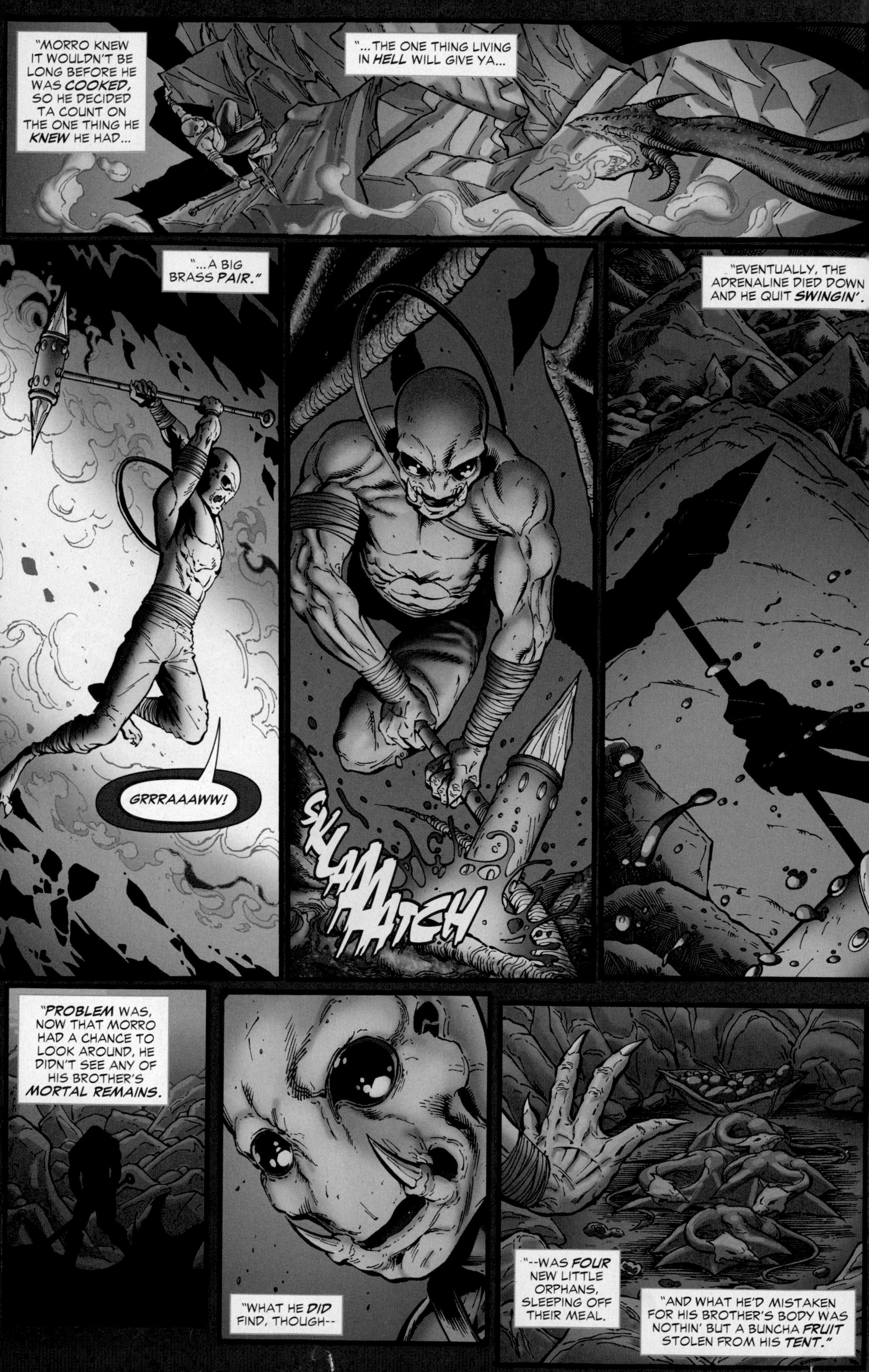
"MORRO KNEW IT WOULDN'T BE LONG BEFORE HE WAS COOKED, SO HE DECIDED TA COUNT ON THE ONE THING HE KNEW HE HAD...
"...THE ONE THING LIVING IN HELL WILL GIVE YA...
"...A BIG BRASS PAIR."
GRRRAAAWW!
SKLAMMATCH
"EVENTUALLY, THE ADRENALINE DIED DOWN AND HE QUIT SWINGIN'.
"PROBLEM WAS, NOW THAT MORRO HAD A CHANCE TO LOOK AROUND, HE DIDN'T SEE ANY OF HIS BROTHER'S MORTAL REMAINS.
"WHAT HE DID FIND, THOUGH--
"--WAS FOUR NEW LITTLE ORPHANS, SLEEPING OFF THEIR MEAL.
"AND WHAT HE'D MISTAKEN FOR HIS BROTHER'S BODY WAS NOTHIN' BUT A BUNCHA FRUIT STOLEN FROM HIS TENT."

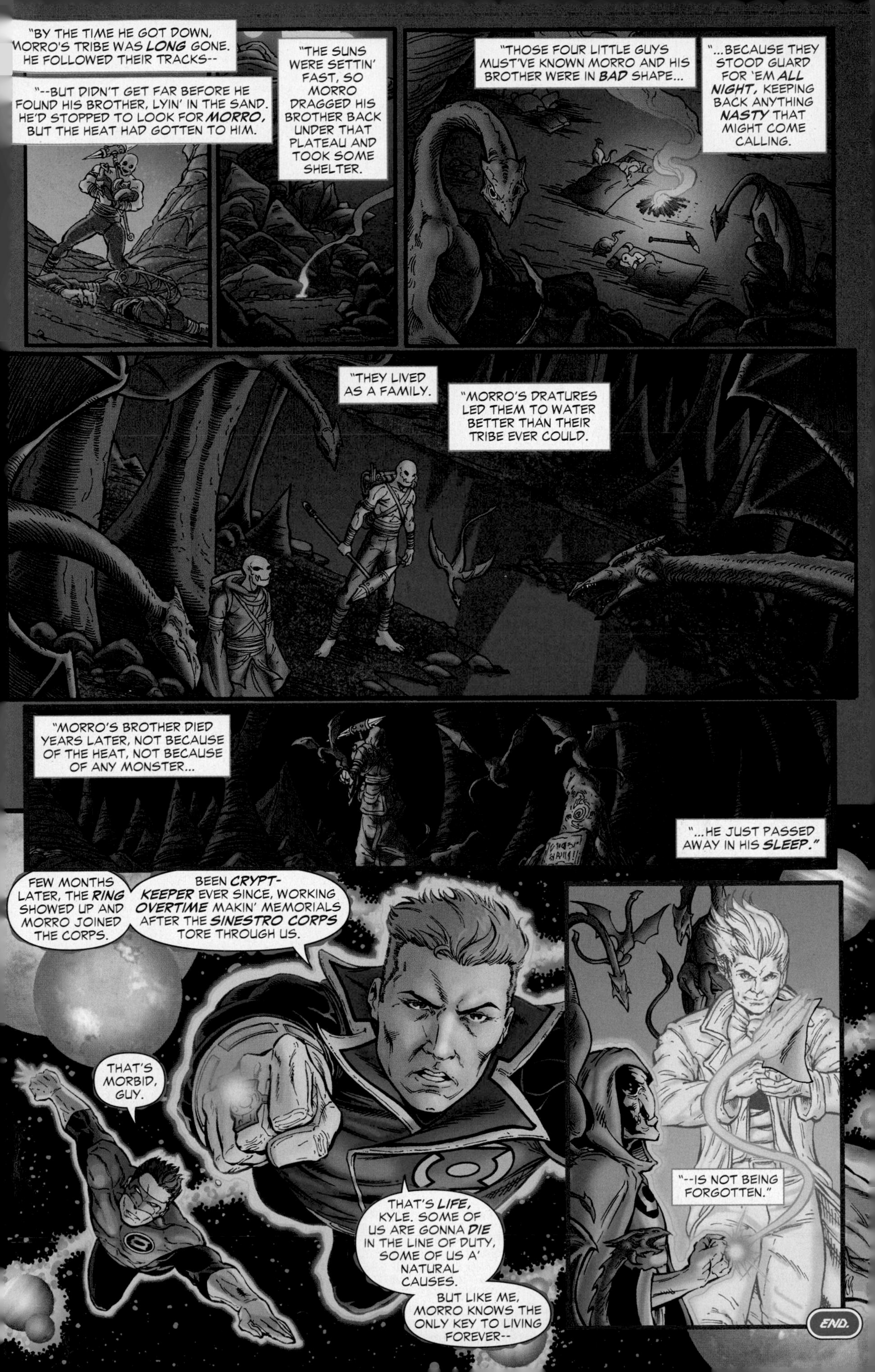
"BY THE TIME HE GOT DOWN, MORRO'S TRIBE WAS LONG GONE. HE FOLLOWED THEIR TRACKS--
"--BUT DIDN'T GET FAR BEFORE HE FOUND HIS BROTHER, LYIN' IN THE SAND. HE'D STOPPED TO LOOK FOR MORRO, BUT THE HEAT HAD GOTTEN TO HIM.
"THE SUNS WERE SETTIN' FAST, SO MORRO DRAGGED HIS BROTHER BACK UNDER THAT PLATEAU AND TOOK SOME SHELTER.
"THOSE FOUR LITTLE GUYS MUST'VE KNOWN MORRO AND HIS BROTHER WERE IN BAD SHAPE...
"...BECAUSE THEY STOOD GUARD FOR 'EM ALL NIGHT, KEEPING BACK ANYTHING NASTY THAT MIGHT COME CALLING.
"THEY LIVED AS A FAMILY.
"MORRO'S DRATURES LED THEM TO WATER BETTER THAN THEIR TRIBE EVER COULD.
"MORRO'S BROTHER DIED YEARS LATER, NOT BECAUSE OF THE HEAT, NOT BECAUSE OF ANY MONSTER...
"...HE JUST PASSED AWAY IN HIS SLEEP."
FEW MONTHS LATER, THE RING SHOWED UP AND MORRO JOINED THE CORPS.
BEEN CRYPT-KEEPER EVER SINCE, WORKING OVERTIME MAKIN' MEMORIALS AFTER THE SINESTRO CORPS TORE THROUGH US.
THAT'S MORBID, GUY.
THAT'S LIFE, KYLE. SOME OF US ARE GONNA DIE IN THE LINE OF DUTY, SOME OF US A' NATURAL CAUSES.
BUT LIKE ME, MORRO KNOWS THE ONLY KEY TO LIVING FOREVER--
"--IS NOT BEING FORGOTTEN."
END.

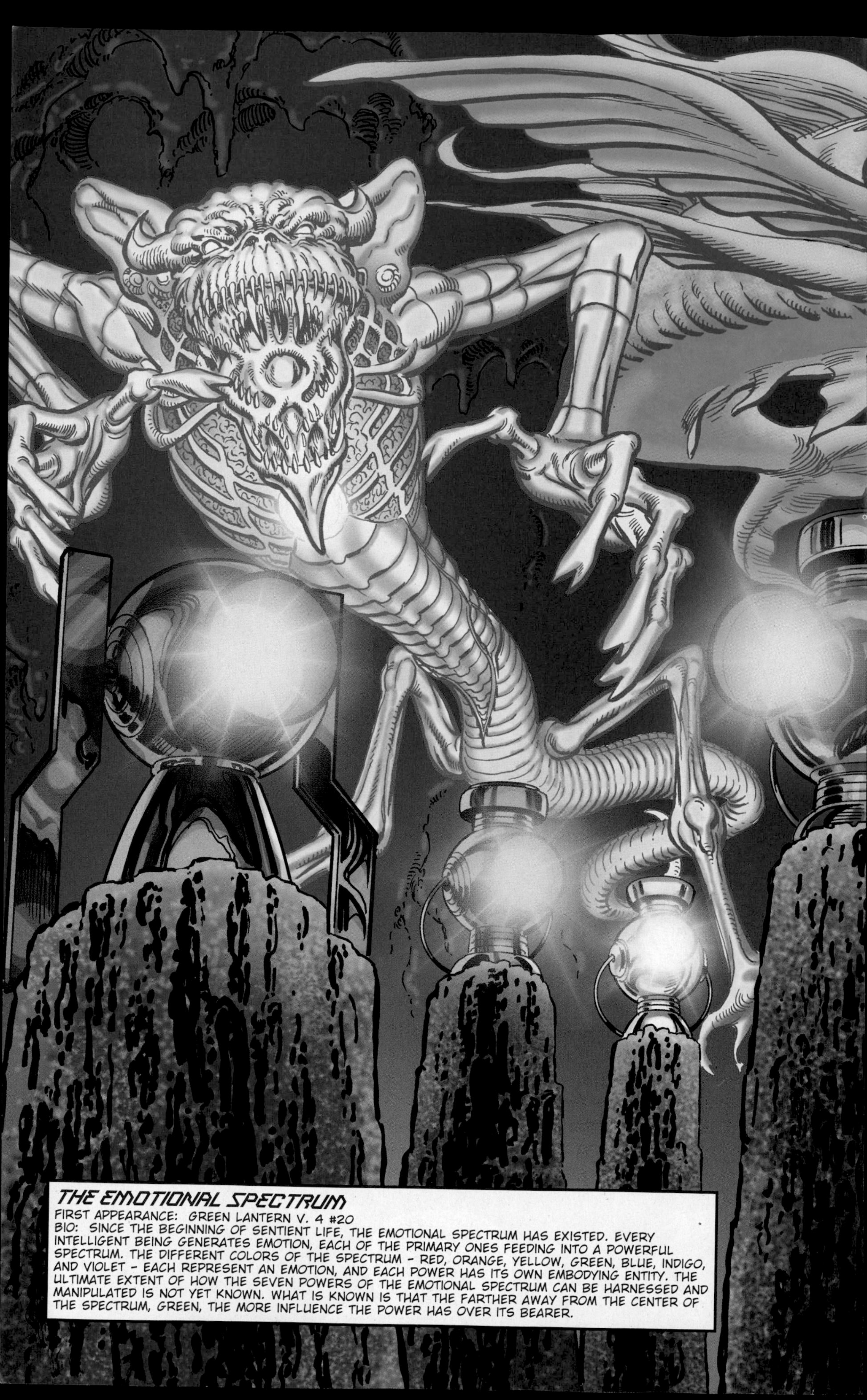
THE EMOTIONAL SPECTRUM
FIRST APPEARANCE: GREEN LANTERN V. 4 #20
BIO: SINCE THE BEGINNING OF SENTIENT LIFE, THE EMOTIONAL SPECTRUM HAS EXISTED. EVERY INTELLIGENT BEING GENERATES EMOTION, EACH OF THE PRIMARY ONES FEEDING INTO A POWERFUL SPECTRUM. THE DIFFERENT COLORS OF THE SPECTRUM - RED, ORANGE, YELLOW, GREEN, BLUE, INDIGO, AND VIOLET - EACH REPRESENT AN EMOTION, AND EACH POWER HAS ITS OWN EMBODYING ENTITY. THE ULTIMATE EXTENT OF HOW THE SEVEN POWERS OF THE EMOTIONAL SPECTRUM CAN BE HARNESSED AND MANIPULATED IS NOT YET KNOWN. WHAT IS KNOWN IS THAT THE FARTHER AWAY FROM THE CENTER OF THE SPECTRUM, GREEN, THE MORE INFLUENCE THE POWER HAS OVER ITS BEARER.

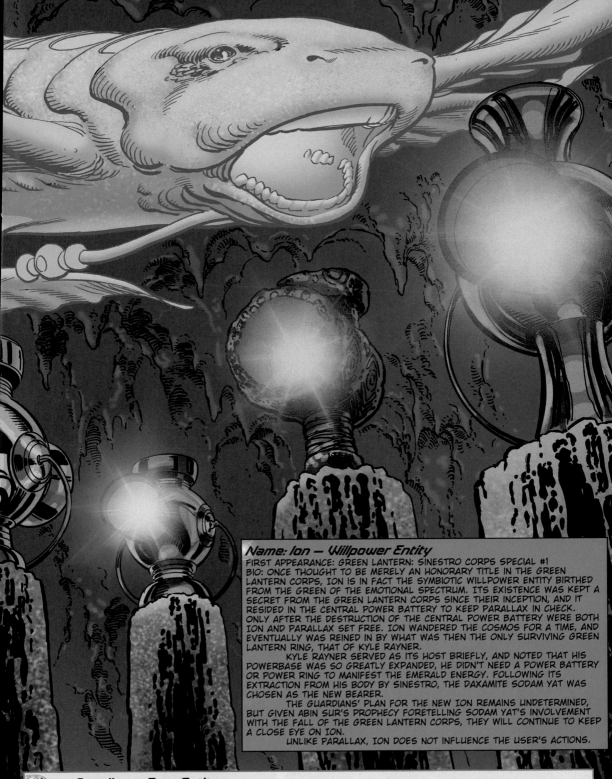

Name: Ion — Willpower Entity

FIRST APPEARANCE: GREEN LANTERN: SINESTRO CORPS SPECIAL #1

BIO: ONCE THOUGHT TO BE MERELY AN HONORARY TITLE IN THE GREEN LANTERN CORPS, ION IS IN FACT THE SYMBIOTIC WILLPOWER ENTITY BIRTHED FROM THE GREEN OF THE EMOTIONAL SPECTRUM. ITS EXISTENCE WAS KEPT A SECRET FROM THE GREEN LANTERN CORPS SINCE THEIR INCEPTION, AND IT RESIDED IN THE CENTRAL POWER BATTERY TO KEEP PARALLAX IN CHECK. ONLY AFTER THE DESTRUCTION OF THE CENTRAL POWER BATTERY WERE BOTH ION AND PARALLAX SET FREE. ION WANDERED THE COSMOS FOR A TIME, AND EVENTUALLY WAS REINED IN BY WHAT WAS THEN THE ONLY SURVIVING GREEN LANTERN RING, THAT OF KYLE RAYNER.

KYLE RAYNER SERVED AS ITS HOST BRIEFLY, AND NOTED THAT HIS POWERBASE WAS SO GREATLY EXPANDED, HE DIDN'T NEED A POWER BATTERY OR POWER RING TO MANIFEST THE EMERALD ENERGY. FOLLOWING ITS EXTRACTION FROM HIS BODY BY SINESTRO, THE DAXAMITE SODAM YAT WAS CHOSEN AS THE NEW BEARER.

THE GUARDIANS' PLAN FOR THE NEW ION REMAINS UNDETERMINED, BUT GIVEN ABIN SUR'S PROPHECY FORETELLING SODAM YAT'S INVOLVEMENT WITH THE FALL OF THE GREEN LANTERN CORPS, THEY WILL CONTINUE TO KEEP A CLOSE EYE ON ION.

UNLIKE PARALLAX, ION DOES NOT INFLUENCE THE USER'S ACTIONS.

Name: Parallax — Fear Entity

FIRST APPEARANCE: GREEN LANTERN: REBIRTH #3

BIO: AS SOON AS SENTIENT BEINGS IN THE UNIVERSE FELT FEAR, PARALLAX WAS BORN. AS FEAR GREW ACROSS THE UNIVERSE, PARALLAX GAINED ITS OWN SENTIENCE, AND BEGAN TRAVELING FROM PLANET TO PLANET TO FEED OFF THE TERROR IT WAS CREATING. THE GUARDIANS FINALLY IMPRISONED PARALLAX WITHIN THE CENTRAL POWER BATTERY, HELD IN PLACE BY THE CONCENTRATION OF WILLPOWER. OVER TIME, THE NAME AND LEGEND OF PARALLAX WAS FORGOTTEN, ONLY REFERRED TO AS THE "YELLOW IMPURITY" WHICH LEFT THE GREEN LANTERN CORPS' RINGS HELPLESS AGAINST ANYTHING YELLOW.

AFTER THE RENEGADE GREEN LANTERN SINESTRO WAS HIMSELF INCARCERATED WITHIN THE CENTRAL POWER BATTERY, HE DISCOVERED AND AWOKE PARALLAX. THE FEAR CREATURE, UNDER SINESTRO'S DIRECTION, REACHED OUT AND INFECTED THE GREEN LANTERN HAL JORDAN AND TOOK POSSESSION OF HIM. WITH THE HELP OF THE SPECTRE, JORDAN BROKE FREE OF PARALLAX, AND THE MONSTER FOUND ITSELF AGAIN WITHOUT A HOST.

SINESTRO TURNED TO A DIFFERENT EARTHMAN AND WAGED A PRIVATE WAR OF TERROR ON KYLE RAYNER TO WEAKEN HIS RESOLVE. WHEN HE WAS AT HIS LOWEST, SINESTRO GRAFTED PARALLAX ONTO HIS SOUL. HAL JORDAN WAS ABLE TO FREE KYLE, AND THE GUARDIANS GANTHET AND SAYD SPLIT PARALLAX INTO FOUR EQUAL PARTS AND PLACED THEM INSIDE THE POWER BATTERIES OF THE FOUR EARTH GREEN LANTERNS.

ONLY TIME WILL TELL HOW LONG THIS WILL DETAIN PARALLAX.

ART BY JERRY ORDWAY.

Name: Star Sapphires

FIRST APPEARANCE: ALL-FLASH COMICS #32

BIO: BILLIONS OF YEARS AGO, THE GUARDIANS OF THE UNIVERSE SUPPRESSED ALL OF THEIR EMOTIONS FOR FEAR THEY WOULD AFFECT THEIR ACTIONS. A TRIBE OF WOMEN SAW THE LOSS OF EMOTION AS BLASPHEMY, AND OPTED TO LEAVE OA RATHER THAN EMBRACE WHAT THEIR COUNTERPARTS ASKED OF THEM.

AFTER A MILLENNIA SEARCHING, THE TRIBE FOUND SOMETHING ON THE PLANET ZAMARON: A VIOLET GEM CREATED OUT OF THE DYING LOVE OF TWO OF THE PLANET'S INHABITANTS. THE GEM WOULD BE WHAT THE GUARDIANS FEARED, MAGNIFYING THE MOST POTENT OF EMOTIONS, LOVE. THE GEM GRAFTED ITSELF ONTO ONE OF THE TRIBE, AND SOON AFTER, THEY BEGAN THEIR EXPERIMENTS ON IT.

THE FORMER OANS PERFECTED THEIR LOVE GEMS AND SENT THEM OUT ACROSS THE STARS. ALWAYS THE IMPULSE CONTAINED IN IT IS CLEAR: BOND WITH THE MATE OF THE SECTOR'S GREEN LANTERN. THE COUPLING OF WILLPOWER AND LOVE GAVE THE STAR SAPPHIRES THE ABILITY TO CRYSTALLIZE EVERY LIVING CELL ON A PLANET'S SURFACE, FORMING A DIAMOND-HARD PROTECTIVE SHELL ACROSS A WORLD. THE ZAMARONS SAW THIS AS THE PERFECT WAY TO PREVENT WARS OF THE FUTURE, SPREADING THEIR LOVE ACROSS THE COSMOS. A STAR SAPPHIRE HAS BEEN SEEN OFTEN ON THE PLANET EARTH, AND IT HAS POSSESSED A NUMBER OF WOMEN CONNECTED TO HAL JORDAN, INCLUDING CAROL FERRIS, DEBORAH CAMILLE DARNELL, AND JILLIAN "COWGIRL" PEARLMAN.

RECENTLY, THE ZAMARONS HAVE BEGUN TO FORGE THEIR OWN RINGS AND BATTERIES, ABANDONING THE GEMS AS THEY DEEMED THEM TOO UNCONTROLLABLE. THEIR ULTIMATE GOAL REMAINS A MYSTERY.

ART BY IVAN REIS AND OCLAIR ALBERT

Name: Cowgirl

FIRST APPEARANCE: GREEN LANTERN V. 4 #1

BIO: LEE PEARLMAN ALWAYS WANTED A DAUGHTER, AND ON THE FOURTH TRY, HE GOT ONE. JILLIAN PEARLMAN WAS BORN AND RAISED WITH HER THREE OLDER BROTHERS ON A HORSE RANCH OUTSIDE OF ABILENE, TEXAS. FROM HER CHILDHOOD ON, ALL JILLIAN WANTED TO DO WAS FLY. SHE LEFT HER FATHER'S RANCH WHEN SHE WAS 19 AND ENLISTED IN THE AIR FORCE, WHERE HER SHARP WIT, COCKY ATTITUDE AND TEXAS ACCENT EARNED HER THE CALL SIGN "COWGIRL."

COWGIRL AND HAL SPENT MONTHS IN A CHECHNYAN PRISON CAMP AFTER THEIR PLANES WERE SHOT DOWN, AN EVENT THAT BROUGHT THEM CLOSER TOGETHER. COWGIRL WAS RECENTLY PLAGUED BY A STAR SAPPHIRE GEM, BUT WAS FREED WITH THE HELP OF HAL AND CAROL FERRIS.

FOLLOWING HER REVELATION TO HAL THAT SHE KNEW HE WAS GREEN LANTERN, THE TWO BEGAN DATING.

ART BY DANIEL ACUNA.

Name: Carol Ferris

FIRST APPEARANCE: SHOWCASE #22

BIO: CAROL FERRIS HAS KNOWN HAL JORDAN SINCE THEY WERE TEN YEARS OLD, WHEN THEY MET ON THE RUNWAY AT HER FATHER'S COMPANY, FERRIS AIR. SHE WITNESSED HAL'S FATHER'S PLANE CRASH ALONGSIDE HAL. YEARS LATER, AFTER CARL FERRIS'S UNEXPECTED EARLY RETIREMENT, CAROL, A PILOT HERSELF, WAS FORCED TO TAKE OVER THE COMPANY. HER HEAD CAME OUT OF THE CLOUDS AND INTO THE ACCOUNTING BOOKS. MANY OF HER FRIENDS SAW THE OUTSPOKEN, HAPPY YOUNG WOMAN THEY KNEW BECOME OVERWHELMED BY THE BUSINESS. IF SHE HAD HAD A CHOICE, SHE WOULD HAVE NEVER STOPPED BEING A PILOT, BUT CAROL ACCEPTED THE ROLE TO HELP HER FATHER THROUGH A DIFFICULT TIME. CAROL AND HAL CLASHED FROM THE VERY BEGINNING OF HIS EMPLOYMENT WITH FERRIS, BUT EVENTUALLY THEY FELL FOR ONE ANOTHER.

HER FEELINGS FOR GREEN LANTERN WERE FOREVER CHANGED WHEN THE ZAMARONS CHOSE CAROL TO BEAR A STAR SAPPHIRE AND BECOME THE GREEN LANTERN'S PERFECT MATE. HAL SEPARATED HER FROM THE STAR SAPPHIRE, BUT OVER THE NEXT FEW YEARS THE GEM WOULD RETURN TO PLAGUE HER AGAIN AND AGAIN. AFTER HAL SEEMINGLY DIED, CAROL MARRIED.

HER MARRIAGE FELL APART SHORTLY AFTER HAL'S COMEBACK. CAROL HAS SINCE RETURNED TO RUN FERRIS AIR, BUT OFTEN MISSES MEETINGS. SHE TAKES HER OWN PLANES ON SHORT, DAREDEVIL FLIGHTS, RECAPTURING HER YOUTH.

ART BY DANIEL ACUNA

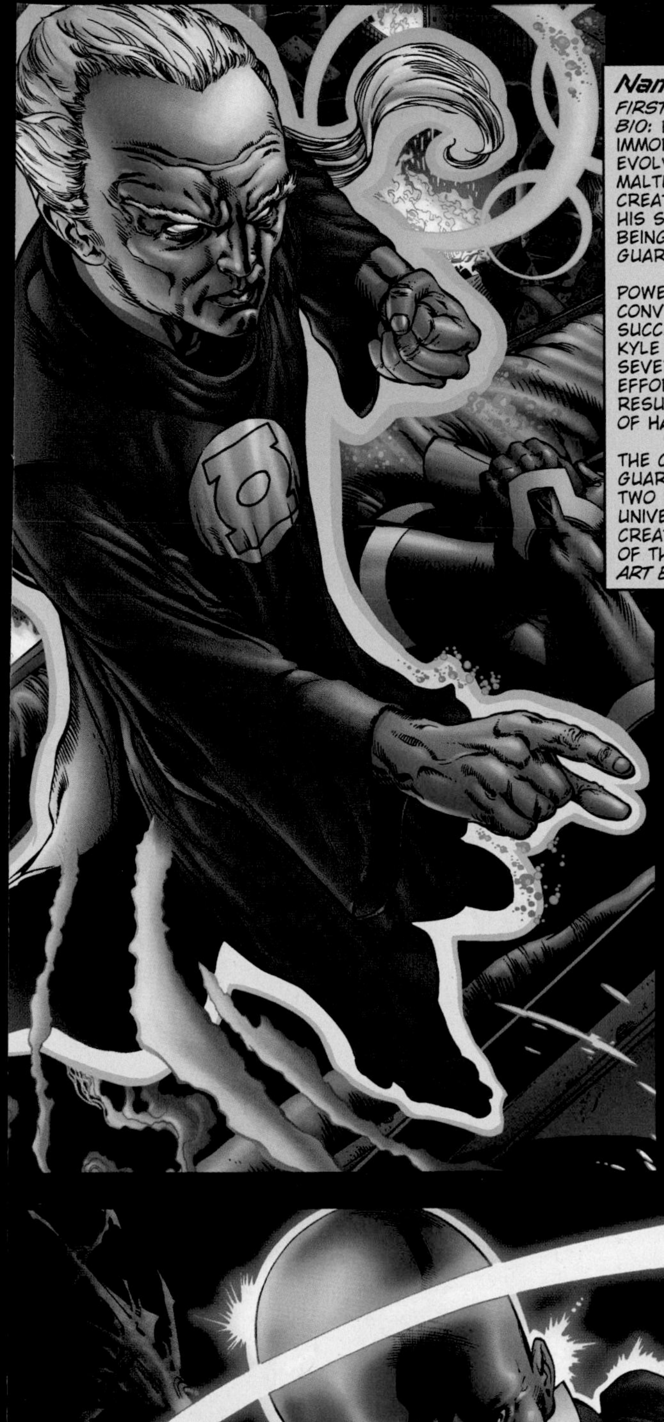

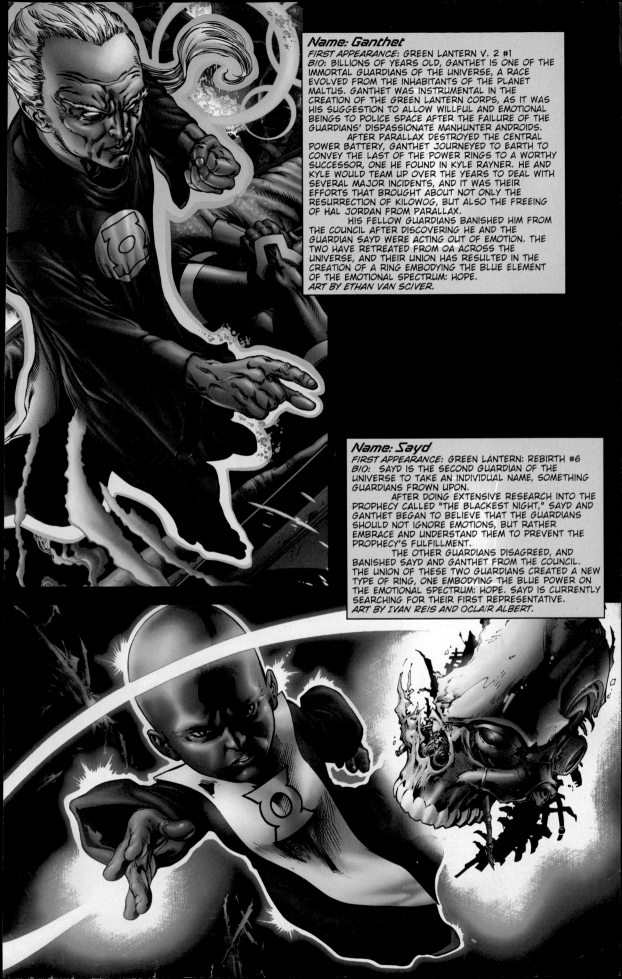

Name: Ganthet

FIRST APPEARANCE: GREEN LANTERN V. 2 #1
BIO: BILLIONS OF YEARS OLD, GANTHET IS ONE OF THE IMMORTAL GUARDIANS OF THE UNIVERSE, A RACE EVOLVED FROM THE INHABITANTS OF THE PLANET MALTUS. GANTHET WAS INSTRUMENTAL IN THE CREATION OF THE GREEN LANTERN CORPS, AS IT WAS HIS SUGGESTION TO ALLOW WILLFUL AND EMOTIONAL BEINGS TO POLICE SPACE AFTER THE FAILURE OF THE GUARDIANS' DISPASSIONATE MANHUNTER ANDROIDS.

AFTER PARALLAX DESTROYED THE CENTRAL POWER BATTERY, GANTHET JOURNEYED TO EARTH TO CONVEY THE LAST OF THE POWER RINGS TO A WORTHY SUCCESSOR, ONE HE FOUND IN KYLE RAYNER. HE AND KYLE WOULD TEAM UP OVER THE YEARS TO DEAL WITH SEVERAL MAJOR INCIDENTS, AND IT WAS THEIR EFFORTS THAT BROUGHT ABOUT NOT ONLY THE RESURRECTION OF KILOWOG, BUT ALSO THE FREEING OF HAL JORDAN FROM PARALLAX.

HIS FELLOW GUARDIANS BANISHED HIM FROM THE COUNCIL AFTER DISCOVERING HE AND THE GUARDIAN SAYD WERE ACTING OUT OF EMOTION. THE TWO HAVE RETREATED FROM OA ACROSS THE UNIVERSE, AND THEIR UNION HAS RESULTED IN THE CREATION OF A RING EMBODYING THE BLUE ELEMENT OF THE EMOTIONAL SPECTRUM: HOPE.
ART BY ETHAN VAN SCIVER.

Name: Sayd

FIRST APPEARANCE: GREEN LANTERN: REBIRTH #6
BIO: SAYD IS THE SECOND GUARDIAN OF THE UNIVERSE TO TAKE AN INDIVIDUAL NAME, SOMETHING GUARDIANS FROWN UPON.

AFTER DOING EXTENSIVE RESEARCH INTO THE PROPHECY CALLED "THE BLACKEST NIGHT," SAYD AND GANTHET BEGAN TO BELIEVE THAT THE GUARDIANS SHOULD NOT IGNORE EMOTIONS, BUT RATHER EMBRACE AND UNDERSTAND THEM TO PREVENT THE PROPHECY'S FULFILLMENT.

THE OTHER GUARDIANS DISAGREED, AND BANISHED SAYD AND GANTHET FROM THE COUNCIL. THE UNION OF THESE TWO GUARDIANS CREATED A NEW TYPE OF RING, ONE EMBODYING THE BLUE POWER ON THE EMOTIONAL SPECTRUM: HOPE. SAYD IS CURRENTLY SEARCHING FOR THEIR FIRST REPRESENTATIVE.
ART BY IVAN REIS AND OCLAIR ALBERT.

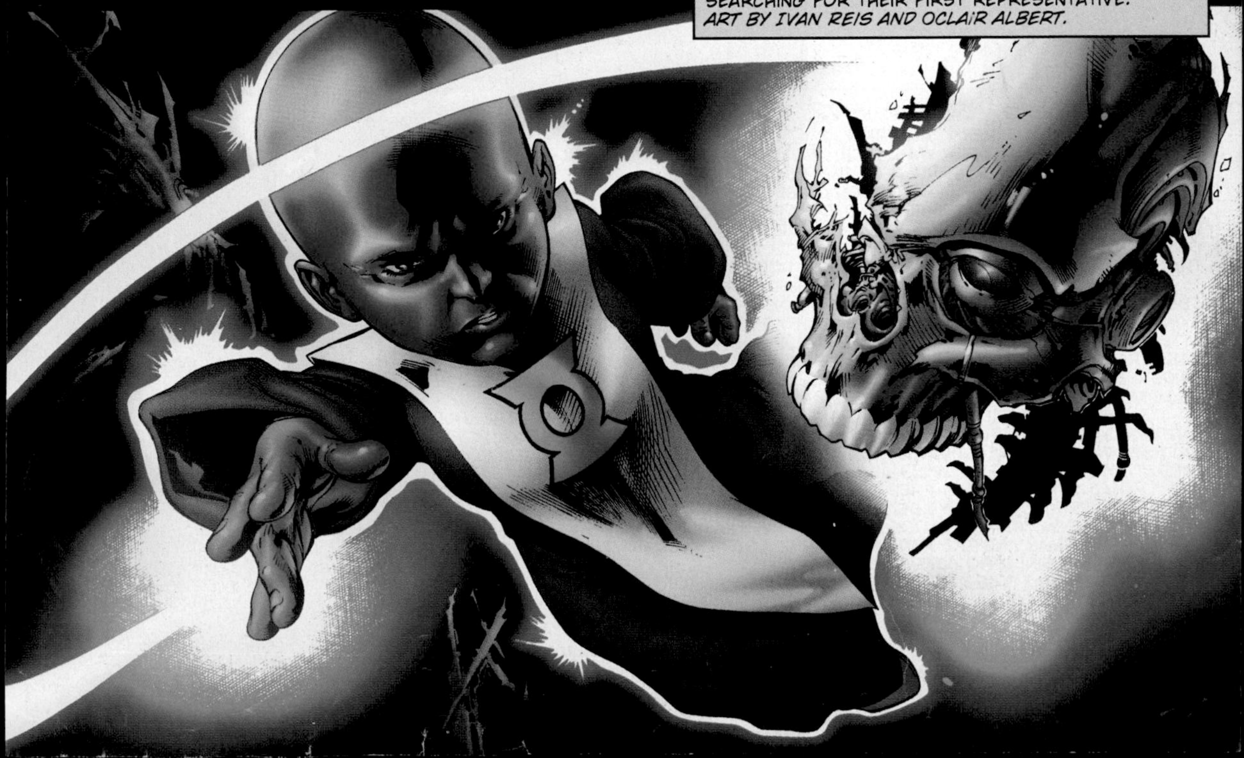

RECENTLY, THE VERY FIRST RENEGADE OF THE GREEN LANTERN CORPS, SINESTRO, CREATED AN ARMY TO INSTILL GREAT FEAR ACROSS THE UNIVERSE. RECRUITED FOR THEIR DEVIANT, EVIL AND TWISTED PSYCHOSES, FROM PLANETS OF EVERY SECTOR IN SPACE, THE MOST HORRIFYING AND VICIOUS SERVE SINESTRO AS MEMBERS OF THE INTERGALACTIC TERRORISTS KNOWN AS THE

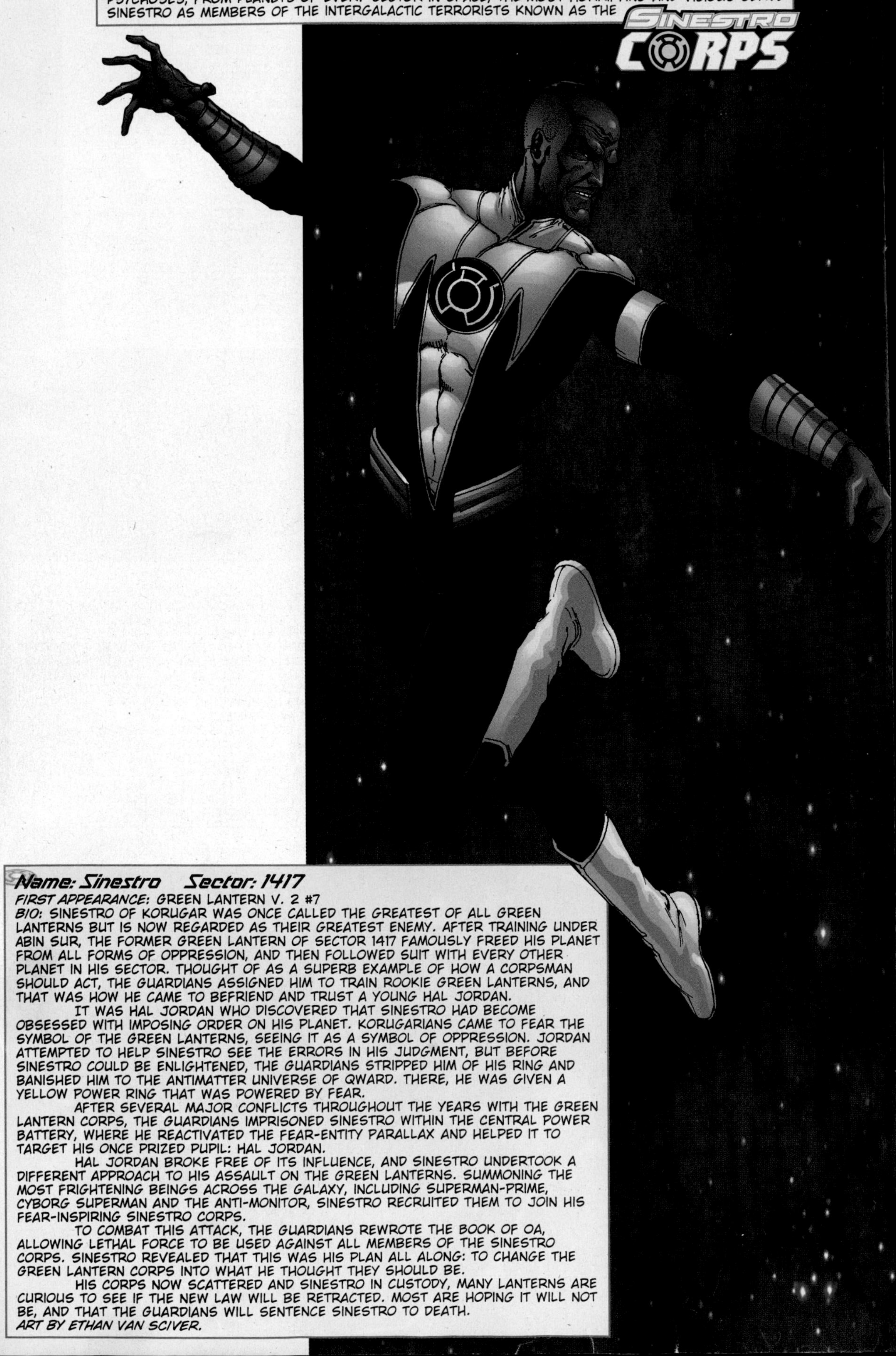
SINESTRO CORPS

Name: Sinestro   Sector: 1417

FIRST APPEARANCE: GREEN LANTERN V. 2 #7

BIO: SINESTRO OF KORUGAR WAS ONCE CALLED THE GREATEST OF ALL GREEN LANTERNS BUT IS NOW REGARDED AS THEIR GREATEST ENEMY. AFTER TRAINING UNDER ABIN SUR, THE FORMER GREEN LANTERN OF SECTOR 1417 FAMOUSLY FREED HIS PLANET FROM ALL FORMS OF OPPRESSION, AND THEN FOLLOWED SUIT WITH EVERY OTHER PLANET IN HIS SECTOR. THOUGHT OF AS A SUPERB EXAMPLE OF HOW A CORPSMAN SHOULD ACT, THE GUARDIANS ASSIGNED HIM TO TRAIN ROOKIE GREEN LANTERNS, AND THAT WAS HOW HE CAME TO BEFRIEND AND TRUST A YOUNG HAL JORDAN.

IT WAS HAL JORDAN WHO DISCOVERED THAT SINESTRO HAD BECOME OBSESSED WITH IMPOSING ORDER ON HIS PLANET. KORUGARIANS CAME TO FEAR THE SYMBOL OF THE GREEN LANTERNS, SEEING IT AS A SYMBOL OF OPPRESSION. JORDAN ATTEMPTED TO HELP SINESTRO SEE THE ERRORS IN HIS JUDGMENT, BUT BEFORE SINESTRO COULD BE ENLIGHTENED, THE GUARDIANS STRIPPED HIM OF HIS RING AND BANISHED HIM TO THE ANTIMATTER UNIVERSE OF QWARD. THERE, HE WAS GIVEN A YELLOW POWER RING THAT WAS POWERED BY FEAR.

AFTER SEVERAL MAJOR CONFLICTS THROUGHOUT THE YEARS WITH THE GREEN LANTERN CORPS, THE GUARDIANS IMPRISONED SINESTRO WITHIN THE CENTRAL POWER BATTERY, WHERE HE REACTIVATED THE FEAR-ENTITY PARALLAX AND HELPED IT TO TARGET HIS ONCE PRIZED PUPIL: HAL JORDAN.

HAL JORDAN BROKE FREE OF ITS INFLUENCE, AND SINESTRO UNDERTOOK A DIFFERENT APPROACH TO HIS ASSAULT ON THE GREEN LANTERNS. SUMMONING THE MOST FRIGHTENING BEINGS ACROSS THE GALAXY, INCLUDING SUPERMAN-PRIME, CYBORG SUPERMAN AND THE ANTI-MONITOR, SINESTRO RECRUITED THEM TO JOIN HIS FEAR-INSPIRING SINESTRO CORPS.

TO COMBAT THIS ATTACK, THE GUARDIANS REWROTE THE BOOK OF OA, ALLOWING LETHAL FORCE TO BE USED AGAINST ALL MEMBERS OF THE SINESTRO CORPS. SINESTRO REVEALED THAT THIS WAS HIS PLAN ALL ALONG: TO CHANGE THE GREEN LANTERN CORPS INTO WHAT HE THOUGHT THEY SHOULD BE.

HIS CORPS NOW SCATTERED AND SINESTRO IN CUSTODY, MANY LANTERNS ARE CURIOUS TO SEE IF THE NEW LAW WILL BE RETRACTED. MOST ARE HOPING IT WILL NOT BE, AND THAT THE GUARDIANS WILL SENTENCE SINESTRO TO DEATH.

ART BY ETHAN VAN SCIVER.

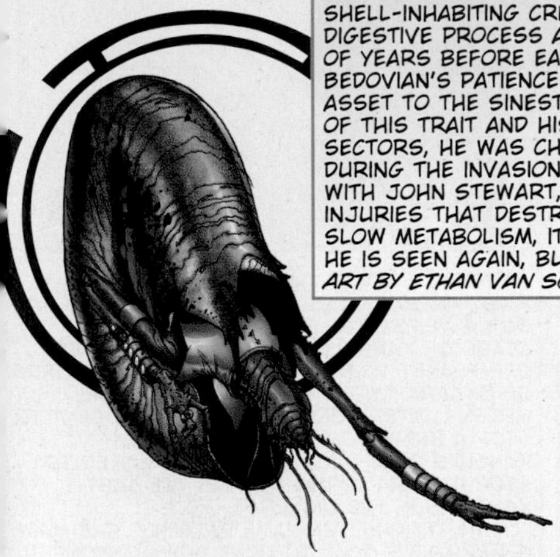

Name: Bedovian Sector: 3

FIRST APPEARANCE: GREEN LANTERN V. 4 #20

BIO: BEDOVIAN IS A DORENVAD, A SHELL-INHABITING CREATURE WHOSE SLOW DIGESTIVE PROCESS ALLOWS IT TO GO HUNDREDS OF YEARS BEFORE EATING ITS NEXT MEAL. BEDOVIAN'S PATIENCE MAKES IT A VALUABLE ASSET TO THE SINESTRO CORPS, AND BECAUSE OF THIS TRAIT AND HIS ABILITY TO SEE ACROSS SECTORS, HE WAS CHOSEN TO ACT AS SNIPER DURING THE INVASION OF OA. DURING THE BATTLE WITH JOHN STEWART, BEDOVIAN SUFFERED INJURIES THAT DESTROYED HIS SHELL. GIVEN ITS SLOW METABOLISM, IT COULD BE YEARS BEFORE HE IS SEEN AGAIN, BUT JOHN DOUBTS THAT.

ART BY ETHAN VAN SCIVER.

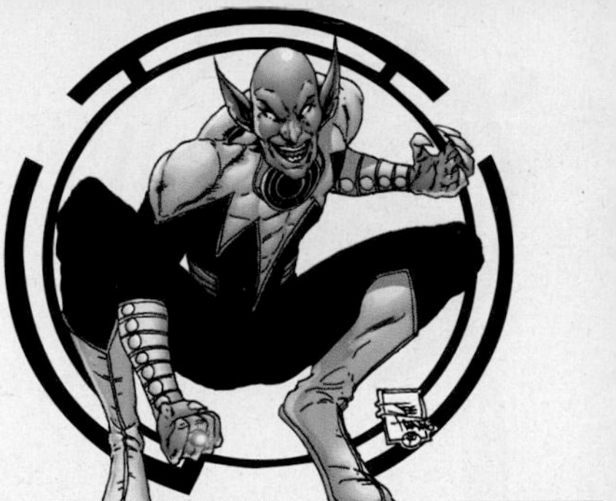

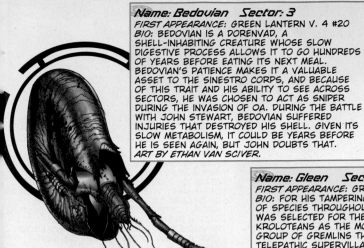

Name: Gleen Sector: 312

FIRST APPEARANCE: GREEN LANTERN V. 4 #5

BIO: FOR HIS TAMPERING WITH THE EVOLUTIONARY PATTERNS OF THOUSANDS OF SPECIES THROUGHOUT THE UNIVERSE, THE KROLOTEAN GREMLIN GLEEN WAS SELECTED FOR THE SINESTRO CORPS. GLEEN IS KNOWN AMONG THE KROLOTEANS AS THE MOST CRUEL AND TWISTED, AND HE WAS PART OF A GROUP OF GREMLINS THAT CHANGED THE HUMAN HECTOR HAMMOND INTO A TELEPATHIC SUPERVILLAIN, EVOLVED THE SHARK INTO THE HUMANOID CARNIVORE AND BEGAN THE EXPERIMENTATION WITH BLACK HAND.

ART BY JOE PRADO.

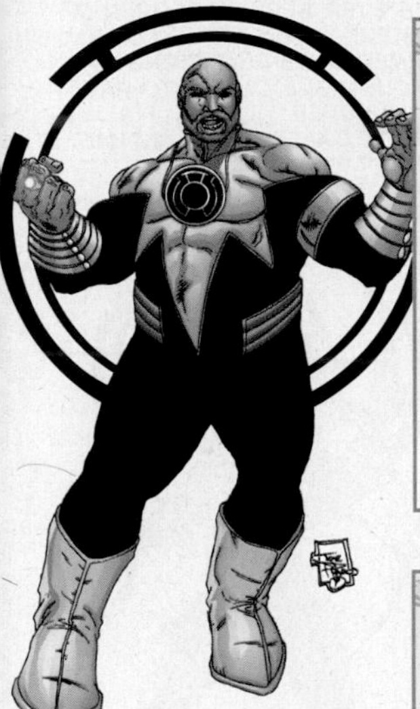

Name: Mallow
Sector: 614

FIRST APPEARANCE: GREEN LANTERN: SINESTRO CORPS SPECIAL #1

BIO: MALLOW HAS LED A BLOODTHIRSTY GROUP OF MARAUDERS FOR THE LAST SIX HUNDRED YEARS, ATTACKING SETTLEMENTS ACROSS THE OUTER PLANETS OF HIS SECTOR. THEY HAVE NEVER LEFT SURVIVORS. THEIR STRONGHOLD, FORT PIERCE, IS LOCATED WITHIN ONE OF THE MOST VIOLENT ASTEROID STORMS IN THE UNIVERSE.

ART BY JOE PRADO.

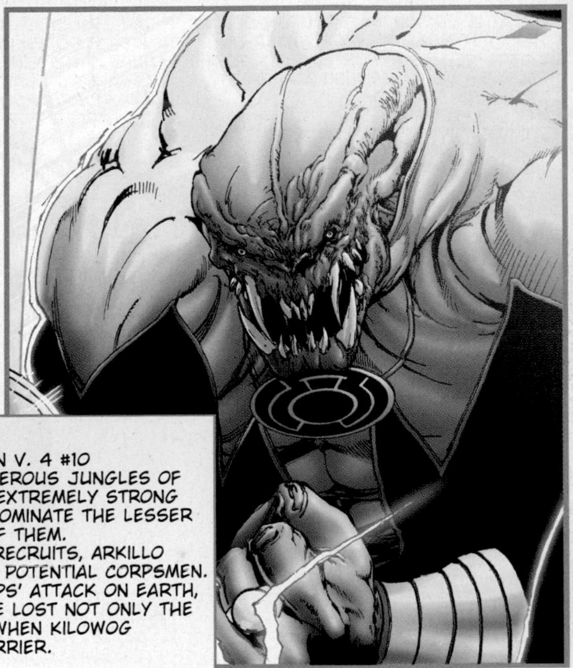

Name: Arkillo Sector: 674

FIRST APPEARANCE: GREEN LANTERN V. 4 #10

BIO: ARKILLO GREW UP IN THE DANGEROUS JUNGLES OF THE PLANET CORISTEEL. ARKILLO IS EXTREMELY STRONG AND HAS USED THIS STRENGTH TO DOMINATE THE LESSER RACES OF THE PLANET AND FEED OFF THEM.

ONE OF SINESTRO'S FIRST RECRUITS, ARKILLO BECAME THE DRILL INSTRUCTOR FOR POTENTIAL CORPSMEN.

DURING THE SINESTRO CORPS' ATTACK ON EARTH, HE FACED OFF AGAINST KILOWOG. HE LOST NOT ONLY THE FIGHT, BUT ALSO HIS RING FINGER, WHEN KILOWOG CRUSHED HIM WITH AN AIRCRAFT CARRIER.

ART BY ETHAN VAN SCIVER.

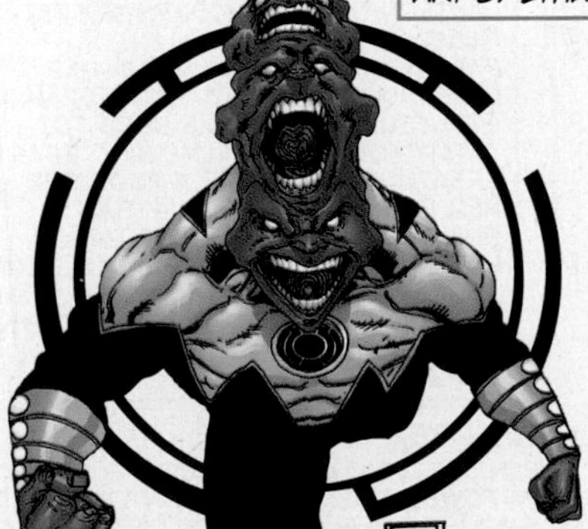

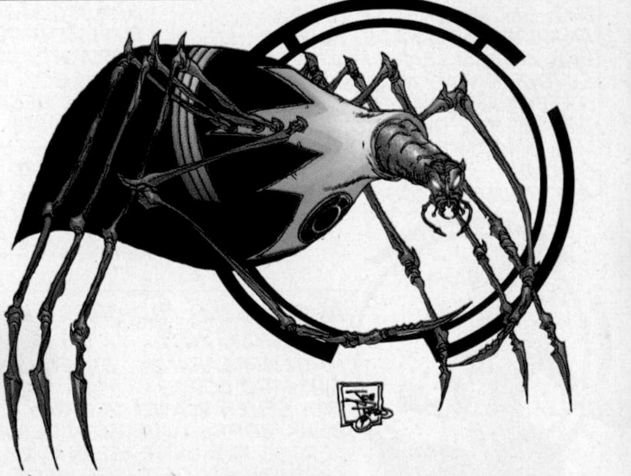

Name: Maash Sector: 863

FIRST APPEARANCE: GREEN LANTERN: SINESTRO CORPS SPECIAL #1

BIO: ORIGINALLY CONCEIVED AS TRIPLETS IN THE WOMB, WHEN MAASH WAS BORN, THE DOCTORS FOUND THAT THE BABIES HAD MERGED TOGETHER INTO ONE BODY. EACH OF MAASH'S THREE FACES HAS A DIFFERENT MIND AND PERSONALITY, AND EACH ONE FIGHTS FOR CONTROL OF THE BODY IT SITS ATOP. TWO OF THEM ARE MURDERERS, EACH KILLING AND MUTILATING THEIR VICTIMS IN DIFFERENT WAYS. OFTEN THE TOPMOST FACE, THE INNOCENT MAN, CAN ONLY WATCH AS HIS OWN BODY COMMITS HEINOUS ACTS. HE DREAMS OF THE DAY HE CAN FINALLY COMMAND HIS BODY. THAT DAY WILL NEVER COME.

ART BY JOE PRADO.

Name: Sirket Sector: 1110

FIRST APPEARANCE: GREEN LANTERN: SINESTRO CORPS SPECIAL #1

BIO: SIRKET IS A BLEEDBUG, AN INSECT THAT LIVES IN THE SPACE BETWEEN DIMENSIONS. HOW IT CAME TO RESIDE ON OUR PLANE IS UNKNOWN, THOUGH MANY HAVE SPECULATED THAT THE ANTI-MONITOR BROUGHT IT TO OUR DIMENSION TO EXPERIMENT ON IT. WHEN SIRKET RUBS ITS MASSIVE FRONT LEGS TOGETHER, THE SOUND IT MAKES CAN DRIVE MEN MAD.

ART BY JOE PRADO.

Name: Setag Retss
Sector: 1155
FIRST APPEARANCE: GREEN LANTERN: SINESTRO CORPS SPECIAL #1
BIO: SETAG RETSS COMES FROM A RACE OF UNDER-REPTILES FOUND IN THE DEPTHS OF THE DARK WATER PLANETS OF THE REXULLUS SYSTEM. SETAG'S RING ENABLES HIM TO BREATHE OUT OF WATER. UPON SEEING THE VAST QUANTITIES OF WATER ON EARTH, HE HAS REPORTED BACK TO HIS PEOPLE – HE HAS FOUND A PERFECT SPAWNING GROUND.
ART BY JOE PRADO.

Name: Yellow Lantern
Sector: 1284
FIRST APPEARANCE: ACTION COMICS #856
BIO: CREATED BY BIZARRO TO PROTECT THE BIZARRO WORLD, YELLOW LANTERN IS A BIZARRO VERSION OF HAL JORDAN. UNAWARE OF HIS OWN POWER, YELLOW LANTERN UNWITTINGLY INCINERATED OVER A DOZEN PEOPLE IN NEW YORK DURING THE SINESTRO CORPS' ASSAULT ON EARTH.
ART BY ERIC POWELL.

Name: Fatality   Sector: 1313
FIRST APPEARANCE: GREEN LANTERN V. 3 #83
BIO: A MEMBER OF THE RULING WARRIOR CLASS OF XANSHI, YRRA CYRNIL WAS SENT OFF-PLANET TO BE TRAINED BY THE WARLORDS OF OKAARA. WHILE SHE WAS THERE, THE GREEN LANTERN JOHN STEWART WAS SENT TO STOP A BLINK-BOMB FROM EXPLODING XANSHI'S CORE, AND BECAUSE HE FAILED TO STOP IT, YRRA CYRNIL BECAME THE LAST XANSHIAN IN THE UNIVERSE.
TAKING THE NAME FATALITY, SHE MADE IT HER LIFE'S GOAL TO HUNT DOWN ANYONE WHO IS, OR HAS EVER BEEN, A MEMBER OF THE GREEN LANTERN CORPS. IT IS NOT KNOWN HOW MANY FORMER GREEN LANTERNS SHE HAS KILLED, THOUGH SHE CLAIMS TO HAVE KILLED OVER A HUNDRED.
ART BY JOE BENITEZ AND VICTOR LLAMAS.

Name: Smithwick
Sector: 1418
FIRST APPEARANCE: GREEN LANTERN: SINESTRO CORPS SPECIAL #1
BIO: SMITHWICK BELIEVES IN ANARCHY AND CHAOS. HE WAS ENRAGED TO LEARN THAT A FELLOW SLYGGIAN WAS A MEMBER OF THE GREEN LANTERN CORPS. SINCE JOINING THE SINESTRO CORPS, HE HAS SWORN TO FIND AND KILL SALAAK.
ART BY JOE PRADO.

Name: DevilDog
Sector: 1567
FIRST APPEARANCE: GREEN LANTERN: SINESTRO CORPS SPECIAL #1
BIO: A CONVICTED ASSASSIN ON AT LEAST 17 DIFFERENT PLANETS, DEVILDOG GAINED NOTORIETY AFTER THE ASSASSINATION OF SAMNI HOY, PRESIDENT OF HIS PLANET. HER BRUTAL DECAPITATION AT DEVILDOG'S HANDS DURING A SECTOR-WIDE LIVE BROADCAST MADE HIM THE MOST WANTED AND FEARED BEING OF SECTOR 1567. VRIL DOX OF THE L.E.G.I.O.N. HAS DIRECTED ALL OF HIS RESOURCES TO FINDING DEVILDOG.
ART BY JOE PRADO.

Name: Kiriazis
Sector: 1771
FIRST APPEARANCE: GREEN LANTERN/SINESTRO CORPS SECRET FILES #1
BIO: KIRIAZIS IS KNOWN FOR HER CRYSTALLINE WEBS, CANNON-SPANNING STRUCTURES THAT SHE USES TO CATCH KORBALLIAN LIGHTNING BEASTS, CREATURES THAT ARE A FOOD FOR HER RACE. SINCE JOINING THE SINESTRO CORPS, KIRIAZIS HAS EXPERIMENTED WITH REFRACTING THE YELLOW ENERGY THROUGH HER BODY TO GENERATE LASER WEBS THAT BIND AND CUT HER VICTIMS.
ART BY JOE PRADO.

Name: Seer Ruggle
Sector: 2700
FIRST APPEARANCE: GREEN LANTERN: SINESTRO CORPS SPECIAL #1
BIO: SEVEN PLANET-DESTROYING BLINK-BOMBS HAVE BEEN DETONATED ACROSS THE UNIVERSE IN THE LAST CENTURY. SIX OF THOSE WERE DESIGNED AND BUILT BY SEER RUGGLE. THE BOMB MISTRESS OF RORC HAS BEEN CONTACTED BY SEVERAL MERCENARY AND TERRORIST ORGANIZATIONS OVER THE YEARS, BUT SHE IS HIGHLY SELECTIVE ABOUT WHICH GROUPS SHE WILL SELL TO. UPON JOINING THE SINESTRO CORPS, SEER RUGGLE GAVE THE CHILDREN OF THE WHITE LOBE A BLINK-BOMB TO SET OFF ON MOGO. SEER WAS EXTREMELY DISAPPOINTED IN THEIR FAILURE.
ART BY JOE PRADO.

Name: Flayt   Sector: 2751
FIRST APPEARANCE: GREEN LANTERN: SINESTRO CORPS SPECIAL #1
BIO: FLAYT IS A TRISTRAM POWER-RAY, LATCHING ONTO THE SIDES OF PASSING SHIPS AND SUCKING THEIR POWER CELLS DRY. FLAYT LEFT HUNDREDS OF SHIPS STRANDED WITHOUT POWER OR LIFE SUPPORT DURING THE TRISTRAM-ZANNER IMPERIAL WAR.
ART BY JOE PRADO.

Name: Mongul
Sector: 2811
FIRST APPEARANCE: SHOWCASE '95 #8
BIO: THE FIRST MONGUL WAS AN INTERGALACTIC WARMONGER WHO SPANNED THE UNIVERSE, WREAKING HAVOC ON UNSUSPECTING PLANETS WITH HIS "WARWORLD." HE SUFFERED MANY DEFEATS, HOWEVER, BY THE HEROES OF THE PLANET EARTH. ALONG WITH THE CYBORG-SUPERMAN, MONGUL WAS RESPONSIBLE FOR THE DESTRUCTION OF COAST CITY.

MONGUL LEFT HIS NAME AND EMPIRE TO HIS SON AND DAUGHTER. MONGUL KILLED HIS SISTER, TIRED OF HER INTERFERENCE. NOW, JUST AS HIS FATHER TOOK AN INTEREST IN EARTH, SO HAS THIS NEW MONGUL. HE HAS SWORN TO MUTILATE THE PLANET'S INHABITANTS TO EXACT REVENGE FOR HIS FATHER'S LIFETIME OF DEFEATS. HIS PROCUREMENT OF A SINESTRO CORPS RING NOW GIVES HIM A FINE TOOL WITH WHICH TO TAKE HIS VENGEANCE.
ART BY JOE PRADO.

Name: Romat-Ru
Sector: 2813
FIRST APPEARANCE: GREEN LANTERN: SINESTRO CORPS SPECIAL #1
BIO: THE XUDARIAN CALLED ROMAT-RU IS ONE OF THE VILEST CREATURES IN THE GALAXY. FOLLOWING HIS ARREST ON A MINOR CHARGE, THE POLICE FORCE SENT TO INVESTIGATE HIS HOUSE FOUND THE BONES OF THOUSANDS OF CHILDREN. AS HE WAS BEING ESCORTED TO HIS LIFE-CELL, THE SINESTRO CORPS RING APPEARED AND RECRUITED HIM.
ART BY JOE PRADO.

Name: Amon Sur   Sector: 2814
FIRST APPEARANCE: GREEN LANTERN V. 3 #162
BIO: SON OF THE GREEN LANTERN ABIN SUR, AMON SUR SPENT YEARS VOWING REVENGE ON HAL JORDAN FOR TAKING POSSESSION OF HIS FATHER'S RING, AN HONOR AMON SUR FELT HE HIMSELF DESERVED. BUT DEEP IN HIS SOUL AMON KNEW HE WOULD NEVER BE ABLE TO GET A GREEN LANTERN RING TO WORK - HE WASN'T CAPABLE OF GENERATING SUCH WILLPOWER. AMON HOPED TO FIND A DIFFERENT WAY TO CARVE A NAME FOR HIMSELF, AND SPENT TIME AS A PART OF THE BLACK CIRCLE CRIME SYNDICATE, WHERE HE PURPORTEDLY KILLED THOUSANDS OF PEOPLE. KYLE RAYNER STOPPED THEIR ACTIVITIES ON EARTH, AND AMON SUR'S HEAD WAS BLOWN OFF.

BUT NOT ALL RACES ARE AS VULNERABLE TO CRANIAL INJURIES AS TERRESTRIALS, AND AMON'S HEAD RECONSTITUTED OVER TIME. LEARNING OF HAL JORDAN'S RETURN, AMON SWORE HE WOULD GET HIS FATHER'S RING BACK AND SENT HUNDREDS OF BOUNTY HUNTERS TO CAPTURE HIM. JORDAN HAD JUST BROKEN FREE OF HIS GRASP WITH THE HELP OF JOHN STEWART WHEN A SINESTRO CORPS RING PRESENTED ITSELF TO HIM.

AMON WAS TRANSPORTED TO QWARD, WHERE LYSSA DRAK GUIDED HIM IN ACTIVATING HIS YELLOW POWER RING. AMON POURED HIS FEAR INTO IT, AND BECAME A FULL MEMBER OF THE SINESTRO CORPS.

IN THE FIGHT IN EARTH'S UPPER ATMOSPHERE, AMON SUR WAS SHOCKED TO LEARN THAT THE GREEN LANTERNS COULD NOW TAKE THE LIVES OF SINESTRO CORPS MEMBERS, AND HE TURNED AND FLED.
ART BY JOE PRADO.

Name: Karu-Sil   Sector: 2815
FIRST APPEARANCE: GREEN LANTERN V. 4 #19
BIO: KARU-SIL WAS BORN INTO A PRIMITIVE TRIBE ON GRAXOS III. WHEN SHE WAS FIVE YEARS OLD, HER PARENTS WERE KILLED DURING A TRIBAL RAID, AND SHE WAS FORCED TO FEND FOR HERSELF IN THE JUNGLE. HUNGRY, SHE KILLED AN ANIMAL, ONLY TO FIND IT WAS ALREADY BEING HUNTED. THE THREE PREDATORS HUNTING IT TOOK HER INTO THEIR PACK. MUTILATING HER FACE IN ORDER TO LOOK MORE LIKE THEM, SHE LIVED WITH THEM FOR YEARS.

WHEN SHE WAS A TEEN, SHE DISCOVERED A BOY FROM A NEARBY TRIBE. ONCE THE SHOCK OF SEEING SOMEONE OF HER OWN SPECIES WORE OFF, SHE KILLED HIM TO BE FOOD FOR HER PACK. THE GREEN LANTERN BLISH, THINKING KARU-SIL WAS BEING ATTACKED BY THE CARNIVORES, INTERVENED, AND KILLED ALL THREE OF THEM. HE THEN TOOK HER TO GRAXOS IV, WHERE SHE WAS INSTITUTIONALIZED. SINESTRO'S POWER RING GAVE HER BACK HER FREEDOM, AS WELL AS HER PACK.

KARU-SIL IS FIERCELY LOYAL TO SINESTRO, AND SHE AND HER PACK WILL DO WHATEVER IS ASKED OF HER.
ART BY ETHAN VAN SCIVER.

Name: Feena Sik
Sector: 2897
FIRST APPEARANCE:
GREEN LANTERN:
SINESTRO CORPS SPECIAL #1
BIO: FEENA SIK WAS A
SECTOR-FAMOUS ARTIST WHEN
SHE DISCOVERED A RITUAL
THAT WOULD BRING HER
PAINTINGS TO LIFE. THE RITUAL
REQUIRED BLOOD, LOTS OF
BLOOD, SO THAT NIGHT FEENA
SIK MURDERED HER HUSBAND
IN THE NAME OF HER "ART." AT
HER NEXT SHOW, THE
PAINTINGS SPRANG TO LIFE,
AND THE CROWD'S AMAZEMENT
TURNED TO HORROR AS THE
ARTWORK BEGAN
SLAUGHTERING EVERYONE. ALL
OF FEENA SIK'S WORKS ARE
CURRENTLY DEEMED
HAZARDOUS AND UNPRINTABLE,
FOR FEAR THAT EVEN ONE OF
HER REPRINTED SKETCHES
COULD COME TO LIFE AND KILL.
ART BY JOE PRADO.

Name: Borialosaurus
Sector: 3001
FIRST APPEARANCE:
GREEN LANTERN:
SINESTRO CORPS
SPECIAL #1
BIO: BORIALOSAURUS IS
THE OLDEST MEMBER OF
THE SINESTRO CORPS. HE
COMES FROM AN ANCIENT
RACE OF CREATURES THAT
WERE ONCE CARNIVOROUS
SEA ANIMALS ON MALTUS
BILLIONS OF YEARS AGO.
HIS KIND WAS ALL BUT
HUNTED OUT OF
EXISTENCE AFTER THEY
ATTACKED AND KILLED
DOZENS OF GUARDIANS.
ART BY JOE PRADO.

Name: Braach Sector: 3064
FIRST APPEARANCE: GREEN LANTERN:
SINESTRO CORPS SPECIAL #1
BIO: BRAACH IS A SELACHIAN, A SHARK-LIKE
RACE THAT TOOK TO THE STARS MILLIONS OF
YEARS AGO. THE CREATURES KNOWN AS
SPACE DOLPHINS ARE BRAACH'S PRIMARY
SOURCE OF FOOD, BUT GIVEN THEIR RARITY,
BRAACH HAS HAD TO GO YEARS WITHOUT
EATING ONE. HE HAS RECENTLY ATTRACTED
THE ATTENTION OF THE BOUNTY HUNTER LOBO,
AND NOT IN A GOOD WAY.
ART BY JOE PRADO.

Name: Scivor Sector: 3106
FIRST APPEARANCE: GREEN LANTERN:
SINESTRO CORPS SPECIAL #1
BIO: POSING AS ONE OF THE TORTURE
GODS OF THE APLIC-TOH, SCIVOR HAS
INFLUENCED THOUSANDS TO MURDER IN
HIS NAME ACROSS HIS SECTOR. HIS
POWERS OF PERSUASION ARE
UNMATCHED. IT IS SAID HE PLANTED
THOUGHTS IN THE MOST INFAMOUS OF
MURDERERS THROUGHOUT THE
UNIVERSE INCLUDING GRAVIK X, KAR
SENIOR AND THE HORGG FAMILY.
ART BY JOE PRADO.

Name: Tri-Eye Sector: 3145
FIRST APPEARANCE: GREEN LANTERN:
SINESTRO CORPS SPECIAL #1
BIO: TRAVELING ACROSS ITS PLANET VIA
A SYSTEM OF CONNECTED UNDERGROUND
TUNNELS, TRI-EYE LIVES AT THE BOTTOM
OF WATERWELLS, SPRINGING UP AND
CAPTURING ITS PREY WHEN THEY COME
TO DRINK. ONCE IN ITS GRASP, TRI-EYE'S
THREE MOUTHS WILL TEAR THROUGH
FLESH AND BONE, LEAVING NO TRACE OF
ITS MEAL BEHIND.
ART BY JOE PRADO.

Name: Snap Trap Sector: 3189
FIRST APPEARANCE: GREEN LANTERN:
SINESTRO CORPS SPECIAL #1
BIO: SNAP TRAP FEEDS ON SPINES, USING HIS HYPNOTIC
EYES TO PULL IN HIS PREY. WHEN HIS VICTIM IS WITHIN
RANGE, HE BRINGS HIS POWERFUL JAWS DOWN TO CRUSH
ITS SKULL AND USES HIS LONG TONGUE TO TEAR THE
SPINE OUT OF ITS BODY. SOMEHOW, HIS VICTIMS ARE
HORRIBLY LEFT ALIVE.
ART BY JOE PRADO.

Name: Sn'Hoj Sector: 3201
FIRST APPEARANCE: GREEN LANTERN:
SINESTRO CORPS SPECIAL #1
BIO: SN'HOJ FLOATS IN DEEP SPACE, ITS BODY ACTING AS
CAMOUFLAGE AGAINST THE STAR FIELD. AS SOON AS A SHIP
PASSES, IT SPRINGS INTO ACTION, BURROWING ITS WAY TO THE
CONTROL UNIT AND DISABLING IT. SN'HOJ THEN ASSIMILATES ANY
TECHNOLOGY THAT IT COULD MAKE USE OF, AND MURDERS THE
CREW. SN'HOJ JOINED THE SINESTRO CORPS IN HOPES OF
FINDING NEW TECHNOLOGIES TO STEAL, AND IT IS RUMORED THAT
IT CO-OPTED OAN TECHNOLOGY DURING THE INVASION OF OA.
ART BY JOE PRADO.

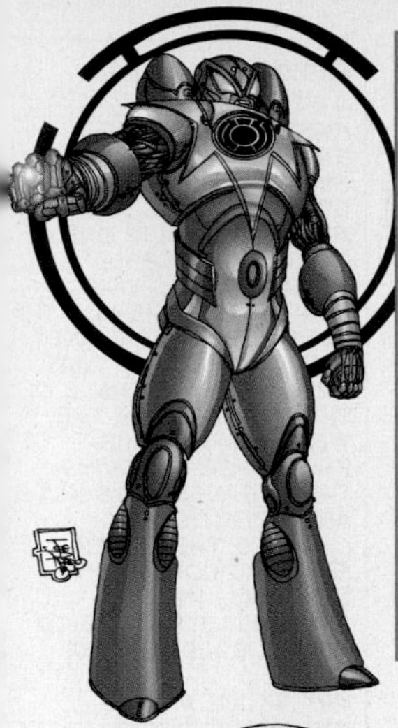

Name: Tekik
Sector: 3281
FIRST APPEARANCE: GREEN LANTERN: SINESTRO CORPS SPECIAL #1
BIO: ON THE PLANET POTTER-59-3, TEKIK WAS A SCIENTIFIC ROBOTIC UNIT WHOSE MASTER GAVE IT EMOTIONS. ANGERED BY ITS LIFE OF ROBOTIC SERVITUDE, TEKIK CREATED A "FEAR CODE," A PROGRAM IT UPLOADED INTO EVERY ROBOT ON THE PLANET SIMULTANEOUSLY. POTTER-59-3 NEVER RECOVERED FROM THE CASUALTIES OF THAT DAY, AND THE PLANET HAS SINCE BEEN ABANDONED AND RENAMED THE "LOST WORLD."
ART BY JOE PRADO.

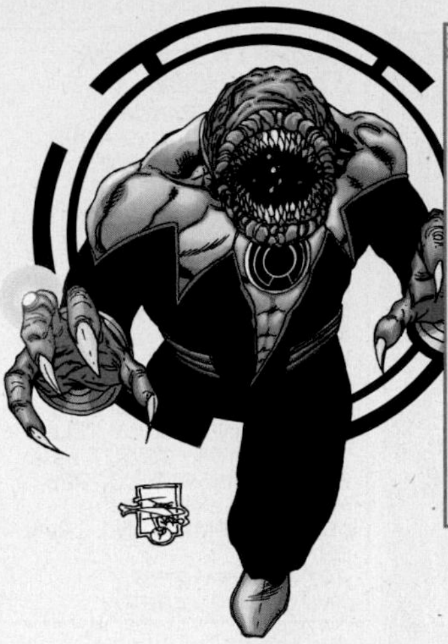

Name: Low
Sector: 3308
FIRST APPEARANCE: GREEN LANTERN: SINESTRO CORPS SPECIAL #1
BIO: LOW IS THE MOST DANGEROUS PARASITE IN THE UNIVERSE. HE CAN SUCK EVERY DROP OF BLOOD FROM NEARLY ANY BEING IN A MATTER OF SECONDS. LOW REPLICATES BY LAYING "EGGS" IN THE BODIES OF THOSE HE FEEDS ON. UP TO A THOUSAND PARASITIC SLUGS CAN BE BORN FROM A SINGLE CARCASS.
ART BY JOE PRADO.

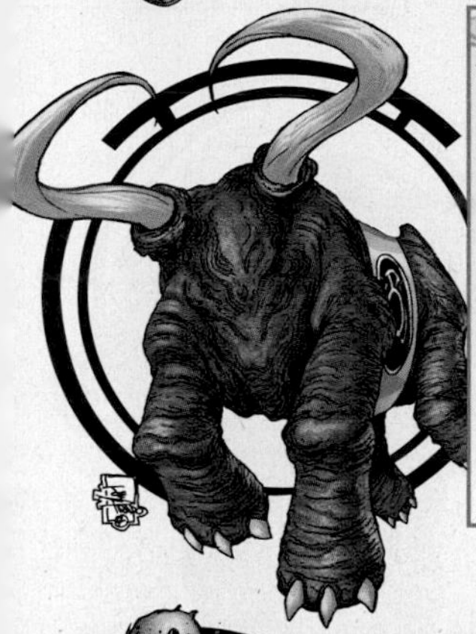

Name: Moose
Sector: 3333
FIRST APPEARANCE: GREEN LANTERN: SINESTRO CORPS SPECIAL #1
BIO: MOOSE WAS ONCE PART OF A MASSIVE PACK OF TROGKIAN MAMMOTHS, GIANT CREATURES WHOSE STAMPEDES TERRORIZED THE PRIMITIVE WORLD OF TROGK. AS MOOSE'S REAL NAME IS UNPRONOUNCEABLE, THE SINESTRO CORPS RING CHOSE THE CLOSEST APPROXIMATION.
ART BY JOE PRADO.

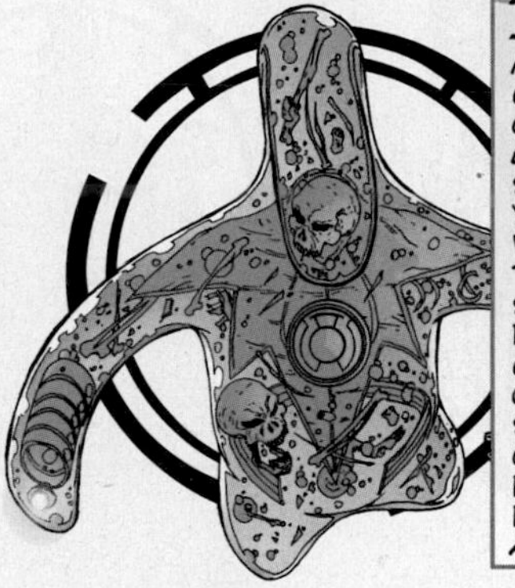

Name: Slushh
Sector: 3376
FIRST APPEARANCE: GREEN LANTERN/SINESTRO CORPS SPECIAL #1
BIO: THE BEING KNOWN AS SLUSHH SPENT MILLIONS OF YEARS TRAPPED BY THE WARLORDS OF PRISUN AT THE BOTTOM OF A RED OIL SEA. SLUSHH IS A POLYMORPHOUS ACIDIC GLOBULAR BEING. ON THE OUTSIDE, HE IS A VISCOUS SHELL, BUT HIS INSIDES ARE COMPOSED OF A CORROSIVE FLUID THAT LIQUEFIES FLESH INSTANTLY.
ART BY JOE PRADO.

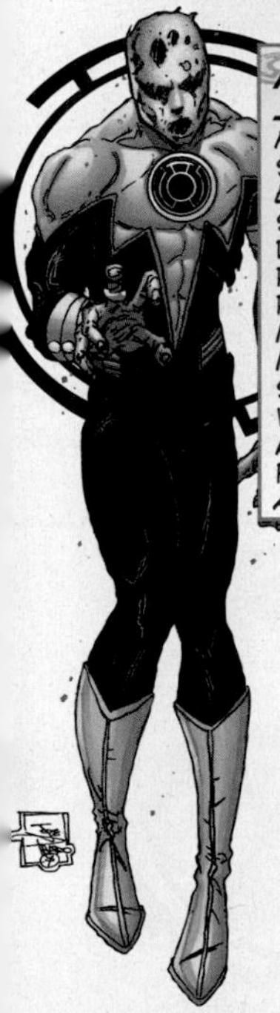

Name: Murr the Melting Man
Sector: 3490
FIRST APPEARANCE: GREEN LANTERN/ SINESTRO CORPS SPECIAL #1
BIO: MURR WAS ONCE AUSIIN SNOW, A SCIENTIST ON THE ASTEROID OUTPOST DW-426. AN ACCIDENT WITH THEIR POWER SOURCE CHANGED AUSIIN'S PHYSIOLOGY, AND HE BECAME A MINDLESS THING WHOSE TOUCH CAN MELT ANY LIVING BEING. OTHER SINESTRO CORPS MEMBERS ARE LEERY WHEN MURR IS AROUND, AND THEY ALWAYS KEEP THEIR PERSONAL FORCE FIELDS UP.
ART BY JOE PRADO.

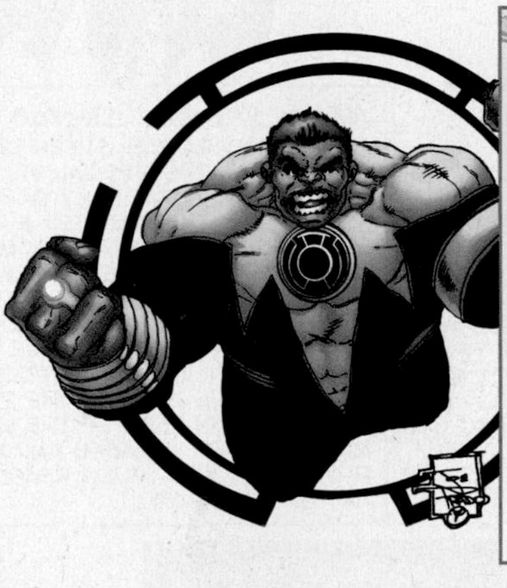

Name: Schlagg-Man
Sector: 3493
FIRST APPEARANCE: GREEN LANTERN: SINESTRO CORPS SPECIAL #1
BIO: A NATIVE OF THE PLANET BISMOLL, SCHLAGG-MAN IS A CAREER CRIMINAL. AFTER HE ONCE BIT THROUGH A POLICEMAN'S NECK, A JUDGE RULED THAT SCHLAGG-MAN'S TEETH BE REMOVED, AND HE HAS SINCE HAD THEM REPLACED WITH BISMOLLIAN STEEL. NOW, HE CAN BITE THROUGH ANYTHING, BE IT A STEEL DOOR OR THE SKULL OF THE JUDGE WHO PULLED OUT HIS TEETH.
ART BY JOE PRADO.

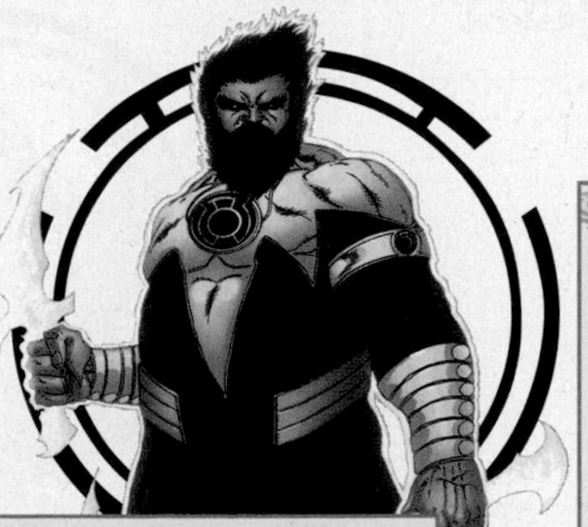

Name: Haasp the Hunter Sector: 3492
FIRST APPEARANCE: GREEN LANTERN: SINESTRO CORPS SPECIAL #1
BIO: BROTHER OF THE GREEN LANTERN HARVID, HAASP TRAVELS THE COSMOS, HUNTING THE MOST RARE AND EXOTIC BREEDS OF SENTIENT RACES AND SELLING THEIR SKINS ON THE BLACK MARKET. AFTER AN ATTEMPT TO MURDER AND SKIN ONE OF THE RAREST SPECIES IN THE UNIVERSE, HIS BROTHER HARVID DEEMED HIM UNSTABLE AND PLACED HAASP INTO AN OAN SCIENCELL. HAASP EVENTUALLY BROKE FREE FROM HIS SCIENCELL AND ESCAPED, AND HE NOW HOLDS A DEEP HATRED FOR HIS BROTHER, WHOM HE HAS DESIGNATED TO BE HIS NEXT BIG HUNT.
ART BY JOE PRADO.

Name: Despotellis Sector: 3497
FIRST APPEARANCE: GREEN LANTERN V. 4 #18
BIO: THE BIO-SENTIENT MICROSCOPIC VIRUS KNOWN AS DESPOTELLIS WAS DEVELOPED ON THE PLANET KHONDRA BY MILITARY SCIENTISTS WHO WERE TRYING TO EVOLVE A HIGHLY EXPERIMENTAL VIRUS FOR USE AS A BIOLOGICAL WEAPON. EACH GENERATION, THE VIRUS WOULD CHANGE, BECOMING STRONGER AND STRONGER UNTIL FINALLY, IT BECAME SELF-AWARE AND ESCAPED. ITS ANGER AT ITS FORCIBLE EVOLUTION WAS GREAT, AND KHONDRA WAS QUARANTINED WITHIN THE HOUR. THE ENTIRE PLANET WAS DEAD WITHIN A DAY.

DESPOTELLIS CREATES NON-SENTIENT COPIES OF ITSELF TO ALLOW IT TO SPREAD, AND CAN DESTROY THESE COPIES AT WILL, LEAVING NO TRACE OF ITSELF IN ITS VICTIMS.

THE GREEN LANTERN SORANIK NATU HAS BEEN STUDYING DESPOTELLIS IN HER LAB SINCE ITS REMOVAL FROM GUY GARDNER'S BODY, AND HOPES TO SOMEDAY CREATE AN ANTIVIRUS THAT WILL COMPLETELY NEUTRALIZE IT.
ART BY ETHAN VAN SCIVER.

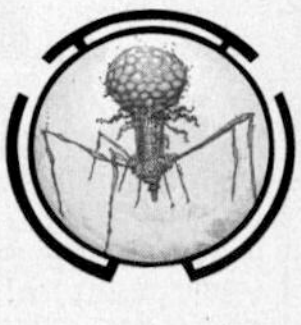

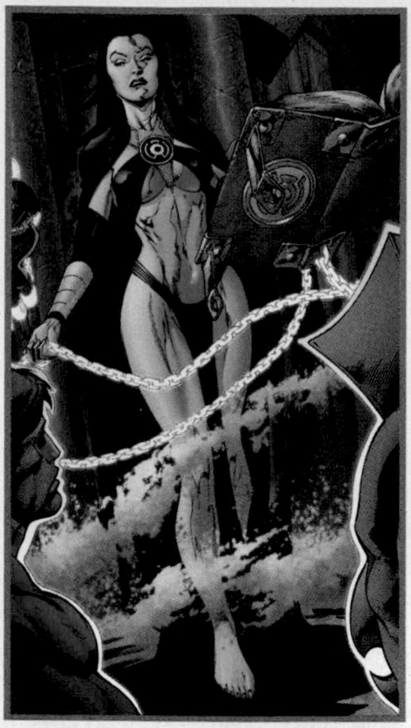

Name: Lyssa Drak
Sector: 3500
FIRST APPEARANCE: GREEN LANTERN V. 4 #18
BIO: LITTLE IS KNOWN ABOUT THE ENIGMATIC LYSSA DRAK, SAVE THAT SHE IS FROM TALOK VII AND IS THE KEEPER OF THE BOOK OF PARALLAX. SEVERAL MEMBERS OF THE GREEN LANTERN CORPS HAVE TRIED TO INTERROGATE HER FOLLOWING HER CAPTURE, BUT SHE INEVITABLY TELLS THEM A STORY ABOUT HER FELLOW SINESTRO CORPS MEMBERS. SHE IS CURRENTLY AWAITING TRIAL ON OA.
ART BY IVAN REIS AND OCLAIR ALBERT.

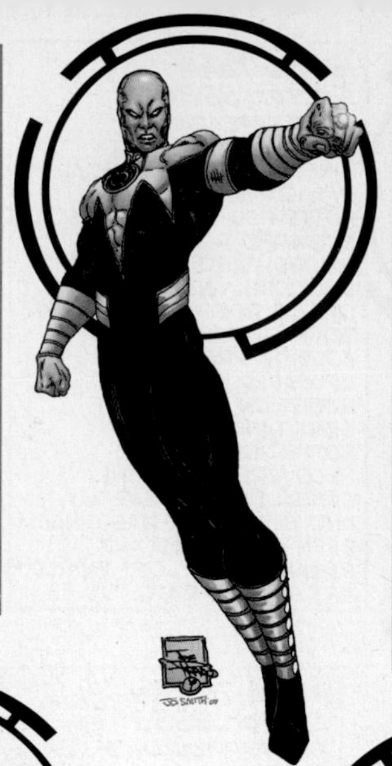

Name: Ampa Nnn
Sector: 3517
FIRST APPEARANCE: GREEN LANTERN: SINESTRO CORPS SPECIAL #1
BIO: AMPA NNN IS ONE OF THE REMORSELESS, SERIAL KILLERS WHO BANDED TOGETHER ON THE SURFACE OF THE PLANET LYTHYL, A SOCIETY THAT EMPHASIZED THE RULE OF THE STRONG OVER THE WEAK. AMPA NNN IS KNOWN FOR REMOVING THE ORGANS OF HIS KILLS AND METICULOUSLY CLEANING THEM. WITH THE SINESTRO CORPS IN UPHEAVAL, HE HAS RETURNED TO LYTHYL TO CONTINUE HIS MURDER SPREE.
ART BY JOE PRADO.

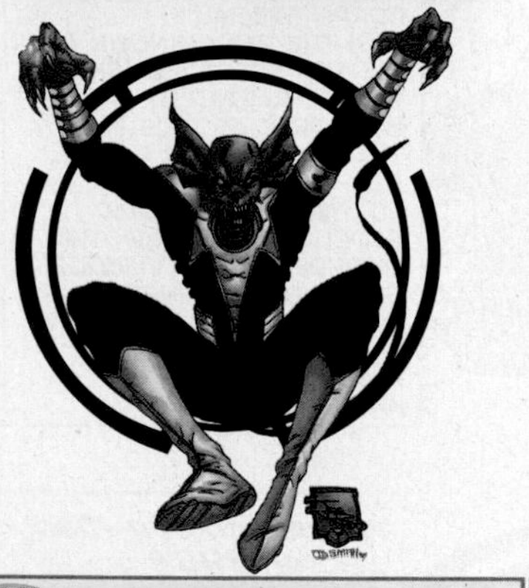

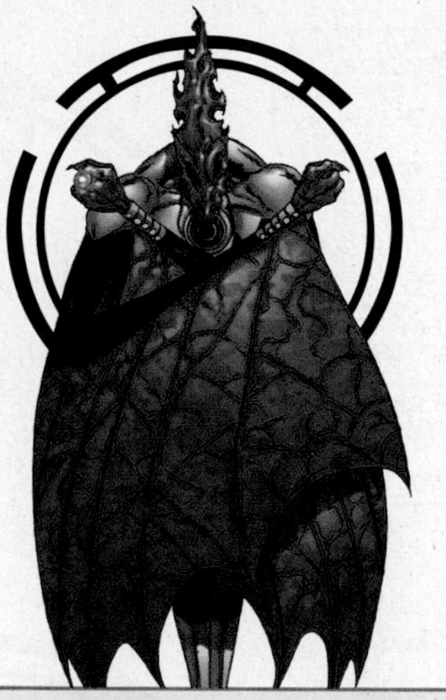

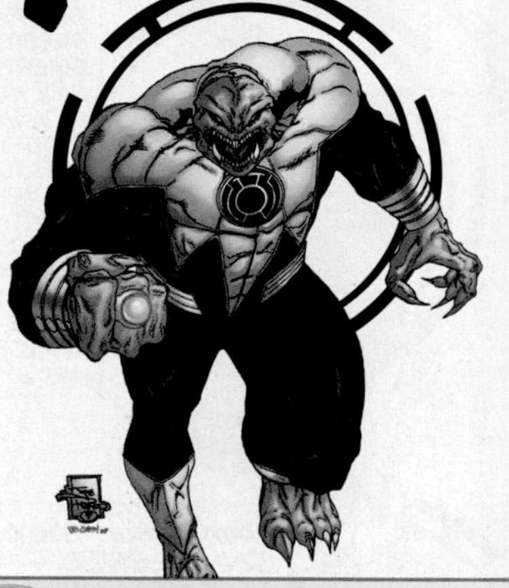

Name: Kretch
Sector: 3545
FIRST APPEARANCE: GREEN LANTERN: SINESTRO CORPS SPECIAL #1
BIO: KRETCH IS A DEMONIC BEING FROM THE HELLFIRE PLANET OF SOH. ABLE TO ERUPT INTO A MASSIVE SUPERNOVA CAPABLE OF CONSUMING WHOLE CITIES, KRETCH SPREADS HIS FIRE FROM WORLD TO WORLD. IF YOU SEE A NEW STAR IN THE SKY, IT IS MOST LIKELY KRETCH ENGULFING YET ANOTHER PLANET IN HIS HELLFIRE.
ART BY JOE PRADO.

Name: Stanch Sector: 3560
FIRST APPEARANCE: GREEN LANTERN: SINESTRO CORPS SPECIAL #1
BIO: STANCH IS THE ONLY ONE OF HIS KIND TO SURVIVE THE POLLUTED SKIES OF THE PLANET GUUSH. THE POISON MADE ITS WAY SLOWLY THROUGH ITS SYSTEM, AND OVER A DECADE, STANCH CHANGED. SPROUTING WINGS OF A PHOTOSYNTHETIC SKIN, THE ONCE-BENEVOLENT CREATURE TOOK TO THE SKIES TO GET ABOVE THE POLLUTION AND LIVE IN SUNLIGHT. NOW, THE PEOPLE OF GUUSH LIVE IN FEAR OF THE LEGENDARY MONSTER THAT ATTACKS AND KILLS WITHOUT RHYME, BUT WITH MUCH REASON.
ART BY JOE PRADO.

Name: Bur'Gunza
Sector: 3561
FIRST APPEARANCE: GREEN LANTERN: SINESTRO CORPS SPECIAL #1
BIO: A MODEL PRISONER ON TAKRON-GALTOS, BUR'GUNZA WAS MERELY BIDING HIS TIME. ON THE DAY HE WAS TO BE RELEASED, ONCE HIS RESTRAINTS WERE REMOVED, HE TURNED ON THE GUARDS AND KILLED OVER FORTY-TWO OF THEM BEFORE HE WAS BROUGHT DOWN.
ART BY JOE PRADO.

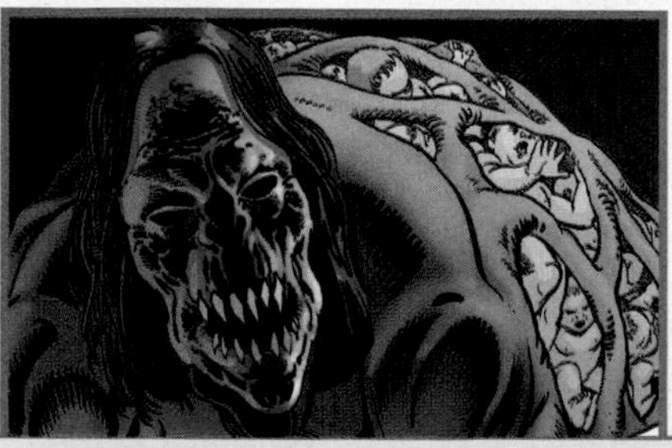

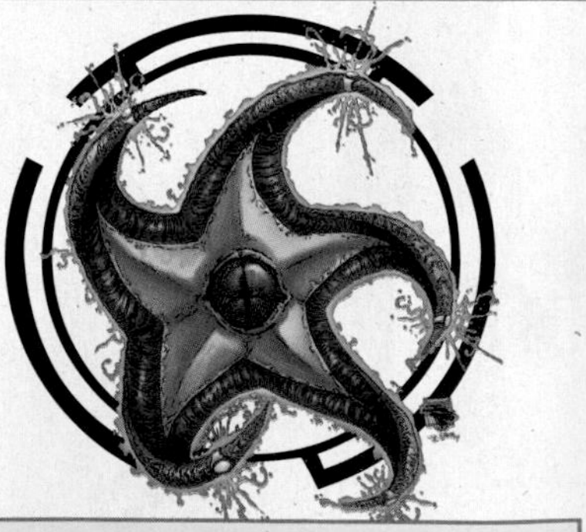

Name: Kryb Sector: 3599
FIRST APPEARANCE: GREEN LANTERN: SINESTRO CORPS SPECIAL #1
BIO: IN THE FAR REACHES OF SECTOR 3599, THE MONSTER KNOWN AS KRYB WAS THOUGHT TO BE MERELY A FRIGHTENING STORY TOLD BY PARENTS TO KEEP THEIR CHILDREN IN BED AT NIGHT. BUT KRYB IS VERY REAL, A CREATURE BENT ON MURDERING PARENTS AND STEALING THEIR INFANT CHILDREN. KRYB'S PURPOSE FOR THESE INFANTS IS UNKNOWN, BUT THERE IS MUCH SPECULATION THAT THEY'RE STILL ALIVE SOMEWHERE. UPON HER INDUCTION INTO THE SINESTRO CORPS, KRYB CHANGED HER PREY, TARGETING GREEN LANTERNS WITH CHILDREN OF THEIR OWN. AFTER LEARNING OF HER COLLECTION, THE GREEN LANTERNS KT21 AND MATOO AND AMNEE PREE BEGAN THEIR PLAN TO FIND HER AND RECLAIM THE ORPHANS OF THE GREEN LANTERN CORPS.
ART BY JERRY ORDWAY.

Name: Starro Sector: Unknown
FIRST APPEARANCE: THE BRAVE AND THE BOLD V. 1 #28
BIO: PART OF A NOMADIC ALIEN RACE KNOWN AS THE STAR CONQUERORS, THE ALIEN STARRO HAS SENT BILLIONS OF PROBES INTO THE UNIVERSE. ONE OF THEM WAS CHOSEN FOR THE SINESTRO CORPS. IT IS UNKNOWN WHAT THE EFFECT OF A YELLOW POWER RING WILL HAVE ON THE MIND OF A LOWLY STAR CONQUEROR, AND ITS RECENT CLASH WITH THE TEEN TITANS DEMONSTRATED THAT IT WAS NOT OPERATING AT FULL CAPACITY. THE STAR CONQUEROR STARRO'S RESPONSE TO LOSING ONE OF ITS PROBES TO THE SINESTRO CORPS IS ALSO UNKNOWN, BUT IT IS DOUBTFUL IT WILL BE POSITIVE.
ART BY JOE PRADO.

Name: Cyborg-Superman   Sector: N/A
FIRST APPEARANCE: ADVENTURES OF SUPERMAN #500
BIO: A BRILLIANT MAN, HANK HENSHAW ALWAYS WANTED TO GO TO SPACE. AFTER YEARS OF TRAINING, HE FOUND HIMSELF PART OF A SPACE SHUTTLE CREW, HIS WIFE AND TWO BEST FRIENDS AT HIS SIDE. MINUTES INTO THEIR JOURNEY, THEIR SHIELDS FAILED AND THEY WERE EXPOSED TO COSMIC RADIATION, WHICH CAUSED UNCONTROLLABLE MUTATIONS IN ALL FOUR OF THEM. HIS TWO FRIENDS DIED FROM THEIR METAMORPHOSES, AND HENSHAW'S WIFE, UNABLE TO COPE WITH HER BODY'S CHANGE, KILLED HERSELF.

HENSHAW BECAME A LIVING ELECTRONIC SIGNAL, ABLE TO MOVE FROM MACHINE TO MACHINE. BLAMING SUPERMAN FOR HIS CONDITION, HE FOLLOWED HIS MOVEMENT BY SATELLITES, EVENTUALLY LEAPING ONTO THE FORTRESS OF SOLITUDE'S COMPUTERS AND LEARNING ALL HE COULD ABOUT THE MAN OF STEEL.

WHEN SUPERMAN SEEMINGLY DIED AT THE HANDS OF DOOMSDAY, HENSHAW STEPPED FORWARD IN A BODY THAT RESEMBLED SUPERMAN'S AND BEGAN A CAMPAIGN TO SMEAR THE KRYPTONIAN'S NAME. HIS PLAN RESULTED IN THE DESTRUCTION OF COAST CITY.

OVER THE NEXT FEW YEARS, CYBORG-SUPERMAN RETURNED AGAIN AND AGAIN, EACH TIME WITH A NEW STRATEGY TO DESTROY KAL-EL. TRAVELING TO THE WORLD BIOT INSIDE THE ROBOTIC BODY OF A MANHUNTER, HENSHAW SAW THAT THEY NEEDED A LEADER, AND HE TOOK COMMAND OF THEM AS THEIR NEW GRANDMASTER. A GROUP OF GREEN LANTERNS, LED BY HAL JORDAN, DESTROYED BIOT, AND HENSHAW AND HIS MANHUNTERS BEGAN CONSTRUCTION OF THEIR NEW BASE, WARWORLD.

CYBORG-SUPERMAN JOINED SINESTRO'S GROUP IN HOPES THAT THE ANTI-MONITOR WOULD BE ABLE TO GIVE HIM THE ONE THING THE EARTH'S HEROES COULDN'T: ETERNAL REST. THE ANTI-MONITOR FAILED, AND HENSHAW'S MANGLED BODY WAS LAST SEEN BACK IN THE HANDS OF HIS OWN MANHUNTERS.
ART BY IVAN REIS AND OCLAIR ALBERT.

Name: Manhunters   Sector: 3601
FIRST APPEARANCE: JUSTICE LEAGUE OF AMERICA V. 1 #140
BIO: THE GUARDIANS OF THE UNIVERSE CREATED THE MANHUNTERS OVER THREE BILLION YEARS AGO, DESIGNING THEM TO POLICE ANY AND ALL WORLDS THAT HELD SENTIENT LIFEFORMS. LACKING EMOTION OR EMPATHY, THEY REBELLED AGAINST THEIR PROGRAMMING AND CAME TO OPPOSE THE GUARDIANS BELIEVING THAT THE ONLY WAY TO ACHIEVE TRUE ORDER IN THE UNIVERSE WAS TO ELIMINATE ALL LIFE. AFTER AN UNSUCCESSFUL ATTACK ON OA, THE MANHUNTERS WERE BANISHED TO THE FAR CORNERS OF THE UNIVERSE.

RECENTLY, THE MANHUNTERS WERE FOUND BEING LED BY THE CYBORG-SUPERMAN IN SPACE SECTOR 3601, A SECTOR OF SPACE WHERE NOTHING EXISTS, SAVE FOR THEIR HOMEWORLD OF BIOT. THEY WERE REVEALED TO HAVE BEEN USING THE BODIES OF GREEN LANTERNS TO POWER THEIR OWN WEAPONS, LEECHING THE EMERALD ENERGY OUT OF A LANTERN'S CELLS. HAL JORDAN DESTROYED BIOT, AND THE MANHUNTERS CONSTRUCTED WARWORLD, WHICH WAS DESTROYED BY THE HEROES OF EARTH IN AN ATTEMPT TO DESTROY THE ANTI-MONITOR.

MANHUNTERS' FACEPLATES LIFT UP TO REVEAL A POWER SKULL UNDERNEATH, WHICH THEY CAN USE AS A POWER-TRANSFER UNIT, EITHER DRAINING OR CHARGING A POWER RING.
ART BY CARLOS PACHECO AND JESUS MERINO.

LIST OF THE DEAD
1-HORKU = SECTOR 2 = ART BY IVAN REIS AND OCLAIR ALBERT.
2-ENKAFOS = SECTOR 2981 = ART BY ANGEL UNZUETA AND PRENTIS ROLLINS.
3-RANX = SECTOR 3272 = ART BY DAVE GIBBONS AND RODNEY RAMOS.
4-RANX BRAIN = SECTOR 3272 = ART BY PATRICK GLEASON AND PRENTIS ROLLINS.

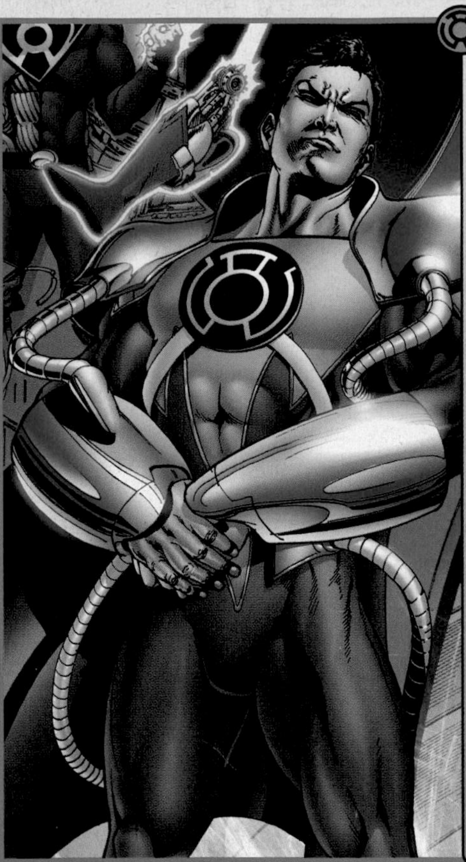

Name: Superman-Prime

FIRST APPEARANCE: DC COMICS PRESENTS #87

BIO: SUPERMAN-PRIME, A.K.A. CLARK KENT, IS FROM A PARALLEL EARTH CALLED EARTH-PRIME THAT HAD NO SUPER-HEROES. THE ADVENTURES OF THE HEROES OF OUR WORLD TOOK PLACE ONLY IN COMIC BOOKS. PRIME WAS ONLY A BOY WHEN HE LEARNED HE HAD POWERS AND WAS KRYPTONIAN LIKE THE SUPERMAN HE GREW UP READING. PRIME WAS RECRUITED BY OUR EARTH'S SUPERMAN TO FIGHT IN THE "CRISIS." AFTER HE LEFT, HE WAS HORRIFIED TO LEARN THAT THE MONSTER KNOWN AS THE ANTI-MONITOR DESTROYED HIS WORLD, INCLUDING LAURIE, THE GIRL HE LOVED. PRIME HELPED DEFEAT THE ANTI-MONITOR AND AFTERWARDS ENTERED A PARADISE DIMENSION, ALONG WITH SUPERMAN AND LOIS LANE FROM EARTH-2, AND ALEXANDER LUTHOR OF EARTH-3. THERE, THEY WATCHED THE EVENTS UNFOLDING ON THE "NEW" EARTH THEY SAVED, AND THEY DIDN'T LIKE WHAT THEY SAW. PRIME BELIEVED HIS CHILDHOOD HEROES HAD BECOME CORRUPT.

PRIME AND THE EARTH-2 SUPERMAN BROKE THROUGH THE BARRIER ONTO OUR EARTH, AND WITH ALEX LUTHOR, THEY BEGAN A CAMPAIGN TO CREATE A PERFECT EARTH. CONFRONTING CONNER KENT, PRIME GOADED HIM INTO A FIGHT, SAYING THAT HE WAS LIVING THE LIFE PRIME SHOULD HAVE HAD. IN THE MIDDLE OF THAT CONFLICT, CONNER SUMMONED THE TEEN TITANS, AND PRIME BEGAN TO MURDER THEM IN HIS RAGE, CLAMING, "YOU'RE MAKING ME LIKE YOU!"

THE FLASHES IMPRISONED PRIME, WHICH IS WHY HE DEVELOPED A PHOBIA FOR SPEEDSTERS (HE NEVER REALLY LIKED FLASH COMICS ANYWAY!). EVENTUALLY, PRIME ESCAPED AFTER CREATING A SOLAR ENERGY-COLLECTING ARMOR SIMILAR TO THE ANTI-MONITOR'S. AGAIN, EARTH'S HEROES STOPPED HIS RAMPAGE - YET NOT UNTIL AFTER PRIME MURDERED THE SUPERMAN OF EARTH-2 WHO HAD BEGUN TO SIDE WITH THESE "CORRUPTED" HEROES.

THE GREEN LANTERNS CREATED A PRISON OUT OF A RED SUN-EATER AND HELD PRIME FOR A YEAR. THE SINESTRO CORPS INVADED OA FOR THE SOLE PURPOSE OF BREAKING OUT PRIME AND THE CYBORG-SUPERMAN. DISCOVERING THAT THE ANTI-MONITOR HAD RETURNED TO ACT AS THE GUARDIAN OF THE SINESTRO CORPS, SUPERMAN-PRIME SWORE WHEN THE ANTI-MONITOR WAS NEAR VICTORY THAT HE WOULD HAVE HIS REVENGE FOR HIS EARTH'S DESTRUCTION. WHEN THE ANTI-MONITOR WAS WOUNDED, PRIME THREW HIS DYING BODY INTO SPACE.

TURNING HIS ATTENTION TO THE GUARDIANS, PRIME ACTUALLY KILLED ONE OF THEM, CAUSING A MASSIVE EXPLOSION OF ENERGY. WHEN THE SMOKE CLEARED, SUPERMAN-PRIME FOUND HIMSELF LOST IN THE NEW MULTIVERSE AND HIS MUSCLES SWOLLEN WITH POWER, GIVING PRIME THE ILLUSION THAT HE HAD FINALLY GROWN INTO A "MAN." HE NOW SEARCHES IN HOPES OF FINDING EARTH-PRIME REBORN.

ART BY ETHAN VAN SCIVER.

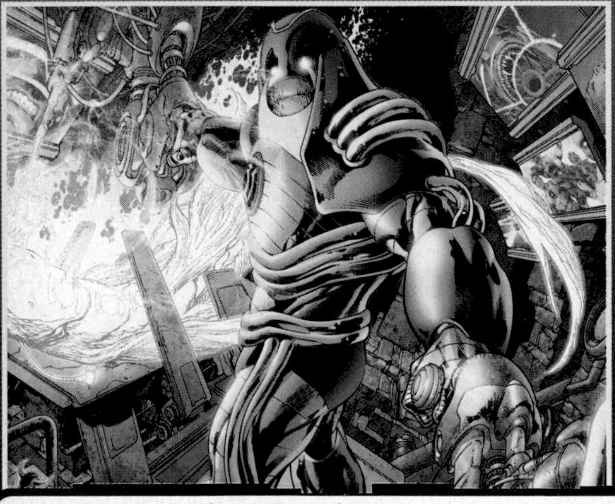

Name: Anti-Monitor Sector: -1

FIRST APPEARANCE: CRISIS ON INFINITE EARTHS #5

BIO: AT THE SAME MOMENT THAT OUR UNIVERSE WAS BORN, THE ANTIMATTER UNIVERSE WAS ALSO CREATED. BILLIONS OF YEARS LATER, THE BEING KNOWN AS THE ANTI-MONITOR BEGAN TAKING POWER. HE CONQUERED THE WEAPONERS OF QWARD, AND FROM THEM HE LEARNED THERE WAS A DIFFERENT UNIVERSE, A POSITIVE MATTER UNIVERSE, AND HE WANTED CONTROL OF IT, TOO.

AFTER A COSMIC ACCIDENT TORE A HOLE BETWEEN THE POSITIVE AND ANTIMATTER UNIVERSE, ANTIMATTER BEGAN FLOODING THE UNIVERSE, RESULTING IN THE INTERDIMENSIONAL "CRISIS." IT TOOK EARTH'S GREATEST HEROES TO STOP THE ANTI-MONITOR, AND TOGETHER, THEY DESTROYED HIM.

WHEN THE 52 UNIVERSES THAT FORM THE MULTIVERSE WERE REBORN, THE ANTI-MONITOR WAS AS WELL, AND HE BECAME THE SINESTRO CORPS' SOLE GUARDIAN. SINESTRO THEN BEGAN HIS PLOT TO DESTROY THE EARTH. HAD HE BEEN SUCCESSFUL, THE MULTIVERSE WOULD HAVE UNRAVELED, LEAVING ONLY THE ANTIMATTER UNIVERSE BEHIND, AND THE ANTI-MONITOR WOULD HAVE RULED ALL ONCE MORE. BUT THE EARTH'S HEROES ONCE AGAIN RALLIED AND DEFEATED THE SINESTRO CORPS, AND SUPERMAN-PRIME BETRAYED THE ANTI-MONITOR, THROWING HIM DEEP INTO SPACE.

THE ANTI-MONITOR CRASHED DOWN ON AN UNKNOWN PLANET. BLACK WALLS SUDDENLY SURROUNDED HIM, AND HE FOUND HIMSELF THE POWER SOURCE OF A BLACK LANTERN.

ART BY IVAN REIS AND OCLAIR ALBERT.

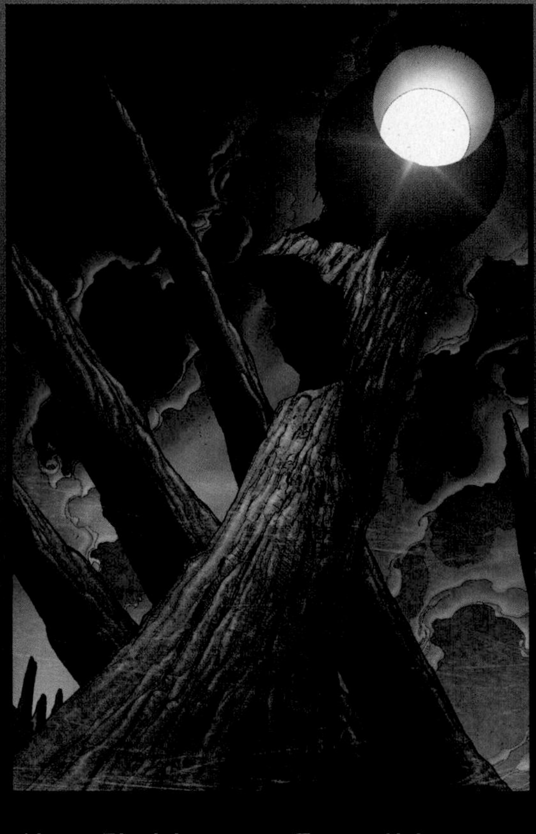

Name: Black Lantern Sector: Unknown

FIRST APPEARANCE: GREEN LANTERN V. 4 #25

BIO: ALL THAT IS KNOWN ABOUT THE BLACK LANTERN IS THAT IT NOW SERVES AS A PRISON FOR THE ANTI-MONITOR. THE BLACK LANTERNS WILL SOON RISE. AND DEATH WILL COME FOR US ALL...

ART BY ETHAN VAN SCIVER.

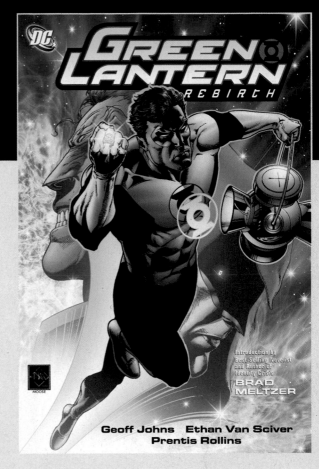

READ MORE ADVENTURES OF YOUR FAVORITE HEROES IN THESE COLLECTIONS FROM DC COMICS:

KINGDOM COME

THE GREATEST SUPER HERO EPIC OF TOMORROW!
KINGDOM COME
ELSEWORLDS
Mark WAID Alex ROSS

Mark Waid and **Alex Ross** deliver a grim tale of youth versus experience, tradition versus change and what defines a hero. KINGDOM COME is a riveting story pitting the old guard — Superman, Batman, Wonder Woman and their peers — against a new uncompromising generation.

WINNER OF FIVE EISNER AND HARVEY AWARDS, INCLUDING BEST LIMITED SERIES AND BEST ARTIST

IDENTITY CRISIS

NEW YORK TIMES BEST-SELLING AUTHOR OF THE ZERO GAME
BRAD MELTZER
RAGS MORALES MICHAEL BAIR
IDENTITY CRISIS
Introduction by JOSS WHEDON, creator of BUFFY THE VAMPIRE SLAYER and FIREFLY
"The IDENTITY CRISIS mystery involves the biggest DC heroes and uses all of Mr. Meltzer's skills as a thriller novelist."
— The New York Times

BRAD MELTZER
RAGS MORALES
MICHAEL BAIR

CRISIS ON INFINITE EARTHS

CRISIS
ON INFINITE EARTHS
MARV WOLFMAN
& GEORGE PÉREZ

MARV WOLFMAN
GEORGE PÉREZ

DC: THE NEW FRONTIER VOLUME 1

DC: The New Frontier
VOLUME ONE
BY DARWYN COOKE WITH DAVE STEWART

DARWYN COOKE
DAVE STEWART

SEARCH THE GRAPHIC NOVELS SECTION OF
www.DCCOMICS.com
FOR ART AND INFORMATION ON ALL OF OUR BOOKS!

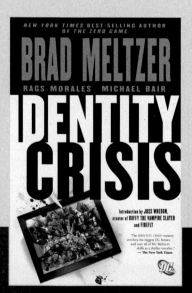